Lecture Notes in Computer Science 1033

Edited by G.

Advisory B.

Lecture Notes in Computer Science   1033

Edited by G. Goos, J. Hartmanis and J. van Leeuwen

Springer

Berlin
Heidelberg
New York
Barcelona
Budapest
Hong Kong
London
Milan
Paris
Tokyo

C.-H. Huang   P. Sadayappan   U. Banerjee
D. Gelernter   A. Nicolau   D. Padua (Eds.)

Languages and Compilers for Parallel Computing

8th International Workshop, LCPC '95
Columbus, Ohio, USA, August 10-12, 1995
Proceedings

 Springer

Series Editors

Gerhard Goos, Karlsruhe University, Germany

Juris Hartmanis, Cornell University, NY, USA

Jan van Leeuwen, Utrecht University, The Netherlands

Volume Editors

Chua-Huang Huang
Ponnuswamy Sadayappan
The Ohio State University, Dept. of Computer and Information Science
Columbus, OH 43210, USA

Utpal Banerjee
Intel Corporation
2200 Mission College Blvd., Santa Clara, CA 95052, RN6-18, USA

David Gelernter
Yale University, Department of Computer Science
51 Prospect St., New Haven, CT 06520, USA

Alex Nicolau
University of California, Dept. of Information and Computer Science
Irvine, CA 92717, USA

David Padua
Center for Supercomputing Research and Development
1308 West Main St., Urbana, IL 61801, USA

Cataloging-in-Publication data applied for
Die Deutsche Bibliothek - CIP-Einheitsaufnahme

Languages and compilers for parallel computing : ...
international workshop ... ; proceedings. - Berlin ; Heidelberg
; New York ; Barcelona ; Budapest ; Hong Kong ; London ;
Milan ; Paris ; Santa Clara ; Singapore ; Tokyo : Springer.
8. Columbus, Ohio, USA, August 10 - 12, 1995. - 1995
  (Lecture notes in computer science ; 1033)
  ISBN 3-540-60765-X
NE: GT

CR Subject Classification (1991): F.1.2, D.1.3, D.3.1, B.2.1, D.3.4

ISBN 3-540-60765-X Springer-Verlag Berlin Heidelberg New York

© Springer-Verlag Berlin Heidelberg 1996
Printed in Germany

Typesetting: Camera-ready by author
SPIN 10512465   06/3142 – 5 4 3 2 1 0   Printed on acid-free paper

Foreword

This volume contains papers presented at the Eighth Annual Workshop on Languages and Compilers for Parallel Computing, which was held in Columbus, Ohio on August 10-12, 1995. This workshop series has traditionally been a forum for the presentation of state-of-the-art research in languages, restructuring compilers, and runtime systems. As in previous years, the workshop attracted participation from leading research groups in the USA, Europe, and Japan.

We are grateful to the large number of people who helped us to organize this year's workshop. The members of the standing program committee — Utpal Banerjee, David Gelernter, Alex Nicolau, and David Padua — had many helpful suggestions and words of advice for us. Tom Fletcher, Sandy Hill, and Marty Marlatt ably assisted us with administrative and financial matters. Our student volunteers Debashis Basak, Donglai Dai, and Ram Kesavan worked tirelessly in helping us organize the workshop and in putting together this volume. We are thankful to the Department of Computer and Information Science at the Ohio State University and the Ohio Supercomputer Center for their financial support, which enabled us to control registration fees for the workshop attendees.

Last, but not least, we wish to thank the large number of referees who helped us evaluate the submitted papers and provided valuable feedback to the authors: Erik Altman, Bill Appelbe, Rajive Bagrodia, Prith Banerjee, Utpal Banerjee, Aart Bik, Rastislav Bodik, Carrie Brownhill, Sid Chatterjee, Andrew Chien, Lynn Choi, Fabien Coelho, Beatrice Creusillet, Benoit deDinechin, Mary Hall, Susan Hinrichs, Joe Hummel, Suresh Jagannathan, L.V. Kale, Peter Knijnenburg, David Kolson, Wei Li, Ziyuan Li, Kathryn McKinley, Sam Midkiff, Alex Nicolau, David Padua, John Plevyak, Sundeep Prakash, Bill Pugh, J. Ramanujam, Jerry Roth, Dale Schouten, Tom Sheffler, Henk Sips, Jaspal Subhlok, Chau-Wen Tseng, Pen Yew.

October 1995

Chua-Huang Huang
P. Sadayappan

Program Co-Chairs

Table of Contents

Line Grain Parallelism I

Array Data-Flow Analysis for Load-Store Optimizations in
Superscalar Architectures 1
    R. Bodik, R. Gupta
    University of Pittsburgh, Pennsylvania

An Experimental Study of an ILP-based Exact Solution Method
for Software Pipelining 16
    E. R. Altman, G. R. Gao
    McGill University, Montreal
    R. Govindarajan
    Memorial University of Newfoundland, St. John's

Insertion Scheduling: An Alternative to List Scheduling for
Modulo Schedulers 31
    B. D. de Dinechin
    CEA Limeil-Valenton, Cesson, France

Interprocedural Analysis

Interprocedural Array Region Analyses 46
    F. Creusillet, F. Irigoin
    Ecole des Mines de Paris, France

Interprocedural Analysis for Parallelization 61
    M. W. Hall
    California Institute of Technology, Pasadena
    B. R. Murphy, S. P. Amarasinghe, S. W. Liao, M. S. Lam
    Stanford University, California

Table of Contents

Fine Grain Parallelism I

Array Data Flow Analysis for Load-Store Optimizations in Superscalar Architectures 1

R. Bodík, R. Gupta
University of Pittsburgh, Pennsylvania

An Experimental Study of an ILP-based Exact Solution Method for Software Pipelining 16

E. R. Altman, G. R. Gao
McGill University, Montreal
R. Govindarajan
Memorial University of Newfoundland, St. John's

Insertion Scheduling: An Alternative to List Scheduling for Modulo Schedulers 31

B. D. de Dinechin
CEA Limeil-Valenton Center, France

Interprocedural Analysis

Interprocedural Array Region Analyses 46

B. Creusillet, F. Irigoin
Ecole des Mines de Paris, France

Interprocedural Analysis for Parallelization 61

M. W. Hall
California Institute of Technology, Pasadena
B. R. Murphy, S. P. Amarasinghe, S.-W. Liao, M. S. Lam
Stanford University, California

Interprocedural Array Data-Flow Analysis for Cache Coherence 81

L. Choi
University of Illinois, Urbana
P.-C. Yew
University of Minnesota, Minneapolis

**An Interprocedural Parallelizing Compiler and Its Support for
Memory Hierarchy Research** 96

T. Nguyen
*Army High Performance Computing Research Center,
Minneapolis*
J. Gu, Z. Li
University of Minnesota, Minneapolis

Program Analysis

V-cal: A Calculus for the Compilation of Data Parallel Languages 111

P. F. G. Dechering, J. A. Trescher, J. P. M. de Vreught,
H. J. Sips
Delft University, The Netherlands

Transitive Closure of Infinite Graphs and Its Applications . . . 126

W. Kelly, W. Pugh, E. Rosser, T. Shpeisman
University of Maryland, College Park

Demand-Driven, Symbolic Range Propagation 141

W. Blume
Hewlett Packard, California
R. Eigenmann
Purdue University, West Lafayette

Fortran 90 and HPF

**Optimizing Fortran 90 Shift Operations on Distributed-Memory
Multicomputers** 161

K. Kennedy, J. Mellor-Crummey, G. Roth
Rice University, Houston

A Loop Parallelization Algorithm for HPF Compilers 176

K. Ishizaki, H. Komatsu
IBM Japan Ltd, Tokyo Research Lab

**Fast Address Sequence Generation for Data-Parallel Programs
Using Integer Lattices** 191

A. Thirumalai, J. Ramanujam
Louisiana State University, Baton Rouge

**Compiling Array Statements for Efficient Execution on Distributed-
Memory Machines: Two-Level Mappings** 209

S. D. Kaushik, C.-H. Huang, P. Sadayappan
The Ohio State University, Columbus

Tools/Libraries

A Communication Backend for Parallel Language Compilers . . 224

J. M. Stichnoth, T. Gross
Carnegie Mellon University, Pittsburgh

Parallel Simulation of Data Parallel Programs 239

S. Prakash, R. Bagrodia
University of California, Los Angeles

**A Parallel Processing Support Library Based on Synchronized
Aggregate Communication** 254

H. G. Dietz, T. M. Chung, T. I. Mattox
Purdue University, West Lafayette

FALCON: A MATLAB Interactive Restructuring Compiler . . . 269

L. De Rose, K. Gallivan, E. Gallopoulos, B. Marsolf,
D. Padua
University of Illinois, Urbana

Fine Grain Parallelism II

**A Simple Mechanism for Improving the Accuracy and Efficiency
of Instruction-Level Disambiguation** 289

    S. Novack, J. Hummel, A. Nicolau
    University of California, Irvine

**Hoisting Branch Conditions - Improving Super-Scalar Processor
Performance** 304

    B. Appelbe, S. Doddapaneni, R. Harmon, P. May, S. Wills,
    M. Vitale
    Georgia Institute of Technology, Atlanta

Integer Loop Code Generation for VLIW 318

    J. Radigan, P. Chang, U. Banerjee
    Intel Architecture Lab, Santa Clara

Loop-Level Optimization

Dependence Analysis in Parallel Loops with i±k Subscripts . . . 331

    S. P. Midkiff
    IBM T.J.Watson Research Center, Yorktown Heights

Piecewise Execution of Nested Data-Parallel Programs 346

    D. W. Palmer, J. F. Prins, S. Chatterjee, R. E. Faith
    University of North Carolina, Chapel Hill

Recovering Logical Structures of Data 362

    M. Cierniak, W. Li
    University of Rochester, New York

Automatic Data Distribution

Efficient Distribution Analysis via Graph Contraction 377

> T. J. Sheffler, R. Schreiber
> *Research Institute for Advanced Computer Science,*
> *California*
> W. Pugh
> *University of Maryland, College Park*
> J. R. Gilbert
> *Xerox Palo Alto Research Center, California*
> S. Chatterjee
> *University of North Carolina, Chapel Hill*

Automatic Selection of Dynamic Data Partitioning Schemes for Distributed-Memory Multicomputers 392

> D. J. Palermo, P. Banerjee
> *University of Illinois, Urbana*

Data Redistribution in an Automatic Data Distribution Tool . . 407

> E. Ayguadé, J. Garcia, M. Gironès, M. L. Grande,
> J. Labarta
> *Universitat Politecnica Catalunya, Spain*

Compiler Models

General Purpose Optimization Technology 422

> T. Cheatham, A. Fahmy, D. C. Stefanescu
> *Harvard University, Cambridge*

Compiler Architectures for Heterogeneous Systems 434

> K. S. McKinley, S. K. Singhai, G. E. Weaver, C. C. Weems
> *University of Massachusetts, Amherst*

Virtual Topologies: A New Concurrency Abstraction for High-
Level Parallel Languages 450

    J. Philbin, S. Jagannathan
    NEC Research Institute, Princeton
    R. Mirani
    Yale University, New Haven

Irregular Computation

Interprocedural Data Flow Based Optimizations for Compilation
of Irregular Problems 465

    G. Agrawal, J. Saltz
    University of Maryland, College Park

Automatic Parallelization of the Conjugate Gradient Algorithm 480

    V. Kotlyar, K. Pingali, P. Stodghill
    Cornell University, Ithaca

Annotations for a Sparse Compiler 500

    A. J. C. Bik, H. A. G. Wijshoff
    Leiden University, The Netherlands

Connection Analysis: A Practical Interprocedural Heap Analysis
for C 515

    R. Ghiya, L. J. Hendren
    McGill University, Montréal

Object Oriented and Functional Parallelism

Language and Run-Time Support for Network Parallel
Computing 534

    P. A. Dinda, D. R. O'Hallaron, J. Subhlok, J. A. Webb,
    B. Yang
    Carnegie Mellon University, Pittsburgh

Agents: An Undistorted Representation of Problem Structure . 551

    J. Yelon, L. V. Kalé
    University of Illinois, Urbana

Type Directed Cloning for Object-Oriented Programs 566

J. Plevyak, A. A. Chien
University of Illinois, Urbana

The Performance Impact of Granularity Control and Functional Parallelism 581

J. E. Moreira
IBM T.J.Watson Research Center, Yorktown Heights
D. Schouten, C. Polychronopoulos
University of Illinois, Urbana

Array Data Flow Analysis for Load-Store Optimizations in Superscalar Architectures*

Rastislav Bodík and Rajiv Gupta

Dept. of Computer Science, University of Pittsburgh, Pittsburgh, PA 15260

Abstract. The performance of scientific programs on superscalar processors can be improved... degraded by memory references that frequently arise... load store operations and while array references... has been developed... for analyzing array elements whose values are repeatedly referenced ... keep live references in place (via loads, stores, and register-to-register shift operations without introducing full/partially redundant... appropriately a detailed value flow analysis of array references is required. We present an analysis framework to efficiently solve various data flow problems required by array load-store operations. The framework determines the collective behavior of recurrent references spread over multiple loop iterations. We also demonstrate how our algorithms can be retargeted for various fine-grain architectures.

1 Introduction

The performance of a superscalar processor is adversely affected by frequent references to memory. Therefore, techniques for effective allocation of registers to scalars have received considerable attention [3]. In scientific programs, a significant fraction of memory accesses arise from references to array elements. In order to reduce the frequency of these memory references, recent research has also considered the assignment of registers to array elements in inner loops [1,6,4,10,11].

The loop in Fig. 1(a) contains references that in turn address the same array element over five consecutive loop iterations. The value of an array element flows among the references forming a live range. As illustrated in Fig. 2, the value of r[i-3] is defined in the *i*th iteration and then redefined or used in the subsequent iterations by the shadowed references. A set of registers can be used to form a pipeline that holds the repeatedly referenced array elements throughout the live range. The definition of A[2*3*j] is a different reference that interferes with the value flow shown in Fig. 2. If two pipeline stages in this pipeline cause the value kept in the register pipeline of additional load operations must be introduced to ensure that values of array elements are available in appropriate registers when needed. A load

* Partially supported by National Science Foundation Presidential Young Investigator Award CCR-9157371 to the University of Pittsburgh and a grant from Hewlett-Packard Laboratories.

Array Data Flow Analysis for Load-Store Optimizations in Superscalar Architectures*

Rastislav Bodík and Rajiv Gupta

Dept. of Computer Science, University of Pittsburgh, Pittsburgh, PA 15260

Abstract. The performance of scientific programs on superscalar processors can be significantly degraded by memory references that frequently arise due to load and store operations associated with array references. Therefore, register allocation techniques have been developed for allocating registers to array elements whose values are repeatedly referenced over one or more loop iterations. To place load, store, and register-to-register shift operations without introducing fully/partially redundant and dead memory operations, a detailed value flow analysis of array references is required. We present an analysis framework to efficiently solve various data flow problems required by array load-store optimizations. The framework determines the collective behavior of recurrent references spread over multiple loop iterations. We also demonstrate how our algorithms can be adapted for various fine-grain architectures.

1 Introduction

The performance of a superscalar processor is adversely affected by frequent references to memory. Therefore, techniques for effective allocation of registers to scalars have received considerable attention [5]. In scientific programs, a significant fraction of memory accesses arise from references to array elements. In order to reduce the frequency of these memory references, recent research has also considered the assignment of registers to array elements in inner loops [1, 3, 4, 10, 11].

The loop in Fig. 1(a) contains references that in turn access the same array element over five consecutive loop iterations. The value of an array element flows among the references forming a live range. As illustrated in Fig. 2, the value of $A[i+4]$ is defined in the kth iteration and then redefined or used in the subsequent iterations by the shadowed references. A set of registers can be used to form a pipeline that holds the repeatedly referenced array elements throughout the live range. The definition of $A[2 \times i]$ is a killing reference that interferes with the value flow shown in Fig. 2 at two points. Since it may redefine the value kept in the register pipeline, additional load operations must be introduced to ensure that values of array elements are available in appropriate registers when needed. Also,

* Partially supported by National Science Foundation Presidential Young Investigator Award CCR-9157371 to the University of Pittsburgh and a grant from Hewlett-Packard Laboratories.

```
1   load R1, A[4]
2   load R2, A[3]
3   load R3, A[2]
4   load R4, A[1]
5   for i in 1...N              i
6       use R2                  ii
7       use R4                  iii
8       if (odd(i)) then        iv
9           use R1              v
10          shift R3, R4
11          shift R2, R3
12          def R2              vi
13          store R2, A[i + 3]  vi
14      else                    vii
15          store R1, A[i + 3]
16          def R2              viii
17          store R2, A[2 × i]  viii
18          shift R3, R4
19          shift R1, R2
20          load R3, A[i + 2]
21      endif                   ix
22      def R1                  x
23  endloop                     xi
24  store R1, A[N + 4]
```

```
i    for i in 1...N
ii       use A[i + 2]
iii      use A[i]
iv       if (odd(i)) then
v            use A[i + 3]
vi           def A[i + 3]
vii      else
viii         def A[2 × i]
ix       endif
x        def A[i + 4]
xi   endloop
```

(a) Source loop.   (b) After the optimization.

Fig. 1. The example.

store operations are inserted to save newly computed values of array elements in memory. Lastly, register-to-register copy operations have to be introduced to shift the contents of the pipeline once per iteration.

In this paper we present an analysis framework to efficiently solve various data flow problems required by the desired load-store optimizations. In the pro-

$i = k$	$i = k+1$	$i = k+2$	$i = k+3$	$i = k+4$
use $A[i+2]$	use $A[i+2]$	use $A[i+2]$	use $A[i+2]$	use $A[i+2]$
use $A[i]$	use $A[i]$	use $A[i]$	use $A[i]$	use $A[i]$
if (odd(i))	if (odd(i))	if (odd(i))	if (odd(i))	if (odd(i))
use $A[i+3]$	use $A[i+3]$	use $A[i+3]$	use $A[i+3]$	use $A[i+3]$
def $A[i+3]$	def $A[i+3]$	def $A[i+3]$	def $A[i+3]$	def $A[i+3]$
else	else	else	else	else
def $A[2 \times i]$	def $A[2 \times i]$	def $A[2 \times i]$	def $A[2 \times i]$	def $A[2 \times i]$
endif	endif	endif	endif	endif
def $A[i+4]$	def $A[i+4]$	def $A[i+4]$	def $A[i+4]$	def $A[i+4]$

Fig. 2. Flow of the value among array elements during any five consecutive loop iterations.

posed method, all references accessing the same element are considered in concert during a window of consecutive iterations similar to that in Fig. 2. The span of the window covers the entire live range of the array references. In addition, killing references that do not interfere with the value flow through the window are ignored, resulting in more precise analysis. For example, the definition of $A[2 \times i]$ kills the value of $A[i+4]$ from the kth iteration only two and four iterations later. Thus, the definition of $A[i + 4]$ and the definition of $A[i + 3]$, when considered together, lead us to conclude that the value for use in reference to $A[i + 2]$ is always available. Due to these properties, the framework exposes precise collective behavior of the recurrent references to which a register pipeline will be allocated. Our work was inspired by the framework of Duesterwald [11] which is based on reference analysis and thus is not capable of determining that two references may in concert generate the same value. To overcome this deficiency, we base our framework on value analysis.

Arbitrary placement of loads and stores may introduce fully/partially redundant loads and fully/partially dead stores which can be precisely characterized as follows.

Definition 1. A load operation, **load** $R, A[i]$, at a program point p is **partially/fully redundant** if, along *some/all paths* leading to p, the value of $A[i]$ is already available in R.

Definition 2. A store operation, **store** $R, A[i]$, at a program point p is **partially/fully dead** if, along *some/all paths* leaving from p, every potential use of the current value of $A[i]$ is read from register R.

We describe the application domain of our framework through load-store optimization which performs partial redundancy elimination (PRE) and partial dead code elimination (PDE) of the memory operations. Figure 1(b) shows the optimal placement of loads, stores, and shifts for the example loop. A load before the use of $A[i]$ would be partially redundant because, if i is odd in the $k + 2^{nd}$ iteration, the value of $A[i + 2]$ was not killed by the definition of $A[2 \times i]$ in this iteration (see Fig. 2). A load is appropriately inserted at line 20 to restore the pipeline in case the value was killed in this iteration. A store placed immediately after the definition of $A[i + 4]$ in the kth iteration would be partially dead because the value is rewritten one iteration later by the definition of $A[i + 3]$. Therefore, the store is delayed to the next iteration and performed at line 15. Shifts are placed in the holes of the live range which results in two operations per iteration, as opposed to four when shifts are placed at the end of the loop body. In summary, the optimized code performs 0/1 load and 1/2 stores per iteration. In contrast, load placement which does not consider PRE and PDE of memory references would perform 2 loads and 2 stores. Existing PRE and PDE techniques have primarily focussed on scalars and thus they do not perform optimization of array references over multiple loop iterations [8, 9, 15, 17].

2 Analyzing Congruent References

This section presents the data flow analysis framework. The analysis considers a group of array references that refer to the same array element during the execution of one or more consecutive loop iterations. Problems such as must availability and must anticipability of a value related to the array element can be solved using the framework. The group of array references being analyzed collectively is termed as a *congruent class* of references. The solution of an analysis of a congruent class of references will be *pictorially* represented using a *stretched loop*. A stretched loop offers a concise view at the window of consecutive iterations shown in Fig. 2 and conceptually illustrates the pattern of the flow of values associated with a congruent class. Figure 3(d) depicts the live range of the example loop; it contains only the references that influence the value, i.e., the references in boxes and the appropriate control statements. The number of loop iterations in the stretched loop for every congruent class is a small constant, typically less than 5, as is suggested by our experiments. Not only is the stretched loop short, but it is also merely an abstract visualization aid. The source loop is never unrolled and the framework computes the solution corresponding to the stretched loop on the source loop itself.

A given loop is analyzed for each array that is referenced in the loop. The references to a given array are divided into disjoint congruent classes based on their index expressions and each congruent class is processed individually, considering killing effects of references from other congruent classes of the same array. Analysis of a congruent class over the length of the stretched loop is sufficient to perform optimizations applicable to the references in the congruent class. Precise definitions of congruence are given below.

Definition 3. References r_1 and r_2 to an array A are **congruent** if they are of the form $r_1 = A[c \times i + k_1]$ and $r_2 = A[c \times i + k_2]$, where i is the normalized loop induction variable and $k_1 \bmod c = k_2 \bmod c$.

Definition 4. A **congruent class** of references to an array A, denoted as $[A, c \times i + k]$, is the largest set of congruent references in the loop of the form $A[c \times i + j]$, such that $j \bmod c = k \bmod c$. For a given loop the references to array A in the loop can be partitioned into disjoint congruent classes.

In Fig. 1(a), the references to array A are divided into two congruent classes. The congruence class $[A, 1 \times i]$ contains references $A[i], A[i+2], A[i+3], A[i+4]$; the congruent class $[A, 2 \times i]$ contains the reference $A[2 \times i]$.

Next, we describe the data flow framework in detail. The framework is able to solve both forward and backward data flow problems. We will present the analysis in the context of forward problems. As illustrated in Fig. 3, the solutions of various analyses span multiple loop iterations. To compute such solutions, we do not explicitly construct a stretched loop. Instead, the solution of an analysis on the conceptual stretched loop is represented in form of a vector associated with each node in the original flow graph. The solutions corresponding to distinct iterations in the stretched loop are computed into distinct positions in the vector.

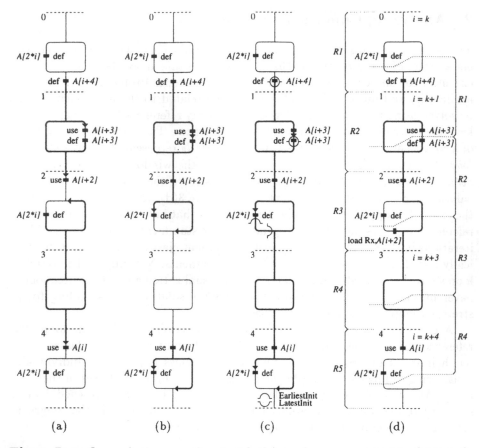

Fig. 3. Data flow solutions on the stretched loop for congruent class $[A, 1 \times i]$: (a) Range of must anticipability of congruent uses; (b) Range of must availability of congruent values; (c) EarliestInit and LatestInit points in the merged range; and (d) Usable congruent live range and shift placement points: naive shift placement on the left, optimal shift placement on the right.

In general, if d is the iteration distance between the lexicographically most distant references in a congruence class, then the stretched loop for the congruent class contains at most $d+1$ consecutive loop iterations which are numbered from 0 to d. Therefore, the size of the solution vector can be at most $d+1$. The size of the solution vector can be reduced by omitting the iterations that contain no array references and kills. For example, in Fig. 3, the iteration numbered 3 can be omitted from the vector. Since a node n in the original loop appears in multiple iterations of the stretched loop, we will use n_i to denote the instance of node n in the ith iteration of the stretched loop.

Since we are mainly interested in problems such as availability of values, the binary lattice $\{\top, \bot\}$, where $\top$ is the greatest element, is used to represent the solutions. The data flow solution value $\top$ indicates that the characteristic of interest holds while the value $\bot$ indicates that characteristic does not hold. The parametric meet operator $\sqcap$ can be either $\wedge$ or $\vee$ where the operator $\wedge$, which is used for must problems, returns the least value and the operator $\vee$, which is used for may problems, returns the highest value.

A straightforward implementation of data flow over the stretched loop requires traversing the loop body $d + 1$ times. However, we present a better approach in which all $d + 1$ iterations in the stretched loop are processed simultaneously using bit-vector operations. We use the chain lattice $\{\top, Cond, \bot\}$ in which $\top$ and $\bot$ have the same meaning as above. The value $Cond$ at node n_i indicates that the solution for n_i is the same as the solution for $start_i$, where $start_i$ is the start node of the loop body in the ith iteration of the stretched loop. In the first step, the algorithm simultaneously processes all $d + 1$ iterations under the assumption that the solution for $start_i$'s is $Cond$. The value $Cond$ is propagated to nodes whose solution depends on the solution of the appropriate $start_i$ node. In the second step, a single pass over the $start_i$'s is used to compute the true solution for $start_i$'s. In the third step again nodes from all $d + 1$ iterations are simultaneously processed such that the $Cond$ solution at each node instance n_i is changed to $\top$ if the solution at $start_i$ is $\top$ and to $\bot$ if the solution at $start_i$ is $\bot$. Therefore, the above solution requires only two passes over all the nodes during which vector operations are performed. Next, we describe the computation of GEN and $KILL$ sets and present the above algorithm in detail.

For a given congruence class C, we define set GEN^C to contain all generating references for class C and $KILL^C$ to contain references that kill values of class C. For the must availability problem, GEN^C contains all congruent definitions and uses from C and $KILL^C$ is the set of definitions that kill values generated by references in C. Shown in Fig. 4(a) is how the placement of references from these two sets on the stretched loop is computed. The computation of the positions in function $position^C$ requires two pieces of information, the iteration number $it(r)$ of every reference r in C and the killing distance between a reference s from C and any other reference r. The iteration number of reference R is equal to the number of the stretched loop segment where r resides.

A single killing reference may kill the flow of the congruent value in various distances from the generating references and hence appear in multiple iterations of the stretched loop. For instance, consider the placement of the killing reference $A[2 \times i]$ in the stretched loop for class $[A, 1 \times i]$ of the example loop. For forward/backward *must* data flow problems, it is sufficient to place the killing reference r, for every congruent reference s, in the single killing point closest to s in the appropriate direction of data flow. The value of k_r^s is the shortest killing distance between reference s and a killing reference r, that is, for $k_r^s - 1$ iterations after the value of s is generated it is *not* killed by reference r. The value of k_r^s can be computed using the simple approach suggested in [11], which is equivalent to computing line intersection. If k_r^s is ∞, then there is no dependence between references r and s. On systems with full dependence analysis, accuracy of a finite k_r^s is verified by any data dependence test such as the *gcd* test [18].

```
procedure Specialize
    for every reference r ∈ GEN^C
        for every i ∈ positions^C(r)
            add r to GEN_i^C
    for every reference r ∈ KILL^C
        for every i ∈ positions^C(r)
            add r to KILL_i^C

function positions^C(r)
    if r ∈ C then P := {it(r)}
    else for every s ∈ C do
        if k_r^s ≠ ∞ then
            P := P ∪ {it(s) + k_r^s}
    return P

function f_{n_i}^C(sol)
    if n contains r ∈ GEN_i^C
        return ⊤
    else if n contains r ∈ KILL_i^C
        return ⊥
    else return sol
```

Step I: Conditional solution
Initialize *start* point in every iteration:
$$IN^C[start][0..d] := (Cond, \ldots, Cond)$$
for each node n in reverse postorder do
    for $i := 0$ to d do (vectorizable loop)
        $IN^C[n][i] := \sqcap_{m \in pred(n)} OUT^C[m][i]$
        $OUT^C[n][i] := f_{n_i}^C(IN^C[n][i])$

Step II: Solution for *start* points
$IN^C[start][0] := \bot$
for $i := 1$ to d
    if $IN^C[start][i] = Cond$ then
        $IN^C[start][i] := IN^C[start][i-1]$

Step III: Resolving cond. solutions
for every node n do
    for $i := 0$ to d do (vectorizable loop)
        if $IN^C[n][i] = Cond$ then
            $IN^C[n][i] := IN^C[start][i]$
        if $OUT^C[n][i] = Cond$ then
            $OUT^C[n][i] := IN^C[start][i]$

(a)   (b)

Fig. 4. Data flow framework for forward problems: (a) $f_{n_i}^C$: flow function for node n_i with respect to congruent class C; and (b) Data flow algorithm.

The *flow function* for a node n corresponding to the ith iteration of the stretched loop is defined in Fig. 4(a). If the node contains a generating (killing) reference, then the flow function returns ⊤ (⊥), otherwise the flow function is the identity function. The computation of the data flow solution using the three step process discussed earlier is shown in Fig. 4(b).

In the above analysis framework, the inner loops of Steps I and III are vectorized using bit-vector operations. Since all congruent classes can be processed simultaneously, only two passes over all the nodes in the loop are required by this algorithm. The solution vector at every node n is represented by two parallel bit vectors in which n_i owns the two i^{th} bits. The encoding of the conditional lattice is $\{\bot = 00, Cond = 01, \top = 11\}$. The runtime complexity of the algorithm is expected to be $O(N)$ bit-vector operations or $O(N^2)$ bit-operations where N is the number of array references in the loop. The bound is low due to typically low values of d_{max}, the length of the longest stretched loop, and d_{sum}, the cumulative length of all stretched loops in the loop, as shown in Sect. 4. The bit-vector implementation and the complexity analysis are elaborated in [2].

The framework can also analyze loops with multiple entries and exits. This is possible because we are interested in determining the flow of values in the stabilized middle portion of the iteration space, not the flow in the first or last iterations which may be excuted only partially, due to multiple entries or exits.

3 The Optimization Algorithms

This section presents the applications of the array data flow framework. First, the optimal load-store placement algorithm is described. Then, we show how the framework can improve software pipelining and discuss architectural support provided by existing architectures which can assist in array register allocation.

3.1 The Load-Store Placement Algorithm

To minimize the number of memory references, loop invariant loads and stores can be moved out of the loop. Here we present algorithms for determining the placement of loads, stores, and shifts operations which cannot be moved out of the loop. Our approach uses virtual register names; a subsequent register allocation phase will map the names to physical registers. Under the assumptions that the branching structure of the program and the ordering of code statements is preserved, the algorithm presented achieves the following characteristics:

1. Minimal number of loads and stores are introduced along every path through the loop and therefore the resulting code performs minimal number of memory related operations for array references. This form of optimality is a direct consequence of employing a formulation for partial redundancy elimination developed by Knoop *et al.* [15].
2. The lengths of array live ranges are minimal, that is, the lengths cannot be shortened without introducing additional memory references.
3. Corresponding to a minimal placement of loads and stores, the placement of register-to-register shift operations introduced is such that the number of shifts executed on an average is minimized.
4. Corresponding to a load, store, and shift placement, the number of virtual registers introduced for a given live range is minimal. Furthermore, the scalar ranges created through the use of virtual registers will be precisely identifiable by a scalar register allocator such as the one presented in [13].

The algorithm consists of five steps: (1) Load placement; (2) Store placement; (3) Shift placement and introduction of virtual registers names in loads, stores, and shift operations; (4) Prologue and epilogue creation to ensure that values are appropriately loaded into and stored out of virtual registers; and (5) Register allocation. Each congruent class is processed separately. The algorithms are applied with respect to a given branching structure and code ordering, that is, we do not modify the branching structure or reorder program statements during these algorithms. However, since arbitrary graphs may prevent code placement optimizations, a dummy node is inserted along every *critical edge*[2] [8, 15].
Load Placement. The main objective of this step is to identify points at which the placement of loads does not introduce partial redundancy. An approach for eliminating partially redundant scalar expressions was developed by

---

[2] A critical edge is an edge leading from a node with more than one successor to a node with more than one predecessor.

Knoop *et al.* [15]. This approach is adapted for application to loads for array references by utilizing the framework introduced in the preceding section.

In order to avoid partial redundancy, we must place loads *as early as necessary* to ensure that later uses can reuse the value and the need for later loads is eliminated. We refer to a point at which a virtual register is initialized as an *initialization point*. To avoid partial redundancy we must consider only those points as initialization points at which the value under consideration is *must anticipable*, that is, there is a use of the value along all paths from the point. Furthermore, if the value under consideration is *must available* at the initialization point, then no load is needed at this point. The initialization points which satisfy the above conditions are called the *earliest initialization* points. Instead of placing loads at earliest points, we compute the *delaylability* of earliest points and insert loads *as late as possible* to shorten the live range during which the values are kept in registers. The resulting points are called *latest initialization* points. This step causes loads to be delayed to the closest use point or to a merge point some of whose incoming paths could not delay their load. The initialization points can be either array uses or array definitions; if the value is being defined at a latest point, then it is directly computed into the appropriate virtual register and no load is required. The above algorithm is summarized in Fig. 5. As we can see, the framework from the preceding section is used to perform *must anticipability*, *must availability*, and *delaylability* analysis. For the example loop of Fig. 1(a), the results of these analyses corresponding to congruence class $[A, 1 \times i]$ are shown in Figs. 3(a), 3(b), and 3(c).

Placement of stores. The values of array references directly computed into virtual registers must be written from the registers to the memory preceding killing uses, congruent loads, and prior to loop termination (assuming the array is used after the loop). The process of placing stores so that partially dead stores are avoided is analogous to the introduction of loads so that partially redundant loads are avoided. A store is partially dead if a later store causes the earlier store to become redundant along a program path. Therefore, the store placement analysis is, with respect to data flow direction, opposite of load placement analysis. While load placement requires backward anticipability, forward availability, and forward delaylability analysis, the placement of stores requires *forward anticipability* and *backward availability* of congruent definitions, and *backward dispatchability* of stores.

Placement of register shifts. Array live ranges longer than one iteration are allocated a set of virtual registers which must shift their values once per iteration using register copy operations so that each reference finds its value in the same register during each loop iteration. Existing techniques [1, 3, 4, 10] place the shifts at the *end* of the loop body, as illustrated in Fig. 3(d). In this example, such a placement requires four copy operations because the iteration boundary crosses the live range four times.

However, when a shift copy is placed in a live range hole, it becomes redundant because the destination register will be reloaded later. Since our data flow framework computes precise shape of live ranges, we can place shifts optimally

---

Definitions:

Let $\mathcal{R}$ be the set of all references to a specific array in a loop and $C \subseteq \mathcal{R}$ a congruent class. Then

$C_{def} \subseteq C$ is the set of defining references in C,

$C_{use} \subseteq C$ is the set of using references in C,

$(\mathcal{R} \setminus C)$ is the set of references in $\mathcal{R}$ that are not in C,

$(\mathcal{R} \setminus C)_{def}$ is the set of defining references in $(\mathcal{R} \setminus C)$, and

$(\mathcal{R} \setminus C)_{use}$ is the set of using references in $(\mathcal{R} \setminus C)$.

Note: $(\mathcal{R} \setminus C)$ is the set of references that may have data dependence on references in C and thus may appear as killing references in the stretched loop for C.

Load Placement:

AnticUseRange $= \{n_i \mid OUT^C_{AnUse}[n][i] = \top\}$

where $OUT^C_{AnUse}[n][i]$ is solution to *must anticip. of congr. uses* (i.e., potential loads) for n_i

Direction: backward $GEN^C = C_{use}$ $KILL^C = C_{def} \cup (\mathcal{R} \setminus C)_{def}$ Meet $= \wedge$

AvailValRange $= \{n_i \mid IN^C_{AvVal}[n][i] = \top\}$

where $IN^C_{AvVal}[n][i]$ is the solution to *must availability of the congruent values* (i.e., congruent references) for n_i

Direction: forward $GEN^C = C$ $KILL^C = (\mathcal{R} \setminus C)_{def}$ Meet operator $= \wedge$

AALoadRange = **AnticUseRange** $\cup$ **AvailValRange**

EarliestInit $= \{n_i \mid \exists m \in pred(n) : n_i \in$ **AALoadRange** $\wedge$

$(m_i \notin$ **AALoadRange** $\vee n_i$ contains r from $C_{def})\}^a$

set of nodes where register initialization achieves minimal number of loads

DelayRange $= \{n_i \mid IN^C_{Del}[n][i] = \top\}$

where $IN^C_{Del}[n][i]$ is the solution to *delaylability* problem for n_i

Direction: forward $GEN^C =$ **EarliestInit** $KILL^C = C$ Meet operator $= \wedge$

LatestInit $= \{n_i \mid \exists m \in succ(n) : n_i \in$ **DelayRange** $\wedge$

$(m_i \notin$ **DelayRange** $\vee n_i$ contains r from $C)\}$

set of nodes where register initialization achieves shortest live ranges

LatestInit$_{def} = \{n_i \in$ **LatestInit** $\mid n$ contains r from $C_{def}\}$

LatestInit$_{load} =$ **LatestInit** $\setminus$ **LatestInit**$_{def}$

Insert **def** R_x to nodes in **LatestInit**$_{def}$,

Insert **load** R_x at the entry of nodes in **LatestInit**$_{load}$ if they contain a reference from C_{use},

Insert **load** R_x at the exit of nodes in **LatestInit**$_{load}$ if they contain a reference from $(\mathcal{R} \setminus C)_{def}$.

^{a} If $n = start$ then end_{i-1} is considered instead of m_i.

Store Placement:

AvailDefRange $= \{n_i \mid IN^C_{AvDef}[n][i] = \top\}$

where $IN^C_{AvDef}[n][i]$ is the solution to *must availability of congruent definitions* (i.e., definitions of registers) for n_i

Direction: forward $GEN^C = C_{def}$ $KILL^C = (\mathcal{R} \setminus C)$ Meet operator $= \wedge$

AnticDefRange $= \{n_i \mid IN^C_{AnDef}[n][i] = \top\}$

where $IN^C_{AnDef}[n][i]$ is the solution to *must anticipability of congruent definitions* (i.e., congruent value redefinitions)

Direction: backward $GEN^C = C_{def}$ $KILL^C =$ **LatestInit**$_{load} \cup (\mathcal{R} \setminus C)_{use}$ Meet $= \wedge$

AAStoreRange = **AvailDefRange** $\cup$ **AnticDefRange**

LatestStore $= \{n_i \mid \exists m \in succ(n) : n_i \in$ **AAStoreRange** $\wedge$

$(m_i \notin$ **AAStoreRange** $\vee n_i$ contains r from **LatestInit**$_{load}\}$

set of nodes where register stores achieve minimal number of stores

DispatchRange $= \{n_i \mid OUT^C_{Disp}[n][i] = \top\}$

where $OUT^C_{Disp}[n][i]$ is the solution to *dispatchability* for n_i

Direction: backward $GEN^C =$ **LatestStore** $KILL^C = C_{def}$ Meet $= \wedge$

EarliestStore $= \{n_i \mid \exists m \in pred(n) : n_i \in$ **DispatchRange** $\wedge$

$(m_i \notin$ **DispatchRange** $\vee n_i$ contains r from $C_{def})\}$

set of nodes where stores achieve earliest stores

Insert **store** R_x at the exit of nodes in **EarliestStore**.

Fig. 5. Load Placement and Store Placement algorithms.

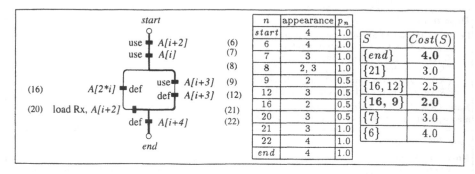

Fig. 6. Shift placement positions in the example loop.

by finding a set of nodes that cut the loop body through the live range holes. The optimal placement (Fig. 3(d)) requires only two copy operations per iteration.

Next, we present an algorithm that places shifts so that the average number of shifts expected to be executed per iteration is minimized. First, the precise live range is determined for a given congruent class using one-pass data flow analysis. Next, the number of times every node appears in the live range is weighted by the node execution probability to obtain the *weighted appearance* of the node. This is a trivial step because each node is attached a vector with live range solutions for each of its $d + 1$ positions in the stretched loop. It suffices to traverse the vector and count the number of vector elements equal to $\top$.

A set of nodes S is a valid candidate for the placement of shifts if *exactly* one node from S is encountered along any path through the loop body. Such set is a generalized dominator [12] of *end*. The shifts are placed into nodes of set S which minimizes the sum of weighted appearances of its members.

The optimal dominator set is identified by means of solving the maximum network flow problem [6]. The network flow is defined by setting the flow capacity of every node n to the weighted appearance of the node. In a network with saturated flow, there exists a set of nodes S that cut the loop body such that the maximum flow from *start* to *end* is equal to the cumulative flow capacity of the nodes in S [6]. Obviously, there is no cut with a lower flow capacity than that of S. Since S collectively dominates *end* and its cost is the minimum among all cuts, S represents the optimal shift placement. An $O(N^3)$ algorithm for the network flow problem exists [6] and, since the number of basic blocks in a loop is typically very small, the algorithm is practical for our purposes.

After the positions of shifts are fixed, the algorithm assigns the names to the registers in the shifts inserted in the range as well as to the anonymous virtual registers inserted in the previous stages. Figure 6 illustrates the computation of costs for several cuts of the loop body in Fig. 1(b). The optimal cut $\{13, 8\}$ requires two shifts. On the other hand, the approach used by Carr [4], which places the shifts at the end of the loop (i.e, at *end*), requires four shifts.

Prologue and epilogue. A *prologue* may be required to initialize the register pipeline prior to entering the loop and an *epilogue* may be required to flush the values from the pipeline after exiting the loop. The prologue contains a sequence of loads for loading values expected in the registers in the loop body during the first iteration. Since the store-elimination algorithm sometimes delays stores of array elements to later iterations, when the loop is exited, the registers may contain values that must be written by generating a series of stores after the loop. For multiple-exit loops, a different epilogue is generated for each exit.

If the newly computed values are not live when the loop is exited, the epilogue is formed by issuing the stores immediately after all definitions in the last k iterations, where k depends on how far the stores have been delayed. This solution handles the case of multiple-exit loops as well.

Register Allocation. Our algorithm determines precise shapes of array element live ranges and splits them into scalar ranges by inserting the shifts. The precision allows a scalar register allocator to use the same register for more array live ranges that do not overlap. For instance, in Fig. 1(b) lines 16 and 17 use register **R2** allocated to the congruent live range. Since the resulting scalar live ranges cross iterations, the allocator developed by Hendren *et al.* [13] is very suitable for subsequent register allocation. To eliminate the register pressure caused by allocating registers to all live ranges, the cost/benefit ratio can be determined for every candidate range, as is done in [4]. When only a part of a live range can be allocated registers, the most beneficial segment of the range can be found with a data flow analysis using our framework, as is done for scalars in the load/store range analysis developed by Kolte and Harrold [16]. Register placement of nested loops is performed in the manner similar to that of [13], starting from the innermost loop and working outward. A nested loop is represented in its enclosing loop by a summary node that references all virtual registers of the inner loop.

3.2 Exploiting Fine-Grain Architectures.

Data Speculative Load in PlayDoh [14]. The algorithm inserts a load after every killing reference that appears in the live range of the congruent value. This load updates the register pipeline in case the killing reference wrote to a memory location that is being stored in a pipeline register. Since upward movement of such a load is not possible, the load latency may complicate scheduling. In this subsection we discuss the utilization of an existing run-time memory disambiguation mechanism [14] for eliminating the load latency and propose a modification to the mechanism.

In Fig. 7(a) the live range of the value $A[i]$ is split by the definition of $A[f(i)]$ and thus a load must be placed at line 4. The PlayDoh architecture [14] offers data speculative load (LDS) and load verification (LDV) instructions that can eliminate latency of the load as is shown in Fig. 7(b). The speculative load is started before the killing store is issued and an entry $\langle address(A[i]), \mathbf{R3} \rangle$ is placed in the processor data speculative log. If $f(i) = i$, then the subsequent store invalidates the entry. If the entry remains valid at line 5, the LDV instruction does not reissue the load.

```
1   do i = 1, n
2       store R1, A[i]
3       store R2, A[f(i)]
4       load R3, A[i]
5   end do
```

```
1   do i = 1, n
2       store R1, A[i]
3       LDS R3, A[i]
4       store R2, A[f(i)]
5       LDV R3, A[i]
6   end do
```

```
1   do i = 1, n
2       store R1, A[i]
3       R3 = R1
4       LOG R3, A[i]
5       store R2, A[f(i)]
6       LDV R3, A[i]
7   end do
```

(a) Load after a kill. (b) LDS/LDV. (c) LOG/LDV.

Fig. 7. The use of data speculative load.

The LDS/LDV pair is ideal for register allocation with congruent references because a killing reference is likely to invalidate the pipeline only a few times per loop execution. However, if the value to be loaded is available when the LDS is issued, the LDS load is redundant. We propose a new instruction LOG which inserts the entry to the log but does not issue the load. The use of LOG (Fig. 7(c)) eliminates the memory traffic related to reloading the killed values. Whether an LDS operation can be replaced by a LOG is decided based on the solution of the must-availability problem solved in the load-placement algorithm.

The LDS operations can be moved upwards so that the LDS load is completed when the LDV operation is issued. The LDS positions are determined in our framework by solving a data flow problem under a numeric chain lattice. The details are beyond the scope of the paper.

Streaming in WM [1]. The WM architecture provides *streaming* load/store instructions that enable vector-like access to array elements with a fixed displacement through a FIFO memory queue. Streaming loads can be used in our register allocation if no two loads in the live range lie on the same path, that is, every congruent value is loaded exactly once. This can be verified from the positions of the loads by a data flow analysis within our framework.

Cyclic Register Files in Cydra 5 [7]. The design of Cydra 5 [7] took into consideration array register allocation and provided a cyclic register file in which it is possible to shift the contents of a subset of registers in one cycle. When cyclic registers are used in load-store elimination, the single shift copy operation can be placed at the end of the loop body and the shift placement algorithm need not be consulted.

Software Pipelining. The minimal length of a software pipeline schedule is governed by resource constraints and loop carried dependencies. To achieve short schedules, it is necessary to consider only the value-based dependencies and eliminate the spurious memory-based dependencies.

Our framework can inexpensively eliminate spurious dependencies as follows. We consider all congruent classes present in the loop. A value-based def-use dependence between any two loop statements a and b exists if there is a def-use path from an instance of a to an instance of b in any of the stretched loops corresponding to the congruent classes. The positions of the statements in the stretched loops are determined based on the array references in the statements.

4   Experiments and Related Work in Optimization

We are currently implementing presented techniques in the PDGCC compiler at the University of Pittsburgh. To verify the usefulness of our optimizations, we have determined by hand the register placement for the Livermore Loops benchmark suite and compared the results to the register placement of the Gnu C compiler (version 2.6.0). The number of loads due to array references was determined by profiling the suite, examining the assembly output of the compiler, and by considering the loads required by the manually optimized kernels. Gcc was unable to eliminate congruent loads across iterations even when loop unrolling, the CSE optimization, and all expensive optimizations were enabled. This implies that PRE of congruent memory references in the presence of conditional control flow is not performed in gcc.

Figure 8 gives the dynamic count of loads before and after the optimization. As we can see, a large fraction of loads are avoided. Since we were only able to optimize simple loops, we did not encounter any opportunities to eliminate stores, or find holes in array live ranges that would enable shift optimization. Figure 8 also gives the values of d_{max}, the largest stretched loop, and d_{sum}, the cumulative length of stretched loops for all congruent classes, for the examined programs. As we can see, the length of the stretched loop is typically small.

Techniques described in [1, 3, 10, 11] do not handle full conditional control flow. The only available method for array PRE is Scalar Replacement of Carr *et al.* [4]. However, we can obtain a superset of their optimizations. For instance, when a congruent definition is killed only outside the stretched loop window, their algorithm considers it to be an unsafe generator for the live range, even though for the register allocation purposes the kill has no effect. Moreover, the algorithm is very complex; eleven data flow problems must be solved to place the loads (we solve only three problems). While we can prove the optimality of our load-placement algorithm, their approach uses heuristic decisions. Also, the prologue created by their algorithm unrolls the loop, whereas ours only places a sequence of loads. As has been shown in Sect. 3.2, the compiler may need to solve various data flow problems to customize the load-store placement for a particular architecture. Our framework allows an easy formulation and provides precise calculation of these problems. Consequently, Carr's algorithm cannot place the shift operations optimally.

Livermore loop no.	1	5	7	11	12	15	20	23
Loads placed by gcc -O2 -funroll-all-loops	1200	3000	1080	2000	2000	52500	8000	50000
Loads placed by our register placement	800	2000	360	1000	1000	35000	6000	40000
Loads eliminated	33%	33%	66%	50%	50%	33%	25%	20%
d_{max}	1	1	6	1	1	1	1	2
d_{sum}	4	4	10	3	3	13	8	10

Fig. 8. Dynamic count of array-related register loads before and after optimization. The maximum and cumulative lengths of stretched loops.

References

1. M.E. Benitez and J.W. Davidson, "Code Generation for Streaming: an Access/Execute Mechanism," *Proceedings of Arch. Support for Programming Languages and Operating Systems-IV*, pages 132-141, 1991.
2. R. Bodik and R. Gupta, "Optimal Placement of Load-Store Operations for Array Accesses in Loops," *Technical report 95–03*, DCS, Univ. of Pittsburgh, 1995.
3. D. Callahan, S. Carr, and K. Kennedy, "Improving Register Allocation for Subscripted Variables," *Proceedings of the SIGPLAN Conference on Programming Language Design and Implementation*, White Plains, New York, pages 53-65, June 1990.
4. S. Carr and K. Kennedy, "Scalar Replacement in the Presence of Conditional Control Flow," *Software-Practice and Experience*, Vol. 24, No. 1, pages 51-77, Jan. 1994.
5. G.J. Chaitin, "Register Allocation and Spilling via Graph Coloring," *Proceedings of the SIGPLAN Symposium on Compiler Construction*, SIGPLAN Notices, vol. 17, no. 6, pages 98-105, June 1982.
6. T.H. Cormen, C.E. Leiserson, and R.L. Rivest, *Introduction to Algorithms*, The MIT Press, Cambridge, Massachusetts, 1990.
7. J.C. Dehnert, P.Y.-T. Hsu, and J.P. Bratt, "Overlapped Loop Support in the Cydra 5," *Proceedings of ASPLOS-III*, pages 26-39, 1989.
8. D.M. Dhamdhere, "Practical Adaptation of the Global Optimization Algorithm of Morel and Renvoise," *ACM Transactions on Programming Languages and Systems*, Volume 13, No. 2, pages 291-294, April 1991.
9. D.M. Dhamdhere, B.K. Rosen and F.K. Zadeck, "How to Analyze Large Programs Efficiently and informatively," *Proc. of the SIGPLAN PLDI*, San Francisco, California, pages 212-223, June 1992.
10. E. Duesterwald, R. Gupta, and M.L. Soffa, "Register Pipelining: An Integrated Approach to Register Allocation for Scalar and Subscripted Variables," *Proc. of International Workshop on Compiler Construction, LNCS 641* Springer Verlag, pages 192-206, Paderborn, Germany, October 1992.
11. E. Duesterwald, R. Gupta, and M.L. Soffa, "A Practical Data Flow Framework for Array Reference Analysis and its Application in Optimizations," *Proc. of ACM SIGPLAN Conference on Programming Language Design and Implementation*, pp.68-77, Albuquerque, New Mexico, June 1993.
12. R. Gupta, "Generalized Dominators and Post-Dominators," *The Nineteenth Annual ACM SIGPLAN-SIGACT Symposium on Principles of Programming Languages*, pages 246-257, Albuquerque, New Mexico, January 1992.
13. L. Hendren, G.R. Gao, E.R. Altman, and C. Mukerji, "A Register Allocation Framework based upon Hierarchical Cyclic Interval Graphs," *Intnl. Workshop on Compiler Construction, LNCS 641* Springer Verlag, pages 176-191, Germany, 1992.
14. V. Kathail, M. Schlansker, and B. Rau, *HPL PlayDoh Architecture Specification: Version 1.0*, HPL-93-80, February, 1994.
15. J. Knoop, O. Ruthing, and B. Steffen, "Optimal Code Motion: Theory and Practice," *ACM TOPLAS*, vol. 16, num. 4, 1117-1155.
16. P. Kolte and M.J. Harrold, "Load/Store Range Analysis for Global Register Allocation," *Proc. of the SIGPLAN Conference on Programming Language Design and Implementation*, Albuquerque, New Mexico, pages 268-277, June 1994.
17. E. Morel and C. Renvoise, "Global Optimization by Suppression of Partial Redundancies," *Communications of the ACM*, Volume 22, No. 2, pages 96-103, 1979.
18. M. Wolfe and U. Banerjee, "Data Dependence and Its Application to Parallel Processing," *Intl. Journal of Parallel Programming*, Vol. 16, No. 2, April 1987.

An Experimental Study of an ILP-based Exact Solution Method for Software Pipelining*

Erik R. Altman

Dept. of Electrical Engineering, McGill University, Montreal, H3A 2A7, Canada

R. Govindarajan

Dept. of Computer Science, Memorial Univ. of Newfoundland, St. John's, A1B 3X5

Guang R. Gao

School of Computer Science, McGill University, Montreal, H3A 2A7, Canada

{erik,govind,gao}@acaps.cs.mcgill.ca

Abstract. *Software pipelining has been widely accepted as an efficient technique for scheduling instructions in a loop body for VLIW and Superscalar processors. Several software pipelining methods based on heuristic approachs have been proposed in the literature. Mathematical formulations based on integer linear programming (ILP) to obtain rate-optimal schedules are also becoming popular. We term formulations such as ILP exact to indicate that they solve a precisely stated optimality problem. By contrast, we term what are generally called "heuristic" methods inexact since they do not guarantee optimality. We do not use the term heuristic, because various heuristics can also be used to guide approaches such as ILP—without losing any optimality.*

In this paper we compare our software pipelining method based on the ILP with three inexact methods. These software pipelining methods are applied to 1008 different loops extracted from a variety of benchmark programs, and their performance, in terms of the computation rate of the loop schedule, the number of registers used, and the execution time of the scheduling method. Compared to the inexact approaches and in terms of computation rate and register requirements, the ILP based scheduling method obtains better schedules in a significant number of test cases. The ILP based method obtained optimal schedules reasonably fast, with a median of less than 3 seconds and a geometric mean of less than 3 seconds. We present a case for the ILP approach and its usefulness in performance critical applications and also as a testbed for evaluating other inexact software pipelining methods.

1 Introduction

In recent years, software pipelining [3, 5, 8, 10, 11, 12, 13, 16, 17, 20, 19] has been gaining increasing attention as an efficient loop scheduling technique from both researchers and practitioners in compiler design. Software pipelining techniques are applicable to both VLIW and Superscalar architectures. Rapid advances in computer architecture — both in hardware and software technology — provide a rich design space to exploit software pipelined schedules. In particular, modern

* This work was supported by research grants from NSERC (Canada) and MICRONET –Network Centers of Excellence (Canada).

processor architectures (superscalar, superpipelined and VLIW) employ multiple function units (**Adder, Multiplier,** etc.) of different types (**integer** vs. **floating-point units**). The function units may or may not be pipelined. Compiler writers face both new opportunities and new challenges in constructing software pipelined schedules which fully exploit the power of available function units and registers. Ideally, one would like to address the following problem:

> *Given a machine M and a loop L with its dependence graph, determine a fastest software pipelined schedule of L on M within the resource and register constraints of M.*

This problem is sometimes called the *modulo scheduling* problem [16] or *cyclic scheduling* problem. The performance of a software-pipelined schedule can be measured by the *initiation rate* of successive iterations. The "fastest schedule" here refers to the schedule with the maximum possible initiation rate under the resource and register constraints. A schedule with the maximum initiation rate is called a *rate-optimal* schedule — in other words, there exist no other schedules which can have a faster computation rate without exceeding the resource and/or register constraints.

There have been many proposed algorithms for modulo scheduling [3, 5, 8, 10, 11, 12, 16, 17, 19, 20]. These algorithms differ in many ways: the objectives to be achieved, the solution methods, the heuristics applied, the quality of produced schedules (measured in computation rate/initiation interval, resources utilized, etc.) and the compile time needed to find the schedule. A comprehensive survey of these methods can be found in [15].

In this paper, we are interested in studying the tradeoffs between modulo scheduling methods which seek exact optimal solutions (perhaps at the expense of extra computing cost) and those which do not. We call the former *exact methods*, and the latter *inexact methods*. We use the name *inexact* for heuristic methods as they have neither precise mathematical optimality criteria nor guarantee optimality. Further, since the general problem is NP hard, both exact and inexact methods employ heuristics in their solution process. Examples of exact methods include integer linear programming (ILP) based software pipelined methods [2, 1, 9, 6]. Examples of inexact methods include Huff's Slack Scheduling [11], Wang, Eisenbeis, Jourdan and Su's FRLC variant of DESP–Decomposed Software Pipelining [19], and Gasperoni and Schwiegelshohn's Modified List Scheduling approach [8], Rau's iterative modulo scheduling algorithms [17] and Ebcioglu's enhanced software pipelining methods [4].

In this paper, we present an evaluation of the exact ILP based solution method proposed by the authors in [2, 9] and compare its results with three inexact solution methods mentioned above: Slack Scheduling, FRLC/DESP, and Modified List Scheduling. A comprehensive set of experiments are performed on 1008 loops from typical benchmark programs such as specint92, specfp92, the livermore loops, and linpack. Six architecture models with different levels of instruction level parallelism are tested with various combinations of function units, both homogeneous and heterogeneous, fully pipelined and unpipelined. The main observations from these experiments are:

- The ILP-based exact method currently in use found optimal schedules reasonably fast — with a geometric mean of computation time less than 5 seconds and a median of 3 seconds.
- The current version of our ILP based exact method spends a considerably longer time in searching for good schedules. But, in a substantial fraction of the test cases the ILP based exact method found a 15% to 20% better schedule compared with the inexact methods, both in time and resource/register usage. Compared to the most competitive inexact method (Slack Scheduling) known to us, the ILP based exact method still generates faster schedules in 14% of cases when using a heterogeneous, pipelined architecture model, and in a significantly larger fraction (45%) of the test cases required fewer registers.

Our conclusion from this study is that exact methods (such as ILP based methods) can be profitably used by compiler writers to evaluate other less expensive inexact methods. By quantitatively comparing the difference between their favorite inexact heuristic and the exact optimal solution, compiler writers can improve their heuristics and achieve better solution methods. With improvements in the efficiency of the exact solution method, it may also become feasible to include them in real compilers as an option for those users who need to use the best possible scheduled code at the expense of longer compile time.

In Section 2, we further develop the differences between exact and inexact methods and introduce how they are applied to software pipelining. In Section 3, we review our ILP formulation for software pipelining — both for pipelined and non-pipelined function units. Experiments are discussed in Section 4, first with evaluation of ILP performance, and then comparing ILP performance to inexact methods. Finally we conclude in Section 5.

2 Why Study ILP Based Exact Scheduling Methods ?

An integer linear programming-based scheduling method represents resource and register constraints as linear inequalities of integer variables, and uses linear functions as objective functions to be optimized. Since the objective functions of an ILP formulation capture optimality criteria precisely, and an optimal solution is sought against such optimality, ILP based formulations and solution algorithms belong to the class of *exact* methods.

Solving a general ILP problem is known to be NP-hard [7]. However, it does have a great advantage in terms of the quality of solutions — ILP solvers usually guarantee they will find an optimal solution if one exists.

In contrast, inexact methods for scheduling do not emphasize a precise mathematical formulation of optimality objective functions. Instead, they focus on finding good (feasible but often suboptimal) solutions fast. Simple heuristics can often be found to guide the solution process and the resulting schedules are quite satisfiable in practice. List scheduling represents one such inexact method widely used in scheduling problems. Similar ideas have been employed in solving modulo scheduling problems [12]. With the success of such (more or less) inexpensive and good inexact methods, questions naturally arise: why bother with exact solution methods such as ILP?

It is our belief that rapid technology advances in microprocessor architectures makes the search for exact optimal solutions ever more important. For example, a simple register spill may cause an expensive memory operation (due to a possible cache miss) — memory stalls incur more performance loss in the presence of the multi-issuing capability. This makes an exact optimal schedule using a minimum number of register more attractive. Furthermore, there are indications that with increasing numbers and types of function units, inexact methods may not able to fully exploit the available instruction-level parallelism.

On the other hand, we have seen continuing progress in designing more efficient ILP algorithms. Various heuristics have been employed to improve their efficiency without compromising their optimality. Such progress, coupled with the rapid advance in the computation power of high-performance workstations, is making ILP solution speed more feasible for practical use.

However, in order to assess the advantage and tradeoffs of ILP based methods for modulo scheduling, we need to perform more comprehensive experimental studies. These studies should be applied to a reasonably large number of real loops with various architecture configurations. They should also be compared quantitatively with other contemporary inexact methods for modulo scheduling. This is the motivation of the present paper.

3 ILP Formulation

In this section we briefly review the exact ILP formulation for the software pipelining problem reported in [2, 9]. Only an overview of the formulation is presented here for the sake of completeness. This overview will also help us introduce the notations and terminology used in the rest of this paper. Readers familiar with [2, 9] can proceed directly to Section 4. Section 3.1 deals with architectures consisting of pipelined function units (FUs). An overview of the formulation for non-pipelined FUs is presented in Section 3.2.

3.1   Pipelined FUs

First, we will consider target architecture consisting of homogeneous pipelined function units, each capable of performing any instruction. Such a description normally characterizes instruction fetch units. Subsequently we will relax this and consider heterogeneous function units where each function unit type, such as **Integer, Floating Point (FP) Add, Load/Store, FP Multiply, FP Divide**, can execute one type of instructions.

The performance of a software-pipelined schedule can be measured by the *initiation rate* of successive iterations. In the following discussion, we often use the reciprocal of the initiation rate, the *initiation interval* T. Let us first establish a lower bound for T — i.e. the shortest initiation interval for a loop under various constraints. It is well known that, the initiation interval is governed by both loop-carried dependences in the dependency graph and the resource constraints presented by the architecture. Under the loop-carried dependence constraint, the shortest initiation interval, T_{dep}, is given by [18]:

$$T_{dep} = \max_{\forall cycles\ C} \left(\frac{\text{total execution time of all nodes in the cycle}}{\text{sum of the dependence distance around the cycle}} \right)$$

Resource constraints (of the architecture) impose a lower bound on the initiation interval as well. If the function units are fully pipelined, then the resource constraint bound is:

$$T_{res} = \frac{\text{number of nodes in the DDG}}{\text{number of FUs}}.$$

Considering both dependence and resource constraints, the lower bound on minimum initiation interval (T_{lb}) for our example with pipelined FUs is

$$T_{lb} = \max\{\lceil T_{dep} \rceil, \lceil T_{res} \rceil\}$$

The smallest iteration period $T_{min} \geq T_{lb}$, for which a resource-constrained schedule exists, is called the rate-optimal period (with the given resource constraints) for the given loop. The initiation rate $\frac{1}{T_{lb}}$ for a given DDG may be improved by unrolling the graph a number of times, though we do not focus on any unrolling in this paper.

To construct a resource-constrained schedule for a loop, we first need to obtain an exact formulation of the software pipelining problem for a given iteration period T. By solving the formulation for successive values of T from T_{lb} until a solution satisfying the constraints is found, we obtain a rate-optimal software pipelined schedule.

In this paper we investigate periodic *linear schedules*, under which the time the various operations begin their execution is governed by a simple linear relationship. That is, under the linear schedule considered in this paper, the j-th instance of a statement i begins execution at time $T \cdot j + t_i$, where $t_i \geq 0$ is an integer offset and T is the initiation interval or the *iteration period* of the given schedule. ($\frac{1}{T}$ is the *initiation rate* of the schedule.)

Dependence constraints between the nodes of the DDG can be expressed as a linear constraint on the values of t_i [18]:

$$t_j - t_i \geq d_i - T \cdot m_{ij}$$

where d_i is the delay of node i, T the period, and m_{ij} the dependence distance or *loop-carried dependence* for arc (i, j).

The resource constraints are represented succinctly in a linear form with the help of a $T \times N$ matrix, $\mathcal{A}$, where T is the period of the schedule and N is the number of nodes in the DDG. The elements of the $\mathcal{A}$ matrix, $\mathcal{A}[t, i]$ are either 0 or 1 depending on whether instruction i is scheduled for execution at time step t in the repetitive pattern.

To make things clearer, consider an example $\mathcal{A}$ matrix with an iteration period $T = 2$ and with six instructions, i_0 to i_5.

$$\mathcal{A} = [a_{t,i}] = \begin{bmatrix} 1 & 0 & 1 & 0 & 0 & 1 \\ 0 & 1 & 0 & 1 & 1 & 0 \end{bmatrix}$$

This $\mathcal{A}$ matrix represents initiation of instruction i_0 at time step 0 in the repetitive pattern, i_1 at time step 1, i_2 at time step 0, and so on. Since each FU is pipelined, we can initiate a new operation in each cycle. Thus, conceptually at least, the FU is required for an instruction only at the time step it is initiated. Thus the sum of each row of the $\mathcal{A}$ matrix represents the number of FUs required at each time step in the repetitive pattern. Hence the resource constraint can be expressed as

$$\sum_{i=0}^{N-1} a_{t,i} \leq F \quad \text{for all } t \in [0, T-1] \tag{1}$$

where F is the number of FUs available in the target architecture.

In order to ensure that each instruction is scheduled exactly once in the repetitive pattern, we require that the sum of each column in the $\mathcal{A}$ matrix to be 1. This can also be expressed as a linear constraint as:

$$\sum_{t=0}^{T-1} a_{t,i} = 1 \quad \text{for all } i \in [0, N-1] \tag{2}$$

Lastly we need to relate the $\mathcal{A}$ matrix and the t_i variables.

$$\mathcal{T} = T \cdot \mathcal{K} + \mathcal{A}^{\text{Transpose}} \times [0, 1, \cdots, T-1]^{\text{Transpose}} \tag{3}$$

where

$$\mathcal{T} = [t_0, t_1, \cdots, t_{N-1}] \quad \text{and} \quad \mathcal{K} = [k_0, k_1, \cdots, k_{N-1}]$$

Intuitively k_i corresponds to the iteration from which the first occurrence of i in the repetitive pattern comes, while $\mathcal{A}^{\text{Transpose}} \times [\cdots]^{\text{Transpose}}$ is the offset of that i from the start of the pattern.

In addition to enforcing resource constraints, we could also simultaneously minimize the number of registers required for the schedule, where registers are modeled by FIFO buffers placed between producer and consumer nodes (instructions). With each instruction i, a buffer size b_i is associated. The buffer b_i is sufficient to hold the data values produced by i until they are consumed by any of the successor nodes of i. In [14], buffer requirements are represented as linear constraints on t_i variables as:

$$T \cdot b_i + t_i - t_j \geq T \cdot m_{ij} \tag{4}$$

Buffer requirements provide a tight upper bound on the total register requirement, and once the buffer assignment is done, a classical graph coloring method can subsequently be performed which generally leads to the minimum register requirement. In this paper, we assume that such a coloring phase will always be performed once the schedule is determined.

The overall objective of our formulation is to minimize the total buffer requirements subject to resource and dependence constraints. The complete ILP formulation is shown in Figure 1.

[ILP Formulation for Pipelined Homogeneous FUs]

$$\text{minimize} \sum_{i=0}^{N-1} b_i$$

subject to

$$\sum_{i=0}^{N-1} a_{t,i} \leq F, \quad \text{for all } t \in [0, T-1] \tag{5}$$

$$T \cdot \mathcal{K} + \mathcal{A}^{\text{Transpose}} \times [0, 1, \cdots, T-1]^{\text{Transpose}} = \mathcal{T} \tag{6}$$

$$T \cdot b_i + t_i - t_j \geq T \cdot m_{ij} \quad \forall i \in [0, N-1] \text{ and } (i, j) \in E \tag{7}$$

$$\sum_{r=0}^{T-1} a_{r,i} = 1 \quad \text{for all } i \in [0, N-1] \tag{8}$$

$$t_j - t_i \geq d_i - T \cdot m_{ij} \quad \forall (i, j) \in E \tag{9}$$

$$b_i \geq 0, t_i \geq 0, k_i \geq 0, \text{ and } a_{r,i} \geq 0 \text{ are integers} \quad \forall i \in [0, N-1], \forall r \in [0, T-1] \tag{10}$$

Fig. 1. ILP formulation

Heterogeneous Function Units: We can extend our ILP formulation to handle heterogeneous function units so as to more realistically model architectures with a variety of function unit types, such as **Integer, Load/Store,** and **Float Divide.** Let us assume that target architecture contains F_r FUs in type r and there are s different types of FUs. The resource constrained lower bound on T is defined as:

$$T_{res}(r) = \frac{\text{number of nodes that execute in FU type } r}{F_r}$$

and the overall T_{res} is

$$T_{res} = \max_r (T_{res}(r)) \quad \text{for all } r \in [0, s-1]$$

For heterogeneous FUs, we need to calculate the resource requirements for each FU type separately. At time step t in the repetitive pattern the resource requirement for FU type r is the sum of the elements in the t-th row of $\mathcal{A}$, but we include only those elements (instructions) which execute on FU type r. For this purpose we introduce the notation $\mathcal{I}(r)$ to represent the set of all instructions that execute in FU type r. Thus, the resource constraint for FU type r can be specified as

$$\sum_{i \in \mathcal{I}(r)} a_{t,i} \leq F_r \quad \text{for all } t \in [0, T-1] \tag{11}$$

Similar constraints for each FU type $r \in [0, s-1]$ are also generated. Using these constraints in the place of the resource constraint (Equation 5) in the ILP formulation, we get an ILP formulation for heterogeneous FUs.

In the following subsection, we show how to extend our formulation to non-pipelined FUs.

3.2 Non-Pipelined Function Units

In the case of non-pipelined and homogeneous FUs, the lower bound T_{res} is given by:

$$T_{res} = \frac{\text{sum of the execution time of all nodes}}{\text{number of FUs}}$$

For non-pipelined architectures with heterogeneous FUs,

$$T_{res} = \max_r \left(T_{res}(r) \right)$$

$$= \max_r \frac{\text{total execution time of nodes that execute in FU type } r}{\text{number of FUs in type } r}$$

In order to estimate the resource requirements with non-pipelined FUs, we need to know not just when each instruction is *initiated* (given by the $\mathcal{A}$ matrix), but also how long it executes. For example, if an instruction i is initiated at time step 2 in the repetitive pattern of length 3, and executes until time step 0, then the FU is required at time steps 2 and 0. Thus we need to define a *usage matrix* $\mathcal{U}$ from the $\mathcal{A}$ matrix to represent the resource usage in non-pipelined FUs.

How do we obtain the $\mathcal{U}$ matrix from $\mathcal{A}$? An instruction i initiated at time t requires the FU until time step $(t + d_i - 1) \bmod T$. Alternatively, we can say that instruction i requires a function unit at time step t if i began execution less than d_i time steps prior to t. Thus we can define $\mathcal{U}[t, i]$ as:

$$\mathcal{U} = u_{t,i} = \sum_{l=0}^{(d_i - 1)} a_{((t-l) \bmod T), i}, \quad \forall t \in [0, T-1], \text{ and } \forall i \in V \tag{12}$$

As an example, for the $\mathcal{A}$ matrix shown below, if instructions i_2, i_3 and i_4 execute in a non-pipelined FU for 2 time units, and instructions i_0, i_1 and i_5 execute for 1 time unit, then the usage matrix $\mathcal{U}$ is:

$$\mathcal{A} = \begin{bmatrix} 1 & 0 & 0 & 1 & 0 & 0 \\ 0 & 1 & 1 & 0 & 0 & 0 \\ 0 & 0 & 0 & 0 & 1 & 1 \end{bmatrix} \quad \text{and} \quad \mathcal{U} = \begin{bmatrix} 1 & 0 & 0 & 1 & 1 & 0 \\ 0 & 1 & 1 & 1 & 0 & 0 \\ 0 & 0 & 1 & 0 & 1 & 1 \end{bmatrix}$$

Or symbolically,

$$\mathcal{U} = \begin{bmatrix} a_{0,0} & a_{0,1} & a_{0,2} + a_{2,2} & a_{0,3} + a_{2,3} & a_{0,4} + a_{2,4} & a_{0,5} \\ a_{1,0} & a_{1,1} & a_{1,2} + a_{0,2} & a_{1,3} + a_{0,3} & a_{1,4} + a_{0,4} & a_{1,5} \\ a_{2,0} & a_{2,1} & a_{2,2} + a_{1,2} & a_{2,3} + a_{1,3} & a_{2,4} + a_{1,4} & a_{2,5} \end{bmatrix}$$

The FU requirement at time step t is the sum of the elements of row t of the $\mathcal{U}$ matrix. Since this should be less than the number of available FUs,

$$\sum_{i=0}^{N-1} u_{t,i} \leq F \quad \text{for all } t \in [0, T-1] \tag{13}$$

Replacing the resource constraint (Equation 5) in the ILP formulation (Figure 1) by Equations 12 and 13, we obtain the ILP formulation for non-pipelined FUs. This formulation can be extended to heterogeneous FUs along lines similar to pipelined FUs as discussed in Section 3.1.

Mapping Instructions to FUs: Unfortunately, the formulation developed in the previous subsection does not completely capture the software pipelining problem for non-pipelined FUs. In particular it may require that an instruction initiated on one FU switch to some other FU during the course of the instruction execution. Since this is not practical, such a schedule is clearly illegal. We will illustrate this problem with the help of an example.

Consider the repetitive pattern shown in Figure 2(a). In this table, each row represents an (relative) iteration number to which the different instructions of a repetitive pattern belong to. We have used the notation $\_i_2$ to indicate that the execution of an instruction continues from the previous time step (in the repetitive pattern). Since the FUs are non-pipelined, $\_i_2$ indicates the need for an FU at a particular time step. If we count the number of instructions in each column of

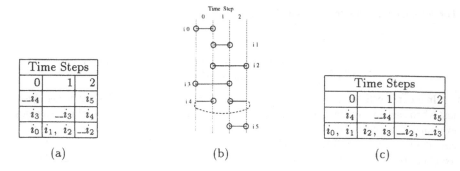

Fig. 2. Repetitive Patterns and Resource Usage

the repetitive pattern we should get the number of FUs required. In fact, this is what Equation 13 captures. Thus for the repetitive pattern shown in Figure 2(a) we expect to require no more than 3 (homogeneous) FUs. Assume that we assign the first FU, FU-1, to instructions i_0 at time 0, to i_1 at time 1 and to i_5 at time 2. We are left with 2 FUs, FU-2 and FU-3, using which we need to execute instructions i_2, i_3 and i_4 each taking 2 time units. Assume FU-2 is assigned to instruction i_3 and FU-3 to instruction i_4. Now we have FU-2 free at time step 2 and FU-3 free at time step 1. Thus instruction i_2 scheduled at time step 1 starts its execution in FU-3, but needs to switch to FU-2 at time step 2. This is impractical and hence the schedule is illegal.

In order to ensure than an instruction initiated in one FU continues to execute in the same FU until completion, we enforce a *fixed FU assignment*. That is, each instruction is assigned to one FU at compile time. In order to maintain optimality, this mapping of instructions to FUs needs to be performed simultaneously with the scheduling of instructions. Thus, the main task here is how to formulate the scheduling and mapping problem in a unified framework.

In [2], we demonstrated how the mapping problem illustrated in Figure 2(b) can be formulated as a graph coloring problem. By considering all pairs of instructions whose resource requirements (as identified from the usage matrix) overlap at any time step in the repetitive pattern, and by assigning different colors (FU's) to overlapping instructions, fixed FU mapping can be accomplished. With the help of the resource usage matrix $\mathcal{U}$ this can be formulated as integer linear constraints in our ILP framework. A schedule obtained by integrating mapping with software pipelining is shown in Figure 2(c). Note that instruction i_0 in time step 0 and i_2 in time steps 1 and 2 can be assigned to FU-1. Similarly instructions i_1 and i_3 can share FU-2 while i_4 and i_5 can be executed in FU-3.

If the target architecture contains heterogeneous (non-pipelined) FUs, then the coloring formulation need only consider all pairs of instructions that execute on the same FU type r. Lastly we require that the color of an instruction i that executes on FU type r be in the range $[1, F_r]$, where F_r is the number of FUs in type r.

4   Performance of ILP Schedules

We have implemented our ILP based software pipelining method on a UNIX workbench. We have experimented on 1008 single-basic-block inner loops extracted from various benchmark programs such as SPEC92 (integer and floating point), linpack, livermore, and the NAS kernels. The DDG's for the loops were obtained by instrumenting a highly optimizing research compiler. We have considered loops with up to 64 nodes in the DDG as in [11]. The DDG's varied widely in size, with a median of 7 nodes, a geometric mean of 8, and an arithmetic mean of 12.

We have assumed the following execution latencies for the various instructions.

Instructions:	Integer	FP Add	Load	Store	Multiply	Divide
Clock cycle(s):	1	3	3	1	4	17

Six different architectural configurations consisting of homogeneous or heterogeneous pipelines with pipelined or non-pipelined execution units were considered.

A1 – 6 pipelined homogeneous FUs

A2 – 4 pipelined homogeneous FUs

A3 – 6 non-pipelined homogeneous FUs

A4 – 4 non-pipelined homogeneous FUs

A5 – pipelined heterogeneous FUs (2 **Integer** FUs and one of **Load/Store, FP Add, Multiply** and **Divide** units.)

A6 – Same as **A5**, but function units are non-pipelined.

The 1008 loops were scheduled for each of these architectures.

4.1 ILP Scheduling Statistics

To solve the ILP's, we used the commercial program, *CPLEX*. In order to deal with the fact that our ILP approach can take a very long time on some loops, we adopted the following approach. *First*, we limited CPLEX to 3 minutes in trying to solve any single ILP, i.e. a maximum of 3 minutes was allowed to find a schedule at a given T. *Second*, initiation intervals from $[T_{min}, T_{min} + 5]$ were tried if necessary. As soon as a schedule was found before $T_{min} + 5$, we did not try any greater values of T.

In a large majority of cases, the ILP approach did find an optimal schedule close to T_{min} as shown in Table 1(a). To be specific, for architectures with homogeneous pipelined FUs (**A1** and **A2**), the ILP approach found an optimal schedule in more than 88% of cases. For non-pipelined homogeneous FUs, an optimal schedule was found in 71% of the cases. Lastly, for architectures with heterogeneous FUs (**A5** and **A6**) it varies from 80% to 85%. For all architectural configurations, in a small fraction of the test cases, the ILP method found a schedule at a T greater than a *possible* T_{min}. That is, in these cases, the obtained schedule is a *possible* optimal schedule. We say a *possible* T_{min} and *possible* optimal schedule here since there is no evidence — CPLEX' 3 minute time limit expired without indicating whether or not a schedule exists for a lower value of T_{min}. Table 1(a) indicates how far the schedule found was from a *possible* optimal schedule.

Next we compare how close the ILP schedules were to the optimal buffer requirement. In deriving minimal buffer, rate-optimal schedules, CPLEX's 3 minutes time limit was sometimes exceeded before finding a buffer optimal schedule using B_{min} buffers. In those cases, we took the best schedule obtained so far. Such schedules may or may not be optimal. There is no evidence, as CPLEX' 3 minute time limit was exceeded. We compare the buffer requirement of this schedule with that of a schedule obtained from the Ning-Gao formulation [14]. We note again that the Ning-Gao formulation obtains minimal buffer, rate optimal schedules using linear programming techniques and does not include resource constraints. Thus the bound obtained from the Ning-Gao formulation is a loose lower bound, and there may or may not exist a resource-constrained schedule with this buffer requirement. However, in order to be conservative, we assume that B_{min} is the Ning-Gao number of buffers in this case.

Table 1(b) shows the quality of ILP schedules in terms of their buffer requirements. Here we consider only those cases where the ILP approach found a schedule (optimal or otherwise). As can be seen from this table, the ILP approach produces schedules that require minimal buffers in 85% to 90% of the cases for architectures involving heterogeneous FUs (pipelined or non-pipelined)

Initiation	Number of Loops					
Interval	**A1**	**A2**	**A3**	**A4**	**A5**	**A6**
$T = T_{min}$	946	882	714	699	854	792
$T = T_{min} + 1$	1	4	37	39	60	9
$T = T_{min} + 2$	0	24	9	10	18	9
$T = T_{min} + 3$	0	4	7	5	13	9
$T = T_{min} + 4$	6	1	1	17	9	9
$T = T_{min} + 5$	0	6	8	5	1	9
No Schedule	55	87	232	233	53	166

(a) Initiation Interval

Buffer	Number of Loops					
Requirements	**A1**	**A2**	**A3**	**A4**	**A5**	**A6**
$B = B_{min}$	916	846	710	696	804	766
$B = B_{min} + 1$	0	1	32	28	33	17
$B = B_{min} + 2$	4	4	21	25	22	8
$B = B_{min} + 3$	1	5	7	8	20	33
$B = B_{min} + 4$	2	21	5	15	20	6
$B = B_{min} + 5$	2	17	1	1	6	6
$B > B_{min} + 5$	28	27	0	2	50	6

(b) Buffer Requirements

Table 1. Schedule Quality

or homogeneous pipelined FUs (6 or 4 FUs). For architectures with homogeneous non-pipelined FUs (**A3** and **A4**) the quality of schedule, in terms of both computation rate $(1/T)$ and buffer requirement is poor compared to all other architectural configurations. This is due to the increased complexity of mapping rather than scheduling. The complexity of mapping instructions to FUs is significantly higher for homogeneous FU than for heterogeneous FUs. This is because, each instruction can potentially be mapped to any of the FUs, and hence the overlap (in execution) of **all pairs of instructions** needs to be considered. On the other hand, in the heterogeneous model, we only need to consider **all pairs of instructions that are executed in the same FU type**.

Finally, how long did it take to get these schedules? We measured the execution time (henceforth referred to as the compilation time) of our scheduling method on a Sun/Sparc20 workstation. The geometric mean, arithmetic mean, and median of the execution time for the 6 architectural configurations are shown in Table 2(a). A histogram of the execution time for various architectural configurations is shown in Figure 2(b). From Table 2(a) we observe that the geometric mean of execution time is less than is less than 2 seconds for architectures with homogeneous pipelined FUs and less than 5 seconds for architectures with heterogeneous FUs. The median of the execution time is less than 3 seconds. Architectural configurations **A3** and **A4** (with homogeneous non-pipelined FUs) required a larger execution time compared to other configurations due to increased complexity in mapping instructions.

It was increasingly difficult for the ILP method to construct schedules for larger DDGs. This raises the question: Is the execution time of the ILP method is a function of the number of nodes of the DDG? To test this, we plotted the execution of the ILP method against the number of nodes in DDGs. Unfortunately, the graphs do no indicate any clear relation between the two. Figure 3 shows the graph for the ILP method for architectures **A1** and **A6**. As can be seen from the Figure, the density (number of points) of the graphs is higher for smaller DDGs.

4.2 Comparison with Inexact Methods

Our extensive experimental evaluation indicates that the ILP approach can obtain the schedule for a large majority of the test cases reasonably quickly. But does the optimality objective and the associated computation cost pay off in terms computation rate or buffer requirement of the derived schedules? It is often argued that existing inexact methods (without any mathematical optimality formulation) do very well and consequently there is no need to find optimal schedules. Our results indicate otherwise.

We consider 3 leading inexact methods for comparative study. They are Huff's Slack Scheduling [11], Wang, Eisenbeis, Jourdan and Su's FRLC [19], and Gasperoni and Schwiegelshohn's

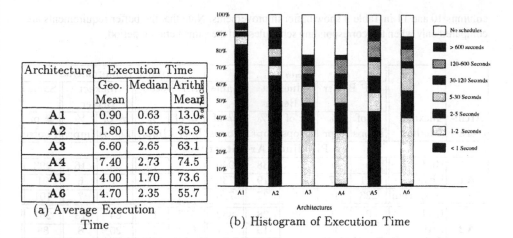

Architecture	Execution Time		
	Geo. Mean	Median	Arith. Mean
A1	0.90	0.63	13.0
A2	1.80	0.65	35.9
A3	6.60	2.65	63.1
A4	7.40	2.73	74.5
A5	4.00	1.70	73.6
A6	4.70	2.35	55.7

(a) Average Execution Time

(b) Histogram of Execution Time

Table 2. Execution Time Statistics for ILP Schedules

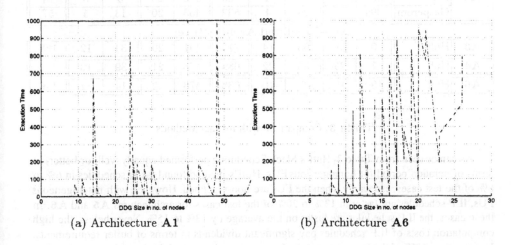

(a) Architecture **A1**

(b) Architecture **A6**

Fig. 3. Execution Time of ILP Method

Modified List Scheduling [8]. In particular, we compare our ILP approach with all 3 scheduling methods for architecture configurations with pipelined FUs. As our implementation of Modified List Scheduling and FRLC does not handle non-pipelined FUs, comparison of the ILP approach is limited to Huff's Slack Scheduling for non-pipelined architectures (**A3**, **A4**, and **A6**).

Table 3 compares the computation rate and buffer requirements of ILP schedules with those of the inexact methods for various architectural configurations. In particular, columns 3 and 4 tabulate the number of loops in which the ILP schedules did better and the mean percentage improvement in T_{min}. Similarly columns 8 and 9 represent the improvements in buffer requirements. Due to the approach followed in obtaining the ILP schedules — restricting the time to solve an ILP problem to 3 minutes and trying a schedule for the next (higher) T value (sub-optimal schedules) — the computation rate and/or the buffer requirements of ILP schedules are greater than the inexact methods in a small fraction of the test cases. Columns 5 and 6 represent, respectively, the number of test loops and the percentage improvement in T_{min} achieved by the inexact methods, while columns 10 and 11 in Table 3 show buffer improvements. Note that the buffer requirements are compared only when the corresponding schedules had the same iteration period.

Archi-tecture	Inexact Method	T_{min}					Buffer Requirements				
		ILP Better		Inexact Better		Same	ILP Better		Inexact Better		Same
		# of Loops	% Impr.	# of Loops	% Impr.	# of Loops	# of Loops	% Impr.	# of Loops	% Impr.	# of Loops
		**Pipelined Architectures**									
	Huff	0	0	7	38	946	618	15	35	16	293
A1	FRLC	211	47	6	19	736	640	24	5	6	91
	Gasperoni	223	48	4	27	726	604	17	13	7	101
	Huff	0	0	39	28	882	557	17	64	13	261
A2	FRLC	18	36	13	19	721	613	25	20	8	88
	Gasperoni	19	35	14	18	699	551	19	39	11	109
	Huff	137	13	35	6	766	210	18	55	11	210
A5	FRLC	250	33	35	4	665	586	29	5	5	74
	Gasperoni	394	26	28	4	533	463	20	13	5	57
		**Non-Pipelined Architectures**									
A3	Huff	0	0	63	14	713	491	20	34	12	188
A4	Huff	1	75	85	22	689	478	21	39	13	172
A6	Huff	190	15	9	10	638	478	22	14	12	146

Table 3. Comparison with Inexact Methods

As can be seen from Table 3, Huff's Slack Scheduling performed equally well (or better) in terms of iteration period for homogeneous FUs. Huff's method found faster schedules in 6% to 8% of the test cases, especially when the FUs are non-pipelined. However, with heterogeneous FUs, ILP schedules are faster in 13% to 20% of the test cases for architectures **A5** and **A6**. In these cases, the ILP schedules are faster on the average by 13% to 15%. Nevertheless, the high computation costs of ILP schedules pay significant dividends in terms of buffer requirements. In more than 45% of the test cases (when the corresponding schedules have the same iteration period), the buffer requirements of ILP schedules are less than those of Huff's Slack Scheduling. The geometric mean of the improvement (in buffer requirements) achieved by the ILP schedules range from 15% to 22%.

Compared to Gasperoni's modified list scheduling and Wang, et al's FRLC method, ILP produced faster schedules in 18% to 40% (or 187 to 394) of the test cases for the various architectural configurations considered. The improvement in T_{min} achieved by the ILP schedules are significant, 26% to 48%. This means that the schedules generated by the ILP method can run 50% faster than those generated by the FRLC method or the modified list scheduling method. The inexact methods score well in a small fraction (3%) of the test cases. Once again the buffer requirements of ILP schedules are better (by 17% to 20%) than its inexact counterparts in 460 to 640 test cases.

The most attractive feature of the inexact methods is their execution time. The execution time for any of the inexact methods was less than 1 second for more than 90% of the loops. The mean execution time was less than 0.25 second for all the architectural configurations. Of the three inexact methods, Huff's Slack Scheduling required slightly more computation time. Unlike the

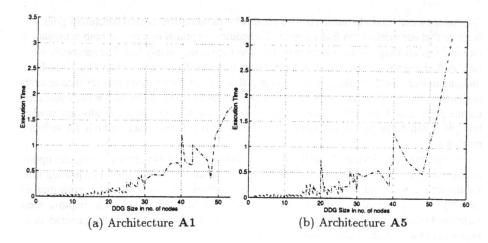

(a) Architecture **A1**   (b) Architecture **A5**

Fig. 4. Execution Time of Huff's Method

ILP method, the execution time of the inexact methods are a function of the number of nodes in the DDG. This is illustrated in Figure 4 for Huff's method.

Our experiments reveal that the ILP-based optimal scheduling method does produce good schedules at the expense of a longer compilation time. With the advent of more efficient ILP solvers, the compilation time is likely to decrease in future. Irrespective of the high compilation costs, our experiments suggest the possible use of the ILP approach for performance critical applications. In the following subsection we present a case for the ILP approach even though the use of such an approach in production compilers is debatable.

4.3   The Case for an ILP based Exact Method

We hope that results presented here section will help the compiler community in the assessment of the ILP based exact method. Despite a reasonably good performance in a large majority of the test cases, the use of ILP based exact methods in production compilers remains questionable. However, in the course of our experiments, we noticed that many loop bodies occur repeatedly in different programs. We developed a tool that analyzes whether two DDGs are similar in the sense that they (1) execute the same operations — or at least execute operations with the same latency that execute on the same function unit, and (2) have the same set of edges and dependence distances between those operations.

We found that out of our 1008 test cases, there are only 415 loops that are unique. One loop body was common to 73 different loops! This being the case, the compiler could use our ILP approach to precompute optimal schedules for the most commonly occurring loops. This scheme could also be tailored to individual users by adding new loops to the database as the compiler encounters them. In fact, the ILP computation could be run in the background, so that the user may get non-optimal code the first time his/her code is compiled, but on later compilations the desired schedule would be in the database.

5   Conclusions

In this paper we presented an experimental evaluation of an ILP based exact method for six different architecture models with varying degrees of instruction-level parallelism and pipelining.

Our experimental results based on 1008 benchmark loops taken from typical benchmark programs indicate that our method can find an optimal schedule — optimal in terms of both computation rate and register usage — for a large majority of test cases reasonably fast. The geometric mean time to find a schedule was less than 5 seconds and the median was less than 3 seconds. Even though our exact method takes longer, it produced schedules with smaller register requirements in more than 50% of the test cases. ILP schedules are faster (better computation rate) than their counterparts in 14% of the test cases (on the average). We believe that the results presented in this paper will be helpful in assessing the tradeoffs of ILP based exact methods for software pipelining.

As mentioned in Section 2, our ILP based method can be used to provide a compiler option to performance critical applications where the user is willing to spend a larger compilation time for the returns achieved during the execution. Our method can also be used for evaluation of existing/newly proposed inexact methods, thus allowing heuristic designers to improve their methods. In the light of these arguments, the experimental results presented in this paper serve as evidence of the usefulness of our exact method.

Acknowledgments

Kemal Ebcioğlu, Mayan Moudgill, and Gabriel M. Silberman were instrumental in completing this paper. We wish to thank Qi Ning, Vincent Van Dongen, and Philip Wong and the anonymous referees for their helpful suggestions. We are thankful to IBM for its technical support, and acknowledge the Natural Science and Engineering Research Council (NSERC) and MICRONET, Network Centres of Excellence, support of this work.

References

1. E.R. Altman. *Optimal Software Pipelining with Function Unit and Register Constraints (In Preparation)*. PhD thesis, McGill University, Montreal, Quebec, 1995.
2. Erik R. Altman, R. Govindarajan, and Guang R. Gao. Scheduling and mapping: Software pipelining in the presence of structural hazards. In *Proc. of the SIGPLAN '95 Conf. on Programming Language Design and Implementation*, La Jolla, Calif., Jun. 18–21, 1995. ACM SIGPLAN.
3. James C. Dehnert and Ross A. Towle. Compiling for Cydra 5. *J. of Supercomputing*, 7:181–227, May 1993.
4. Kemal Ebcioglu and Toshio Nakatani. A new compilation technique for parallelizing loops with unpredictable branches on a VLIW architecture. In David Gelernter, Alexandru Nicolau, and David Padua, editors, *Languages and Compilers for Parallel Computing*, Res. Monographs in Parallel and Distrib. Computing, chapter 12, pages 213–229. Pitman Pub. and the MIT Press, London, England, and Cambridge, Mass., 1990. Selected papers from the Second Work. on Languages and Compilers for Parallel Computing, Urbana, Ill., Aug. 1–3, 1989.
5. Alexandre E. Eichenberger, Edward S. Davidson, and Santosh G. Abraham. Minimum register requirements for a modulo schedule. In *Proc. of the 27th Ann. Intl. Symp. on Microarchitecture*, pages 75–84, San Jose, Calif., Nov. 30–Dec.2, 1994. ACM SIG-MICRO and IEEE-CS TC-MICRO.
6. P. Feautrier. Fine-grain Scheduling under Resource Constraints. In *Seventh Annual Workshop on Languages and Compilers for Parallel Computing*, Ithaca, USA, Aug 1994.
7. M. R. Garey and D. S. Johnson. *Computers and Intractability: A Guide to the Theory of NP-Completeness*. W. H. Freeman and Company, New York, N. Y., 1979.

8. F. Gasperoni and U. Schwiegelshohn. Efficient algorithms for cyclic scheduling. Res. Rep. RC 17068, IBM TJ Watson Res. Center, Yorktown Heights, NY, 1991.

9. R. Govindarajan, Erik R. Altman, and Guang R. Gao. Minimizing register requirements under resource-constrained rate-optimal software pipelining. In *Proc. of the 27th Ann. Intl. Symp. on Microarchitecture*, pages 85–94, San Jose, Calif., Nov. 30–Dec.2, 1994. ACM SIGMICRO and IEEE-CS TC-MICRO.

10. P.Y.T. Hsu. Highly concurrent scalar processing. Technical report, University of Illinois at Urbana-Champagne, Urbana, IL, 1986. Ph.D. Thesis.

11. Richard A. Huff. Lifetime-sensitive modulo scheduling. In *Proc. of the SIGPLAN '93 Conf. on Programming Language Design and Implementation*, pages 258–267, Albuquerque, N. Mex., Jun. 23–25, 1993. ACM SIGPLAN. *SIGPLAN Notices, 28(6)*, Jun. 1993.

12. Monica Lam. Software pipelining: An effective scheduling technique for VLIW machines. In *Proc. of the SIGPLAN '88 Conf. on Programming Language Design and Implementation*, pages 318–328, Atlanta, Georgia, Jun. 22–24, 1988. ACM SIGPLAN. *SIGPLAN Notices, 23(7)*, Jul. 1988.

13. Soo-Mook Moon and Kemal Ebcioğlu. An efficient resource-constrained global scheduling technique for superscalar and VLIW processors. In *Proc. of the 25th Ann. Intl. Symp. on Microarchitecture*, pages 55–71, Portland, Ore., Dec. 1–4, 1992. ACM SIGMICRO and IEEE-CS TC-MICRO.

14. Q. Ning and G. R. Gao. A novel framework of register allocation for software pipelining. In *Conf. Rec. of the Twentieth Ann. ACM SIGPLAN-SIGACT Symp. on Principles of Prog Languages*, pages 29–42, Charleston, S. Carolina, Jan. 10–13, 1993.

15. B. R. Rau and J. A. Fisher. Instruction-level parallel processing: History, overview and perspective. *J. of Supercomputing*, 7:9–50, May 1993.

16. B. R. Rau and C. D. Glaeser. Some scheduling techniques and an easily schedulable horizontal architecture for high performance scientific computing. In *Proc. of the 14th Ann. Microprogramming Work.*, pages 183–198, Chatham, Mass., Oct. 12–15, 1981. ACM SIGMICRO and IEEE-CS TC-MICRO.

17. B. Ramakrishna Rau. Iterative modulo scheduling: An algorithm for software pipelining loops. In *Proc. of the 27th Ann. Intl. Symp. on Microarchitecture*, pages 63–74, San Jose, Cal, Nov 30–Dec 2, 1994. ACM SIGMICRO & IEEE-CS TC-MICRO.

18. Raymond Reiter. Scheduling parallel computations. *J. of the ACM*, 15(4):590–599, Oct. 1968.

19. J. Wang and E. Eisenbeis. A new approach to software pipelining of complicated loops with branches. Res. rep. no., Institut Nat. de Recherche en Informatique et en Automatique (INRIA), Rocquencourt, France, Jan. 1993.

20. Nancy J. Warter, John W. Bockhaus, Grant E. Haab, and Krishna Subramanian. Enhanced modulo scheduling for loops with conditional branches. In *Proc. of the 25th Ann. Intl. Symp. on Microarchitecture*, pages 170–179, Portland, Ore., Dec. 1–4, 1992. ACM SIGMICRO and IEEE-CS TC-MICRO.

Insertion Scheduling: An Alternative to List Scheduling for Modulo Schedulers

Benoît Dupont de Dinechin
bd3@limeil.cea.fr

CEA Limeil-Valenton center, department of Applied Mathematics,
94195 Villeneuve StGeorges cedex, France

Abstract. The list scheduling algorithm is a popular scheduling engine used in most, if not all, industrial instruction schedulers. However this technique has several drawbacks, especially in the context of modulo scheduling. One such problem is the need to restart scheduling from scratch whenever scheduling fails at the current value of the initiation interval. Another problem of list scheduling is that the order in which the instructions are selected for scheduling is constrained to be a topological sort of the scheduling graph, minus the loop-carried dependencies.

We present a new instruction scheduling technique, suitable for block scheduling and modulo scheduling, which addresses these restrictions, while allowing efficient implementations. The technique is fully implemented, as part of a software pipeliner we developed for an experimental version of the Cray T3D™ cft77 Fortran compiler.

Introduction

Instruction scheduling problems are a subcase of deterministic scheduling problems. That is, given a set of *tasks*, whose resource requirements are represented by *reservation tables*, and a *scheduling graph*, whose arcs materialize the precedence constraints between the tasks, build a schedule which satisfies the precedence and the resource constraints, while simultaneously minimizing a cost criterion. In the case of instruction scheduling, the tasks correspond to the instructions. The scheduling graph includes the control dependencies, along with the data dependencies which arise from the reads and the updates of the memory cells and of the processor registers. The cost criterion is the schedule length.

The main heuristic available to schedule acyclic scheduling graphs is the list scheduling algorithm [1], which is used under some form in most if not all instruction schedulers. List scheduling however has several drawbacks in the setting of instruction scheduling, which can be summarized as:

- List scheduling does not work on cyclic scheduling graphs unless it is significantly extended. The required extensions, sketched in [11], are cumbersome enough to motivate extensive research especially in the area of modulo scheduling [13], where cyclic scheduling graphs arise frequently because of the loop-carried dependencies.

- Even after it is extended[1], list scheduling requires that the instructions are issued in a topological sort order of the scheduling graph, minus the loop-carried dependencies. This is necessary to prevent deadlock, because once an instruction is issued, it is never moved at a later step. Being constrained by a topological sort order prevents useful scheduling orders from being used, such as lowest slack first which performs best in the case of recurrent loops.
- List scheduling is greedy, for the ready tasks are scheduled as early as possible. As a result, the use of a value returned from memory is often separated from the corresponding LOAD by the minimum memory latency. This feature makes the performance of the resulting schedule very sensitive to unpredictable delays, such as cache misses. In addition, it is difficult to direct the scheduling process in order to optimize a second criterion beyond schedule length, such as cumulative register lifetimes, or maximum register pressure.

Our insertion scheduling technique allows the instructions to be issued in any convenient order, and at any date which is within their current margins. Unlike techniques by Huff [10] or by Rau [13], this capability is achieved without resorting to backtracking. The other advantage of our technique, compared to the various extensions of list scheduling, is that we do not need to restart the modulo scheduling process from scratch, whenever scheduling fails at a given value of the initiation interval. In this respect our technique is "faster" than list scheduling in the setting of modulo scheduling. All that is currently required for the technique to apply is the satisfaction of the following conditions:

- The delays associated with each precedence constraint are non-negative.
- The scheduling graph without its loop-carried dependencies is cycle-free.
- The resource constraints of each instruction can be represented as *regular reservation tables*, or equivalently as *reservation vectors* [5].

The restrictions on the scheduling graph are not an issue, since they must already hold for list scheduling to succeed. Our restriction on the resource constraints is assumed in [7], and is implicitly carried by the gcc processor description [14].

We use *regular reservation tables* for approximating the resource requirements of each task because it makes the correctness proofs of section 2.2 simpler. A regular reservation table is a reservation table where the ones in each row start in the leftmost column, and are all adjacent. Of course these reservation tables may also have rows filled with zeroes. The regular reservation tables are in turn compactly represented as *reservation vectors*. In figure 1, we illustrate the relationships between a reservation table, a regular reservation table, and a reservation vector, for the conditional stores of the DEC Alpha 21064.

The main restriction of regular reservation tables is not that the ones in every row must be left-justified, for collisions between two reservation tables do not change if a given row is justified the same amount in both tables. Rather, it has

---

[1] Plain list schedulers maintain the left margins, because the "ready set" is recomputed every time an instruction is issued. Extended list schedulers maintain the left margins *and* the right margins, in order to handle cycles in the scheduling graph.

	0	1	2	3	4
bus1					
bus2	1				
abox		1			
cond			1	1	1
bbox					
ebox					
imul					
iwrt					
fbox					
fdiv					
fwrt					

	0	1	2
bus1			
bus2	1		
abox	1		
cond	1	1	1
bbox			
ebox			
imul			
iwrt			
fbox			
fdiv			
fwrt			

bus1	0
bus2	1
abox	1
cond	3
bbox	0
ebox	0
imul	0
iwrt	0
fbox	0
fdiv	0
fwrt	0

Fig. 1. A reservation table, a regular reservation table, and a reservation vector.

to do with the fact that the ones must be adjacent in each row. However these restrictions do not appear to be a problem in practice. For instance the only instructions of the 21064 where regular reservation tables are slightly inaccurate are the integer multiplications, and the floating-point divisions.

The paper is organized as follows: Section 1 provides background about block scheduling and modulo scheduling. Section 2 demonstrates insertion scheduling on an example, then exposes the theoretical results upon which the technique is based. Section 3 reports the results we currently achieve on the Livermore loops, for less and less constrained scheduling graphs.

1 Instruction Scheduling

1.1 Block Scheduling

We start by introducing some terminology. Formally, a non-preemptive deterministic scheduling problem is defined by $(\mathcal{S}, \mathcal{C}, r, \mathcal{F})$ where:

- $\mathcal{S} \stackrel{\text{def}}{=} \{\sigma_i\}_{0 \leq i \leq N}$ is a set of $N + 1$ tasks, including a dummy "start" task σ_0 which is always scheduled at date zero;
- $\mathcal{C} \stackrel{\text{def}}{=} \{t_{j_k} - t_{i_k} \geq \alpha_k\}_{1 \leq k \leq M}$, called the *precedence constraints*, is a set of M inequalities involving the start times $\{t_i\}_{0 \leq i \leq N}$ of the tasks;
- $r \stackrel{\text{def}}{=} (r_1, r_2, \ldots, r_p)^T$ is a vector describing the total availabilities of the *renewable resources*;
- $\mathcal{F} \stackrel{\text{def}}{=} \{f^1, f^2, \ldots, f^N\}$ are N *reservation functions* such that $\forall t < 0 : f^i(t) = 0$, $\forall t \geq 0 : f^i(t) \geq 0$, describing for each task its use of the renewable resources.

Each reservation function f^i takes as input the time elapsed from the start of task σ_i, and returns a vector describing its use of resources at that time. Any solution of the scheduling problem satisfies the precedence constraints, and the *resource constraints*:

$$\forall t : \sum_{i=1}^{N} f^i(t - t_i) \leq r$$

We call *central problem* a scheduling problem with no resource constraints. A central problem associated to a given deterministic scheduling problem contains all the precedence constraints of that problem, and eventually some other constraints of the form $\{t_i = S_i\}$. A *partial central schedule* of a central problem P is a map from n tasks to schedule dates $\{\sigma_{i_j} \mapsto S_{i_j}\}_{1 \leq j \leq n}$, with $1 \leq n \leq N$, such that $P \wedge \{t_{i_1} = S_{i_1}\} \ldots \wedge \{t_{i_n} = S_{i_n}\}$ is not empty. We shall denote $\{S_{i_j}\}_{1 \leq j \leq n}$ such a map. A *partial schedule*, also denoted $\{S_{i_j}\}_{1 \leq j \leq n}$, is a partial central schedule of the central problem associated with the deterministic scheduling problem, such that the resource constraints are also satisfied for $\{\sigma_{i_j}\}_{1 \leq j \leq n}$.

The *margins* are another useful notion we shall borrow from operations research. Given a feasible central problem P, the *left margin* t_i^- of a task σ_i is the smallest positive value of τ such that the central problem $P \wedge \{t_i \leq \tau\}$ is feasible. Likewise, assuming that the schedule length is constrained by some kind of upper bound L (which may be equal to $+\infty$), the *right margin* t_i^+ of task σ_i is the largest positive value of τ such that the central problem $P \wedge \{t_i \geq \tau\} \wedge_{1 \leq j \leq N} \{t_j \leq L\}$ is feasible. Intuitively, margins indicate that there is no central schedule $\{S_i\}_{1 \leq i \leq N}$ of length below L such that $S_i < t_i^-$, or $S_i > t_i^+$. Following Huff [10], we also define the *slack* of a task σ_i as $t_i^+ - t_i^-$.

An alternate representation of the precedence constraints $\mathcal{C}$ of a deterministic scheduling problem is a valued directed graph $\mathcal{G} \stackrel{\text{def}}{=} [\mathcal{S}, \mathcal{E}] : t_{j_k} - t_{i_k} \geq \alpha_k \in \mathcal{C} \Leftrightarrow (\sigma_{i_k}, \sigma_{j_k}, \alpha_k) \in \mathcal{E}$, called the *scheduling graph*. Since equality constraints of the form $\{t_i = S_i\}$ can be represented by the pair of arcs $((\sigma_0, \sigma_i, S_i), (\sigma_i, \sigma_0, -S_i))$, a central problem is equivalent for all practical purposes to a scheduling graph. Margins are easily computed from the scheduling graph by applying a variation of the Bellman shortest path algorithm. This algorithm has an $O(MN)$ running time, where N is the number of nodes and M the number of arcs in the graph.

Block scheduling, also called local code compaction, involves restricted versions of the non-preemptive deterministic scheduling problems, where each instruction is associated to a task. The restrictions are:

- The time is measured in processor cycles and takes integral values.
- The values α_k are non-negative integers.
- The total resource availabilities vector r is 1, so it is not explicated.

A popular representation of the reservation functions f^i are the so-called *reservation tables* $[f^i(j)]$, where $f^i(j)$ is the boolean vector describing the use of the resources j cycles after the instruction σ_i has been issued.

However, block scheduling involves more than taking advantage of these restrictions. In particular, on VLIW or superscalar processors outfitted with several ALUs, floating-point operators, and memory ports, an instruction can be associated to one of several reservation tables upon issue. In the following, a task shall refer to an instruction which has been assigned a reservation table. Issuing an instruction means assigning a reservation table to it, and scheduling the corresponding task. Scheduling a task in turn means including it in a partial schedule. A valid *instruction schedule*, denoted $\{S_i\}_{1 \leq i \leq N}$, is a partial schedule such that every instruction is associated to a task.

```
                              σ₀ ≡ enterblk $LL00008
                              σ₁ ≡ ldt f(5), i(32)
  do i = 1, n                 σ₂ ≡ mult/d F(3), f(5), f(6)
      sam = sam + x(i)*y      σ₃ ≡ addt/d F(4), f(6), F(4)
  end do                      σ₄ ≡ addq i(32), +8, i(32)
                              σ₅ ≡ subq i(33), +1, i(33)
                              σ₆ ≡ ble i(33), $LL00009
                              σ₇ ≡ br izero, $LL00008
```

Fig. 2. The sample source code and its translation.

1.2 Modulo Scheduling

Modulo scheduling is an advanced cyclic scheduling technique formulated for the purpose of constructing software pipelines [13]. The fundamental idea of modulo scheduling is that the *local schedule*[2] [12] of the software pipeline can be created by solving a simple extension of the block scheduling problem, called the *modulo scheduling problem*. More precisely, let us denote as T the software pipeline initiation interval. This value, unknown when scheduling starts, represents the number of machine cycles which separate the initiation of two successive loop iterations. Obviously, the lower T, the better the schedule.

The scheduling graph of the modulo scheduling problem is derived from the scheduling graph of the corresponding block scheduling problem, by including the loop-carried dependencies. Such extra arcs take the form $(\sigma_{i_k}, \sigma_{j_k}, \alpha_k - \beta_k T)$, where $\alpha_k \geq 0$, and where $\beta_k > 0$, denoted Ω in [12], is the collision distance of the loop-carried dependency. Likewise, the reservation function $f^i(t)$ of each task σ_i is replaced by the corresponding *modulo reservation functions* $\sum_{k=0}^{+\infty} f^i(t - t_i - kT)$, so the resource constraints now become the *modulo resource constraints*:

$$\forall t : \sum_{i=1}^{N} \sum_{k=0}^{+\infty} f^i(t - t_i - kT) \leq r$$

It is apparent that modulo scheduling is more difficult to implement in practice than block scheduling, for the precedence constraints, as well as the resource constraints, now involve the unknown parameter T. Moreover:

- Because of the loop-carried dependencies, the scheduling graph may contain cycles, which prevent plain list scheduling to be used.
- The modulo reservation functions have an infinite extent, so scheduling may fail for a given value of T even if there are no cycles in the scheduling graph.

Throughout the paper, we shall illustrate our techniques by applying them to the code displayed in figure 2. On the left part, we have the source program, while the translation in pseudo DEC Alpha assembly code by the Cray cft77 MPP compiler appears on the right. The scheduling graph in the case of modulo scheduling is displayed in figure 3. This scheduling graph contains many fake dependencies, related to the lack of accurate information at the back-end level. For instance, arcs $(\sigma_4, \sigma_6, 0)$ and $(\sigma_6, \sigma_4, -T)$ are def-use and use-def of the

---

[2] The schedule of any particular loop body execution, required to build the pipeline.

Source	Sink	Value	Type		Source	Sink	Value	Type
$\sigma_1 \equiv$ ldt	$\sigma_2 \equiv$ mult/d	3	def_use f(5)		$\sigma_4 \equiv$ addq	$\sigma_4 \equiv$ addq	1-T	def_use i(32)
$\sigma_1 \equiv$ ldt	$\sigma_4 \equiv$ addq	0	use_def i(32)		$\sigma_4 \equiv$ addq	$\sigma_6 \equiv$ ble	0	def_use i(32)
$\sigma_1 \equiv$ ldt	$\sigma_7 \equiv$ br	0	use_def pc		$\sigma_4 \equiv$ addq	$\sigma_7 \equiv$ br	0	use_def pc
$\sigma_2 \equiv$ mult/d	$\sigma_1 \equiv$ ldt	-T	use_def f(5)		$\sigma_5 \equiv$ subq	$\sigma_5 \equiv$ subq	1-T	def_use i(33)
$\sigma_2 \equiv$ mult/d	$\sigma_3 \equiv$ addt/d	6	def_use f(6)		$\sigma_5 \equiv$ subq	$\sigma_6 \equiv$ ble	1	def_use i(33)
$\sigma_2 \equiv$ mult/d	$\sigma_7 \equiv$ br	0	use_def pc		$\sigma_5 \equiv$ subq	$\sigma_7 \equiv$ br	0	use_def pc
$\sigma_3 \equiv$ addt/d	$\sigma_2 \equiv$ mult/d	-T	use_def f(6)		$\sigma_6 \equiv$ ble	$\sigma_3 \equiv$ addt/d	-T	use_def F(4)
$\sigma_3 \equiv$ addt/d	$\sigma_3 \equiv$ addt/d	6-T	def_use F(4)		$\sigma_6 \equiv$ ble	$\sigma_4 \equiv$ addq	-T	use_def i(32)
$\sigma_3 \equiv$ addt/d	$\sigma_6 \equiv$ ble	0	def_use F(4)		$\sigma_6 \equiv$ ble	$\sigma_5 \equiv$ subq	-T	use_def i(33)
$\sigma_3 \equiv$ addt/d	$\sigma_7 \equiv$ br	0	use_def pc		$\sigma_6 \equiv$ ble	$\sigma_7 \equiv$ br	0	def_use pc
$\sigma_4 \equiv$ addq	$\sigma_1 \equiv$ ldt	2-T	def_use i(32)		$\sigma_7 \equiv$ br	$\sigma_6 \equiv$ ble	-T	def_use pc

Fig. 3. The arcs of the scheduling graph for the sample loop.

register i_{32} which would be removed if the back-end could tell that i_{32} is dead upon loop exit. We keep these fake dependencies here because they offer the opportunity to expose interesting aspects of our scheduling technique.

Under the traditional approach to modulo scheduling, scheduling is not performed parametrically with T. Rather, lower bounds on the admissible T are computed, and their maximum T_{glb} is used as the first value of T. The lower bounds usually considered are the bound set by resource usage, denoted here $T_{resource}$, and the bound $T_{recurrence}$ set on the initiation interval by the recurrence cycles. Then, the construction of a valid local schedule is attempted for increasing values of T, until success is achieved.

Failure happens whenever there is no date, within the margins of the instruction currently selected for issuing, such that scheduling a corresponding task at this date would not trigger resource conflicts with the already issued instructions.

2 Insertion Scheduling

In the following, we assume that $\{S_{i_j}\}_{1 \leq j \leq n}$, $\{S'_{i_j}\}_{1 \leq j \leq n}$ are two maps from tasks $\{\sigma_{i_j}\}_{1 \leq j \leq n}$ to schedule dates, and define $\{\phi_{i_j}, \tau_{i_j}, \phi'_{i_j}, \tau'_{i_j}, \delta_{i_j}\}_{1 \leq j \leq n}$ as:

$$\forall j \in [1, n] : \begin{cases} S_{i_j} = \phi_{i_j}T + \tau_{i_j} \wedge 0 \leq \tau_{i_j} < T \\ S'_{i_j} = \phi'_{i_j}T' + \tau'_{i_j} \wedge 0 \leq \tau'_{i_j} < T' \\ \delta_{i_j} = \tau'_{i_j} - \tau_{i_j} \end{cases}$$

2.1 An Intuitive Presentation

Let us denote the *frame* and the *offset* of an instruction σ_{i_j}, scheduled at S_{i_j} in a partial (local) schedule $\{S_{i_j}\}_{1 \leq j \leq n}$ for initiation interval T, the respective integers ϕ_{i_j} and τ_{i_j}. By definition of a partial schedule, $n - 1 < N$ instructions $\{\sigma_{i_j}\}_{1 \leq j < n}$ are already issued. Trying to issue the instruction σ_{i_n} at date S_{i_n}, with S_{i_n} within the current margins of σ_{i_n}, yields the following alternative:

- Either there are no resource conflicts between σ_{i_n} issued at S_{i_n}, and the $n - 1$ already issued instruction. Then $\{S_{i_j}\}_{1 \leq j \leq n}$ is a new partial schedule at initiation interval T.

– Or there are resource conflicts between σ_{i_n} issued at S_{i_n}, and some of the already issued instruction. We take as the new partial schedule $\{S'_{i_j}\}_{1 \le j \le n}$, such as the frames are left unchanged, while the offsets are increased by $\delta_{i_j} \stackrel{\text{def}}{=} \tau'_{i_j} - \tau_{i_j}, 0 \le \delta_{i_j} \le T' - T$.

The first case is easily folded in the second by taking $\delta_{i_j} = 0$ and $T' = T$.

In a traditional list scheduling based modulo scheduler, if there is no S_{i_n} within the current margins of σ_{i_n} which does not trigger resource conflicts, then scheduling has failed at T and must be restarted from scratch at $T' > T$. In our case, such failure never happens, because we are free to choose for S_{i_n} any value within the margins of σ_{i_n}, whether conflicting or not. Indeed the results of the paper show that there is a simple and systematic way of computing the δ_{i_j}, and the new initiation interval T', every time a new instruction σ_{i_n} is issued.

To be more specific, we basically proceed as follows. Starting from $T = T_{glb}$, we build the local schedule by issuing the instructions one by one, in any convenient order. At step n, in order to issue a particular instruction σ_{i_n}, we choose an issue date within its current margins. From this issue date, two numbers Δ^- and Δ^+ are computed. How we actually obtain the values of Δ^- and Δ^+ is explained in §2.3. Then we compute the $\{\delta_{i_j}\}_{1 \le j \le n}$ and $T' \stackrel{\text{def}}{=} T + \Delta$ as follows:

$$\begin{cases} \delta_{i_n} \stackrel{\text{def}}{=} \Delta^- \\ \forall j \in [1, n-1]: \text{ if } \sigma_{i_j} \in I^+ \text{ then } \delta_{i_j} \stackrel{\text{def}}{=} \Delta^- + \Delta^+ \text{ else } \delta_{i_j} \stackrel{\text{def}}{=} 0 \\ \Delta \stackrel{\text{def}}{=} \Delta^- + \Delta^+ \end{cases}$$

Here I^-, I^+ are sets defined by $I^- \cup I^+ = \{\sigma_{i_1}, \ldots, \sigma_{i_{n-1}}\}, I^- \cap I^+ = \emptyset$, and $\sigma_{i_j} \in I^+$ iff $\sigma_{i_n} \prec \sigma_{i_j}$. The partial order $\prec$ on $\{\sigma_{i_j}\}_{1 \le j \le n}$ is itself defined by:

$$\forall j, k \in [1, n], j \ne k : \sigma_{i_j} \prec \sigma_{i_k} \iff \begin{vmatrix} \tau_{i_j} < \tau_{i_k} \\ \tau_{i_j} = \tau_{i_k} \wedge \phi_{i_j} > \phi_{i_k} \\ \tau_{i_j} = \tau_{i_k} \wedge \phi_{i_j} = \phi_{i_k} \wedge \sigma_{i_j} \rightsquigarrow \sigma_{i_k} \end{vmatrix}$$

In the above formula, $\sigma_{i_j} \rightsquigarrow \sigma_{i_k}$ denotes the fact that σ_{i_j} precedes σ_{i_k} in the transitive closure of the loop-independent precedence constraints of the scheduling graph. This relation is safely approximated by taking the lexical order of the instructions in the program text.

Application of the insertion scheduling process to our example is best illustrated by displaying the *modulo issue table* after each issuing step. The issue table is the global reservation table where the individual reservation tables of the already issued instruction are ORed in, at the corresponding issue dates. The modulo issue table displays the issue table modulo the current initiation interval T, and is the only representation needed in modulo scheduling to manage the resource constraints. On our example, the initial value of T is $T_{recurrence} = 6$, because of the critical cycle $((\sigma_2, \sigma_3), (\sigma_3, \sigma_2))$.

Instruction σ_1 is selected first for issuing, and is issued at date $S_1 = 0$. This results in the modulo issue table displayed top, far left, in figure 4. Likewise, σ_2 is issued without resource conflicts at $S_2 = 3$ (top, center left in figure 4). Then

bus1	0	1	2	3	4	5
bus1	σ_1					
bus2						
abox	σ_1					
cond	σ_1					
bbox						
ebox						
imul						
iwrt						
fbox						
fdiv						
fwrt						

	0	1	2	3	4	5
bus1	σ_1					
bus2					σ_2	
abox	σ_1					
cond	σ_1					
bbox						
ebox						
imul						
iwrt						
fbox				σ_2		
fdiv						
fwrt				σ_2		

	0	1	2	3	4	5	6
bus1	σ_1						
bus2						σ_3 σ_2	
abox	σ_1						
cond	σ_1						
bbox							
ebox							
imul							
iwrt							
fbox						σ_3 σ_2	
fdiv							
fwrt						σ_3 σ_2	

	0	1	2	3	4	5	6
bus1	σ_1						
bus2						σ_3 σ_2 σ_6	
abox	σ_1						
cond	σ_1						
bbox							σ_6
ebox							σ_6
imul							
iwrt							
fbox						σ_3 σ_2	
fdiv							
fwrt						σ_3 σ_2	

	0	1	2	3	4	5	6	7
bus1	σ_1							σ_4
bus2					σ_3 σ_2 σ_6			
abox	σ_1							
cond	σ_1							
bbox							σ_6	
ebox							σ_6 σ_4	
imul								
iwrt								σ_4
fbox				σ_3 σ_2				
fdiv								
fwrt				σ_3 σ_2				

	0	1	2	3	4	5	6	7
bus1	σ_1							σ_4
bus2					σ_3 σ_2 σ_6 σ_7			
abox	σ_1							σ_7
cond	σ_1							
bbox							σ_6 σ_7	
ebox							σ_6 σ_4	
imul								
iwrt								σ_4
fbox				σ_3 σ_2				
fdiv								
fwrt				σ_3 σ_2				

	0	1	2	3	4	5	6	7
bus1	σ_1					σ_5		σ_4
bus2					σ_3 σ_2 σ_6 σ_7			
abox	σ_1							σ_7
cond	σ_1							
bbox							σ_6 σ_7	
ebox						σ_5	σ_6 σ_4	
imul								
iwrt						σ_5		σ_4
fbox				σ_3 σ_2				
fdiv								
fwrt				σ_3 σ_2				

Fig. 4. Construction of the modulo issue table

σ_3 is selected for issuing. The only date currently within its margins is $S_3 = 9$, which yields $\phi_3 = 1, \tau_3 = 3$. However, scheduling σ_3 at $S_3 = 9$ would result in a resource conflict with σ_2, since $\tau_2 = 3$ and because both instructions happen to use the same resources. Here $\sigma_3 \prec \sigma_2$, for $\tau_3 = \tau_2 \wedge \phi_3 > \phi_2$, hence $I^- = \{\sigma_1\}$, and $I^+ = \{\sigma_2\}$. The values are $\Delta^- = 0, \Delta^+ = 1$, hence $T' = T + \Delta^- + \Delta^+ = 7$, $\delta_1 = \delta_3 = 0$, and $\delta_2 = 1$. This yields the modulo issue table displayed top, center right in figure 4. After that σ_6 is selected and issued at $S_6 = 12 \Rightarrow \phi_6 = 1 \wedge \tau_6 = 5$, without resource conflicts (top, far right in figure 4).

Then σ_4 is selected for issuing at $S_4 = 5 \Rightarrow \phi_4 = 0 \wedge \tau_4 = 5$. Here we have a perfect illustration that we are not constrained to issue the instructions in a topological sort order of the scheduling graph, for the latter includes the arc $(\sigma_4, \sigma_6, 0)$ (figure 3), while σ_6 is already issued. Returning to σ_4, it conflicts with σ_6. The condition $\tau_4 = \tau_6 \wedge \phi_4 < \phi_6$ implies that $\sigma_6 \in I^- = \{\sigma_1, \sigma_2, \sigma_3, \sigma_6\}$, while $I^+ = \emptyset$. We have $\Delta^- = 1, \Delta^+ = 0$, and this yields $T' = 8, \delta_1 = \delta_2 = \delta_3 = \delta_6 = 0, \delta_4 = 1$. The resulting modulo issue table is displayed bottom, left in figure 4. After that, σ_7 and σ_5 are issued without resource conflicts, to yield respectively the bottom, center and bottom, right modulo issue tables in figure 4.

The resulting software pipeline appears in figure 5. This is a **while**-type software pipeline [2] (no epilog), which speculatively executes $\sigma_1', \sigma_2', \sigma_4'$ of the next iteration. Although a **FOR**-type software pipeline does not ask for a speculative execution support, it requires to know which register variable is the loop counter, an information not easily available in a back-end. Two iterations are overlapped, with a local schedule length L of 15 cycles, and an initiation interval T of 8 cy-

```
           $PROLOG
  σ₁       [0]  ldt f(5), i(32)
           [1]
           [2]
           [3]
  σ₂       [4]  mult/d F(3), f(5), f(6)
           [5]
  σ₄       [6]  addq i(32), +8, i(32)
           $LL00008
           [7]
  σ₁′      [8]  ldt f(5), i(32)
           [9]
           [10]
  σ₃       [11] addt/d F(4), f(6), F(4)
  σ₂′, σ₅  [12] mult/d F(3), f(5), f(6)  subq i(33), +1, i(33)
  σ₆       [13] ble i(33), $LL00009
  σ₄′, σ₇  [14] addq i(32), +8, i(32)    br izero, $LL00008
           $LL00009
```

Fig. 5. The resulting while software pipeline.

cles. A block scheduler would schedule the loop body in 12 cycles, so pipelining significantly improves the performance of our sample loop, even though we did not remove the fake dependencies from the scheduling graph.

2.2 The Main Results

The following result states precisely the conditions that must be met by the δ_{i_j} in order to preserve the precedence constraints of the scheduling graph.

Theorem 1. *Let* $\{S_{i_j}\}_{1 \leq j \leq n}$ *be a partial central schedule of a central problem* P *at initiation interval* T. *Let* $\{S'_{i_j}\}_{1 \leq j \leq n}$ *be* n *integers such that:*

$$\forall j, k \in [1, n]: \begin{cases} \phi_{i_j} = \phi'_{i_j} \\ 0 \leq \delta_{i_j} \leq \Delta \\ \tau_{i_j} < \tau_{i_k} \implies \delta_{i_j} \leq \delta_{i_k} \\ \tau_{i_j} = \tau_{i_k} \wedge \phi_{i_j} > \phi_{i_k} \implies \delta_{i_j} \leq \delta_{i_k} \\ \tau_{i_j} = \tau_{i_k} \wedge \phi_{i_j} = \phi_{i_k} \wedge \sigma_{i_j} \rightsquigarrow \sigma_{i_k} \implies \delta_{i_j} \leq \delta_{i_k} \end{cases}$$

Then $\{S'_{i_j}\}_{1 \leq j \leq n}$ *is a partial central schedule of* P *at initiation interval* $T' \stackrel{def}{=} T + \Delta$.

Proof: Let $(\sigma_i, \sigma_j, \alpha_k - \beta_k T)$ be a precedence constraint of P. From the definition of a precedence constraint, $S_j - S_i \geq \alpha_k - \beta_k T \Leftrightarrow \phi_j T + \tau_j - \phi_i T - \tau_i \geq \alpha_k - \beta_k T$. Given the hypothesis, our aim is to show that $\phi_j T' + \tau'_j - \phi_i T' - \tau'_i \geq \alpha_k - \beta_k T'$.

Dividing the former inequality by T and taking the floor yields $\phi_j - \phi_i + \lfloor \frac{\tau_j - \tau_i}{T} \rfloor \geq -\beta_k$, since all α_k values are non-negative. We have $0 \leq \tau_i < T$, $0 \leq \tau_j < T$, hence $0 \leq |\tau_j - \tau_i| < T$ and the value of $\lfloor \frac{\tau_j - \tau_i}{T} \rfloor$ is -1 or 0. Therefore $\phi_j - \phi_i \geq -\beta_k$.

$\phi_j - \phi_i = -\beta_k$: We only need to show that $\tau'_j - \tau'_i \geq \alpha_k$. Since $\alpha_k \geq 0$, we have $\tau_j \geq \tau_i$. Several subcases need to be distinguished:

$\tau_i < \tau_j$: We have $\delta_j \geq \delta_i \Leftrightarrow \tau'_j - \tau_j \geq \tau'_i - \tau_i \Leftrightarrow \tau'_j - \tau'_i \geq \tau_j - \tau_i \geq \alpha_k$.

$\tau_i = \tau_j \wedge \phi_i \neq \phi_j$: Either $\phi_i > \phi_j$, or $\phi_i < \phi_j$. The latter is impossible, for $\beta_k = \phi_i - \phi_j$, and since all β_k are non-negative. From the hypothesis, $\tau_i = \tau_j \wedge \phi_i > \phi_j$ yields $\delta_j \geq \delta_i$, so the conclusion is the same as above.

$\tau_i = \tau_j \wedge \phi_i = \phi_j$: Since $\beta_k = \phi_i - \phi_j = 0$, there is no precedence constraint unless $\sigma_i \rightsquigarrow \sigma_j$. In this case taking $\delta_j \geq \delta_i$, works like in the cases above.

$\phi_j - \phi_i > -\beta_k$: Let us show that $(\phi_j - \phi_i + \beta_k)T' + \tau'_j - \tau'_i - \alpha_k \geq 0$. We have $\phi_j - \phi_i + \beta_k \geq 1$, so $(\phi_j - \phi_i + \beta_k)T' \geq (\phi_j - \phi_i + \beta_k)T + \Delta$. By hypothesis we also have $\tau_i \leq \tau'_i \leq \tau_i + \Delta$, and $\tau_j \leq \tau'_j \leq \tau_j + \Delta$, so $\tau'_j - \tau'_i \geq \tau_j - \tau_i - \Delta$. Hence $(\phi_j - \phi_i + \beta_k)T' + \tau'_j - \tau'_i - \alpha_k \geq (\phi_j - \phi_i + \beta_k)T + \Delta + \tau_j - \tau_i - \Delta - \alpha_k = (\phi_j - \phi_i + \beta_k)T + \tau_j - \tau_i - \alpha_k \geq 0$. $\qquad \square$

The conditions involving the ϕ_{i_j} and $\rightsquigarrow$ may seem awkward, but are in fact mandatory for the theorem to be useful in an instruction scheduler. Consider for instance the more obvious condition $\tau_{i_j} \leq \tau_{i_k} \Rightarrow \tau'_{i_j} - \tau_{i_j} \leq \tau'_{i_k} - \tau_{i_k}$ as a replacement for the three last conditions of theorem 1. Then $\tau_{i_j} = \tau_{i_k}$ implies $\tau'_{i_j} = \tau'_{i_k}$, by exchanging i_j and i_k. Such a constraint makes scheduling impossible if σ_{i_j} and σ_{i_k} happen to use the same resource.

A result similar to theorem 1 holds for the modulo resource constraints of a partial schedule, assuming reservation vectors $\{\rho_i\}_{1 \leq i \leq N}$ can be used. By definition, the reservation vector ρ^i associated to task σ_i is such that ρ_l^i equals the number of ones in the l-th row of the (regular) reservation table of σ_i.

Theorem 2. Let $\{S_{i_k}\}_{1 \leq k \leq n}$ be a partial schedule satisfying the modulo resource constraints at T, assuming reservation vectors. Let $\{S'_{i_k}\}_{1 \leq k \leq n}$ be such that:

$$\forall j, k \in [1, n] : \begin{cases} \phi_{i_j} = \phi'_{i_j} \\ 0 \leq \delta_{i_j} \leq \Delta \\ \tau_{i_j} < \tau_{i_k} \Longrightarrow \delta_{i_j} \leq \delta_{i_k} \end{cases}$$

Then $\{S'_{i_k}\}_{1 \leq k \leq n}$ taken as a partial schedule satisfies the modulo resource constraints at initiation interval $T' \stackrel{def}{=} T + \Delta$.

Proof: Thanks to the reservation vectors, the satisfaction of the modulo resource constraints at T by the partial schedule $\{S_{i_k}\}_{1 \leq k \leq n}$ is equivalent to [5]:

$$\forall i, j \in \{i_k\}_{1 \leq k \leq n}, i \neq j, \forall l : t_j - t_i \geq \rho_l^i - (\lfloor \frac{t_i - t_j}{T} \rfloor + 1)T \wedge t_i - t_j \geq \rho_l^j + \lfloor \frac{t_i - t_j}{T} \rfloor T$$

These constraints look exactly like precedence constraints of the scheduling graph, save the fact that the β values are now of arbitrary sign. Since the sign of the β values is only used in the demonstration of theorem 1 for the cases where $\tau_i = \tau_j$, which need not be considered here because they imply no resource collisions between σ_i and σ_j, we deduce from the demonstration of theorem 1 that the modulo resource constraints at T' are satisfied by $\{S'_{i_k}\}_{1 \leq k \leq n}$ taken as a partial schedule. $\qquad \square$

2.3 A Simple Implementation

To compute the values Δ^- and Δ^+, we need to define an operation $\odot$ between two reservation vectors, and the function *issuedelay*, as:

$$\begin{cases} \rho^i \odot \rho^j \overset{\text{def}}{=} \lambda\rho^i.\lambda\rho^j.\max(\text{if } \rho^i_l \neq 0 \wedge \rho^j_l \neq 0 \text{ then } \rho^i_l \text{ else } 0) \\ \textit{issuedelay}(\sigma_i, \sigma_j, d) \overset{\text{def}}{=} \lambda\sigma_i.\lambda\sigma_j.\lambda d.\max((\rho^i \odot \rho^j) - d, 0) \end{cases}$$

It is apparent that the function *issuedelay* computes the minimum value δ such that issuing σ_i at date t, and issuing σ_j at date $d + \delta$, does not trigger resource conflicts between σ_i and σ_j. In fact *issuedelay* emulates the behavior of a scoreboard in the target processor. Now, computing Δ^- and Δ^+ is a simple matter given the following formulas:

$$\begin{cases} \Delta^- \overset{\text{def}}{=} \max(\max_{\sigma_j \in I^-} \textit{issuedelay}(\sigma_j, \sigma_{i_n}, \tau_{i_n} - \tau_j), \max_{\sigma_j \in I^+} \textit{issuedelay}(\sigma_j, \sigma_{i_n}, \tau_{i_n} - \tau_j + T)) \\ \Delta^+ \overset{\text{def}}{=} \max(\max_{\sigma_j \in I^-} \textit{issuedelay}(\sigma_{i_n}, \sigma_j, \tau_j + T - \tau_{i_n}), \max_{\sigma_j \in I^+} \textit{issuedelay}(\sigma_{i_n}, \sigma_j, \tau_j - \tau_{i_n})) \end{cases}$$

That is, we take for Δ^- the minimum value such that σ_{i_n} scheduled at $\tau_{i_n} + \Delta^-$ would not conflict on a resource basis with the tasks σ_j in I^-, if they were scheduled at the respective dates τ_j, nor with the tasks σ_j in I^+, if they were scheduled at the respective dates $\tau_j - T$. Likewise, Δ^+ is the minimum value such that σ_{i_n} scheduled at $\tau_{i_n} - \Delta^+$ would not conflict on a resource basis with the tasks σ_j in I^-, if they were scheduled at the respective dates $\tau_j + T$, nor with the tasks σ_j in I^+, if they were scheduled at the respective dates τ_j.

Intuitively, Δ^- is meant to be the number of wait cycles needed by σ_{i_n} in order to avoid resource conflicts with the instructions issued *before* it in an actual software pipeline. And the value Δ^+ is meant to be the number of wait cycles needed by the instructions issued *after* σ_{i_n} in an actual software pipeline.

Theorem 3. *Let $\{S_{i_j}\}_{1 \leq j < n}$ be a partial schedule at initiation interval T of a modulo scheduling problem. Let S_{i_n} be a date within the margins of σ_{i_n}, and $I^-, I^+, \Delta^-, \Delta^+$ be defined as above. Let us define the $\{\delta_{i_j}\}_{1 \leq j \leq n}$ and T' by:*

$$\begin{cases} \delta_{i_n} \overset{\text{def}}{=} \Delta^- \\ \forall j \in [1, n-1]: \text{ if } \sigma_{i_j} \in I^+ \text{ then } \delta_{i_j} \overset{\text{def}}{=} \Delta^- + \Delta^+ \text{ else } \delta_{i_j} \overset{\text{def}}{=} 0 \\ T' \overset{\text{def}}{=} T + \Delta^- + \Delta^+ \end{cases}$$

Then $\{S'_{i_j}\}_{1 \leq j \leq n}$ is a partial schedule at T' of the modulo scheduling problem.

Proof: From theorem 1, the partial schedule $\{S'_{i_j}\}_{1 \leq j \leq n}$ satisfies the precedence constraints at T'. From theorem 2, $\{S'_{i_j}\}_{1 \leq j < n}$ also satisfies the modulo resource constraints at T'. The way we compute Δ^- and Δ^+ guarantees that σ_{i_n} does not conflict with $\{\sigma_{i_j}\}_{1 \leq j < n}$. Therefore $\{S'_{i_j}\}_{1 \leq j \leq n}$ also satisfies the modulo resource constraints at T'. □

We are now in position to describe in a more formal way the process of insertion scheduling, where every instruction σ_i, $i \in [1, N]$ is issued only once, and eventually moved at later steps if its offset τ_i happens to be modified after the current initiation interval T_n is increased. To be more specific:

Step 0 A central problem, called P_0, of the modulo scheduling problem, is built and solved. In the process the minimum value $T_{recurrence}$ of the initiation interval T such that P_0 is feasible is computed. We may also compute a lower bound $T_{resource}$ set by resource constraints on the initiation interval, and take $T_0 \stackrel{\text{def}}{=} T_{glb} = \max(T_{recurrence}, T_{resource})$.

Step n The not yet issued instructions are ranked according to a heuristic order[3], and the one with the highest rank, denoted σ_{i_n}, is issued as follows:

1. From the central problem $P_{n-1} \stackrel{\text{def}}{=} P_0 \wedge \{t_{i_1} = S_{i_1}^{n-1}\} \wedge \ldots \wedge \{t_{i_{n-1}} = S_{i_{n-1}}^{n-1}\}$, compute the left margin $t_{i_n}^-$, and the right margin $t_{i_n}^+$, of σ_{i_n}. Any safe approximation of the margins is actually sufficient.

2. Choose an issue date S_{i_n} for σ_{i_n}, with $S_{i_n} \in [t_{i_n}^-, t_{i_n}^+]$ (this choice guarantees that the central problem $P_{n-1} \wedge \{t_{i_n} = S_{i_n}\}$ is still feasible at initiation interval T_{n-1}), and assign a reservation table to σ_{i_n}.

3. Find $\{\delta_{i_j}\}_{1 \leq j < n}$, δ_{i_n}, satisfying the conditions of theorem 1, and also the modulo resource constraints for the tasks $\{\sigma_{i_j}\}_{1 \leq j \leq n}$, at the dates $\{S_{i_j}^n \stackrel{\text{def}}{=} \phi_{i_j}^{n-1} T_n + \tau_{i_j}^{n-1} + \delta_{i_j}\}_{1 \leq j < n} \cup \{S_{i_n}^n \stackrel{\text{def}}{=} \phi_{i_n} T_n + \tau_{i_n} + \delta_{i_n}\}$, for $T_n \stackrel{\text{def}}{=} T_{n-1} + \max_{1 \leq j \leq n} \delta_{i_j}$. For instance apply theorem 3.

4. Move tasks $\sigma_{i_1}, \ldots \sigma_{i_n}$ at dates $S_{i_1}^n, \ldots S_{i_n}^n$, that is, build the central problem $P_n \stackrel{\text{def}}{=} P_0 \wedge \{t_{i_1} = S_{i_1}^n\} \wedge \ldots \wedge \{t_{i_n} = S_{i_n}^n\}$, from $P_{n-1} \wedge \{t_{i_n} = S_{i_n}\}$.

At step n, ϕ_{i_n} and τ_{i_n} are defined by: $S_{i_n} = \phi_{i_n} T_{n-1} + \tau_{i_n} \wedge 0 \leq \tau_{i_n} < T_{n-1}$, while $\phi_{i_j}^n$ and $\tau_{i_j}^n$ are defined $\forall j \in [1, n]$ by: $S_{i_j}^n = \phi_{i_j}^n T_n + \tau_{i_j}^n \wedge 0 \leq \tau_{i_j}^n < T_n$.

3 Implementation and Experimentations

3.1 About the Implementation

Our implementation currently uses the capabilities of the simplex scheduling framework [3, 4] for solving the central problems $P_0, P_1, \ldots P_N$ generated by the insertion scheduling process, but simplex scheduling is by no means required. Any method able to compute a safe approximation of the margins of the unscheduled instructions, such as a variation of the Bellman shortest path algorithm, does work. Although simplex scheduling is quite heavy, with insertion scheduling we are able to achieve $O(MN)$ experimental running times, where M is the number of arcs in the scheduling graph, and N the number of instructions to schedule [5]. The current estimator formula for our running times are $0.12MN$ ms, a tenfold improvement over the numbers reported in [5].

The insertion scheduling implementation under the simplex scheduling framework is hooked to the back-end of the Cray cft77 compiler for the Cray T3D™. We currently have a main problem with this organization, which prevent our pipeliner from being used in a purely automatic fashion, and tested on large

---

[3] The order currently used in our implementation is lowest slack first.

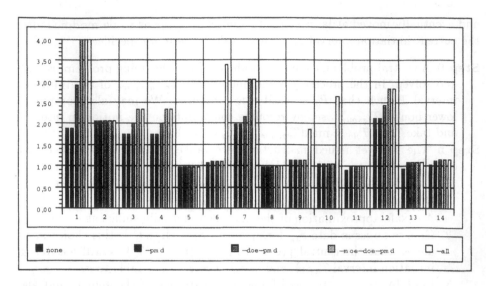

Fig. 6. Performance ratios between software pipelined, and block scheduled, code.

test suites: no high-level information is available in the back-end which could be used to remove the fake dependencies. So in order to have any pipelining effect at all, we print the scheduling graph, flag the various dependencies which should be removed, and we pipeline the result. This manual editing implies that the pipelined code is not put back in the compiler, so currently the pipelined code is not register-assigned. Nonetheless the current implementation provides enough information to estimate the benefits of software pipelining on the DEC Alpha 21064, as shown in the next section.

3.2 Pipelining the Livermore Loops

In the series of experimentations displayed in figure 6, we plot the performance ratios between the software pipelined code, and the corresponding block scheduled code[4] with memory dependencies computed like in the --pmd case below, for the 14 Livermore loops. For each loop, we run the pipeliner five times, with the following set of options:

none the scheduling graph is taken as computed at the back-end level.

--pmd a more precise computation of the memory dependencies is performed.

--doe--pmd in addition to the above, arcs related to the use by the exit branch of variables dead after the loop are removed from the scheduling graph.

--moe--doe--pmd in addition to the above, modulo expansion is performed, with the effect of removing more arcs from the scheduling graph.

--all in addition to the above, the recurrence cycles related to multiple uses of the same induction variable are removed from the scheduling graph.

---

[4] Min-length scheduling of the loop body, no pipelining.

The reasons pipelining does not perform well on some of the loops are independent from insertion scheduling. Loops 5, 6 and 11 are first-order linear recurrences. Loops 8 has a large body (111 instructions), while loops 13 and 14, which have a medium-size body (70 and 54 instructions), are also partially recurrent. So, for the cases it should be applied to, software pipelining under our insertion scheduling implementation yields twofold to fourfold improvements. Even though these improvements assume no cache misses, and are computed before register assignment, it is apparent that pipelining is highly effective. Also, very accurate scheduling graphs are needed before interesting speedups are achieved.

Summary and Conclusions

There is a widespread belief that software pipelining is a solved problem, since the modulo scheduling technique is almost 15 year old [12]. Actually software pipelining works either on idealized VLIW models, or for pure vector loops on specific architectures, where every cycle can be removed from the scheduling graph [11, 6]. Making software pipelining work on realistic machine models (multiple specialized functional units, non-unit latencies), from the output of a real compiler (which contains many fake recurrence cycles), is not that simple. The recent approaches to software pipelining are a testimony of this situation:

- Decomposed software pipelining techniques, initiated by Gasperoni & Schwiegelshohn [8] and Wang & Eisenbeis [15], focus on reducing modulo scheduling problems with cyclic graphs to a minimum-length scheduling problem on an acyclic scheduling graph, which is then solved with plain list scheduling.
- Integer linear programming techniques, investigated by Feautrier [7], and by Govindarajan et al. [9], optimally solve the modulo scheduling problem for simple machine models, at the expense of high running times.
- Enhancements of the modulo scheduling technique, by Rau [13] and by Huff [10], incrementally maintain for each not yet issued instructions its margins, that is, the earliest date and the latest date the instruction can be issued at without violating the precedence constraints. These approaches also ask for a backtracking capability in order to work around deadlock situations.

Our approach is loosely related to the decomposed software pipelining techniques [8, 15], where *row numbers* and *column numbers* corresponding respectively to our offsets and our frames are defined. Although we deal with frames and offsets, we do not *decompose* the modulo scheduling process into computing the offsets of all instructions, then all the frames, or conversely. Rather, we issue the instructions one by one, assigning to each of them a constant frame, and an offset which is eventually increased later. In this way, we achieve fast modulo scheduling for a realistic processor, while allowing advanced scheduling techniques such as lifetime-sensitive scheduling [4] to be easily applied [5]. So in this respect our technique compares with recent work by Rau[13] and by Huff[10], but we achieve equivalent or better results without resorting to backtracking.

Moreover, the ability exposed by our technique to modulo schedule the instructions in any convenient order, combined with the freedom it gives of issuing the instructions at any date within their current margins, is a powerful asset. This distinctive feature of insertion scheduling is to our knowledge not matched by any other scheduling technique. We expect this advantage to become apparent in the area of combined software pipelining / register assignment.

References

1. T. L. Adam, K. M. Chandy, J. R. Dickson "A Comparison of List Schedules for Parallel Processing Systems" *Communications of the ACM*, Vol. 17, no. 12, Dec. 1974.
2. B. Dupont de Dinechin "StaCS: A Static Control Superscalar Architecture" *MICRO-25 / 25th Annual International Symposium on Microarchitecture*, Portland, Dec. 1992.
3. B. Dupont de Dinechin "An Introduction to Simplex Scheduling" PACT'94, Montreal, Aug. 1994.
4. B. Dupont de Dinechin "Simplex Scheduling: More than Lifetime-Sensitive Instruction Scheduling" *PRISM research report 1994.22*, available under anonymous ftp to ftp.prism.uvsq.fr, July 94.
5. B. Dupont de Dinechin "Fast Modulo Scheduling Under the Simplex Scheduling Framework" *PRISM research report 1995.01*, available under anonymous ftp to ftp.prism.uvsq.fr, Jan 95.
6. C. Eisenbeis, D. Windheiser "Optimal Software Pipelining in Presence of Resource Constraints" *PaCT-93*, Obninsk, Russia, Sept. 1993.
7. P. Feautrier "Fine-Grain Scheduling Under Resource Constraints" *7th Annual Workshop on Lang. and Compilers for Parallel Computing, LNCS*, Ithaca, NY, Aug 1994.
8. F. Gasperoni, U. Schwiegelshohn "Scheduling Loops on Parallel Processors: A Simple Algorithm with Close to Optimum Performance" *Parallel Processing: COMPAR'92-VAPP V*, LNCS 634, June 1992.
9. R. Govindarajan, E. R. Altman, G. R. Gao "Minimizing Register Requirements under Resource-Constrained Rate-Optimal Software Pipelining" *MICRO-27 / 27h Annual International Symposium on Microarchitecture*, San Jose, Dec. 1994.
10. R. A. Huff "Lifetime-Sensitive Modulo Scheduling" *Proceedings of the SIG-PLAN'93 Conference on Programming Language Design and Implementation*, Albuquerque, June 1993.
11. M. Lam "A Systolic Array Optimizing Compiler" *Ph. D. Thesis*, Carnegie Mellon University, May 1987.
12. B. R. Rau, C. D. Glaeser "Some Scheduling Techniques and an Easily Schedulable Horizontal Architecture for High Performance Scientific Computing" *IEEE / ACM 14th Annual Microprogramming Workshop*, Oct. 1981.
13. B. R. Rau "Iterative Modulo Scheduling: An Algorithm for Software Pipelining Loops" *IEEE / ACM 27th Annual Microprogramming Workshop*, San Jose, California, Nov. 1994.
14. M. D. Tiemann "The GNU Instruction Scheduler" *Cygnus Technical Report*, available at URL http://www.cygnus.com/library-dir.html, Jul 1989.
15. J. Wang, C. Eisenbeis "Decomposed Software Pipelining: a New Approach to Exploit Instruction Level Parallelism for Loop Programs" *IFIP WG 10.3*, Orlando, Florida, Jan. 1993.

Interprocedural Array Region Analyses

Béatrice CREUSILLET, François IRIGOIN*

Ecole des Mines de Paris/CRI

Abstract. Many program optimizations require exact knowledge of the
sets of array elements that are referenced in or that flow between statements or procedures. Some examples are array privatization, generation
of communications in distributed memory machines, or compile-time optimization of cache behavior in hierarchical memory machines.
Exact array region analysis is introduced in this article. These regions
exactly represent the effects of statements and procedures upon array
variables. To represent the flow of these data, we also introduce two new
types of array region analyses: IN and OUT regions.
The intraprocedural propagation is presented, as well as a general linear
framework for interprocedural analyses, that handles array reshapes.

Introduction

The efficient compilation of scientific programs for massively parallel machines,
hierarchical memory machines or fault-tolerant computing environments requires
a precise intra- and inter-procedural analysis of array data flow.

A recent type of analysis [9] has opened up wide perspectives in this area.
It provides an exact analysis of array data flow, originally in monoprocedural
programs with static control. This last constraint has since been partially removed [14, 8], to the detriment of the accuracy of the results. Furthermore, this
method does not allow interprocedural analyses, and its complexity makes it
unpracticable for large programs.

Another approach is to calculate conservative summaries of the effects of
procedure calls on sets of array elements [19, 6]. They allow the analysis of
large programs, thanks to their low complexity (in practice). But since these
analyses are flow insensitive, and since they do not precisely take into account
the modifications of the values of integer scalar variables, they are not accurate
enough to handle powerful optimizations.

In PIPS [12], the Interprocedural Parallelizer of Scientific Programs developed at Ecole des Mines de Paris, we have extended Triolet's array regions [19]
to calculate *exact* summaries of the effects of statements and procedures on sets
of array elements [3]. The resulting READ/WRITE regions are already used to efficiently compile HPF [7]. However, they cannot be used to compute array data
flow, and are thus insufficient for optimizations such as array privatization.

We therefore introduce two new types of exact regions: for any statement
or procedure, IN regions contain its imported array elements, and OUT regions

* E-mail: {creusillet,irigoin}@cri.ensmp.fr

represent its set of live array elements. For a massively parallel machine, these regions could be used to calculate the communications before and after the execution of a piece of code. They can also be used to privatize array sections [3]. For a hierarchical memory machine, they provide the sets of array elements that are used or reused, and hence could be prefetched (IN regions) or kept (OUT regions) in caches; the array elements that do not appear in these sets, and that are accessed in the current piece of code, are only temporaries, and should be handled as such. For fault-tolerant systems, *checkpointing* [13] is a software solution that regularly saves the current state: as they provide the set of elements that will be used in further computations, IN and OUT regions could be used to reduce the amount of data to be saved.

This paper is organized as follows. In Section 1, we review the necessary background. Section 2 presents array regions and the operators to manipulate them. Their intra- and interprocedural propagation is detailled in Sections 3 and 4. IN and OUT regions are then introduced in Section 5.

1 Prerequisites and Notations

In PIPS the parallelization process is divided into several phases, either analyses or program transformations. *Intraprocedural analyses* are performed on the *hierarchical control flow graph* [12] of the routines. The nodes of these graphs correspond to the FORTRAN language control structures (DO, IF, sequence of instructions, assignement, call, ...), or are themselves flat control flow graphs, when a fragment of code is unstructured (use of GOTOs). *Interprocedural analyses* propagate information over the program *call graph*. This graph is assumed acyclic, according to the FORTRAN standard, and the analyses can be performed bottom-up or top-down.

Two auxiliary analyses are of interest in the remainder of this paper: *transformers* and *preconditions* [11].

Transformers abstract the effects of instructions upon the values of integer scalar variables by giving an affine approximation of the relations that exist between their values before and after the execution of a statement or procedure call. In equations they are designated by T, whereas in programs they appear under the form T(args) {pred}, where args is the list of modified variables, and pred gives the non trivial relations existing between the initial values (suffixed by #init) and the new values of variables. Figure 1 shows the transformers corresponding to each instruction.

Preconditions are predicates over integer scalar variables. They hold just before the execution of the corresponding instruction. In Figure 1, they appear as P(vars) {pred}, where vars is the list of modified variables since the beginning of the current routine, because preconditions abstract the effects of the routine from its entry point to the current instruction.

Transformers are propagated upward, while preconditions are propagated downward. And if T_1 and P_1 correspond to the instruction S_1, and P_2 to the instruction S_2 immediately following S_1, then $P_2 = T_1(P_1)$.

```
C  T(K) {K == 3}                    C  P() {}
   K = 3                               K = 3
C  T(K) {}                          C  P(K) {K==3}
   K = FOO(N)                          K = FOO()
C  T(K) {K == K#init + 1}           C  P(K) {}
   CALL INC1(K)                        CALL INC1(K)
                                    C  P(K) {}
```

Fig. 1. Transformers and preconditions

In the remainder of this paper, we shall use the following notations: for a statement S_k, σ_k is a store preceding it, and T_k its corresponding transformer.

2 Regions: Definitions and Operators

An array region is a set of array elements described by equalities and inequalities defining a convex polyhedron [19]. Two other characteristics have been introduced in PIPS to represent the effects of statements and procedures upon array elements:

- the *action* upon the elements of the region; READ (R) for a use or WRITE (W) for a definition;
- the *approximation* of the region; MAY if the region is an overapproximation of the set of array elements actually referenced in the corresponding piece of code; MUST if the region exactly represents this set (*exact* region).

For instance, the region:

$$\texttt{<A}(\phi_1,\phi_2)\texttt{-W-MUST-}\{\phi_1\texttt{==I}, \ \phi_1\texttt{==}\phi_2\}\texttt{>}$$

where ϕ_1 and ϕ_2 respectively represent the first and second dimensions of A, corresponds to a use of element A(I,I).

In order to summarize array accesses, and to propagate the summaries along control flow paths, we need several operators: union, intersection, difference, and unary operators.

Union The union operator is used to merge two elementary regions. Unfortunately, the union of two convex polyhedra is not necessarily a convex polyhedron. The operator $\bar{\cup}$ we use instead is the convex hull. It may generate points that do not belong to the original polyhedra. In this case, the resulting region is MAY region. The third column in Table 1 gives the approximation of the resulting region against the characteristics of the initial regions.

Intersection The intersection of two convex polyhedra is a convex polyhedron. It follows that the intersection of two MUST regions is a MUST region. The impact of the approximations of the initial regions is summarized in the fourth column of Table 1.

R_1	R_2	$R_1 \,\bar\cup\, R_2$	$R_1 \cap R_2$	$R_1 \ominus R_2$
MUST	MUST	MUST, iff exact convex hull	MUST	$\bar\cup\,(R_1 \cap \bar R_2)$, MUST iff exact
MUST	MAY	MUST, iff $R_2 \subseteq R_1$	MAY	R_1, MUST iff $R_1 \cap R_2 = \emptyset$
MAY	MUST	MUST, iff $R_1 \subseteq R_2$	MAY	$\bar\cup\,(R_1 \cap \bar R_2)$, MAY
MAY	MAY	MAY	MAY	R_1, MAY

Table 1. Binary operators on regions

Difference The difference of two convex polyhedra is not necessarily a convex polyhedron. The chosen operator $\ominus$ gives an over-approximation of the actual difference of the original regions. Its features are described in Table 1, Column 5.

Translation from one store to another The linear constraints defining a region often involve integer scalar variables from the program (e.g. ϕ_1==I). Their values, and thus the region, are relative to the current store. If we consider the statement I = I + 1, the value of I is not the same in the stores preceding and following the execution of the instruction. Thus, if the polyhedron of a region is ϕ_1==I before the execution of I = I + 1, it must be ϕ_1==I-1 afterwards.

To apply one of the preceding operators to two regions, they must be relative to the same store. We shall call $\mathcal{T}_{\sigma_1 \to \sigma_2}$ the transformation of a region relative to the store σ_1 into a region relative to the store σ_2.

This transformation has been described in [3]. Very briefly, it consists in adding to the predicate of the region, the constraints of the transformer that abstracts the effects of the program between the two stores. The variables of the original store (σ_1) are then eliminated. The only variables that remain in the resulting polyhedron all refer to the store σ_2. Thus, two transformations, $\mathcal{T}_{\sigma_k \to \sigma_{k+1}}$ and $\mathcal{T}_{\sigma_{k+1} \to \sigma_k}$, correspond to the transformer T_k associated to statement S_k, depending on the variables that are eliminated.

For instance, let us assume that σ_1 is the store preceding statement I = I + 1, σ_2 the store following it, and $\{\phi_1$==I#init$\}$ the predicate of a region relative to σ_1. We first add the transformer corresponding to the statement (T(I) {I==I#init+1}). This gives the predicate $\{\phi_1$==I#init, I==I#init+1$\}$. We then eliminate I#init, because it refers to σ_1. We obtain $\{\phi_1$==I-1$\}$, which is relative to σ_2.

The elimination of a variable from a convex polyhedron may introduce integer points that do not belong to the actual projection. Ancourt or Pugh [2, 16] have proposed conditions under which this elimination is exact. They do not apply in our case because program entities must be considered as parameters (symbolic constants) for the polyhedron, and not as variables.

For instance, the elimination of I from $\{\phi_1$==I, I<=J$\}$ gives $\{\phi_1$<=J$\}$. It satisfies the usual conditions for an exact projection. However, these two polyhedra do not describe the same region. The first contains only one element, uniquely defined by the value of I in the current store, even if we do not know it. Whereas the second contains all the elements such that ϕ_1 is smaller than the current value of J.

On the contrary, the elimination of I from $\{2\phi_1 == 3I, 2I == J\}$, which gives $\{4\phi_1 == 3J\}$, is usually considered inexact. In our case, and referring to a given store, ϕ_1 is uniquely defined in both cases by the values of the variables appearing in both polyhedra.

Since this is not the purpose of our paper, we refer the reader to [3] for conditions of the exact elimination of a symbolic constant from a polyhedron, and their verification. When these conditions are not met, the elimination is performed, but the original region becomes a MAY region.

Sometimes, we shall need to eliminate all but one variable (e.g. i). $\mathcal{T}_{\sigma_1 \to \sigma_2 \setminus i}$ will denote the corresponding transformation.

Elimination of loop indices or ϕ variables During the propagation of regions in a linear block of instructions, a loop index is considered as a normal program entity. It receives a particular treatment only when propagating regions towards the outside or the inside of the corresponding loop, because it then successively takes a whole range of values (iteration space), instead of a single one. Thus, the elimination of a loop index from the polyhedron of a region is exact if the following conditions are met:

1. the expressions of the lower and upper bounds are affine;
2. the absolute value of the increment is equal to 1;
3. the conditions of Ancourt or Pugh for an exact projection are met.

The first two conditions ensure that the iteration space can be described exactly by a convex polyhedron over the program entities (i.e. $lb \leq i \leq ub$ if lb and ub respectively are the upper and lower bounds of the loop index). We shall designate by $proj_i$ the elimination of loop index i.

We also need to eliminate ϕ variables from regions during their interprocedural propagation. These entities are variables in the usual sense: their elimination is exact if the conditions of Ancourt or Pugh are met.

Constraining regions predicate In order to have more information on ϕ variables, the constraints of the preconditions are systematically added to the predicate of the region. This is particularly useful when merging two regions. For instance, $\{\phi_1 == I\} \; \bar{\cup} \; \{\phi_1 == J\} = \{\}$. If we add the current preconditions (e.g. $\{I == J\}$) to the original regions, we obtain $\{\phi_1 == I, I == J\}$ instead of $\{\}$. This operation increases the accuracy of the analysis, without modifying the definition of regions. Furthermore, since preconditions include some IF conditions, regions are powerful enough to disprove interprocedurally conditional dependencies.

3 Intraprocedural Propagation

In this section, we detail the computation of READ and WRITE regions for the main structures of the FORTRAN language: assignment, sequence of complex instructions, DO loop. As an illustration, we shall consider the contrived example of Figure 2.

```
K = FOO()                              SUBROUTINE INC1(I)
DO I = 1,N                             I = I + 1
   DO J = 1,N                          END
      WORK(J,K) = J + K
   ENDDO
   CALL INC1(K)
   DO J = 1,N
      WORK(J,K) = J*J - K*K
      A(I) = A(I)+WORK(J,K)+WORK(J,K-1)
   ENDDO
ENDDO
```

Fig. 2. Sample program

3.1 Assignment

The reference on the left hand side of the assignment is converted into a WRITE region, whereas on the right hand side, each reference is converted into an elementary READ region. These regions are exact (MUST regions) if and only if the indices expressions are affine functions of the program variables.

When there are several references for a particular array on the right hand side, the corresponding regions are merged using $\bar{\cup}$ in order to obtain a summary.

> For instance, for the instruction A(I) = A(I)+WORK(J,K)+WORK(J,K-1) in our working example, elementary READ regions are:
>
> $$<A(\phi_1)-R-MUST-\{\phi_1==I, \; 1<=I<=N, \; 1<=J<=N\}>$$
> $$<WORK(\phi_1,\phi_2)-R-MUST-\{\phi_1==J, \; \phi_2==K, \; 1<=I<=N, \; 1<=J<=N\}>$$
> $$<WORK(\phi_1,\phi_2)-R-MUST-\{\phi_1==J, \; \phi_2==K-1, \; 1<=I<=N, \; 1<=J<=N\}>$$
>
> By merging the two regions concerning array WORK, we finally obtain:
>
> $$<A(\phi_1)-R-MUST-\{\phi_1==I, \; 1<=I<=N, \; 1<=J<=N\}>$$
> $$<WORK(\phi_1,\phi_2)-R-MUST-\{\phi_1==J, \; K-1<=\phi_2<=K, \; 1<=I<=N, \; 1<=J<=N\}>$$

3.2 Sequence of Instructions

Our purpose is to calculate the regions R_B associated to the whole sequence $B = S_1, \ldots, S_n$, that is to say a summary of all the read and write references occuring in statements $S_1, \ldots, S_n$ of B.

We assume that the READ/WRITE regions of the instructions of B are known. We denote them as R_k for each statement S_k, with no distinction between READ and WRITE regions, since their propagation is identical, as we shall see later.

The region R_k is relative to the store σ_k preceding the execution of S_k. Thus, we cannot simply merge the $R_k, k \in [1..n]$ by using $\overline{\cup}$. We must first convert them into the same store. Since we know the transformer T_k corresponding to the instruction S_k, we can determine the transformation $T_{\sigma_{k+1} \to \sigma_k}$, and hence recursively compute the region R'_k associated with the subsequence $S_k, \ldots, S_n$, by using the following equations:

$$R'_k = R_k \ \overline{\cup} \ T_{\sigma_{k+1} \to \sigma_k}(R'_{k+1}), \ \forall k \in [1..n-1] \tag{1}$$
$$R'_n = R_n$$

And finally, $R_B = R'_1$.

In Equation 1, $T_{\sigma_{k+1} \to \sigma_k}(R'_{k+1})$ represents all the references read and written by instructions $S_{k+1}, \ldots, S_n$. These regions are relative to σ_k because of the use of $T_{\sigma_{k+1} \to \sigma_k}$. Thus, it is legal to merge them with regions R_k. The result contains the elements read and written by instructions S_k and $S_{k+1}, \ldots, S_n$, which is the definition of R'_k.

As an illustration, let us consider the body of the I loop in our example. We are interested in the read and written references to array WORK. We assume that we know the regions associated to both J loops:

> `<WORK(`ϕ_1,ϕ_2`)-W-MUST-{1<=`ϕ_1`<=N,` ϕ_2`==K, 1<=I<=N}>`

for the first loop, and for the second:

> `<WORK(`ϕ_1,ϕ_2`)-W-MUST-{1<=`ϕ_1`<=N,` ϕ_2`==K, 1<=I<=N}>`
> `<WORK(`ϕ_1,ϕ_2`)-R-MUST-{1<=`ϕ_1`<=N, K-1<=`ϕ_2`<=K, 1<=I<=N}>`

We cannot simply merge these regions because the value of K is modified by a call to INC1. The transformer that abstracts the effects of this call is T(K) {K==K#init+1}. We add its constraint to the regions corresponding to the second loop, and eliminate the variable K which refers to the store immediately following the call. This gives:

> `<WORK(`ϕ_1,ϕ_2`)-W-MUST-{1<=`ϕ_1`<=N,` ϕ_2`==K#init+1, 1<=I<=N}>`
> `<WORK(`ϕ_1,ϕ_2`)-R-MUST-{1<=`ϕ_1`<=N, K#init<=`ϕ_2`<=K#init+1, 1<=I<=N}>`

These regions are relative to the store preceding the call. Since no integer scalar variables appearing in the constraints are modified by the first J loop, the regions are also relative to the store preceding the execution of the first J loop. Thus, it is legal to merge them with the regions corresponding to the first J loop, after renaming K#init into K. It follows:

> `<WORK(`ϕ_1,ϕ_2`)-W-MUST-{1<=`ϕ_1`<=N, K<=`ϕ_2`<=K+1, 1<=I<=N}>`
> `<WORK(`ϕ_1,ϕ_2`)-R-MUST-{1<=`ϕ_1`<=N, K<=`ϕ_2`<=K+1, 1<=I<=N}>`

3.3 DO Loop

We want to compute the regions R_L corresponding to the DO loop L, knowing the regions of its body. They are not only functions of the value i of loop index

I, but also of the variables modified in the loop body (collectively denoted as v). Hence, we denote them as $R(i, v)$.

These v variables are themselves functions of the loop index. We must then eliminate them to obtain regions that are functions of the sole loop index (and of course of variables that do not vary in the loop body). This is achieved by using operator $\mathcal{T}_{\sigma_i \to \sigma_L \setminus I}$, σ_L being the store preceding the loop and σ_i the store preceding the iteration such that $I = i$. This operator is based on the transformer of the loop body, which represents the loop invariant (when it is computable). Then the loop index is eliminated using operator $proj_I$.

The computation of the regions of a DO loop can finally be summarized by the following equation:

$$R_L = proj_I(\mathcal{T}_{\sigma_i \to \sigma_L \setminus I}(R(i, v)))$$

As an example, let us consider the I loop in Figure 2. We have seen in the previous section that the regions of the loop body concerning read accesses to the array WORK are:

$$<\text{WORK}(\phi_1, \phi_2)\text{-R-MUST-}\{1<=\phi_1<=N, K<=\phi_2<=K+1, 1<=I<=N\}>$$

They are functions of the loop index I and of the variable K, the value of which is modified in the loop body. The transformer giving the loop invariant is T(I,K) {K==K#init+I-1} (K#init is the value of K before the execution of the loop). We add its constraint to the previous region, and eliminate K (not I, because it is the loop index). After renaming K#init into K, it gives:

$$<\text{WORK}(\phi_1, \phi_2)\text{-R-MUST-}\{1<=\phi_1<=N, K+I-1<=\phi_2<=K+I, 1<=I<=N\}>$$

We then eliminate the loop index. This elimination is exact because the lower and upper bounds are affine, the value of the increment is 1, and the projection is exact in the usual meaning. We finaly obtain:

$$<\text{WORK}(\phi_1, \phi_2)\text{-R-MUST-}\{1<=\phi_1<=N, K<=\phi_2<=K+N\}>$$

4 Interprocedural Propagation

The interprocedural propagation of array regions is a backward analysis; the summary regions of the called subroutine are translated from the callee's name space into the caller's name space. Because of array reshaping, this operation is not straightforward.

Let us first consider the translation from a formal to an actual array. In [18], Triolet gave conditions to perform the translation by only changing the name of the array, possibly adding equalities between ϕ variables and the array reference indices at call site, and projecting the polyhedron onto the name space of the caller. These conditions are that the formal array is either similar to the actual array, or a *subarray* of the actual array, for instance a single column of a matrix.

By examining the Perfect Club Benchmarks [4], we found these conditions to be too restrictive. In particular, they cannot handle offsets in declarations, general offsets in the references at call site, and array reshaping is treated in a very

```
subroutine FOO(C,n)                <M(φ1,φ2)-IN-MUST-{1<=φ1<=n1,1<=φ2<=n2}>
dimension C(n,100,100)                  subroutine BAR(M,n1,n2)
call BAR(C,n,300)                       dimension M(n1,n2)
```

Fig. 3. Interprocedural propagation

few cases. In order to handle the general case, we have chosen to use *subscript values* as they are described in the FORTRAN standard [1]. The subscript value of an array element is its *rank* in the array, given the fact that array elements are held in *column order*. Definition 1 expresses the fact that two corresponding elements of the actual and formal arguments must have the same subscript values, more or less the offset of the actual argument.

Notations In the remainder of this section, we shall use the following notations:
P is the calling routine, Q the called routine.

A_Q is the formal array, of dimension q, of lower and upper bounds $lq_1, \ldots, lq_q$ and $uq_1, \ldots uq_q$. The elements of A_Q are described by ϕ variables.

A_P is the corresponding actual array, of dimension p, of lower and upper bounds $lp_1, \ldots, lp_p$ and $up_1, \ldots up_p$; $op_1, \ldots, op_p$ are the indices of the reference at the call site[2]. The elements of A_P are described by ψ variables.

Definition 1. Let the *subscript value equation* be:

$$
\begin{aligned}
(\psi_1 - lp_1) + \sum_{i=2}^{p}[(\psi_i - lp_i)\prod_{j=1}^{i-1}(up_j - lp_j)] - (offset - 1) \\
= (\phi_1 - lq_1) + \sum_{i=2}^{q}[(\phi_i - lq_i)\prod_{j=1}^{i-1}(uq_j - lq_j)]
\end{aligned}
\tag{2}
$$

with $offset = 1 + (op_1 - lp_1) + \sum_{i=2}^{p}[(op_i - lp_i)\prod_{j=1}^{i-1}(up_j - lp_j)]$. □

In the example of Figure 3, we have $A_Q = $ M, $q = 2$, $lq_1 = lq_2 = 1$, $uq_1 = $ n1, and $uq_2 = $ n2 for the called procedure; $A_P = $ C, $p = 3$, $lp_1 = lp_2 = lp_3 = 1$, $up_1 = $ n, $up_2 = up_3 = 100$ for the calling subroutine; and $op_1 = op_2 = op_3 = 1$ because call BAR(C, n, 300) is equivalent to call BAR(C(1,1,1), n, 300). And $C(\psi_1,\psi_2,\psi_3)$ corresponds to $M(\phi_1, \phi_2)$ if and only if:

$$(\psi_1 - 1) + (\psi_2 - 1) \times n + (\psi_3 - 1) \times n \times 100 = (\phi_1 - 1) + (\phi_2 - 1) \times n1$$

When the subscript value equation is affine, it can be used to propagate array regions, by simply adding it to the summary region corresponding to A_Q, and eliminating ϕ variables.

Unfortunately, subcript values of arrays of two or more dimensions are seldom affine functions of ϕ or ψ variables. In our example, the equation contains several non linear terms. In order to decrease the degree of equation (2), we take into account the possible relations between the first common dimensions of the two arrays. For that purpose, we give two more definitions.

---

[2] CALL $Q(A_P(op_1, \ldots, op_p))$.

Definition 2. We say that arrays A_P and A_Q *have similar d-th dimension* iff:
$d = 1$ or A_P and A_Q have similar $(d-1)$-th dimension,
and $op_d = lp_d$,
and $up_d - lp_d = uq_d - lp_d$. □

Definition 3. We define the *partial subscript value equation of rank d* to be:

$$(\psi_1 - lp_d) + \sum_{i=d+1}^{p}[(\psi_i - lp_i)\prod_{j=d+1}^{i-1}(up_j - lp_j)] - (offset_d - 1)$$
$$= (\phi_d - lq_d) + \sum_{i=d+1}^{q}[(\phi_i - lq_i)\prod_{j=d+1}^{i-1}(uq_j - lq_j)] \tag{3}$$

with $offset_d = 1 + (op_d - lp_d) + \sum_{i=d+1}^{p}[(op_i - lp_i)\prod_{j=d+1}^{i-1}(up_j - lp_j)]$. □

Algorithm The principle of the translation of a summary region R corresponding to A_Q into a region corresponding to A_P is the following:

1. $d = 1$
2. `while` $d \leq min(p,q)$ `and` A_P `and` A_Q `have same` d-`th dimension do`
    add $\psi_d - lp_d = \phi_d - lq_d$ to R
    $d = d + 1$
3. `if` $d <= p$ `and` $d <= q$ *(not all common dim. have been translated)*
    add the partial subscrit value equation (3) of rank d to R
4. `else` *(all common dimensions have been translated)*
    `if` $d <= p$ `and` $d > q$ (remaining dimensions of A_P)
    `forall` $i \in [d..p]$ add $\psi_d = op_d$ to R
5. `forall` $i \in [1..p]$ add $lp_i \leq \psi_i \leq up_i$ to R
6. `eliminate` ϕ `variables from` R
7. `project the polyhedron of` R `onto the name space of` P

Step 2 consists in translating the similar common dimensions of P and Q. Two cases may appear: either one or more common dimensions have not been translated, and we must use the partial subscript value equation for the remaining dimensions (Step 3); or all common dimensions are similar, and if the actual array has more dimensions than the formal one, the remaining ψ variables are equal to the array element indices at the call site (Step 4). At Step 5, we add the bounding constraints on ψ variables. The polyhedron of R then describes the relations between ϕ and ψ variables. Steps 6 and 7 complete the translation.

At Steps 2, 3, 4, and 5, the constraints that are added to the polyhedron of R may not be affine. In that case, they are not added to the polyhedron, and the translation is considered inexact. The translated region is then a MAY region. Steps 6 and 7 may also yield a MAY region, as we have seen in Section 2. □

In our example, since n1 = n, we can add $\psi_1 = \phi_1$ to the region. Then, we build the partial subscript values equation of rank 2, which is linear:

$$(\psi_2 - 1) + (\psi_3 - 1) \times 100 = (\phi_2 - 1)$$

Step 5 then adds $\{1 \leq \psi_1 \leq n, 1 \leq \psi_2 \leq 100, 1 \leq \psi_3 \leq 100\}$. Step 6 eliminates the ϕ variables. We obtain the following region:

$$<C(\psi_1,\psi_2,\psi_3)-\text{IN-MUST}-$$
$$\{1<=\psi_1<=n, \ 1<=\psi_2+100\psi_3-100<=n2, \ 1<=\psi_2<=100,1<=\psi_3<=100\}>$$

We finally substitute n2 by its value (300).

Regions concerning arrays in COMMONs are handled similarly, except that *offset* becomes the relative offset of the arrays in the COMMON data layout.

The previous algorithm has several advantages, especially over [5, 10]:

1. the first dimensions of the array are treated separately; even if the remaining partial subscript value equation is not affine, these dimensions are translated, and the resulting region is more precise, even if it is a MAY region; moreover, this leads to constraints that are simpler than with the full subcript value equation;
2. the partial subscript value equation may be affine, even if the complete subscript value equation is not linear;
3. we think that most cases that arise and that can be solved using Maslov's method [15] can also be solved by our algorithm; for instance, the translation from A(N,M,L) to B(N,M,L) yields the equation $\psi_1 + N\psi_2 + NM\psi_3 = \phi_1 + N\phi_2 + NM\phi_3$ which he gives as an example; we solve it by simply verifying that all three dimensions are similar;
4. this framework is very well suited to handle arrays in COMMONs, because their data layout and the array bounds are known at compile time.

But we also know its limitations. It cannot solve some very frequent problems such as translating V(N*N) into A(N,N) (neither do the other methods). In a near future, we intend to extend our approach to handle more cases.

5 IN and OUT Regions

READ and WRITE regions summarize the exact effects of statements and procedures upon array elements. They do not represent the flows of array elements, which are necessary to test the legality of many optimizations. For that purpose, we introduce two new types of regions: IN and OUT regions, that take array kills [17] into account.

IN regions contain the array elements, the values of which are (MUST) or may be (MAY) *imported* by the current piece of code. These are the elements that are read before being possibly redefined by another instruction of the same fragment. In Figure 2, in the body of the second J loop, the element WORK(J,K) is read, but its value is not imported because it is previously defined in the same iteration. On the contrary, the element WORK(J,K-1) is imported from the first J loop.

OUT regions corresponding to a piece of code contain the array elements that it defines, and that are (MUST) or may be (MAY) used afterwards, in the continuation. These are the *live* or *exported* array elements. In the program of Figure 2, the first J loop exports all the elements of the array WORK it defines towards the second J loop, whereas the elements of WORK defined in the latter are not exported towards the next iterations of the I loop.

The interprocedural propagation of IN regions is similar to that of READ/WRITE regions. Its a backward propagation: IN regions corresponding to a formal parameter are translated into regions corresponding to its actual parameter, at each call site. On the contrary, the propagation of OUT regions on the call graph is a forward propagation: actual parameters are translated into formal ones at each call site, and the resulting regions are merged to form a unique summary, which is the OUT regions of the procedure. This propagation is performed using the same principles as those presented in Section 4. In the remainder of this section, we shall limit ourselves to the intraprocedural computation of IN and OUT regions for a single instruction, or a sequence of instructions.

5.1 Computation of IN Regions

IN regions of an assignment are identical to the corresponding READ regions because the values of the referenced elements cannot come from the assignement itself.

We are now interested in the region IN_B corresponding to the sequence of instructions $B = S_1, \ldots, S_n$, and relative to the store $\sigma_B = \sigma_1$ preceding the execution of B. It is the set of array elements that are read by the instructions of B, and the values of which do not come from previous instructions of B.

For each instruction S_k, we denote its WRITE and IN regions as W_k and IN_k; they are relative to the store σ_k preceding S_k, and are supposed to be known.

IN'_k also represents the IN region corresponding to the subsequence $S_k, \ldots S_n$. IN_B is then defined by:

$$\begin{cases} IN_B = IN'_1 \\ IN'_k = IN_k \ \bar{\cup} \ [\mathcal{T}_{\sigma_{k+1} \to \sigma_k}(IN'_{k+1}) \ominus W_k], \ \forall \, k \in [1..n-1] \\ IN'_n = IN_n \end{cases}$$

$\mathcal{T}_{\sigma_{k+1} \to \sigma_k}$ translates the IN regions corresponding to $S_{k+1}, \ldots, S_n$ in the same store σ_k as the WRITE and IN regions of S_k. $\mathcal{T}_{\sigma_{k+1} \to \sigma_k}(IN'_{k+1}) \ominus W_k$ represents the regions imported by the subsequence $S_{k+1}, \ldots, S_n$, but not defined by Statement S_k. Merged with IN_k, they give the set of elements that are read by the sequence $S_k, \ldots, S_n$ before being possibly redefined by any other statements of the same subsequence. This is exactly the definition of IN'_k.

As an illustration, let us consider the body of the second J loop. The READ and IN regions of its instructions concerning the array WORK are[3]:

```
C  S₁:
C  <WORK(φ₁,φ₂)-W-MUST-{φ₁==J,  φ₂==K}>
   WORK(J,K) = J*J - K*K
C  S₂:
C  <WORK(φ₁,φ₂)-IN-MUST-{φ₁==J, K-1<=φ₂<=K}>
   A(I) = A(I) + WORK(J,K) + WORK(J,K-1)
```

---

[3] Without the constraints from the preconditions, since integer scalar variables are not modified in this loop body.

Thus, we successively have :

$$IN'_2 = IN_2 = \texttt{<WORK}(\phi_1,\phi_2)\texttt{-IN-MUST-}\{\phi_1\texttt{==J, K-1<=}\phi_2\texttt{<=K}\}\texttt{>}$$
$$IN'_1 = IN_1 \ \bar{\cup} \ (IN'_2 \ominus W_1) = \varnothing \ \bar{\cup} \ (IN'_2 - W_1)$$
$$= \texttt{<WORK}(\phi_1,\phi_2)\texttt{-IN-MUST-}\{\phi_1\texttt{==J,} \ \phi_2\texttt{==K-1}\}\texttt{>}$$

Finaly, $IN_B = IN'_1$ contains the sole element $\texttt{WORK(J,K-1)}$.

5.2 Computation of OUT Regions

OUT regions are propagated top-down along the hierarchical control flow graph. Thus, the region OUT_B corresponding to the sequence B is supposed to be known; and we are interested in the regions OUT_k ($k \in [1..n]$) corresponding to each instruction S_k of B. These regions contain the array elements written by the current instruction, and the values of which are used by the next instructions, inside and outside the sequence.

We call OUT'_k the set of array elements defined by the subsequence $S_1, \ldots, S_k$, and the values of which are exported outside of B. The equations defining $OUT_k, k \in [1..n]$ are then:

$$\left\{ \begin{array}{l} OUT'_n = \mathcal{T}_{\sigma_B \to \sigma_n}(OUT_B) \\ OUT_n = W_n \cap OUT'_n \\ OUT'_k = \mathcal{T}_{\sigma_{k+1} \to \sigma_k}(OUT'_{k+1} \ominus W_{k+1}), \ \forall \, k \in [1..n-1] \\ OUT_k = W_k \cap [\, OUT'_k \ \bar{\cup} \ \mathcal{T}_{\sigma_{k+1} \to \sigma_k}(IN'_{k+1})\,], \ \forall \, k \in [1..n-1] \end{array} \right.$$

OUT_B is the OUT region corresponding to $B = S_1, \ldots, S_N$. It is relative to the store σ_B preceding the execution of the sequence. Therefore, $\mathcal{T}_{\sigma_B \to \sigma_n}(OUT_B)$ is the region corresponding to $S_1, \ldots, S_n$, but relative to the store σ_n preceding S_n. This is exactly the definition of OUT'_n. Thus $OUT'_n = \mathcal{T}_{\sigma_B \to \sigma_n}(OUT_B)$.

The elements exported by the subsequence $S_1, \ldots, S_k$ towards the outside of B, are those that exported by the subsequence $S_1, \ldots, S_{k+1}$ towards the outside of B, minus the elements exported by the instruction S_{k+1}. The corresponding OUT regions must be relative to the store σ_k, which gives:

$$OUT'_k = \mathcal{T}_{\sigma_{k+1} \to \sigma_k}(OUT'_{k+1} - W_{k+1})$$

Finaly, the OUT region of instruction S_k contain the elements written by S_k and exported towards the outside of B ($W_k \cap OUT'_k$), to which we must add the region written by S_k and exported towards $S_{k+1}, \ldots, S_n$ ($W_k \cap \mathcal{T}_{\sigma_{k+1} \to \sigma_k}(IN'_{k+1})$). We obtain:

$$OUT_k = W_k \cap [\, OUT'_k \ \bar{\cup} \ \mathcal{T}_{\sigma_{k+1} \to \sigma_k}(IN'_{k+1})\,]$$

Let us consider as an illustration the body of the second J loop, in Figure 2. Its WRITE and IN regions concerning the array WORK are the following:

```
C S1
C <WORK(φ1,φ2)-W-MUST-{φ1==J, φ2==K}>
    WORK(J,K) = J*J - K*K
C S2
C <WORK(φ1,φ2)-IN-MUST-{φ1==J, K-1<=φ2<=K}>
    A(I) = A(I)+WORK(J,K)+WORK(J,K-1)
```

Moreover, we assume that $OUT_B = \varnothing$. Then, we successively have:

$$
\begin{aligned}
OUT_2' &= OUT_B = \varnothing \\
OUT_2 &= W_2 \cap OUT_2' = \varnothing \\
OUT'1 &= OUT_2' - W_2 = \varnothing \\
OUT_1 &= W_1 \cap (OUT_1' \;\bar{\cup}\; IN_2') = W_1 \cap IN_2' \\
&= \texttt{<WORK(}\phi_1\texttt{,}\phi_2\texttt{)-W-MUST-\{}\phi_1\texttt{==J, }\phi_2\texttt{==K\}>} \\
&\quad \cap\ \texttt{<WORK(}\phi_1\texttt{,}\phi_2\texttt{)-IN-MUST-\{}\phi_1\texttt{==J, K-1<=}\phi_2\texttt{<=K\}>} \\
&= \texttt{<WORK(}\phi_1\texttt{,}\phi_2\texttt{)-W-MUST-\{}\phi_1\texttt{==J, }\phi_2\texttt{==K\}>}
\end{aligned}
$$

The first instruction exports the element it defines towards the second one, which exports nothing.

6 Conclusion

We have presented the analysis of exact READ/WRITE array regions. They provide an effective way to exactly represent the effects of statements and procedures upon array elements. Whereas the regions initially defined by Triolet [19] are over-approximations of the effects of procedures.

Since READ/WRITE regions cannot be used to compute the flow of array elements, we have introduced two new types of array region. IN and OUT regions represent the sets of array elements that are imported or exported by the corresponding code fragment. IN regions contain the locally upward exposed read elements, and are thus different from the usual upward-exposed read references.

We also provide a general linear framework for the interprocedural propagation of exact regions. It handles array reshapes, even in COMMONs that do not have the same data layout.

The current implementation covers all the intraprocedural structures of the FORTRAN language, along with the interprocedural propagation. A first series of experiments carried on the Perfect Club benchmarks has proven the practicality of the analysis in terms of time and memory space, in spite of the exponential complexity of the operators on polyhedra.

More experiments are needed to determine if the representation of IN and OUT regions in polyhedral form is precise enough to perform optimizations such as array privatisation, generation of communications in distributed memory machines, or compile-time optimization of cache behavior in hierarchichal memory machines. Other representations are being considered, such as finite unions of polyhedra, or polyhedra with holes.

Acknowledgments

We are very thankful to Corinne Ancourt, William Pugh, Fabien Coelho, Pierre Jouvelot, Alexis Platonoff and the referees for their careful reading, and helpful comments.

References

1. *American National Standard Programming Language FORTRAN ANSI X3.9-1978, ISO 1539-1980*, 1983.
2. Corinne Ancourt and François Irigoin. Scanning polyhedra with DO loops. In *Symposium on Principles and Practice of Parallel Programming*, April 1991.
3. Béatrice Apvrille-Creusillet. Régions exactes et privatisation de tableaux (exact array region analysis and array privatization). Master's thesis, Université Paris VI, France, September 1994. Available via http://www.cri.ensmp.fr/~creusil.
4. M. Berry et al. The PERFECT Club benchmarks: Effective performance evaluation of supercomputers. Technical Report CSRD-827, CSRD, University of Illinois, May 1989.
5. Michael Burke and Ron Cytron. Interprocedural dependence analysis and parallelization. ACM SIGPLAN NOTICES, 21(7):162–175, July 1986.
6. D. Callahan and K. Kennedy. Analysis of interprocedural side effects in a parallel programming environment. *Journal of Parallel and Distributed Computing*, 5:517–550, 1988.
7. Fabien Coelho. Compilation of I/O communications for HPF. In *Frontiers'95*, February 1995. Available via http://www.cri.ensmp.fr/~coelho.
8. Jean-François Collard. Automatic parallelization of while-loops using speculative execution. *International Journal of Parallel Programming*, 23(2):191–219, 1995.
9. Paul Feautrier. Dataflow analysis of array and scalar references. *International Journal of Parallel Programming*, 20(1):23–53, September 1991.
10. Mary Hall, Brian Murphy, Saman Amarasinghe, Shih-Wei Liao, and Monica Lam. Overview of an interprocedural automatic parallelization system. In *Fifth International Workshop on Compilers for Parallel Computers*, pages 570–579, June 1995.
11. François Irigoin. Interprocedural analyses for programming environments. In *Workshop on Environments and Tools for Parallel Scientific Computing*, September 1992.
12. François Irigoin, Pierre Jouvelot, and Rémi Triolet. Semantical interprocedural parallelization: An overview of the PIPS project. In *International Conference on Supercomputing*, June 1991.
13. Chung-Chi Jim Li, Elliot M. Stewart, and W. Kent Fuchs. Compiler-assisted full checkpointing. *Software : Practice and Experience*, 24(10):871–886, October 1994.
14. Vadim Maslov. Lazy array data-flow analysis. In *Symposium on Principles of Programming Language*, pages 311–325, January 1994.
15. Vadim Maslov and William Pugh. Simplifying polynomial constraints over integers to make dependence analysis more precise. Technical Report CS-TR-3109.1, University of Maryland, College Park, February 1994.
16. William Pugh. A practical algorithm for exact array dependence analysis. COMMUNICATIONS OF THE ACM, 35(8):102–114, August 1992.
17. William Pugh and David Wonnacott. Eliminating false data dependences using the omega test. In *International Conference on Programming Language Design and Implementation*, pages 140–151, June 1992.
18. Rémi Triolet. Interprocedural analysis for program restructuring with Parafrase. Technical report 538, CSRD, University of Illinois, December 1985.
19. Rémi Triolet, Paul Feautrier, and François Irigoin. Direct parallelization of call statements. In *Symposium on Compiler Construction*, 1986.

Interprocedural Analysis for Parallelization

Mary W. Hall†,

Brian R. Murphy, Saman P. Amarasinghe,
Shih-Wei Liao, Monica S. Lam

Computer Systems Laboratory †Computer Science Dept.
Stanford University   California Institute of Technology
Stanford, CA 94305   Pasadena, CA 91125

Abstract. This paper presents an extensive empirical evaluation of an interprocedural parallelizing compiler, developed as part of the Stanford SUIF compiler system. The system incorporates a comprehensive and integrated collection of analyses, including privatization and reduction recognition for both array and scalar variables, and symbolic analysis of array subscripts. The interprocedural analysis framework is designed to provide analysis results nearly as precise as full inlining but without its associated costs. Experimentation with this system on programs from standard benchmark suites demonstrate that an integrated combination of interprocedural analyses can substantially advance the capability of automatic parallelization technology.

1 Introduction

Symmetric shared-memory multiprocessors, built out of the latest microprocessors, are now a widely available class of powerful machines. As hardware technology advances make pervasive parallel computing a possibility, compilers which can extract parallelism from sequential codes become important tools to simplify parallel programming. Unfortunately, today's commercially available parallelizing compilers are not effective at getting good performance on multiprocessors [3, 19]. These compilers tend to be successful in parallelizing only innermost loops. Parallelizing just inner loops is not adequate for multiprocessors for two reasons. First, inner loops may not make up a significant portion of the sequential computation, thus limiting the parallel speedup by limiting the amount of parallelism. Second, synchronizing processors at the end of inner loops leaves little computation occurring in parallel between synchronization points. The cost of frequent synchronization and its associated load imbalance can potentially overwhelm the benefits of parallelization.

If compilers are to successfully locate outer, coarse-grain parallel loops, two improvements are needed. First, parallelizing compilers must incorporate ad-

This research was supported in part by DARPA contracts N00039-91-C-0138 and DABT63-91-K-0003, the NASA HPCC program, an NSF Young Investigator Award, an NSF CISE postdoctoral fellowship, a fellowship from Intel Corporation, and a fellowship from AT&T Bell Laboratories.

vanced array analyses, generalizing techniques currently only applied to scalar variables. For example, the compiler must recognize opportunities for *array privatization*, whereby storage-related dependences on array variables are eliminated by making a private copy of the array for each processor. As another example, the compiler must recognize opportunities to parallelize *array reductions*, such as computations of a sum, product, or maximum over array elements.

A second essential requirement for recognizing coarse-grain parallel loops is that procedures must not pose a barrier to analysis. One way to eliminate procedure boundaries is to perform inline substitution—replacing each procedure call by a copy of the called procedure—and perform analysis in the usual way. This is not a practical solution for large programs, as it is inefficient in both time and space. Interprocedural analysis, which applies data-flow analysis techniques across procedure boundaries, can be much more efficient as it analyzes only a single copy of each procedure. However, progress in interprocedural analysis has been inhibited by the complexity of interprocedural systems and the inherent tradeoff between performing analysis efficiently and obtaining precise results.

We have developed an automatic parallelization system that is fully interprocedural, and incorporates all standard analyses included in today's parallelizers, such as data dependence analysis, analyses of scalar values such as induction variable recognition, and scalar dependence and reduction recognition. In addition, the system employs analyses for array privatization and array reduction recognition. This system has allowed extensive empirical evaluation of automatic parallelization of three standard benchmark suites, demonstrating significant improvements over previous interprocedural parallelization systems and the technology available in commercial systems.

This paper describes the components of this system, and the interprocedural analysis framework in which they were developed. The key distinguishing features of this system are as follows. First, the interprocedural analysis is designed to be practical while providing nearly the same quality of analysis as if the program were fully inlined. Second, the array analysis incorporates a mathematical formulation of array reshapes at procedure boundaries, supporting changes in dimension between actual and corresponding formal parameters. Third, the system recognizes interprocedural array reductions. Finally, because the system has been used in an extensive empirical evaluation, the implementations of all the analysis techniques extend previous work to meet the demands of parallelizing real programs.

The remainder of the paper is organized into seven sections. Section 2 compares our work with other automatic parallelization systems. In Section 3, we present the interprocedural analysis framework and algorithm. Sections 4 and 5, describe the analysis of scalar variables and array variables, presented as instantiations of the analysis framework from Section 3. Section 6 describes how the interprocedural array analysis is extended to recognize array reductions. The final two sections discuss experiences with this system and conclude.

2 Related Work

In the late 1980s, a series of papers presented results on interprocedural parallelization analysis [9, 15, 20]. Their common approach was to determine the sections of arrays that are modified or referenced by each procedure call, enabling parallelization of some loops containing calls whenever each invocation modifies array elements distinct from those that are referenced or modified in other invocations. These techniques were shown to be effective in parallelizing linear algebra libraries. More recently, the FIDA system was developed at IBM to obtain more precise array sections through partial inlining of array accesses [10] (see Section 7).

Irigoin et al. developed an interprocedural analysis system, called PIPS, that is part of an environment for parallel programming [12]. More recently, PIPS has been extended to incorporate interprocedural array privatization [11, 5]. PIPS is most similar to our work, but lacks three important features: (1) path-specific interprocedural information such as obtained through selective procedure cloning, (2) interprocedural reductions, and (3) extensive interprocedural scalar data-flow analysis such as scalar privatization.

The Polaris system at University of Illinois is also pushing the state of the art in parallelization technology [2]. The most fundamental difference between our system and Polaris is that Polaris performs no interprocedural analysis, instead relying on full inlining of the programs to obtain interprocedural information. The Polaris group has demonstrated that good coverage (fraction of the program parallelized) can be obtained automatically. Although they report that full inlining is feasible on eight medium-sized programs, this approach will likely have difficulty parallelizing large loops containing thousands of lines of code.

3 Interprocedural Framework

Parallelization depends upon the solution of a large number of data-flow analysis problems, which share many commonalities. Traditional data-flow analysis frameworks help reduce development time and improve correctness by capturing these common features in a single tool [13]. In an interprocedural setting, a framework is even more important because of the complexity of collecting and managing information about all the procedures in a program.

We use FIAT [6], a tool which encapsulates the common features of interprocedural analysis, in combination with the Stanford SUIF compiler to constitute our interprocedural parallelization system. The FIAT system has been described previously, but we have extended the system to obtain precise flow-sensitive interprocedural results through the combination of two techniques which we now describe. We have also added to the system a mathematical formulation of array reshapes (see Section 5.2) in order to support interprocedural array analysis. This section describes FIAT's parameterized templates that drive the parallelization analysis.

Region-Based Flow-Sensitive Analysis. To capture precise interprocedural information requires a *flow-sensitive* analysis approach, which derives analysis results along each possible control flow path through the program. Precise and efficient flow-sensitive interprocedural analysis is difficult because information flows into a procedure both from its callers (representing the *calling context* in which the procedure is invoked) and from its callees (representing the effects of the invocation). For example, in a straightforward interprocedural adaptation of traditional iterative analysis, analysis might be carried out over a program representation called the *supergraph* [16], where individual control flow graphs for the procedures in the program are linked together at procedure call and return points. Iterative analysis over this structure is slow because the number of control flow paths through which information flows increases greatly. Such analysis also loses precision by propagating information along *unrealizable paths* [14]; the analysis may propagate calling context information from one caller through a procedure and return the side-effect information to a different caller. In our system, we use a region-based analysis that solves the problems of unrealizable paths and slow convergence. We perform analysis efficiently in two passes over the program.

Selective Procedure Cloning. For procedures invoked on multiple distinct paths through a program, traditional interprocedural analysis forms a conservative approximation of the information entering the procedure that is correct for all paths. Such approximations can affect the precision of analysis if a procedure is invoked along paths that contribute very different information. Path-specific interprocedural information has previously been obtained either by inline substitution or by tagging data-flow sets with a path history through the call graph, incurring a data-flow set expansion problem corresponding to the code explosion problem of inlining [8, 16, 17, 18]. To avoid such excessive space usage, we utilize path-specific information only when it may provide opportunities for improved optimization. Our system incorporates *selective procedure cloning*, a program restructuring in which the compiler replicates the analysis results for a procedure to analyze it in the context of distinct calling environments [4]. By applying cloning *selectively* according to the unique data-flow information it exposes, we can obtain the same precision as full inlining without unnecessary replication.

3.1 The Region Graph

The region-based analysis aggregates information at the boundaries of program regions: basic blocks, loop bodies and loops (restricted to DO loops), procedure calls, procedure bodies, and procedures. We use a program representation called the *region graph* to represent the loop nesting and procedure nesting of the program. The region graph is a directed graph whose nodes represent regions and whose edges represent nesting relationships. With each region is associated an *immediate subregions graph*, a directed flow graph consisting of immediately nested regions and control flow edges between them.

Each region has a single entry node. To simplify presentation, we primarily describe analyses with regions that also have a single exit. (The actual analysis framework implementation is more general. Irreducible graphs are supported in the scalar data-flow analysis described in Section 4, although the array analysis approximates when graphs are irreducible or when loops contain multiple exits.)

3.2 Data-Flow Functions

The first phase of any program analysis using this framework yields a transfer function for each region in a problem-specific form. For each analysis, a representation for transfer functions $\mathcal{T}$ with the following operations must be provided:

- Extract basic block transfer function ($\mathcal{T} = \text{BasicBlockTF}(b)$)
- Composition ($\circ$)
- Meet ($\bigwedge$), with identity value ($\top$)
- Iteration ($\mathcal{T}^i$): yield effect after i iterations, where i is the loop's normalized index variable.
- Closure ($\mathcal{T}^*$): eliminate the most recent loop index variable to describe the effect of the entire loop.
- RetMap($\mathcal{T}$, *callsite*): map procedure transfer function into caller space

The first phase computes relative information that summarizes the behavior of each region. To compute absolute information, a second phase may optionally be performed. The second phase determines absolute information on entry to each procedure and region, using the transfer functions found in the first phase to propagate a problem-specific data-flow value. A representation for this value must be provided, along with the following operations:

- Context of program (input value $\bot$)
- Meet ($\bigwedge$), with identity value ($\top$)
- Apply transfer function to a data-flow value to yield another
- CallMap(*val*, *callsite*): map call context into procedure space
- Filter(*val*, *Proc*): remove information not relevant to *Proc*
- Partition(val_1, val_2): equivalence relation on procedure contexts

3.3 Algorithm

A region-based analysis, as shown in Figure 1, proceeds in one or two phases. In the first phase, we analyze each procedure independent of its calling environment to obtain a transfer function $\mathcal{T}_P$; this transfer function is used (with appropriate parameter mapping) at call sites when analyzing callers. The second phase propagates data-flow values, applying them to the transfer functions from the previous phase, to yield the data-flow input to each region. The two-phase region-based analysis is similar to what is traditionally called interval-based analysis, where the intervals of interest are loops and procedure bodies.

/* PHASE 1: Derive Transfer Functions */
for each *procedure* P from bottom to top over call graph:
    for each *region* R from innermost to outermost:
        if R is a basic block, compute $\mathcal{T}_R = \text{BasicBlockTF}(R)$
        if R is a loop with body R',
            $\mathcal{T}_{R,R'} = \mathcal{T}_{R'}^{i}$ for this loop's normalized index variable i
            $\mathcal{T}_R = \mathcal{T}_{R,R'}^{*}$
        if R is a call at site cs to procedure with body R',
            $\mathcal{T}_R = \text{RetMap}(\mathcal{T}_{R'}, cs)$ /* map parameters */
        if R is a loop body or procedure body,
            for a forward data-flow problem,
                for each immediate subregion R',
                    compute $\mathcal{T}_{R,R'}$ = transfer function from entry of R to entry of R'
                by finding least solution to (for all R'):

$$\mathcal{T}_{R,R'} = \bigwedge_{p\,\in\,pred(R')} \mathcal{T}_p \circ \mathcal{T}_{R,p}$$
$$\mathcal{T}_R = \mathcal{T}_{\text{Exit}(R)} \circ \mathcal{T}_{R,\text{Exit}(R)}$$

            for a backward data-flow problem,
                for each immediate subregion R',
                    compute $\mathcal{T}_{R,R'}$ = transfer function from exit of R to exit of R'
                by finding least solution to (for all R'):

$$\mathcal{T}_{R,R'} = \bigwedge_{s\,\in\,succ(R')} \mathcal{T}_s \circ \mathcal{T}_{R,s}$$
$$\mathcal{T}_R = \mathcal{T}_{\text{Entry}(R)} \circ \mathcal{T}_{R,\text{Entry}(R)}$$

/* PHASE 2: Derive Procedure Contexts using Transfer Functions */
/*   and propagate data flow information to regions */
$\mathcal{C}_{\text{Entry}(Program)} = \{\perp\}$
for each *procedure* P from top to bottom over call graph,
    let $\mathcal{C}$ be the union of calling contexts on incoming edges
    let $\mathcal{C}' = \{\text{Filter}(c, P) \mid c \in \mathcal{C}\}$
    let $\mathcal{P}$ be the equivalence classes of $\mathcal{C}'$ with respect to Partition
    for each partition $p \in \mathcal{P}$
        $\mathcal{V}_{p,P} = \bigwedge_{c\,\in\,p} c$
        for each region R in P from outermost to innermost,
            for each subregion R' of R,
                $\mathcal{V}_{p,R'} = \mathcal{T}_{R,R'}(\mathcal{V}_{p,R})$
            if R is a call at site cs with corresponding call graph edge e,
                add context $\text{CallMap}(\mathcal{V}_{p,R}, cs)$ to edge e /* map parameters */

Fig. 1. Region-Based Interprocedural Analysis Framework

Phase 1: Calculating Region Transfer Functions For each region R from innermost loop to outermost loop, and from bottom to top in the call graph, we compute its transfer function $\mathcal{T}_R$. A basic block's transfer function is derived directly (using the BasicBlockTF function). The transfer function of a procedure call takes the procedure body's transfer function and maps it to the caller space, renaming variables in its representation (using the RetMap operation).

The transfer function for a loop applies the Iteration operation to the transfer function of its loop body $\mathcal{T}_{R'}$ to obtain a transfer function $\mathcal{T}_{R,R'}$ representing the effect of i iterations of the body, where i is the loop's normalized index variable. The final transfer function showing the total effect of the loop is obtained by using the Closure operation to eliminate the iteration counter i.

For loop bodies and procedure bodies, deriving the transfer function involves the transfer functions of its immediate subregions. In a forward data-flow problem, for each subregion R', we compute $\mathcal{T}_{R,R'}$, the transfer function from the entry of R to the entry of R'. This calculation results from a meet over the predecessors of R'. If the immediate subregions graph is cyclic, then an iterative solution may be required to find the transfer function. Otherwise, the subregions are simply visited in the appropriate (reverse postorder) order within the region. The final transfer function for the loop body or procedure body is derived by composing the transfer function $\mathcal{T}_{R,\mathrm{Exit}(R)}$ for the subregion that represents the exit from region R, with the transfer function $\mathcal{T}_{\mathrm{Exit}(R)}$ of that region.

Data-flow problems that require a backward propagation within the intervals are analogous. For an acyclic subregion graph, a postorder traversal over the subregions derives transfer functions $\mathcal{T}_{R,R'}$ to describe the effects from the exit of R up to the exit of R'.

Phase 2: Deriving Calling Contexts and Computing Final Values. For a two-phase problem, the second phase of the algorithm derives the data-flow input to each procedure and its subregions. This phase of the analysis is performed top-down over the call graph and from outermost to innermost loops within each procedure body. For a procedure, the analysis derives the set of calling contexts $\mathcal{C}$ contributed by calls to the procedure. Instead of performing a meet operation over all of the calling contexts, the analysis partitions these contexts into equivalence classes under the Partition relation according to their data-flow information before meeting only the contexts within each equivalence class.

The number of partitions is reduced by first using a Filter to eliminate from the data-flow values information not relevant to the called procedure. (We describe an example of this filtering in Section 4.)

Each partition defines a data-flow input value $\mathcal{V}_{p,P}$, the meet of the calling contexts in that partition. For each partition, the analysis applies the transfer functions to this data-flow value to propagate information from outermost to innermost to yield the input to inner regions. For a region R representing a procedure call, the analysis adds to the corresponding call graph edge the calling context $\mathcal{V}_{p,R}$. It is important to note that our analysis does not actually generate cloned procedure bodies, but merely replicates their data-flow information for the purposes of analysis.

4 Scalar Data-Flow Analysis

Scalar data-flow analysis is crucial for parallelizing loops. Analyses of scalar variables in a loop are necessary both to detect and eliminate scalar dependences and to support precise analysis of array accesses. Array analysis support is provided by an interprocedural symbolic analysis and a separate inequality constraint propagation.

4.1 Support for Array Analysis: Interprocedural Symbolic Analysis

To precisely represent the array accesses in a loop (using an analysis such as the one to be described in Section 5) requires that array indices be rephrased in terms which are valid throughout the loop. Using traditional program analyses, a set of analyses of integer variable values is needed: constant propagation, induction and loop-invariant variable detection, and common subexpression recognition.

Our system provides the effect of such analyses through a single symbolic analysis, which is performed interprocedurally. For example, to parallelize the following loop:

```
     K = J + 1
        DO 10 I=1,N
           A(J) = A(K)
           J = J + 2
           K = K + 2
     10 CONTINUE
```

the array index expressions in terms of loop-varying variables (J and K) are mapped into expressions in terms of normalized (base 0) loop indices and loop invariants. In this particular loop, a new loop-invariant variable J_0 is introduced to refer to the value of J on entry to the loop and a base-0 iteration count variable i is introduced, local to the loop body. J is found to have a value $J_0 + 2i$ and K a value $J_0 + 2i + 1$. Substituting these values into the array indices allows comparison of the portions of array A read and written by the loop.

The symbolic analysis determines for each variable appearing in an array access a symbolic value: an arbitrary expression describing its value in terms of constants, loop-invariant variables, and normalized loop indices, if possible.

Array dependence analysis typically only handles affine array indices precisely; nevertheless, the symbolic values resulting from the symbolic analysis may be non-affine. In some cases our system is currently unable to make use of this non-affine information. In one common case of non-affine array indices—those resulting from a higher-order induction variable—we extract additional information which can be provided in an affine form, as discussed below.

Representation: Symbolic Maps More formally, a symbolic value expression *sym* is either *Unknown* or an arbitrary arithmetic/conditional expression in terms of constants, variables, and loop indices. A *symbolic map*

$$SM = \{< var_1, sym_1 >, \ldots\}$$

binds variables var_i to symbolic descriptions of their values sym_i. A symbolic map associated with a region R may be either *relative* or *absolute*. In a *relative* map, variables within bound values refer to their values on entry to R; in an *absolute* map, no bound value may contain a variable modified within R.

For convenience below, we define an operation $SM(sym)$ on symbolic map SM and symbolic value sym, which yields *Unknown* if sym contains a var_i not bound in SM, and otherwise yields sym with every occurrence of a var_i bound by SM replaced by the bound value sym_i.

Region-Based Analysis We obtain absolute value maps describing variable values at every program point in two passes, as a region-based data-flow analysis. A bottom-up pass through the program derives the transfer function for each region, as a relative value map that describes variable values at each immediate subregion in terms of entry variable values. A subsequent top-down pass through the program propagates to each region a symbolic context, an absolute map describing actual variable values on region entry in terms of enclosing loop indices and invariants.

Phase 1: Transfer Functions The symbolic behavior of a region R is a relative map SM_R describing every variable's value on exit in terms of enclosing loop indices and variable values on entry to R. The following operations are defined:

- BasicBlockTF(b): forms a map showing the effect of the block on every program variable: unmodified variables are mapped to themselves, modified variables are mapped to a symbolic value expression representing the value on exit in terms of the values on entry. New variables are introduced to represent the values of certain operations with unknown results (e.g., load from memory, I/O read). These variables are limited in scope to the nearest enclosing loop or procedure body.
- Composition ($\circ$): apply SM_2 to every bound value in SM_1:
$$SM_1 \circ SM_2 = \{< var_i, SM_2(sym_i) > \ | < var_i, sym_i > \in SM_1\}$$
- Meet ($\bigwedge$), with identity element $\top_{SM}$:
$$SM_1 \wedge SM_2 = \{< var, sym > \ | \ sym = (SM_1 \cap SM_2)(var)\}$$
- Iteration: SM^i finds loop invariants and induction variables and rephrases them in terms of the given index variable i. Auxiliary maps SM_0^i (loop invariants) and SM_1^i (induction variables) are used to compute SM^i, as follows:
$$SM_0^i = \{< var, var > \ | < var, var > \in SM\}$$
$$SM_1^i = \{< var, var + i * c > \ | < var, var + c > \in SM, c = SM(c)\}$$
$$SM^i = \{< var, sym > \ | sym = (SM_0^i \cup SM_1^i)(var)\}$$
gives the net change after i iterations of the loop, and includes loop invariant and induction variable recognition.
- Closure: SM^* substitutes an expression *if* $lb \leq ub$ *then* $\lceil (ub - lb)/step \rceil + 1$ *else* 0 for the most recent loop index variable i throughout SM.
- RetMap(SM, *callsite*): maps formals to actuals everywhere in SM.

Phase 2: Symbolic Calling Contexts. The symbolic context of a region R is an absolute map SM_R describing each live variable's value on entry to R in terms of loop invariants and loop indices of enclosing loops.

- Context on entry to program: the initial symbolic context $\perp$ maps all variables to *Unknown*.
- Meet ($\bigwedge$), identity ($\top$): as for relative maps.
- Apply transfer function: Relative map SM_1 is applied to an absolute map SM_2 to derive a new absolute map: $SM_1(SM_2) = SM_1 \circ SM_2$.
- CallMap(SM, *callsite*): map actuals to formals everywhere in SM.
- Filter(SM, *Proc*): Eliminate from the map all bindings of variables with no upwards-exposed reads in *Proc*.
- Partition(SM_1, SM_2): Only identical maps are equivalent.

Cloning. We employ selective procedure cloning based on the values in the map. Currently, the filter function eliminates from the map relations on variables that have no upwards-exposed reads in the called procedure; this significantly reduces the amount of replication in the analysis.

Higher-order Induction Variable Support The closure operation can be extended to recognize higher order induction variables, such as a variable incremented inside a triangular loop. Such variables are not uncommon in scientific codes as linearized array subscripts. To handle 2nd-order induction variables, we extend the iteration operator with an auxiliary SM_2^i map, as follows:

$$SM_2^i = \{< var, var + c_1 * (i * (i-1))/2 + c_2 * i > \mid$$
$$< var, var + c_1 * i + c_2 > \in SM' \circ (SM_0^i \cup SM_1^{i-1}),$$
$$c_1 = SM(c_1), \ c_2 = SM(c_2)\}$$
$$SM^i = \{< var, sym > \mid sym = (SM_0^i \cup SM_1^i \cup SM_2^i)(var)\}$$

Unfortunately, the resulting closed form of a second-order induction variable which is thus introduced is non-affine and not directly useful to the affine parallelization tests used in array analysis. For this reason, the analysis in this case introduces a new variable x, whose scope is limited to the loop body, and in place of the non-affine expression $var + c_1 * (i * (i-1))/2 + c_2 * i$, we use the affine expression $var + x$.

When the array analysis performs a comparison between two accesses containing x, the additional affine information is provided that if, for example, $c_1 \geq 0$ and $c_2 \geq 0$, then for iteration $i = i'$ we have $x = x'$ and for iteration $i = i''$ we have $x = x''$ such that if $i' < i''$ then $x' \leq x'' + c_1 + c_2$. Similar useful affine information can be provided under other conditions on c_1 and c_2. This approach enables one commonly occurring case of non-affine symbolic values in array subscripts to be handled without an expensive extension to the array analysis.

4.2 Inequality Constraints

The symbolic analysis described thus far can only determine equality constraints between variables. Since array analysis also benefits from knowledge of loop bounds and other control-based contextual constraints on variables (e.g., if predicates), which may contain inequalities, a separate top-down pass carries loop and predicate constraints to relevant array accesses. Equality constraints determined by the symbolic analysis are used to rephrase each predicate in loop-invariant terms, if possible. The control context is represented by a set of affine inequalities in the form discussed in Section 5.

4.3 Scalar Parallelization Analysis

A number of standard analyses ensure that scalar variables do not limit the parallelism available in a loop. These analyses locate scalar dependences, locate opportunities for scalar reduction transformations and determine privatizable scalars. We apply these analyses interprocedurally. A simple flow-insensitive mod-ref analysis[1] detects scalar dependences and, with a straightforward extension, provides the necessary information to locate scalar reductions. A flow-sensitive live-variable analysis, discussed below, allows detection of privatizable scalar variables. The flow-sensitive symbolic analysis of Section 4.1 also finds induction and loop-invariant integer variables, which can then be privatized.

Live Variable Analysis. We solve a standard live-variable problem interprocedurally through a two-phase region-based backward analysis. In Phase 1, the transfer function for each region is computed as a pair of sets: Gen set, containing variables with upwards exposed reads in the region, and $Kill$ set, containing variables written in the region. In Phase 2, the set of live variables on entry to a region is determined from the set of live variables on exit of the region: $Live_{entry} = (Live_{exit} - Kill) \cup Gen$.

For loops containing returns and breaks, the situation is somewhat complicated, since there is not just a single exit. A single transfer function is not sufficient to describe the behavior of a region with multiple exits in a backward data-flow problem. Instead, we summarize the behavior of a loop body by three transfer functions—from *loop body* exit, from *loop* exit, and from *enclosing procedure* exit. A loop is described by just two transfer functions—from *loop* exit and from *procedure* exit. A single transfer function still suffices to describe a procedure. In other respects the analysis is straightforward.

5 Analysis of Array Variables

The array analysis locates loops that carry no data dependences on array elements or that can be safely parallelized after array privatization. The system, when integrated with the reduction recognition and scalar data-flow analysis, performs an array data-flow analysis based on systems of linear inequalities to analyze affine array access functions. This approach is driven by the need to compute both data dependences and value-based dependences for array privatization in a framework that is suitable for flow-sensitive interprocedural analysis. An important feature of the array data-flow analysis is the use of summaries, which describe subarrays accessed by a region of the code; summaries eliminate the need to perform $\mathcal{O}(n^2)$ pairwise dependence tests for a loop containing n array accesses. This efficiency consideration may be unimportant within a single procedure, but is crucial when analyzing large loops that may span multiple procedures and have hundreds of array accesses.

5.1 Representation: Summaries

We represent each array access by a system of integer linear inequalities. An *array summary* is a set of such systems. For example, consider the following loop nest.

$$
\left.\left.\begin{array}{l}
\texttt{DO 10 I = 1, N} \\
\quad \texttt{DO 10 J = 1, M} \\
\qquad \texttt{A(J + 1, 2 * I)} \; = \; \dots \; \} \, W_1
\end{array} \right\} W_2 \right\} W_3
$$

The region of array A written by a single execution of the statement is represented by set containing one system of inequalities, parameterized by the program variables M and N, and normalized loop index variables i and j:

$$
W_1 = \left\{ (w_1, w_2) \; \middle| \; \left\{ \begin{array}{l} 0 \le j \le \texttt{M} - 1, \; w_1 = j + 2, \\ 0 \le i \le \texttt{N} - 1, \; w_2 = 2i + 2 \end{array} \right\} \right\}
$$

The included contextual constraints on program variables and loop indices are provided by the scalar context analysis.

Intuitively, a set is necessary because different accesses to an array may refer to distinctly different regions of the array. Mathematically, many of the operators applied to array summaries result in non-convex regions, which cannot be precisely described with a single system of inequalities. To maintain efficiency, we merge systems of inequalities whenever we can guarantee no loss of information will result. The following basic operations are defined on array summaries. Operations marked * are not exact.

- **Empty?** $(A = \emptyset) = \forall_{a \in A} (a = \emptyset)$. A set of systems is empty iff all systems in the set are empty. A system of inequalities is empty if there are no integer solutions that satisfy the system. We use a Fourier-Motzkin pair-wise elimination technique with branch-and-bound to check for the existence of an integer solution to a system of inequalities. If no solution exists, the system is empty.
* **Contained?** $A \subseteq B = \forall_{a \in A} \exists_{b \in B} (a \subseteq b)$. A set of systems is contained in another, iff each system in the first set is contained in a single system in the other set. This is conservative as it may return a false negative. A system of inequalities a is contained in a system of inequalities b if and only if a combined with the negation of any single inequality of b is empty.

- **Union** $A \cup B = \{c \mid c \in A \text{ or } c \in B\}$. The union of two sets of systems simply unions the two sets, then simplifies the set using the following two heuristics:
  - If there are two systems a and b in the set such that $a \subseteq \cdot b$, then a is removed from the set.
  - If two systems are rectilinear and adjacent, they are combined to form a single system.

  In practice, these heuristics keep the sets a manageable size and increase the precision of the *Contained?* operator. Since the union of two convex regions can result in a non-convex region, a set is necessary to maintain the precision of the union operator.
- **Intersection** $A \cap B = \{a \cap b \mid a \in A \text{ and } b \in B \text{ and } a \cap b \neq \emptyset\}$. The intersection of two sets of systems is the set of all non-empty pairwise intersections of their elements. Intersection of two systems of inequalities simply concatenates the inequalities of the two systems.
- * **Subtraction** $A \sim B = \{a \sim b_1 \sim \ldots \sim b_n \mid a \in A \text{ and } B = \{b_1 \ldots b_n\}\}$. The subtraction of two sets of systems subtracts all systems of the second set from each system in the first. Two systems are subtracted using a heuristic: $a \sim b$ is exact when $a \cap b = \emptyset$ or $a \subseteq b$ or both are simple rectilinear systems; otherwise it is approximated as a.
- **Projections** $Proj(A, v)$ eliminates the variable v from the constraints of all the systems in set A by applying the Fourier-Motzkin elimination technique to each system. Each system $a \in A$ can be viewed as the integer points inside a n-dimensional polytope whose dimensions are the variables of a and whose bounds are given by the inequalities of a; this polytope is projected into a lower-dimensional $(n-1)$ space where the integer solutions of all remaining dimensions remain unchanged. One use of projection is to summarize the effects of array accesses within a loop. For example, for the system of inequalities representing the access to array A shown above, projections are used to generate systems of inequalities representing the array accesses for each loop in the nest. In some cases, eliminating a variable may result in a larger region than the actual region. In the example, eliminating the constraint $w_2 = 2\mathtt{i} + 2$ will lose the information that w_2 must be even. For this reason, analysis introduces an auxiliary x in W_3 to retain this constraint.

$$W_2 = Proj(W_1, \mathtt{j}) = \left\{ (\mathtt{w_1}, \mathtt{w_2}) \left| \left\{ \begin{array}{l} 0 \leq \mathtt{i} \leq \mathtt{N} - 1, \ w_2 = 2\mathtt{i} + 2 \\ 2 \leq w_1 \leq \mathtt{M} + 1 \end{array} \right\} \right. \right\}$$

$$W_3 = Proj(W_2, \mathtt{i}) = \left\{ (\mathtt{w_1}, \mathtt{w_2}) \left| \left\{ \begin{array}{l} 2 \leq w_2 \leq 2\mathtt{N}, \ w_2 = 2x \\ 2 \leq w_1 \leq \mathtt{M} + 1 \end{array} \right\} \right. \right\}$$

5.2 Array Reshapes

Interprocedural array analysis must provide precise results in the presence of *array reshapes* at procedure boundaries, as when a slice of an array is passed into a procedure, and as in *linearization*, when a multi-dimensional array in one procedure is treated as a linear array in another. In the following example, FOO passes BAR the Kth column of the array X. This 10000-element vector from FOO, is manipulated as a 100×100 array in BAR.

```
SUBROUTINE FOO                    SUBROUTINE BAR(Y)
INTEGER X(10000, 10)              INTEGER Y(100, 100)
    ....                              DO 9 I= 1,100
CALL BAR(X(1, K))                     DO 9 J= 1,50
                                         Y(I,J) = ...
                                9    CONTINUE
```

Mapping an array summary from callee to caller is not a simple rename operation. We perform this mapping by deriving inequalities for the indices of the actual parameter in terms of the indices of the formal parameter and use the projection operation to eliminate the formal parameter's indices.

We formalize the mapping of summary S for an n-dimensional formal array parameter F, where $A(a_1, \ldots, a_m)$ is passed at the call site and actual A is an m-dimensional array, using the mapping function:

$$\mathcal{M}(S, F, A, a_1, \ldots, a_m) = \{(j_1, \ldots, j_m) \mid Proj\left(\{b_F \cap b_A \cap r_{FA}\} \cap S, \{i_1, \ldots, i_n\}\right)\}$$

Where

- $i_1, \ldots, i_n$ are variables representing the indices of accesses to array F.
- $j_1, \ldots, j_m$ are variables representing the indices of accesses to array A.
- b_F is the set of bounds for the array F given by its type declaration. (Note that the exact bounds of the outermost dimension are not required.)
- b_A is the set of bounds for the array A given by its type declaration.
- r_{FA} describes the conditions under which an access $F(i_1, \ldots, i_n)$ in the procedure and an access $A(j_1, \ldots, j_m)$ in the callee refer to the same location. This occurs when the memory offset of $F(i_1, \ldots, i_n)$ is equal to the memory offset of $A(j_1, \ldots, j_m)$ minus the memory offset of $A(a_1, \ldots, a_m)$. This relationship between memory offsets is represented as an equality relation; other known facts about variables used in the equality may be included in the system.

For the FOO, BAR example the mapping function is calculated using:

$$b_F = \left\{ \begin{array}{c} 1 \leq j_1 \leq 100 \\ 1 \leq j_2 \leq 100 \end{array} \right\}, \qquad b_A = \left\{ \begin{array}{c} 1 \leq i_1 \leq 10000 \\ 1 \leq i_2 \leq 10 \end{array} \right\},$$

$$r_{FA} = \left\{ \begin{array}{c} 100 * (j_2 - 1) + (j_1 - 1) = 10000 * (i_2 - K) + (i_1 - 1) \\ 1 \leq K \leq 10 \end{array} \right\}$$

Thus when when using the mapping function on the summary of the array Y at the start of subroutine BAR:

$$\mathcal{M}\left(\left\{(j_1, j_2) \middle| \left\{ \begin{array}{c} 1 \leq j_1 \leq 100 \\ 1 \leq j_2 \leq 50 \end{array} \right\}\right\}, Y, X, 1, K\right) = \left\{(i_1, i_2) \middle| \left\{ \begin{array}{c} 1 \leq i_1 \leq 5000 \\ i_2 = K \\ 1 \leq K \leq 10 \end{array} \right\}\right\}$$

This approach handles precisely cases where complex numbers in one procedure are treated as real numbers in another by modeling a complex number as an array with two elements. Some reshapes are not handled precisely. If array dimensions are unknown, for example, there is no linear relationship between the indices of the actual and formal parameters, and unless the unknown dimensions are identical, we must approximate.

5.3 Region-Based Analysis

The analysis of an array variables computes four distinct sets for each program region. These sets are used by both the dependence and privatization tests to determine the safety of parallelization. The data-flow sets for a given region R are informally defined as follows:

W_R –   *Write*: portions of arrays possibly written within region R
M_R –   *Must Write*: portions of arrays always written within region R
R_R –   *Read*: portions of arrays possibly read within region R
E_R –   *Exposed Read*: portions of arrays whose reads are possibly upwards exposed to the beginning of R

These sets are together computed as a 4-tuple transfer function using a backwards region-based analysis as described in Section 3. Because just the transfer function itself is needed, the second phase of the region-based framework can be omitted.

Transfer Functions. The side-effect transfer function of a region R on a particular array is represented as the 4-tuple

$$S_R =< W_R, M_R, R_R, E_R >$$

where the elements are the sets informally defined as described above. The following operations are defined on S tuples:

- BasicBlockTF(b): result of composing read and write accesses in block b. Read access: $S =< \emptyset, \emptyset, \{a\}, \{a\} >$. Write access: $S =< \{a\}, \{a\}, \emptyset, \emptyset >$. where a is a system describing the access indices, rewritten in loop-relative terms (from symbolic analysis), with relevant inequality constraints added.
- Composition: $S_1 \circ S_2 =< W_1 \cup W_2, M_1 \cup M_2, R_1 \cup R_2, E_1 \cup (E_2 \sim M_1) >$.
- Meet: $S_1 \wedge S_2 =< W_1 \cup W_2, M_1 \cap M_2, R_1 \cup R_2, E_1 \cup E_2 >$.
- Identity element: $\top_S =< \emptyset, \emptyset, \emptyset, \emptyset >$.
- Iteration: $S^i = S$. The given loop index variable i is used to perform dependence and privatization tests, as in the following section.
- Closure: $S^* =< Proj(W, L), Proj(M, L), Proj(R, L), Proj(E, L) >$, where L contains the loop index i and other loop-modified variables.
- RetMap$(S, callsite) =< \mathcal{M}(W, \ldots), \mathcal{M}(M, \ldots), \mathcal{M}(R, \ldots), \mathcal{M}(E, \ldots) >$, as discussed in Section 5.2.

5.4 Dependence and Array Privatization Tests

To determine if array accesses allow the parallelization of a loop with index i, dependence and privatization tests are performed on the summary sets for the loop body R:

- There is no loop-carried:
  - *True Dependence* iff $W_R|_j^{i_1} \cap R_R|_j^{i_2} \cap \{i_1 < i_2\} = \phi$
  - *Anti Dependence* iff $W_R|_i^{i_1} \cap R_R|_i^{i_2} \cap \{i_1 > i_2\} = \phi$

- *Output Dependence* iff $W_R|_i^{i_1} \cap W_R|_i^{i_2} \cap \{i_1 < i_2\} = \phi$
  - *Array Privatization* is possible iff $W_R|_i^{i_1} \cap E_R|_i^{i_2} \cap \{i_1 < i_2\} = \phi$

A loop may be safely parallelized if there are no loop-carried true, anti or output dependences. The array privatization test is applied only to the variables that are involved in dependences to determine if privatization will eliminate these dependences.

Our formulation of array privatization is an extension of Tu and Padua's algorithm[21]. Tu and Padua recognize an array as privatizable only if there are *no* upwards-exposed reads within the loop. Our algorithm is more general in that upwards-exposed reads are acceptable as long as they do not overlap writes in other iterations of the same loop.

5.5 Generating Executable Code With Array Privatization

It is straightforward to generate parallelized code for loops for which there are no dependences, but in the presence of array privatization, the system must ensure that initial and final values of the array are copied to and from the private copies.

If an array has upwards-exposed read regions, the compiler must copy these regions into the private copy prior to execution of the parallel loop. If an array is live on exit of the loop, then after a parallel execution of the loop the array must contain the same values as those obtained had the loop been executed sequentially; we do not test array liveness on exit, so we limit privatization to those cases where every iteration in the loop writes to exactly the same region of data. To do so the analysis performs the following test to finalize a loop whose index i has upper bound ub: If $W = M|_i^{ub}$, the last loop iteration is peeled, and this final iteration writes to the original array. Earlier iterations write to a private copy of the array. No peeling is necessary if the compiler can guarantee that the last processor executes the last iteration. Then the compiler can generate code which simply writes to private copies in all the processors except the last one.

6 Array Reduction Recognition

A reduction occurs when a location is updated on each loop iteration with the result of a commutative and associative operation applied to its previous contents and some data value. A loop containing a reduction may be safely parallelized since the ordering of the commutative updates need not be preserved.

We have implemented a simple, yet powerful approach to recognizing reductions, in response to the common cases we have encountered in experimenting with the compiler. The reduction recognition, which is integrated with the array analysis described in the previous section, finds reductions involving general commutative updates to array elements, possibly spanning multiple procedures.

6.1 Reduction Recognition

We currently recognize reductions on scalar variables and array locations involving the operations $+$, $*$, MIN, and MAX. MIN (and, equivalently, MAX) reductions of the form if (a(i) < tmin) tmin = a(i) are also supported.

The system looks for commutative updates to a single location A of the form $A = A$ op ..., where A is either a scalar variable or an array location and op is one of the operations listed above. This approach allows any commutative update to a single array location to be recognized as a reduction, even without information about the array indices. We illustrate this point with an example sparse matrix-vector multiply found in the NAS sample benchmark cgm:

```
      DO 200 J = 1, N
         XJ = X(J)
         DO 100 K = COLSTR(J) , COLSTR(J+1)-1
            Y(ROWIDX(K)) = Y(ROWIDX(K)) + A(K) * XJ
100      CONTINUE
200   CONTINUE
```

Our system correctly determines that updates to Y are reductions on the outer loop, even though Y is indexed by another array ROWIDX and so the array access functions for Y are not affine expressions.

The reduction recognition analysis first locates commutative updates in a loop body; it verifies that the only other reads and writes in the loop to the same location are also commutative updates of the same type described by op. A loop is parallelized if all dependences involve variables whose only accesses are reduction operations of identical type.

In terms of our data-flow analysis algorithm, reduction recognition is initialized by examining the code for commutative updates to the same array location. Whenever an array element is involved in a commutative update, the array analysis derives summaries for the read and written subarrays and marks the system of inequalities as a reduction of the type described by op. When meeting two systems of inequalities during the interval analysis, the reduction types are also met. The resulting system of inequalities will only be marked as a reduction if both reduction types are identical.

6.2 Generating Executable Code With Reductions

For each variable involved in a reduction, the compiler makes a private copy of the variable for each processor. The executable code for the loop containing the reduction manipulates the private copy of the reduction variable in three separate parts. First, the private copy is initialized prior to executing the loop with the identity element for op (e.g., 0 for $+$). Second, the reduction operation is applied to the private copy within the parallel loop. Finally, the program performs a global accumulation following the loop execution whereby all non-identity elements of the local copies of the variable are accumulated into the original variable. Synchronization locks are used to guard accesses to the original variable to guarantee that the updates are atomic.

Programs	Loops w/ calls	Parallel (Fida)	Parallel (SUIF)
SPEC89:			
doduc	19	2	7
matrix300	11	0	8
nasa7	8	0	0
tomcatv	0	0	0
PERFECT:			
adm	35	*	4
arc2d	1	0	0
bdna	9	0	1
dyfesm	21	0	6
flo52q	9	7	7
mdg	7	0	2
mg3d	12	0	0
ocean	12	0	0
qcd	40	0	0
spec77	35	*	18
track	18	1	1
trfd	6	0	0
Total	234	10	54

Fig. 2. Static loop count comparison of our system with FIDA.

7   Experience with this System

This system has been used as an experimental platform in an extensive empirical evaluation of the effectiveness of automatic parallelization technology. The full results are presented elsewhere [7], but we present a few highlights in this section.

We have compared the results of our interpocedural analysis with the FIDA system (Full Interprocedural Data-Flow Analysis), an interprocedural system that performs precise flow-insensitive array analysis [10] (see Section 2). The FIDA system was the first to measure how interprocedural analysis on full applications (from the PERFECT and SPEC89 benchmark suites) affects the number of parallel loops that the system can automatically recognize. We compare how many loops containing procedure calls are parallelized using the two systems in Figure 2. The SUIF system is able to locate greater than 5 times more parallel loops than FIDA. This marked difference is due to the additional array analysis techniques employed in our system, and the tight integration with comprehensive interprocedural scalar analysis.

As part of our evaluation, we have measured the importance of the individual techniques employed in this system but not available in current commercial systems. In particular, we have measured how much the advanced array analyses for privatization and reduction recognition and the interprocedural array analysis on advanced array analyses impact the results of parallelization. We have found that these techniques are essential to achieving any speedup on three of the twelve SPEC92FP programs, four of the eight NAS sample benchmarks and two of the thirteen PERFECT benchmarks.

8 Conclusions

This paper has described the analyses in a fully interprocedural automatic parallelization system. This system has been used in an extensive experiment that has demonstrated that interprocedural data-flow analysis, array privatization and reduction recognition are key technologies that greatly improve a parallelizing compiler's ability to locate coarse-grain parallel loops. Through our work, we discovered that the effectiveness of an interprocedural parallelization system depends on the strength of all the individual analyses, and their ability to work together in an integrated fashion. This comprehensive approach to parallelization analysis is why our system has been much more effective at automatic parallelization than previous interprocedural systems and commercially available compilers.

For some programs, our analysis is sufficient to find the available parallelism. For other programs, it seems impossible or unlikely that a purely static analysis could discover parallelism—either because correct parallelization requires dynamic information not available at compile time or because it is too difficult to analyze. In such cases, we might benefit from some support for run-time parallelization or user interaction. The aggressive static parallelizer we have built will provide a good starting point to investigate these techniques.

Acknowledgements. The authors wish to thank Patrick Sathyanathan and Alex Seibulescu for their contributions to the design and implementation of this system, and the rest of the SUIF group, particularly Jennifer Anderson and Chris Wilson, for providing support and infrastructure upon which this system is built.

References

1. J. P. Banning. An efficient way to find the side effects of procedure calls and the aliases of variables. In *Proceedings of the Sixth Annual Symposium on Principles of Programming Languages*. ACM, January 1979.
2. B. Blume, R. Eigenmann, K. Faigin, J. Grout, Jay Hoeflinger, D. Padua, P. Petersen, B. Pottenger, L. Rauchwerger, P. Tu, and S. Weatherford. Polaris: The next generation in parallelizing compilers. In *Proceedings of the Seventh Annual Workshop on Languages and Compilers for Parallel Computing*, August 1994.
3. W. Blume and R. Eigenmann. Performance analysis of parallelizing compilers on the Perfect Benchmarks programs. *IEEE Transactions on Parallel and Distributed Systems*, 3(6):643–656, November 1992.
4. K. Cooper, M.W. Hall, and K. Kennedy. A methodology for procedure cloning. *Computer Languages*, 19(2), April 1993.
5. B. Creusillet and F. Irigoin. Interprocedural array region analyses. In *Proceedings of the 8th International Workshop on Languages and Compilers for Parallel Computing*. Springer-Verlag, August 1995.

6. M. W. Hall, J. Mellor-Crummey, A. Carle, and R. Rodriguez. FIAT: A framework for interprocedural analysis and transformation. In *Proceedings of the Sixth Workshop on Languages and Compilers for Parallel Computing*, Portland, OR, August 1993.

7. M.W. Hall, S.P. Amarasinghe, B.R. Murphy, S. Liao, and M.S. Lam. Detecting coarse-grain parallelism using an interprocedural parallelizing compiler. In *Proceedings of Supercomputing '95*, December 1995.

8. W.L. Harrison. The interprocedural analysis and automatic parallelization of Scheme programs. *Lisp and Symbolic Computation*, 2(3/4):179–396, October 1989.

9. P. Havlak and K. Kennedy. An implementation of interprocedural bounded regular section analysis. *IEEE Transactions on Parallel and Distributed Systems*, 2(3):350–360, July 1991.

10. M. Hind, M. Burke, P. Carini, and S. Midkiff. An empirical study of precise interprocedural array analysis. *Scientific Programming*, 3(3):255–271, 1994.

11. F. Irigoin. Interprocedural analyses for programming environments. In *NSF-CNRS Workshop on Evironments and Tools for Parallel Scientific Programming*, September 1992.

12. F. Irigoin, P. Jouvelot, and R. Triolet. Semantical interprocedural parallelization: An overview of the PIPS project. In *Proceedings of the 1991 ACM International Conference on Supercomputing*, Cologne, Germany, June 1991.

13. J. Kam and J. Ullman. Global data flow analysis and iterative algorithms. *Journal of the ACM*, 23(1):159–171, January 1976.

14. W. Landi and B.G. Ryder. A safe approximate algorithm for interprocedural pointer aliasing. In *SIGPLAN '92 Conference on Programming Language Design and Implementation*, SIGPLAN Notices 27(7), pages 235–248, July 1992.

15. Z. Li and P. Yew. Efficient interprocedural analysis for program restructuring for parallel programs. In *Proceedings of the ACM SIGPLAN Symposium on Parallel Programming: Experience with Applications, Languages, and Systems (PPEALS)*, New Haven, CT, July 1988.

16. E. Myers. A precise inter-procedural data flow algorithm. In *Conference Record of the Eighth Annual Symposium on Principles of Programming Languages*. ACM, January 1981.

17. M. Sharir and A. Pnueli. Two approaches to interprocedural data flow analysis. In S. Muchnick and N.D. Jones, editors, *Program Flow Analysis: Theory and Applications*. Prentice Hall Inc, 1981.

18. O. Shivers. *Control-Flow Analysis of higher-order languages*. PhD thesis, Carnegie Mellon University, School of Computer Science, Pittsburgh, PA, May 1991.

19. J. P. Singh and J. L. Hennessy. An empirical investigation of the effectiveness of and limitations of automatic parallelization. In *Proceedings of the International Symposium on Shared Memory Multiprocessors*, Tokyo, Japan, April 1991.

20. R. Triolet, F. Irigoin, and P. Feautrier. Direct parallelization of call statements. In *Proceedings of the SIGPLAN '86 Symposium on Compiler Construction*, SIGPLAN Notices 21(7), pages 176–185. ACM, July 1986.

21. P. Tu and D. Padua. Automatic array privatization. In *Proceedings of the Sixth Workshop on Languages and Compilers for Parallel Computing*, Portland, OR, August 1993.

Interprocedural Array Data-Flow Analysis for Cache Coherence *

Lynn Choi[1] and Pen-Chung Yew[2]

[1] Center for Supercomputing Research and Development, University of Illinois,
Urbana, IL 61801-1351, USA
[2] Department of Computer Science, University of Minnesota, Minneapolis,
MN 55455-0519, USA

Abstract. *The presence of procedures and procedure calls introduces side effects, which complicate the analysis of stale reference detection in compiler-directed cache coherence schemes [4, 3, 10]. Previous compiler algorithms use the invalidation of an entire cache at procedure boundary [5, 8] or inlining [8] to avoid reference marking interprocedurally. However, frequent cache invalidations will result in poor performance since locality can not be exploited across the procedure boundary. Also, the inlining is often prohibitive due to both its code expansion and increase in its compilation time and memory requirements. In this paper, we introduce an improved intraprocedural and interprocedural algorithms for detecting references to stale data. The intraprocedural algorithm can mark potential stale references without relying on any cache invalidation or inlining at procedure boundaries, thus avoiding unnecessary cache misses for subroutine local data. The interprocedural algorithm performs bottom-up and top-down analysis on the procedure call graph to further exploit locality across procedure boundaries.*

1 Introduction

Procedure calls introduce complications in most global compiler analysis and complicate optimizations due to its side effects and potential aliasing caused by parameter passing. Stale access detection [5, 10] is a compile time analysis to identify potential references to stale data in compiler-directed coherence schemes [4, 3, 10]. By identifying these potential stale references at compile time, cache coherence can be maintained by forcing those references to get up-to-date data directly from the main memory, instead of from the cache. In stale reference detection, procedure boundaries force all previous algorithms [5, 8] to use conservative approaches such as cache invalidation or inlining to avoid reference marking across procedure calls.

In this paper, we develop both intraprocedural and interprocedural compiler algorithms, both of which can perform stale reference detection without relying on either invalidation or inlining. The algorithm is based on a combination of

---

* This work is supported in part by the National Science Foundation under Grant No. MIP 89-20891, MIP 93-07910.

interval and def-use chain data-flow analysis performed on a modified program control flow graph which represents both parallel program constructs as well as procedure control flow. To obtain more precise array access information, we compute the array region referenced by each array reference. The interprocedural algorithm performs bottom-up and top-down analysis on the procedure call graph to exploit cache locality across procedure boundaries. The first bottom-up *side effect analysis* eliminates side effects by summarizing the access information at each call site. The second top-down *context analysis* allows the context information of a procedure to be visible by passing the summary access information of its previous activation records. The compiler marking algorithms developed here are general enough to be applicable to other compiler-directed coherence schemes [3, 4].

We also propose a new condition for a stale access which identifies the memory reference sequences leading to stale accesses at compile time. The condition considers RAW (read-after-write) and WAW (write-after-write) dependencies caused by multi-word cache lines.

1.1 Parallel execution model

The execution of a parallel program can be viewed as a sequence of *epochs*. An epoch is either a parallel loop (*parallel epoch*) or a serial section of the code (*serial epoch*) between parallel loops. The figure 1 shows an example program and its epochs at runtime.

A *task* is a unit of computation that gets scheduled and assigned to a processor at runtime. In a serial epoch, a single task is executed on a single processor. In a parallel epoch, multiple tasks are scheduled and executed on multiple processors concurrently. Therefore, each task boundary corresponds to an epoch boundary where processor scheduling occurs. Synchronizations are assumed at each epoch boundary and at every synchronization points, memory should be made up-to-date by writing back to memory. Barrier synchronizations are used at the end of parallel epochs.

1.2 Memory reference patterns for stale references

Let's first define the ordering of events which leads to a stale reference. The following sequence of events creates a stale access [17]: (1) a read/write to a memory location x by the processor i; (2) a write to x by another processor j ($\neq i$); (3) a read of x by the processor i. The first read or write reference will create an initial cache copy of the data x in processor i, and the second write reference will create a new copy of x in processor j's cache, making the copy in processor i's cache stale. The following read of x by processor i becomes a stale reference.

With multi-word cache lines, there can be implicit dependences due to line aliasing. Let's assume a 2-word cache line containing variables x and y. Assume that processor i's read reference to variable y in epoch a causes a cache miss. An entire cache line is fetched into the cache, creating a copy for each variable. However, in the same epoch a, another processor j ($\neq$ i) writes to the variable x.

The write creates a new cache copy in processor j's cache, making the cache copy in the processor i stale. The following reference to the variable x by processor j in epoch b ($> a$) becomes a stale reference. The read-write dependence between the variables in the same cache line creates a false sharing effect. With write-allocate policy, similar situations can occur for a write reference. These causes implicit RAW(read-after-write) or WAR(write-after-read) dependences between the two tasks in the same epoch even for doall types of parallel loops. To handle the line aliasing with multi-word cache lines, the sequence of events (1) a write, (2) one or more epoch boundaries, and (3) a read is sufficient to create a potential stale reference. We call this sequence of events a *stale reference sequence*.

1.3 Coherence mechanism and hardware support

In our cache coherence scheme, each epoch is assigned a unique epoch number which is similar to the version number in previous schemes [3, 6, 7, 14]. The epoch number is stored in an n-bit register in each processor, called *epoch counter* ($R_{counter}$), and is incremented at the end of every epoch by each processor individually. Every word in a cache is associated with an n-bit timetag that records the epoch number when the cache copy is created. The timetag is updated with the value of the current epoch counter during a cache miss or a write operation. On a cache line reload (either due to a read miss or a write-allocate), the timetags for the remaining words of the cache line are assigned the value, $R_{counter}$ - 1, to avoid the line aliasing problem (refer to section 1.2).

In addition to normal read and write operations, one extra memory operation, called Time-Read, is required to support our coherence scheme. A Time-Read is a special cache read operation to check for a potential stale access. A Time-Read is similar to a Read except that it is augmented with an *offset*. The *offset* indicates the number of epoch boundaries between the current epoch and the epoch in which the data was last updated. On a Time-Read, in addition to checking the address tag and the valid bit, the timetag of the cache word is tested to determine a cache hit. If (1) timetag $\geq$ ($R_{counter}$ - offset), which checks whether the cache copy is up-to-date, (2) the address tag matches, and (3) the valid bit is set, then we have a cache hit. For correct coherence enforcement, the compiler needs to generate appropriate memory and cache management operations. First, the compiler should insert the epoch counter increment operation at the end of each epoch. Second, potential stale read references need to be identified and issued as Time-Read operations. For such references, the compiler also needs to calculate their offset values.

Consider the program example in figure 1(a). Since a copy of Y is modified by a processor in epoch 1, any read reference to the variable Y in the following epochs is a potential stale access and should be issued as a Time-Read. The Time-Read operation to Y in epoch 2 will have an offset 1 since the last write occurs in epoch 1 while the Time-Read operations in epoch 3 are assigned an offset 2. Note that the read references to X in epoch 4 are not marked as Time-Read. Treating an array as a single variable, the compiler will mark read references to X in both epoch 3 and epoch 4 as potentially stale since the variable X is modified in epoch

2 and read in the following epochs. However, a careful array flow analysis will mark these read references in epoch 4 as safe because the array regions accessed in epoch 2 and epoch 4 are distinct, so the array elements addressed by the read references to X in epoch 4 have not been modified. All the references to the variable W are safe because the variable W is read-only. The staleness of the data is determined at runtime by using this Time-Read instruction because it will check whether the cache data is created after the most recent write by checking the condition (1).

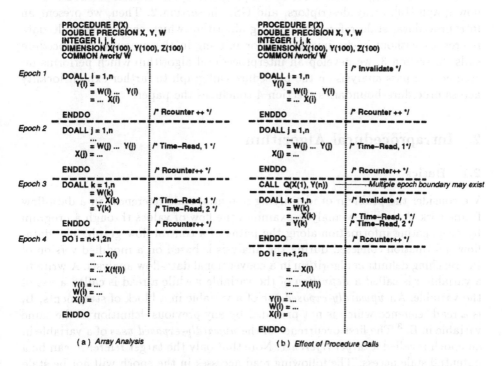

Fig. 1. A program example of compiler marking of Time-Reads.

Effect of procedure calls Procedure calls complicate the analysis of stale reference detection. Let's look at the program example in figure 1(b) where a procedure CALL statement is inserted between the epoch 2 and the epoch 3. Since FORTRAN uses call-by-reference parameter passing mechanism, the parameters X and Y can be modified in the procedure Q. Moreover, all the global COMMON variables such as W in the example can also be modified in the procedure Q. This complicates the analysis of stale reference detection since an intraprocedural algorithm does not have the access information from the procedures called. In addition, this also causes another problem at the beginning of procedure since any global COMMON variables and formal parameters could have been previously modified before entering the procedure. To avoid the complications caused by procedure calls, previous algorithms [5, 8] use cache invalidation both at the beginning of a procedure and after each call site. Since the algorithms assume a clean cache at procedure boundaries, their analysis can guarantee the correctness of reference marking. However, note that such invalidations cause unnecessary cache misses for global COMMON variables and parameters as well as for subroutine local variables. Frequent invalidations at procedure boundaries will degrade cache performance significantly because it limits the scope of locality within procedural boundaries. From our execution-driven simulations on Perfect benchmarks [8], the performance degradation could be significant especially if a program contains many small procedures.

In the following, we first describe our program representation methods: epoch flow graph [10], array descriptors, and GSA in section 2. Then, we present an intraprocedural stale reference marking algorithm which can detect stale data references without cache invalidation or inlining in the presence of procedure calls. In section 3, we develop an interprocedural algorithm which performs incremental 2-pass analysis on the procedure call graph to further exploit locality across procedure boundaries. Section 4 concludes the paper.

2   Intraprocedural Algorithm

2.1   Basics

We consider the problem of identifying potential stale references in a data-flow framework. A data-flow analysis examines the flow of values through a program by propagating information along the paths of a control flow graph. The data-flow information collected during the analysis is based on a modified version of the reaching definition algorithm in a conventional data-flow analysis. A write to a variable v is called a *definition* of the variable v while a read is called a *use* of the variable. An *upwardly-exposed use* of a variable in a block of statements, B, is a read reference which is not preceded by any previous definition of the same variable in B. [3] The first occurrence of the *upwardly-exposed uses* of a variable in an epoch is called a *target reference*. Note that only the target reference can be a potential stale access. The following read accesses in the epoch will not be stale because the cache copy will have been made up-to-date by the target reference if it was stale. The rest of the memory references can thus be marked as regular reads or writes.

From the stale reference sequence in section 1.2, we now need to look for the following def-use chains to determine a potential stale data reference: (1) a definition, (2) one or more epoch boundaries, and finally (3) a target reference.

Data structure for array references The data sets propagated during the flow analysis are implemented as sets of data descriptors. For each memory reference, we associate a data descriptor D, which contains the following fields.

- **name(D)** the variable name
- **subarray(D)** the region of the variable being referenced

---

[3] A block B can be either an epoch or a procedure in our analysis.

– **offset(D)** the offset for the Time-Read operation

The subarray field represents the region of the array that are accessed by the array reference. The notion of subarray we use is an extension to the *regular section* used in [2, 12]. A subarray consists of a subscripted variable and one or more ranges for each index in the subscript expression. A range includes expressions for the lower bound, upper bound and stride. The offset field keeps track of the number of epoch boundaries crossed for each definition propagated.

Gated single assignment (GSA) form GSA is an extension of static single assignment (SSA) form. Like SSA, GSA automatically renames the variable, so we can determine whether the two array references are referring to the same element of X by comparing their index expressions. Similarly, by representing the subarray fields in the GSA form, we can perform subarray operations involving symbolic loop bounds. In addition, GSA allows a backward demand-driven symbolic analysis to compute values and conditions across the confluence points [16]. Figure 2 shows the example program and its GSA form which will be used throughout the discussion in this section.

Because the epoch boundary information is essential in identifying potential stale references, we include parallel constructs in our control flow graph, called the *epoch flow graph* [10].

Epoch flow graph Let the directed graph $G = (V, E)$ represent a control flow graph where V is a set of statements, and E is a set of directed edges, representing the control flow between nodes in V. We define the *epoch flow graph* $G' = (V \cup S, E')$ where $E' = E - \{e: e \text{ is the back edge from the end of a parallel loop to the beginning of the loop}\} - \{e: e \text{ is the edge from the beginning of a parallel loop to the outside of the loop}\} + \{e: e \text{ is the edge from the end of a parallel loop to the outside of the loop}\}$. S is called the *start node* and is inserted at the beginning of the epoch flow graph. We divide the edges into two types. The edge into the beginning of a parallel loop and the edge exiting a parallel loop are called *scheduling edges*. The scheduling edges convey the epoch boundary information. The remaining edges are called *control flow edges*. In addition, the following definitions are used in this section.

- *Head Node*: A statement which has an incoming *scheduling* edge. The start node is a special head node which does not have any incoming *scheduling* edge.
- *Tail Node*: A statement which has an outgoing *scheduling* edge.
- *Epoch Level*: A subset L of an epoch flow graph G' that includes only a single head node H, and all the nodes and edges that have a directed path from H without crossing a scheduling edge. The set L is called the *epoch level from H*. There is an one-to-one relationship between a head node and an epoch level. Multiple tail nodes can exist in L. A directed path from H to each tail node T is called an *epoch from H to T*.

```
PROCEDURE P(x)                            PROCEDURE P(x)
DOUBLE PRECISION x, y                      DOUBLE PRECISION x, y
INTEGER*4 i, num                           INTEGER*4 i, num
DIMENSION x(200), y(200)                   DIMENSION x(200), y(200)
COMMON /work/ y                            COMMON /work/ y

S1        PRINT *, 'PROGRAM START'          PRINT *, 'PROGRAM START'
CSRD$ PARALLEL (i)                    CSRD$ PARALLEL (i)
S2        DO i = 1, 100, 1                  DO i1 = 1, 100, 1
                                            y1 = <MU>(y0, y2)
                                            x1 = <MU>(x0, x2)
S3        x(i) = i                          x2(i1) = <ALPHA>(x1, i1)
S4        y(i) = i                          y2(i1) = <ALPHA>(y1, i1)
S5        ENDDO                             ENDDO
S6        DO num = 1, 10, 1                 DO num1 = 1, 10, 1
                                            y3 = <MU>(y1, y6)
                                            x3 = <MU>(x1, x7)
                                            i2 = <MU>(i1, i4)
S7        IF (15+5*num.LE.30) THEN          IF (15+5*num1.LE.30) THEN
S8        DO i = 1, 15+5*num, 1             DO i3 = 1, 15+5*num1, 1
                                            y4 = <MU>(y3, y5)
                                            x4 = <MU>(x3, x5)
S9        CALL Q(x(1), y(1))                CALL Q(x4(1), y4(1))
S10       y(i) = x(i+(15+5*num))           y5(i3) = <ALPHA>(y4,
                                              x4(i3+(15+5*num1)))
S11       x(i+i) = x(i+(15+5*num))         x5(i3+i3) = <ALPHA>(x4,
                                              x4(i3+(15+5*num1)))
S12       ENDDO                             ENDDO
S13       ELSE                              ELSE
CSRD$ PARALLEL (i)                    CSRD$ PARALLEL (i)
S14       DO i = 1, 15+5*num, 1            DO i5 = 1, 15+5*num1, 1
                                            x8 = <MU>(x3, x9)
S15       x(14+i+5*num) =                  x9(14+i5+5*num1) =
            x((-1)+i)+y(14+i+5*num)          <ALPHA>(x8, x8((-1)+i5)
                                             +*y3(14+i5+5*num1))
S16       ENDDO                             ENDDO
S17       ENDIF                            ENDIF
                                            y6 = <GA>(15+5*num1.LE.30, y4, y3)
                                            x6 = <GA>(15+5*num1.LE.30, x4, x8)
                                            i4 = <GA>(15+5*num1.LE.30, i3, i5)
S18       x(15+5*num) = (15+5*num)+1       x7(15+5*num1) = <ALPHA>(x6,
                                              (15+5*num1)+1)
S19       ENDDO                             ENDDO
S20       PRINT *, 'PRINT RESULT'           PRINT *, 'PRINT RESULT'
S21       DO i = 101, 200, 1               DO i6 = 101, 200, 1
S22       PRINT *, x(i), y(i)               PRINT *, x3(i6), y3(i6)
S23       ENDDO                             ENDDO
S24       STOP                              STOP
S25       END                               END
```

Fig. 2. A program example and its GSA form

Figure 3 shows the control flow graph for the program example in figure 2 and its corresponding epoch flow graph. Note that the notion of an epoch is *dynamic* in that a section of code can belong to different epochs at runtime depending on the branch taken. For example, in figure 3, the statement S17 can belong to the epoch from S17 to S23 (The epoch consists of nodes S17, S18, S6, S19, S20, S21, S22 and S23) or the epoch from S6 to S13 (The epoch consists of nodes S6, S7, S8, S9, S10, S11, S8, S16, S17, S18, S6, S7, S12, and S13 if S9 does not contain any parallel loop.).

2.2 Overall algorithm

First, we transform the source program to a GSA form, which is used to refine symbolic analysis involving array references. Then, we construct the *epoch flow graph*, which contains the epoch boundary information as well as the control flows of the program. Given a source program unit and its epoch flow graph G, we mark target references in each epoch for potential stale references. After marking the

88

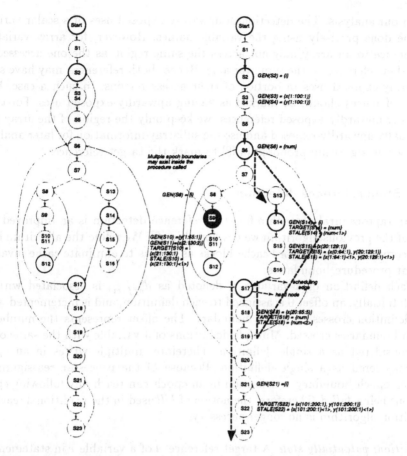

Fig. 3. The control flow graph and the corresponding epoch flow graph for the program example. A bold arc denotes a scheduling edge while a normal arc denotes a flow edge. Head nodes are represented as bold nodes. Call sites are denoted as shaded nodes. The bold-dotted paths show two instances of the epoch where statement S17 can belong at runtime. The epoch flow graph also shows the set of definitions GEN(S), TARGET(S), and STALE(S) computed for each statement according to the intraprocedural algorithm.

target reference, regions of array that are referenced in each epoch are computed. Then, a stale reference detection algorithm determines the existence of stale memory reference sequences and compute offsets for the target references.

If a stale reference sequence is found for a target reference, the reference is marked as a Time-Read operation. Finally, we transform the program in its GSA form back to the original program with the reference marking information.

Target reference marking For our analysis, we are interested in finding only the first occurrence of the upwardly-exposed uses. To simplify the discussion, we refer only the first occurrence of upwardly-exposed uses as an upwardly-exposed use. Therefore, a read following a read will not be marked as an upwardly exposed use in our analysis. The detection of upwardly-exposed uses of a scalar variable can be done precisely using the variable names. However, for array variables, a reference to an array may not access the same region as the one accessed by an earlier reference to the same variable. Hence, both references may have some upwardly-exposed uses in portion of their access regions. In such a case, both array references should be marked as having upwardly-exposed uses. For those partially upwardly-exposed references, we keep only the region of the array that is actually upwardly-exposed and use the subarray information for later analysis. We use the algorithm proposed in [8] to mark the target references.

2.3 Stale reference detection

The intraprocedural algorithm for stale reference detection is an improved version of the previous algorithm we developed in [8]. We refine the algorithm both to accommodate multi-word cache blocks as well as to eliminate cache invalidation at procedure boundaries.

Each definition of a variable v, denoted as d^v_{offset}, is associated with an *offset*. Initially, an offset 0 is assigned to each definition, and is incremented when the definition crosses an epoch boundary. The offset represents the number of epoch boundaries crossed. Multiple definitions of a variable with the same offset are considered as a single definition. Therefore, multiple writes in an epoch are considered as a single definition. Because of the processor reassignments at each epoch boundary, a definition in an epoch can reach any following epoch without being *killed*. Therefore, the notion of *kill* used in the traditional reaching definition algorithm is no longer necessary.

Definition: potentially stale A target reference u of a variable v in statement S1 is *potentially stale* if there is a directed path in the epoch flow graph from a definition d of variable v in statement S2 to S1 including at least one scheduling edge.

When a definition reaches a target reference across at least one scheduling edge, there should exist the sequence of events from (1) to (3), and the target reference to v should be marked as potential stale and be issued as a Time-Read operation. Since we increment the offset of a definition when we propagate the definition across epoch boundaries, the offset of the definition shows the number of epoch boundaries crossed since the write, and used as an offset for the Time-Read operation.

For each statement S, we define the following sets.

- $GEN(S)_{offset}$ is the set of definitions generated by S. Since all the definitions created in S are assigned the same offset, the offset can be denoted collectively for S as $GEN(S)_{offset}$.
- $IN(S)$ is a set of definitions reaching the beginning of S, $IN'(S) = \bigcup_P OUT'(P)$ where P is a predecessor of S.
- $OUT(S)$ is a set of definitions reaching the end of S, $OUT(S) = IN(S) \cup GEN(S)_0$.

– *STALE(S)* is a subset of TARGET(S) where there exists a definition reaching at the beginning of S across epoch boundaries, STALE(S) = {use u of the variable v: $u \in$ TARGET(S) and $\exists$ a definition d of the variable v in IN(S) where offset(d) > 0 and (subarray(u) $\cap$ subarray(d)) $\neq \phi$ }.

Complications in the presence of procedure calls The presence of procedures and procedure calls introduces the following complications in this intraprocedural algorithm for the stale reference detection.

– **side effect** The execution of a procedure can have a side effect on variables at the point from which the procedure is called. The variables include the actual parameters given at the call site as well as the global variables visible to both the calling procedure and called procedure.
– **hidden context** Any of the global variables and formal parameters could have been read or written previously at the beginning of the procedure.
– **aliases** The third issue is the static and dynamic aliases caused by call-by-reference parameter passing and EQUIVALENCE statement of FORTRAN.
  1. **static alias** EQUIVALENCE statement causes distinct variables to refer to the same memory location. Since the alias relationship is fixed in any instantiation of the procedure, we call it *static* alias. In our algorithm, all the static aliases are treated as a single variable.
  2. **dynamic alias** The call-by-reference parameter passing mechanism associated with procedure calls in FORTRAN can cause two distinct variables to refer to the same memory location. The aliases makes our analysis no longer valid even if we invalidate the cache at procedure boundaries. However, ANSI FORTRAN does not allow programs written with aliases. Therefore, we do not consider the dynamic aliases in the following algorithm. If aliases do occur in a source program, then we use selective inlining if possible, or treat all the aliased variables as a single variable.

The intraprocedural algorithm works as follows. [4] Because of the unknown context information, we assume all the formal parameters and global variables have been previous modified at the beginning of procedure. This is accomplished by keeping track of minimum offset from the beginning of a procedure. For a target reference which does not have a reaching definition inside a procedure, we issue a Time-Read with the minimum offset, implying the data item referenced can be potentially modified before entering the procedure. This is an improvement over previous algorithms [5, 8] which use cache invalidation at the procedure beginning since only global and formal variables are affected by the unknown context information. We propagate definitions through the flow graph and increment their offsets when they cross the scheduling edges. Note that for procedure CALL statements, we purposely insert all the actual parameters and global variables in its OUT set, implying that those variables can be modified at the call site. Without having any information for the procedure called, we have

---

[4] The more detail algorithm is presented in [9].

to assume that an entire array can be modified by the procedure. Note that this lack of information also affects the analysis of the subroutine local variables since the offset can be unnecessarily too small if the procedure call has at least one parallel epoch inside. This small offset can result in unnecessary cache misses at runtime. This is because the epoch counter will be incremented at runtime by the number of epochs inside the procedure, which will cause Time-Reads to miss due to the conservative offset values. For each target reference, whenever there is a reaching definition in IN(S) with an offset greater than 0, the target reference is marked as a Time-Read operation. To refine stale reference marking for an array reference, we take the intersection of subarrays of a reaching definition and the target reference. When there exists a definition whose intersection with the target reference has nonempty subarrays, the target reference is marked as a Time-Read and its offset is determined by taking the minimum of all the offsets of such definitions. Figure 3 shows the result of reference marking for the program example in figure 2.

3 Interprocedural Analysis

Until now, the algorithm presented assumes program units, i.e. single procedures, and therefore single flow graphs. The obvious drawback of such an algorithm is that it can not exploit locality across procedure boundaries. To further exploit locality, we need to look at an entire program rather than a program unit at a time. To perform the interprocedural analysis, we use a *procedure call graph*, which is the basic data structure for the interprocedural analysis.

Definition: procedure call graph Let a directed multigraph $G = (V, E)$ represent a call graph where V is a set of procedures, and E is a set of directed edges. An edge from node p to node q exists if procedure p can invoke procedure q.

We extend the procedure call graph to contain the following summary information for each procedure.

 - Procedure name, code size (number of lines)
 - Numbers/types of formal parameters and global variables
 - Numbers/types of actual parameters for each call site (call site information)
 - Summary side effect information (OUT set of callee for each call site)
 - Summary context information (IN set of caller at the beginning of procedure)
 - Number of minimum epoch boundaries in a procedure

3.1 Side effect analysis

Figure 4 shows the overall structure of interprocedural analysis. It consists of 2 passes on the procedure call graph: the bottom-up side effect analysis pass and the top-down context analysis pass. [5]

---

[5] A complete algorithm is presented in [9].

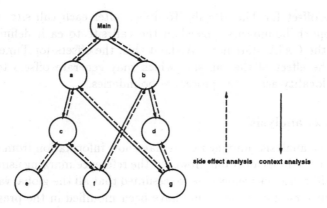

Fig. 4. An example of procedure call graph and the overall structure of the two-pass interprocedural analysis.

The side effect analysis combines intraprocedural analysis with a bottom-up scan of the procedure call graph to eliminate the side effects caused by each call site. The side effect of each call site is summarized by the OUT set computed from the called procedure. We first start at the bottom of the procedure call graph. We apply the intraprocedural algorithm described in section 2 for all the leaf procedures. This can be performed without considering side effects since those procedures do not include procedure calls. After performing the intraprocedural analysis, we summarize the information and attach the summary side effect information to the procedures which have call sites to the current procedure. Note that this requires the translation of the summary information from callee's context to caller's context. The summary side effect information should contain the following information for each actual parameter and global variable.

- whether the variable is modified or not
- the number of epoch boundaries from the last write (offset)
- the region of array that have been modified (subarray)

Note that all the above information can be represented by OUT set of the procedure called, which is already computed by the intraprocedural analysis. Since a procedure can have multiple return points, the summary information requires merging the OUT sets of all the return points. This can be accomplished by taking the conservative union of all the OUT sets and by taking the minimum offset among the OUT sets for each actual parameter. Since we need the side effect information only for actual parameters and global variables, we eliminate the information for subroutine local variables from the summary information. By using the summary information, we add the translated OUT set from the callee to the OUT set of the CALL statement in a caller.

In addition to the above information, the minimum number of epoch boundaries crossed during the execution of the callee is necessary. This is because we need to consider the number of epoch boundaries crossed inside a call site to compute the offset for Time-Reads. To do so, after each call site, we add the number of epoch boundaries crossed in the call site to each definition in the OUT set of the CALL statement. Without this, the offsets for Time-Reads will not reflect the effect of the call site, which may generate offsets too small to capture the locality across the procedure boundaries.

3.2 Context analysis

The side effect analysis summarizes the data-flow information from the descendants of the procedure call graph. However, the reference marking using only such analysis is still conservative because we assumed that all the global variables and formal parameters of each procedure have been modified in the previous epoch before entering the procedure. This is due to the unknown context information for the activation records that invoke the current procedure. To eliminate this conservative assumption caused by such hidden context, we need to perform the second pass, the context analysis.

We start from a main procedure. Since the main procedure does not have any context at the beginning, the previous bottom-up analysis already generates the precise result for the main program unit. But, we still need to propagate the context information of the main program unit to all its call sites. Generally, for each call site, we need to propagate the context information of the caller to the callee. The context information in our analysis can be represented by the IN set of CALL statement at each call site. This context propagation allows the IN set at the beginning of the callee to be replaced by the IN set of the CALL statement. Since the context information is necessary only for formal parameters and global variables of the callee, we only propagate the summary context information for those variables. In opposite to the side effect analysis, at this time we need to translate the IN set information from caller's context to callee's context.

Note that there can be multiple callers to a procedure. So, we need to merge the context information from multiple call sites. This is achieved by taking the union of all the IN sets from the call sites and by taking the minimum offset among multiple callers for each actual parameter and global variable. This is necessary unless we clone the procedure for each call site (different code for each case), which, in the worst case, produces the same effect as the inlining.

Using the summary context information, we can refine the conservative reference marking in the previous bottom-up analysis. With the context information, we need to compute more precise (larger) offset for each Time-Read, or eliminate a Time-Read operation completely if there has been no previous update to the variable referenced. To do so, in side effect analysis, we mark all the Time-Reads issued as a result of hidden context (Time-Reads that does not have a reaching definition inside the procedure and all its call sites). Note that for the context analysis, we only need to update the reference marking results for those references. For other Time-Reads, they are already precise with the side effect analysis alone.

Using the bottom-up and top-down analyses, we can eliminate many redundant computation by performing minimal number of computation (twice) per program unit. In addition, our top-down analysis updates the reference marking results only for necessary cases, allowing incremental updates. Note that during the top-down pass, for each procedure, we don't have to propagate the data-flow information again since the summary context information is enough to refine reference marking. We only need to add the offset of each variable in the summary context information at the beginning of a procedure to the Time-Reads for those variables. For the Time-Reads marked which do not have definitions in the summary context, we could eliminate the Time-Reads completely since there have been no previous update to the variable referenced by those Time-Reads.

In addition, this two-pass analysis allows separate compilation. We don't need to load an entire program in memory for the interprocedural analysis. We only need to load a procedure at a time as well as the procedure call graph with the summary information. This two-pass interprocedural algorithm allows incremental flow analysis without losing any preciseness. We also can limit the scope of the analysis on a level-by-level basis rather than the entire call graph.

4 Conclusion

We propose improved compiler algorithms for detecting stale data references in the presence of procedures calls. Procedure calls can introduce side effects at a call site and hidden context at the beginning of a procedure, which can limit compiler-directed coherence schemes [2, 4, 3, 10, 13, 14] to exploit locality only within procedure boundaries. Previous algorithms use cache invalidation [5, 8] or selective inlining [8] to solve the problem. However, invalidation at procedure boundaries incur significant performance penalty especially if a program contains many small procedures in its critical path. Inlining allows the most precise analysis but often prohibitive due to its potential code size expansion as well as the compile time increase. By detecting target references, we propose an improved compiler algorithm which avoids the invalidation at procedure boundaries. We selectively issue Time-Reads only for procedure parameters and global COMMON variables which are shared by multiple procedures. By doing so, the procedure boundary will not affect the access of subroutine local data. We also propose an interprocedural algorithm which can exploit locality across procedure boundaries. It performs interprocedural analysis according to a bottom-up and a top-down order of the procedure call graph. The bottom-up side effect analysis replaces each call site with summary side effect information from its descendants while the top-down context analysis propagates the context of predecessors to each procedure, generating the context information for its intraprocedural analysis. This two-pass algorithm eliminates redundant data-flow computation for each program unit by doing minimal number of computation per program unit. In addition, the top-down pass updates the reference marking result of the side effect analysis incrementally, minimizing the compilation time. We are currently implementing these algorithms on the Polaris parallelizing compiler [15].

References

1. R. Ballance, A. Maccabe, and K. Ottenstein. The Program Dependence Web: a Representation Supporting Control- Data- and Demand-Driven Interpretation of Imperative Languages. *Proceedings of the SIGPLAN '90 Conference on Programming Language Design and Implementation*, pages 257–271, June 1990.

2. D. Callahan and K. Kennedy. Analysis of Interprocedural Side Effects in a Parallel Programming Environment. *Journal of Parallel and Distributed Computing*, 5:517–550, 1988.

3. Hoichi Cheong. Life Span Strategy - A Compiler-Based Approach to Cache Coherence. *Proceedings of the 1992 International Conference on Supercomputing*, July 1992.

4. Hoichi Cheong and Alex Veidenbaum. A Cache Coherence Scheme with Fast Selective Invalidation. *Proceedings of The 15th Annual International Symposium on Computer Architecture*, page 299, June 1988.

5. Hoichi Cheong and Alexander V. Veidenbaum. Stale Data Detection and Coherence Enforcement Using Flow Analysis. *Proceedings of the 1988 International Conference on Parallel Processing*, I, Architecture:138–145, August 1988.

6. Hoichi Cheong and Alexander V. Veidenbaum. A Version Control Approach To Cache Coherence. *Proceedings of 1989 ACM/SIGARCH International Conference on Supercomputing*, June 1989.

7. T. Chiueh. A Generational Approach to Software-Controlled Multiprocessor Cache Coherence. *Proceedings 1993 International Conference on Parallel Processing*, 1993.

8. Lynn Choi and Pen-Chung Yew. Eliminating Stale Data References through Array Data-Flow Analysis. *CSRD Technical Report No. 1425*, April. 1995.

9. Lynn Choi and Pen-Chung Yew. Interprocedural Array Data-Flow Analysis for Cache Coherence. *CSRD Technical Report No. 1427*, May. 1995.

10. Lynn Choi and Pen-Chung Yew. A Compiler-Directed Cache Coherence Scheme with Improved Intertask Locality. *Proceedings of the Supercomputing'94*, November 1994.

11. Mary W. Hall. Managing Interprocedural Optimization. Technical report, Rice University, Dept. of Computer Science, April 1991. Ph.D. Thesis.

12. Paul Havlak. Interprocedural Symbolic Analysis. Technical report, Rice University, Dept. of Computer Science, May 1994. Ph.D. Thesis.

13. A. Louri and H. Sung. A Compiler Directed Cache Coherence Scheme with Fast and Parallel Explicit Invalidation. *Proceedings of the 1992 International Conference on Parallel Processing*, I, Architecture:I–2–I–9, August 1992.

14. S. L. Min and J.-L. Baer. A Timestamp-based Cache Coherence Scheme. *1989 International Conference on Parallel Processing*, I:23–32, 1989.

15. D. A. Padua, R. Eigenmann, J. Hoeflinger, P. Peterson, P. Tu, S. Weatherford, and K. Faign. Polaris: A New-Generation Parallelizing Compiler for MPPs. In *CSRD Rept. No. 1306*. Univ. of Illinois at Urbana-Champaign., June, 1993.

16. P. Tu and D. Padua. Gated SSA Based Demand-Driven Symbolic Analysis. *CSRD Technical Report No. 1336*, Feb. 1994.

17. A. V. Veidenbaum. A Compiler-Assisted Cache Coherence Solution for Multiprocessors. *Proceedings of the 1986 International Conference on Parallel Processing*, pages 1029–1035, August 1986.

An Interprocedural Parallelizing Compiler and Its Support for Memory Hierarchy Research *

Trung Nguyen[†]   Junjie Gu   Zhiyuan Li

[†]Army High Performance Computing Research Center
Department of Computer Science
University of Minnesota, Minneapolis MN 55455, USA

Abstract. We present several new compiler techniques employed by our interprocedural parallelizing research compiler, *Panorama*, to improve loop parallelization and the efficiency of memory references. We first present an overview of the compiler and its associated memory architecture simulation environments. We then present an interprocedural array dataflow analysis, using *guarded array regions*, for automatic array privatization, an interprocedural static profile analysis, and a graph reduction algorithm for parallel task assignment and data allocation which aims at reducing remote memory references while maintaining loop parallelism.

1 Introduction

In recent years, researchers see a growing interest in shared-memory multiprocessors with multi-level memories which provide private caches and/or non-uniform memory accesses (NUMA) [14, 15, 28]. In order to deliver the power of such machines to ordinary programs written by a wide range of programmers, it is important for the compilers to improve their ability to automatically identify parallelism in ordinary programs. Moreover, the compilers need to generate parallel machine code that can efficiently use the memory hierarchy by reducing remote memory references and by hiding the memory latency. In order to achieve these goals, we have developed new interprocedural analysis techniques in a source-to-source, parallelizing research Fortran compiler, Panorama. This compiler has the following important new features:

- An interprocedural symbolic array dataflow analysis for array privatization, loop parallelization and memory reference optimizations.
- An interprocedural static profile analysis which estimates *workload variance* to guide the decision on static vs. dynamic scheduling for parallel loops and *reference costs* to guide data allocation and task assignment.
- A graph reduction algorithm for data allocation and task assignment to improve data locality while maintaining loop parallelism.
- Marking on *coherence writes* for efficient use of cache coherence mechanisms.

* Sponsored in part by U.S. Army, Army Research Laboratory, Army HPC Research Center. No official endorsement should be inferred. This work is also supported in part by National Science Foundation, grant CCR-9210913, and by Computing Devices, International.

1.1 An overview of the compiler

One of the main challenges to parallelizing compilers is to exploit parallelism at very high levels of the program. Symbolic relations and dataflow information often need to be propagated between procedure boundaries during program analysis. We find it useful to construct a graph that can represent the program's control flow globally and interprocedurally, and use this graph to efficiently propagate the information that is needed by the compiler. Our *hierarchical supergraph* (HSG) [10] is similar to HSCG [13] adopted by the PIPS project. (Our compiler and the PIPS compiler are perhaps the only two research compilers which utilize such interprocedural flow graphs for interprocedural analysis.) The HSG is a composition of the flow subgraphs of all routines in a program. Each call statement is represented by a node, termed a *call node*, while each DO loop is represented by a *loop node*. Therefore, the resulting graph contains three kinds of nodes – basic block nodes, loop nodes and call nodes. An IF condition itself forms a single basic block. Call nodes and loop nodes are compound nodes which have their attached flow subgraphs describing the control flow within the called routines and the DO loops. Due to the nested structures of DO loops and routines, a hierarchy is derived among the HSG nodes, with the flow subgraph at the highest level representing the main program. Note that the flow subgraph of a routine is never duplicated for different calls to the same routine.

Based on the HSG, the compiler computes interprocedural scalar use-def chains[18]. Combining such chains with local expression trees, we in effect obtain an interprocedural version of the *value graphs* which are proposed by Reif and Lewis[25]. The value graphs are used in our compiler for transforming array subscripts and loop control expressions into linear expressions in terms of loop indices and symbolic terms that are loop invariants. After performing a traditional data dependence analysis, the compiler puts DO loops in three categories: parallelizable, sequential (because the main part of the loops' bodies are covered by large *flow dependence* cycles), and those requiring further examination after *array privatization*[17, 22, 30, 31]. Array privatization may eliminate *output dependences* and *anti-dependences* due to memory conflicts and it is widely recognized as a key to loop parallelization. After array privatization, the compiler re-performs an interprocedural data dependence analysis to recognize new parallelizable loops.

The Panorama compiler employs several compiler techniques to enable an efficient use of multi-level memories. Where load imbalance is not a risk, the compiler statically allocate tasks and data to increase data locality, while maintaining parallelism. However, since static scheduling bears the risk of load imbalance, the compiler identifies loop candidates for static scheduling by symbolically estimating the *workload variance* among parallel loop iterations. By performing static task assignment and data allocation simultaneously, remote memory references may be reduced. Among related works, Anderson and Lam's work [1] has the closest objective to ours. However, our method is different from [1] in that we do not re-distribute data and that we use a refined cost model which incorporates communication costs for individual arrays with respect to individual loops. Our method does not always attempt to totally eliminate remote memory references. Instead, our compiler attempts to *reduce* the number of remote memory references, based on a symbolic estimate of the potential penalty due to remote references for each parallel DO loop. In addition, for shared-memory multiprocessors with private caches, the compiler identifies write references which do not cause cache incoherence and thereby reduce expensive coherence actions. We shall discuss our static task profile analysis in Section 3 and a graph reduction algorithm for performing task assignment and data allocation in Section 4. Our strategy for reducing coherence actions has been presented in a previous paper[24]. Therefore, we shall not address this issue further in this paper.

To study the effectiveness of the compiler analysis, we are currently developing compiler modules for generating parallel codes for the Silicon Graphics Power Challenge and the Cray T3D supercomputer. At the same time, we use the compiler to generate traces which drive various simulators. A trace-generation pass is integrated into Panorama to annotate each memory reference and/or each operation in the program generated by the source-to-source translation. When the new program is compiled and executed, an annotated trace, which include both memory references and ALU operations, is produced. A data reference in the trace is either a memory reference or a register reference. A memory reference is due to either a declared variable or a compiler generated temporary. Each memory reference can be annotated with any information that the simulator may need, such as the memory address, the processor issuing the reference, and whether the reference is a read, a coherence write, or a non-coherence write[24]. During the annotation process, a memory map assigning variables to virtual addresses is created. In addition to annotating memory references and ALU operations, the annotator also inserts markers to identify parallel loops and their chosen scheduling method in the trace. The trace is then fed to an architectural simulator which generates statistics including execution time, cache miss ratio, and network traffic. Previous experimental results using this methodology are reported in [19, 23, 24]. A limitation of our trace-generation facility is the lack of sub-traces generated by the execution of library routines. In order to characterize memory activities more precisely while retaining the information provided by parallelizing compilers, we are exploring methods to combine our compiler-annotated traces with library routine traces that can be extracted by tools such as pixie [27]. The simulation issue will not be discussed further in this paper.

In the remainder of the paper, we expand the discussion of some of the techniques listed above. In addition, we present preliminary results of the Panorama compiler in section 5. We summarize our discussions in section 6.

2   Array dataflow analysis for loop parallelization

Previous works on array dataflow analysis for parallelization follow two paths. The first path pursues the goal of computing reaching-definitions for each individual array reference. Feautrier [6] suggests to establish a *source function* for each read reference to indicate which definition defines the value for each distinct array element. Maydan et al [22, 21] simplify Feautrier's method by using a Last-Write-Tree(LWT) for simpler cases. These works ignore IF statements and routine calls. Maslov [20] extends Feautrier's work by handling affine IF conditions and symbolic terms. His work, however, does not handle routine calls and does not address the issue of how to obtain the applicable IF conditions and symbolic expressions for each array reference. The use of source functions for computing reaching-definitions typically results in the need for integer programming to determine the feasibility of an arbitrary set of inequalities. Several researchers, including Gross and Steenkiste [9], Rosene [26], and Granston and Veidenbaum [8], in an apparent attempt to avoid potentially expensive symbolic manipulations and integer programming, have adopted *regular array regions* for their computation of reaching definitions. Although regular array regions cover only restricted array shapes, their operations, such as union, intersection, and difference, can be quite straightforward and efficient. Duesterwald et al [5] have examined cases in which they can compute the dependence distance for each reaching definition within a loop. These works, however, do not take IF conditions and routine calls into account. Works in the second path do not attempt to compute reaching-definitions for each individual array reference. They concern themselves of the array dataflow problem for program parallelization only, for which a *summary* approach seems sufficient and efficient. Array modifications and *upward-exposed uses* are summarized for code segments, e.g. loop iterations. Works by Li [17] and Tu and Padua [30, 31] follow this second path. Our recent work continues to follow this path and extends the previous works by taking IF conditions and call statements into account. A recent paper [10] describes our work on this topic in details. We present only an outline in this section.

It is worth mentioning that the summary approach has previously been used by Triolet and Irigoin [29], Callahan, Kennedy, Balasundrum and Havlak [2, 4, 12], and more recently, Graham et al [7], to compute data dependences instead of dataflow. Their works summarize all array uses while ours summarizes upward-exposed uses which are essential for array privatization. It is also worth mentioning that a recent work by Tu and Padua [31] handles certain IF conditions which contain symbolic terms present in array subscripts and loop limits. Our work is not restricted to such IF conditions. Since our experiments [10] and previous works [3] suggest that the lack of the handling of IF conditions, symbolic expressions, and call statements can significantly handicap parallelizing compilers, the Panorama compiler deals with all these three aspects. In order to take account of IF conditions under which an array reference is issued and to represent the set operation results in the presence of symbolic terms, we adopt a reference predicate which further qualifies a regular array region, called a *guarded array region*(GAR). Graham et al [7] use a similar representation, but they do not summarize upward-exposed uses.

2.1 Guarded array regions

In this section, we assume that the program contains no recursive calls and that a DO loop does not contain GOTO statements which make premature exits.

We also assume that the HSG contains no cycles created by backward GOTO statements. Our implementation, however, does take care of multiple exits in DO loops and backward GOTO statements, making conservative estimates when necessary. In the flow subgraph of a loop node, the back edge from the exit node to the entry node is deliberately deleted, as it conveys no additional information for array summaries. Under the above assumptions and treatment, the HSG is a hierarchical *dag* (directed acyclic graph).

A GAR contains a regular array region and a guard. In the following, we define the regular array regions first and then define GAR's.

Definition A *regular array region* of array A is denoted by $A(r_1, r_2, \cdots, r_m)$, where m is the dimension of A and r_i, $i = 1, \cdots, m$, is a range in the form of $(l : u : s)$ in which l, u, s are symbolic expressions. The triple $(l : u : s)$ represents all values from l to u with step s. An empty regular array region is represented by $\emptyset$ and an unknown regular array region is represented by Ω.

Definition A *guarded array region* (GAR) is a tuple $[P, R]$ which contains a *regular array region* R and a guard P, where P is a predicate that specifies the condition under which R is accessed. We use Δ to denote a guard whose predicate cannot be written explicitly, i.e. an unknown guard. If both $P = \Delta$ and $R = \Omega$, we say the GAR $[P, R]$ equals Ω (unknown). Similarly, if either P is *False* or R is $\emptyset$, we say $[P, R]$ is $\emptyset$.

The predicate defined above is represented in the form of the conjunctive normal form (CNF). To keep as much information as possible, the predicate is marked as unknown only if all its conjunctive terms are marked as unknown. A conjunctive term, which is a disconjunction of relational expressions, is marked as unknown only if all the relationals are marked as unknown. Similarly, a multi-dimensional regular array region is marked as unknown only if all its dimensions are marked as unknown (see [10] for details).

For any given program segment, we use GAR's to summarize the sets listed below, which are important to our array dataflow analysis for array privatization and loop parallelization. Since we use guards, all these sets are exact sets unless the GAR's contain unknown components.

- UE – The set of the upward-exposed array elements which are used within this segment and take values defined outside this segment.
- UE_i – For an arbitrary iteration i of a DO loop, the set of the upward-exposed array elements which are used within this iteration and take values defined outside this iteration.
- MOD – The set of array elements written within this segment.
- MOD_i – For an arbitrary iteration i of a DO loop, the set of the array elements written within this iteration.
- $MOD_{<i}$ – For an arbitrary iteration i of a DO node, the set of the array elements written within the iterations prior to i.
- $MOD_{>i}$ – For an arbitrary iteration i of a DO node, the set of the array elements written within the iterations following i.

2.2 Operations on GAR's

The Panorama compiler requires three kinds of operations on GAR's, namely, union, intersection, and difference. These operations in turn are based on union, intersection, and difference operations on regular array regions as well as logical operations on predicates. Since symbolic terms may appear in both arithmetic expressions and predicates, we implement a GAR simplifier and a predicate simplifier to simplify GAR's and predicates. Hence, the operations on GAR's are composed of two simplifiers and array region operations based on basic arithmetic and logical expression operations. Due to the space limit, we discuss only the top-level operations and refer the readers to [10] for more details. Given two GAR's, $T_1 = [P_1, R_1]$ and $T_2 = [P_2, R_2]$, we have the following:

- $T_1 \cap T_2 = [P_1 \wedge P_2, R_1 \cap R_2]$
- $T_1 \cup T_2 = [P_1 \wedge P_2, R_1 \cup R_2] \cup [P_1 \wedge \overline{P_2}, R_1] \cup [\overline{P_1} \wedge P_2, R_2]$
  The above formula can be simplified in the following three common cases:
  - If $P_1 \Rightarrow P_2$, the union becomes $[P_1, R_1 \cup R_2] \cup [\overline{P_1} \wedge P_2, R_2]$.
  - If $P_2 \Rightarrow P_1$, the union becomes $[P_2, R_1 \cup R_2] \cup [P_1 \wedge \overline{P_2}, R_1]$.
  - If $R_1 = R_2$, the result is $[P_1 \vee P_2, R_1]$.
- $T_1 - T_2 = [P_1 \wedge P_2, R_1 - R_2] \cup [P_1 \wedge \overline{P_2}, R_1]$

2.3 Summary algorithms

Suppose we want to check whether loop L is parallel. Let $g(s, e)$ be the HSG of the subgraph of loop L, where s is the starting node and e is the exit node. Let $UE(n)$ and $MOD(n)$ represent the upward-exposed use set and mod set for node n respectively, and let $UE\_IN(n)$ and $MOD\_IN(n)$ represent the upward-exposed use set and mod set, respectively, at the entry point of node n for the subgraph containing node n. These sets are all represented by GAR's. The compiler performs the following recursive algorithm, $gar\_summary$:

1. Summarize all basic block nodes within $g(s, e)$.
   For each basic block node n, we calculate the $MOD(n)$ and $UE(n)$ sets for arrays within node n. All predicates in GAR's of $MOD(n)$ and $UE(n)$ are set to True.
2. Summarize all compound nodes.
   (a) *Call nodes.* For a call node n, let the subgraph of the call node be $g'(s, e)$. The compiler recursively applies $gar\_summary$ to $g'(s, e)$, which summarizes the references to global arrays and arrays parameters. The returning results are mapped back to the actual arguments of the procedure call (reshape if necessary). The mapping results become $MOD(n)$ and $UE(n)$.
   (b) *Loop nodes.* For a loop node n, let the subgraph of the loop node be $g'(s, e)$. The compiler recursively applies $gar\_summary$ to $g'(s, e)$. Let $UE_{i'}(n)$ and $MOD_{i'}(n)$ represent the MOD and UE sets of $g'(s, e)$, which contain modification GAR's and upward-exposed use GAR's in one loop iteration indexed by i'. The sets $MOD_{i'}(n)$ and $(UE_{i'}(n)$

- $MOD_{<i'}(n))$ are then expanded across the i' index range to form $MOD(n)$ and $UE(n)$ for loop node n. (Details for this expansion are explained in [10]).

3. Propagate the array dataflow information.

   From node e to s, the *gar_summary* algorithm traverses the nodes in $g(s,e)$ in a reverse topological order. During the summary propagation, the following flow equations are used:

   $$MOD\_IN(n) = MOD(n) \cup (\bigcup_{p \in succ(n)} MOD\_IN(p))$$
   $$UE\_IN(n) = UE(n) \cup (\bigcup_{p \in succ(n)} UE\_IN(p) - MOD(n))$$

   Note that the set of successors of the exit node succ(e) is $\emptyset$. When applying the flow equations, we need to handle the following situations.

   - If n is a basic block containing an IF-condition, add the condition to the guard of each GAR in $MOD\_IN(n)$ and $UE\_IN(n)$.
   - If any expression in the $MOD\_IN(n)$ and $UE\_IN(n)$ contains a variable that is defined within n, then that variable must be substituted by the right-hand side of the defining statement within n. If the right-hand side is too complicated, the expression is marked as unknown. If a variable is defined by a procedure or a function, we propagate information through the subgraph of this procedure or function.

For a call node, the above algorithm produces the MOD and UE sets of $g(s,e)$, where MOD equals $MOD\_IN(s)$ and UE equals $UE\_IN(s)$. For a loop node, the algorithm produces the MOD_i and UE_i sets instead. The $MOD_{<i}$, $MOD_{>i}$ and MOD sets are obtained by three different expansions of MOD_i. These sets are then used for array privatization and loop parallelization as described below.

The general technique for array privatization is discussed in [17, 22, 30]. The most important condition to permit the privatization of array A in loop L is the absence of loop-carried dataflow due to A in L. Loop-carried dataflow due to array A in loop L does not exist if and only if $MOD_{<i} \cap UE_i = \emptyset$.

The essence of loop parallelization is to prove the absence of loop-carried dependences. For a given DO loop L with index i, if none of the GAR's is marked as unknown, then the existence of different types of loop-carried dependences can be detected as follows:

- loop-carried flow dependences: They exist if and only if $UE_i \cap MOD_{<i} \neq \emptyset$.
- loop-carried anti- dependences: They exist if and only if $UE_i \cap MOD_{>i} \neq \emptyset$.
- loop-carried output dependences: They exist if and only if $MOD_i \cap (MOD_{<i} \cup MOD_{>i}) \neq \emptyset$.

If any GAR is marked as unknown, then these conditions are conservative.

3 Static Task Profile

In this phase of the compiler, we statically create a profile of each parallel loop in terms of the variance in operation counts between the iterations. A loop with low variance is to be scheduled statically to take advantage of memory reference optimizations. By varying the threshold value for choosing static scheduling, and comparing the performance of the resulting scheduling choices, we can arrive at a heuristic to choose a desirable threshold value at compile time. The analysis to determine the variances of parallel loops is presented below.

Some of the operations in the parallel loop body may be affected by IF conditions or inner loop bounds which contain the loop index. We call the number of such operations as the *loop-variant* part of the operation count and call the number of the other operations the *loop-invariant* part. In order to estimate the degree of load imbalance, we use the compiler to estimate the relative significance of the loop-variant part.

The compiler first marks the HSG nodes, in a top-down manner, as belonging to either the loop-invariant or the loop-variant part. The compiler identifies the IF nodes (basic block nodes that contain only IF conditions) whose IF conditions depend on the parallel loop index and marks the operations belonging to any branches of such IF nodes as loop-variant. The compiler also identifies the inner sequential loops whose loop bounds depend on the parallel loop index and marks all the operations within such loops as loop-variant. All other operations are marked as loop-invariant. We then estimate the loop invariant part of the operation count as follows.

Each node b in the HSG has $COUNT(b) = (min_b, max_b)$ which represents the minimum and the maximum operation counts of the node. The following operations may be performed on such tuples:

- $COUNT(i) + COUNT(j) = (min_i + min_j, max_i + max_j)$,
  where i and j are two nodes in the HSG. The add operator is used for summing the counts on a path in the HSG.
- $Merge(COUNT(b_1), COUNT(b_2), ..., COUNT(b_n)) =$
  $(MIN(min_{b_1}, min_{b_2}, ..., min_{b_n}), MAX(max_{b_1}, max_{b_2}, ..., max_{b_n}))$,
  where b_1 to b_n are nodes in the flow graph. This $Merge$ operator is used to join the counts of different paths in the HSG.

In addition to $COUNT$, a sequential DO loop node also has two numbers ($ITER_{min}$ and $ITER_{max}$) to indicate the number of iterations that the loop will be executed. If the loop iteration's lower bound and upper bound are not functions of an index variable of an outer loop, then $ITER_{min}$ is the same as $ITER_{max}$. Both $ITER_{min}$ and $ITER_{max}$ may be symbolic expressions.

To estimate the workload variance of parallel loops, the following steps are performed:

1. Summarize the loop-invariant counts:
   - For each basic block node b, which belongs to the loop-invariant part, obtain $COUNT(b)$. Note that the minimum and the maximum operation counts of a basic node are the same.
   - For each compound node n, recursively apply the following steps:
     (a) For each node b in the flow subgraph of n, calculate:
         - $C_{in}(b)$: The minimum and maximum operation counts before the entry of node b.

- $C_{out}(b)$: The minimum and maximum operation counts after the exit of node b.

The above counts are found by solving the following flow equations, starting with the entry node of the subgraph of n and towards the exit node:

- $C_{in}(b) = Merge_p(C_{out}(p)|_{p \text{ is a predecessor of } b})$
- If b was marked as loop-invariant then

$$C_{out}(b) = C_{in}(b) + COUNT(b)$$

else

$$C_{out}(b) = C_{in}(b).$$

Initially, C_{in} and C_{out} are empty for all nodes except the entry node which has $C_{out}(entry) = COUNT(entry)$.

(b) Summarize the compound node by setting its $COUNT$ to $C_{out}(exit)$. If the compound node is a loop node, set $COUNT(loop) = C_{out}(exit)*ITER_{min}$. Note that $ITER_{min}$ is the same as $ITER_{max}$ for the DO loop since the DO loop is in the invariant part.

$COUNT(B)$, where B is a parallel loop compound node, gives the minimum and maximum estimates of the loop-invariant part of the operation count, denoted by INV_{min} and INV_{max} respectively.

2. Summarize the loop-variant counts. The loop-variant part is estimated similarly to the loop-invariant part, except that if b was marked as loop-variant then

$$C_{out}(b) = C_{in}(b) + COUNT(b)$$

else

$$C_{out}(b) = C_{in}(b).$$

Also, when summarizing a loop node, set

$$COUNT(loop) = (min(C_{out}(exit))*ITER_{min}, max(C_{out}(exit))*ITER_{max})$$

where $min(C_{out}(exit)$ and $max(C_{out}(exit)$ refer to the minimum and the maximum counts of $C_{out}(exit)$, respectively. $COUNT(B)$, where B is a node for a parallel loop, gives the minimum and maximum estimates of the loop-variant part of the operation count, denoted by VAR_{min} and VAR_{max} respectively.

3. Finally, for the parallel loop represented by compound node B, the coefficient of variance, cov, in operation counts between the loop iterations is estimated as:

$$cov = \sigma/\mu$$

where $\sigma = (VAR_{max}(B) - VAR_{min}(B))/2$ and $\mu = 1/2(INV_{min}(B) + INV_{max}(B) + VAR_{min}(B) + VAR_{max}(B))$. At this point, we may reach three possible situations:

- cov evaluates to a constant.
- Some symbolic terms remain when calculating cov but we can determine the range for cov by using one of the existing techniques[11].

- There are some unknown symbolic terms and, hence, we know nothing about *cov*. In this case, either the user chooses a scheduling method for this loop or the compiler selects a default scheduling method.

4 Task assignment and data allocation

After the compiler identifies the loops that have little or no variance in operation counts, we assume an abundance of *virtual processors* (VP's) and assign the parallel loop iterations to the VP's. Of course, the VP's are eventually folded to the physical processors available for the program execution. Under the NUMA model, each physical processor has a local memory module that is accessible by all processors. For our purpose, we regard each VP as having its own memory module as well. Concurrent with the assignment of parallel loop iterations, we allocate array data to memory modules. Our goal here is to find heuristics that maximize the local memory accesses without sacrificing parallelism. Currently, we consider only single level parallel loops. For multiple loop nests, we select one level as a parallel loop and sequentialize the others. For a multi-dimensional array, our algorithm will automatically select which dimension to be distributed among the VP's. Since data allocation and the assignment of parallel loop iterations are interrelated, they are considered at the same time.

This problem can be broken down into two optimization levels:

1. Optimizing the *orientation* of the data allocation and the assignment of the parallel iterations. Suppose the VP's are numbered from 1 to N. For data allocation, orientation means whether we should allocate the elements of an array along with the increasing order of the VP's or in the decreasing order. Likewise, the orientation of the iteration assignment can be in the increasing or decreasing order.
2. Optimizing the *displacement* of the chosen orientations. Displacement means how far, if any, we should shift the data assignment or the iteration assignment to the left or right. If the optimal displacement is small, then its effect is not as important as choosing a good orientation because it can usually be covered by the effect of practical data cache block sizes which are greater than one word.

The heuristics for choosing the orientations are as follows. We create a *connection graph* $CG(d, a, e)$ where d is the set of vertices each of which represents a parallel loop in the program, a is the set of vertices each of which represents an array name, and e is the set of undirected edges each of which connects a vertex in a to a vertex in d if the array represented by a is referenced in the parallel loop represented by d. The connection graph indicates which arrays and which loops should be considered together when determining the orientations.

For each connected component in CG, we first construct an undirected, weighted *orientation graph* OG. This graph augments the *component affinity graph* [16] by adding nodes which represent parallel loops to handle task assignment. Each node in OG represents an orientation choice, increasing or decreasing, for either an array A, or a loop L. Thus, each array A or loop L that appears in the connection graph generates two nodes, A^+ and A^-, or L^+ and L^-, in OG. Suppose an array A is referenced within a loop L. Their orientation choices, say A^+ and L^+, normally result in a number of A references that are likely to be local, which we call as the *mismatch cost*. An edge is drawn between A^+ and L^+ with an annotation of this mismatch cost. The mismatch cost is estimated symbolically from the HSG in a way similar to the estimate of the operation counts discussed in the last section. For a multi-dimensional array, the dimension of the array is also labeled along with the orientation, for example, $A^{+,2}$. An n-dimensional array will have $2n$ nodes representing the dimensions of the array and the orientation in each dimension. Figure 1 shows a simple OG example. In this graph, an edge is drawn between the node $L1^+$ and the node A^+ and

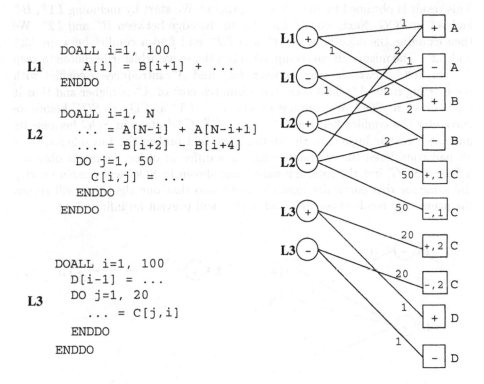

```
      DOALL i=1, 100
L1       A[i] = B[i+1] + ...
      ENDDO

      DOALL i=1, N
L2       ... = A[N-i] + A[N-i+1]
         ... = B[i+2] - B[i+4]
         DO j=1, 50
            C[i,j] = ...
         ENDDO
      ENDDO


      DOALL i=1, 100
         D[i-1] = ...
L3       DO j=1, 20
            ... = C[j,i]
         ENDDO
      ENDDO
```

Fig. 1. Example of an OG. The circles represent loop nodes while the boxes represent array nodes.

another edge is drawn between $L1^-$ and A^-, each with a mismatch cost of 1. These two edges indicate that if the orientations of loop $L1$ and array A are different, then there will be one remote reference to A by each VP.

After constructing OG, we attempt to find a subgraph, SOG, which contains only one node for each loop or each array and whose edges have the maximum total mismatch cost. This problem is NP-hard and we use the following heuristics for its solution. The desired subgraph SOG initially contains an arbitrary node from OG. Incrementally with a breadth-first traversal, we add to SOG the neighbors of the nodes which are already in SOG, together with the connecting edges. During this process, whenever we find that adding a new node to SOG will create a conflict, we sum the mismatch costs for each node over all its edges excluding those connecting to nodes which conflict with nodes in the current SOG. We then remove one of the conflicting nodes which has the smaller mismatch costs. If the two costs are equal, then an arbitrary choice is made to break the tie. We continue to construct SOG until all edges incident to the nodes in SOG have been considered. The final SOG gives the orientation decision.

Figure 2 shows an example of a final subgraph for OG in Figure 1, and the corresponding orientation decision is A^-, B^+, $C^{+,1}$, D^+, $L1^+$, $L2^+$ and $L3^+$. This result is obtained by the following process. We start by including $L1^+$, B^+ and A^+ in SOG. Next, we add $L2^+$ due to the edge between B^+ and $L2^+$. We then examine the edge between A^+ and $L2^-$ and find a conflict between $L2^+$ and $L2^-$. The mismatch cost comparison is a tie, so we arbitrarily choose to keep $L2^+$ in SOG. Next, the edge between $L2^+$ and A^- introduces a conflict with the existing node A^+. This time, the mismatch cost of A^- is higher and thus it replaces A^+ in SOG. We continue to add $C^{+,1}$, $L3^+$ and D^+ to SOG before we encounter the conflict between $C^{+,1}$ and $C^{+,2}$. $C^{+,1}$ stays in SOG because its mismatch cost is higher. In the above, if we had broken the ties differently or we had considered the candidate edges in a different order, we might obtain a different SOG, but the total mismatch cost shown in SOG will remain exactly the same for this particular example. Note also that our algorithm will record the previously resolved conflicts and thus it will prevent an infinite loop.

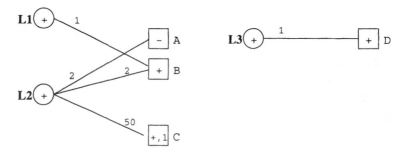

Fig. 2. The resulting subgraph SOG for the OG in Figure 1.

The displacements of the array allocation and iterations to processors assignment are determined using similar heuristics as above, using a *displacement graph* which is similar to the orientation graph. However, instead of only two possible orientations for each node, we may have many possible displacements for each array and each loop. To reduce the complexity of the subgraph building problem, we group references to each array into different displacement patterns

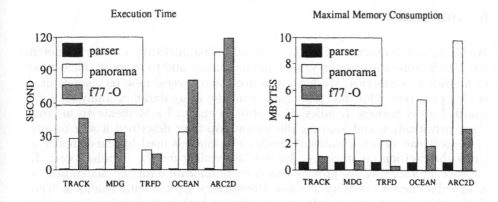

Fig. 3. Comparison between Panorama and F77 concerning resource utilization (The 'parser' bar includes the Panorama parser only.)

and choose only d (where d is a small number) dominant patterns for that array according to the number of references found in those patterns. Again, we attempt to find a subgraph which contains only one node for each loop or each array and the total mismatch cost is maximum.

5 Experimental results

Preliminary experimental results regarding the capability of our interprocedural array dataflow analysis for array privatization can be found in [10]. Here we show data, in Figure 3, regarding the efficiency of the compiler both in its memory use and its execution time, since it is important to demonstrate that such an ambitious interprocedural parallelizing compiler can be implemented efficiently so as to be practical. We expect most readers to be familiar with the efficiency of F77 Fortran compilers on Unix systems. Hence, we compare the memory requirement and execution time of the Panorama compiler with those of the F77 optimizing compiler that generates object codes (with the -O option) on Sun Sparc 2. Also, since the Fortran parser in Panorama is similar to other Fortran 77 parsers, we also compare the memory requirement and execution time between the whole Panorama and its parser only. The running time of Panorama is shorter for most programs than F77 with option -O, which suggests that the time spent by Panorama is quite acceptable. The memory requirement of Panorama is also quite acceptable for modern workstations. For example, it takes ten megabytes to compile ARC2D which has 2465 source lines excluding comments. The maximal memory utilization of Panorama is, however, considerably larger than that of F77 because the array summary information and interprocedural scalar information can occupy quite a large amount of memory. Nonetheless, the memory requirement of Panorama seems considerably smaller than most of other research prototypes.

6 Summary

We have given an overview of our interprocedural parallelizing compiler, Panorama, a research prototype to improve loop parallelization and to support efficient use of multi-level memories. We have also presented several new techniques used in this prototype. Our interprocedural symbolic array dataflow analysis, using guarded array regions, handles IF conditions and call statements to improve array privatization and loop parallelization. We have described a way to estimate workload variance statically. Such an estimate is used by the compiler to guide the decision on static vs. dynamic scheduling for the parallel loops. To improve data locality, we provide heuristics to allocate data and assign task so as to reduce remote memory accesses. Preliminary experimental results indicate that such an ambitious compiler can be efficient both in its memory use and its execution time.

References

1. J. M. Anderson and M. S. Lam. Global optimizations for parallelism and locality on scalable parallel machines. In *Proc. ACM SIGPLAN Conf. on Prog. Lang. Design and Imp.*, pages 112–125, June 1993.
2. V. Balasundaram. A mechanism for keeping useful internal information in parallel programming tools: The data access descriptor. *J. of Parallel and Distributed Computing*, 9:154–170, 1990.
3. W. Blume and R. Eigenmann. Symbolic analysis techniques needed or the effective parallelization of perfect benchmarks. Technical report, Dept. of Computer Science, University of Illinois, 1994.
4. D. Callahan and K. Kennedy. Analysis of interprocedural side effects in a parallel programming environment. In *ACM SIGPLAN '86 Symp. Compiler Construction*, pages 162–175, June 1986.
5. E. Duesterwald, R. Gupta, and M. L. Soffa. A practical data flow framework for array reference analysis and its use in optimizations. In *Proc. ACM SIGPLAN Conf. on Prog. Lang. Design and Imp.*, pages 68–77, June 1993.
6. P. Feautrier. Dataflow analysis of array and scalar references. *International Journal of Parallel Programming*, 2(1):23–53, February 1991.
7. S.L. Graham, S. Lucco, and O. Sharp. Orchestrating interactions among parallel computations. In *Proc. ACM SIGPLAN Conf. on Prog. Lang. Design and Imp.*, pages 100–111, June 1993.
8. E.D. Granston and A.V. Veidenbaum. Detecting redundant accesses to array data. In *Proc. Supercomputing '91*, November 1991.
9. T. Gross and P. Steenkiste. Structured dataflow analysis for arrays and its use in an optimizing compiler. *Software – Practice and Experience*, 20(2):133–155, February 1990.
10. J. Gu, Z. Li, and G. Lee. Symbolic array dataflow analysis for array privatization and program parallelization. In *Proc. Supercomputing '95*, December 1995.
11. W. H. Harrison. Compiler analysis of the value ranges for variables. *IEEE Trans. on Software Engineering*, SE-3(3):243–250, May 1977.
12. P. Havlak and K. Kennedy. An implementation of interprocedural bounded regular section analysis. *IEEE Trans. on Par. and Dist. Systems*, 2(3), 1991.

13. F. Irigoin, P. Jouvelot, and R. Triolet. Semantical interprocedural parallelization: An overview of the pips project. In *Proc. Int. Conf. on Supercomputing*, pages 244–251, 1991.

14. D. J. Kuck, E. S. Davidson, D. J. Lawrie, and A. H. Sameh. Parallel supercomputing today and the Cedar approach. *Science*, 231:967–974, February 1986.

15. D. Lenoski, K. Gharachorloo, J. Laudon, A. Gupta, J. Hennessy, M. Horowitz, and M. Lam. The Stanford DASH multiprocessor. *Computer*, pages 63–79, March 1992.

16. J. Li and M. Chen. The data alignment phase in compiling programs for distributed-memory machines. *J. Par. and Dist. Computing*, 13:213–221, 1991.

17. Z. Li. Array privatization for parallel execution of loops. In *Proc. Int. Conf. on Supercomputing*, July 1992.

18. Z. Li. Propagating symbolic relations on an interprocedural and hierarchical control flow graph. Technical Report CSci-93-87, University of Minnesota, 1993.

19. Z. Li and T. N. Nguyen. An empricial study of the work load distribution under static scheduling. In *Proc. Int. Conf. on Par. Processing*, volume II: Software, St. Charles, IL, 1994.

20. V. Maslov. Lazy array data-flow dependence analysis. In *Proc. of Annual ACM Symp. on Principles of Programming Languages*, pages 331–325, Jan. 1994.

21. D. E. Maydan. *Accurate Analysis of Array References*. PhD thesis, Stanford University, October 1992.

22. D. E. Maydan, S. P. Amarasinghe, and M. S. Lam. Array data-flow analysis and its use in array privatization. In *Proc. of the 20th ACM Symp. on Principles of Programming Languages*, pages 2–15, January 1993.

23. T. N. Nguyen, Z. Li, and D. J. Lilja. Efficient use of dynamically tagged directories through compiler analysis. In *Proc. Int. Conf. on Par. Processing*, volume II: Software, pages 112–119, St. Charles, IL, 1993.

24. T. N. Nguyen, F. Mounes-Toussi, D. J. Lilja, and Z. Li. A compiler-assisted scheme for adaptive cache coherence enforcement. In *Proc. Int. Conf. on Par. Arch. and Compilation Techniques*, pages 69–78, 1994.

25. J. H. Reif and H. R. Lewis. Symbolic evaluation and the global value graph. In *Conf. Record of the Fourth ACM Symp. on Principles of Programming Languages*, pages 104–118, 1977.

26. C. Rosene. Incremental dependence analysis. Technical Report CRPC-TR90044, PhD thesis, Computer Science Department, Rice University, March 1990.

27. M. D. Smith. Tracing with pixie. Technical Report CSL-TR-91-497, Stanford University, November 1991.

28. P. Stenstrom, J. Truman, and A. Gupta. Comparative performance evaluation of cache-coherent NUMA and COMA architectures. In *Proc. Int. Sym. on Comp. Arch.*, pages 80–91, 1992.

29. R. Triolet, F. Irigoin, and P. Feautrier. Direct parallelization of CALL statments. In *ACM SIGPLAN '86 Sym. on Compiler Construction*, pages 176–185, July 1986.

30. P. Tu and D. Padua. Automatic array privatization. In *Proc. Lang. and Compilers for Par. Computing*, pages 500–521, August 1993.

31. P. Tu and D. Padua. Gated SSA-Based demand-driven symbolic analysis for parallelizing compilers. In *Proc. Int. Conf. on Supercomputing*, pages 414–423, July 1995.

V-cal: a Calculus for the Compilation of Data Parallel Languages

P.F.G. Dechering*   J.A. Trescher
J.P.M. de Vreught   H.J. Sips

Delft University of Technology, Faculty of Applied Physics
The Netherlands
Email: BoosterTeam@cp.tn.tudelft.nl

Abstract. *V-cal* is a calculus designed to support the compilation of data parallel languages that allows to describe program transformations and optimizations as semantics preserving rewrite rules. In *V-cal* the program transformation and optimization phase of a compiler is organized in three independent passes: in the first pass a set of rewrite rules are applied that attempt to identify the potential parallelism of an algorithm. In the second pass program parts amenable to parallelization or algorithm substitution are replaced by their semantically equivalent parallel counterparts. Finally, a set of rules are applied that map the parallelized program to the target architecture in a way that makes efficient use of the given resources.

Data parallel languages provide a programming model that abstracts from parallelism, communication, and synchronization. To be able to express optimizing transformations in *V-cal* parallelism, communication, and synchronization are made explicit by the means of dedicated operators that represent these concepts in a machine independent way. In this paper we describe the operators and transformation rules that allow to implement the first two passes of a *V-cal* engine. We show that our approach leads to a flexible compiler design that allows to experiment with different optimization strategies and heuristics.

1 Introduction

Traditional compilers for data parallel languages advocate the 'one tool does all' approach: parsing, optimizing, and code generation are strongly interweaved and they are often hard-coded in the compiler. In the compiler that we have constructed, we have taken a different approach where all these phases are handled by separate tools.

There are several advantages of this approach over the 'one tool does all' approach:

- The different tools are easier to develop, to maintain, and to extend because they do just a single job. There is no interweaving with other tools.

---

* Author is affiliated to NWO and is sponsored by SION.

– It is easier to replace the individual tools. A change in the front end means that a different language can be translated. Choosing a different target machine will mean that the back end must be changed.

The disadvantage of our approach is a little drop in speed of the compiler due to the overhead of running several tools. Each tool has to parse its input and generate its output. In our opinion the flexibility of the new approach outweights the minor decrease in speed.

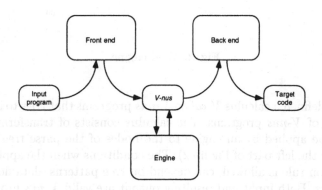

Fig. 1. Overview of the *Booster* compiler

Our experimental compiler consists of three tools (see Figure 1) [Trescher 94]: a front end that parses the input program, an optimizer that operates on an intermediate language, and a back end that generates target code. Our input language is an experimental data parallel language called *Booster* [Breebaart 95, Paalvast 89].

The front end only parses the input program and checks the static semantics of the program. The front end does not try to do any optimizations. The output of the front end is a program in the intermediate language *V-nus*.

Since *V-nus* is the interface between all tools, we have several requirements for such an intermediate language:

– *V-nus* is self contained. A *V-nus* program is the *only* information that is exchanged between the different tools.
– *V-nus* must be suitable for the definition of a calculus.
– *V-nus* must be expressive enough to describe all constructs of the input language and of the target language. Furthermore *V-nus* must be able to describe the topology at a high level.
– Since all tools must parse or generate *V-nus* code, the language must be extremely simple such that only little time is lost while parsing and generating *V-nus* code.

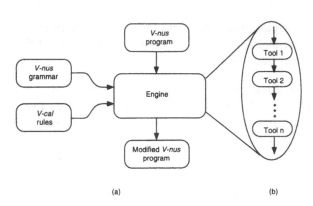

Fig. 2. *V-cal* engine

We have defined a calculus *V-cal* on *V-nus* programs that tries to improve the performance of *V-nus* programs. The calculus consists of transformation rules that are to be applied by an engine to the nodes of the parse tree of a *V-nus* program (see the left part of Figure 2). The conditions when the application of a transformation rule is allowed, can depend on tree patterns, data flow analysis, and heuristics. Both input and resulting output are valid *V-nus* programs.

As an advantage of this approach the optimizing engine can be implemented by a set of dedicated tools. As illustrated by the blow up in the right part of Figure 2 each of these tools reads a *V-nus* program, performs a particular type of optimization and then generates a modified *V-nus* program. The final *V-nus* program resulting from this process will then form the input of the back end. Its job is to make a direct translation from *V-nus* to the target code. Just like the front end it does not do any optimizations.

Before we get into the details of *V-nus* and *V-cal*, we will first discuss related work like *Fidil*, *F-Code*, and the ψ-*calculus*. The emphasis of the paper will be on the transformation rules found in *V-cal*. There are three kinds of transformation rules in *V-cal*: a set of parallelism identifying rules, a set of communication handling rules, and a set of topology dependent rules. In the final section we will discuss our approach.

2 Related Work

Research on compilers that generate distributed code from sequential or data parallel algorithms concentrates on problems in the area of scientific computing, where shared arrays have to be distributed among the private memories of different machines. In particular methods that extent FORTRAN [ISO/IEC 91] by array constructs and means to specify a decomposition of an array have been studied extensively [Callahan 88] [André 90] [Hiranandani 92] [Zima 90].

While these approaches promise immediate advances of the state of practice, it is also acknowledged that many algorithms described in a few pages of mathematics oftenly result in large FORTRAN programs which make it difficult to experiment with simple variations of the algorithm, or to port such a program to a variety of architectures [Semenzato 90]. Several experimental approaches have been proposed that address these problems by more fundamental algorithmic, semantical, or linguistic considerations [Jesshope 93] [Hilflinger 93] [Mullin 93].

One characteristic of these approaches is to extend the usual notion of array types to provide arrays with more general index sets, e.g. *maps* in *Fidil*, *selective assignments* in *F-Code*, *Psi Reductions* in the ψ-*calculus*, and the *view* concept of *Booster* [Paalvast 89]. The second characteristic is a formal approach to the definition of the language semantics and compilation process.

F-Code [Jesshope 93] is a formally defined language that was developed to represent the semantics of data parallel processing, as well as data managment and control primitives of imperative languages. *F-Code* was designed as an intermediate language for compilers to act as a portable software platform with the purpose to foster an architecture independent programming model. In contrast to our work on *Booster* and *V-cal* that tries to facilitate research on novel programming paradigms and associated compiler technology, *F-Code* supports the rapid implementation of data parallel languages.

Like *Booster*, *Fidil* [Hilflinger 93] extends the semantic domain of FORTRAN-like algebraic languages with facilities for construction, composition, and refinement of index sets —called *domains*— and for performing computations on functions defined over these domains —called *maps*. Additionally, it provides capabilities for defining operators and for performing higher order operations on functions.

Fidil is an attempt to automate much of the routine book-keeping that forms a large part of many programs involving for instance PDEs, and to bring the semantic level of these programs closer to that at which the algorithms are originally conceived. However, the versatile nature of maps, like that of views in *Booster*, is a potential source of inefficiency. A set of techniques to reduce or eliminate it have been described in [Semenzato 90], and it would be interesting to obtain performance figures on realistic programs that evaluate these techniques.

In [Mullin 93] a calculus on arrays, called the ψ-*calculus*, is given that is capable of transforming a high level single massively parallel operation on arrays into a low level version optimized for a given parallel architecture. The ψ-*calculus* is just like *V-cal* based on operations acting on the indexing scheme of arrays. Given a data structure, a communication pattern, and a topology of the parallel machine the ψ-*calculus* is able to compute an efficient memory mapping with respect to some cost function.

In *V-cal* this information is in general not known during compile time. In some cases we will need to resort to default parameters to compute a mapping. The ψ-*calculus* could be embedded as an auxiliar calculus at the lowest level of *V-cal*. In such a framework *V-cal* would be used for the higher level constructs (like control flow) and establishing the parameters needed for the ψ-*calculus*, which in turn could compute a good mapping scheme.

3 The calculus *V-cal*

The view calculus *V-cal* came into existence due to the creation of the language *Booster*. *V-cal* is intended to be a calculus for supporting the compilation of a high level data parallel language like *Booster*. We have chosen to use an intermediate language, called *V-nus*, to express the program patterns on which the calculus will work. The calculus consists of a set of rewrite rules for *V-nus*. The left-hand side specifies a program pattern while the right-hand side defines its replacement. We say that a rule matches a program construct if the rule is defined for this program construct. If a rule matches a program construct it will replace this program construct by that of the right-hand side. Of course the program, after rewriting, will be semantically equivalent with the original program.

V-cal can be divided into three classes of rewrite rules. The first class of rewrite rules is the set of rules that will initially be used when *V-cal* is applied to a *V-nus* program. This set of parallelism identifying rules will be used to rewrite program constructs such that parallelism can be improved. Construct substitutions and loop distributions are examples of this class of rules. The second class of rules in *V-cal* will handle the use of communication statements. These communication handling rules will introduce, move or remove statements needed for the transport of data. At this level data distribution information will not be used and therefore the communication statements only specify at what point in the program data is needed, synchronization is required, or a redistribution has to be performed. Finally, in the topology dependent rules information can be used about the ownership of data, the data distribution and the topology. In this paper we will focus on the first and second class of *V-cal* rules. Current research is focussed on investigating *V-cal* on the third level.

A calculus specification consists of a language definition (i.c. *V-nus*) and the use and definition of rewrite rules (i.c. the *V-cal* rules) which we introduce in the following sections. We aim at achieving an engine that reads a program and a specification of a calculus, and will result in a modified program. Note that the definition of the language is an integral unit of the specified calculus. This is depicted in Figure 2 of the previous section.

3.1 Definition of *V-nus*

V-nus is a framework for the denotational semantics of programs written in high level programming languages, such as *Booster* or FORTRAN. Each *V-nus* expression can be represented by a function on states in the denotational semantics [Dechering 95]. Once a program is converted into *V-nus* we can apply the rules of the calculus *V-cal* in order to gain a more efficient *V-nus* program. We aim at the compilation for a SPMD machine and therefore the rules of *V-cal* will focus on the effective exploration of potential parallelism. It is not necessary to have a notion of parallelism in the program that was the source of the *V-nus* program.

We will now demonstrate the syntax and semantics of the intermediate language *V-nus* with an example. From the set of high level programming languages we are only able to compile *Booster* programs to *V-nus*, for this moment. Therefore we will present the semantics of *V-nus* by showing how to translate a *Booster* program to *V-nus*. The syntax of *V-nus* corresponds to data structures of the functional language Miranda [Turner 85]. Suppose we have the following assignment in *Booster*:

    A [i:0..2] := 7+13;

We assume A to be a one-dimensional array. This statement assigns the value 7 + 13 to the elements A [0], A [1] and A [2]. Translating this to *V-nus* we get:

    (s, iteration [(i,3)] [(s', assignment (A, [i]) (7,+,13))]])

A statement in the *V-nus* language is represented by a tuple consisting of a statement handle (s) and a description of the action (iteration ...). The *V-nus* representation of the *Booster* statement is denoted as an iteration of an assignment. The assignment uses a constructor with two items. The first item represents the structure ((A, [i])) for which the assignment must be performed. The second one is the expression ((7,+,13)) that is assigned.

Several statements that occur in a sequence in a *Booster* program will result in a statement list in *V-nus*. Consider the following *Booster* program:

    V {i:n} <- A [i,i];
    V | |= 1;
    B [i:1..m-1] := B [i-1] + B [i+1];
    ITER i OVER 3 DO
        P(A,i);
    END;

The symbol '<-' denotes that the corresponding statement is a *view statement*. This means that the elements V[0],...,V[n-1] are references to A[0,0],...,A[n-1,n-1] respectively. The symbol '| |=' denotes a parallel assignment. The assignment is performed in such a way that no element is used as a target before it is used as a source. The symbol ':=' denotes a sequential assignment. Such an assignment is performed in a predefined order of the normalized index space. In this case a lexicographical order is used. The compiler will try to convert this such that as much parallelism as possible is incorporated. Furthermore, we made the following assumptions: n and m are defined integers, A is declared as an array of dimension n by n, B is declared as an array of dimension m, and P is some procedure having two formal arguments.

The next statement list is an example of the *V-nus* representation of the above program fragment.

    [(s1, view [(i,n)] V (A, [i,i])),
    (s2, forall [(i,n)]
        [(s21, assignment (V, [i]) 1)]),

```
(s3, iteration [(i,(m,-,2))]
    [(s31, assignment (B, [(i,+,1)]) ((B, [i]),+,(B, [(i,+,2)])))]],
(s4, iteration [(i,3)]
    [(s41, procedurecall P ([(k,n)],(A, [k])) i)])]
```

Note that the cardinality list (for instance, the list [(i,(m,-,2))]) is normalized such that the index space, denoted by a cardinality list, starts with zero.

3.2   Effects of using *V-cal.*

Based on the language *V-nus* a set of transformation rules can be used in order to replace certain program constructs by semantically equivalent program constructs. The calculus *V-cal* consists of a set of transformation rules and a strategy that prescribes the use of the rules. We will illustrate the use of some *V-cal* rules of the first class, the parallelism identifying rules, by a small demonstration, based on an example from [Zima 90], where sequential code is transformed to code suited for the purpose of parallelism. Below the intermediate results are presented after each application of a transformation rule. The *Booster* program we start with is:

```
ITER i OVER 100 DO
    x := 5+i;
    A [x] := B [x+1] + C [x];
    E [i] := F [i+1] * A [x];
END;
```

Translating this to *V-nus* we obtain the following statement list:

```
[(s1, iteration [(i,100)]
    [(s11, assignment (x, []) (5,+,i)),
    (s12, assignment (A, [x]) ((B, [(x,+,1)]),+,(C, [x]))),
    (s13, assignment (E, [i]) ((F, [(i,+,1)]),*,(A, [x])))])]
```

Applying scalar forward substitution to this *V-nus* program we get:

```
[(s1, iteration [(i,100)]
    [(s11, assignment (x, []) (5,+,i)),
    (s12, assignment (A, [(5,+,i)]) ((B, [((5,+,i),+,1)]),+,(C, [(5,+,i)]))),
    (s13, assignment (E, [i]) ((F, [(i,+,1)]),*,(A, [(5,+,i)])))])]
```

If we consider this as the whole program we may apply useless code elimination. The result is:

```
[(s1, iteration [(i,100)]
    [(s12, assignment (A, [(5,+,i)]) ((B, [((5,+,i),+,1)]),+,(C, [(5,+,i)]))),
    (s13, assignment (E, [i]) ((F, [(i,+,1)]),*,(A, [(5,+,i)])))])]
```

The expression evaluator can reduce some expressions at compile time such that the program may be replaced by:

```
[(s1, iteration [(i,100)]
    [(s12, assignment (A, [(5,+,i)]) ((B, [(6,+,i)]),+,(C, [(5,+,i)]))),
    (s13, assignment (E, [i]) ((F, [(i,+,1)]),*,(A, [(5,+,i)])))])]
```

By using data dependence information we can perform a loop distribution with the following result:

```
[(s1, iteration [(i,100)]
    [(s12, assignment (A, [(5,+,i)]) ((B, [(6,+,i)]),+,(C, [(5,+,i)])))]),
 (s2, iteration [(i,100)]
    [(s13, assignment (E, [i]) ((F, [(i,+,1)]),*,(A, [(5,+,i)])))])]
```

Again by using data dependence information we can replace both loops by a parallel loop such that we end up with:

```
[(s1, forall [(i,100)]
    [(s12, assignment (A, [(5,+,i)]) ((B, [(6,+,i)]),+,(C, [(5,+,i)])))]),
 (s2, forall [(i,100)]
    [(s13, assignment (E, [i]) ((F, [(i,+,1)]),*,(A, [(5,+,i)])))])]
```

3.3 The specification of transformation rules

In this section we will describe some of the *V-cal* rules. In order to be able to apply rules to a *V-nus* program we need some mechanism to express how these rules will be applied. Therefore we introduce a notion of a 'strategy'. The description of a strategy prescribes which transformation rules will be used and how these are applied (order, kind of tree-walk, etc.). Most of the work for this strategy is still on going and we will hope to get inspiration from the vast body of work that has been done on attribute grammars, pattern matched program transformations, and rewrite systems.

In our opinion a strategy for *V-cal* encompasses the following elements: tree traversals, rule selections, and matching criteria. The engine will walk several times through the tree as is described in the tree traversals (like the traversals used in attribute grammars [Deransart 88]): e.g. in depth first order, in breadth first order, in a (static) sweep, or in a (dynamic) visit. Each walk/pass through the tree can be done by using a different traversal. Depending on the pass only a certain selection of the rules will be candidates for application to the tree nodes.

Our engine tries to compute a closure of those rules when applied to the nodes of the tree. The actual application of the rule can be restricted by matching criteria. Besides that the node must match the pattern of the rule, we can also limit the times a rule is performed to a node and we can also limit the number of nodes to which a rule may be applied.

In this paper we will concentrate on the way transformation rules can be defined in *V-cal*. Furthermore, for the implementation of *V-cal* data dependence information is needed. Techniques to compute this kind of information are described in [Li 94, Zima 90] and is out of the scope of this paper.

The kind of transformation rules can be divided into three classes as is explained in the introduction of Section 3. Examples of the first class have been presented in Section 3.2. We will start showing how we can incorporate transformation rules like 'loop distribution' and 'construct substitution' in *V-cal*. Consider the loop distribution function $LD : Statements \rightarrow Statements$ defined as:

$$LD((s, \text{iteration } cardinalities \; statements \;)) ,$$
$$(s', \text{iteration } cardinalities \; block1 \;),(s'', \text{iteration } cardinalities \; block2 \;) \quad (1)$$
$$\text{if } Distributive(cardinalities, \; block1, \; block2)(ddi)$$

The italic items like *cardinalities*, *statements* etc. (except for the function name) are variables representing all possible instantiations at that place. These are defined by the grammar describing *V-nus* [Dechering 95]. Here *statements* is assumed to be the concatenation of *block1* followed by *block2*. Note that splitting *statements* into two consecutive blocks such that an optimal loop distribution can be performed, may heavily depend on the order of the statements represented by *statements*. This desirable order can be achieved by applying *V-cal* rules that reorder statement lists. The function *Distributive* determines whether the given loop distribution is semantically valid or not. For such a computation the data dependence information is needed which is represented by the variable *ddi* (see also [Zima 90]).

In the same way we can define a transformation rule that replaces an iteration loop with a **forall** loop. The construct substitution function $CS : Statement \rightarrow Statement$ will perform such a replacement in the following way:

$$CS((s, \text{iteration } cardinalities \; statements \;)) ,$$
$$(s, \text{forall } cardinalities \; statements \;)$$
$$\text{if not } (DD(cardinalities, \; statements, \; statements)(ddi) \text{ and} \quad (2)$$
$$DU(cardinalities, \; statements, \; statements)(ddi))$$

Here the functions *DD* and *DU* determine for the given two statement lists if a define-define dependence or a define-use dependence exists respectively. As with the loop distribution rule, these dependencies can easily be computed by using the scalar analysis information. For the ease of this paper we will overload the *DD* and *DU* functions such that *cardinalities* is not always needed and *statements* may also be statement handles.

As said before, the second class of transformation rules define where some kind of communication is needed in order to gain parallelism. This kind of parallelism takes care of a correct use of the data needed for a certain computation. Using this class of rules we abstract from the information about the distribution of data. Also the rule that determines the tasks for the individual processors, called a computes-rule, is not available for these communication handling rules. In the third class of *V-cal* rules the data distribution is known and information can be obtained about the owner of certain data. Based on the ownership of data the computes-rule can be specified. For instance, we may specify the 'owner computes-rule'. This means that if the data on the left-hand side of an assignment is owned by process x then the computation of the right-hand side will be performed by process x. So, we come up with the following communication primitives for the communication handling rules:

- **want** *sh ds*. This statement denotes that the data structure *ds* is needed for the execution of the statement indicated by *sh*. In the third level of *V-cal* this statement is translated to 'send' and 'receive' primitives dependent on the ownership of the wanted data.
- **synchronize** *sh ds*. This one is needed to tell that the data structure *ds* is changed by statement *sh*. Also a synchronize is translated to 'send' and 're-ceive' primitives in the third level of *V-cal* when the computes-rule is defined.
- **redistribute** *dh*. When redistribution of data is needed, this statement can be used to specify which data structure needs to be redistributed.

Here '*sh*', '*ds*', and '*dh*' stand for 'statement handle', 'data structure', and 'data structure handle' resp. The communication primitives are introduced when the basic statements of *V-nus* are processed; i.e. the assignment and the view. The communication insertion function $CI : Statements \rightarrow Statements$ defines the *V-cal* rule that inserts the mentioned communication primitives as follows:

$$CI((s, \text{view } cardinalities \; dh \; rhs)) ,$$
$$(s, \text{view } cardinalities \; dh \; rhs),(s_1, \text{redistribute } dh)$$

$$CI((s, \text{assignment } lhs \; rhs)) ,$$
$$(s_1, \text{want } s \; ds_1), \dots , (s_n, \text{want } s \; ds_n),$$
$$(s, \text{assignment } lhs \; rhs),$$
$$(s_m, \text{synchronize } s \; lhs) \tag{3}$$

where the data structures $ds_1, ..., ds_n$ are used in *rhs*.

The next set of rules we need consists of moving the communication primitives. An improvement of efficient parallelism can be achieved by reducing the number of communications without reducing the grain of parallelism. For instance, we can lift the **want** statements out of a **forall** loop and let them execute before en-tering the loop. The **synchronize** statements can be executed when the loop has finished. The *V-cal* rule for a communication lift $CL : Statements \rightarrow Statements$ will do the job.

$$CL((s_1, \text{forall } cardinalities \; statements)) ,$$
$$(s_0, \text{want } s \; d'), (s_1, \text{forall } cardinalities \; statements')$$
$$\text{if } Occurs((s_0, \text{want } s \; d), statements) \tag{4}$$
$$\text{where } statements' = statements \setminus (s_0, \text{want } s \; d)$$
$$\text{and } d' = cardinalities \cdot d.$$

The variable *statements'* represents the statement list *statements* without the statement **want** *s d*. The data structure d' represents all elements of d that are referenced by *cardinalities*. The function *Occurs* checks whether the first argu-ment appears in the second. The synchronize statements can be moved backwards in the same way such that *CL* is also defined as

$CL((s_1, \text{forall } cardinalities\ statements\ ))$,
   $(s_1, \text{forall } cardinalities\ statements'\ )$, $(s_2, \text{synchronize } s\ d'\ )$
     if $Occurs((s_2, \text{synchronize } s\ d\ ), statements)$ (5)
where $statements' = statements \setminus (s_2, \text{synchronize } s\ d\ )$
and $d' = cardinalities \cdot d$.

When a **synchronize** statement or a **want** statement is found in a **forall** loop it can unconditionally be moved outside the loop. The semantics of an iteration loop requires an extra check on dependencies between the statements in the loop before a communication statement can be put before or after the loop. Suppose a communication statement c within an iteration loop is necessary for the transport of some data structure d. Say d is changed by a statement s. Then c may be placed outside the loop if d will not be used by another statement (instance) in the loop. The rule performing such a replacement of the communication statements must therefore check for a define-use dependence as follows:

$CL((s_1, \text{iteration } cardinalities\ statements\ ))$,
   $(s_0, \text{want } s\ d'\ )$, $(s_1, \text{iteration } cardinalities\ statements'\ )$
     if $Occurs((s_0, \text{want } s\ d\ ), statements)$ and
     there does not exist an $s' \in statements$ such that
          $DU(cardinalities, s, s')(ddi)$ (6)
where s as well as s' are statement handles
and $statements' = statements \setminus (s_0, \text{want } s\ d\ )$
and $d' = cardinalities \cdot d$.

In the same way we can define the transformation for placing a **synchronize** after the finishing of the iteration loop.

$CL((s_1, \text{iteration } cardinalities\ statements\ ))$,
   $(s_1, \text{iteration } cardinalities\ statements'\ )$, $(s_2, \text{synchronize } s\ d'\ )$
     if $Occurs((s_2, \text{synchronize } s\ d\ ), statements)$ and
     there does not exist an $s' \in statements$ such that
          $DU(cardinalities, s, s')(ddi)$ (7)
where s as well as s' are statement handles
and $statements' = statements \setminus (s_2, \text{synchronize } s\ d\ )$
and $d' = cardinalities \cdot d$.

Note that the define-use dependence check may be too restrictive for some loops. In case the 'define' and 'use' are carried out by the same process, it is possible to place the communication statements outside the loop. However, the function CL then has to check for the owner of the specific data. This kind of program transformations will not be performed at this level of the calculus.

We are aiming at large program pieces that can execute in parallel without any interaction. In order to get this we want to use rules that separate a **want**-**synchronize** pair as far as possible. So, next we present how **want** and **synchronize** statements may skip over statements. For now, we only focus on an upward move of the want statements in the *V-nus* program, and a downward move of the synchronize statements. We define the communication move rule *CM*: *Statements* → *Statements* as follows:

$$CM((s_1, \text{ statement }),(s_2, \text{ want } s \ d \ )) \ ,$$
$$(s_2, \text{ want } s \ d \ ),(s_1, \text{ statement }) \tag{8}$$
$$\text{if not } DU(s_1, s_2)(ddi)$$

The opposite move for a synchronize is then defined as:

$$CM((s_1, \text{ synchronize } s \ d \ ),(s_2, \text{ statement })) \ ,$$
$$(s_2, \text{ statement }),(s_1, \text{ synchronize } s \ d \ ) \tag{9}$$
$$\text{if not } DU(s_1, s_2)(ddi)$$

Since a synchronize statement may cause storing a value of some data structure in a certain memory location, we see the data structure, used by a synchronize, as a 'define' of that data structure. Of course it is necessary to check for a define-use dependence in the above *V-cal* rule.

3.4 The application of transformation rules

Now that we have defined a strategy, we can apply the rules to a *V-nus* program. The tree-walker will try to match a given rule one or several times to parts of the program. Based on the type of a part of the *V-nus* program and the signature of the *V-cal* rules it can be decided whether applying a rule makes sense or not. The example of using *V-cal*, which was given in section 3.2, resulted in:

```
(s1, forall [(i,100)]
    [(s12, assignment (A, [(5,+,i)]) ((B, [(6,+,i)]),+,(C, [(5,+,i)])))]),
(s2, forall [(i,100)]
    [(s13, assignment (E, [i]) ((F, [(i,+,1)]),*,(A, [(5,+,i)])))])
```

This example can now be extended by using a strategy that prescribes to use a 'communication insertion' (3) for each statement in the program and then lift the want statements out of the loop by using *V-cal* rule (4), and lift the synchronize statements by using *V-cal* rule (5). An intermediate result is:

```
(t1, want s12 ([(i,100)],(B, [(6,+,i)]))),
(t2, want s12 ([(i,100)],(C, [(5,+,i)]))),
(s1, forall [(i,100)]
    [(s12, assignment (A, [(5,+,i)])
        ((B, [(6,+,i)]),+,(C, [(5,+,i)])))]),
(t3, synchronize s12 ([(i,100)],(A, [(5,+,i)]))),
(t4, want s13 ([(i,100)],(F, [(i,+,1)]))),
(t5, want s13 ([(i,100)],(A, [(5,+,i)]))),
(s2, forall [(i,100)]
    [(s13, assignment (E, [i]) ((F, [(i,+,1)]),*,(A, [(5,+,i)])))]),
(t6, synchronize s13 ([(i,100)],(E, [i])))
```

To increase the grain of parallelism the want statement t4 may be skipped over the statements t3 and s1 as is defined by the 'communication move' rule (8). The above program will then be transformed into the final form:

(t1, want s12 ([[(i,100)],(B, [(6,+,i)])])),
(t2, want s12 ([[(i,100)],(C, [(5,+,i)])])),
(t4, want s13 ([[(i,100)],(F, [(i,+,1)])])),
(s1, forall [(i,100)]
    [(s12, assignment (A, [(5,+,i)])
        ((B, [(6,+,i)]),+,(C, [(5,+,i)])))]),
(t3, synchronize s12 ([[(i,100)],(A, [(5,+,i)]))),
(t5, want s13 ([[(i,100)],(A, [(5,+,i)])])),
(s2, forall [(i,100)]
    [(s13, assignment (E, [i]) ((F, [(i,+,1)]),*,(A, [(5,+,i)])))]),
(t6, synchronize s13 ([[(i,100)],(E, [i])))

In this example only forall loops were involved. A more complex demonstration of *V-cal* rules handles an iteration loop. In the next example we show a replacement of some communication statements out of an iteration loop. Consider the following *V-nus* program:

(s1, iteration [(i,100)]
    [(s11, assignment (A, [i]) (B, [i])),
    (s12, assignment (C, [(i,+,1)]) ((C, [i]), +, (C, [(i,+,2)])))])

Inserting the communication statements into this program by using the *V-cal* rule (3) will result in:

(s1, iteration [(i,100)]
    [(t1, want s11 (B, [i])),
    (s11, assignment (A, [i]) (B, [i])),
    (t2, synchronize s11 (A, [i])),
    (t3, want s12 (C, [i])),
    (s12, assignment (C, [(i,+,1)]) ((C, [i]), +, (C, [(i,+,2)]))),
    (t4, synchronize s12 (C, [i]))])

One can easily verify that no define-use dependence exists between s11 and any other statement or statement instance. Though there is a define-use dependence between the statement instances of s12. So, applying both rule (4) and (5) once to this program we see that the communication statements for s11 can be placed outside the loop. Those for s12 cannot due to the dependencies. In the loop body we can use rule (9) such that the assignments can be executed sequentially without interference of a communication primitive. Using the *V-cal* rules will therefore lead to:

(t1, want s11 ([[(i,100)], (B, [i]))),
(s1, iteration [(i,100)]
    [(t3, want s12 (C, [i])),

```
        (s11, assignment (A, [i]) (B, [i])),
        (s12, assignment (C, [(i,+,1)]) ((C, [i]), +, (C, [(i,+,2)]))),
        (t4, synchronize s12 (C, [i]))]),
    (t2, synchronize s11 ([(i,100)], (A, [i])))
```

Note that the want statement in the loop body only retrieves one element at a time; the want statement that is placed out of the loop body now retrieves all the elements (B, [i]) that will be used in the subsequent iteration. In a similar way the synchronize statement in the loop differs from the one outside the loop.

4 Discussion

In this paper we have described the compiler based on *V-nus* and *V-cal*. The compiler is structured into three independent tools. The flexibility of this compiler design has several advantages.

Since *Booster* uses abstractions known from many high level data parallel languages it should be straightforward to use our compiler as a back end for a language as *HPF* [HPFF 93]. The *V-cal* engine is written in TXL (see [Cordy 93]) which allows rapid prototyping. This means that we can 'plug & play' with transformation rules and with the strategy in which order these rules are applied. Rewriting our compiler for a different target machine involves rewriting the back end and most likely extending the topology dependent rules. Since *V-cal* rules preserve semantics, existing rules (if properly defined) need not be replaced.

In the near future we want to extend the parallelism identifying and the communication handling rules, and we also like to make a start with the topology dependent rules. We will perform several theoretical and practical tests on the set of rules that we have developed. The general parallelism identifying rules can be tested with the results found in the literature. Beside the theoretical comparison the entire set of rules needs to be tested on a large number of programs relevant to the field of computational science.

We hope that our compiler will be used by the research community as a tool to experiment with different transformation rules and strategies.

References

[André 90] F. André, J. Pazat, H. Thomas *Pandore: A System to Manage Data Distribution*, in Proc. 1990 Intl. Conf. on Supercomputing, The Netherlands, 1990.

[Breebaart 95] L.C. Breebaart, P.F.G. Dechering, A.B. Poelman, J.A. Trescher, J.P.M. de Vreught, and H.J. Sips, *The Booster Language, A Working Paper 1.0*, Computational Physics report series CP–95–02, Delft University of Technology, 1995.

[Callahan 88] D. Callahan and K. Kennedy *Compiling Programs for Distributed-Memory Multiprocessor*, The Journal of Supercomputing, 2:151-169, 1988.

[Cordy 93] J. Cordy, I. Carmichael, *The TXL Programming Language, Syntax and Informal Semantics*, Version 7, Department of Computing and Information Science, Queens University at Kingston, txl@qucis.queensu.ca, 1993.

[Dechering 95] P.F.G. Dechering, *The Denotational Semantics of Booster*, Computational Physics report series CP–95–05, Delft University of Technology, 1995.

[Deransart 88] P. Deransart, M. Jourdan, B. Lorho, *Attribute grammars, definitions, systems and bibliography*, vol. 323 of Lecture Notes in Computer Science, Springer Verlag, 1988

[Hiranandani 92] S. Hiranandani et. al. *Compiling Fortran-D for MIMD Distributed-Memory Machines*, Communications of the ACM, 35(8):66-80, August, 1992.

[Hilflinger 93] P. Hilflinger P. Colella *Fidil Reference Manual*, Report No. UCB/CSG 93-759, 1993.

[HPFF 93] High Performance Fortran Forum, *High Performance Fortran, Language Specification, Version 1.0*, Rice University, Houston, Texas, 1993.

[ISO/IEC 91] ISO/IEC *Information technology — Programming languages — Fortran*, ISO/IEC standard 1539, 1991.

[Jesshope 93] C. Jesshope et. al. *F-code and its implementation: a Portable Software Platform for Data Parallelism*, in Proc. 4. Intl. Workshop on Compilers for Parallel Computers, Delft 1993, The Netherlands.

[Li 94] J. Li and M. Wolfe. Defining, Analyzing and Transforming Program Constructs. *IEEE Parallel and Distributed Technology*, pages 32–39, 1994.

[Mullin 93] L.M.R. Mullin, D.R. Dooling, E.A. Sandberg, and S.A. Thibault. *Formal Method in Scheduling, Routing, and Communication Protocol*, Fourth International Workshop on Compilers for Parallel Computers, Delft University of Technology, 1993.

[Paalvast 89] E. Paalvast, H. Sips *A High-level Language for the Description of Parallel Algorithms*, in Proc. of Parallel Computing '89, North Holland Publ., 1989.

[Semenzato 90] L. Semenzato and P. Hilflinger *Arrays in Fidil*, in: L. M. R. Mullin, M. Jenkins, G. Hains, R. Bernecky, G. Gao, *Arrays, Functional Languages, and Parallel Systems*.

[Trescher 94] J.A. Trescher, P.F.G. Dechering, A.B. Poelman, J.P.M. de Vreught, and H.J. Sips, *A Formal Approach to the Compilation of Data Parallel Languages*, in K. Pingali, U. Banerjee, D. Gelernter, A. Nicolau, and D. Padua, editors, *Languages and Compilers for Parallel Computing*, pages 155 – 169, Springer-Verlag, 1994.

[Turner 85] D. Turner. Miranda: a Non-strict Functional Language with Polymorphic Types. In J.P. Jouannaud, editor, *Functional Programming Languages and Computer Architecture*, volume 201 of *Lecture Notes in Computer Science*. Springer-Verlag, 1985.

[Wolfe 89] M. Wolfe *Optimizing Supercompilers for Supercomputers*, MIT Press, Cambridge, Massachusetts, 1989.

[Zima 90] H. Zima and B. Chapman *Supercompilers for Parallel and Vector Computers*, ACM Press, 1990.

Transitive Closure of Infinite Graphs and its Applications

Wayne Kelly, William Pugh, Evan Rosser and Tatiana Shpeisman

Department of Computer Science
University of Maryland, College Park, MD 20742
{wak,pugh,ejr,murka}@cs.umd.edu

Abstract. *Integer tuple relations can concisely summarize many types of information gathered from analysis of scientific codes. For example they can be used to precisely describe which iterations of a statement are data dependent of which other iterations. It is generally not possible to represent these tuple relations by enumerating the related pairs of tuples. For example, it is impossible to enumerate the related pairs of tuples in the relation $\{[i] \rightarrow [i+2] \mid 1 \leq i \leq n-2 \}$. Even when it is possible to enumerate the related pairs of tuples, such as for the relation $\{[i,j] \rightarrow [i',j'] \mid 1 \leq i,j,i',j' \leq 100 \}$, it is often not practical to do so. We instead use a closed form description by specifying a predicate consisting of affine constraints on the related pairs of tuples. As we just saw, these affine constraints can be parameterized, so what we are really describing are infinite families of relations (or graphs). Many of our applications of tuple relations rely heavily on an operation called transitive closure. Computing the transitive closure of these "infinite graphs" is very different from the traditional problem of computing the transitive closure of a graph whose edges can be enumerated. For example, the transitive closure of the first relation above is the relation $\{ [i] \rightarrow [i'] \mid \exists \beta \text{ s.t. } i'-i = 2\beta \wedge 1 \leq i \leq i' \leq n \}$. As we will prove, transitive closure is not computable in the general case. We have developed algorithms that produce exact results in most commonly occurring cases and produce upper or lower bounds (as necessary) in the other cases. This paper will describe our algorithms for computing transitive closure and some of its applications such as determining which inter-processor synchronizations are redundant.*

1 Introduction

This paper proposes a new general purpose abstraction called tuple relations, that is capable of concisely summarizing many kinds of information gathered from analysis of scientific codes. We provide a number of operations on these tuple relations including a particularly powerful one called transitive closure. We will show how transitive closure leads to simple and elegant solutions to several program analysis problems.

An *integer tuple relation* is a relation whose domain consists of integer k-tuples and whose range consists of integer k'-tuples, for some fixed k and k'. An integer k-tuple is simply a point in $\mathcal{Z}^k$. The following is an example of a relation from 1-tuples to 2-tuples:

$$\{ [i] \rightarrow [i',j'] \mid 1 \leq i = i' = j' \leq n \}$$

One possible use of tuple relations is to concisely and accurately represent the data dependences in a program. For example, the relation given above describes the data dependences from statement 1 to statement 2 in the program shown in Figure 1.

```
              do 2 i = 1, n
    1             a(i,i) = 0
              do 2 j = 1, i
    2             b(i,j) = b(i,j) + a(i,j)
```

Fig. 1. Example program

We use the term *dependence relation* rather than tuple relation when they describe data dependences. A dependence relation is a much more powerful abstraction that the traditional dependence distance or direction abstractions. The above program has dependence distance (0), but that doesn't tell us that only the last iteration of j loop is involved in the dependence. This type of additional information is crucial for determining the legality of a number of advanced transformations [3].

Tuple relations can also be used to represent other forms of ordering constraints between iterations that don't necessarily correspond to data dependences. For example, we can construct relations that represent which iterations will be executed before which other iterations. We will see later how taking the transitive closure of these relations is a key element in removing redundant synchronizations within loops. In the case of perfectly nested loops with the entire loop body considered as an atomic statement, doing so is not prohibitive expensive and gives us more power than any of the previous papers on this topic. We also describe exact methods for removing redundant synchronization for the more general case of imperfectly nested loops with synchronization occurring between individual statements. But just because our methods might be capable of computing this exactly doesn't mean that they can or should only be used in this way. It is a relatively straight forward process to extend our exact method into a framework in which accuracy can be traded off for efficiency.

As a third application of relations, we show how they can be used to compute closed form expressions for induction variables.

The next section describes the general form of the relations that we can handle, and the operations that we can perform on them. The remainder of the paper deals with the transitive closure operation. First, we describe how transitive closure of relations leads to simple and elegant solutions to several program analysis problems. We then describe the algorithms we use to compute transitive closure.

2   Tuple Relations

The class of scientific codes that is amenable to exact analysis generally consists of for loops with affine loop bounds, whose bodies consist of accesses to scalars and arrays with affine subscripts. The following general form of an integer tuple relation is therefore expressive enough to represent most information derived during the analysis of such programs:

$$\{[s_1,\ldots,s_k] \to [t_1,\ldots,t_{k'}] \mid \bigvee_{i=1}^{n} \exists \alpha_{i1},\ldots,\alpha_{im_i} \text{ s.t. } F_i \}$$

where the F_i's are conjunctions of affine equalities and inequalities on the input variables $s_1 \ldots, s_k$, the output variables $t_1,\ldots,t_{k'}$, the existentially quantified

operation	Description	Definition
$F \cap G$	Intersection of F and G	$x \rightarrow y \in F \cap G \Leftrightarrow x \rightarrow y \in F \wedge x \rightarrow y \in G$
$F \cup G$	Union of F and G	$x \rightarrow y \in F \cap G \Leftrightarrow x \rightarrow y \in F \vee x \rightarrow y \in G$
$F - G$	Difference of F and G	$x \rightarrow y \in F - G \Leftrightarrow x \rightarrow y \in F \wedge x \rightarrow y \notin G$
$range(F)$	Range of F	$y \in range(F) \Leftrightarrow \exists x \text{ s.t. } x \rightarrow y \in F$
$domain(F)$	Domain of F	$x \in domain(F) \Leftrightarrow \exists y \text{ s.t. } x \rightarrow y \in F$
$F \times G$	Cross product of F and G	$x \rightarrow y \in (F \times G) \Leftrightarrow x \in F \wedge y \in G$
$F \circ G$	Composition of F and G	$x \rightarrow z \in F \circ G \Leftrightarrow \exists y \text{ s.t. } y \rightarrow z \in F \wedge x \rightarrow y \in G$
$F \bullet G$	Join of F and G	$x \rightarrow y \in (F \bullet G) \Leftrightarrow x \rightarrow y \in (G \circ F)$
$F \subseteq G$	F is subset of G	$x \rightarrow y \in F \Rightarrow x \rightarrow y \in G$

Table 1. Operations on tuple relations

variables $\alpha_{i1}, \ldots, \alpha_{im_i}$ and symbolic constants. These relations can be written equivalently as the union of a number of simpler relations, each of which can be described using a single conjunct:

$$\bigcup_{i=1}^{n} \{[s_1, \ldots, s_k] \rightarrow [t_1, \ldots, t_{k'}] \mid \exists \alpha_{i1}, \ldots, \alpha_{im_i} \text{ s.t. } F_i \}$$

Table 1 gives a brief description of some of the operations on integer tuple relations that we have implemented and use in our applications. The implementation of these operations is described elsewhere [2] (see also http://www.cs.umd.ed u/projects/omega or ftp://ftp.cs.umd.edu/pub/omega)

In addition to these operations we have also implemented and use in our applications the *transitive closure* operator:

$$x \rightarrow z \in F^* \Leftrightarrow x = z \vee \exists y \text{ s.t. } x \rightarrow y \in F \wedge y \rightarrow z \in F^*$$

and *positive transitive closure* operator:

$$x \rightarrow z \in F^+ \Leftrightarrow x \rightarrow z \in F \vee \exists y \text{ s.t. } x \rightarrow y \in F \wedge y \rightarrow z \in F^+$$

In previous work[4], we developed algorithms for a closely related operation called affine closure. Affine closure is well suited to testing the legality of reordering transformations and is generally easier to compute than transitive closure. But many of our applications require the full generality of transitive closure.

Unfortunately, the exact transitive closure of an affine integer tuple relation may not be affine. In fact, we can encode multiplication using transitive closure:

$$\{[x, y] \rightarrow [x + 1, y + z]\}^* \text{ is equivalent to: } \{[x, y] \rightarrow [x', y + z(x' - x)] \mid x \leq x'\}$$

Adding multiplication to the supported operations allows us to pose undecidable questions. Transitive closure is therefore not computable in the general case.

3 Applications

This section describes a number of applications of tuple relations and demonstrates the importance of the transitive closure operator.

Original program:
```
do i = 1, 3
  do j = 1, 4
    a(i,j)=a(i-1,j)+a(i,j-1)+a(i-1,j-1)
```

Dependence pattern:

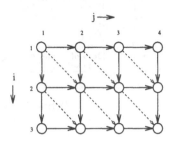

Program with posts and waits inserted:
```
doacross i = 1, 3
  doacross j = 1, 4
    if (1<i) wait(1,i-1,j)
    if (1<j) wait(2,i,j-1)
    if (1<i and 1<j) wait(3,i-1,j-1)
    a(i,j)=a(i-1,j)+a(i,j-1)+a(i-1,j-1)
    if (i<3) post(1,i,j)
    if (j<4) post(2,i,j)
    if (i<3 and j<4) post(3,i,j)
```

Fig. 2. Example of redundant synchronization

3.1 Simple Redundant Synchronization Removal

A common approach to executing scientific programs on parallel machines is to distribute the iterations of the program across the processors. If there are no dependences between iterations executing on different processors then the processors can execute completely independently. Otherwise, the processors will have to synchronize at certain points to preserve the original sequential semantics of the program. On a shared memory system, the simplest way to achieve the necessary synchronization is to place a **post** statement after the source of each dependence and a corresponding **wait** statement before the sink of each dependence. Figure 2 shows the results of inserting **posts** and **waits** for the given example. As this example demonstrates, and is often the case, many of the posts and waits inserted by this approach are redundant. In this example, we can see that the explicit synchronization that results from the dependence from the write of a(i,j) to the read of a(i-1,j-1) is redundant, since the appropriate execution ordering will always be achieved due to a chain of explicit synchronizations that result from the other two dependences.

The problem then is to identify which dependences need to be explicitly synchronized. In this section, we restrict ourselves to a simple case of this problem where: the loops are perfectly nested, the granularity of synchronization is between entire iterations of the loop body (i.e., all **posts** occur at the end of the loop body and all **waits** occur at the start of the loop body), and we assume each iteration may execute on a different processor. This is the class of problems considered by some related work [6] in this area. We will show how our approach improves on the related work in this limited domain, then in Section 3.3, we will show how to extend the approach to the more general problem.

We first compute a dependence relation d that represents the data dependences between different iterations of the loop body (see Figure 3 for an example). Each of these dependences will have to be synchronized either explicitly or implicitly. The transitive closure, d^+, of this relation will contain all pairs of iterations that are linked by a chain of synchronizations of length one or more. The relation $d^+ \circ d$, which we denote d^{2+}, therefore contains all pairs of iterations that are linked by a chain of synchronizations of length **two** or more and will therefore not have to be explicitly synchronized. So, the dependences that we do have to explicitly synchronize are $d - d^{2+}$. Note that this is equivalent to computing the transitive reduction of d. An example of the technique is presented in Figure 3, an example from [1].

```
doacross i ...
    doacross j ...
        a(i+3,j)=b(i-1,j-1)+ ...
        b(i,j) = ...
        ... = b(i-2,j+1)+c(i-1,j-1)
        c(i,j) = a(i,j) + z(i,j)
```

$$d = \{[i,j] \rightarrow [i+3,j]\} \cup \{[i,j] \rightarrow [i+2,j-1]\} \cup \{[i,j] \rightarrow [i+1,j+1]\}$$

$$d^{2+} = \{[i,j] \rightarrow [i',j-i+i'-3] \mid i \le i'-3\} \cup$$
$$\{[i,j] \rightarrow [i',j'] \mid i+2j = i'+2j' \wedge j' \le j-2\} \cup$$
$$\{[i,j] \rightarrow [i',j'] \mid \exists \beta \text{ s.t. } j+i' = i+j'+3\beta \wedge 6+i+j' \le j+i' \wedge 3+i+2j \le i'+2j'\} \cup$$
$$\{[i,j] \rightarrow [i',j-i+i'] \mid i \le i'-2\} \cup$$
$$\{[i,j] \rightarrow [i',j'] \mid 3+i+2j = i'+2j' \wedge j' \le j\} \cup$$
$$\{[i,j] \rightarrow [i',j'] \mid \exists \beta \text{ s.t. } j+i' = i+j'+3\beta \wedge 3+i+j' \le j+i' \wedge 6+i+2j \le i'+2j'\}$$

$$d - d^{2+} = \{[i,j] \rightarrow [i+2,j-1]\} \cup \{[i,j] \rightarrow [i+1,j+1]\}$$

The dependence from the write of a(i+3,j) to the read of a(i,j) is found redundant.

Fig. 3. Example of determining dependences that must be explicitly synchronized

In cases where more complex dependence relations cause the transitive closure calculation to be inexact, we can still produce useful results. We can safely subtract a lower bound on the 2+ closure from the dependences and still produce correct (but perhaps conservative) synchronization.

Our approach improves on related work in the following ways:

1. We use tuple relations as an abstraction for data dependences rather than the more traditional dependence distance representation. This allows us to handle non-constant dependences, which previous work is not able to do (see Figure 4).

2. Using dependence relations also allows us to use our algorithm for nested loops without having to make special checks in boundary cases. Related work builds an explicit graph of a subset of the iteration space, with each node representing an iteration of the loop body, and each edge representing a dependence [6]. Redundancy is found either through taking the transitive closure or reduction of this graph, or using algorithms that search a subgraph starting at the first iteration. In a one-dimensional loop, provided all dependence distances are constant, it is simple to find a small subgraph such that if a dependence is redundant in the subgraph, it is redundant throughout the iteration space. But in a nested loop, the existence of negative inner dependence distances (such as (1,-2)) can result in *non-uniformly* redundant synchronizations [1]. A chain of synchronizations may exist within part of the iteration space, but at the edges of the iteration space, the chain may travel outside the bounds of the loops, and so intermediate iterations in the chain do not execute; thus it is difficult to find a small graph that finds all uniform redundancy. Figure 5 shows an example of finding an alternate path to handle the boundary cases. Methods that search a small graph, but which may miss some redundancy when nesting is greater than 2 have been developed[6].

Because we start with more precise dependence information, we do not have the same problem. No out-of-bounds iteration is in the range or domain of any dependence relation. Thus, we never need to worry that the 2+ closure will contain chains that are illegal at the edges of the iteration space. At the

```
doacross i = 1, n
    doacross j = 1, m
        A(i,j+2*i) = A(i,j) + Z(i,j)
        B(i,j) = B(i,j-4) + Y(i,j)
```

$d_{11} = \{[i,j] \to [i, 2i+j] \mid 1 \le i \le n \land 2i+j \le m \land 1 \le j\}$

$d_{22} = \{[i,j] \to [i, j+4] \mid 1 \le i \le n \land 1 \le j < m\}$

$d = d_{11} \cup d_{22}$

$d^+ = \{[i,j] \to [i,j'] \mid \exists \beta \ \text{s.t.} \ j' = j + 4\beta \land 1 \le i \le n \land 1 \le j \le j' - 4 \land j' \le m\} \cup$
$\qquad \{[i,j] \to [i, 2i+j] \mid 1 \le i \le n \land 2i+j \le m \land 1 \le j\}$

$d^{2+} = d^+ \circ d$

$\qquad = \{[i,j] \to [i,j'] \mid \exists \beta \ \text{s.t.} \ j + 4\beta = 2i + j' \land 1 \le i \le n \land j' \le m \land 1 \le j \land 4 + 2i + j \le j'\} \cup$
$\qquad \{[i,j] \to [i, 4i+j] \mid 1 \le i \le n \land 4i+j \le m \land 1 \le j\} \cup$
$\qquad \{[i,j] \to [i,j'] \mid \exists \beta \ \text{s.t.} \ j + 4\beta = j' \land 1 \le i \le n \land 1 \le j \le j' - 8 \land j' \le m\}$

$d - d^{2+} = \{[i,j] \to [i, 2i+j] \mid 1 \le i \le 3, n \land 2i + j \le m \land 1 \le j\} \cup$
$\qquad \{[i,j] \to [i, 2i+j] \mid \exists \beta \ \text{s.t.} \ 0 = 1 + i + 2\beta \land 5 \le i \le n \land 1 \le j \land 2i + j \le m\} \cup$
$\qquad \{[i,j] \to [i, j+4] \mid 2 \le i \le n \land 1 \le j \le m - 4\}$

We find that d_{11} does not need to be enforced when i > 3 and i is even (and thus 2i is a multiple of 4.)

Fig. 4. Example of non-constant dependence distances and partial redundancy

same time, since the 2+ closure contains all chains of two or more ordering constraints, all possible alternate paths are contained in it.

3. When a dependence is only partially redundant, we produce the conditions under which it needs to be explicitly enforced, and we can use that information to conditionally execute synchronization.

3.2 Testing the Legality of Iteration Reordering Transformations

Optimizing compilers reorder the iterations of statements so as to expose or increase parallelism and to improve data locality. An important part of this process is determining for each statement, which orderings of the iterations of that statement will preserve the semantics of the original code. Before we decide

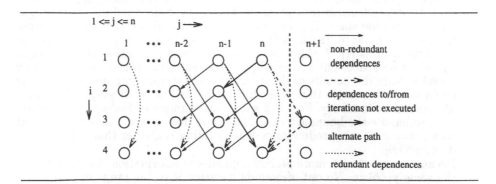

Fig. 5. Finding alternate paths at boundaries; (3,0) is redundant when n > 1

which orderings will be used for other statements, we can determine necessary conditions for the legality of an ordering for a particular statement by considering the direct self dependences of that statement. For example, it is not legal to interchange the i and j loops for statement 1 in Example 1 in Figure 6 because of the direct self dependence from $a(i-1, j+1)$ to $a(i, j)$. It is legal, however, to interchange the i and j loops for statement 2.

We can obtain stronger legality conditions by considering transitive self dependences, as is demonstrated by Example 2 in Figure 6. In this example, executing the i loop in reverse order is legal for both statements with respect to direct self dependences (there aren't any), but is not legal with respect to transitive self dependences.

To compute all transitive dependences we use an adapted form of the Floyd-Warshall algorithm for transitive closure. The algorithm is modified because we need to characterize each edge, not simply determine its existence. We denote by d_{pq}, the data dependences from statement s_p to statement s_q. The algorithm is shown in Figure 7. In an iteration of the k loop, we update all dependences to incorporate all transitive dependences through statements $1..k$. The key expression in the algorithm is $d_{rq} \circ (d_{rr})^* \circ d_{pr}$. We include the $(d_{rr})^*$ term because we want to infer transitive dependences of the following form:

> If there is a dependence from iteration i_1 of statement s_p to iteration i_2 of statement s_r and a chain of self dependences from iteration i_2 to iteration i_3 and finally a dependence from iteration i_3 to iteration i_4 of statement s_q then there is a transitive self dependence from iteration i_1 to iteration i_4.

In [5] we describe a framework for unifying iteration reordering transformations that uses a legality test similar to those described above.

3.3 General Redundant Synchronization Removal

In this section, we consider a more general form of the problem described in Section 3.1. We no longer require the loops to be perfectly nested, the granularity of synchronization is now between iterations of particular statements (i.e. posts and waits occur immediately before and after the statements they are associated with) and we know how iterations will be distributed to the physical processors. For example, we might know that iterations are distributed to a virtual processor array via a data distribution and the owner computes rule, and the virtual processor array is folded onto the physical processor array in say a blocked fashion.

For each pair of statements p and q, we construct a relation c_{pq} that represents all ordering constraints on the iterations that are guaranteed to be satisfied in the distributed program. Such ordering constraints come from two sources:

```
      do i = 1, n                                do 2 i = 1, 4
          do j = 1, m                  1             a(i) = b(i)
1             a(i,j) = a(i,j) + a(i-1,j+1)  2             b(i) = a(i-1)
2             b(i,j) = b(i,j) + a(i,j)
```

Example 1   Example 2

Fig. 6. Examples of direct and transitive self dependences

```
for each statement r
    for each statement p
        for each statement q
            d_pq = d_pq ∪ d_rq ∘ (d_rr)* ∘ d_pr
```

Fig. 7. Modified Floyd-Warshall algorithm

1. If there is a data dependence from iteration i of statement p to iteration j of statement q (denoted $i \rightarrow j \in d_{pq}$), then i is guaranteed to be executed before j in any semantically equivalent distributed version of the program.
2. If iteration i of statement p and iteration j of statement q will be executed on the same physical processor (denoted $s_p(i) = s_q(j)$), and iteration i is executed before iteration j in the original execution order of the program (denoted $i \prec_{pq} j$), then i is guaranteed to be executed before j in the distributed program.

Combining these ordering constraints gives:

$$c_{pq} = d_{pq} \cup \{i \rightarrow j \mid i \prec_{pq} j \wedge s_p(i) = s_q(j)\}$$

Unlike in Section 3.1, we cannot determine which dependences need not be explicitly synchronized simply by computing $(c_{pq})^{2+}$. A synchronization may be redundant because of a chain of synchronizations through other statements. To determine such chains of ordering constraints, we first apply the algorithm in Figure 7 substituting c_{pq} for d_{pq} and producing c'_{pq}. This gives us all chains of ordering constraints of length **one** or more. We then find all chains of ordering constraints of length **two** or more using:

$$c''_{pq} = \bigcup_{r \in \{statements\}} c_{rq} \circ c'_{pr}$$

We do not need to explicitly synchronize iterations if they will be executed on the same physical processor, or if there is a chain of ordering constraints of length **two** or more. Therefore the only dependences that we have to synchronize explicitly are:

$$d_{pq} - \{i \rightarrow j \mid s_p(i) = s_q(j)\} - c''_{pq}$$

If the number of physical processors is not known at compile time, the expression $s_p(i) = s_q(j)$ may not be affine. In such cases, we can instead use the stricter requirement that the two iterations will execute on the same virtual processor. This expression is always affine for the class of programs and distribution methods that we are able to handle and is a sufficient condition for the two iterations to be executed on the same physical processor. So, any redundancy that we find based on this stronger requirement can be safely eliminated.

Related work[7, 8, 1] addresses the case of synchronization between statements using methods similar to those used for the simple case. All of the methods build an explicit graph of a subset of the iteration space, with each node representing an iteration of a statement. Redundancy is found either by searching the graph[1] or using transitive closure of the graph[7, 8]; dependences are restricted to constant distances; and the problem regarding boundary cases still exists. These methods search a small graph which finds all redundancy when nesting level is 2, but may miss some redundancy when the nesting level is greater[1].

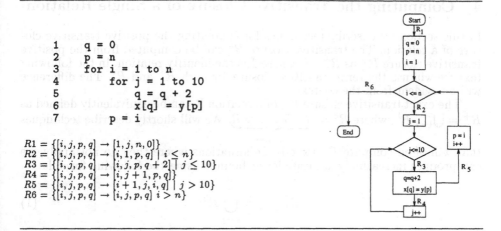

Fig. 8. Induction Variable Example

None of the above methods consider non-perfectly nested loops, and they do not use information regarding distribution. One previous technique has the ability to generate the conditions under which a non-uniformly redundant dependence must be enforced[8], but the authors indicate that their technique may require taking transitive closure of a large subset of the iteration space.

3.4 Induction Variables

Tuple relations and the transitive closure operation can also be used to compute closed form expressions for induction variables. We will use the program in Figure 8 as an example. In this example, we will be using 4-tuples because there are four scalar variables of interest in this program: i, j, n and m. For each edge in the control flow graph, we create a *state transition* relation which summarizes the change in value of the scalars as a result of executing the code in the control flow node corresponding to that edge and the conditions under which execution occurs (see Figure 8). To investigate the state of the scalar variables at statement 6, we could use the algorithm in Figure 7 to compute (along with other things) all transitive edges from the start node to the node containing statement 6. Alternatively, we can directly calculate:

$$R_1 \bullet (R_2 \bullet (R_3 \bullet R4)^* \bullet R_5)^* \bullet R_2 \bullet (R_3 \bullet R_4)^* \bullet R_3$$

Which in this case evaluates to:

$$\{[i, j, p, q] \rightarrow [i', j', i' - 1, 20i' + 2j' - 20] \mid 2 \leq i' \leq n \land 1 \leq j' \leq 10\} \cup$$
$$\{[i, j, p, q] \rightarrow [1, j', n, 2j'] \mid 1 \leq j' \leq 10 \land 1 \leq n\}$$

From this result, we can deduce that at line 6 we can replace the induction variable p with (i=1?n:i-1) and the induction variable q with 20i+2j-20.

This general approach has uses other that induction variable recognition, such as deriving or proving assertions about scalar variables. The fact that we could use transitive closure to potentially completely describe the effect of arbitrary programs consisting of loops and conditionals with affine bounds and conditions and assignment statements involving affine expressions further demonstrates that transitive closure cannot always be computed exactly, since such analysis is known to be uncomputable.

4 Computing the Transitive Closure of a Single Relation

In this section we describe techniques for computing the positive transitive closure of a relation. The transitive closure R^* can be computed from the positive transitive closure R^+ as $R^+ \cup I$, where I is the identity relation. In the following text we will use the term transitive closure for both R^+ and R^*. The difference will be evident from the context.

The exact transitive closure R^+ of a relation R can be equivalently defined as $R^+ = \bigcup_{k=1}^{\infty} R^k$, where $R^k = \underbrace{R \circ R \circ \ldots \circ R}_{k \ times}$. We will shortly describe techniques that will often compute R^+ exactly. In situations where they do not apply, we can produce increasingly accurate lower bounds using the following formula:

$$R^+_{LB(n)} = \bigcup_{k=1}^{n} R^k \qquad (1)$$

In some cases $R^+_{LB(n)} = R^+$ for all n greater than some small value. The following theorem allows us to determine when a lower bound is equal to the exact transitive closure:

Theorem 1. *For all relations P and R such that $R \subseteq P \subseteq R^+$ the following holds: $P = R^+$ if and only if $P \circ R \subseteq P$.*

Proof. The "only if" part is trivial. To prove the "if" part we will prove by induction on k that $R^k \subseteq P$. The assumption $R \subseteq P$ proves the base case. If $R^k \subseteq P$ then $R^{k+1} = (R^k \circ R) \subseteq (P \circ R) \subseteq P$. Since $R^+ = \bigcup_{k=1}^{\infty} R^k$ and $\forall k \geq 1, R^k \subseteq P$, we know that $R^+ \subseteq P$. Thus $P = R^+$. $\square$

Corollary 2. $R^+_{LB(n)} = R^+$ iff $R^+_{LB(n)} \circ R \subseteq R^+_{LB(n)}$.

Thus, one approach to computing transitive closure would be to compute more and more accurate lower bounds until the result becomes exact. Although this technique works in some cases, there is no guarantee of termination. For example, the exact transitive closure of $R = \{[i] \rightarrow [i+1]\}$ cannot be computed using this approach. Thus more sophisticated techniques are required. Section 4.1 describes techniques that work in the special case of relations that can be described by a single conjunct. Section 4.2 describes techniques for the general case, making use of the techniques used for the single conjunct case.

4.1 Single Conjunct Relations

For a certain class of single conjunct relations, the transitive closure can be calculated straightforwardly. Consider the following example:

$$R = \{[i_1, i_2] \rightarrow [j_1, j_2] \mid j_1 - i_1 \geq 2 \wedge j_2 - i_2 = 2 \wedge \exists \alpha \ s.t. \ j_1 - i_1 = 2\alpha\}$$

For any $k \geq 1$ the relation R^k can be calculated as:

$$R^k = \{[i_1, i_2] \rightarrow [j_1, j_2] \mid j_1 - i_1 \geq 2k \wedge j_2 - i_2 = 2k \wedge \exists \alpha \ s.t. \ j_1 - i_1 = 2\alpha\}$$

By making k in the above expression existentially quantified, we get the union of R^k for all $k > 0$; that is, R^+:

$$\{[i_1, i_2] \rightarrow [j_1, j_2] \mid \exists k > 0 \ s.t. \ j_1 - i_1 \geq 2k \wedge j_2 - i_2 = 2k \wedge \exists \alpha \ s.t. \ j_1 - i_1 = 2\alpha\}$$

$$
\begin{aligned}
R &= \{[i_1, i_2] \rightarrow [j_1, j_2] \mid j_1 - i_1 = 1 \wedge j_2 - i_2 \geq 2 \wedge 1 \leq i_1, j_1, j_2 \leq n \wedge \\
& \quad i_1 \leq i_2 \leq n\} \\
d &= \{[i_1, i_2] \rightarrow [j_1, j_1] \mid j_1 - i_1 = 1 \wedge j_2 - i_2 \geq 2\} \\
d^+ &= \{[i_1, i_2] \rightarrow [j_1, j_2] \mid i_1 < j_1 \wedge j_2 - i_2 \geq 2(j_1 - i_1)\} \\
Domain(R) &= \{[i_1, i_2] \mid 1 \leq i_1 \leq i_2 \leq n - 2\} \\
Range(R) &= \{[j_1, j_2] \mid 2 \leq j_1 < j_2 \leq n\} \\
h &= \{[i_1, i_2] \rightarrow [j_1, j_2] \mid 1 \leq i_1 \leq i_2 \leq n - 2 \wedge 2 \leq j_1 < j_2 \leq n\} \\
D_+ &= \{[i_1, i_2] \rightarrow [j_1, j_2] \mid 1 \leq i_1 \leq i_2 \wedge i_1 < j_1 \wedge j_2 \leq n \wedge \\
& \quad j_2 - i_2 \geq 2(j_1 - i_1)\}
\end{aligned}
$$

D_+ is lexicographically forward and $D_+ \subseteq R \circ D_+ \cup R$, thus $R^+ = D_+$.

Fig. 9. Example of calculating transitive closure of a single conjunct relation

This method can be used for any relation that only contains constraints on the differences between the corresponding elements of the input and output tuples. We call such relations *d-form relations*.

Definition 3. A relation R is said to be in *d-form* iff it can be written as:

$$
\{[i_1, i_2, \ldots i_m] \rightarrow [j_1, j_2 \ldots j_m] \mid \forall p, 1 \leq p \leq m, \; L_p \leq j_p - i_p \leq U_p \wedge \\
\exists \alpha_p \text{ s.t. } j_p - i_p = M_p \, \alpha_p \}
$$

where L_p and U_p are constants and M_p is an integer.

The transitive closure of a *d-form* relation is:

$$
\{[i_1, i_2, \ldots i_m] \rightarrow [j_1, j_2 \ldots j_m] \mid \exists k > 0 \text{ s.t. } \forall p, 1 \leq p \leq m \\
L_p k \leq j_p - i_p \leq U_p k \wedge \exists \alpha_p \text{ s.t. } j_p - i_p = M_p \, \alpha_p \} \tag{2}
$$

For any relation R that is not in *d*-form, it is relatively easy to compute a *d*-form relation d such that $R \subseteq d$. For each $p \in \{1, \ldots, m\}$, we introduce a new variable equal to $j_p - i_p$ and project away all other variables. We then look for upper and lower bounds and stride constraints on this variable. So, it is always possible to compute a *d*-form relation that is a superset of R, since in the worst case we can set M_p to 1, L_p to $-\infty$ and U_p to $+\infty$. We can then use d^+ as an upper bound on R^+ since for any two relations R_1 and R_2, if $R_1 \subseteq R_2$ then $R_1^+ \subseteq R_2^+$. To improve this upper bound we can restrict the domain and range of d^+ to those of R by computing $D_+ = d^+ \cap h$, where $h = Domain(R) \times Range(R)$.

In most of our applications the relations R and D_+ have the property of being *lexicographically forward*.

Definition 4. A relation A is lexicographically forward iff $\forall x \rightarrow y \in A, 0 \prec y - x$ ($y - x$ is lexicographically positive).

This property is often known in advance, but even if it isn't, it can be easily determined via simple satisfiability tests. For lexicographically forward relations we can check whether the upper bound is an exact transitive closure using the following theorem:

Theorem 5. $\forall$ *lexicographically forward relations* P, R : $R^+ \subseteq P \Rightarrow (P = R^+ \Leftrightarrow P \subseteq (R \cup R \circ P))$.

Proof. Assume $(P \subseteq (R \cup R \circ P))$. We will show that $(P \subseteq R^+)$. Let $x \to z$ be in P. We will show by induction on $z - x$ that $x \to z$ is in R^+. The base case $x = z$ is vacuous. If $x \to z \in R$ then $x \to z \in R^+$. Otherwise, $\exists y$ s.t. $x \to y \in P \wedge y \to z \in R$. Because P and R are lexicographically forward, $z - x \succ z - y$. Thus, by induction hypothesis, $y \to z \in R^+$, and, consequently $x \to z \in R^+$. So we have $(P \subseteq (R \cup R \circ P)) \Rightarrow (P \subseteq R^+)$. $R^+ \subseteq P$ is in the theorem assumption, so we have $(P \subseteq (R \cup R \circ P)) \Rightarrow (P = R^+)$. The reverse statement $(P = R^+) \Rightarrow (P \subseteq (R \circ P \cup R))$ is trivial. $\square$

Corollary 6. *If D_+ is lexicographically forward, then*

$$D_+ = R^+ \text{ iff } D_+ \subseteq (R \cup R \circ D_+) \tag{3}$$

We collected statistics for all of the examples given in this paper, plus about 2000 other real-life examples of transitive closure that arose from our applications This test showed that 97% of single conjunct closures performed in these examples were computed exactly.

4.2 Multiple Conjunct Relations

Computing a lower bound on the transitive closure of a relation with more than one conjunct via a naive application of Equation 1 is prohibitively expensive due to the possible exponential growth in the number of the conjuncts. We have developed techniques that try to limit this growth. We first describe how to compute the transitive closure of a two conjunct relation; then we show how to generalize this technique for relations with an arbitrary number of conjuncts.

Computing the Transitive Closure of Two-conjunct Relations Let R be a two-conjunct relation, $R = C_1 \cup C_2$. The transitive closure of R is:

$$(C_1 \cup C_2)^+ = C_1^+ \cup (C_1^* \circ C_2 \circ C_1^*)^+ \tag{4}$$

If $C_1^* \circ C_2 \circ C_1^*$ is a single conjunct relation, its closure can be calculated using the techniques described in the Section 4.1. $C_1^* \circ C_2 \circ C_1^*$ will be a single conjunct relation provided that C_1^* is a single conjunct relation, since the composition of two single conjunct relations is always a single conjunct relation. Unfortunately, C_1^* is often not a single conjunct relation even if C_1^+ is. To overcome this difficulty, we use a single conjunct approximation of C_1^*, that we will denote $C_1^?$ and call *?-closure*. We try to select an $C_1^?$ that has the following desirable property

$$C_1^* \circ C_2 \circ C_1^* \equiv C_1^? \circ C_2 \circ C_1^? \tag{5}$$

Our choice of $C_1^?$ will not depend on C_2, so there is only hope, not a guarantee, of satisfying this property. If this hope is realized then we can use $C_1^?$ instead of C^* in Equation 4. If not, it may still be possible to limit the number of conjuncts in $(C_1 \cup C_2)^+$ through the use of $C_1^?$ if $C_1^* \circ C_2 \equiv C_1^? \circ C_2$ or $C_2 \circ C_1^* \equiv C_2 \circ C_1^?$.

Testing the property described in Equation 5 directly is rather expensive, so we instead use the following cheaper but possibly conservative test. If $(C_1^? - C_1^+)$ is convex (which is often the case) and $(C_1^? - C_1^+) \circ C_2 \circ (C_1^? - C_1^+) \equiv C_2$ then we know that the property described in Equation 5 holds, otherwise we assume it doesn't. This test succeeded in all of the 2000 plus examples described earlier.

Input: $R = \bigcup_{i=1}^{m} C_i$

Output: R^+ or R_{LB}^+

Invariant: $(R^+ \supseteq T \cup W^+) \wedge (exact \Rightarrow R^+ = T \cup W^+)$
$T = \emptyset;\ W = R;\ exact = true$

while not $(W = \emptyset$ or "accept W as W_{LB}^+") **do**
   choose a conjunct $A \in W$; remove A from W
   if A^+ is known **then**
      $T = T \cup A^+$
      $W_{new} = \emptyset$
      for all conjuncts $C_i \in W$ **do**
         if $(A^? - A^+) \circ C_i \circ (A^? - A^+) \equiv C_i$ **then** $W_{new} = W_{new} \cup (A^? \circ C_i \circ A^?)$
         else if $C_i \circ (A^? - A^+) \equiv C_i$ **then** $W_{new} = W_{new} \cup (C_i \circ A^?) \cup (A^+ \circ C_i \circ A^?)$
         else if $(A^? - A^+) \circ C_i \equiv C_i$ **then** $W_{new} = W_{new} \cup (A^? \circ C_i) \cup (A^? \circ C_i \circ A^+)$
         else $W_{new} = W_{new} \cup (C_i \circ A^+) \cup (A^+ \circ C_i) \cup (A^+ \circ C_i \circ A^+) \cup C_i$
      endfor
      $W = W_{new}$
   else
      $T = T \cup A_{LB}^+$
      $W = (W \circ A_{LB}^+) \cup (A_{LB}^+ \circ W \cup A_{LB}^+) \circ (W \circ A_{LB}^+) \cup W$
      $exact = false$
endwhile
if $(W = \emptyset$ and $exact = true)$ or $(T \cup W) \circ (T \cup W) \subseteq (T \cup W)$ **then**
   $R^+ = T \cup W$
else
   $R_{LB}^+ = T \cup W$

Fig. 10. The algorithm for computing transitive closure

Heuristics for Computing ?-closure We try to compute ?-closure for a relation R only if R^+ is an exact single conjunct relation. The $R^?$ that we compute will be a superset of R^+ but a proper subset of R^* since it will not include all elements in I. Property 5 will often still hold since these missing elements from I are also often not in the domain or range of C_2.

For a d-form relation d (see Section 4.1) we compute $d^?$ as:

$$\{[i_1, i_2, \ldots i_m] \rightarrow [j_1, j_2 \ldots j_m] \mid \exists k \geq 0 \text{ s.t. } \forall p, 1 \leq p \leq m \atop L_p k \leq j_p - i_p \leq U_p k \wedge \exists \alpha_p \text{ s.t. } j_p - i_p = M_p \alpha_p)\} \tag{6}$$

For a relation R s.t. $R^+ = D_+$, we use $R^? = d^? \cap h'$, where $h' = (Domain(R) \cup Range(R)) \times (Domain(R) \cup Range(R))$. In other cases we assume that $?-closure$ cannot be computed and let $R^?$ be the empty relation.

Computing the Transitive Closure of Multiple Conjunct Relations
The transitive closure of a relation with an arbitrary number of conjuncts can be computed similarly to the transitive closure of a relation with two conjuncts. Let R be a m-conjunct relation $R = \bigcup_{i=1}^{m} C_i$. Its transitive closure is:

$$R^+ = C_1^+ \cup (C_1^* \circ \bigcup_{i=2}^{m} C_i \circ C_1^*)^+ = C_1^+ \cup (\bigcup_{i=2}^{m} C_1^* \circ C_i \circ C_1^*)^+$$

For $i \in \{2, \ldots, m\}$, $C_1^* \circ C_i \circ C_1^*$ can be computed using the techniques described in the two conjunct case. After all these terms are computed, the same algorithm can be applied recursively to compute the transitive closure of their union. The algorithm is shown in Figure 10. The algorithm will terminate when the transitive

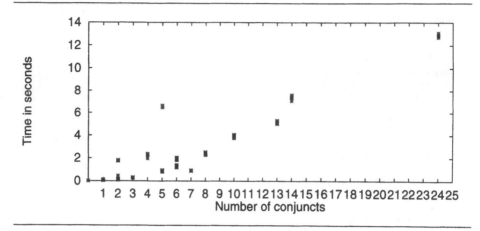

Fig. 11. Relationship between number of conjuncts and computation time

closure has been computed exactly or when we are willing to accept the current approximation as a lower bound. In many cases, what we accept as a lower bound turns out to be exact after all, and can be proved to be so using Theorem 1. We computed the exact transitive closure in 99% of the examples described earlier. An example of a transitive closure calculation using this algorithm is shown in Figure 12.

The order in which we consider the conjuncts in a relation can significantly affect the performance of our algorithm. One heuristic that we use is to consider first those conjuncts C_i for which we can find a $C_i^?$ that satisfies Equation 5. In some cases, pre-computing the positive transitive closure of some of the conjuncts in the original relation (i.e. replacing C_i by C_i^+) can also simplify the calculations.

The algorithm in Figure 10 allows us to compute the exact transitive closure of a multiple conjunct relation or its lower bound. If an upper bound is required, it can be calculated in a manner similar to that of a single conjunct relation.

The time required to compute transitive closure obviously increases with the number of conjuncts in the original relation. Figure 11 shows this relationship for the set of examples described earlier.

5 Conclusion

We have presented a number of applications for the transitive closure of tuple relations. These applications include:

- Avoiding redundant synchronization of iterations executing on different processors.
- Precisely describing which iterations of a statement are data dependent on which other iterations, and using this information to determine which iteration reordering transformations are legal.
- Computing closed form expressions for induction variables.

We also presented algorithms for transitive closure that produce exact results in most commonly occurring cases and produce upper or lower bounds (as necessary) in the other cases. Our experiments show that we produce exact results for most of the programs we have considered. We believe that the applications

$$R \qquad = \{[i,j] \to [i',j+1] \mid 1 \le i,j,j+1 \le n \wedge i' = i\} \cup$$
$$\{[i,n] \to [i+1,1] \mid 1 \le i, i+1 \le n\}$$
$$C_1^+ \qquad = \{[i,j] \to [i,j'] \mid 1 \le j < j' \le n \wedge 1 \le i \le n\}$$
$$C_1^? \qquad = \{[i,j] \to [i,j'] \mid 1 \le j \le j' \le n \wedge 1 \le i \le n\}$$
$$C_1^? \circ C_2 \circ C_1^? = \{[i,j] \to [i+1,j']' \mid 1 \le i < n \wedge 1 \le j \le n \wedge 1 \le j' \le n\}$$
Since, $\qquad C_1^? \circ C_2 \circ C_1^? \equiv C_1^* \circ C_2 \circ C_1^*$
$$(C_1^* \circ C_2 \circ C_1^*)^+ = (C_1^? \circ C_2 \circ C_1^?)^+$$
$$= \{[i,j] \to [i',j'] \mid 1 \le i < i' \le n \wedge 1 \le j, j' \le n\}$$
$$R^+ \qquad = C_1^+ \cup (C_1^* \circ C_2 \circ C_1^*)^+$$
$$= \{[i,j] \to [i',j'] \mid (1 \le j < j' \le n \wedge 1 \le i \le n \wedge i = i')\} \cup$$
$$\{[i,j] \to [i',j'] \mid (1 \le i < i' \le n \wedge 1 \le j \le n \wedge 1 \le j' \le n)\}$$

Fig. 12. Example of transitive closure calculation

described in this paper are only a small subset of the possible applications of this general purpose program abstraction and set of operations.

References

1. Ding-Kai Chen. *Compiler Optimizations for Parallel Loops With Fine-Grained Synchronization*. PhD thesis, Dept. of Computer Science, U. of Illinois at Urbana-Champaign, 1994. Also available as CSRD Report 1374.
2. Wayne Kelly, Vadim Maslov, William Pugh, Evan Rosser, Tatiana Shpeisman, and David Wonnacott. The Omega Library interface guide. Technical Report CS-TR-3445, Dept. of Computer Science, University of Maryland, College Park, March 1995.
3. Wayne Kelly and William Pugh. A framework for unifying reordering transformations. Technical Report CS-TR-3193, Dept. of Computer Science, University of Maryland, College Park, April 1993.
4. Wayne Kelly and William Pugh. Finding legal reordering transformations using mappings. In *Lecture Notes in Computer Science 892: Seventh International Workshop on Languages and Compilers for Parallel Computing*, Ithaca, NY, August 1994. Springer-Verlag.
5. Wayne Kelly and William Pugh. A unifying framework for iteration reordering transformations. In *Proceedings of the IEEE First International Conference on Algorithms And Architectures for Parallel Processing*, Brisbane, Australia, April 1995.
6. V.P. Krothapalli and P. Sadayappan. Removal of redundant dependences in DOACROSS loops with constant dependences. In *Proc. of the 3rd ACM SIGPLAN Symposium on Principles and Practice of Parallel Programming*, pages 51–60, July 1991.
7. S.P. Midkiff and D.A. Padua. Compiler algorithm for synchronization. *IEEE Trans. on Computers*, C-36(12):1485–1495, 1987.
8. S.P. Midkiff and D.A. Padua. A comparison of four synchronization optimization techniques. In *Proc. 1991 IEEE International Conf. on Parallel Processing*, pages II-9 – II-16, August 1991.

Demand-Driven, Symbolic Range Propagation*

William Blume
Hewlett Packard
Cupertino, California

Rudolf Eigenmann
Purdue University
West Lafayette, Indiana

Abstract. To effectively parallelize real programs, parallelizing compilers need powerful symbolic analysis techniques [13, 6]. In previous work we have introduced an algorithm called range propagation [4] that provides such capabilities. Range propagation has been implemented in Polaris, a parallelizing Fortran compiler being developed at the University of Illinois [7]. Because the algorithm is relatively expensive and several compilation passes make use of it, we have studied opportunities for increasing its efficiency. In this paper we present an algorithm that provides range analysis on-demand. We have implemented this algorithm in Polaris as well, and have measured its effectiveness.

1 Introduction

Range propagation was developed for the Polaris parallelizing compiler in response to our observed need of compilation passes to determine and reason about the values and expressions that program variables can take on.

The algorithm centers upon the computation and manipulation of *ranges*, which are lower and upper bound expressions for the value of a given variable at a given program statement.

Range propagation inludes two algorithms that depend on each other: one that can compare expressions and one that can derive upper and lower bounds of variables from the program text. The latter uses abstract interpretation [10] for analyzing the program.

As an example, suppose the data-dependence test wishes to compare the expression $x * y - 1$ with $-y$. Upper and lower bound analysis has determined that $x = [y : 10]$ and $y = [1 : \infty]$. It did this by analyzing all assignments to these variables and factoring in additional contraints imposed by control statements such as IF and DO statements. The goal of the comparison algorithm is to prove that the difference $d = expression_1 - expression_2 = [x * y + y - 1 : x * y + y - 1]$ is either always positive or always negative and, hence, either $expression_1 > expression_2$ or $expression_1 < expression_2$ holds. First, it replaces x with $[y : 10]$, getting $d = [[y : 10] * y + y - 1 : [y : 10] * y + y - 1]$. Simplifying leads to $d = [y^2 + y - 1 : 11 * y - 1]$. At this point it cannot yet determine whether the range of d is always positive or negative. The next step replaces y with

* This work was done at the University of Illinois at Urbana-Champaign under support by Army contract DABT63-92-C-0033. This work is not necessarily representative of the positions or policies of the U.S. Army or the government.

$[1 : \infty]$, getting $d = [[1 : \infty]^2 + [1 : \infty] - 1 : 11 * [1 : \infty] - 1]$. After simplifying, $d = [1 : \infty]$. Now, the lower bound of d is an integer greater than zero, and hence $x * y - 1 > -y$. The techniques used to determine the substitution order of variables and to simplify the substituted ranges are described in [4].

One issue is that the compiler usually modifies the program between different applications of range propagation, requiring repeated recomputations of the program's ranges. Because of this, a significant fraction of a compiler's execution time can be spent performing range propagation.

To lower these costs, we have developed a demand-driven algorithm for performing range propagation. It can compute the range for a particular variable when that range is requested by the compilation pass, as opposed to a conventional data-flow algorithm that computes all ranges at once. Since many restructuring techniques only need to know a small subset of the ranges of all variables, a demand-driven algorithm should greatly reduce the costs of range propagation.

2 Determining upper and lower bounds of variable values

The range propagation algorithm computes the range of each variable at each point of the program. A range is simply a symbolic lower bound and a symbolic upper bound on the values that a variable may take.

Since one cannot always statically compute the exact range that all variables may take in a program, range propagation computes a conservative approximation of the range of a variable. The lower bound of this approximation is always guaranteed to be smaller than or equal to the actual lower bound while the upper bound of this approximation is always guaranteed to be larger than or equal to the actual upper bound.

We break up the problem of computing the ranges of a variable at a particular statement into two sub-problems: the computation of the *control ranges* of the variable, and the computation of the *data ranges* of the variable. The final range for the variable is simply the intersection of its control and data ranges. The control ranges of a variable are those ranges computed from the constraints imposed by the control flow of the program, such as from IF or DO statements. The data ranges of a variable are those ranges computed from the assignments to that variable. We compute the control and data ranges separately because control ranges are much cheaper to compute.

The top-level function get_range for the demand-driven range propagation algorithm is shown in Figure 1. It stores its results in a global structure named R, so that future invocations of this function can reuse these results rather than recomputing. This storing and reusing values to avoid recomputation is called **memoization** [17, 1]. The algorithm simply checks whether the range for the given variable and statement already exists in R, computes and stores the range if it does not, then returns the range. The range is computed by intersecting the data and control ranges returned by get_control_range and get_data_range, two functions that will be described in Sections 3 and 4, respectively.

```
function get_range(s : statement, v : variable) : range
    if (R(s, v) has not been defined) then
        c ← get_control_range(s, v)
        d ← get_data_range(v)
        R(s, v) ← c ∩ d
    end if
    return R(s, v)
end function
```

Fig. 1. The demand-driven range propagation algorithm

Notation used in this paper: A **control-flow graph** (CFG) of a program is a directed graph. Each vertex in the CFG corresponds to a statement in the program and an edge between two vertices indicates that the second statement may be immediately executed after the first statment. An edge is said to be a **back-edge** if the order of the source of the edge is larger than the order of the sink of the edge, under a depth first ordering of the CFG.[2] Vertex u **dominates** vertex v if and only if every path from *start* to v pass through vertex u. Vertex u **strictly dominates** vertex v if and only if u dominates v and u does not equal v. Vertex u is the **immediate dominator** of vertex v if and only if u strictly dominates v and there is no vertex w such that u strictly dominates w and w strictly dominates v. See Aho, Sethi, and Ullman [2] for more details on these definitions.

Similar dominance relationships can be defined for the control-flow edges in the program. For example, a control-flow edge dominates a statement if all paths from *start* to that statement pass through that control-flow edge. In this paper, we would say that a control-flow edge is an **immediate dominating control-flow edge** (or `icdom(s)`) of a statement (s) if that edge is the immediate dominator of the statement.

Our demand-driven range propagation algorithm assumes that programs are in **Static Single Assignment** (SSA) form. A program is in SSA form when every variable within it has at most one defining statement. Programs are translated into SSA form by inserting ϕ-*functions* and renaming variables. A ϕ-**function**, denoted as $v \leftarrow \phi(w_1, w_2, \ldots, w_n)$, is a special assignment to a variable v that is inserted at a join in the control flow where at least two definitions of v reach this join. The ϕ-function has an argument for each entering control-flow edge of this join. The ith argument (w_i) corresponds to the value that the variable assigned by the ϕ-function (v) would take if the control-flow of the program took the ith control-flow edge to reach the join node, (i.e., $v = w_i$). An efficient algorithm to translate programs into SSA form is described in [12]. In this paper, we will assume that the function **def**(v) would return the single statement in the program that defines v.

---

[2] Our definition of back-edges is wider than the definition of back-edges given in other papers, (i.e., we define more edges to be back-edges than they do). We have defined back-edges differently so that if one deleted all the back-edges from a graph, the graph is guaranteed to be acyclic, even if the original graph is irreducible.

```
function get_control_range(s : statement, v : variable) : range
    if (icdom(s) is not defined) then
        return [−∞ : ∞]
    else
        return get_control_range1(icdom(s), v)
    end if
end function

function get_control_range1(e : control-flow edge, v : variable) : range
    if (C(e, v) has not been defined) then
        c ← get_local_control_range(e, v)
        p ← get_control_range(source(e), v)
        C(e, v) ← c ∩ p
    end if
    return C(e, v)
end function
```

Fig. 2. The demand-driven control range propagation algorithm

3 Computing control ranges

3.1 Needed functionality

Our demand-driven control range propagation algorithm assumes that the immediate dominating control-flow edge is known for each statement and that the program is in SSA form. The function `icdom(s)` will represent the immediate dominating control-flow edge of the statement s. A linear-time algorithm for computing dominators has been developed by Harel [14]. Alternatively, one can approximate the dominating control-flow edges from the statement dominators, which must be computed when translating into SSA form.

To compute the control ranges of a program, we will assume that there exists a function `get_local_control_ranges(e, v)`, which computes and returns the range of a given variable v at a given control-flow edge e computed from the control constraints imposed by the source statement of that edge. For example, `get_local_control_ranges(e, v)` would return $[a : ∞]$, if e is the exiting control flow edge for the **then** case of the statement `IF (V .GE. A) THEN`. If there are no control flow constraints imposed on that variable for that control-flow edge, then the function returns the unconstrained range $[−∞ : ∞]$.

3.2 Algorithm

The algorithm for demand-driven control range propagation is shown in Figure 2. This algorithm is composed of two mutually recursive functions: a function that computes the control range that holds for the entry of a given statement, and a function that computes the control range that holds after taking a given control-flow edge. Intuitively, these functions compute the control range of a given variable and statement (or control-flow edge) by intersecting the ranges that hold for the variable for all the dominating control-flow edges of the given statement (or control-flow edge). The control range of a statement is simply the control range that holds after passing through that statement's immediately dominating control-flow edge, (i.e., icdom(s)). As discussed in [8], this is more efficient but slightly more conservative than intersecting the control ranges of all incoming control flow edges. If the statement does not have an immediately dominating control-flow edge, then its result is the unconstrained range $[-\infty : \infty]$. The control range for a control-flow edge is the control range that is imposed by the edge, (i.e., the result of get_local_control_range), intersected with the control range for the source statement of that edge. The result is stored in the data structure C so as to avoid needless recomputation, (i.e., it memoizes).

Although recursive, the functions in Figure 2 are guaranteed to terminate. By definition of immediately dominating control-flow edges, the source of icdom(s) must strictly dominate statement s. Since the graphical representation of the dominator relationship is a tree, the algorithm will eventually reach a statement that does not have an immediately dominating control-flow edge.

3.3 Time complexity

The worst case time taken by the algorithm in Figure 2 is bounded by $O(c|S|)$, where c is the time taken to perform an intersection, (which equals the time taken to perform a constant number of symbolic expression comparisons), and $|S|$ is the number of statements in the program. However, from the extensive use of memoization, (i.e., storing computed values into C and reusing them), the worst case time taken to compute the range for every variable at every statement is $O(c|S||V|)$, where $|V|$ is the number of scalar variables in the program. Since a non-demand-driven algorithm would also take at least $O(c|S||V|)$ time, (since such an algorithm would have to visit each (statement, variable) pair in the program), the demand-driven algorithm is at most as expensive as a non-demand-driven algorithm, ignoring a constant factor.

3.4 Optimizations

By design of the algorithm, the time taken to compute a single control range is dependent upon the number of control-flow edges that dominate the given statement s. The number of dominating control-flow edges of a statement can be very large ($O(|S|)$). However, only a few of these edges add new constraints, (e.g., edges exiting IF or DO statements or from ASSERT directives). Because of this, our algorithm creates and uses a sparse form of the icdom function, where this sparse form returns the most immediate dominating control-flow edge that adds at least one range to one variable.

We have implemented an algorithm for computing the sparse immediate dominating control-flow edge of a statement. It simply traces back through all the

```
type node_ptr = pointer to d_range_node
type node = structure
    var : variable
    value : range          = ⊤ (assignment stmt.); [−∞ : ∞] (otherwise)
    old_value : range      = ⊤
    committed : boolean     = false (assignment stmt.); true (otherwise)
    prev : set of node_ptr  = ∅
    next : set of node_ptr  = ∅
end structure
```

Fig. 3. Fields and initial values of a **node** structure

statement's dominating control flow edges, using the `icdom` relationship, until it finds an edge that adds a control range to at least one variable. A global structure is used to memoize the result of this computation so that the algorithm would not recompute it in future calls.

4 Computing data ranges

The algorithm for computing ranges originating from the program's data flow is much more complex than the algorithm for computing ranges originating from constraints imposed by the control flow. This additional complexity arises from the need to iterate to a fixed point, (i.e., perform data-flow analysis), to compute the data ranges.

4.1 Data-flow graph

To allow the algorithm to cleanly and efficiently perform data flow analysis on a program in a demand-driven manner, we create and iterate over a data-flow graph that contains only the information needed to compute the desired range. Each node in this data-flow graph represents a variable and its data range. An edge exists from the node for variable x to the node for variable y if and only if the computation of the range of x depends upon the range of y. One node in this graph, denoted as *root*, is the node for the variable of the requested data range. All other nodes in the graph that we need to iterate over are reachable from *root*.

The fields of a single node of this graph are shown in Figure 3. *value*, *old_value*, *prev*, and *next* are working fields for the node. Once the final value has been determined, *committed* is set to true, which "freezes" the node's value and, in this way, memoizes the node's range.

With the exception of the initialization of the *value* field, all the initializations are straightforward. The initial range assigned to the *value* field is determined from the single definition point of the variable, which is given by the program's SSA representation. If the variable's definition is not an assignment statement, (e.g., the variable is a formal parameter, an argument to a procedure call, or an

function get_data_range(v : **variable**) : **range**
    $root \leftarrow$ get_node(v)
    return $root.value$
end function

function get_node(v : **variable**) : node_ptr
    if ($D(v)$ has not been defined) **then**
        $root \leftarrow$ create_node(v)
        $D(v) \leftarrow root$
        call add_children_to_node($root$)
        // Node $root$ is now fully-initialized
        if (all uncommitted nodes reachable from $root$ have been fully initialized) **then**
            compute_data_ranges($root$)
            commit_data_ranges($root$)
        end if
    end if
    return $D(v)$
end function

Fig. 4. The demand-driven data range propagation algorithm

procedure add_children_to_node(x : node_ptr)
    if (**def**(v) is an assignment statement) **then**
        for each variable w in rhs of **def**(v) **do**
            $y \leftarrow$ get_node(w)
            $x.next \leftarrow x.next \cup \{y\}$
            $y.prev \leftarrow y.prev \cup \{x\}$
        end for
    end if
end procedure

Fig. 5. Algorithm to create children for a data-flow graph node.

I/O statement), then its range is set to the unconstrained range $[-\infty : \infty]$ and committed. Otherwise, its value is set to the undefined range denoted $\top$.

4.2 Algorithm

The top-level of the algorithm for computing data ranges is shown in Figure 4. This algorithm simply calls the function **get_node** to build and iterate over a data-flow graph whose root is the node for the given variable, then returns the computed range stored in this root node.

The function **get_node** has two responsibilities. One of these responsibilities is to build a data-flow graph. More specifically, it creates a node for the given variable as well as data-flow subgraphs for the variables that the given variable's range may depend on. The function **create_node**, creates the node for the given variable, as shown in Figure 3. The function **add_children_to_node**, which is

```
procedure commit_data_ranges(root : node_ptr)
    for each uncommitted node x reachable from root do
        x.committed ← true
    end for
end procedure
```

Fig. 6. Algorithm to commit data ranges in the data-flow subgraph rooted at *root*

shown in Figure 5, creates nodes for the variables that the current node depends upon and adds edges between this current node and the newly created nodes by updating their *next* and *prev* fields. These other nodes are created by recursive calls to get_node. The global array D is used to memoize created nodes for future reuse.

The other responsibility of function get_node is to compute and commit the data ranges for the data-flow subgraph under construction. It does this eagerly, whenever the subgraph contains all nodes that it reaches (and hence it contains all variables needed for the analysis of this subgraph). We determine this state of the subgraph using Tarjan's *strong-connect* algorithm.

This eagerness to compute and commit data ranges as early as possible is one of the inherent properties of the algorithm. The reason for this eager computation of ranges is that it maximizes the number of committed ranges that a particular range may depend on, which improves the accuracy of the ranges computed by function compute_data_ranges_phase. Computing and committing data ranges early also minimizes the number of *poisoned* ranges generated. Poisoned ranges will be discussed in Section 5.

The point in algorithm get_node where the subgraph under construction is ready for computing the data ranges can be thought of as where "all uncommitted nodes reachable from *root* have been fully initialized", whereby the nodes are marked "initialized" as indicated by the comment line. The function get_node computes and commits the ranges of this subgraph by calling functions compute_data_ranges and commit_data_ranges. The implementation of compute_data_ranges will be described in the next subsection. The implementation of commit_data_ranges is shown in Figure 6. This algorithm sets the *committed* field to true for all (uncommitted) nodes in the subgraph rooted at *root*. By committing these nodes, it memoizes the ranges contained in these nodes, so that future invocations of get_data_range will return the ranges in these nodes rather than recomputing them.

4.3 Computing data ranges from a data-flow graph

The main function for computing data ranges is shown in Figure 7. It calls the function compute_data_ranges_phase twice in order to compute the ranges of ϕ-functions in two phases: the *widening phase* and the *narrowing phase*. These two phases are discussed in [8]. Briefly, the widening phase applies some conservative operations in order to guarantee termination of the algorithm in loop situations. The narrowing phase follows for regaining some of the accuracy lost

```
procedure compute_data_ranges(root : node_ptr)
    compute_data_ranges_phase(root, WIDENING_PHASE)
    compute_data_ranges_phase(root, NARROWING_PHASE)
end procedure
```

Fig. 7. Algorithm to compute data ranges from the given graph.

$$[a : b] \cup [c : d] \Rightarrow [\min(a, c) : \max(b, d)] \tag{1}$$

$$[a : b] \cap [c : d] \Rightarrow [\max(a, c) : \min(b, d)] \tag{2}$$

$$[a : b] \bigtriangledown [c : d] \Rightarrow [\text{if } a = c \text{ then } a \text{ else } -\infty :$$
$$\text{if } b = d \text{ then } b \text{ else } \infty] \tag{3}$$

$$[a : b] \bigtriangleup [c : d] \Rightarrow [\text{if } a \neq -\infty \text{ then } a \text{ else } c :$$
$$\text{if } b \neq \infty \text{ then } b \text{ else } d] \tag{4}$$

Table 1. Basic operations used by the range propagation algorithm.

by the widening operations. In Section 4.4 we will illustrate this mechanism in an example.

The implementation of function **compute_data_ranges_phase** is shown in Figure 8. It performs an iterative data-flow analysis upon all uncommitted nodes in the data-flow graph. More specifically, it initially inserts all uncommitted nodes on the priority queue *work_list*. It then repeatedly removes a node from *work_list*, updates that node's data range, then adds all nodes to *work_list* that depend upon its data range, (i.e., the nodes in *x.prev*), if its data range has changed. The algorithm quits only when the *work_list* becomes empty. To minimize the number of updates performed upon the graph's nodes, the nodes in *work_list* should be ordered by a topological order of the data-flow graph, ignoring any back-edges, (that is, in rPOSTORDER, as described in [16]).

The data range (r) of a node x, whose variable's (v) definition contains a ϕ-function, is computed by unioning ($\cup$) the ranges of the arguments of its ϕ-function. The semantics of the union operator is given in Table 1. This union results in a range whose lower bound is the minimum of the lower bounds of the argument's ranges and whose upper bound is a maximum of the upper bounds of the arguments' ranges. An argument's range (s) is the intersection ($\cap$) of the argument's current data range and the control range holding for the argument's control-flow edge.[3]

A node whose variable's definition is not a ϕ-function, is initially assigned a single-element data range whose bounds are equal to the right-hand-side of the variable's definition.

For both types of nodes the algorithm then replaces all variables of uncom-

---

[3] By construction of ϕ-functions, each argument of a ϕ-function corresponds to one of the entering control-flow edges of the ϕ-function's basic block.

```
procedure compute_data_ranges_phase(root : node_ptr, phase : phase_type)
    work_list ← all uncommitted nodes that are reachable from root
    while (work_list is not empty) do
        x ← dequeue(work_list)
        v ← x.var
        if (rhs of def(v) is a φ-function) then
            r ← ⊤
            for each edge e entering def(v) do
                y ← node in x.next associated with edge e
                s ← y.value ∩ get_control_range1(e, y.var)
                r ← r ∪ s
            end for
            if (def(v) has an entering back edge in CFG and x.old_value ≠ ⊤) then
                if (phase = WIDENING_PHASE) then
                    r ← x.value ▽ r
                else    // (phase = NARROWING_PHASE)
                    r ← x.value △ r
                end if
            end if
        else
            b ← rhs of def(v)
            r ← [b : b]
        end if
        for each node y ∈ x.next such that y.committed = false do
            s ← y.value ∩ get_control_range(def(v), y.var)
            r ← r with all occurrences of variable y.var replaced with s
        end for
        x.old_value ← x.value
        x.value ← r
        if (x.old_value ≠ x.value) then
            work_list ← work_list ∪ x.prev
        end if
    end while
end procedure
```

Fig. 8. Algorithm to compute data ranges for nodes whose definitions are φ-functions.

mitted nodes in their range with the ranges that these variables assume at the given statement. As a result of this replacement step, only committed range values appear in the ranges being computed. This way, ranges being computed cannot be self-referential, which would introduce difficulties in the algorithm. A self-referential range is a range assigned to a variable v, where after repeated replacements of variables in the range with those variables' ranges, its symbolic value contains variable v. An example of a directly self-referential range is $x = [1 : x + 1]$. An example of indirectly self-referential ranges is the pair of ranges $x = [1 : y]$ and $y = [1 : x + 1]$. Such self-referential ranges are not very useful because self-referential bounds typically add no constraint information to variables. For example, in the range $x = [1 : x + 1]$ the upper bound adds no

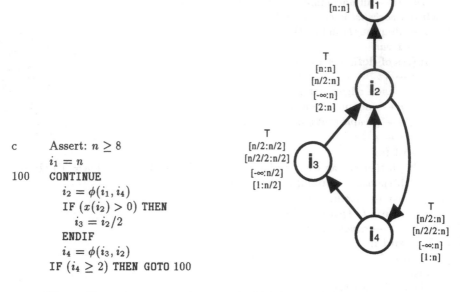

```
c       Assert: n ≥ 8
        i₁ = n
100     CONTINUE
        i₂ = φ(i₁, i₄)
        IF (x(i₂) > 0) THEN
            i₃ = i₂/2
        ENDIF
        i₄ = φ(i₃, i₂)
        IF (i₄ ≥ 2) THEN GOTO 100
```

Fig. 9. Example program fragment in SSA form and its data-flow graph

information, since all it says is $x \leq x+1$, which is always true. Hence, this range is equivalent to the simpler range $x = [1 : \infty]$. Another problem with directly or indirectly self-referential ranges is that the expression comparison algorithm, which is briefly described in the introduction, has difficulties determining a good order to substitute variables with ranges, resulting in more variable substitutions and less accurate results.

Furthermore, the replacement mechanism simplifies the termination test of the data-flow algorithm. The algorithm terminates if all nodes are processed without changing their range value. Such a change is easy to detect if the range includes only variables with fixed (i.e., committed) values.

The replacement scheme comes at the cost of some inaccuracy. We can regain some of this accuracy by "undoing" the replacement at the end of the range computation. This is further discussed in [8].

4.4 Example

As an example of how function **get_data_range** works, suppose that we wish to compute the data range for variable i_4 in the Fortran code fragment shown in Figure 9. For this example, the function call **get_data_range**(i_4) creates and iterates over the data-flow graph shown in figure 9. Function **get_range_data** invokes **compute_data_ranges** (and **commit_data_ranges**) twice in this example; once to compute the range of i_1, and once to compute the ranges for i_2, i_3, and i_4. This is because $\{i_1\}$ and $\{i_2, i_3, i_4\}$ are strongly-connected components of the data flow graph, and function **get_node** computes and commits all nodes in a created subgraph as soon as it is fully formed, (i.e., is a strongly-connected component).

The ranges listed alongside each node in the graph represent the values that the node's *value* field take while function compute_data_ranges_phase iterates to a fixed point. To give the reader an understanding of how these ranges are computed, we will describe how the data range was computed for the node for variable i_2. Initially, on entry to compute_data_ranges, the range of i_2 is the undefined range $\top$. In the widening phase, the first visit to i_2[4] sets its value to the union of the ranges of i_1 and i_4, both intersected with the control range of their incoming control-flow edge. The control range of i_1 is the unconstrained range $[-\infty : \infty]$ since there is no control-flow constraints on i_1 coming from the statement before the CONTINUE statement. The control range for i_4 comes from the IF statement, and is $[2 : \infty]$ because of the condition ($i_4 \geq 2$) in the IF statement. That leads to the formula for the range of i_2:

$$i_2 = (i_1 \cap [-\infty : \infty]) \cup (i_4 \cap [2 : \infty]) = i_1 \cup (i_4 \cap [2 : \infty])$$

So the value of the range of i_2 on the first visit to its node is $[n : n] \cup (\top \cap [2 : \infty]) = [n : n]$. Since the range of i_2 has changed, predecessors of node i_2 (i.e., i_1 and i_4), are placed in the work list and the algorithm continues. When the algorithm returns to i_2, the range of i_3 would have been updated to $[i_2/2 : i_2/2] = [[n : n]/2 : [n : n]/2] = [n/2 : n/2]$, and i_4 would have been updated to $[n/2 : n/2] \cup [n : n] = [n/2 : n]$. At this point, the new range for i_2 is $[n : n] \cup ([n/2 : n] \cap [2 : \infty]) = [n/2 : \infty]$. On the third visit to i_2, the algorithm determines its range to be $[n : n] \cup ([n/2/2 : n] \cap [2 : \infty]) = [n/2/2 : n]$. Now, since i_2 is a loop header node, the algorithm also applies the widening operator ($\triangledown$) to this result, getting $[n/2 : n] \triangledown [n/2/2 : n] = [-\infty : n]$. On the fourth visit to i_2, the algorithm would find that the range of i_2 is $[-\infty : n] \triangledown ([n : n] \cup ([-\infty : n] \cap [2 : \infty])) = [-\infty : n] \triangledown [2 : n] = [-\infty : n]$. Since the range of i_2 has not changed, the algorithm will not put i_2's successors on the work list, causing the widening phase to stop. Note, that the widening operator, which is applied after two visits to a node, has caused the value to become stable. However, it has introduced an overly conservative lower bound. Function compute_data_range would then enter the narrowing phase. In the narrowing phase, the narrowing operator ($\triangle$) would be applied to the range of i_2 instead of the widening operator. Thus the narrowing phase, on its first visit to i_2, would compute the range of i_2 to be $[-\infty : n] \triangle ([n : n] \cup ([-\infty : n] \cap [2 : \infty])) = [-\infty : n] \triangle [2 : n] = [2 : n]$. On its second visit of i_2, the computed range of i_2 would also be $[2 : n]$, causing the narrowing phase to stop.

When function get_data_range(i_4) completes, it will have computed and committed the data ranges $i_1 = [n : n]$, $i_2 = [2 : n]$, $i_3 = [i_2/2 : i_2/2]$ [5], and $i_4 = [1 : n]$. So, the function get_data_range will return $[1 : n]$.

---

[4] In this example, we will use a variable's name to represent both the variable and the data-flow node for that variable.

[5] The range $i_3 = [i_2/2 : i_2/2]$ was created in the loop at the end of function compute_data_ranges.

5 Handling union and intersection operations

In our presentation of the algorithms to compute control and data ranges, we have not addressed the complexities associated with making the union or intersection of two ranges. Both of these operations form the bounds of the resulting range by taking the minimum or maximum of the bounds of their two arguments. Simplifying these minimum and maximum expressions typically requires symbolic expression comparisons, which in turn can perform several get_range operations.

5.1 Control ranges

Handling this recursion in the control range computation algorithm in Figure 2 is not difficult. One only needs to initialize $C(e, v)$, (i.e., the memoized control range of variable v at control-flow edge e), to the unconstrained range $[-\infty : \infty]$ and allow the intersection operation to use only control ranges to compare bounds when simplifying the range. Initially setting the control range of the current variable and statement to $[-\infty : \infty]$ ensures termination, since this assignment guarantees that any recursive invocation of get_control_range will not attempt to compute the control range for this variable, statement pair. Because the intersection operator can generate many recursive calls to get_control_range, the worst case time complexity of the algorithm in Figure 2 would be $O(c|S||V|)$.

5.2 Data ranges

A simple way to handle the recursion caused by union and intersection operations performed in the algorithm compute_data_ranges_phase in Figure 8 is to allow these operations to use only control ranges to simplify their results. Since the computation of control ranges will never invoke get_data_range, the algorithm is guaranteed to terminate. The worst case time complexity of the algorithm remains unchanged.

However, by using only control ranges to perform unions and intersections when computing data ranges, the resulting data ranges may lead to overly conservative results. This is because the widening operator may replace partially unsimplified range bounds with $\pm\infty$. Thus, it is desirable to be able to use data ranges in these simplifications as well. Unfortunately, avoiding infinite recursions is complex. We handle this problem by assigning a variable's node a timestamp when we create it in create_node. This timestamp, which is associated with a particular invocation of get_data_range, is used to identify when a node belongs to an older invocation of get_data_range. The functions compute_data_ranges, compute_data_ranges_phase and commit_data_ranges are allowed to only visit nodes created by the current invocation of get_data_range. Additionally, if the function compute_data_ranges_phase attempts to access the data range of a uncommitted node created by a previous invocation of get_data_range, it would use the range $[-\infty : \infty]$ for that node's data range. Also, any node that uses the range of a node created by an older invocation of get_data_range is marked as *poisoned.* Poisoned nodes are nodes that cannot be memoized, (i.e., their values will not be stored in the global data structure), nor committed, since their data ranges may be overly conservative. Instead, they are deleted from the data-flow graph on the exit of **get_data_range**. Any node that uses the data range of a poisoned node is itself poisoned.

6 Performance

The time complexities of the algorithms are discussed in [8]. In this paper we show that our demand-driven range propagation algorithm is efficient for real programs, even when called many times. All optimizations described in the previous sections have been implemented in these algorithms. These times taken to compute all control and data ranges in a program are displayed in Table 2. The *code* column displays the name of each Fortran code examined. These codes were taken from the Perfect Benchmarks, which is a suite of Fortran 77 programs representing applications in a number of areas in engineering and scientific computing [3]. The *Number of lines* column displays the number of lines in each code after being converted into SSA form. The *Computing control ranges* and *Computing data ranges* columns give the total times taken to compute every control and data range respectively in each of the codes. The *Merging data and control ranges* column shows the time taken to intersect all the control and data ranges in the program, as done by the top-level algorithm described in Section 2. The total time to compute all the ranges in the program is just the sum of these columns. All timings are user times measured on a Sparc 10, using g++ 2.6.3 with the flag -O.

Code	Number of lines	Computing data ranges (s)	Computing control ranges (s)	Merging data and control ranges (s)
ARC2D	3573	2.4	1.3	1.4
BDNA	5960	3.8	5.4	4.3
FLO52	3348	3.9	4.9	2.7
MDG	1487	0.7	1.9	1.1
OCEAN	3142	8.0	4.6	25.3
TRFD	965	1.7	4.9	17.6

Table 2. Time taken in seconds to compute all data and control ranges, and to merge all data and control ranges on a Sparc 10 workstation.

As Table 2 has shown, computing all data and control ranges is very efficient. However, merging them can be expensive. This cost of merging them together arises from the intersection operation in the function **get_range**. In our experience, much of this time in computing and merging control and data ranges is spent computing the intersection and union of ranges. This cost arises from the fact that the symbolic expression comparison algorithm is used to simplify the intersection and union of ranges, and this algorithm can be expensive. However, unions and intersections are very cheap if one of their arguments is $[-\infty : \infty]$

Table 2 has shown that the demand-driven range propagation algorithm is efficient for computing all ranges in a program. However, it says little about the costs of computing a single range. The demand-driven range propagator may need to compute the values of other control and data ranges to determine the value of a certain range. In the worst case, every data and control range may need to be computed.

To determine the efficiency of the demand-driven range propagation algorithm for computing a single range, we have measured the number of control and data ranges computed by the algorithm to determine this range. Since the running time of the algorithm is proportional to the number of ranges it needs to compute, the fraction of computed control and data ranges computed out of the set of all control and data ranges should roughly indicate what fraction of the execution times shown in Table 2 that a typical range computation takes.

We have collected both the average and the maximum number of data and control ranges computed for a single invocation of get_control_range from Figure 2 and get_data_range from Figure 4. Tables 3 and 4 displays these results. These numbers were computed by requesting each control or data range in a program, then counting the number of control and data ranges created by each request. All memoized ranges, (i.e., the ranges stored in R, C, and D, from functions get_range, get_control_range, get_data_range), were cleared before each request for a control or data range. Ideally, the average and maximum number of control ranges created should be one when a single control range is requested. Also, the ideal average and maximum number of data ranges created should be one and the ideal average and maximum number of control and poisoned ranges created should be zero when a data range is requested.

Code	No. control ranges	No. computed Avg.	Max.
ARC2D	10227	1.9	5
BDNA	27285	2.7	8
FLO52	35094	2.6	11
MDG	4152	2.4	7
OCEAN	94819	2.4	37
TRFD	9994	3.1	21

Table 3. Average and maximum number of control ranges computed when computing a single control range.

Examining Table 3, one can see that typically only two or three control ranges need to be computed to determine the value of a single control range. This low number is mostly due to the use of the sparse icdom optimization, as described in Section 3. This sparse `icdom` relationship usually causes the algorithm in Figure 2 to compute the control ranges for only the control-flow statements, (e.g., `IF` and `DO` statements) that enclose the current statement. Since our test programs do not have deeply nested control flow, it is not surprising that the average number of computed control ranges is small.

One can roughly determine the cost of computing a control range by dividing the total time taken by `get_control_range`, as shown in Table 2, by the total number of control ranges in the program, as shown in column *No. control ranges* in Table 3, then multiplying this result by the number of ranges computed for that control range. Doing this, we find that the average control range computation takes about a few hundred microseconds, and the longest control range computation takes about a few milliseconds. Thus, we feel confident to claim that computing a single control range using a demand-driven algorithm is very efficient.

Code	No. data ranges	Control Avg.	Control Max.	Data Avg.	Data Max.	Poisoned Avg.	Poisoned Max.
ARC2D	1002	2.9	31	2.4	20	0.1	24
BDNA	1431	5.5	47	3.9	29	1.3	40
FLO52	1142	22.9	243	9.8	97	2.8	54
MDG	436	4.0	20	2.9	11	1.1	49
OCEAN	1529	10.5	201	6.6	64	0.4	30
TRFD	521	8.4	68	4.4	21	0.2	6

Table 4. Average and maximum number of control ranges, data ranges, and poisoned data ranges computed when computing a single data range.

Table 4 displays the average and maximum number of control, data, and poisoned ranges computed per data range.[6] The overall average and maximum cost of computing a data range can be approximated by adding these averages and maximums respectively. This table shows that computing a data range typically causes the algorithm to compute several data and control ranges, possibly many data and control ranges in the worst case. Additionally, the large discrepancies between the averages and the maximums indicate that the costs of computing a data range may vary greatly. Despite the potentially large number of data ranges computed, the average and maximum data and control ranges computed is still a small fraction of the total number of control and data ranges in the program. Thus, a demand-driven data range computation algorithm is still more efficient than its non-demand-driven counterpart.

---

[6] Poisoned ranges are overly conservative data ranges computed by a recursive call to `get_data_range`. Unlike control and data ranges, poisoned ranges are not memoized, so they may be repeatedly recomputed when computing a data range. We count such ranges multiple times, once per computation, in the table. See Section 4 for more details.

We can determine the rough cost of computing a data range by dividing the total time taken by get_data_range by the total number of data ranges in the program, then multiplying by the number of data and poisoned ranges ranges computed for that data range. Doing this, one can determine that the average time taken to compute a data range is a few tens of milliseconds, and the worst case time is a few hundreds of milliseconds for real codes.

If one finds the cost of computing a single data range to be too expensive, one can sometimes compute and use only control ranges. We have found that using only control ranges, coupled with symbolic constant propagation and induction variable substitution, provides sufficient information for applications of range propagation by parallelizing compilers on some Fortran programs. This is because such transformations transform most expressions in a program into expressions made up of only symbolic constants and enclosing loop indices, and one only needs to know the constraints imposed upon these loop indices and symbolic constants to compare or compute the ranges of such expressions.

7 Related work

The idea for representing program constraints as ranges was first proposed by Harrison [15] for array bounds checking and program verification. Bourdoncle [9] greatly improves the accuracy of the integer range propagation algorithm by Harrison, through the use of abstract interpretation [10]. However, Bourdoncle's algorithm does not generate symbolic ranges. Neither Harrison's nor Bourdoncle's algorithms are demand-driven, nor do they use a sparse data-flow representation of a program, such as SSA form or definition-use chains.

Cousot and Halbwachs [11] present a different method to compute and propagate constraints through a program. In their technique, sets of constraints between variables are represented as a convex polyhedron in the n-space of variable values. Because of this representation, all constraints are restricted to the form of affine inequality relationships, (e.g., $5 * x + 2 * y \leq 2$). Abstract interpretation is used to compute the convex polyhedron of variable constraints for each statement and each control-flow edge of the program.

They are more accurate in the computation and propagation of affine variable constraints than our algorithm. However, they cannot handle non-affine variable constraints, such as $a < b * c$. Additionally, by using a convex hull representation to compute variable constraints, their algorithm cannot benefit from a sparse data-flow representation of a program. Because of this, their algorithm can be much less efficient than ours. Also, their convex hull representation prevents one from creating a demand-driven version of their algorithm that is not overly complex.

Tu and Padua [18] also present a demand-driven, symbolic expression comparison and constraint propagation technique, based on an extension of SSA called gated SSA form. Their technique compares expressions by repeatedly substituting variables with their constant symbolic values until the two expressions differ by only an integer constant. The values to substitute are determined by

158

a demand-driven analysis of the program. Variants of ϕ-functions, which can be substituted in other expressions, are used to represent ranges of values. (These variants of ϕ-functions are simply ϕ-functions extended to contain conditional predicates that indicate which of their arguments should be their result.) Rewrite rules are used to simplify expressions containing such ϕ-functions.

The differences between our algorithm and theirs are mainly due to the two different applications. Their algorithm was designed to compare the bounds of array sections for array privatization [19]. Because conditional array definitions and uses occur in a significant fraction of important loop nests, flow-sensitive analysis is essential to successfully perform such comparisons. This capability was included in their algorithm. On the other hand, the bounds being compared are usually very similar to each other, requiring the substitution of only a few variables with their constant values to make the two bounds equal each other, except for a constant offset. On the other hand, range propagation was orignally designed for dependence testing. Our symbolic data dependence test, called the Range Test [5], often needs to compare expressions that are more complicated and dissimilar to each other than the expressions compared for array privatization. Because of this, more constraint information and a more powerful expression comparator is needed to compare such expressions. Also, dependence testing requests many more constraints, making memoization much more important. Therefore a memoization mechanism was included in our algorithm while not in Tu's. In our experience, conditionally defined constants and constraints do not significantly improve the effectiveness of dependence testing. Because of these differences, Polaris includes implementations of both range propagation and Tu's and Padua's gated-SSA demand-driven analysis. In future work, we will attempt to merge the two algorithms.

8 Conclusions

We have developed a demand-driven range propagation algorithm and have shown it to be efficient for computing a single range as well as many ranges. Because of its efficiency, it is feasible to use range propagation at many points in a compiler without a serious degradation of the compiler's performance, even though the program may be modified between these points. Since these ranges can be used to perform symbolic expression comparisons and range computation of expressions, and these operations enable powerful symbolic analyses, demand-driven range propagation can significantly increase the effectiveness of parallelizing and optimizing compilers.

References

1. H. Abelson, G. J. Sussman, and J. Sussman. *Structure and Interpretation of Computer Programs.* The MIT Press, 1985.
2. Alfred V. Aho, Ravi Sethi, and Jeffrey D. Ullman. *Compilers: Principles, Techniques, and Tools.* Addison-Wesley, Reading, Mass., 1986.

3. M. Berry, D. Chen, P. Koss, D. Kuck, L. Pointer, S. Lo, Y. Pang, R. Roloff, A. Sameh, E. Clementi, S. Chin, D. Schneider, G. Fox, P. Messina, D. Walker, C. Hsiung, J. Schwarzmeier, K. Lue, S. Orszag, F. Seidl, O. Johnson, G. Swanson, R. Goodrum, and J. Martin. The Perfect Club Benchmarks: Effective Performance Evalution of Supercomputers. *Int'l. Journal of Supercomputer Applications, Fall 1989*, 3(3):5–40, Fall 1989.

4. William Blume and Rudolf Eigenmann. Symbolic Range Propagation. *Proceedings of the 9th International Parallel Processing Symposium, April 1995.*

5. William Blume and Rudolf Eigenmann. The Range Test: A Dependence Test for Symbolic, Non-linear Expressions. *Proceedings of Supercomputing '94, Washington D.C., November 1994*, pages 528–537.

6. William Blume and Rudolf Eigenmann. An Overview of Symbolic Analysis Techniques Needed for the Effective Parallelization of the Perfect Benchmarks. *Proceedings of the 1994 International Conference on Parallel Processing*, pages II233 – II238, August, 1994.

7. William Blume, Rudolf Eigenmann, Keith Faigin, John Grout, Jay Hoeflinger, David Padua, Paul Petersen, Bill Pottenger, Lawrence Rauchwerger, Peng Tu, and Stephen Weatherford. Polaris: Improving the Effectiveness of Parallelizing Compilers. *Proceedings of the Seventh Workshop on Languages and Compilers for Parallel Computing, Ithaca, New York; also: Lecture Notes in Computer Science 892, Springer-Verlag*, pages 141–154, August 1994.

8. William Joseph Blume. *Symbolic Analysis Techniques for Effective Automatice Parallelization.* PhD thesis, Univ. of Illinois at Urbana-Champaign, Cntr. for Supercomputing Res. & Dev., June 1995.

9. Francqis Bourdoncle. Abstract Debugging of Higher-Order Imperative Languages. *Proceedings of the ACM SIGPLAN '93 Conference on Programming Language Design and Implementation*, pages 46–55, June 1993.

10. Partrick Cousot and Radhia Cousot. Abstract Interpretation: A unified Lattice Model for Static Analysis of Programs by Construction or Approximation of Fixpoints. *Proceedings of the 4th Annual ACM Symposium on Principles of Programming Languages*, pages 238–252, January 1977.

11. Patrick Cousot and Nicolas Halbwachs. Automatic Discovery of Linear Restraints Among Variables of a Program. In *Proceedings of the 5th Annual ACM Symposium on Principles of Programming Languages*, pages 84–97, 1978.

12. Ron Cytron, Jeanne Ferrante, Barry K. Rosen, Mark N. Wegman, and F. Kenneth Zadeck. Efficiently Computing Static Single Assignment Form and the Control Dependence Graph. *ACM Transactions on Programming Languages and Systems*, 13(4):451–490, October 1991.

13. Mohammad Haghighat and Constantine Polychronopoulos. Symbolic Dependence Analysis for High-Performance Parallelizing Compilers. *Parallel and Distributed Computing: Advances in Languages and Compilers for Parallel Processing, MIT Press, Cambridge, MA*, pages 310–330, 1991.

14. D. Harel. A linear time algorithm for finding dominators in a flow graph and related problems. *Proceedings of the 17th ACM Symposium of Theory of Computing*, pages 185–194, May 1985.

15. William H. Harrison. Compiler Analysis of the Value Ranges for Variables. *IEEE Transactions on Software Engineering*, SE-3(3):243–250, May 1977.

16. Matthew S. Hecht and Jeffrey D. Ullman. A Simple Algorithm for Global Data Flow Analysis Problems. *SIAM Journal on Computing*, 4(4):519–532, December 1975.

17. D. Maydan, J. Hennessy, and M. Lam. Efficient and exact data dependence analysis. In *SIGPLAN NOTICES: Proceedings of the ACM SIGPLAN 91 Conference on Programming Language Design and Implementation, Toronto, Ontario, Canada, June 26-28*, pages 1–14. ACM Press, 1991.
18. Peng Tu and David Padua. Gated SSA-Based Demand-Driven Symbolic Analysis for Parallelizing Compilers. *Proceedings of the 9th ACM International Conference on Supercomputing, Barcelona, Spain, July 1995.*
19. Peng Tu and David Padua. Automatic Array Privatization. In Utpal Banerjee-David GelernterAlex NicolauDavid Padua, editor, *Proc. Sixth Workshop on Languages and Compilers for Parallel Computing, Portland, OR. Lecture Notes in Computer Science.*, volume 768, pages 500–521, August 12-14, 1993.

Optimizing Fortran 90 Shift Operations on Distributed-Memory Multicomputers *

Ken Kennedy, John Mellor-Crummey, and Gerald Roth **

Department of Computer Science MS#132, Rice University, Houston, TX 77005-1892

Abstract. When executing Fortran 90 style data-parallel array operations on distributed-memory multiprocessors, intraprocessor data movement due to shift operations can account for a significant fraction of
the execution time. This paper describes a strategy for minimizing data
movement caused by Fortran 90 CSHIFT operations and presents a compiler technique that exploits this strategy automatically. The compiler
technique is global in scope and can reduce data movement even when
a definition of an array and its uses are separated by control flow. This
technique supersedes those whose scope is restricted to a single statement. We focus on the application of this strategy on distributed-memory
architectures, although it is more broadly applicable.

1 Introduction

High-Performance Fortran (HPF)[11], an extension of Fortran 90, has attracted
considerable attention as a promising language for writing portable parallel programs. Programmers express data parallelism using Fortran 90 array operations
and use data layout directives to direct partitioning of the data and computation
among the processors of a parallel machine.

For HPF to gain acceptance as a vehicle for parallel scientific programming,
it must achieve high performance on problems for which it is well suited. To
achieve high performance on a distributed-memory parallel machine, an HPF
compiler must do a superb job of translating Fortran 90 data-parallel operations
on arrays into an efficient sequence of operations that minimize the overhead
associated with data movement.

Interprocessor data movement on a distributed-memory parallel machine is
typically far more costly than movement within the memory of a single processor. For this reason, much of the prior research on minimizing data movement
has focused on the interprocessor case. However, although interprocessor data
movement is more costly per element, the number of elements moved within the
memory of a single processor may be much larger, causing the cost of local data

---

* This research supported in part by the NSF Cooperative Research Agreement Num-
ber CCR-9120008.
** Supported in part by the IBM Corporation through the Graduate Resident Study
Program.

movement to be dominant. Johnsson previously has noted that "eliminating the local data motion by separating the set of data that must move between nodes from the data that stays within local memory may yield a significant performance improvement" [12]. The cost of local data movement becomes more important for distributed arrays as the partition size per processor increases.

In this paper, we focus on the problem of minimizing the amount of intra-processor data movement when computing Fortran 90 array operations. To make our technique as generally applicable as possible, we handle array assignment statements where the right-hand side consists of a call to a Fortran 90 shift intrinsic. The technique can handle all such assignment statements, even when the definition of the array and its uses are separated by control flow. Such a technique supersedes those that are restricted to a single statement.

In the next section we briefly review the Fortran 90 shift operators and their execution cost on distributed-memory machines. In Section 3, we describe the *offset array* strategy for reducing intraprocessor data movement associated with shift operations on arrays with BLOCK or CYCLIC(K) distributions. We also present some empirical results to show the potential profitability of applying the offset array optimization. Section 4 describes a global SSA-based analysis algorithm that restructures programs to use offset arrays where profitable. We close with a look at related work.

2   Fortran 90 Shift Operators

The Fortran 90 circular shift operator CSHIFT(ARRAY, SHIFT, DIM) returns an array of the same shape, type, and values as ARRAY, except that each rank-one section of ARRAY crossing dimension DIM has been shifted circularly SHIFT times. The sign of SHIFT determines the shift direction. The end-off shift operator EOSHIFT(ARRAY, SHIFT, BOUNDARY, DIM) is identical to CSHIFT except for the handling of boundaries. For the rest of the paper we focus on optimizing CSHIFT operations although our techniques can be generalized to handle EOSHIFT as well.

2.1   Sources of CSHIFT Operations

For HPF, optimizing CSHIFT operations is important since CSHIFT operations are ubiquitous in stencil-based dense array computations for which HPF is best suited. Besides CSHIFT operations written by users, compilers for distributed-memory machines commonly insert them to perform data movement needed for operations on array sections that have different processor mappings [14, 15]. For example, given the statement X(2:255) = X(1:254) + X(2:255) + X(3:256) the CM Fortran compiler would translate it into the following statement sequence, where the temporary arrays match the size and distribution of X:

```
ALLOCATE TMP1, TMP2
TMP1 = CSHIFT(X,SHIFT=-1,DIM=1)
TMP2 = CSHIFT(X,SHIFT=+1,DIM=1)
```

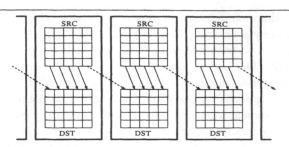

Fig. 1. DST = CSHIFT(SRC,SHIFT=-1,DIM=2)

```
X(2:255) = TMP1(2:255) + X(2:255) + TMP2(2:255)
DEALLOCATE TMP1, TMP2
```

For the rest of the paper, we assume that all CSHIFT operations in a program are explicit (either user-written, or inserted where appropriate during an earlier phase of HPF compilation), that each call to CSHIFT occurs as a singleton operation on the right-hand side of an assignment statement, and that each CSHIFT in our intermediate form is applied only to a whole array. All other occurrences of CSHIFT can be translated into the required form by factoring expressions and introducing array temporaries.

2.2 CSHIFT Operations on Distributed-Memory Machines

When a distributed array is shifted across a distributed dimension, two major actions take place:

1. Data elements that must be shifted across processing element (*PE*) boundaries are sent to the neighboring PE. This is the interprocessor component of the shift. The dashed lines in Fig. 1 represent this data movement for arrays distributed in a BLOCK fashion.
2. Data elements that stay within the memory of the PE must be copied to the appropriate locations in the destination array. This is the intraprocessor component of the shift. The solid lines in Fig. 1 represent this data movement.

Assuming a BLOCK distribution and that each PE contains a 2D subgrid of size $(g \times g)$, a shift amount of d, $d < g$, consists of an interprocessor move of d columns (of size g), and an intraprocessor move of $g - d$ columns. The cost of such a shift operation is described by the following model [8]:

$$T_{\text{shift}} = g\,(g - d)\,t_{\text{onpe}} + C_{\text{onpe}} + g\,d\,t_{\text{offpe}} + C_{\text{offpe}} \qquad (1)$$

where t_{onpe} and t_{offpe} represent the time to perform an intraprocessor and interprocessor copy respectively, and C_{onpe} and C_{offpe} represent the startup time (or latency) for each type of copy. Table 1[3] presents measured values for each of

---
[3] From Fatoohi [8], ©1993 ACM.

Table 1. Measured cost of communication parameters for a 32-bit word (in μsec).

Parameter	CM2	MPP	MP-1	610C
t_{offpe}	9.0	3.2	2.7	3.2
C_{offpe}	20.0	13.4	41.9	7.2
t_{onpe}	0.7	-	5.6	9.0
C_{onpe}	35.0	-	59.1	18.0

the model's parameters for four different SIMD machines. Different models are required for the cases $d = g$ and $d > g$. CYCLIC(K) distributions also require a different model which include a parameterization for the blocking factor.

The instances in which we are most interested occur when d is small compared to g. For such cases Equation (1) is $O(g^2 \, t_{\text{onpe}})$ and the execution time T_{shift} is dominated by the cost of the intraprocessor copies, even when $t_{\text{onpe}} \ll t_{\text{offpe}}$.

3 Offset Arrays

The goal of the work described here is to eliminate the intraprocessor copying associated with a Fortran 90 `CSHIFT` operation when it is safe to do so. When we can determine that the intraprocessor copying of a `CSHIFT` is unnecessary, we can transform the program to perform only the interprocessor copying and rewrite references to the shift's destination array to refer to the source array with indexing adjusted by the shift amount. We call such a destination array an *offset array*. In the following subsections, we present criteria for determining when offset arrays are safe and profitable and present the code transformations that avoid intraprocessor copying by exploiting offset arrays.

To hold the data that must move between PEs, we use *overlap areas* [9]. Overlap areas are subgrid extensions to hold data received from neighboring PEs. To limit the impact of allocating this permanent storage, we place an upper bound on their size. This upper bound should be set at compile-time by a heuristic that considers the machine characteristics along with the expected size of the subgrids.

3.1 Criteria for Offset Arrays

Given an assignment statement `DST = CSHIFT(SRC,SHIFT,DIM)` within our intermediate representation, the array `DST` may be treated as an offset array if the following criteria can be verified for this statement at compile time:

1. The source array `SRC` is not modified while this definition of `DST` is *live*.
2. The destination array `DST` is not partially modified[4] while `SRC` is *live*.

---

[4] Any partial modification will require a copy of the shifted array SRC and so we simply go ahead and make the copy at the point of the shift. Any full modification of DST which *kills* the whole array does not require the copy of SRC and thus DST may still be treated as an offset array up to the point of the killing definition.

From the work on copy elimination in functional and higher-order programming languages [17], we know that the above two criteria are necessary and sufficient conditions for when the two objects can share the same storage. However, the sharing of storage may not always be profitable. To insure profitability, we add the following efficiency criteria:

3. The SRC array and the DST array are distributed in the same BLOCK (or CYCLIC(K)) fashion and are aligned with one another.
4. The values SHIFT and DIM are compile-time scalar constants.
5. The amount of interprocessor data must fit within the bounds placed on the size of the overlap areas.
6. For each use of DST that is reached by the given definition, all the definitions of DST that reach that use are identical offset arrays of the same source array SRC.

These efficiency criteria may be relaxed if we are willing to generate multiple versions of code for statements that use the array DST, and then select the appropriate version depending upon run-time conditions. However, due to the drawbacks of multiple versions of code, in particular code growth, we consider these additional criteria as important.

3.2 Offset Array Optimization

Once we have determined that the destination array of the assignment statement DST = CSHIFT(SRC,SHIFT,DIM) may be an offset array, we perform the following transformations on the code. First we replace the shift operation with a call to a routine that moves the interprocessor data into the appropriate overlap area: CALL OFFSET_SHIFT(SRC,SHIFT,DIM). We then replace all uses of the array DST, that are reached from this definition, with a use of the array SRC. The newly created references to SRC carry along special annotations representing the values of SHIFT and DIM. In the examples that follow, the annotations are represented by a superscripted vector where the DIM-th element contains the value SHIFT; e.g., $SRC^{<\cdots,SHIFT,\cdots>}$. Finally, when creating subgrid loops during the code generation phase, we alter the subscript indices used for the offset arrays. The array subscript used for the offset reference to SRC is identical to the subscript that would have been generated for DST with the exception that the DIM-th dimension has been incremented by the SHIFT amount.

It is possible that offset arrays are themselves used in other shift operations. If these shift operations also meet all of the criteria to be an offset array then the above transformations can again be applied. We call such arrays *multiple-offset arrays*. If one dimension is shifted multiple times, the SHIFT amounts are simply added together.

As an example, consider the 5-point stencil routine in Fig. 2(a). The expected intermediate representation in Fig. 2(b) is achieved by separating the communication operations from the computational operations. Once we have determined that the temporary arrays T1–T4 can be offset arrays, we perform the above

```
SUBROUTINE FIVE_PT(a,b,n)
REAL, DIMENSION(n,n) :: a,b
!HPF$ DISTRIBUTE(BLOCK,BLOCK)::a,b
REAL cc,cn,ce,cw,cs
COMMON cc,cn,ce,cw,cs

b = cc * a
& + cn * cshift(a,-1,1)
& + cs * cshift(a,+1,1)
& + cw * cshift(a,-1,2)
& + ce * cshift(a,+1,2)


RETURN
END
```

(a) Original program

```
SUBROUTINE FIVE_PT(a,b,n)
REAL, DIMENSION(n,n) :: a,b
REAL, ALLOCATABLE :: t1,t2,t3,t4
DIMENSION(:,:) :: t1,t2,t3,t4
!HPF$ DISTRIBUTE(BLOCK,BLOCK)::a,b
!HPF$ ALIGN WITH a :: t1,t2,t3,t4
REAL cc,cn,ce,cw,cs
COMMON cc,cn,ce,cw,cs

ALLOCATE(t1(n,n),t2(n,n),
&        t3(n,n),t4(n,n))
t1 = cshift(a,-1,1)
t2 = cshift(a,+1,1)
t3 = cshift(a,-1,2)
t4 = cshift(a,+1,2)
b = cc * a
& + cn * t1
& + cs * t2
& + cw * t3
& + ce * t4
DEALLOCATE(t1,t2,t3,t4)
RETURN
END
```

(b) Intermediate representation

```
SUBROUTINE FIVE_PT(a,b,n)
REAL, DIMENSION(n,n) :: a,b
!HPF$ DISTRIBUTE(BLOCK,BLOCK)::a,b
REAL cc,cn,ce,cw,cs
COMMON cc,cn,ce,cw,cs

CALL offset_cshift(a,-1,1)
CALL offset_cshift(a,+1,1)
CALL offset_cshift(a,-1,2)
CALL offset_cshift(a,+1,2)
b = cc * a
```
$$\& + cn * a^{<-1,0>}$$
$$\& + cs * a^{<+1,0>}$$
$$\& + cw * a^{<0,-1>}$$
$$\& + ce * a^{<0,+1>}$$
```

RETURN
END
```

(c) Offset array transformations

```
SUBROUTINE FIVE_PT(a,b,n)
REAL,DIMENSION(n/p,n/p) :: b
REAL,DIMENSION(0:n/p+1,0:n/p+1)::a
REAL cc,cn,ce,cw,cs
COMMON cc,cn,ce,cw,cs

CALL offset_cshift(a,-1,1)
CALL offset_cshift(a,+1,1)
CALL offset_cshift(a,-1,2)
CALL offset_cshift(a,+1,2)
do j=1,n/p
  do i=1,n/p
    b(i,j) = cc * a(i,j)
&          + cn * a(i-1,j)
&          + cs * a(i+1,j)
&          + cw * a(i,j-1)
&          + ce * a(i,j+1)
  enddo
enddo

RETURN
END
```

(d) Final node program

Fig. 2. Offset array optimization on a 5-point stencil computation.

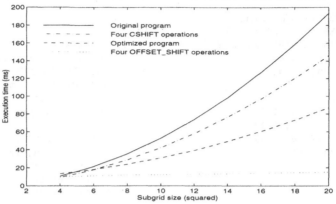

Fig. 3. Timings for 5-point stencil computation on 16K MasPar MP-1.

set of transformations. Fig. 2(c) shows the program after the first two transformation steps have been completed. The third step is performed during subgrid loop generation and is shown in Fig. 2(d).

To demonstrate the usefulness of this optimization, we have compiled and executed the code from Fig. 2 on a MasPar MP-1 with 16K processors. Figure 3 compares the execution times of the original program displayed in Fig. 2(a) and the optimized program shown in Fig. 2(d) for varying subgrid sizes. The figure shows that the program exploiting offset arrays gives a speed-up of a factor of two for the larger subgrid sizes. The figure also displays the time to execute the four CSHIFTs of Fig. 2(b) and the four calls to OFFSET_SHIFT of Fig. 2(d). We can see that the amount of execution time that is spent performing the four CSHIFT operations is actually more than the time spent performing the desired computation. In fact, the CSHIFT operations account for 75% of the total execution time for the largest subgrid. The corresponding number for the OFFSET_SHIFT operations is 17%.

4 Offset Array Analysis

Our algorithm for determining offset arrays relies upon the *static single assignment* (SSA) intermediate representation [7]. For our purposes, the SSA representation is an analysis framework which is used in conjunction with the control flow graph. Within SSA, modifications and uses of arrays are represented with UPDATE and REFERENCE operators, respectively. Since we are analyzing Fortran 90D programs, we have enhanced these operators to handle array sections by incorporating regular section descriptors (RSDs) [1].

In addition to the SSA graph, we generate an interference graph [3]. The interference graph indicates those SSA variables with overlapping live ranges, and is used to check for violations of criteria 1 or 2. The graph is built in the usual manner, but with one exception: all ϕ-functions occurring at the same merge point are considered to be executed simultaneously. This prevents the detection of spurious interferences that may prevent the use of offset arrays across merge points. We also enhance the accuracy of the interference graph by exploiting the RSDs in UPDATE operations to identify statements that *kill* the entire array.

4.1 Offset Array Algorithm

In this section, we present our algorithm for identifying offset arrays and transforming the program to reference them. In describing the algorithm, we typically refer to the SSA variable names rather than their CFG counterparts. The algorithm is shown in Fig. 4.

We begin by traversing the CFG in a reverse depth-first order looking for shift operations. Upon encountering a shift operation which satisfies criteria 3–5, we check the interference graph to see if criterion 1 is not violated. If all the required criteria are satisfied, then it is safe for the destination array to be an offset array. Given such a shift operation, we rename the destination array DST_i by giving it the same SSA name as the source array SRC_j. The new name is annotated as described in Section 3.2. By using the same name we do not violate the spirit of SSA. This is because the shift really does not create any new values but rather just specifies a new indexing method for existing values. We change the use of the SHIFT intrinsic into a use of the OFFSET_SHIFT routine, and update the interference graph by renaming the changed variable.

After we make this change, we propagate the information in an optimistic manner. This will insure that criterion 6 is satisfied wherever possible. This is accomplished by simply following the SSA def-use edges and replacing all uses of DST_i with uses of $SRC_j^{<\cdots,SHIFT,\cdots>}$. Depending upon the type of use, further propagation may be possible. Several different cases must be handled during this propagation; we discuss them next. When the propagation of a change has completed, we continue the traversal of the program looking for the next offsetable array. The reverse depth-first traversal order is important so that multiple-offset arrays can be correctly handled in a single pass of the program.

As stated in the previous paragraph, we propagate the offset array information by changing all uses of the original destination array DST_i into uses of the new offset array $SRC_j^{<\cdots,SHIFT,\cdots>}$. Since we are dealing with arrays, these uses can only occur in three places: a REFERENCE operation, an UPDATE operation, or a ϕ-function. If this change is propagated into an array REFERENCE operator, there are no more opportunities for propagation. If the use is at an UPDATE operator we propagate the offset array through the operation when possible. It is valid to propagate through the UPDATE as long as it does not violate criterion 2 and does not realign or redistribute the array. The propagation is accomplished by generating a new instance of the SRC array, call it SRC_k, to be the target of the UPDATE operation in place of the existing DST array instance. This new SRC_k receives the same annotations as $SRC_j^{<\cdots,SHIFT,\cdots>}$, and then is propagated to all its uses in a similar manner. If it is not possible to propagate through the UPDATE operation then a copy of the offset array may be required prior to the

Procedure *Offset_Arrays*
Input: *CFG*, the control flow graph for the procedure.
Output: *CFG* optimized with offset arrays.
/* See Fig. 5 for auxiliary routines. */

$SSA = Create\_SSA\_Form(CFG)$
$IG = Build\_Interference\_Graph(SSA, CFG)$

for each SHIFT operation *stmt* in a depth-first traversal of the *CFG* **do**
    push *stmt* onto stack *S*
endfor

while stack *S* is not empty **do**
    pop *stmt* off of stack *S*
    switch (*stmt*)

      case SHIFT operation: $Dst_{Dsub} = shift(Src_{Ssub}^{Sanot}, shift, dim)$:
        if criteria 3, 4, or 5 is violated **then break endif**
        if $Check\_Interferences(Dst_{Dsub}, Src_{Ssub}, IG)$ **then break endif**
        calculate new annotation *Nanot* from *Sanot*, *shift*, and *dim*
        replace *stmt* with $Src_{Ssub}^{Nanot} = offset\_shift(Src_{Ssub}^{Sanot}, shift, dim)$
        call $Replace\_Uses(Dst_{Dsub}, Src_{Ssub}^{Nanot}, S)$
        call $Update\_Graphs(Dst_{Dsub}, Src_{Ssub}^{Nanot}, SSA, IG)$
        break

      case ϕ-function: $Dst_{Dsub} = \phi(Lvar_{Lsub}^{Lanot}, Rvar_{Rsub}^{Ranot})$:
        if criteria 3 is violated **then break endif**
        if $Lvar^{Lanot} \neq Rvar^{Ranot}$ **then break**
        elseif $Dst_{Dsub} = Lvar_{Lsub}$ or $Dst_{Dsub} = Rvar_{Rsub}$ **then break**
        elseif $Lvar_{Lsub}^{Lanot} = Rvar_{Rsub}^{Ranot}$ **then**
          $New_{Nsub} = Lvar_{Lsub}$
        else
          $New_{Nsub} = Find\_Phi(Lvar_{Lsub}, Rvar_{Rsub}, stmt)$
        endif
        if $Check\_Interferences(Dst_{Dsub}, New_{Nsub}, IG)$ **then break endif**
        replace *stmt* with $New_{Nsub}^{Lanot} = \phi(Lvar_{Lsub}^{Lanot}, Rvar_{Rsub}^{Ranot})$
        call $Replace\_Uses(Dst_{Dsub}, New_{Nsub}^{Lanot}, S)$
        call $Update\_Graphs(Dst_{Dsub}, New_{Nsub}^{Lanot}, SSA, IG)$
        break

      case UPDATE operation: $Dst_{Dsub} = Update(Lvar_{Lsub}^{Lanot}, section, values)$:
        if criteria 3 is violated **then break endif**
        $New_{Nsub} = Gen\_Next\_SSA\_Var(Lvar)$
        if $Check\_Interferences(Dst_{Dsub}, New_{Nsub}, IG)$ **then break endif**
        replace *stmt* with $New_{Nsub}^{Lanot} = Update(Lvar_{Lsub}^{Lanot}, section, values)$
        call $Replace\_Uses(Dst_{Dsub}, New_{Nsub}^{Lanot}, S)$
        call $Update\_Graphs(Dst_{Dsub}, New_{Nsub}^{Lanot}, SSA, IG)$
        break

    endswitch
endwhile

call $Insert\_Copies(CFG, SSA)$
return *CFG*

Fig. 4. Offset array propagation algorithm

Function $Check\_Interferences(Dst_{Dsub}, Src_{Ssub}, IG)$
/* Return TRUE if there exists an interference between */
/* Dst_{Dsub} and some Src_i, $i \neq Ssub$. */

Procedure $Replace\_Uses(Dest, Src, S)$
/* Replace each reference to $Dest$ with a reference to Src. */
/* If the use is in a ϕ-function or **UPDATE** operation, then */
/* push operation on stack S. */

Procedure $Update\_Graphs(Old, New, SSA, IG)$
/* Replace node Old with node New in both SSA and IG. */

Function $Find\_Phi(Lvar_{Lsub}, Rvar_{Rsub}, stmt)$
/* Find the ϕ-function merging $Lvar_{Lsub}$ and $Rvar_{Rsub}$ */
/* at the same merge point as $stmt$ and return it. */
/* If it does not exist, return a new instance of $Lvar$. */

Fig. 5. Auxiliary procedures.

UPDATE. This copy is inserted by a subsequent phase which we describe in the next subsection.

When propagating an offset array into a ϕ-function, in addition to verifying criteria 1 and 3, it is only valid to continue the propagation if the other input to the ϕ-function is an equivalent offset array (see criterion 6). Two offset arrays are equivalent if they are from the same SSA family and have identical annotations. The one exception to this rule is if a cycle has been created (*i.e.*; one of the inputs to the ϕ-function, when its annotation is removed, is the same SSA variable being defined by the ϕ-function). When it is possible to propagate through the ϕ-function, we need to select the correct SSA variable to receive the definition of this ϕ-function. If the ϕ-function happens to be merging identical values, we simply use one of its inputs as the target variable. Otherwise we look for a ϕ-function at the same merge point whose inputs are the unannotated variables of the current ϕ-function. If found, we use the SSA variable that it defines, otherwise we generate a new instance of the SSA variable in the same manner as we did for **UPDATE**. In any case, the variable is annotated with the same annotation as the input variables and is propagated forward. If it is not possible to propagate through a ϕ-function, then array copy statements must be inserted on the appropriate branches leading to the ϕ-function. These copies are added by the *Insert_Copies* routine, which is the last function called by the *Offset_Arrays* procedure and which we describe next.

4.2 Inserting Array Copies

Once we have found all the offset arrays and propagated them as far as possible through the program, it may be necessary to insert some array copy statements to maintain the original semantics. The copy statements may be needed at points where an offset array is used to define, via an **UPDATE** operation or a ϕ-function, a non-offset array.

Procedure *Insert_Copies*(*CFG*, *SSA*, *stmt_set*)
/* *stmt_set* is produced in *Offset_Arrays* as described */

for each *stmt* in *stmt_set* **do**
  switch (*stmt*)

    case UPDATE operation: $Dst_{Dsub} = Update(Lvar_{Lsub}^{Lanot}, section, values)$:
      if (*section* does not specify the entire array) **then**
        insert $Dst = Lvar^{Lanot}$ immediately preceding *stmt* in *CFG*
      endif
      break

    case ϕ-function: $Dst_{Dsub} = \phi(Lvar_{Lsub}^{Lanot}, Rvar_{Rsub}^{Ranot})$:
      if (*Lanot* ≠ nil) **then** /* *Rvar* is handled similarly. */
        insert $Dst = Lvar^{Lanot}$ on appropriate branch in *CFG*
        /* optimize placement when possible. */
      endif
      break

  endswitch
endfor
return

Fig. 6. Algorithm to insert array copy statements.

It is quite easy to determine the statements that may require a copy while we are propagating offset arrays in the *Offset_Arrays* procedure. To track these statements, we maintain a set of such statements (the code has been omitted from Fig. 4). An UPDATE operation which is processed by the algorithm but determined not to be offsetable is added to the set. A ϕ-function which is determined not to be offsetable is also added to the set. If the ϕ-function is later determined to actually be offsetable (after the other input parameter has been processed), then it is removed from the set. The use of *pruned-SSA form*, where dead ϕ-functions have been eliminated, can greatly reduce the number of ϕ-functions added to the set.

After the propagation of offset arrays has completed, the procedure *Insert_Copies*, shown in Fig. 6, is called to add the required array copies to the program. It examines each statement in the set that was produced to determine if an array copy is actually needed and to select the best placement for it. If the array copy is truly required, it will take as input the offset array and will define the array originally used by the statement. This copy statement will perform all the intraprocessor data movement that was avoided at the shift operation. Note however that no interprocessor data movement is required.

Given an UPDATE operation from the set, an array copy statement is not required if the UPDATE is a *killing* definition. Otherwise, we insert an array copy immediately preceding the UPDATE.

For a ϕ-function which defines a non-offset array, an array copy statement will need to be generated for each input parameter that is an offset array. In general, the copy statements are placed on the appropriate branches leading to the merge point represented by the ϕ-function. It is possible to optimize this placement in the case of some loop structures. If a copy must be made for the array values coming around from the previous iteration but there is no use within the loop of the values defined by the ϕ-function, then it is possible to move the array copy out of the loop by placing it on the loop exit branch. The copy is moved to the shallowest nesting level such that it still dominates all uses. This is advantageous in situations where it is allowable for an array to be an offset array inside a loop nest but not outside. The full copy is only performed when the loop nest is exited rather than on each iteration.

The insertion of such array copy statements into the program raises a concern. We must answer the question of whether these inserted copy statements can generate more data movement than was specified in the original program. The following lemmas and theorem state that this is not possible.

Lemma 1. *Given a copy statement C created for an offset array* SRC^{anot} *which was generated by a set of* **OFFSET_SHIFT** *operations* $\{S_1, S_2, S_3, \ldots\}$, *any path from the beginning of the program (Root) to C must go through at least one S_i.*

Proof. Assume there exists a path P_1: $Root \xrightarrow{*} C$ that does not contain an **OFFSET_SHIFT** operation S_i. Since C is an inserted copy statement for an offset array, there must exist an **OFFSET_SHIFT** operation S_j and a path P_2: $S_j \xrightarrow{*} C$. Since both P_1 and P_2 end at C, and P_1 does not contain S_j (by assumption), then there must exist a merge point X that joins P_1 and P_2 prior to C. X must contain a ϕ-function which merges the values of SRC^{anot} generated at S_j with the other values of SRC that reach C along $Root \xrightarrow{*} X$. But our algorithm only propagates an offset array through a ϕ-function when the ϕ-function merges identical offset arrays. Thus there must exist an **OFFSET_SHIFT** operation S_i identical to S_j on $Root \xrightarrow{*} X$ which contradicts our original assumption. $\Box$

Lemma 2. *C cannot be more deeply nested than all $S_i \in \{S_1, S_2, S_3, \ldots\}$.*

Proof. Assume C is contained in a loop which does not contain an **OFFSET_SHIFT** operation S_i. Since C is an inserted copy statement for an offset array, there must exist an **OFFSET_SHIFT** operation S_j outside the loop and a path P: $S_j \xrightarrow{*} C$. The path P must contain a ϕ-function to merge the values reaching C from S_j with those that reach C from the back edge of the loop. By the same argument used in the proof of Lemma 1, there must exist an **OFFSET_SHIFT** operation S_i within the loop that reaches the back edge of the loop, thus contradicting our original assumption. $\Box$

Theorem 3. *An inserted copy statement C is never executed more often than $\{S_1, S_2, S_3, \ldots\}$, the set of* **OFFSET_SHIFT** *operations which generated the offset array for which the copy statement was required.*

Proof. The theorem follows directly from the preceding two lemmas. $\Box$

4.3 Cost Analysis

During our offset array algorithm each SSA def/use edge is processed at most once. Thus our algorithm is guaranteed to terminate. This also means that our algorithm is quite efficient. The cost of the algorithm is actually dominated by the cost of generating SSA form and building the interference graph, both of which are $O(n^2)$ in the worst case (although building SSA is $O(n)$ in practice [7]). Once these structures are built, the rest of the algorithm is linear. Finding offsetable arrays is $O(n)$ and their propagation through the program is $O(e)$. In addition, the checking of interferences is $O(i)$. Here n is the size of the program, e is the number if edges in the SSA graph, and i is the number of edges in the interference graph.

5 Related Work

Stencil Compiler: The stencil compiler [2, 4] for the CM-2 avoids the memory-to-memory copying for shift operations that occur within specific, stylized, array-assignment statements. These statements, or *stencils*, must be in the form of a weighted sum of circularly-shifted arrays. Not only does the compiler eliminate intraprocessor data movement for these statements, it also optimizes interprocessor data movement by using the CM-2's multidimensional and bidirectional interconnect, and exploits hand-optimized library microcode to minimize data movement between local memory and registers. However, use of this special-purpose compiler requires that the user identify these stylized assignment statements in the source program and separate them into their own subroutine.

Our compiler scheme is a superset of the stencil compiler. We hoist all shift operations, whether implicit or explicit, out of expressions and assign them to array temporaries. This allows us to handle all shift operations, whether part of larger expression or not, in a uniform manner. Since hoisted temporaries have short life spans and thus never have conflicting uses, we will always be able to make them into offset arrays.

Currently we do not plan to exploit multidimensional and bidirectional communication, since they are exclusive to the CM-2's slicewise model. Although, it would not be difficult to scan adjacent communication operations looking for opportunities. Our context partitioning optimization [13] groups together as many such operations as possible, thus maximizing the possibilities of finding such opportunities.

Finally, to match the performance of the stencil compiler, we would exploit a highly-optimizing node compiler to perform final code generation. Such a compiler would consider the memory hierarchy and attempt to minimize data movement between local memory and registers [5].

Scalarizing Compilers: Previous work on Fortran 90D [6], like the stencil compiler, is capable of avoiding some intraprocessor data movement for stylized expressions. In this case, the expressions have to use array syntax. The compiler translates the array syntax expressions into equivalent Fortran 77D code using FORALL statements. It is then the job of the Fortran 77D back end, using dependence information, to determine the exact amount of interprocessor communication required. Unfortunately, any call to CSHIFT, whether in an assignment statement or as part of an expression, still makes a full copy of the array. As with the stencil compiler, our work is a superset of this work.

Functional Languages: Functional and many high-level languages have value semantics, and thus do not have the concept of state and variable as in Fortran. Naive compilation of such languages causes the insertion of many copy operations of aggregate objects to maintain program semantics. It is imperative that compilers for such languages eliminate a majority of the unnecessary copies if they hope to generate efficient code. This task is known as *copy optimization*.

Schwartz [17] characterizes the task of copy optimization as the destructive use (reuse) of an object v at a point P in the program where it can be shown that all other objects that may contain v are *dead* at P. He then develops a set of *value transmission functions* that can be used to determine the safety of a destructive use within the language SETL.

Gopinath and Hennessy [10] address the problem of copy elimination by *targeting*, or the proper selection of a storage area for evaluating an expression. For the lambda calculus extended with array operation constructs, they develop a set of equations which, when solved iteratively to a fixpoint, specify targets for array parameters and expressions. Unfortunately, solving their equations to a fixpoint is at least exponential in time.

Schnorf *et al.* [16] describe their efforts to eliminate aggregate copies in the single-assignment language SISAL. Their work analyzes edges in a data flow graph and attempts to determine when edges, representing values, may share storage. Our work has some similarities to parts of their work.

6 Conclusion

In this paper, we have presented a unified framework for analyzing and optimizing shift operations on distributed-memory multicomputers. The framework is capable of handling all such operations, whether written by the user or generated internally by the compiler. This work supersedes prior work by others that only handled shifts embedded within expressions. And although this paper has concentrated on distributed-memory machines, the optimizations presented are also applicable to scalar and shared-memory machines.

7 Acknowledgments

We'd like to thank Cliff Click, Paul Havlak, and Mike Paleczny for the many fruitful discussions regarding our usage of SSA. We'd also like to thank Ralph Brickner for sharing some of his knowledge on compiling stencils.

References

1. J. R. Allen. *Dependence Analysis for Subscripted Variables and Its Application to Program Transformations*. PhD thesis, Dept. of Computer Science, Rice University, April 1983.
2. R. G. Brickner, W. George, S. L. Johnsson, and A. Ruttenberg. A stencil compiler for the Connection Machine models CM-2/200. In *Proceedings of the Fourth Workshop on Compilers for Parallel Computers*, Delft, The Netherlands, December 1993.
3. P. Briggs. *Register Allocation via Graph Coloring*. PhD thesis, Dept. of Computer Science, Rice University, April 1992.
4. M. Bromley, S. Heller, T. McNerney, and G. Steele, Jr. Fortran at ten gigaflops: The Connection Machine convolution compiler. In *Proceedings of the SIGPLAN '91 Conference on Programming Language Design and Implementation*, Toronto, Canada, June 1991.
5. S. Carr. *Memory-Hierarchy Management*. PhD thesis, Dept. of Computer Science, Rice University, September 1992.
6. A. Choudhary, G. Fox, S. Hiranandani, K. Kennedy, C. Koelbel, S. Ranka, and C.-W. Tseng. Unified compilation of Fortran 77D and 90D. *ACM Letters on Programming Languages and Systems*, 2(1-4):95-114, March–December 1993.
7. R. Cytron, J. Ferrante, B. Rosen, M. Wegman, and K. Zadeck. Efficiently computing static single assignment form and the control dependence graph. *ACM Transactions on Programming Languages and Systems*, 13(4):451-490, October 1991.
8. R. Fatoohi. Performance analysis of four SIMD machines. In *Proceedings of the 1993 ACM International Conference on Supercomputing*, Tokyo, Japan, July 1993.
9. M. Gerndt. Updating distributed variables in local computations. *Concurrency: Practice and Experience*, 2(3):171-193, September 1990.
10. K. Gopinath and J. L. Hennessy. Copy elimination in functional languages. In *Proceedings of the Sixteenth Annual ACM Symposium on the Principles of Programming Languages*, Austin, TX, January 1989.
11. High Performance Fortran Forum. High Performance Fortran language specification. *Scientific Programming*, 2(1-2):1-170, 1993.
12. S. L. Johnsson. Language and compiler issues in scalable high performance scientific libraries. In *Proceedings of the Third Workshop on Compilers for Parallel Computers*, Vienna, Austria, July 1992.
13. K. Kennedy and G. Roth. Context optimization for SIMD execution. In *Proceedings of the 1994 Scalable High Performance Computing Conference*, Knoxville, TN, May 1994.
14. K. Knobe, J. Lukas, and M. Weiss. Optimization techniques for SIMD Fortran compilers. *Concurrency: Practice and Experience*, 5(7):527-552, October 1993.
15. G. Sabot. A compiler for a massively parallel distributed memory MIMD computer. In *Frontiers '92: The 4th Symposium on the Frontiers of Massively Parallel Computation*, McLean, VA, October 1992.
16. P. Schnorf, M. Ganapathi, and J. Hennessy. Compile-time copy elimination. *Software—Practice and Experience*, 23(11):1175-1200, November 1993.
17. J. T. Schwartz. Optimization of very high level languages – I. Value transmission and its corollaries. *Computer Languages*, 1(2):161-194, 1975.

A Loop Parallelization Algorithm for HPF Compilers

Kazuaki Ishizaki and Hideaki Komatsu

IBM Tokyo Research Laboratory, IBM Japan Ltd.
1623-14 Shimotsuruma, Yamato, Kanagawa 242, Japan
Email: ishizaki@trl.ibm.co.jp

Abstract. This paper presents a formalized loop parallelization algorithm for effectively extracting parallelism from data to be allocated to processors with array decomposition directives, in languages such as High Performance Fortran (HPF). We define a communication dependence vector that shows data dependence among processors, and use it in our algorithm to formalize and unify the detection of vector prefetch communication and vector pipeline communication for loop parallelization. The paper also presents a method, based on our algorithm for generating vector communications. We implemented the algorithm in our HPF compiler and carried out experiments with two applications on an IBM RS/6000 Scalable POWERparallel System.

1 Introduction

High Performance Fortran (HPF) [1] is an extension of Fortran that support data-parallel programming. To be successful, an HPF compiler must be able to generate highly efficient codes from an HPF program. To generate efficient Single-Program Multiple-Data (SPMD) codes [2] for MIMD distributed memory machines, it is important to parallelize loops and optimize communications.

Preliminary-proposed compilers [3, 4, 5, 6, 7] for distributed memory machines use different communication optimization algorithms. Among these algorithms, message vectorization is the key to optimization [8]. When there is a difference in a data decomposition between the left-hand side operand and a right-hand side operand, or anti dependence between the source operand and the sink operand, a vector prefetch communication [9, 10] is known as a communication optimization. When there is true dependence between the source operand and the sink operand, a vector pipeline communication [11] is known as a communication optimization.

Both communication optimizations are implemented in the Fortran-D compiler [3]. These optimization algorithms classify messages into three types. According to the type of message, the compiler generates either vector prefetch communication or vector pipeline communication. However, the algorithm used in the Fortran-D compiler is not formalized, and algorithms for detecting vector prefetch communication and vector pipeline communication are not unified. To our knowledge, no unified algorithm has been reported so far.

This paper presents a loop parallelization algorithm, formalized by using logical operations of vectors, which provide information on data dependence and communication. To provide information on data dependence, we define a true dependence vector and an anti dependence vector. These are extensions of a dependence vector [12]. We also define a communication dependence vector, in order to show combined information on data dependence and communication. The difference between a dependence vector and a communication dependence vector is as follows. A dependence vector shows that the execution order of the iterations is constrained by their data dependence. On the other hand, a communication dependence vector shows that the execution order of the iterations is constrained by the communication among processors.

Our algorithm uses a communication dependence vector to unify the detection of vector prefetch communication and vector pipeline communication for loop parallelization. Our algorithm is applied from the outermost loop to the innermost loop until all operands have been vectorized or no loop nest is parallelized.

This paper also presents a method for generating vector communications, based on the result of our loop parallelization algorithm.

Our algorithm has the following three advantages:

1. It can unify the detection of vector prefetch communications and vector pipeline communications that satisfy data dependence among processors.
2. It is applied from the outermost loop to the innermost loop until all operands have been marked as requiring either vector prefetch communication or vector pipeline communication, or no loop nest is parallelized.
3. It generates the correct code even for the loop nests that have any component of true dependences is negative.

To realize the first of these advantages, we define a communication dependence vector that shows the data dependence among processors, and use it for parallelizing loops and classifying communication methods. Our algorithm uses logical vector operations and a transformation of vector space. It is simple and efficient.

To realize the second advantage, we extract vector communications from loop nests and generate them at the outermost possible loop level. Since our algorithm is applied from the outermost loop, it is easy to generate vector communications at the outermost possible loop level. Even when a loop nest is not fully parallelized, the communication for operands can be vectorized at a level further out than the level of a parallelized loop nest.

The reason for the third advantage is that we suspect that other preliminary-proposed algorithms do not consider the case for the loop nest that has any component of true dependences is negative, unlike our algorithm.

The structure of this paper is as follows. In Sect. 2, we define an anti dependence vector and a true dependence vector, and parallelizable loop nests using them. In Sect. 3, we give an algorithm for loop parallelization, using a communication dependence vector. In Sect. 4, we discuss our algorithm in comparison with other preliminary-proposed algorithms. In Sect. 5, we give the performance results of experiments using our algorithm. In Sect. 6, we summarize related work. In Sect. 7, we present our conclusions.

2 Parallelizable Loop Nests

In this section, we define a true dependence vector and an anti dependence vector, which are the extensions of a dependence vector, and we also define parallelizable loop nests using the true dependence vector and the anti dependence vector.

2.1 Data Dependence

Goff [13] stated that data dependence exists between two statements S_1 and S_2 if there is a path from S_1 to S_2 and both statements access the same location in memory. There are four types of data dependence:

True Dependence occurs when S_1 writes to a memory location that S_2 later reads.

Anti Dependence occurs when S_1 reads a memory location that S_2 later writes to.

Output Dependence occurs when S_1 writes to a memory location that S_2 later writes to.

Input Dependence occurs when S_1 reads a memory location that S_2 later reads.

In this paper, we focus on true dependence and anti dependence. We do not need to worry about input dependence, since there is no constraint on the execution order of two read operands. If there is output dependence between different loop iterations, we cannot parallelize the loop nest.

2.2 True Dependence and Anti Dependence Vectors

A dependence vector shows that the execution order of iterations is constrained by their data dependence.

We use the definition of the dependence vector $\vec{d}$ given in [12].

Definition 1. Let an index vector in an n-nested loop be $\vec{p} = (p_1, p_2, ..., p_n)$, where p_i is the ith loop index, counting from the outermost loop to the innermost loop. A dependence vector $\vec{d}$ is defined as follows:

$$D = \left\{ \vec{d} \mid \vec{d} = \vec{p}' - \vec{p}, \text{ data dependence from } \vec{p} \text{ to } \vec{p}' \right\}$$

$$\vec{d} = (d_1, d_2, ..., d_n), d_i = \left[d_i^{\min}, d_i^{\max} \right], d_i^{\min} \in Z \cup \{-\infty\}, d_i^{\max} \in Z \cup \{\infty\}$$

In d_i, we use the notation '+' for $[1, \infty]$ and '-' for $[-\infty, -1]$.

In conventional compilers, dependence vectors show a partial order, since all dependences in the loop are satisfied. We distinguish between true dependence and anti dependence, because we classify different methods of communication according to the type of data dependence. We classify dependence vectors into two types: true dependence vectors and anti dependence vectors.

Definition 2. A *true dependence vector* $\vec{d}_t$ shows that an execution order is constrained by true dependence. An *anti dependence vector* $\vec{d}_a$ shows that an execution order is constrained by anti dependence.

Examples are given in Fig. 1. In the rest of paper, we use the example shown in Fig. 1 (a) for our loop parallelization algorithm.

```
        REAL A(100, 100)                            REAL A(100, 100)
*HPF$   PROCESSORS P(2,2)                   *HPF$   PROCESSORS P(2,2)
*HPF$   DISTRIBUTE (BLOCK,BLOCK) onto P::A,B *HPF$  DISTRIBUTE (BLOCK,BLOCK) onto P::A,B
        DO 10 J = 2, 99                              DO 10 T = 1, 10
          DO 10 I = 2, 99                              DO 10 J = 2, 99
            A(I,J) = A(I-1,J)+A(I+1,J)                   DO 10 I = 2, 99
10      CONTINUE                                           A(I,J) = A(I-1,J)+A(I+1,J)
                                             10        CONTINUE
```

$$\vec{d}_t(A(I,J), A(I-1,J)) = \{(0,1)\}$$

$$\vec{d}_a(A(I,J), A(I+1,J)) = \{(0,1)\}$$

(a)

$$\vec{d}_t(A(I,J), A(I-1,J)) = \{(+,0,1)\}$$

$$\vec{d}_t(A(I,J), A(I+1,J)) = \{(+,0,-1)\}$$

$$\vec{d}_a(A(I,J), A(I+1,J)) = \{(+,0,1)\}$$

$$\vec{d}_a(A(I,J), A(I-1,J)) = \{(+,0,-1)\}$$

(b)

Fig. 1. Examples of true dependence and anti dependence vectors

2.3 Parallelizable Loop Nests

We define parallelizable loop nests as loop nests that can be executed in parallel after vector communications have been performed. In the following definitions, "an operand that has an anti dependence vector" means the source operand of an arc that has anti dependence. "An operand that has a true dependence vector" means the sink operand of an arc that has true dependence.

Definition 3. *Parallelizable loop nests* include only the following five types of operands:

1. An operand that has no data dependence
2. An operand that has no data dependence among processors
3. An operand that has only an anti dependence vector among processors
4. An operand that has only a true dependence vector among processors. Let D_t be a set of the true dependence vectors, and let it satisfy the following condition:

$$\forall \vec{d} \in D_t : (\forall i:1 \le i \le n : d_i \ge 0)$$

5. An operand that has only a true dependence vector among processors. Let D_t be a set of the true dependence vectors, and let it satisfy the following condition:

$$\forall \vec{d}_1, \vec{d}_2 \in D_t : \left(\left(\exists i:1 \le i \le n : d_{1i} < 0 \right) \text{ and } \left(\begin{array}{l} \forall j:i < j \le n : \\ \left(\text{sign}(d_{1j}) = \text{sign}(d_{2j})\right) \text{or} \left(d_{1j} = 0\right) \text{or} \left(d_{2j} = 0\right) \end{array} \right) \right)$$

The reasons for which each of the above operands is parallelizable are, respectively,

1. An operand has no data dependence, and therefore the operand is executed in parallel among processors.
2. An operand has data dependence kept in processors, and therefore the operand is executed in parallel if data dependence is satisfied within each processor.
3. An operand has only an anti dependence vector among processors. In this case, the operand is executed in parallel after vector prefetch communication has been performed before the loop.

4. An operand has a true dependence vector among processors. If the value of all the elements in the true dependence vector are non-negative, the true dependence vector spans iteration space. In this case, the operand is executed in a pipelined fashion.

5. An operand has a true data dependence among processors. If an elemental value in the ith dimension of the true dependence vector is negative, the operand on the iteration space between $i+1$ and n is executed in a pipelined fashion. In this case, the degree of parallelism is smaller than the others.

3 Algorithm for Loop Parallelization

In this section, we discuss an algorithm for detecting the parallelizable loop nests specified in Definition 3, and for classifying the optimal communication method of the operands in the loop and the manner in which the loop should be executed. Our loop parallelization algorithm, like those of other compilers, is based on extracting vector communication from loop nests. It is structured in the following nine steps:

3.1 (STEP 1) Specifying the Scope of a Loop Nest

First, the compiler tries to parallelize a loop nest from the outermost loop, in order to extract the maximal parallelism. Therefore, it sets the parallelization scope to the whole loop nest.

In 3.8 (STEP 8), if the compiler classifies the loop nest as one that cannot be executed in parallel, it reduces the depth of the loop nest by one, and attempts to parallelize a subnest of the loop.

In the following steps, we use the example shown in Fig. 1 (a). In the example, the compiler sets the scope to the doubly nested loop.

3.2 (STEP 2) Calculating the Dependence Vectors

The compiler analyzes the data dependence [13, 14] in the specified loop nest. Precise information on data dependence is more important than in conventional compilers, because it is the basis of our loop parallelization. The compiler uses it to calculate the true dependence vector and the anti dependence vector for each referenced operand in the loop nest.

In the example, the compiler generates an anti dependence vector $\vec{d_a} = (0,1)$ on A(I+1, J) and a true dependence vector $\vec{d_t} = (0,1)$ on A(I-1, J).

3.3 (STEP 3) Partitioning the Iteration Space

For a loop to be executed in parallel, its iteration space is partitioned and each iteration sub-space is allocated to a single processor. In this paper, we apply the owner-computes rule [11, 15]. The left-hand side of each assignment statement in a loop nest is used to calculate the iteration space that enables a processor to store local data.

The limitation of our implementation is that a subscript function in the operands must be a linear function of a single index variable (SIV) [13], because we use a regular section descriptor (RSD) [3].

In the example, the partitioned index is calculated as follows:

```
Processor 1:   (J,I) = ([ 2:50:1],[ 2:50:1])
Processor 2:   (J,I) = ([ 2:50:1],[51:99:1])
Processor 3:   (J,I) = ([51:99:1],[ 2:50:1])
Processor 4:   (J,I) = ([51:99:1],[51:99:1])
```

3.4   (STEP 4) Communication Analysis

The compiler analyzes the region of the operands that causes nonlocal data access when the content of a partitioned iteration space is executed in the loop nest. Our communication analysis has a limitation, since we use an RSD, a subscript function in the operands must be a linear function of a SIV. This limitation is not serious limitation, however, since in many programs most index variables are known to be SIV. For addition, our algorithm recognizes any triangular subscript function as a linear function of a SIV at the inner loop level.

The compiler analyzes each right-hand side reference by a partitioned iteration space to a decomposed array. The reference is subtracted from the information on the array, to check whether it accesses nonlocal data. The result shows a vector representation of arrays with triplets on each dimension, called a communication region, as in the following definition:

Definition 4. The *communication region* E in an *m*-dimension array is defined as follows:

$$
E = \left\{ \vec{e} \mid \vec{e} = (e_1, e_2, \ldots, e_m), e_i = [lower{:}upper{:}step] \text{ is an iteration set} \atop \text{for communication} \right\}
$$

In the example, the communication regions for the two right-hand side operands are calculated as follows:

$$
\texttt{A(I-1,J)}: \ E=([50{:}50{:}1], \varnothing), \quad \texttt{A(I+1,J)}: \ E=([51{:}51{:}1], \varnothing)
$$

3.5   (STEP 5) Generating a Communication Vector

We need communication information to be represented on the basis of the iteration space, since we need to analyze whether communication is required by either anti dependence or true dependence. The true dependence vector and the anti dependence vector are represented on the basis of the iteration space. We translate communication information based on the array dimension into information based on the iteration space, and therefore define the communication vector $\vec{b}$ as being represented on the basis of the iteration space.

Definition 5. The *communication vector* $\vec{b} = (b_1, b_2, \ldots, b_n)$, $b_i = 1$ or 0, is defined as a vector in which each elemental value, which may be 1 or 0, indicates whether inter-processor communication exists, according to each dimension of a loop nest.

In order to generate communication vectors, the compiler matches each expression f_i in the operand $A(f_1, f_2, ..., f_m)$ with a vector in the iteration space $(I_1, I_2, ..., I_n)$, using the following algorithm:

```
for i = 1 to n
    found = false
    b_i = 0
    for j = 1 to m
        if (I_i ⊂ f_j) then
            if (e_j ≠ ∅) then
                b_i = 1
            endif
            found = true
        endif
    endfor
    if not found then
        for j = i+1 to n
            b_j = 1
        endfor
        break
    endif
endfor
```

Fig. 2. Algorithm for generating a communication vector

In the example, the communication vectors for the two right-hand side operands are generated as follows:

$$A(I-1, J): \vec{b} = (0, 1), \quad A(I+1, J): \vec{b} = (0, 1)$$

3.6 (STEP 6) Generating a Communication Dependence Vector

We analyze communication by requiring either true dependence or anti dependence. We define the communication dependence vector $\vec{c}$ on the basis of the iteration space.

Definition 6. Let the *communication dependence vector* $\vec{c}$ be a vector in which the value of each element indicates whether inter-processor communication occurs, by anti dependence or true dependence. The communication dependence vector $\vec{c}$ consists of a *true communication dependence vector* $\vec{c}_t$ and an *anti communication dependence vector* $\vec{c}_a$.

We derive a communication dependence vector from a true dependence vector d_t, an anti dependence vector d_a, and a communication vector $\vec{b}$ as follows.

$$\left(\vec{c}_t = (c_{t1}, c_{t2}, ... c_{tm}), \ c_{ti} = \begin{cases} d_{ti} \ (\text{if } b_i = 1) \\ 0 \ (\text{if } b_i = 0) \end{cases} \right) \left(\vec{c}_a = (c_{a1}, c_{a2}, ... c_{an}), \ c_{ai} = \begin{cases} d_{ai} \ (\text{if } b_i = 1) \\ 0 \ (\text{if } b_i = 0) \end{cases} \right)$$

The difference between a dependence vector and a communication dependence vector is as follows. A dependence vector shows that the execution order of the iterations is constrained by their data dependence on each processor and among processors. On the other hand, a communication dependence vector shows that the execution order of the iterations is constrained by their communication among processors.

In the example, the communication vectors for the two right-hand side operands are generated as follows:

$$A(I-1,J): \vec{C}_a = \varnothing, \ \vec{C}_t = (0,1), \quad A(I+1,J): \vec{C}_a = (0,1), \vec{C}_t = \varnothing$$

3.7 (STEP 7) Classification of Communication Methods

The compiler classifies optimal communication methods into four categories by using the communication dependence vector:

1. *No communication*
2. *Prefetch communication*: vector prefetch communication is used before execution of a loop
3. *Pipeline communication*: vector pipeline communication is used to trigger execution of a loop
4. *Synchronous communication*: each iteration with communication is executed in a loop

We now give an algorithm for classifying communication methods for each operand in Fig. 3. Let C_t be a set of true communication dependence vectors in a loop.

```
IF (b⃗ = 0) THEN
   "no communication"
ELSE
   SELECT
      CASE (c⃗ₜ = 0) :
         "prefetch communication"
      CASE (c⃗ₐ = 0) & (∀c⃗ ∈ Cₜ:(∀i:1 ≤ i ≤ n: cᵢ ≥ 0))
                         or
(c⃗ₐ = 0) & | ∀c⃗₁,c⃗₂ ∈ Cₜ:| (∃i:1 ≤ i ≤ n: c₁ᵢ < 0)and | (∀j:i < j ≤ n: (sign(c₁ⱼ) = sign(c₂ⱼ))or(c₁ⱼ = 0)or(c₂ⱼ = 0)) | | |  :
         "pipeline communication"
      OTHERWISE
         "synchronous communication"
   END SELECT
END IF
```

Fig. 3. Algorithm for classifying communication methods

The algorithm detects vector prefetch communication and vector pipeline communication in a uniform manner, using a communication dependence vector.

In the algorithm, if an operand in a loop has both $\vec{c}_a$ and $\vec{c}_t$, the loop is not executed in parallel, since the communication is not vectorized. To exploit parallelism, we suggest that an array decomposition of the operand should be changed into a decomposition that makes $\vec{c}_t$ empty. In other words, if d_{ti} is not zero, data decomposition of the *i*th dimension in the array should be collapsed. We give an example in Sect. 4.

In the example, the communication vectors for the two right-hand side operands are generated as follows:

```
A(I-1,J): pipeline communication
A(I+1,J): prefetch communication
```

3.8 (STEP 8) Classification of Loop Execution Modes

We define loop execution modes as follows:

1. *DO PARALLEL*: a loop is executed in parallel
2. *DO PIPELINE*: a loop is executed in pipelined fashion
3. *DO SYNCHRONOUS*: a loop is not executed in parallel or in pipelined fashion

The computation and communication for each mode are shown in Fig. 4. Solid lines denote computation, and dotted arrows denote communication.

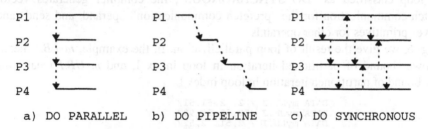

a) DO PARALLEL   b) DO PIPELINE   c) DO SYNCHRONOUS

Fig. 4. Execution modes

A loop execution mode is classified as "DO PARALLEL" if all the operands in the loop are classified as "no communication" or "prefetch communication."

A loop execution mode is classified as "DO PIPELINE" if one or more the operands in the loop are classified as "pipeline communication" and the others arc classified as "no communication" or "prefetch communication."

A loop execution mode is classified as "DO SYNCHRONOUS" if one or more "synchronous communication" operands are included in the loop. In this case, the compiler reduces the depth of the loop nest by one and tries to parallelize a subnet of a loop, as described in Sect. 3.1 (STEP 1). If there are "prefetch communication" operands, vector prefetch communications are generated at the current loop nest level and the operands are excluded from the set of operands that will be tested in the next step of the loop parallelization. It is easy to generate prefetch communications in the outer loop nest, since our algorithm starts loop parallelization from the outermost loop nest.

In Fig. 5, we give the result of classification of loop modes for the example.

```
        DOPIPE 10 J = 2, 99
          DOPIPE 10 I = 2, 99
            A(I,J) = A(I-1,J)+A(I+1,J)
     10 CONTINUE
```

Fig. 5. Classification of loop execution modes for the example

3.9 (STEP 9) Generating Vector Communications

This section briefly describes how we generate vector communications using the loop execution modes classified in Sect. 3.8.

For "prefetch communication" in a loop classified as "DO PARALLEL" or "DO PIPELINE," the compiler generates vector prefetch communication, which we call PREFETCH, at the loop nest level that the communication method is classified as belonging to. In this communication, the processor that owns the data referenced by another processor sends them and the processor referencing the data receives them before a loop.

For "pipeline communication" in a loop classified as "DO PIPELINE", the compiler generates a vector receive, which we call PRERECV, before a loop, and generates a vector send, which we call POSTSEND, after a loop. POSTSEND transfers the data that is written in a loop and that is going to be used in the succeeding processor. PRERECV receives data that is going to be read in a loop from the preceding processor.

In a loop classified as "DO SYNCHRONOUS", the compiler generates vector prefetch communication for the "prefetch communication" operand, and sends and receives primitives for other operands.

In Fig. 6, we give the result of loop parallelization. In the example, *myLB.I* means the lower bound of partitioned iteration in loop index I, and *myUB.I* means the upper bound of partitioned iteration in loop index I.

```
      DATA myLB.J / 2, 2,51,51/
      DATA myUB.J /50,50,99,99/
      DATA myLB.I / 2,51, 2,51/
      DATA myUB.I /50,99,50,99/

      PREFETCH for A(I+1,J)
      PRERECV for A(I-1,J)
      DOPIPE 10 J = myLB.J(pID),myUB.J(pID)
        DOPIPE 10 I = myLB.I(pID),myUB.I(pID)
          A(I,J) = A(I-1,J)+A(I+1,J)
   10 CONTINUE
      POSTSEND for A(I-1,J)
```

Fig. 6. A parallelized loop for the example

4 Discussion

In this section, we compare our algorithm with other preliminary-proposed algorithms. There are two major differences. One is to generate an incorrect code for the loop nest that has any components of true dependences is negative. The other is not to transform the loop nest in our algorithm.

4.1 Generating Vector Communications

An example is given in Fig. 7. We assume that the array decomposition is (BLOCK, BLOCK) in the example. The proposed algorithm [3] parallelizes the loop nests solely according to the level of true dependence. In this case, it generates vector pipeline communication for A(I-1,J-1) and A(I+1, J-1) before the J loop. This is an incorrect code and deadlock occurs, because the loop nest has any component of true dependences is negative.

```
        REAL A(100, 100)
        DO 10 J = 2, 99
          DO 10 I = 2, 99
            A(I,J) = A(I-1,J-1)+A(I-1,J+1)+
    c                A(I+1,J-1)+A(I+1,J+1)
 10     CONTINUE
```

$$\vec{d}_t(A(I,J), A(I-1,J-1)) = \{(+,1,1)\}, \vec{d}_t(A(I,J), A(I+1,J-1)) = \{(+,1,-1)\}$$

$$\vec{d}_a(A(I,J), A(I-1,J+1)) = \{(+,1,-1)\}, \vec{d}_a(A(I,J), A(I+1,J+1)) = \{(+,1,1)\}$$

Fig. 7. Example for parallelization

Our algorithm parallelizes the loop nests on the basis of a communication dependence vector which shows that the execution order of the iterations is constrained by communication. In this case, this doubly nested loop is not parallelized, because the true communication dependence vectors are (1,1) and (1,-1). This does not satisfy Definition 3-4.

To exploit parallelism, we suggest that the array decomposition of the operand should be changed into the decomposition that makes $\vec{c}_t$ empty. In other words, if d_{ti} is not zero, the data decomposition of the ith dimension in the array must be collapsed. In the example, the first dimension of the array must be collapsed.

We assume that the array decomposition is (*, BLOCK) in the example. Our algorithm detects that the doubly nested loop can be pipelined, because all communication dependence vectors are (1,0). In Fig. 8, we give the result of the loop parallelization.

```
        PREFETCH for.A(I-1,J+1)
        PREFETCH for A(I+1,J+1)
        PRERECV for A(I-1,J-1)
        PRERECV for A(I+1,J-1)
        DOPIPE 10 J = myLB.J(pID),myUB.J(pID)
          DOPIPE 10 I = 2, 99
            A(I,J) = A(I-1,J-1)+A(I-1,J+1)+
    c                A(I+1,J-1)+A(I+1,J+1)
 10     CONTINUE
        POSTSEND for A(I-1,J-1)
        POSTSEND for A(I+1,J-1)
```

Fig. 8. Parallelized loop nest

Actually, there is no parallelism in the code. We have to exploit coarse-grain pipeline parallelism [8] by applying the strip-mining and loop interchange. We will discuss it in Sect. 4.2.

4.2 Loop Transformations

Some of the preliminary-proposed algorithms, such as Fortran D and PARADIGM algorithms [17], attempt loop transformations, such as strip-mining and loop interchange, for coarse-grain pipelining.

Our algorithm generates vector pipeline communication at the outermost possible loop nest. The vector communication can be put at an inner loop nest that has been strip-mined to exploit coarse-grain parallelism. Our current implementation does not support these loop transformations for the following reason. The reason is that determining optimal block size is difficult. The block size for strip-mining is discussed in other papers [16, 17]. In [16], however, none of them describe how to determine optimal block size automatically. In [17], the automatic selection of the block size in multidimensional data distributions is discussed, but this function is not integrated into the compiler. To exploit coarse-grain parallelism, we plan to support strip-mining in our algorithm.

To exploit parallelism, we plan to implement other loop transformations, such as loop reversal.

5 Experiments

In this section, we give the results of our experiments. To measure the effectiveness of our algorithm, we applied it to two applications.

5.1 Environment

For our experiments, we used an IBM RISC System/6000 Scalable POWERparallel System (SP) Thin Node. Each processor on the SP has 128MB of memory. A high-performance switch with a bi-directional peak bandwidth of 40MB/s is used to connect 32 processors. For a message passing library, we used the user-space communication protocol in the IBM Message Passing Library [18], which is included in the IBM Parallel Environment [19].

We have implemented our algorithm in our HPF compiler, compiled two applications, and executed them on the SP. One was a shallow water code [20], about 500 lines in length, for measuring the capability to detect vector prefetch communications. The other was a successive over relaxation (SOR) code, about 100 lines in length, for measuring the capability to detect vector pipeline communications.

5.2 Results

We ran the shallow water code, for 513×513 arrays in the distribution (*, block). The performance results are shown in Fig. 9 (a). In the shallow water code, all the detected communications were prefetch communications, and consequently a good performance was achieved.

We then ran the SOR code, for 1000×1000 arrays, in the distribution (block, block). The performance results are shown in Fig. 9 (b). The SOR code does not include a convergence check, because our intention was to show the effectiveness of vector pipeline communications. Therefore the speed-up ratio is further than $5.5 (= \sqrt{30}) : 1$ when 30 processors are used. In general, the performance is worse than this result indicates, because the typical SOR code includes a convergence check.

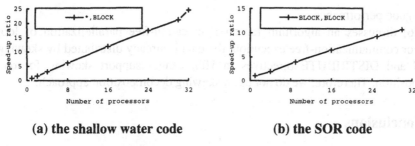

| (a) the shallow water code | (b) the SOR code |

Fig. 9. Results of the performance

6 Related Work

Much work has been done on parallelizing loop nests by extracting vector communication in compilers.

Two pioneer compilers for distributed memory machines, Crystal [21] and Id Nouveau [11], extract vector prefetch communication from a program with single-assignment semantics. Some HPF compilers, such as xHPF [22] and ADAPTOR [23] parallelize loop nests, and the loops are executed in parallel.

The Fortran-D compiler [3] can detect pipeline communication by means of cross-processor dependences [16]. However, its optimization algorithm is not formalized, and it separates the detection of vector prefetch communication and vector pipeline communication. In contrast, we unify the detection of two vector communications (that is, prefetch and pipeline), and formalize our algorithm using a communication dependence vector. Actual implementation of Fortran-D compiler supports BLOCK and CYCLIC distributions only in one dimension. Our compiler supports BLOCK and CYCLIC distributions in multi-dimensions.

The Fortran-D compiler supports coarse-grain pipelining to overlap computation and communication. Our algorithm, however, does not support it because its policy is to reduce the number of synchronizations in a loop nest. We will support coarse-grain pipelining for one-dimensional distribution.

The Fortran90D compiler [6] can parallelize only Fortran90 constructs, such as array operations and forall statements. It supports multi-dimensional distributions, but it does not attempt to parallelize Fortran77 DO loops.

The SUIF compiler [4] automatically parallelizes sequential programs. Amarasinghe [24] discusses algorithms that minimize communication across loops and exploit pipeline communication. These algorithms are separate, and are not discussed alongside true dependence and anti dependence. In our algorithm, we distinguish between true dependence and anti dependence.

Anderson [25] discusses a method for exploiting parallelism by data redistribution. Data redistribution requires communication and thus it is costly. If the optimal data distribution is different for each loop in a program, a large amount of communication is required for the whole program. In contrast, our algorithm parallelizes loop nests from the user-specified data distribution. This approach gives a fairly good performance.

Lim [26] discusses an algorithm for communication-free parallelization of loop nests. For communication-free execution, the data is already distributed by skewing. ALIGN and DISTRIBUTE directives in HPF cannot support skewing for data decomposition. Therefore, we do not use a skewing decomposition approach.

7 Conclusions

This paper has presented a formalized algorithm for effectively extracting parallelism among processors from loop nests by using a communication dependence vector. Both prefetch communication and pipeline communication are handled by a uniform framework to detect data dependence among processors. We also presented a method to generate communications. The experimental results obtained by applying our algorithm showed a good performance.

8 Acknowledgments

We are grateful to Toshio Nakatani for supporting our research and providing helpful suggestions for this paper. We are also grateful to Osamu Gohda, Gyo Ohsawa, Toshio Suganuma, and Takeshi Ogasawara for implementing our HPF compiler and for participating in helpful discussions. We also thank the referees for their helpful comments and suggestions.

References

1. High Performance Fortran Forum, High Performance Fortran Language Specification, Version 1.0, Technical Report, Rice University, CRPC-TR92225, 1992
2. Darema F., George D., Norton V., and Pfister G.: A Single Program Multiple Data Computational Model for EPEX/FORTRAN, Parallel Computing, Vol. 7, pp. 11-24, 1988
3. C. W. Tseng: An Optimizing Fortran D Compiler for MIMD Distributed-Memory Machines, PhD thesis, Rice University, CRPC-TR93291, 1993
4. Stanford SUIF Compiler Group: SUIF: A Parallelizing and Optimizing Research Compiler, Technical Report, Stanford University, CSL-TR-94-620, 1994
5. H. P. Zima, H. J. Bast, and M. Gerndt: SUPERB: A Tool for Semiautomatic MIMD/SIMD Parallelization, Parallel Computing, Vol. 6, pp. 1-18, 1988
6. Z. Bozkus, A. Choudhary, G. Fox, T. Haupt, S. Ranka : Fortran90D/HPF Compiler for Distributed Memory MIMD Computers: Design, Implementation, and Performance Results, Proceedings of Supercomputing '93, pp. 351-360, 1993
7. P. Banerjee, J. A. Chandy, M. Gupta, J. G. Holm, A. Lain, D. J. Palermo, S. Ramaswamy: The PARADIGM Compiler for Distributed-Memory Message Passing Multicomputers, In Proceedings of the First International Workshop on Parallel Processing, pp. 322-330, 1994
8. S. Hiranandani, K. Kennedy, and C. W. Tseng: Compiling Fortran D for MIMD Distributed-Memory Machines, Communications of the ACM, Vol. 35, pp. 66-80, 1992

9. V. Balasundaram, G. Fox, K. Kennedy, and U. Kremer: An Interactive Environment for Data Partitioning and Distribution, In Proceedings of the 5th Distributed Memory Computing Conference, pp. 1160-1170, 1990

10. M. Gerndt: Updating Distributed Variables in Local Computations, Concurrency: Practice & Experience, Vol. 2, No. 3, pp. 171-193, 1990

11. A. Rogers and K. Pingali: Process Decomposition through Locality of Reference, Conference on Programming Language Design and Implementation, pp. 69-80, 1989

12. M. E. Wolfe and M. S. Lam: A Loop Transformation Theory and an Algorithm to Maximize Parallelism, IEEE Transactions on Parallel and Distributed Systems, Vol. 2, No. 4, pp. 452-471, 1991

13. G. Goff, K. Kennedy, and C. W. Tseng: Practical Dependence Testing, Proceedings of the ACM SIGPLAN '91 Conference on Programming Language Design and Implementation, pp. 15-29, 1991

14. M. J. Wolfe: Optimizing Supercompilers for Supercomputers, The MIT Press, 1989

15. D. Callahan and K. Kennedy: Compiling Programs for Distributed-Memory Multiprocessors, Journal of Supercomputing, Vol. 2, pp. 151-169, 1988

16. S. Hiranandani, K. Kennedy, and C. W. Tseng: Evaluating Compiler Optimizations for Fortran D, Journal of Parallel and Distributed Computing, Vol. 21, pp. 27-45, 1994

17. D. J. Palermo, E. Su, J. A. Chandy, P. Banerjee: Communication Optimizations used in the PARADIGM Compiler for Distributed-Memory Multicomputers, In Proceedings of the 23rd International Conference on Parallel Processing, pp. II:1-10, 1994

18. IBM AIX Parallel Environment - Parallel Programming Subroutine Reference Release 2.0, SH26-7228-01, IBM Corporation, 1994

19. IBM AIX Parallel Environment - Operation and Use Release 2.0, SH26-7230-01, IBM Corporation, 1994

20. R. K. Sato and P. N. Swarztrauber: BenchMarking the Connection Machine 2, Proceedings of Supercomputing '88, 1988

21. J. Li and M. Chen: Compiling Communication Efficient Programs for Massively Parallel Machines, IEEE Transactions on Parallel and Distributed Systems, Vol. 2, No. 3, pp. 361-376, 1991

22. Applied Parallel Research: xHPF: User's Guide (Version 2.0), 1995

23. T. Brandes: ADAPTOR Language Reference Manual Version 2.0, German National Research Center for Computer Science, 1994

24. S. P. Amarasinghe, J. M. Anderson, M. S. Lam, and A.W. Lim: An Overview of a Compiler for Scalable Parallel Machines, Proceedings of the 6th Workshop on Languages and Compilers for Parallel Computing, 1993

25. J. M. Anderson and M. S. Lam: Global Optimizations for Parallelism and Locality on Scalable Parallel Machines, Conference on Programming Language Design and Implementation, 1993

26. A. W. Lim and M. S. Lam: Communication-Free Parallelization via Affine Transformation, Proceedings of the 7th Workshop on Languages and Compilers for Parallel Computing, 1994

Fast Address Sequence Generation for Data-Parallel Programs Using Integer Lattices

Ashwath Thirumalai and J. Ramanujam

Dept. of Electrical & Computer Engineering
Louisiana State University, Baton Rouge, LA 70803
({ash,jxr}@gate.ee.lsu.edu)

Abstract. In data-parallel languages such as High Performance Fortran and Fortran D, arrays are mapped to processors through a two step process involving alignment followed by distribution. A compiler that generates code for each processor has to compute the sequence of local memory addresses accessed by each processor and the sequence of sends and receives for a given processor to access non-local data. In this paper, we present a novel approach based on integer lattices. The set of elements referenced can be generated by integer linear combinations of basis vectors. Our linear algorithm determines the basis vectors as a function of the mapping. Using the basis vectors, we derive a loop nest that enumerates the addresses, which are points in the lattice generated by the basis vectors. Experimental results show that our approach is better than that of a recent linear time solution to this problem.

1 Introduction

Programming massively parallel distributed memory machines involves partitioning data and computation across processors. Languages such as Fortran D [4], Vienna Fortran [2] and High Performance Fortran (HPF) [7] include directives—such as align and distribute—that describe how data is distributed among the processors in a distributed-memory multiprocessor. For example, in HPF, arrays are mapped to processors in two steps: in the first step, arrays are *aligned* to an abstract discrete Cartesian grid called a *template;* the template is then distributed onto the processors. The effect of this two-level mapping onto p processors is to create p disjoint pieces of the array, with each processor being able to address only data items in its locally allocated piece. Thus, a HPF compiler must generate code for each processor (node code) that accesses only locally owned pieces directly, and inserts communication for non-local accesses.

In order to generate node code for each processor, we need to know the sequence of local memory addresses accessed by each processor and the sequence of sends and receives for a given processor to access non-local data. A regular access pattern in terms of the global data structure can appear to be irregular within each locally allocated piece. For example, an array section $A(\ell : h : s)$ exhibits a regular access sequence of stride s; but with an HPF-style data mapping, the access sequence can become irregular. In this paper we present efficient algorithms for generating local memory access patterns for the various processors given the alignment of arrays to a template and the distribution of the template onto the processors. Our solution is based on viewing the access sequence as an integer lattice, and involves the derivation of a suitable set of basis vectors for the lattice. Given the lattice basis, we enumerate the lattice by using loop nests; this allows us to generate efficient code that incurs negligible runtime overhead in determining the access pattern. Chatterjee *et al.* [3] presented an $O(k \log k)$ algorithm (where k is the block size – see Section 2 for definition) for this problem; ours is an $O(k)$ algorithm. Recently, Kennedy *et al.* [9] have also presented an $O(k)$ algorithm. Experiments demonstrate that our algorithm is 2 to 9 times faster than the algorithm of Kennedy *at al.* and 13 to 60 times faster than the algorithm in Chatterjee *et al.*

---
[1] Supported in part by an NSF Young Investigator Award CCR–9457768, and NSF grant CCR–9210422, and by the Louisiana Board of Regents through contract LEQSF (1991-94)-RD-A-09.

Processor 0		Processor 1		$\cdots$	Processor $p-1$		
0 $\cdots$	$k-1$	k	$\cdots$ $2k-1$	$\cdots$	$(p-1)k$	$\cdots$	$pk-1$
pk $\cdots$	$(p+1)k-1$	$(p+1)k$	$\cdots$ $(p+2)k-1$	$\cdots$	$(2p-1)k$	$\cdots$	$2pk-1$
$\vdots$ $\vdots$	$\vdots$	$\vdots$	$\vdots$ $\vdots$	$\vdots$	$\vdots$	$\vdots$	$\vdots$

(a): Layout of an array distributed CYCLIC(k) onto p processors.

Global index (Processor m)	mk	$\cdots$	$mk+k-1$	$(p+m)k$	$\cdots$	$(p+m+1)k-1$	$\cdots$
Local index (Processor m)	0	$\cdots$	$k-1$	k	$\cdots$	$2k-1$	$\cdots$

(b): Local layout of array shown in Fig. 1(a) in Processor m.

Fig. 1. Global and local addresses for data mappings

This paper is organized as follows. In Section 2, we present the problem setting and discuss related work. Section 3 outlines our approach using lattices and presents key mathematical results which are used later in the paper. In Section 4, we present our linear algorithm for determining basis vectors, and contrast it with the algorithm of Kennedy *et al*. In Section 5 we show how to determine address sequences by lattice enumeration using loop nests. We show how to use the lattice basis vectors derived in Section 4 to generate a loop nest that determines the address sequence. Section 6 discusses optimizations applied to the loop enumeration strategy presented in Section 5, specifically the GO-LEFT and GO-RIGHT schemes. Section 7 demonstrates the efficacy of our approach using experimental results comparing our solution to those of Chatterjee *et al*. and Kennedy *et al*. Section 8 concludes with a summary and points to further research directions.

2   Background and Related Work

We consider an array A identically aligned to the template T; this means that if, $A(i)$ is aligned with $T(ai+b)$, then the alignment stride $a=1$ and the alignment offset $b=0$. Further let this template be distributed in a block-cyclic fashion with a block size of k across p processors. This is also known as a CYCLIC(k) distribution [7]. If $k=1$, the distribution is called CYCLIC, and if $k=\frac{N}{p}$, where N is the size of the template, the distribution is called a BLOCK distribution. We assume that arrays have a lower limit of zero, and processors and local addresses are numbered from zero onward. This mapping of the elements of A to the processor memories is shown in the Fig. 1(a). Though the elements of A are stored in the processor memories in a linear fashion as shown in Fig. 1(b), we adopt a two-dimensional view of the storage allocated for the array as shown in Fig. 1(a). We view the global addresses as being organized in terms of courses; each course consists of pk elements. In the two-dimensional view we adopt, the first dimension denotes the course number (starting from zero), and the second dimension denotes the offset from the beginning of the course.

An array section in HPF is of the form $A(\ell:h:s)$, where s is the access stride, and ℓ and h are the lower and upper bounds, respectively. Given an array statement with HPF-style data mappings, it is our aim to generate the address sequence for the different processors.

Consider the case of an array aligned identically to a template that is distributed CYCLIC(4) onto 3 processors, which is accessed with a stride of 7 (p=3, k=4 and

Processor 0				Processor 1				Processor 2			
0^0	1	2	3	4	5	6	7^3	8	9	10	11
12	13	14^6	15	16	17	18	19	20	21^5	22	23
24	25	26	27	28^8	29	30	31	32	33	34	35^{11}
36	37	38	39	40	41	42^{14}	43	44	45	46	47
48	49^{17}	50	51	52	53	54	55	56^{16}	57	58	59
60	61	62	63^{23}	64	65	66	67	68	69	70^{22}	71
72	73	74	75	76	77^{25}	78	79	80	81	82	83
84^{28}	85	86	87	88	89	90	91^{31}	92	93	94	95

Fig. 2. Layout of array A for $p = 3$ and $k = 4$ along with the global and local addresses of the accessed elements in $A(0 : 95 : 7)$ $(s = 7)$; Superscripts denote local addresses.

s=7). Fig. 2 shows the allocation of the array elements along with the corresponding global addresses. The array elements accessed are marked and the corresponding local addresses are shown in Fig. 2. While the global access stride is constant (7 in this case), the local access sequence does not have a constant stride on any processor. For example, the local addresses of elements accessed in processor 1 are $3, 8, 14, 25, 31, \ldots$. The address generation problem is to enumerate this sequence.

Several papers have addressed this code generation problem. Koelbel [10] derived techniques for compile-time address and communication generation for BLOCK and CYCLIC distribution for non-unit stride accesses. Chatterjee *et al.* [3] derived a technique that identifies a repeating access pattern, which is characterized as a finite-state machine. Their $O(k \ log \ k)$ algorithm involves a solution of k linear Diophantine equations to determine the pattern of address accessed, followed by sorting these addresses to derive the accesses in linear order. In this paper, we show that sorting the elements is not required to generate the addresses in lexicographic order. In an exhaustive study of this problem, Stichnoth [13] presented a framework to enumerate local addresses and generation of communication sets. Gupta *et al.* [6] derived the *virtual-block* and *virtual-cyclic* schemes. The virtual block (cyclic) scheme views the global array as a union of several cyclically (block) distributed arrays. The virtual cyclic scheme does not preserve the access order in the case of DO loops (this is not a problem for parallel array assignments). Ancourt *et al.* [1] use a linear algebra framework to generate code for fully parallel loops in HPF and do not exploit the repetition of the access sequence. Recently, Kennedy *et al.* [9] derived an $O(k)$ algorithm that determines the basis vectors by locating $2k - 1$ addresses accessed using the solutions of $2k - 1$ linear Diophantine equations. The improvement over [3] comes from avoiding the sorting step at the expense of solving an additional set of $k - 1$ linear Diophantine equations. In this paper, we show that solving $2k - 1$ equations is not required. Our algorithm requires finding only $\min(s, k + 1)$ addresses that are accessed by the array section. In addition, our lattice enumeration algorithm (given the basis vectors) is different from and faster than [9].

3 A Lattice Based Approach for Address Generation

In this section we present a novel technique based on integer lattices for the address generation problem presented in the previous section. We first show that the accessed array elements of an array section belong to an integer lattice. We then provide a linear time algorithm to obtain the basis vectors of the integer lattice. We then go on to use these basis vectors to generate a loop nest that determines the access sequence. The problem of basis determination forms the core of code generation for HPF array statements; thus, a fast solution for this problem improves the performance of several facets of an HPF compiler. In this section we also provide a few optimizations of our basis determination algorithm.

3.1 Assumptions

We present our approach to address generation for an alignment stride, $a = 1$. For $a > 1$, we use an approach similar to the one developed in [3], which involves two applications of our algorithm. Therefore, we do not discuss non-unit alignment strides. Communication sets for array statements can be derived by two applications of our algorithm for address generation [14, 15].

We assume that A is identically aligned to the template T. As it is evident from Fig. 1(a), we assign a block of k cells of the template to each of the p processors and then wrap around and assign the rest of the cells in a similar fashion. As mentioned earlier, we treat the global address space as a two dimensional space and every element of an array $A(i)$ has an address of the form $(x, y) = (i \operatorname{div} pk, i \bmod pk)$ in this space. Here x gives the course number to which this element belongs and y gives the offset of the element in that course. We refer to the two-dimensional view of an array A as A_{2D}; this notation is used throughout this paper.

3.2 Lattices

We use the following definitions of a lattice and its basis [5].

Definition 1. A set of points $x_1, x_2, \cdots, x_k$ in $\mathbb{R}^n$ is said to be *independent* if these points do not belong to a linear subspace of $\mathbb{R}^n$ of dimension less than k.

For $k = n$, this is equivalent to the condition that the determinant of the matrix X whose columns are $x_i, i = 1, \ldots, n$ is non-zero, *i.e.*, $det([x_1 x_2 \cdots x_n]) \neq 0$. Now we state the following definition from the theory of lattices [5]; see [5] for a proof.

Definition 2. Let $b_1, b_2, \cdots, b_n$ be n independent points. Then the set Λ of points q such that
$$q = u_1 b_1 + u_2 b_2 + \cdots + u_n b_n$$
(where $u_1, \ldots, u_n$ are integers) is called a lattice. The set of vectors $b_1, \cdots, b_n$ is called a basis of Λ. A matrix $B = b_1 b_2 \cdots b_n$ is called a basis matrix.

Definition 3. Let Λ be a discrete subspace of $\mathbb{R}^n$ which is not contained in an $(n - 1)$-dimensional linear subspace of $\mathbb{R}^n$. Then Λ is a lattice.

We refer to the set of global addresses (elements) over all processors accessed by $A(\ell : h : s)$ with distribution parameters (p, k) as $\Gamma = \langle A(\ell : h : s), p, k \rangle$. We refer to the set of local addresses accessed by processor m in executing its portion of $A(\ell : h : s)$ with distribution parameters (p, k) as Γ_m. By construction, Γ is a discrete subgroup of $\mathbb{R}^2$ and in general, is not contained in a 1-dimensional linear subspace of $\mathbb{R}^2$; if a single vector can be used to generate the elements accessed, our algorithm handles this as a special case. Thus, without loss of generality, $\Gamma = \langle A(\ell : h : s), p, k \rangle$ is a lattice. Similarly Γ_m is also a lattice.

In order to find the sequence of local addresses accessed on processor m, one needs to:

1. find a set of basis vectors of the lattice Γ_m; and
2. enumerate the points in Γ_m using integer linear combinations of the basis vectors.

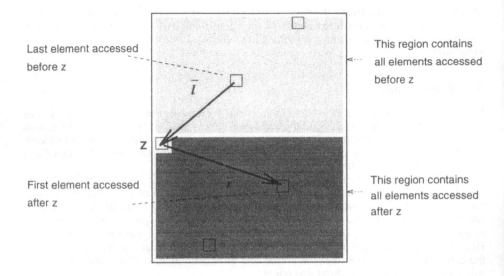

Fig. 3. Explanation of basis determination

Our solution to Step 1 (presented in Section 4) uses the fact that a basis for the lattice can be computed from a knowledge of some of the points in the lattice. Our solution to Step 2 (presented in Section 5) uses the fact that if (with a given origin) every point in the lattice can be generated as non-negative integer linear combinations of a suitable pair of basis vectors, then these points can be enumerated by a two-level loop (each level with a step size of 1); in addition, this two-level nest can be derived by applying the linear transformation B^{-1} where B is the basis of the lattice.

Definition 4. A basis B of the lattice Λ is called an *extremal basis* if the set of points $\mathbf{q}$ that belong to Λ can be written as

$$\mathbf{q} = u_1\mathbf{b_1} + u_2\mathbf{b_2} + \cdots + u_n\mathbf{b_n}$$

where $u_1, \ldots, u_n$ are non-negative integers.

This paper presents an algorithm for determining an extremal basis of the array section lattice $\langle A(\ell : h : s), p, k \rangle$ and shows how to use the extremal basis to generate the address sequence efficiently.

4 Determination of Basis Vectors

In this section, we show how to derive a pair of extremal basis vectors for the lattice Γ_m. In order to do that, we state a key result that allows us to find a basis for the lattice given a set of points in the lattice.

Result 5. Let $\mathbf{b_1}, \mathbf{b_2}, \cdots, \mathbf{b_n}$ be independent points of a lattice Λ in $\mathbb{R}^n$. Then Λ has a basis $\{\mathbf{a_1}, \mathbf{a_2}, \cdots, \mathbf{a_n}\}$ such that

$$\mathbf{b_i} = \sum_{k=1}^{i} u_{ki}\mathbf{a_k} \qquad (i = 1, \ldots, n)$$

where $u_{ii} > 0$ and $0 \le u_{ki} < u_{ii}$ $(k < i; i = 1, \ldots, n)$. In addition, the set of points $\{b_1, b_2, \cdots, b_n\}$ is a basis of the lattice Λ if and only if $u_{ii} = 1$.

While this result allows us to decide if a given set of independent points form a basis of the lattice, it is not constructive. But for $n = 2$, we derive the following theorem which allows us to construct a basis for the array section lattice on processor m. We use the vector o to refer to the origin of the lattice.

Theorem 6. *Let b_1 and b_2 be independent points of a lattice Λ in $\mathbb{R}^2$ such that the closed triangle formed by the vertices o, b_1 and b_2 contains no other points of Λ. Then $\{b_1, b_2\}$ is a basis of Λ.*

Proof. Let $\{a_1, a_2\}$ be any basis of Λ. From Result 5, we can write

$$b_1 = u_{11}a_1$$
$$b_2 = u_{12}a_1 + u_{22}a_2$$

where $u_{11} > 0, u_{22} > 0$ and $0 \le u_{12} < u_{22}$. Based on the hypothesis, the side of the triangle connecting vertices o and b_1 does not contain other points of Λ. Therefore, $u_{11} = 1$.

Let us assume that $u_{22} > 1$. If $u_{12} = 0$, the triangle formed by o, b_1 and b_2 contains the point $a_2 \in \Lambda$; similarly, if $u_{12} \ge 1$, the triangle formed by o, b_1 and b_2 contains the point $a_1 + a_2 \in \Lambda$. This contradicts our hypothesis. Hence, $u_{22} = 1$. Since, $u_{11} = u_{22} = 1$, it follows from Result 1 that the vectors b_1 and b_2 form a basis of Λ. $\square$

Thus, in order to determine a basis of the array section lattice on processor m, we need to find three points (one of which can be considered as the origin without loss of generality) not on a straight line such that the triangle formed by them contains no other points belonging to the lattice. Let x_1, x_2, and x_3 be three consecutively accessed elements of the array section lattice on processor m. If x_1, x_2, and x_3 are independent points (do not lie on a straight line), then the vectors $x_2 - x_1$ and $x_3 - x_2$ form a basis for Γ_m. Recall that we view the array layout as consisting of several courses on each processor with each course consisting of k elements; this allows us to refer to each of the k columns on a processor. For the array section $A(\ell : h : s)$, let c_f be the first column in which an element is accessed and let c_l be the last column in which an element is accessed. Let z_f be some element accessed in column c_f and let z_l be some element accessed in column c_l by a processor. Let x^{prev} denote the element accessed immediately before x in lexicographic order on a processor, and x^{next} denote the element accessed immediately after x in linear order on a processor. We do not discuss the case where z_f and z_f^{next} (or z_f^{prev}) are in the same column. This case is handled separately and is easily detected by our technique.

Theorem 7. *The set of points $\{z_f^{prev}, z_f, z_f^{next}\}$ generate a basis of Γ_m.*

Proof. From Theorem 6, the set of points $\{z_f^{prev}, z_f, z_f^{next}\}$ generate a basis of Γ_m if there are no lattice points in the triangle enclosing them and if they are independent. By construction, these are consecutive points in the lattice Γ_m and therefore, there no lattice points in the triangle (if any) enclosing them. Suppose these are not independent, *i.e.*, they lie on a straight line. This implies one of the following two cases:

Case (a): $\text{Column}(z_f^{prev}) < \text{Column}(z_f) < \text{Column}(z_f^{next})$.
Case (b): $\text{Column}(z_f^{next}) < \text{Column}(z_f) < \text{Column}(z_f^{prev})$.

Neither of these cases hold, since $\text{Column}(z_f) = c_f$ is the first column on processor m in which any element is accessed. Therefore, the three points are independent. Hence the result. $\square$

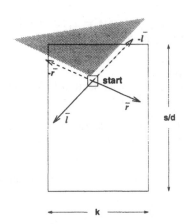

Fig. 4. No lattice point is a non-positive linear combinations of basis vectors

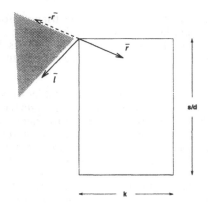

Fig. 5. No lattice points in region spanned by vectors **l** and **-r**

Similarly, the set of points $\{z_1^{prev}, z_1, z_1^{next}\}$ also generate a basis of Γ_m. We use the set $\{z_f^{prev}, z_f, z_f^{next}\}$. We refer to the vector $z_f - z_f^{prev}$ as $\mathbf{l} = (l_1, l_2)$ and the vector $z_f^{next} - z$ as $\mathbf{r} = (r_1, r_2)$. Again by construction, $l_1 > 0$, $r_2 > 0$, $l_2 < 0$ and $r_1 \geq 0$. This is illustrated in Fig. 3 on p. 5.

4.1 Basis Determination Algorithm

In order to obtain a basis for the lattice, we need to find three points belonging to the lattice not on a straight line such that the triangle formed by them contains no other lattice point. Chatterjee *et al.* [3] suggested a way to locate lattice points by solving linear Diophantine equation for each column with accessed elements. For details on their derivation refer [3]. The smallest solution of each of these solvable equations gives the smallest array element accessed in the corresponding column on a processor. Using this we show that we can obtain a basis for an array section lattice which generates the smallest element in each column that belongs to Γ_m by solving only two linear Diophantine equations.

The first two consecutive points accessed on a given column and the first point accessed on the next solvable column form a triangle that contains no other points.

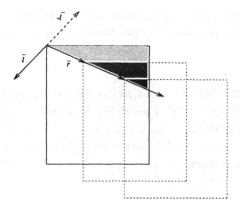

Fig. 6. No lattice points in region spanned by vectors -**l** and **r**

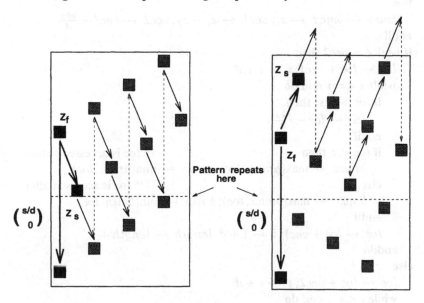

Fig. 7. Starting points in the columns generated by the vectors $\left(\frac{s}{d}, 0\right)$ and $z_s - z_f$.

Again, let c_f be the first column in which an element is accessed on a processor. Let z_f be the first element accessed in column c_f. Since the access pattern on a given processor repeats after $\frac{pks}{\text{GCD}(s,pk)}$ elements, the point accessed immediately after z_f in column c_f is $z_f + \frac{pks}{\text{GCD}(s,pk)}$. Now if c_s is the second column in which an element is accessed on the processor, and z_s is the first element accessed in it, then without loss of generality $z_f, z_f + \frac{pks}{\text{GCD}(s,pk)}$ and z_s form a basis for the array section lattice. Hence the vectors $\left(\frac{s}{d}, 0\right)$ and $z_s - z_f$ form a pair of basis vectors of the array section lattice.

The elements z_f and z_s can be obtained by solving the first two solvable Diophantine equations in the algorithm (Lines 4 and 6) shown in Fig. 8. Fig. 7 shows the basis vectors generated as explained above whereas Fig. 8 gives an outline of how the new basis

Input: Layout parameters (p, k), regular section $(\ell : h : s)$, processor number m.

Output: *start* address, *end* address, length, basis vectors $\mathbf{r} = (r_1, r_2)$ and $\mathbf{l} = (l_1, l_2)$
    for m.

Method:

1    $(d, x, y) \leftarrow$ EXTENDED-EUCLID(s, pk); $length \leftarrow 2$; $start \leftarrow h + 1$

2    $amax \leftarrow -1$; $bmin \leftarrow \frac{pks}{d}$; $i \leftarrow d\lceil \frac{km - \ell}{d} \rceil$; $i\_end \leftarrow km - \ell + k - 1$

3   **if** $i > i\_end$ **then return** $\perp, \perp, 0, \perp, \perp, \perp, \perp$ /* No element */

4    $amin \leftarrow bmax \leftarrow z_f \leftarrow \ell + \frac{s}{d}(ix + pk\lceil \frac{-ix}{pk} \rceil)$; $i \leftarrow i + d$

5   **if** $i > i\_end$ **then return** $z_f, z_f, 1, \perp, \perp, \perp, \perp$ /* One element */

6    $z_s \leftarrow \ell + \frac{s}{d}(ix + pk\lceil \frac{-ix}{pk} \rceil)$

7   **if** $z_s < z_f$ **then**

8       $amin \leftarrow amax \leftarrow z_s$; $vec2 \leftarrow z_s - z_f$; $vec1 \leftarrow \frac{pks}{d} + vec2$

9   **else**

10      $bmin \leftarrow bmax \leftarrow z_s$; $vec1 \leftarrow z_s - z_f$; $vec2 \leftarrow vec2 - \frac{pks}{d}$

11   **endif**

12   **if** $vec1 <= vec2$ **then**

13      $loc \leftarrow loc + vec1$; $i \leftarrow i + d$

14   **while** $i <= i\_end$ **do**

15   **if** $loc > last$ **then**

16          $loc \leftarrow loc - \frac{pks}{d}$

17   **endif**

18   **if** $loc < z$ **then**   /* loc is accessed before z */

19          $amax \leftarrow \max(amax, loc)$; $amin \leftarrow \min(amin, loc)$

20   **else**   /* loc is accessed after z */

21          $bmax \leftarrow \max(bmax, loc)$; $bmin \leftarrow \min(bmin, loc)$

22   **endif**

23        $loc \leftarrow loc + vec1$; $i \leftarrow i + d$; $length \leftarrow length + 1$

24   **enddo**

25   **else**

26      $loc \leftarrow loc + vec2$; $i \leftarrow i + d$

27   **while** $i <= i\_end$ **do**

28   **if** $loc < first$ **then**

29          $loc \leftarrow loc + \frac{pks}{d}$

30   **endif**

31   **if** $loc < z$ **then**   /* loc is accessed before z */

32          $amax \leftarrow \max(amax, loc)$; $amin \leftarrow \min(amin, loc)$

33   **else**   /* loc is accessed after z */

34          $bmax \leftarrow \max(bmax, loc)$; $bmin \leftarrow \min(bmin, loc)$

35   **endif**

36        $loc \leftarrow loc + vec2$; $i \leftarrow i + d$; $length \leftarrow length + 1$

37   **enddo**

38   **endif**

39   COMPUTE_VECTORS $z_f, p, k, s, d, amin, amax, bmin, bmax$

40   **return** $start, end, length - 1, l_1, l_2, r_1, r_2$

Fig. 8. Algorithm for determining basis vectors

Input: $z_f, p, k, s, d, amin, amax, bmin, bmax$.

Output: The *start* memory location, *end* memory location and the basis

vectors $\mathbf{r} = (r_1, r_2)$ and $\mathbf{l} = (l_1, l_2)$ for processor m.

Method:

1   **if** $amin = z_f$ **and** $amax = -1$ **then**   /* above is empty */

2      $l_1 \leftarrow \lfloor \frac{z_f}{pk} \rfloor + \frac{s}{d} - \lfloor \frac{bmax}{pk} \rfloor$; $l_2 \leftarrow z_f \bmod k - bmax \bmod k$

3      $r_1 \leftarrow \lfloor \frac{bmin}{pk} \rfloor - \lfloor \frac{z_f}{pk} \rfloor$; $r_2 \leftarrow bmin \bmod k - z_f \bmod k$

4   **else if** $bmin = \frac{pks}{d}$ **and** $bmax = z_f$ **then**   /* below is empty */

5      $l_1 \leftarrow \lfloor \frac{z_f}{pk} \rfloor - \lfloor \frac{amax}{pk} \rfloor$; $l_2 \leftarrow z_f \bmod k - amax \bmod k$

6      $r_1 \leftarrow \lfloor \frac{amin}{pk} \rfloor + \frac{s}{d} - \lfloor \frac{z_f}{pk} \rfloor$; $r_2 \leftarrow amin \bmod k - z_f \bmod k$

7   **else**   /* above & below not empty */

8      $l_1 \leftarrow \lfloor \frac{z_f}{pk} \rfloor - \lfloor \frac{amax}{pk} \rfloor$; $l_2 \leftarrow z_f \bmod k - amax \bmod k$

9      $r_1 \leftarrow \lfloor \frac{bmin}{pk} \rfloor - \lfloor \frac{z_f}{pk} \rfloor$; $r_2 \leftarrow bmin \bmod k - z_f \bmod k$

10   **endif**

11   start $\leftarrow amin$

12   end $\leftarrow bmax$

13   **return** $start, end, l_1, l_2, r_1, r_2$

Fig. 9. COMPUTE_VECTORS subroutine for basis vectors determination algorithm

vectors could be used to access the smallest array element accessed in each column for the case where $\mathbf{z}_s$ lies on a course above or below $\mathbf{z}_f$. Our basis determination algorithm works as follows. First we use the new basis to walk through the lattice to enumerate all the points on the lattice before the pattern starts to repeat. Then we use these points to locate the three independent points $\mathbf{z}_f^{\text{prev}}$, $\mathbf{z}_f$, $\mathbf{z}_f^{\text{next}}$ that form a triangle that contains no other lattice point. Using these three points we obtain the new basis of the lattice which we use to walk through the lattice in lexicographic order. Thus, we now need to solve only two Diophantine equations to generate the basis of the array section lattice that enumerates the points accessed in lexicographic order. This new basis determination algorithm performs substantially better than that proposed by Kennedy *et al.* for large values of k.

4.2 Extremal Basis Vectors

In this section, we show that the basis vectors generated by our algorithm in Fig. 8 form an extremal set of basis vectors.

Theorem 8. *The lattice Γ_m (the projection of the array section lattice on processor m) contains only those points which are non-negative integer linear combinations of the basis vectors $\mathbf{l}$ and $\mathbf{r}$.*

Proof. Let $\mathbf{z}$ be the starting point of the lattice Γ_m. As $\mathbf{r}$ and $\mathbf{l}$ are the basis vectors of the lattice, any point $\mathbf{q}$ belonging to the lattice can be written as

$$\mathbf{q} = \mathbf{z} + v_1 \mathbf{l} + v_2 \mathbf{r}$$

where $\mathbf{r} = (r_1, r_2)$ and $\mathbf{l} = (l_1, l_2)$. Also, $l_1 > 0, l_2 < 0, r_1 \geq 0$ and $r_2 > 0$ by construction. Suppose $\mathbf{q} \in \Gamma_m$ and that either one or both of v_1 and v_2 are negative integers. There are two cases to consider:

Case (1): $(v_1 < 0$ and $v_2 < 0)$ $v_1 l_1 + v_2 r_1 < 0$

As both v_1 and v_2 are negative, it is clear from Fig. 4 that $\mathbf{q}$ lies in the region above the start element $\mathbf{z}$. This contradicts our earlier assumption that $\mathbf{z}$ is the start element on processor m. Hence, $v_1 < 0$ and $v_2 < 0$ cannot be true.

Case (2): $(v_1 < 0$ or $v_2 < 0)$

Without loss of generality we assume that the start element $\mathbf{z}$ on a processor lies in the first non-empty column.

Let $v_1 \geq 0$ and $v_2 < 0$. As shown in Fig. 5, $\mathbf{q}$ lies in the region to the left of $\mathbf{z}$ since $v_1 l_2 + v_2 r_2 < 0$. This contradicts our assumption that $\mathbf{q} \in \Gamma_m$. Hence $v_1 \geq 0$ and $v_2 < 0$ cannot be true.

If $v_1 < 0$ and $v_2 \geq 0$, then the next element accessed after the origin is either $\mathbf{z} + \mathbf{r}$ or $\mathbf{z} + \mathbf{r} - \mathbf{l}$. If the next accessed element of Γ_m is $\mathbf{z} + \mathbf{r} - \mathbf{l}$, then this point should be located on a course above $\mathbf{z}$ or on a course below $\mathbf{z}$. If this element is located on a course above $\mathbf{z}$, it would not be a point in the lattice Γ_m. If this element is located on a course below $\mathbf{z}$, then this element is lexicographically closer to $\mathbf{z}$ than the point $\mathbf{z} + \mathbf{r}$ which is impossible (due to the construction of $\mathbf{r}$). By the above arguments (as can be seen in Fig. 6), we have shown that the next element accessed after $\mathbf{z}$ can only be $\mathbf{z} + \mathbf{r}$. A repeated application of the above argument rules out the presence of a lattice point in the shaded regions in Fig. 6. If $\mathbf{z}$ is not in the first accessed column on processor m, similar reasoning can be used for the vector $\mathbf{l}$. Hence, the result. □

4.3 Improvements to the algorithm

If $s < k$, it is sufficient to find only $s + 1$ lattice points instead of k lattice points (as in [9]) in order to derive the basis vectors. Our implementation uses this idea. Line 1 of the algorithm in Fig. 8 is the extended Euclid step which requires $O(\log min(s, pk))$ time. Lines 2 thru 40 require $O(min(s, k))$ time. Thus, the basis generation part of our algorithm is $O(\log min(s, pk) + min(s, k))$; the basis generation portion of the algorithm in Kennedy *et al.* [9] is $O(\log min(s, pk) + k)$. We note that the address enumeration part of both the algorithms is $O(k)$. Experiments have shown that the basis determination part dominates the total time in practice. Thus, our algorithm is superior to that of Kennedy *et al.* [9].

5 Address Sequence Generation by Lattice Enumeration

As mentioned earlier, we will treat the global address space as a two dimensional space, and each element of an array $A(i)$ has an address of the form $(x, y) = (i \text{ div } pk, i \bmod pk)$ in this space. We refer to the two-dimensional view of an array A as A_{2D}. The sequence of the array elements accessed (course by course) in a processor can be obtained by strip mining the loop corresponding to $A(\ell : h : s)$ with a strip length of pk and appropriately restricting the inner loop limits. In the following analysis we assume that $\ell = 0$ and $h = N - 1$. At the end of this section we will show how the code generated for $A(0 : N - 1 : s)$ can be used to generate the code for $A(\ell : h : s)$. The code for the HPF array section $A(0 : N - 1 : s)$ that iterates over all the points in the two dimensional space shown in Fig. 1(a) could be written as follows:

```
do i = 0, ⌊ N-1/pk ⌋
  do j = 0, pk - 1
    A_2D(i, j) = ·······
  end do
end do
```

We apply a loop transformation to the above loop nest to obtain the points of the lattice. Since the access pattern repeats after the first $\left(\frac{s}{d}\right)$ courses, we limit the outer loop in the above loop nest to iterate over the first $\left(\frac{s}{d}\right)$ courses only. In this case the global address of the first element allocated to the processor memory is mk, where m is the processor number. So in order to obtain the sequence of local addresses on processor m, we need to apply the loop transformation to the following modified code:

```
do i = 0, (s/d − 1)
    do j = mk, mk + k − 1
        A2D[i, j] = ···
    end do
end do
```

The basis matrix for the lattice as derived in the last section is $B = \begin{bmatrix} l_1 & r_1 \\ l_2 & r_2 \end{bmatrix}$. Hence the transformation matrix T is of the form

$$T = B^{-1} = \frac{1}{\Delta} \begin{bmatrix} r_2 & -r_1 \\ -l_2 & l_1 \end{bmatrix},$$

where $\Delta = l_1 r_2 - l_2 r_1 = s$ (since $l_1 > 0, r_1 \geq 0, l_2 \leq 0$, and $r_2 > 0$). The loop bounds can be written as follows:

$$\begin{bmatrix} -1 & 0 \\ 1 & 0 \\ 0 & -1 \\ 0 & 1 \end{bmatrix} \begin{bmatrix} i \\ j \end{bmatrix} \leq \begin{bmatrix} 0 \\ \frac{s}{d} - 1 \\ -mk \\ mk + k - 1 \end{bmatrix} \implies \begin{bmatrix} -1 & 0 \\ 1 & 0 \\ 0 & -1 \\ 0 & 1 \end{bmatrix} BB^{-1} \begin{bmatrix} i \\ j \end{bmatrix} \leq \begin{bmatrix} 0 \\ \frac{s}{d} - 1 \\ -mk \\ mk + k - 1 \end{bmatrix}$$

$$\begin{bmatrix} -1 & 0 \\ 1 & 0 \\ 0 & -1 \\ 0 & 1 \end{bmatrix} \begin{bmatrix} l_1 & r_1 \\ l_2 & r_2 \end{bmatrix} \begin{bmatrix} u \\ v \end{bmatrix} \leq \begin{bmatrix} 0 \\ \frac{s}{d} - 1 \\ -mk \\ mk + k - 1 \end{bmatrix}$$

where $\begin{bmatrix} u \\ v \end{bmatrix} = B^{-1} \begin{bmatrix} i \\ j \end{bmatrix}$ and u and v are integers. Therefore, $\begin{bmatrix} i \\ j \end{bmatrix} = \begin{bmatrix} l_1 u + r_1 v \\ l_2 u + r_2 v \end{bmatrix}$. We now use Fourier-Motzkin elimination [17] on the following system of inequalities to solve for integral u and v:

$$-l_1 u - r_1 v \leq 0$$

$$l_1 u + r_1 v \leq \frac{s}{d} - 1$$

$$-l_2 u - r_2 v \leq -mk$$

$$l_2 u + r_2 v \leq mk + k - 1$$

If $r_1 > 0$ we have the following inequalities for u and v:

$$\left\lceil \frac{(-mk - k + 1)r_1}{s} \right\rceil \leq u \leq \left\lfloor \frac{(\frac{s}{d} - 1)r_2 - mkr_1}{s} \right\rfloor$$

$$\left\lceil \max\left(\frac{mk - ul_2}{r_2}, \frac{-ul_1}{r_1} \right) \right\rceil \leq v \leq \left\lfloor \min\left(\frac{mk + k - 1 - ul_2}{r_2}, \frac{\frac{s}{d} - 1 - ul_1}{r_1} \right) \right\rfloor$$

The node code for processor m if $r_1 > 0$ is:

```
do u = ⌈(−mk−k+1)r₁/s⌉, ⌊(s/d−1)r₂−mkr₁/s⌋
    do v = ⌈max(mk−ul₂/r₂, −ul₁/r₁)⌉, ⌊min(mk+k−1−ul₂/r₂, s/d−1−ul₁/r₁)⌋
        A2D[l₁u + r₁v, l₂u + r₂v] = ······
    end do
end do
```

If $r_1 = 0$ we have the following inequalities for u and v:

$$0 \le u \le \frac{r_2}{s}\left(\frac{s}{d} - 1\right)$$

$$\left\lceil \frac{mk - ul_2}{r_2} \right\rceil \le v \le \left\lfloor \frac{mk + k - 1 - ul_2}{r_2} \right\rfloor$$

The node code for processor m if $r_1 = 0$ is:

do $u = 0, \frac{(\frac{s}{d}-1)r_2}{s}$

   do $v = \left\lceil \frac{mk-ul_2}{r_2} \right\rceil, \left\lfloor \frac{mk+k-1-ul_2}{r_2} \right\rfloor$

      $A_{2D}[l_1u, l_2u + r_2v] = \cdots\cdots$

   end do

end do

Example 1: Code generated for the case where $\ell = 0$, $p = 3$, $k = 4$ and $s = 11$ for processor 1. The set of addresses generated by the algorithm in Fig. 8 is $\{88, 77, 66, 55\}$. Also $z = 88$, $amin = 55$, $amax = 77$, $bmin = 132$ and $bmax = 88$. Since the *below* section is empty we execute lines 5 and 6 of the algorithm in Fig. 9. So our algorithm returns $\mathbf{l} = (1, -1)$ and $\mathbf{r} = (8, 3)$ as the basis vectors. The access pattern is shown in Fig. 10. The node code to obtain the access pattern for processor 1 is:

do $u = \left\lfloor \frac{-56}{11} \right\rfloor, \left\lfloor \frac{-2}{11} \right\rfloor$

   do $v = \left\lceil \max\left(\frac{4+u}{3}, \frac{-u}{8}\right) \right\rceil, \left\lfloor \min\left(\frac{7+u}{3}, \frac{10-u}{8}\right) \right\rfloor$

      $A_{2D}[u + 8v, -u + 3v] = \cdots\cdots$

   end do

end do

Next we show the iterations of the nested loop and the elements accessed; the elements indeed are accessed in lexicographic order.

u	$v_{lb} = \left\lceil \max\left(\frac{4+u}{3}, \frac{-u}{8}\right) \right\rceil$	$v_{ub} = \left\lfloor \min\left(\frac{7+u}{3}, \frac{10-u}{8}\right) \right\rfloor$	accessed elements
-5	1	0	
-4	1	1	$(4, 7)$
-3	1	1	$(5, 6)$
-2	1	1	$(6, 5)$
-1	1	1	$(7, 4)$

Converting the global two-dimensional address of the accessed elements to local addresses we get the local access pattern $\{19, 22, 25, 28\}$ on processor 1.

6 Optimization of Loop Enumeration: GO-LEFT and GO-RIGHT

A closer look at Fig. 10 reveals that even if we generated code that enumerates the points belonging to a family of parallel lines along the vector (l_1, l_2) by moving from one parallel line to the next along the vector (r_1, r_2), we would still access the elements in lexicographic order. Clearly, in this example, the above enumeration turns out to be more efficient than the earlier enumeration. We refer to this new method of enumeration as GO-LEFT, as we enumerate all points on a line along the vector (l_1, l_2) before we move to the next line along the other basis vector. For the same reasons, we refer to the earlier method of enumeration as GO-RIGHT. Next we show that the GO-LEFT method also enumerates elements in lexicographic order. If B (as shown in Section 5) is the basis matrix for the GO-RIGHT case then the basis for the GO-LEFT case is $B_L = \begin{bmatrix} r_1 & l_1 \\ r_2 & l_2 \end{bmatrix}$.

Processor 0				Processor 1				Processor 2			
⟦0⟧	1	2	3	4	5	6	7	8	9	10	⟦11⟧
12	13	14	15	16	17	18	19	20	21	⟦22⟧	23
24	25	26	27	28	29	30	31	32	⟦33⟧	34	35
36	37	38	39	40	41	42	43	⟦44⟧	45	46	47
48	49	50	51	52	53	54	⟦55⟧	56	57	58	59
60	61	62	63	64	65	⟦66⟧	67	68	69	70	71
72	73	74	75	76	⟦77⟧	78	79	80	81	82	83
84	85	86	87	⟦88⟧	89	90	91	92	93	94	95
96	97	98	⟦99⟧	100	101	102	103	104	105	106	107
108	109	⟦110⟧	111	112	113	114	115	116	117	118	119
120	⟦121⟧	122	123	124	125	126	127	128	129	130	131
⟦132⟧	133	134	135	136	137	138	139	140	141	142	⟦143⟧

Fig. 10. Global addresses of the accessed elements of array A along with the 2-dimensional view for the case $p = 3$, $k = 4$ and $s = 11$.

Hence the transformation matrix in the GO-LEFT case is $B_L{}^{-1}$. Next, we show that for the pair of basis vectors obtained using the algorithm shown in Fig. 8, the GO-LEFT scheme is always legal.

Theorem 9. *Given a point $\mathbf{q}$ belonging to the lattice Γ_m and a pair of extremal basis vectors $\mathbf{l}$ and $\mathbf{r}$ obtained using the algorithm in Fig. 8, then on applying $B_L{}^{-1}$ as a transformation we maintain the access order.*

Proof. Since $\mathbf{l}$ and $\mathbf{r}$ are extremal basis vectors,

$$\mathbf{q} = \mathbf{z} + v_1\mathbf{l} + v_2\mathbf{r}$$

where $\mathbf{z}$ is the starting point of Γ_m and v_1 and v_2 are positive integers. So $\mathbf{q}^{next}$ could either be $\mathbf{q} + \mathbf{r}$ or $\mathbf{q} + \mathbf{l}$ or $\mathbf{q} + \mathbf{l} + \mathbf{r}$.

Let us assume that $\mathbf{q} + \mathbf{r} \in \Gamma_m$ and $\mathbf{q} + \mathbf{l} \in \Gamma_m$. This implies that $\mathbf{q} + \mathbf{r} + \mathbf{l} \in \Gamma_m$. With this assumption we can have the two following cases,

Case 1: $\mathbf{q} + \mathbf{r}$ is lexicographically closer to $\mathbf{q}$ than $\mathbf{q} + \mathbf{l}$.
Case 2: $\mathbf{q} + \mathbf{l}$ is lexicographically closer to $\mathbf{q}$ than $\mathbf{q} + \mathbf{r}$.

In Case 1, $\mathbf{q} + \mathbf{l}$ is lexicographically closer to $\mathbf{q}$ than $\mathbf{q} + \mathbf{r}$. So it should be clear that $\mathbf{q} + \mathbf{r}$ should be lexicographically closer to $\mathbf{q} + \mathbf{l}$ than to $\mathbf{q}$, which is impossible (due to the construction of $\mathbf{r}$ and $\mathbf{l}$). Hence our assumption that $\mathbf{q} + \mathbf{r} \in \Gamma_m$ and $\mathbf{q} + \mathbf{l} \in \Gamma_m$ is not true. A similar argument can be used to show that out initial assumption is incorrect for Case 2 also.

From the above arguments, we conclude that given the starting point of Γ_m, we maintain the lexicographic order of the points accessed by repeatedly adding $\mathbf{l}$ until we run out of Γ_m and then add a $\mathbf{r}$ and continue adding $\mathbf{l}$ until we run out of Γ_m again and so on. So the access order does not change on using B_L as the basis matrix, *i.e.*, applying $B_L{}^{-1}$ as the transformation. □

From the above theorem it is clear that GO-LEFT is always legal for the pair of basis vectors obtained using the algorithm shown in Fig. 8.
    The loop nest for $r_1 \neq 0$ is:

$$\textbf{do}\ u = \left\lceil \tfrac{mkl_1}{s} \right\rceil, \left\lfloor \frac{(\frac{s}{d}-1)(-l_2)+(mk+k-1)l_1}{s} \right\rfloor$$

$$\textbf{do}\ v = \left\lceil \max\left(\frac{(mk+k-1)-ur_2}{l_2}, \frac{-ur_1}{l_1} \right) \right\rceil, \left\lfloor \min\left(\frac{mk-ur_2}{l_2}, \frac{\frac{s}{d}-1-ur_1}{l_1} \right) \right\rfloor$$

$$A_{2D}[r_1 u + l_1 v, r_2 u + l_2 v] = \cdots\cdots$$

$$\textbf{end do}$$
$$\textbf{end do}$$

The node code for processor m if $r_1 = 0$ is:

$$\textbf{do}\ u = \left\lceil \tfrac{mkl_1}{s} \right\rceil, \left\lfloor \frac{(\frac{s}{d}-1)(-l_2)+(mk+k-1)l_1}{s} \right\rfloor$$

$$\textbf{do}\ v = \left\lceil \max\left(\frac{(mk+k-1)-ur_2}{l_2}, 0 \right) \right\rceil, \left\lfloor \min\left(\frac{mk-ur_2}{l_2}, \frac{\frac{s}{d}-1}{l_1} \right) \right\rfloor$$

$$A_{2D}[l_1 v, r_2 u + l_2 v] = \cdots\cdots$$

$$\textbf{end do}$$
$$\textbf{end do}$$

Next, we need to decide when it is beneficial to use GO-LEFT. The amount of work that needs to be done to evaluate the inner loop bounds is the same for each outer loop iteration in both the enumeration methods. So an enumeration that results in fewer outer loop iterations is the scheme of choice. The number of elements accessed per line in the two cases is a function of the block size k and second components of the basis vectors. If $r_2 \leq -l_2$, we use GO-RIGHT; else, we use GO-LEFT.

Example 2: Code generated for the case where $\ell = 0$, $p = 3$, $k = 4$ and $s = 11$ for processor 1 when we choose to GO-LEFT. The basis vectors obtained by running through the algorithms shown in Fig. 8 are $\mathbf{l} = (1, -1)$ and $\mathbf{r} = (8, 3)$. Hence the resulting node code for processor 1 is:

$$\textbf{do}\ u = \left\lceil \tfrac{4}{11} \right\rceil, \left\lfloor \tfrac{17}{11} \right\rfloor$$

$$\textbf{do}\ v = \max(3u - 7, -8u), \min(3u - 4, 10 - 8u)$$

$$A_{2D}[8u + v, 3u - v] = \cdots\cdots$$

$$\textbf{end do}$$
$$\textbf{end do}$$

Here we observe that unlike the previous example, we scan all the elements along a single line rather than 4 different lines. Clearly in this case going left is the better choice.

6.1 Implementation

We observe from the example in Sections 5 and 6 that the code generated for GO-RIGHT enumerates the points that belong to a family of parallel lines, *i.e.*, along the vector $\mathbf{r}$, by moving from one parallel line to the next within the family along the vector $\mathbf{l}$ and the code generated for GO-LEFT enumerates the points that belong to a family of parallel lines along the vector $\mathbf{l}$, by moving from one parallel line to the next within the family along the vector $\mathbf{r}$. So in the code derived in Section 5, the outer loop iterates over the set of parallel lines while the inner loop iterates over all the elements accessed in each line on a given processor.

From the previous example it can be seen that we may scan a few empty lines (*i.e.*, lines on which no element is accessed) in the beginning and the end. This can be avoided by evaluating a tighter lower bound for the outer loop using the *start* and *end* elements evaluated in the algorithm shown in Fig. 8. The start line u_{start} and end line u_{end} can be evaluated as follows (using GO-RIGHT enumeration scheme):

$$l_1 u_{start} + r_1 v_{start} = start\ \text{div}\ pk - \ell\ \text{div}\ pk$$

$$l_2 u_{start} + r_2 v_{start} = start\ \text{mod}\ pk - \ell\ \text{mod}\ pk$$

$$\text{Hence,}\quad u_{start} = \frac{r_2(start\ \text{div}\ pk - \ell\ \text{div}\ pk) - r_1(start\ \text{mod}\ pk - \ell\ \text{mod}\ pk)}{s};$$

$$u_{end} = \frac{r_2(end \text{ div } pk - \ell \text{ div } pk) - r_1(end \bmod pk - \ell \bmod pk)}{s}.$$

The inner loop of the node code evaluates the start element for each iteration of the outer loop *i.e.*, each line traversed. In our implementation of the loop enumeration we use the start element of the previous line traversed to obtain the start element of the next line. This eliminates the expensive integer divisions involved in evaluating the start elements on the different lines. A simple algorithm for GO-RIGHT followed by us is given below.

1. Scan all the elements on the first line (u_{start}), starting at the *start* element and then adding **r** until there are no more elements on this processor.
2. From the previous start add **l** and then add **r** as many times as necessary till you get back onto the processor space. The element thus obtained is the start for the new line. Starting at this element keep adding **r** until you run out of the processor space. Repeat this until the line immediately before the last line (u_{end}).
3. Obtain the start point on the last line as before. Scan all the elements along the line from the start by adding **r** until you reach the *end* element.

The algorithm for GO-LEFT is given below.

1. Scan all the elements on the first line (u_{start}), starting at the *start* element and then adding **l** until there are no more elements on this processor.
2. From the previous start add **r** and then add **l** as many times as necessary till you get back onto the processor space. The element thus obtained is the start for the new line. Starting at this element keep adding **l** until you run out of the processor space. Repeat this until the line immediately before the last line (u_{end}).
3. Obtain the start point on the last line as before. Scan all the elements along the line from the start by adding **l** until you reach the *end* element.

7 Experimental Results

We performed experiments on our pattern generation algorithm on a Sun Sparcstation 10. We used the acc compiler using the -fast optimization switch; the function gettimeofday() was used to measure time. When computing time for 32 processors, we timed the code that computes the access pattern for each processor, and report the maximum time over all processors. We experimented with block sizes in powers of 2 ranging from 4 to 1024 for 32 processors. The total times for the two different implementations ("Right" and "Zigzag") of the algorithm in [9] and our algorithm include basis and table generation times. Tables 1(a)–1(c) show the total times for the above three algorithms and the total time for pattern generation for the algorithm proposed by Chatterjee *et al.* [3] (referred to as "Sort" in the tables). For very small block sizes, all the methods have comparable performance. At block sizes from 16 onward, our solution outperforms the other three. For higher block sizes, our pattern generation algorithm performs 2 to 9 times faster than the two Rice [9] algorithms. For larger block sizes, if $s < k$, our algorithm is 6 to 9 times faster than the Rice algorithms because of the need to find $s + 1$ lattice points, instead of k lattice points, in order to find the basis vectors. In addition, for larger block sizes, experiments indicate that address enumeration time (given the basis vectors) for our algorithm is less than that of [9]. From our choice of enumeration, we decide to use GO-LEFT for $s = pk - 1$ and use GO-RIGHT for $s = pk + 1$. Since the algorithms in [9] do not exploit this enumeration choice, our algorithm performs significantly better. In addition, our algorithm is 13 to 60 times faster than the approach of Chatterjee *et al.* [3] for large block sizes.

8 Summary and Conclusions

The success of data parallel languages such as High Performance Fortran and Fortran D critically depends on efficient compiler and runtime support. In this paper we presented efficient compiler algorithms for generating local memory access patterns and interprocessor communication sets for the various processors (node code) given the alignment of arrays to a template and a CYCLIC(k) distribution of the template onto the processors. Our solution is based on viewing the access sequence as an integer lattice, and involves the derivation of a suitable set of basis vectors for the lattice. The basis vector determination algorithm is $O(\log min(s, pk) + min(s, k))$ and requires finding $min(s + 1, k)$ points in the lattice. Kennedy *et al.*'s algorithm for basis determination is $O(\log min(s, pk) + k)$ and requires finding $2k - 1$ points in the lattice. Our loop nest based technique used for address enumeration chooses the best strategy as a function of the basis vectors, unlike [9]. Experimental results comparing the times for our basis determination technique and that of Kennedy *et al.* shows that our solution is 2 to 9 times faster for large block sizes. Experiments on several platforms indicate the efficacy of our approach. Work is in progress on the problem of incremental generation of access sequences and communication sets.

Acknowlegdments We thank Nenad Nedeljkovic, Ajay Sethi and Arun Venkatachar for their comments on an earlier draft of this paper.

References

1. A. Ancourt, F. Coelho, F. Irigoin and R. Keryell. A linear algebra framework for static HPF code distribution. In *Proc. of the 4th Workshop on Compilers for Parallel Computers*, Delft, The Netherlands, December 1993.
2. B. Chapman, P. Mehrotra, and H. Zima. Programming in Vienna Fortran. *Scientific Programming*, 1(1):31–50, Fall 1992.
3. S. Chatterjee, J. R. Gilbert, F. J. E. Long, R. Schreiber, and S.-H. Teng. Generating local addresses and communication sets for data parallel programs. In *Proc. of ACM Symposium on Principles and Practices of Parallel Programming*, pages 149–158, May 1993.
4. G. Fox, S. Hiranandani, K. Kennedy, C. Koelbel, U. Kremer, C. Tseng, and M. Wu. Fortran D Language Specification. Technical Report CRPC-TR90079, Rice University, Dec. 1990.
5. P. M. Gruber and C. G. Lekkerkerker. *Geometry of numbers*. North-Holland Mathematical Library Volume 37, North-Holland, Amsterdam, 1987 (Second Edition).
6. S. K. S. Gupta, S. D. Kaushik, C.-H. Huang, and P. Sadayappan. On compiling array expressions for efficient execution on distributed-memory machines. Technical Report OSU-CISRC-94-TR19, The Ohio State University, April 1994.
7. High Performance Fortran Forum. High Performance Fortran language specification. *Scientific Programming*, 2(1-2):1–170, 1993.
8. S. Hiranandani, K. Kennedy, J. Mellor-Crummey, and A. Sethi. Compilation techniques for block-cyclic distributions. In *Proc. ACM Intl. Conf. Supercomputing*, July 1994.
9. K. Kennedy, N. Nedeljkovic, and A. Sethi. A linear-time algorithm for computing the memory access sequence in data-parallel programs. In *Proc. of Fifth ACM SIGPLAN Symposium on Principles and Practice of Parallel Programming*, Santa Barbara, CA, July 1995.
10. C. Koelbel. Compile-time generation of communication for scientific programs. In *Supercomputing '91*, pages 101–110, Nov. 1991.
11. C. Koelbel, D. Loveman, R. Schreiber, G. Steele, and M. Zosel. *High Performance Fortran Handbook*. The MIT Press, 1994.
12. J. Ramanujam. Non-unimodular transformations of nested loops. In *Proc. Supercomputing 92*, pages 214–223, Nov. 1992.
13. J. M. Stichnoth. Efficient compilation of array statements for private memory multicomputers. Technical Report CMU-CS-93-109, Carnegie-Mellon University, Feb. 1993.
14. A. Thirumalai and J. Ramanujam. Code generation and optimization for array statements in HPF. Technical Report ECE-TR-94-11-02, Louisiana State University, Nov. 1994.
15. A. Thirumalai and J. Ramanujam. Address sequence generation for data-parallel programs using integer lattices. Technical Report ECE-TR-95-04-03, Louisiana State University, Apr. 1995.
16. A. Thirumalai and J. Ramanujam. An efficient compile-time approach to compute address sequences in data parallel programs. In *Proc. 5th International Workshop on Compilers for Parallel Computers*, Malaga, Spain, pp. 581-605, June 1995.
17. Michael Wolfe. *High performance compilers for parallel computing*. Addison-Wesley Publishing Co., 1996.

Table 1. Times (in μs) for our technique (Loop), Right and Zigzag of Rice [9] and the Sort approach [3] on a Sun Sparcstation 10

(a) $p = 32; s = 7$ and $s = 99$

Block Size	$s = 7$				$s = 99$			
k	Loop	Right	Zigzag	Sort	Loop	Right	Zigzag	Sort
4	26	23	23	27	51	47	47	51
8	34	34	35	47	61	59	59	71
16	33	31	32	67	56	58	58	93
32	36	46	47	152	56	64	64	170
64	47	81	84	460	77	91	98	469
128	41	126	131	844	100	149	152	865
256	53	236	245	1639	118	256	276	1657
512	80	465	487	3224	122	454	471	3226
1024	108	892	940	6373	159	889	918	6397

(b) $p = 32; s = k - 1$ and $s = k + 1$

Block Size	$s = k - 1$				$s = k + 1$			
k	Loop	Right	Zigzag	Sort	Loop	Right	Zigzag	Sort
4	24	23	23	27	35	31	31	35
8	34	34	35	47	29	26	27	39
16	29	33	33	69	32	33	33	69
32	36	45	45	154	38	45	45	155
64	69	84	87	460	70	82	90	459
128	97	142	141	853	98	135	144	853
256˙	154	256	255	1642	155	240	255	1642
512	268	487	486	3220	269	459	487	3220
1024	498	946	945	6377	499	894	947	6377

(c) $p = 32; s = pk - 1$ and $s = pk + 1$

Block Size	$s = pk - 1$				$s = pk + 1$			
k	Loop	Right	Zigzag	Sort	Loop	Right	Zigzag	Sort
4	23	21	21	25	21	19	19	23
8	24	24	24	37	22	22	23	35
16	28	31	31	67	25	29	30	65
32	34	45	45	155	31	43	44	147
64	48	73	72	450	43	72	74	449
128	75	128	128	844	67	129	132	845
256	129	240	239	1633	114	243	250	1638
512	237	465	464	3211	210	475	487	3222
1024	455	912	911	6369	403	935	960	6394

Compiling Array Statements for Efficient Execution on Distributed-Memory Machines: Two-level Mappings

S. D. Kaushik, C.-H. Huang, and P. Sadayappan

Dept. of Computer and Information Science,
The Ohio State University,
Columbus, OH 43210.
{kaushik,chh,saday}@cis.ohio-state.edu

Abstract. In languages such as High Performance Fortran (HPF), array statements are used for expressing data parallelism. In compiling array statements for distributed-memory machines, efficient enumeration of local index sets and communication sets is important. The virtual processor approach, among several other methods, has been proposed for efficient enumeration of these index sets. In this paper, using simple mathematical properties of regular sections, we extend the virtual processor approach to address the memory allocation and index set enumeration problems for array statements involving arrays mapped using the two-level mapping supported by HPF. Performance results on the Cray T3D are presented to demonstrate the efficacy of the extensions and identify various tradeoffs associated with the proposed method.

1   Introduction

Languages such as High Performance Fortran (HPF) [3, 10], Fortran-D [4], and Vienna Fortran [1] provide a programming environment which allows annotation of single address space programs with distribution directives specifying the mapping of arrays to processors of a distributed-memory machine. For compiling the array statement:

$$B(l_2 : u_2 : s_2) = \mathcal{F}(A(l_1 : u_1 : s_1)) \tag{1}$$

in the context of an HPF program, a processor must determine which elements of $B(l_2 : u_s : s_2)$ are allocated to it, the order in which these elements are located in its local memory, the processors from which it must receive non-local data and the elements corresponding to the non-local data in local memory. Efficient methods for enumerating the following index sets for a processor p reduces the associated indexing overhead.

- Local index set of p: set of local indices of the array elements of B on p whose values will be evaluated by the array statement.
- Send processor set of p: set of processors to which p has to send data.
- Send data index set of p to processor q: set of local indices of the array elements resident on p but needed by processor q.

- Receive processor set of p: set of processors from which p has to receive data.
- Receive data index set of p from processor q: set of local indices of the array elements needed by p but resident on q.

If the arrays have only block or cyclic distributions, then the data index sets and the processor sets can be characterized using regular sections for closed forms [5, 9]. However, for the general block-cyclic distribution, closed form characterization of these sets using simple regular sections is not possible.

Several approaches have addressed the efficient execution of array statements involving block-cyclically distributed arrays. A *virtual processor approach* to efficiently enumerate the data index sets and processor sets is presented in [5, 7]. The approach is based on viewing a block-cyclic distribution as a block (or cyclic) distribution on a set of virtual processors, which are cyclically (or block-wise) mapped to physical processors. Closed forms in terms of regular sections are developed for the index sets for block and cyclically distributed arrays. These closed forms are then used in the virtual processor domain for efficient enumeration of the communication and local index sets. The problem of local index set identification was addressed by Chatterjee et al. [2] using a *finite-state machine* (FSM) to traverse the local index space. Stichnoth et al. [11] address the problem of index set and processor set identification. The formulation proposed has similarities to an instance of the virtual processor approach. The implementation of the Fortran-D compiler at Rice University is being extended to handle arrays with block-cyclic distributions [6]. An approach similar to the FSM approach [2] for determining the local memory access sequence is used and efficient algorithms for computing the FSM for frequently occuring cases are presented. A linear-time algorithm for constructing the FSM which improves the asymptotic complexity of the algorithm presented in [6] was presented in [8]. The key idea behind the construction is the recognition that the local index space for a block-cyclically distributed array is an integer lattice spanned by a basis of dimensionality two. An approach for the local index set and communication set enumeration based on identifying the basis for the integer lattice and exploiting pattern repetition in the send and receive sets was presented in [12].

HPF supports a two-level mapping of data arrays to the abstract processor grid. The language introduces a Cartesian grid referred to as a *template*. Arrays are *aligned* to the template at a stride and initial offset and the templates are *distributed* onto the abstract processor array using regular data distributions. For instance, an array $A(0 : N - 1)$ can be aligned with a template T such that $A(i)$ is aligned with $T(ci + a)$. Due to the distribution of the template, the array A is divided into subarrays, each subarray residing in the local memory of one of the processors. The portion of the array A located in a processor's local memory is referred to as A_loc in the SPMD node program generated by an HPF compiler. If memory for the local array is allocated for all the template cells mapped to the processor, then the introduction of a non-unit stride c in the array-template mapping creates "holes" in the array A_loc of each processor. These holes should be removed by allocating memory only for those template cells with which array elements are aligned. The indexing methods presented in [5, 7] are directly applicable for an array statement involving arrays which are distributed using a two-level mapping when existence of holes in the local memory arrays is acceptable. Suppose array $A(m_1 : n_1)$ is aligned with template T_1 using a stride c_1 and an offset a_1 and $B(m_2 : n_2)$ is aligned with template T_2 using a stride c_2 and an offset a_2. The array statement in Eq. 1, is equivalent to the following array statement in terms of the sections of the templates T_1 and T_2:

$$T_2(a_2 + l_2 c_2 : a_2 + u_2 c_2 : s_2 c_2) = \mathcal{F}(T_1(a_1 + l_1 c_1 : a_1 + u_1 c_1 : s_1 c_1)) \quad (2)$$

The methods developed in [5, 7], when applied to the array statement in Eq. 2, will construct the data index sets and local index sets in terms of the local indices of T_1 and T_2. In this paper, we extend the virtual processor approach to enumerate the index sets for array statements involving arrays distributed using two-level mappings with non-unit alignment stride and for which memory allocation with hole compression is performed. The hole compression affects *how* the array elements are placed in the local memory of a processor and not *which* array elements are mapped to a processor. Thus, the processor send and receive sets derived using the techniques for one-level mappings for the array statement in Eq. 2 are equal to those for the two-level mappings. We concern ourselves only with the enumeration of the modified data and local index sets.

In this paper, we will refer to two forms of allocation for the local array in a processor's memory - one with hole compression and the other without. Since the local array allocation without hole-compression is equivalent to allocating memory for the portion of the distributed template T assigned to a processor, we refer to such a local array as T_loc. The local array allocation with hole-compression corresponds to storing only elements of the array A and such a local array is referred to as A_loc. The compression of holes in the local arrays complicates the indexing for the array statement. Specifically two problems have to be addressed:

- *Local Memory Allocation:* Determining the exact amount of the memory to be allocated for the distributed array in a processor's local memory.
- *Index Translation:* The closed forms developed in [5, 7] for data and local index sets are expressed as simple regular sections in terms of indices of T_loc. New closed forms in terms of indices of A_loc for enumerating the send and receive data index sets and the local index set are to be developed.

To illustrate the above problems consider the array section $A(0 : 36 : 3)$ of the array $A(0 : 37)$ aligned with template T at a stride three and offset zero as shown in Fig. 1. The distributed array is shown in Fig. 1(a) and the elements belonging to the array section $A(0 : 36 : 3)$ are marked with boxes. Local memory allocation performed on basis of the template is shown in Fig. 1(b), while allocation with hole-compression performed is shown in Fig. 1(c). After hole compression, each processor will have a different number of array elements mapped to it and ideally a different amount of local memory should be allocated per processor. The local index set on processor 0 corresponding to the array section $A(0 : 36 : 3)$ consists of the indices $\{0, 6, 21, 27\}$ in T_loc and the indices $\{0, 2, 7, 9\}$ in A_loc.

Processor 0		Processor 1		Processor 2		Processor 3	
0	1	2		3		4	5
6		7		8	9	10	
11		12	13	14		15	
16	17	18		19		20	21
22		23		24	25	26	
27		28	29	30		31	
32	33	34		35		36	37

(a)

T_loc Index t	0	1	2	3	4	5	6	7	8	9	10	11	12	13	14	15	...
P_0	0		1			6			11			16			17		...
P_1			2		7				12		13				18		...
P_2				3		8			9				14			19	...
P_3	4			5			10				15			20		21	...

(b)

A_loc Index	0	1	2	3	4	5	6	7	8	9
P_0	0	1	6	11	16	17	22	27	32	33
P_1	2	7	12	13	18	23	28	29	34	
P_2	3	8	9	14	19	24	25	30	35	
P_3	4	5	10	15	20	21	26	31	36	37

(c)

Fig. 1. Memory allocation for array mapped using a two-level mapping with non-unit stride.

Our approach for extending the virtual processor approach is based on the observations:

1. For block and cyclically distributed templates the set of array elements mapped to a processor can be represented by a simple regular section.
2. The array indices represented by a simple regular section in the uncompressed array T_loc can be represented by a simple regular section in the compressed array A_loc.

For block and cyclically distributed templates, the first observation facilitates the memory allocation for each processor. It also helps construct a scheme for mapping a template cell with which an array element is aligned to an element of the compressed array. Furthermore, for block and cyclically distributed templates, the data index sets and local index sets for the array statement in Eq. 2, can be expressed as simple regular sections of the uncompressed local arrays T_1_loc and T_2_loc. From the second observation, it follows that a similar scheme can be used for array statements involving arrays mapped using a two-level mapping with non-unit stride and a compressed local memory allocation.

In this paper, for block and cyclically distributed templates, using the regular section characterization of the template cells mapped to a processor p, we develop a regular section characterization of the array elements located on p. This regular section characterization is used to determine the exact amount of memory to be allocated for the distributed array on processor p. Next, we develop a procedure for performing the translation between the local template section and the local array section. Using this procedure, the parameterized closed forms for the send and receive data index sets and the local index sets for one-level mappings developed in [5, 7] can be extended to those for the two-level mappings. Using the results for the block and cyclically distributed arrays, the virtual processor approach for handling block-cyclically distributed templates is extended. The key idea in the extension is to look upon the local array as a two-dimensional array with one dimension corresponding to the virtual processor index and the other corresponding to the local index space of the virtual processor.

This paper is organized as follows. Closed forms expressions for identifying the size of memory to be allocated and a procedure for translating the data and local index sets of T_loc to obtain the corresponding sections of the compressed array A_loc are developed in Section 2. Extensions to the virtual processor approach for two-level mappings are provided in Section 3. Performance results on a Cray T3D are provided in Section 4. Section 5 provides conclusions.

2 Block and Cyclically Distributed Templates

The evaluation of the regular section characterization of the array elements mapped to a processor uses several results about the intersection, translation, expansion, and compression of regular sections. For details of these results the reader is referred to [7]. In this section, we address the memory allocation and indexing problem for block and cyclically distributed templates. Consider an array $A(m_1 : n_1)$ aligned with a template $T(q_1 : r_1)$ at a stride c and an offset a. Let the template T be distributed over P processors using either a block or a cyclic distribution. The elements of the template T assigned to a processor p due to the distribution can be represented by a regular section $T(l_p : u_p : s_p)$. where

$$l_p = pb, \quad u_p = \min(pb + b - 1, r_1), \quad s_p = 1, \quad b = \lceil \frac{r_1 - q_1 + 1}{P} \rceil,$$

if the template is distributed using a block distribution, or

$$l_p = q_1 + p, \quad u_p = r_1, \quad s_p = P,$$

if the template is distributed using a cyclic distribution.

2.1 Memory Allocation

Array $A(m_1 : n_1)$ is aligned with T using an offset a and a stride c. Thus the regular section $T(a + m_1c : a + n_1c : c)$ consists of all the template cells to which elements of A are aligned. Without loss of generality, we assume that $a + m_1c \geq q_1$ and $a + n_1c \leq r_1$. Since $T(l_p : u_p : s_p)$ consists of all the template cells located on processor p, all the template cells on processor p which have array elements aligned with them are given by

$$T(l_{pa} : u_{pa} : s_{pa}) = T(l_p : u_p : s_p) \cap T(a + m_1c : a + n_1c : c).$$

The array elements in the array section $A(l : u : s)$ are aligned with the template cells in the template section $T(a + lc : a + uc : sc)$. Thus if $T(l : u : s)$ represents a section of the template T such that an array element is aligned with every element of $T(l : u : s)$, then the array section corresponding to this template section is given by $A\left(\frac{l-a}{c} : \frac{u-a}{c} : \frac{s}{c}\right)$. It is necessary that c divides s; otherwise it is not possible that every element of $T(l : u : s)$ has an element of the array aligned with it. Now all the template cells on processor p which have array elements aligned with them are included in $T(l_{pa} : u_{pa} : s_{pa})$. Thus $A\left(\frac{l_{pa}-a}{c} : \frac{u_{pa}-a}{c} : \frac{s_{pa}}{c}\right)$ consists of all the array elements located on processor p. We have obtained a regular section characterization of the elements of A located on processor p due to the two-level distribution of array A.

The memory allocation problem can be solved in a straightforward fashion. Since the array section $A\left(\frac{l_{pa}-a}{c} : \frac{u_{pa}-a}{c} : \frac{s_{pa}}{c}\right)$ consists of

$$N_{loc} = \left\lfloor \left(\frac{u_{pa}-a}{c} - \frac{l_{pa}-a}{c}\right) / \left(\frac{s_{pa}}{c}\right) \right\rfloor$$

elements, it is sufficient to allocate the compressed local array on processor p as $A\_loc(0 : N_{loc} - 1)$. The array element $A(\frac{l_{pa}-a}{c} + i\frac{s_{pa}}{c})$ is mapped to the element $A\_loc(i)$. Let $l_a = \frac{l_{pa}-a}{c}$, $u_a = \frac{u_{pa}-a}{c}$, and $s_a = \frac{s_{pa}}{c}$. We refer to l_a, u_a and s_a as the *distribution parameters* of the array A on processor p. The values of the distribution parameters are used in the index translation between a local template section and a local array section as shown in Section 2.2.

2.2 Index Set Translation

For block and cyclically distributed arrays, the local index sets and data index sets for the array statement in Eq. 2, can be expressed as simple regular sections of the uncompressed local array T_loc [5]. We now show that a regular section in T_loc corresponds to a regular section in A_loc for block and cyclically distributed templates and develop a strategy for performing the translation. Let $T\_loc(l' : u' : s')$ be the local template section representing a data or local index set. Depending on the distribution of the template, $T\_loc(l' : u' : s')$ will correspond to a global template $T(l : u : s)$. For a block distribution where $b = \lceil \frac{r_1 - q_1 + 1}{P} \rceil$, we have:

$$l = l' + q_1 + pb, \quad u = u' + q_1 + pb, \quad s = s'.$$

For the cyclically distributed template we have

$$l = q_1 + p + l'P, \quad u = q_1 + p + u'P, \quad s = s'P$$

Furthermore, the techniques developed in [5, 7] guarantee that every cell in the template section $T(l : u : s)$ has an array element aligned with it. Thus the section of array elements represented by the template cells is $A\left(\frac{l-a}{c} : \frac{u-a}{c} : \frac{s}{c}\right)$. As shown in Section 2.1, the array section $A(l_a : u_a : s_a)$ consists of all the elements of array A located on processor p. Thus the array section $A\left(\frac{l-a}{c} : \frac{u-a}{c} : \frac{s}{c}\right)$ must be a subsection of this section. The first element of $A\left(\frac{l-a}{c} : \frac{u-a}{c} : \frac{s}{c}\right)$ has the same global index as $A(l_a + ic_a)$, where $i = \frac{\frac{l-a}{c} - l_a}{c_a}$. Since $A(l_a + ic_a)$ is mapped to $A\_loc(i)$, the first element of the section $A\left(\frac{l-a}{c} : \frac{u-a}{c} : \frac{s}{c}\right)$ will map to $A\_loc\left(\frac{\frac{l-a}{c} - l_a}{c_a}\right)$. The stride between consecutive elements of $A\left(\frac{l-a}{c} : \frac{u-a}{c} : \frac{s}{c}\right)$ in A_loc is $\frac{s/c}{c_a} = \frac{s}{c_a c}$. Thus the local template section, $T\_loc(l' : u' : s')$ will map to the following section of the compressed array A_loc:

$$T\_loc(l' : u' : s') \rightarrow A\_loc\left(\frac{\frac{l-a}{c} - l_a}{c_a} : \frac{\frac{u-a}{c} - l_a}{c_a} : \frac{s}{c_a c}\right)$$

Once the distribution parameters l_a and c_a for the distributed array A have been evaluated, any data index set or local index set in T_loc can be translated to obtain the corresponding index set in A_loc. The above formulas are instantiated to obtain specific closed forms for block and cyclically distributed templates in [7].

3 Virtual Processor Approach for Two-Level Mappings

We now extend the memory allocation scheme and the index translation scheme to block-cyclically distributed templates using the virtual processor approach. For details of the virtual processor approach the reader is referred to [5, 7]. The virtual processor approach is based on viewing a block-cyclic distribution as a block (or cyclic) distribution on a set of virtual processors, which are cyclically (or block-wise) mapped to the physical processors. These views are referred to as *virtual-block* or *virtual-cyclic* views depending on whether a block or cyclic distribution of the array on the virtual processors is used. The closed forms developed for the block and cyclically distributed arrays, are used for computing the data and local index sets in the local index space of the virtual processors, and then extended to the local index space of the physical processor to which the virtual processor is mapped. For one-level mappings, this translation between the local index spaces of the virtual processor and physical processor can be performed in a straightforward fashion. However, for arrays mapped using a two-level mapping with non-unit stride and local memory allocation performed only for array elements, this translation is not straightforward.

For arrays distributed using one-level mapping, under the virtual block view, the block-cyclic distribution is viewed as a block distribution in the virtual processor domain, i.e., one block of array elements is owned by each virtual processor. The virtual processors are then cyclically distributed among the physical processors. Thus the total number of elements per virtual processor, except possibly the last virtual processor, is identical for all the virtual processors. The offset of the origin of the index space of a virtual processor v into the index space of a physical processor p to which it is mapped is equal to the number of virtual processors mapped to p with index lower than v, times the number of array elements per virtual processor. The stride in the virtual processor index space does not change in the physical processor index space. For two-level mappings with hole-compression, this translation is not straightforward, as the number of array elements per virtual processor need not be identical for all the virtual processors. Hence, while the results developed in the previous section, for memory allocation and index translation for block and cyclically distributed templates can be directly applied to obtain the corresponding index sets in the compressed local array of each virtual processor, a scheme for translating these sections to the compressed index space of the physical processors is required.

A similar problem arises for the virtual-cyclic view. Under the virtual cyclic view, a block-cyclic distribution is viewed as a cyclic distribution on a set of virtual processors which are distributed in a block-wise fashion onto the physical processors. Thus the origin of the index space of a virtual processor v in the index space of the physical processor p to which it is mapped is fixed at v div b for a $cyclic(b)$ distribution. Furthermore, a unit stride between the elements in the virtual processor index space, corresponds to a fixed stride b in the physical processor index space where b is the block size of the block-cyclic distribution. Thus for one-level mappings, a regular section in the virtual processor local index space can be translated to the physical processor local index space in a straightforward fashion. Under the two-level mapping with hole compression, each virtual processor may not have the same number of elements or any elements at all. Hence it is possible that both the origin and the stride of the virtual processor's index space in the physical processor's space may change.

Our approach for addressing these problems is based on allocating the local array as a two-dimensional array, wherein the virtual processor index varies along one dimension and the index within the local index space of the virtual processor varies along the other dimension. We now describe the details of memory allocation and indexing for the two virtual views.

3.1 Virtual Block View

Consider an array $A(m_1 : n_1)$ aligned with a template $T(q_1 : r_1)$ at a stride c and an offset a. The template is distributed using a $cyclic(b)$ distribution onto P processors. Under the virtual block view, the array is assumed to be block distributed on $VP = \lceil \frac{r_1 - q_1 + 1}{b} \rceil$ virtual processors. The compressed local array is allocated such that the local index within the virtual processor index space varies along one dimension, while the virtual processor index varies along the other. The local memory allocation for each virtual processor is performed such that memory is allocated only for those template cells which have array elements aligned with them. The techniques developed in Section 2 can be used for performing the allocation. For instance, the two-dimensional local memory allocation for the array $A(0 : 37)$ (Fig. 1), is illustrated in Fig. 2. The two-dimensional allocation corresponds to performing a hole compression within a block. Since each virtual processor may not have equal number of array elements and since Fortran allows memory allocation for only rectangular arrays, some holes may still exist in the local array. These holes can be eliminated if a separate allocation for the exact amount of memory is performed for each virtual processor as opposed to allocating a two-dimensional array for the entire local array.

v	Proc. 0	
v_0	0	1
v_4	6	
v_8	11	
v_{12}	16	17
v_{16}	22	
v_{20}	27	
v_{24}	32	33

v	Proc. 1	
v_1	2	
v_5	7	
v_9	12	13
v_{13}	18	
v_{17}	23	
v_{21}	28	29
v_{25}	34	

v	Proc. 2	
v_2	3	
v_6	8	9
v_{10}	14	
v_{14}	19	
v_{18}	24	25
v_{22}	30	
v_{26}	35	

v	Proc. 3	
v_3	4	5
v_7	10	
v_{11}	15	
v_{15}	20	21
v_{19}	26	
v_{23}	31	
v_{27}	36	37

Fig. 2. Two-dimensional Local Memory Allocation for array mapped using a two-level mapping with non-unit stride under virtual block view.

Under the virtual block view each block of template cells corresponds to a virtual processor. Due to the stride and offset in the alignment, it is possible that virtual processors mapped to a physical processor do not have any array elements mapped to them. Clearly no memory should be allocated for these virtual processors. Depending on the relationship between the alignment stride and the block size, it is possible to allocate memory only for the virtual processors which have array elements mapped to them. If $c \le b$, then each virtual processor $v \in ((cm_1 + a) \text{ div } b : (cn_1 + a) \text{ div } b)$ has at least one element of the array mapped to it. Let $v_l = (cm_1 + a) \text{ div } b$ and $v_u = (cn_1 + a) \text{ div } b$. Since the set of virtual processors on a processor p is $(p : VP : P)$, the virtual processors on p with array elements allocated to them are

$$(v_l : v_u) \cap (p : VP : P) = (\max(v_l + (p - v_l) \bmod P, p) : \min(v_u, VP) : P). \quad (3)$$

We allocate memory for these virtual processors and use the techniques from Section 2 to determine the allocation for each virtual processor. If $c > b$, then each virtual processor has at most one element each and we allocate memory for every virtual processor. However, this case does not occur frequently and the virtual cyclic view would be used instead of the virtual block view.

Given a template section, $T(l : u : s)$ the characterization of the active virtual processors on a processor, can be performed using techniques similar to those presented in [5, 7]. Depending on the set of virtual processor for which memory has been allocated, some translation of this set of active virtual processors will have to be performed [7]. We now describe the allocation scheme for the virtual-cyclic view.

3.2 Virtual Cyclic View

Consider array $A(m_1 : n_1)$ aligned with a template $T(q_1 : r_1)$ at a stride c and an offset a. The template T is distributed using a $cyclic(b)$ distribution. Under a virtual-cyclic view, the template is assumed to have a cyclic distribution on $VP = \min(P*b, r_1 - q_1 + 1)$ virtual processors, which are block-wise distributed to P processors. The local array is allocated such that dimension zero corresponds to the local index within virtual processor index space, while dimension one corresponds to the virtual processor index. For instance the two-dimensional local memory allocation for the array $A(0 : 37)$(Fig. 1), is illustrated in Fig. 3.

Proc. 0				Proc. 1			Proc. 2				Proc. 3			
v_0	0	16	32	v_4	12	28	v_8	8	24		v_{12}	4	20	36
v_1	11	27		v_5	7	23	v_9	3	19	35	v_{13}	15	31	
v_2	6	22		v_6	2	18	34	v_{10}	14	30		v_{14}	10	26	
v_3	1	17	33	v_7	13	29	v_{11}	9	25		v_{15}	5	21	

Fig. 3. Two-dimensional Local Memory Allocation for array mapped using a two-level mapping with non-unit stride under the virtual cyclic view.

Similar to the virtual block view, it is possible that some virtual processors under the virtual cyclic view may not have any array elements mapped to them. The template cells located on a virtual processor v have indices $(q_1 + v : r_1 : P*b)$. Thus if v has any array elements mapped to it, then the intersection $(q_1 + v : r_1 : P * b) \cap (a + m_1 c : a + n_1 c : c)$ is not empty. Hence based on on the requirement for the non-empty intersection of two regular sections, a virtual processor v may have array elements mapped to it if $\gcd(c, P * b)|(q_1 + v - a - m_1 c)$ [7]. The first virtual processor v_f on a processor p can be found by noting that the $v_f \in (p * b : p * b + b - 1)$ and $\gcd(c, P * b)|(q_1 + v_f - a - m_1 c)$. Thus we have

$$v_f = p * b + ((-p * b - q_1 + a + m_1 c) \bmod \gcd(c, P * b))$$

The set of virtual processors on p to which array elements are possibly mapped is thus given by the regular section

$$(v_f : \min(p * b + b - 1, a + n_1 c - q_1) : \gcd(c, P * b)) \tag{4}$$

Local memory allocation is performed only for these virtual processors.

Given a template section, $T(\tilde{l} : \tilde{u} : c * s)$ the characterization of the active virtual processors on a processor, i.e., the set of virtual processors to which elements of the template section are mapped, can be performed using techniques similar to those presented in [5, 7]. Depending on the set of virtual processors for which memory has been allocated, some translation and compression of this set of active virtual processors will need to be performed [7]. We now evaluate the potential merits of the local memory allocation scheme with hole compression.

4 Performance Results

In this section, we present experimental results of the performance evaluation of the virtual processor approach for handling arrays mapped using a two-level mapping with non-unit stride and for the memory allocation scheme with hole compression. The experiments were performed on a 32-processor Cray T3D. The time required by each processor to execute the node program for an array assignment statement was measured and the maximum time among all processors reported. Times were measured using the rtclock() wall clock timer.

The goals of the performance measurement were to determine how the local memory allocation and indexing strategy with hole-compression performed with respect to that without hole compression. The basis for the performance comparison were the following performance metrics:

- *Table generation time:* The time for the generation of the index sets for the execution of the array statement.
- *Memory allocation time:* The time for determining the size of memory to be allocated for local memory arrays. While memory allocation for the storage scheme without hole compression is straightforward, memory allocation for the indexing scheme with hole compression involves some additional computation at allocation time.
- *Memory wastage:* The amount of memory which would be allocated under the two schemes but would never be used. This is the number of holes introduced due to allocating memory for template cells which do not have any array elements aligned with them.
- *Array statement execution time:* The time for the execution of the array statement. The modification of the storage pattern in the local array due to hole-compression leads to a change in the spatial locality characteristics for the array statement execution.

Hole compression leads to a modification of only the local index sets and send and receive data index sets. The processor sets for the execution of the array statement are unchanged. Hence, to evaluate the performance of the hole-compression technique we consider an array statement which would lead to no communication and focus only on the enumeration of the local index sets. The conclusions derived from the performance results for the local index sets, would be equally applicable to the schemes for enumerating the send and receive data

Table 1. Comparison of table generation times for indexing schemes for $cyclic(720)$ distributed template using virtual block view. $P = 32, M = 23040$.

s	$c = 2$		$c = 3$		$c = 5$		$c = 6$		$c = 8$	
	Non	Com	Non	Com	Non	Com	Non	Com	Non	Com
1	6	17	9	28	14	41	15	49	19	64
2	11	30	15	50	23	79	27	96	34	124
3	16	42	21	72	33	116	39	138	50	184
4	19	57	27	97	43	154	50	186	66	251
5	23	70	33	116	52	189	62	228	82	299
6	27	82	39	138	63	231	74	269	98	357
8	35	103	51	186	82	301	98	369	129	477

Non - without hole compression, Com - with hole compression

index sets. To reduce the number of independent parameters, we measured various times for the execution of an array assignment statement of the form:

$$A(0 : M * s - 1 : s) = x * A(0 : M * s - 1 : s) + y.$$

The numbers x and y are double precision floating point numbers (eight bytes). The double precision floating point array A is aligned with a template T with offset zero $(a = 0)$ and a stride $c > 0$. The template T is distributed using a $cyclic(b)$ distribution. Thus the equivalent array statement in the template index space is

$$T(0 : M * c * s - 1 : c * s) = x * T(0 : M * c * s - 1 : c * s) + y.$$

The parameter M gives the number of elements in the array section. For our experiments, we kept the number of active elements M fixed at 23040 and $P = 32$ processors were used. The varying parameters were: block size b, alignment stride c, and the array statement stride s. The empirical values for the memory allocation time, the table generation time, memory wastage, and array statement execution time were obtained for various values of b, c, and s. The values of the block size b considered were equally spaced between the block $(b = \lceil \frac{M*c*s}{P} \rceil)$ and the cyclic $(b = 1)$ distribution. All the reported times are in microseconds. Due to lack of space we present only the performance figures for a $cyclic(720)$ distribution with virtual block view. For other performance figures refer to [7].

Table 1 presents the table generation times. For all the data points considered it can be observed that the table generation time for the indexing scheme with hole-compression is greater than that for the scheme without hole-compression. This behavior is expected as the indexing scheme with hole compression has to perform an addition index translation from the local template index space to the compressed local array index space for every virtual processor which owns elements of the array section. For the block-cyclic distributions under the virtual block view the table generation time increases with increasing array section stride s and alignment stride c. This follows by noting that the template is $T(0 : M * c * s - 1)$ and under the virtual block view, a block of size b belongs to a virtual processor. Thus for a fixed block size b, the number of virtual processors mapped to a processor increases with increasing s and c and the table generation overhead increases with increasing number of virtual processors.

Table 2. Comparison of execution times for indexing schemes for $cyclic(720)$ distributed template using virtual block view. $P = 32, M = 23040$.

s	$c = 2$		$c = 3$		$c = 5$		$c = 6$		$c = 8$	
	Non	Com	Non	Com	Non	Com	Non	Com	Non	Com
1	92	60	155	58	193	60	195	60	194	64
2	191	95	195	98	201	103	203	106	205	112
3	194	157	201	161	208	170	213	172	220	182
4	194	197	203	202	218	215	220	218	234	235
5	201	199	208	208	223	222	235	226	244	241
6	203	202	213	206	235	224	242	242	251	252
8	205	208	220	210	245	245	252	257	286	292

Non - without hole compression, Com - with hole compression

Table 2 presents the execution times for the statement. The Cray T3D has a direct mapped data cache with 256 lines of size 32 bytes each. Thus four double floating point numbers should fit into a single cache line and spatial locality will be exploited when the effective access stride is less than four. For the virtual block view and for the data points at which the stride s is less than four the indexing scheme with hole compression performs better than that without hole compression. The smaller the stride, the greater the improvement. This follows by noting that the effective access stride for the allocation scheme with hole compression is s while that for the allocation scheme without hole compression is $c * s$. When the effective stride is greater that four both schemes have nearly equal performance.

For all the cases except for the case in which the template is distributed using a $cyclic(80)$ distribution, under the local memory allocation scheme with hole compression, no memory is wasted. The amount of memory wasted under the allocation scheme with no hole compression increases with alignment stride c and section stride s. This follows by noting that the template has $M * c * s$ elements and the array has $M * s$ elements. The percentage of memory wasted is $\frac{c-1}{c} * 100\%$.

We now present the memory allocation time for the indexing scheme with hole compression. This represents the time for performing the additional computation for identifying the section of array elements mapped to a virtual processor and evaluating the distribution parameters for each virtual processor. This computation is performed at compile-time for statically allocated arrays and at run-time for dynamically allocated arrays. Since the memory allocation time for the allocation scheme without hole-compression is negligible, we present only the allocation times for the allocation scheme with hole compression. (Tables 3 presents the memory allocation times. For the block-cyclic distribution under a

Table 3. Memory allocation time for allocation schemes with hole-compression for $cyclic(720)$ distributed template using virtual block view. $P = 32, M = 23040$.

s	$c = 2$	$c = 3$	$c = 5$	$c = 6$	$c = 8$
1	24	35	46	52	63
2	34	52	75	89	136
3	22	69	104	120	155
4	51	88	113	155	283
5	56	105	163	270	250
6	66	121	189	309	379
8	80	238	336	381	470

virtual block-view, the allocation time increases with increasing stride s and c. This increase occurs primarily due to an increase in the number of virtual processors $\left(\frac{M*c*s}{b}\right)$ which leads to an increase in the total amount of computation to be performed.

On the basis of the presented data we can make the following conclusions about the allocation and indexing schemes with and without hole compression.

- The allocation scheme with hole compression requires greater allocation time than the scheme without hole compression. However, for most the cases considered, the hole-compression scheme eliminates nearly all holes and leads to significant savings in memory usage.
- The table generation time for the execution of the array statement for the indexing scheme with hole-compression is greater than that for the scheme without hole-compression. However, the scheme with hole compression often has better execution times than that without hole compression primarily due to better spatial locality.

5 Conclusions

In this paper, we have addressed the memory allocation and index set enumeration problem for arrays mapped using a two-level mapping with non-unit stride to a set of processors. Using simple mathematical properties of regular sections we identified the regular section of array elements mapped to a processor for block and cyclically distributed arrays. This regular section characterization identifies the exact amount of the memory required on the processor for block and cyclically distributed arrays. Furthermore, it facilitates the index set translation from the local template space to the local array space. We have identified methods for extending these techniques to the virtual processor approach for handling block-cyclically distributed arrays. Extensive experimental evaluation on the Cray T3D demonstrates that while the scheme with hole will require additional computation at compile time, it leads to significant savings in memory used. Furthermore, while the table generation times for the execution of the array statement, would increase, the time for execution of the array statement is reduced due to an improvement in spatial locality.

Acknowledgments

We would like to thank the Ohio Supercomputer Center for access to the Cray T3D.

References

1. B. M. Chapman, P. Mehrotra, and H. P. Zima. Vienna Fortran – a Fortran language extension for distributed memory multiprocessors. In J. Saltz and P. Mehrotra, editors, *Language, Compilers and Runtime Environments for Distributed Memory Machines*, pages 39–62. 1992.
2. S. Chatterjee, J. R. Gilbert, F. J. E. Long, R. Schreiber, and S.-H. Teng. Generating local addresses and communication sets for data parallel programs. In *Proc. of ACM Symposium on Principles and Practices of Parallel Programming*, pages 149–158, May 1993.
3. High Performance Fortran Forum. High Performance Fortran language specification version 1.0. Technical Report CRPC-TR92225, Rice University, May 1993.
4. G. Fox, S. Hiranandani, K. Kennedy, C. Koelbel, U. Kremer, C.-W. Tseng, and M. Wu. Fortran-D language specification. Technical Report TR-91-170, Dept. of Computer Science, Rice University, Dec. 1991.
5. S. K. S. Gupta, S. D. Kaushik, C.-H. Huang, and P. Sadayappan. On compiling array expressions for efficient execution on distributed-memory machines. *Journal of Parallel and Distributed Computing*, 1995. To appear.
6. S. Hiranandani, K. Kennedy, J. Mellor-Crummey, and A. Sethi. Advanced compilation techniques for Fortran D. Technical Report CRPC-TR-93-338, Center for Research on Parallel Computation, Rice University, Oct. 1993.
7. S. D. Kaushik. *Compile-Time and Run-Time Strategies for Array Statement Execution on Distributed-Memory Machines.* PhD thesis, Department of Computer and Information Science, The Ohio State University, Mar. 1995.
8. K. Kennedy, N. Nedeljkovic', and A. Sethi. A linear-time algorithm for computing the memory access sequence in data-parallel programs. Technical Report CRPC-TR94485-S, Center for Research on Parallel Computation, Rice University, Oct. 1994.
9. C. Koelbel. Compile-time generation of communication for scientific programs. In *Proc. of Supercomputing '91*, pages 101–110, Nov. 1991.
10. C. Koelbel, D. Loveman, R. Schreiber, G. Steele, and M. Zosel. *High Performance Fortran Handbook.* The MIT Press, 1994.
11. J. M. Stichnoth. Efficient compilation of array statements for private memory multicomputers. Technical Report CMU-CS-93-109, School of Computer Science, Carnegie Mellon University, Feb. 1993.
12. A. Thirumalai and J. Ramanujam. Code generation and optimization for array statments in HPF. Technical Report TR-94-12-02, Dept. of Electrical and Computer Engineering, Louisiana State University, 1994.

A Communication Backend for Parallel Language Compilers

James M. Stichnoth and Thomas Gross

Carnegie Mellon University

Abstract. Generating good communication code is an important issue for all compilers targeting parallel or distributed systems. However, different compilers for the same parallel system usually implement the communication generation routines (e.g., message buffer packing) independently and from scratch. As a result, these compilers either pursue a simple approach (calling a standard runtime library), which does not do justice to the capabilities of the system, or they incur high development costs. This paper describes a way to separate the communication issues from other compilation aspects (e.g., determining the distribution of data and computation). This organization places the responsibility for communication issues with the *communication backend*, and this backend can be shared by different compilers. It produces code that is customized for each communication step, based on the exact data distribution and the characteristics of the target parallel system. This approach has several advantages: (1) The communication backend can be shared by multiple compilers, e.g., for different parallel languages. (2) The communication backend provides a way to integrate regular and irregular communication, e.g., as required to deal with irregular codes. (3) Retargeting of a parallel compiler is simplified, since the communication backend deals with the interface to communication (and the single-node compiler). (4) The communication backend can optimize the code, e.g., by constant folding and constant propagation. Code produced by the communication backend is always at least as fast as library code, but the customization has the potential to significantly improve performance depending on what information is known at compile time.

1 Introduction

The standard model for compiling a program written in a parallel language like HPF for a specific parallel system involves two distinct phases. The first phase deals with all parallel aspects of mapping the application onto a parallel system. This phase starts with a program without explicit communication, and produces a program with explicit communication operations. Depending on the implementation strategy of the compiler, this phase may consist of multiple sub-phases, rely on user directives or hints, or use trace information. The second phase of the compiler deals with all single-node aspects of a program, including producing object code.

When mapping an application onto a parallel or distributed system, there exists a wide choice of mappings, and one of the research topics in compiling for parallel systems is how to find good data and computation mappings. Ideally, a compiler finds a mapping

This research was sponsored by the Advanced Research Projects Agency/CSTO monitored by SPAWAR under contract N00039-93-C-0152 and by an Intel Graduate Fellowship.

so that there is no communication, but in practice, realistic applications include some amount of communication. These communication operations determine the scalability of a program (i.e., its efficiency when using more processors).

In this paper, we discuss an approach to deal with whatever communication a compiler decides to perform. That is, we structure the first phase of the parallelizing compiler so that generating communication operations is done by the *communication backend*. The communication backend starts with data distributions that are decided upon elsewhere. It generates code for whatever communication is required to adhere to the chosen distributions. Deciding on the distribution for an object, mapping computations onto the various processors of the system, and making tradeoffs between different distributions are all issues that are dealt with by other parts of the compilation tool chain.

The motivation for the development of this communication backend is provided by two tools developed at Carnegie Mellon. The Fx compiler [3, 11] translates a dialect of High Performance Fortran (HPF) for a variety of parallel systems and communication libraries (iWarp, PVM, Paragon/OSF, Paragon/SUNMOS, T3D). Archimedes [7] is a domain-specific compiler to support the solution of PDEs on parallel systems; its first major users are our collaborators on a Grand Challenge application in the Department of Civil Engineering at CMU. Archimedes targets iWarp and the Paragon, and a retarget to other platforms is under development.

During the development of these compilers, and during our efforts to retarget them as new parallel systems became available, we observed that producing good communication code is far from easy, even if the distributions of the data are known at compile time. Retargeting a compiler can be accomplished easily if performance is no objective, but this approach is not acceptable to our sophisticated users (who tend to point out any inefficiencies). Furthermore, we noticed that the requirements for Fx (dealing with regular computations) and Archimedes (dealing with irregular computations) are not vastly different; we discuss this point later in this paper. Although the communication requirements of these compilers differ in many details, there exists a common structure, provided that we can separate the issue of deciding on the mappings from the issue of generating communication operations. Although this decision to use a separate communication backend required revising part of the Fx compiler (which had been retargeted already to a few systems), this new structure results in a significant long-term savings. At this time, a first prototype of the communication backend is operational.

2 Problem Statement

We use the term *parallel language compiler* (or *language compiler* for short) to refer to the compiler that decides on the distribution of data and computation. Then, the communication backend processes the output of this compiler. For example, the parallel language compiler system may select different data distributions for an array A. When it is necessary to switch from one distribution to another, a specific *communication step* is required to move the data from the old distribution to conform with the new distribution. Usually, it is impossible to move all the data of A at once. Instead, a number of *communication operations* are needed. Each communication operation moves a block of A; a block may be as small as a single item. There may exist many choices to implement the communication operations, depending on the properties of target machine, like the memory system architecture [10], the interconnect topology, or the support for collective operations.

A number of applications can be expressed in a language like HPF that is based on regular array statements. A regular array statement is one like $A = B + C$ where all arrays have regular (i.e., block-cyclic) distributions. HPF allows only regular distributions (i.e., block, cyclic, and block-cyclic), but although there exists a compact (regular) representation of the communication required for such a statement, the communication operations can be quite complicated (see [8] for a discussion of this topic). A straightforward approach yields poor communication code, which directly impacts performance. To optimize the communication code, it may be possible to exploit that the number of processors is known at compile time, or that the dimensions of an array are known at compile time, etc.; in each case, it is possible to customize the communication operations.

Regular array statements are not sufficient to describe all applications of interest. Two important examples of irregularity are use of an indexing vector (e.g., $A[IA[1 : n]] = B[1 : n]$), or array operands with irregular distributions (e.g., a *mapped* distribution). Irregular distributions are not part of HPF, but are necessary for tools like Archimedes. Many other problems involve computations with indexed accesses to arrays. The communication required to deal with such problems is *irregular*, in the sense that there is no concise, regular description of how data has to be moved. As discussed later, executing such an irregular array statement requires multiple communication operations.

In summary, then, the objectives for this communication backend are (1) unify dealing with regular and irregular communication; (2) allow retargeting to different parallel or distributed systems, and allow use by multiple compilers; and (3) produce efficient communication operations.

3 Array Statements as a Communication Abstraction

When we decouple the communication generation from the source language, we must make the important decision of the method of abstracting a communication step. The set of choices forms a spectrum. At one end of the spectrum is simplicity, and at the other end is expressibility. We must find a point in this spectrum that represents a reasonable tradeoff between the two extremes.

On the "simple" end of the spectrum, communication might be represented as a simple reference of an array element. In this abstraction, the language compiler takes sequential code, extracts the individual array references, and passes the names of the individual arrays, along with the subscripts, to the communication backend. While this interface is extremely simple, the expressibility is quite lacking. There is no way to represent the movement of aggregate data structures, since data movement is expressed essentially at the element level.

On the "expressible" end of the spectrum, we could imagine passing an entire loop nest, or perhaps some sort of dataflow graph, to the communication backend. The backend would perform analysis on this loop nest or graph and try to produce optimal parallel communication code that obeyed correctness constraints imposed by, e.g., data dependences. There are two problems with this approach. First, it would be difficult to come up with a representation that could adequately express the operations allowed by the parallel language, and it might also be cumbersome for the parallel language compiler to analyze its input code and convert it to the necessary format. Second, the communication backend would be burdened with performing a great deal of analysis on the input code passed on by the parallel language compiler. This analysis would duplicate work in this compiler and is therefore beyond the scope of our effort.

As an engineering compromise, we choose the *array assignment statement* as the level of communication abstraction. An array assignment statement is a Fortran-90 style assignment involving whole arrays or array sections. An example of such a statement is $A[1 : n] = B[1 : 2n : 2]$. Such array statements allow the concise description of the communication needs of the parallel language compiler. Note that we use the format of array assignment statements, but go beyond the restrictions on distributions embraced by data-parallel languages. To support the irregular computations of a compiler like Archimedes, we must widen the class of distributions that we allow.

There are three types of array assignment statements, serving three general purposes. The first type performs local computations or initializations, as in $A[2 : n - 1] = 0$. Another example is $A = B$, where A and B are known to have the same distribution. Although this kind of statement may not involve actual communication, it still needs to be handled by the communication backend, as discussed below. The second type of assignment statement is a redistribution, such as $A = B$, where arrays A and B have different distributions. The third type, and the most general, is one that performs actual computation as well as communication, such as $A = B + C$. For this type of statement, we use the owner-computes rule, which means that we temporarily redistribute B and C to have the same distribution as A, and then perform the local computation. All three statement types are handled by the communication backend, regardless of whether communication is actually involved.

There are several reasons that motivate our choice of array statements as a communication abstraction. First, these three types of array assignment statements are powerful enough to express parallelism for some important classes of problems, and to express the communication requirements for a wide variety of computations. Array assignment statements are succinct yet highly expressive when considered in conjunction with the wide spectrum of distribution possibilities. Second, array assignment statements are far easier for a compiler to analyze than loop nests. Third, the calling interface for passing the communication requirements from the parallel language compiler to the communication backend is far simpler than other options.

Array assignment statements have another important property: they can express both regular and irregular communication. A simple array assignment statement like $A = B$, where all arrays have regular distributions, results in a regular communication pattern. When either array has an irregular distribution, irregular communication results. In addition, when there is an indexing vector present, as in $A[IA[1 : n]] = B[1 : n]$, the same kind of irregular communication results, as the communication pattern is dependent on the contents of the indexing vector IA. This kind of array statement is powerful enough to express the communication requirements of many irregular programs, such as those written for Archimedes. Our communication backend uses many of the same techniques of regular communication generation to produce the communication for irregular array statements.

If the array statement involves computation, then some part of the tool chain must generate the appropriate code for this computation. At first thought, one might argue that it should be the parallel language compiler's responsibility to deal with the computation phase of an array assignment statement. This compiler should allocate the temporaries, invoke the communication backend to move the arrays into the temporaries, and then generate the code for the local computation on each processor. However, to perform the local computation requires knowledge of the global-to-local array index mapping function, and knowledge of other features managed by the communication backend, such as the format of the runtime distribution descriptors. For this reason, the communication backend must additionally generate code to perform the computation phase. This same argument holds for the first type of array assignment statement described above (e.g., $A = B$ where both arrays have the same distribution). Even though there is no communication, only the communication backend knows the global-to-local mapping function.

The communication backend cannot do all the computation, though. Imagine for instance an HPF "independent" loop. Although the communication backend can be used to temporarily redistribute the data arrays so that they are all aligned, the loop body contains references to array elements. The loop body may include any type of computation, and it is simply infeasible to try to incorporate all computational possibilities into the communication backend. Thus the parallel language compiler must compile the loop body, including applying the local memory mapping function to the array references. The communication backend provides an interface for performing the mapping, as well as methods for attempting to minimize the number of explicit mappings that need to be performed. For example, when advancing to the next local loop iteration, the local memory indices usually just increment by one; thus the parallel language compiler need not perform explicit local memory mappings for every loop iteration.

3.1 Compiling Array Statements

Here we give an overview of the process of generating the communication for both regular and irregular array assignment statements. First, some terminology: an *array section* is a set of array elements specified by a subscript triplet $(f : l : s)$, specifying the array elements beginning with index f, going no higher than l, and with access stride s. An *ownership set* is the set of array elements owned by a particular processor, as defined by the array distribution.

Regular The canonical regular array assignment statement is $A[f : l : s] = B[f : l : s]$, where A and B have block-cyclic distributions. (Block and cyclic are special cases of block-cyclic.) We reduce the problem to determining the portion of B that a particular source processor, s, sends to a particular destination processor, d. Let OA be the ownership set for d of array A, and let OB be the ownership set for s of array B. These block-cyclic ownership sets can be expressed compactly as a disjoint union of regular sections.

The set of elements of B that are sent is the intersection of three sets: $OA \cap OB \cap (f : l : s)$. In other words, s can only send elements that it owns, that are owned by d, and that are included in the array section in the assignment statement. (If the left-hand side section is different from right-hand side section, a simple linear mapping is applied to part of the intersection.)

We have developed algorithms [9] for efficient computation of these set intersections. These algorithms form the basis of the communication generation in Fx. Significant performance benefits are seen when one or both arrays have either block or cyclic distributions, because block and cyclic ownership sets are just regular sets, rather than unions of regular sets.

Irregular Array assignment statements can also be used to express irregular communication. There are two canonical irregular array statements. The first is $A[IA[f : l : s]] = B[f : l : s]$, where A, B, and IA all have regular distributions. The second is $A = B$, where one of the arrays has an irregular distribution. The index-to-processor mapping of the irregular distribution is typically given in a map array. Because the length of the map array is the same as that of the data array, the map array must itself be distributed, usually with a regular (most often block) distribution. Analysis of these two example statements is similar, interchanging only the index array and the map array.

In this paper we will not describe details of the communication generation for irregular array assignment statements. We note, however, that the regular section intersection techniques described above form an essential part of the irregular statement analysis. The important issue is that the array assignment statement can form a communication abstraction for both regular and irregular communication.

3.2 Example

A critical part of any communication step is identifying (and collecting) the local data that must be moved to another processor. This *buffer packing* code may involve a number of costly runtime operations, e.g., modulo, division, and floor/ceiling. Fig. 1 shows the code produced for the array assignment $A[1 : n : sa] = B[1 : n : sb]$, where A has a block distribution and B has a cyclic distribution, both over "numproc" processors. In the absence of information about the parameters, we obtain code as shown.

Fig. 2 depicts the customized code for filling the buffers that can be produced by the communication backend if all the parameters are known. The value of "n" has been instantiated to 1024×1024, "numproc" is 64, and "sa" and "sb" are both 1. (The actual transfer of data after buffer packing is the same in this case, and is therefore not shown.) In this case, the buffer packing code has been significantly optimized.

3.3 Alternatives

Compilers (and users writing programs) for a parallel system have a number of options to deal with communication. We distinguish between three different approaches: libraries, the inspector model, and use of a separate backend for communication. In this section, we briefly describe the approaches and discuss their advantages and disadvantages.

Libraries A popular approach for communication generation is to design a single large library function (or perhaps a small number of functions) that generates communication for any array assignment statement. The language compiler then only needs to parse

```
/* Find: g2 = gcd(sb,numproc) = sb*x2 + numproc*y2 */
euclid(&x2, &y2, &g2, sb, numproc);
stride = (sb * numproc) / g2;
if ((cellid < numproc) && (proc < numproc)) {
  bufptr = 0;
  last = MIN(n - 1,
    sb * floor(MIN(n - 1,
                ((dest * (((n + numproc) - 1) / numproc)) +
                (((n + numproc) - 1) / numproc)) - 1) / sa));
  lmlast = floor((last - cellid) / numproc);
  lower = MAX(sb * ceil((dest * blksize) / fx_sa), cellid);
  if ((cellid % g2) == 0) {
    r = ((cellid * (x2 * sb)) / g2);
    first = lower + mod(r - lower, stride);
    lmfirst = (first - cellid) / numproc;
    for (i=lmfirst; i<=lmlast; i += sb / g2)
      buf[bufptr++] = b[i];
  }
}
```

Fig. 1. Non-customized buffer packing code.

```
bufptr = 0;
last = (dest * 16384) + 16383;
lmlast = (last - cellid) / 64;
lower = MAX(dest * 16384, cellid);
first = lower + mod(cellid - lower, 64);
lmfirst = (first - cellid) / 64;
for (i=lmfirst; i<=lmlast; i++)
  buf[bufptr++] = b[i];
```

Fig. 2. Optimized buffer packing code.

the array assignment statement and generate a parameter list to be passed to this library routine at run time. This approach suffers for a number of reasons:

- The arrays in the assignment statement could have an arbitrary number of dimensions. When generating code to pack/unpack communication buffers, we need a loop nest whose depth is proportional to the number of dimensions. This kind of variable-depth loop nest is notoriously difficult to write in C, often leading the function writer to impose arbitrary restrictions such as limiting the number of dimensions handled.
- It is extremely difficult to write a general-purpose function that efficiently handles all cases. The communication code can be significantly improved when we know certain properties of the assignment statement; e.g., the arrays all have block or cyclic distributions, the access stride of a regular section is 1, or the dimension size

is an even multiple of the number of processors over which it is distributed. In these cases and more, a general-purpose buffer-packing routine will probably generate highly suboptimal code.

– Another complication arises when the array reference mixes scalar subscripts and array sections. For example, $A[i, 1 : n]$ must be treated differently from $A[1 : n, i]$. Having to deal with this complication can be another large headache for the function writer.

– As a result of the above points, the single runtime function usually ends up a collection of many special-purpose routines. These specialized routines are usually added in an ad-hoc manner, as the need arises. As such, there exists no practical way of optimizing the communication routines. Furthermore, extra effort is spent at run time deciding which of the many special cases this statement might be.

For these reasons, we have decided against the library approach for communication generation.

Inspector Model Another approach for communication generation is based on the *inspector-executor* model, which forms the basis of the communication interface in the CHAOS runtime libraries [12]. This model is motivated by the observation that for many irregular computations, the elements of an array that participate in a communication step are often known only at runtime. So instead of attempting to compute the array elements involved in a communication step a priori, the compiler generates code that is executed before a communication step takes place. This inspector code finds out, at runtime, which array elements have to be moved to another processor. This information is then cached to save execution time in future invocations; if there has been no change in the data layout, the inspector phase can be skipped. Ruehl and Annaratone [6] extend this model to include symbolic analysis.

If absolutely no information about the communication requirements is known to the compiler (or communication backend), such an inspector-based approach may be the only option. However, in cases where such information exists, a communication backend is able to optimize at compile time, whereas an inspector-executor loop discovers this information only at runtime.

Customized Code Generation The third approach, customized code generation, involves compile-time generation of the communication code. This method can be viewed as a compile-time instantiation of the right set of communication library functions. Here, for every array assignment statement, the communication backend takes all compile-time information into account and generates a customized routine to perform the communication. Useful compile-time information includes:

– Whether the distribution of a particular array dimension is block, cyclic, or block-cyclic. Although block and cyclic distributions are just special cases of the general block-cyclic distribution, substantial performance gains are possible when a distribution is known to be either block or cyclic.

– Constant regular section (i.e., a Fortran-90 *subscript triplet*) bounds. This knowledge especially pays off when the access stride is known to be 1.

– Other distribution parameters, such as the number of processors or the block size of a block-cyclic distribution.

The main disadvantage of the customized approach over the library approach is that the customized backend is much harder to build. While it is relatively straightforward to convert an array assignment statement into a single procedure call, it is far from easy to generate customized code. This approach requires a substantial compiler framework, such as expression manipulation routines and constant folding. Nevertheless, customized code is guaranteed to be at least as good as library code, since in the worst case, one could simply generate the library routine blindly. Our communication backend takes the approach of generating customized code.

4 Details of the Communication Backend

We now discuss aspects of the design of our communication backend, which uses the customized code generation approach. The aspects discussed include details of retargeting to new parallel systems and language compilers, caching and reuse of communication patterns, and extensibility to add support for new data types and operators.

4.1 Optimization

The most critical portion of the regular communication generation routines, and the portion whose performance is most strongly affected by the code generation techniques of the communication backend, is the step of packing data into buffers. Other details, such as the actual low-level transfer of data across the communication network, are not nearly as susceptible to optimization by the communication backend and are not discussed here. The ultimate goal of the buffer packing optimization routines is to produce the simplest code to be executed at run time, thus minimizing the runtime overhead, especially overhead that occurs inside loops.

The communication generation routines for regular array assignment statements are based on algorithms derived for the most general regular array statements. To optimize these routines, the backend needs to instantiate compile-time constants and simplify the resulting expressions. We begin the optimization process by selecting the general purpose buffer-packing code segment. This first step involves making a decision regarding the code template that should serve as the basis for further optimizations. Unfortunately, there is no single master template that can be used in all cases; the choice depends on whether the distributions of the LHS and RHS arrays are block, cyclic, or the general block-cyclic. We have derived more specialized and efficient routines for when a distribution is known to be the simpler block or cyclic type; the general block-cyclic routines cannot be readily simplified to these specialized versions. Because each of the two arrays can have one of three types of distributions, the communication backend has nine possible code segments to choose from. These buffer-packing code segments are written in a completely general form, assuming that no information (e.g., array sizes, distribution block sizes, number of processors) is known at compile time.

After selecting the distribution-specific code segment, the rest of the optimizations are applied to the code: constant folding, constant/copy propagation, dead code elimination, and a new technique called interval folding.

Constant folding is integrated into the basic expression manipulation routines, which use a simple rule-based approach to find expressions susceptible to folding. To perform dead code elimination and constant/copy propagation, we form a flow graph from the buffer-packing code template, and we apply standard dataflow algorithms to the flow graph.

From a performance perspective, it could be argued that dead code elimination, constant folding, and constant/copy propagation are unnecessary, since these functions would also be performed by the optimizing C compiler that compiles the communication backend's output. However, from a software engineering point of view, these optimizations are necessary, as they help the communication backend developer identify bugs and evaluate the quality of the code being generated.

The final optimization, interval folding, is a new and simple but extremely effective optimization in the context of regular communication generation. To describe this optimization, we begin by observing that there are some variables and expressions that we know can take on only a limited range of values. For example, if the parallel system has 64 processors, we know that the *procid* variables is in the range $[0 : 63]$. As another example, even if we don't know the precise value of the distribution block size, we know it must be positive. Many expressions can be simplified based on these intervals.

We define our intervals in terms of two parameters: a lower bound and an upper bound, both of which are integer constants. A constant c has the interval $[c : c]$. We define a simple algebra for manipulating intervals across the expression operators. For example, if a has the interval $[a_l : a_h]$ and b has the interval $[b_l : b_h]$,

- $a + b$ has the interval $[a_l + b_l : a_h + b_h]$
- $a - b$ has the interval $[a_l - b_h : a_h - b_l]$
- $\max(a, b)$ has the interval $[\max(a_l, b_l) : \max(a_h, b_h)]$
- When $b_l > 0$, $\lfloor a/b \rfloor$ has the interval $[\lfloor a_l/b_h \rfloor : \lfloor a_h/b_l \rfloor]$
- Multiplication and division are slightly more complex in general, as the results depend on the sign of the input bounds.

There are two ways in which expressions can be simplified using interval information. The first involves the min and max operations. Continuing the examples above, if $a_h \leq b_l$, then $\min(a, b) = a$. Likewise, if $a_l \geq b_h$, then $\max(a, b) = a$. The second simplification occurs when the lower bound and the upper bound are equal, in which case the expression just folds to the value of the upper/lower bound. As a somewhat typical example of this case, when there are 64 processors, $\lfloor (1024 - procid)/64 \rfloor$ folds to the value 15. This particular example arises naturally as part of the computation involving a 1024-element array block-distributed over 64 processors.

Our representation of intervals (i.e., a constant lower and upper bound) could be extended in a few ways. One extension is to include a stride value as well. For example, if p has the interval $[0 : 63]$, then $2p + 1$ has the interval $[1 : 127 : 2]$. We have found at least one example, involving block-cyclic distributions, in which this extension would lead to improved output. Another extension is to allow non-constant bounds on expressions. This extension would allow more optimizations when the number of processors is not known at compile time.

4.2 Reuse

Use of the communication backend is not limited to parallelizing Fortran compilers. Any parallel language that uses arrays for bulk storage (as opposed to, say, pointer-based structures) can use the communication compiler as its communication backend. There are two aspects of reuse: targeting a different language compiler to the communication backend, and retargeting the communication backend to a different parallel or distributed system.

Retargeting to Different Architectures The communication backend is designed to produce code for a wide variety of target architectures. When we talk about different architectures, we also include architecture-independent communication interfaces such as PVM or MPI. The backend defines a set of low-level communication routines (e.g., sending/receiving a message, broadcasting a value, barrier synchronization), so that only this small set of routines needs to be rewritten when moving to a new architecture.

There is another architecture dependent aspect of the communication backend that may need to rewritten for each target system, due to efficiency concerns. This aspect is the buffer packing/unpacking routines. Although the communication backend generates portable C code for buffer packing, the single-node optimizing C compiler might not be good enough to make the most effective use of the processor. In such a system, it would be desirable to rewrite these routines as hand-coded assembly loops.

Retargeting to Different Parallel Languages One of the fundamental design goals of the communication backend is portability, i.e., the ability to support multiple parallel compilers. This is one of the novel aspects of the communication backend. We do not want to lock our work into our own (or any other) HPF-like compiler. In fact, we do not even want to limit ourselves to Fortran as a base language. Thus we have abstracted the communication generation routines into a form that, with a little effort, can be integrated into any array-based language compiler.

Because the language compiler and the communication backend need to interact at compile time, we need a set of "interface routines" that convert internal expressions back and forth between the two compilers. Expressions are represented as a binary tree whose leaves consist of constants, symbols, function calls, and array references. Other information attached to symbols includes type information, array dimension sizes, and distribution information. These interface routines, which must be rewritten for every parallel language compiler, have the job of deconstructing the expression tree of one compiler and producing a tree for the other compiler.

One low-level aspect of the interface routines deserves to be mentioned. At least one language, Fortran, is incompatible with C (the language that the communication backend generates code in), with respect to its notion of row-major versus column-major memory layout of arrays. This incompatibility is easily reconciled by the interface routines. When an array is created, the dimension size list must be reversed, and the subscript lists of array references must also be reversed.

4.3   Caching of Communication Patterns

In general, irregular communication patterns are data-dependent; thus we cannot determine until run time what they will be. The pattern is dependent on either the contents of an indexing vector or the contents of a distribution array, which describes an irregular mapping of array elements to processors. The fact that indexing vectors and distribution arrays are large and therefore distributed means that extra global communication steps are required to perform the final communication analysis. In general, each indexing vector and each irregularly distributed array incurs a need for one additional global communication step. If possible, we would like to find ways to eliminate these extra global communications.

Frequently, these indexing vectors and irregular distributions reflect the physical aspects of the problem being simulated. The physical aspects often remain unchanged over many iterations of a loop, and thus the associated distributions and indexing vector contents also remain unchanged. Therefore, repeating the communication analysis will yield the same final communication pattern. This means that the communication backend can save a significant amount of work by caching and reusing the communication pattern.

The problem for the communication backend is that it only sees one communication statement at a time, and thus has no knowledge about how indexing vectors and distribution arrays might be changing between different loop iterations. The communication backend must be certain that the data describing the communication pattern has not changed since it was last cached. One possible solution is for the communication backend to maintain copies of all relevant variables, and then check these variables to determine whether any have changed since the last execution. The problem with this solution is that there is simply too much state to be saved. For example, if the array assignment statement includes an indexing vector, the communication backend must internally save the entire contents of the vector. Furthermore, because the vector is probably distributed, each processor must check to make sure its portion of the vector has not changed, and a global reduction over these values must be performed so that all processors know whether any processor's values have changed. This is probably more work than we want to do, especially given that better alternatives exist.

To address this problem, we look at the execution of the program at a higher level than individual statements. Only the parallel language compiler has this kind of global picture, so it must help out with the caching decisions. For some programs, the parallel language compiler can determine that the physical structure of the problem, and hence the values of the communication parameters such as indexing vectors, never changes throughout the computation. For this type of communication, the parallel language compiler can direct the communication backend always to use the cached pattern (except of course during the first iteration, before the communication cache is warmed up). Other programs might be highly adaptive, where the communication pattern changes every iteration, in which case the parallel language compiler can direct the communication backend never to even bother trying to cache.

The more interesting cases fall between these two extremes. For example, slightly adaptive algorithms might refine the structure only every few iterations, or in a purely data-dependent fashion, such as when the error exceeds a certain threshold. Here, we can reuse a communication pattern most of the time, but not always. To address this issue, the parallel language compiler can add code that tracks changes to the parameters in question. For the above examples, it might simply maintain a flag telling whether or not a refinement occurred during the current iteration. This flag would be passed to the communication routine at run time to tell whether to reuse the previous communication pattern.

The language compiler has to decide at what level of granularity it will attempt to track changes to the parameters. If tests are inserted too far inside loop nests, the overhead of tracking changes might outweigh the caching benefits. On the other hand, if the language compiler is overly conservative and inserts checks too high in the loop nest, communication pattern reuse might happen less often than otherwise possible. Discussion of loop instrumentation techniques is beyond the scope of this paper.

Communication pattern reuse can also be useful for regular communication [2]. For example, while block and cyclic distributions are fairly simple to generate communication for, communication induced by the more general block-cyclic distribution can be considerably more expensive to determine. In this kind of communication pattern, caching can yield a significant performance improvement. For regular communication, it may turn out to be best for the communication backend to track all parameter changes, since there are far fewer such parameters than for irregular communication.

4.4 Extensibility

Building a standalone communication backend provides interesting challenges, primarily relating to the fact that we cannot anticipate or hope to accommodate all possible parallel language compilers. The first step in addressing this problem was to define the interface routines. Having interface routines addresses the fact that virtually all compilers use a different data structure for representing expressions than the communication backend uses.

But there is a more subtle problem. Many parallel languages will use operators (e.g., plus, minus, mod) that the communication backend does not support, or data types that the backend does not support. There is no way in general for the interface routines to handle this problem. Thus we plan to make the communication backend extensible so that code can be added to handle new operators and types.

To give a concrete example, suppose that the communication backend were written only to interface with parallel C-like languages, and that we wanted to integrate it with an HPF compiler. The backend would need to be extended to deal with Fortran's "complex" data type (disregarding the fact that the current prototype of the communication backend already treats complex as a first-class data type).

Recall that in addition to handling communication, the backend produces code to do some amount of computation as well. Extending the communication portion is fairly simple: we need only inform the backend what the size of the data type is, so that it knows how many words to move around at run time. Extending the computation portion is somewhat trickier. The user needs to provide C code that will be emitted when computation on data arrays needs to happen at run time. In the example of the complex data type, the user must provide code for performing complex additions, complex multiplications, etc. When adding a new operator, code must be provided to perform the operation on each of the data types. The code can be provided in terms of a function call, or preferably a macro.

A more ambitious goal for communication backend extensibility is to provide a mechanism for giving programmers a well-defined interface for adding new types of distributions. We are currently exploring the possibilities of adding this functionality.

5 Related Work

To our knowledge, ours is the only system that generates customized communication code at compile time for array assignment statements. The other systems described below use either the runtime library approach or the inspector-executor model for communication generation.

In terms of the low-level buffer packing algorithm, our method is closest to that of Sadayappan et al. [4]. Our method of representing ownership sets corresponds to their *virtual cyclic* ownership representation. A substantially different approach was pioneered by Chatterjee et al. [1], and improved upon by Thirumalai and Ramanujam [13], as well as Kennedy, Nedeljkovic, and Sethi [5]. This approach uses a *finite state machine* to generate tables which are used for address generation. All of these methods are applicable only for regular array assignment statements.

Most systems for irregular communication are based on the inspector-executor method. CHAOS [12] is the predominant such system; parallel programs must be converted into an inspector-executor style, and the resulting code is linked against the CHAOS runtime libraries to do the communication and memory management. The Vienna Fortran Compilation System [14] allows the specification of irregular computations, and then automatically transforms the program into a version that invokes CHAOS.

6 Concluding Remarks

Optimizing communication is important, since the communication behavior of an application has a direct impact on performance and scalability. Communication operations are on the critical path for many regular problems. Sometimes it is possible to overlap communication and computations for these problems. However, for irregular problems, any overlap is difficult or impossible to realize, since the exact details of the communication may depend on the results of the computation steps.

A separate communication backend is a practical solution for parallel compilers that map regular and irregular computations. It provides a clean abstraction between the parallel language compiler, which deals with issues like deciding on a suitable data layout and distribution of the computations, and the communication system.

A communication backend allows us to reuse the generation of communication operations for different parallel compilers. The effort lowers the implementation cost of a parallel compiler; given such a backend, it is much easier to explore different approaches to data partitioning, automatic alignment, etc. At the same time, the communication backend provides one central place to apply communication optimizations, and all compilers can benefit from them.

Acknowledgements

We appreciate the contributions by our colleagues Peter Dinda, Susan Hinrichs, David O'Hallaron, Jonathan Shewchuk, Peter Steenkiste, Tom Stricker, Jaspal Subhlok, and Po-Jen Yang.

References

1. S. Chatterjee, J. Gilbert, F.J.E. Long, R. Schreiber, and S.-H. Teng. Generating local addresses and communication sets for data-parallel programs. In *Proceedings of 4th PPoPP*, pages 149–158, San Diego, CA, May 1993.
2. P. Dinda and D. O'Hallaron. The impact of address relation caching on the performance of deposit model communication. In *Third Workshop on Languages, Compilers, and Run-Time Systems for Scalable Computers*, 1995. To appear.
3. T. Gross, D. O'Hallaron, and J. Subhlok. Task parallelism in a High Performance Fortran framework. *IEEE Parallel and Distributed Technology*, 2(3):16–26, Fall 1994.
4. S. Gupta, S. Kaushik, S. Mufti, S. Sharma, C. Huang, and P. Sadayappan. On compiling array expressions for efficient execution on distributed-memory machines. In *Proceedings of ICPP*, , St. Charles, IL, August 1993. IEEE.
5. K. Kennedy, N. Nedeljkovic, and A. Sethi. A linear-time algorithm for computing the memory access sequence in data-parallel programs. In *Proceedings of 5th PPoPP*, pages 102–111, Santa Barbara, CA, July 1995.
6. R. Ruehl and M. Annaratone. Parallelization of Fortran code on distributed-memory parallel processors. In *Proc. Intl. Conf. on Supercomputers*. ACM, Jne 1990.
7. E. J. Schwabe, G. E. Blelloch, A. Feldmann, O. Ghattas, J. R. Gilbert, G. L. Miller, D. R. O'Hallaron, J. R. Shewchuk, and S. Teng. A separator-based framework for automated partitioning and mapping of parallel algorithms for numerical solution of pdes. In *Proceedings of the 1992 DAGS/PC Symposium*, pages 48–62, June 1992.
8. J. Stichnoth, D. O'Hallaron, and T. Gross. Generating communication for array statements: Design, implementation, and evaluation. *Journal of Parallel and Distributed Computing*, 21(1):150–159, 1994.
9. James M. Stichnoth. Efficient compilation of array statements for private memory multicomputers. Technical Report CMU-CS-93-109, School of Computer Science, Carnegie Mellon University, February 1993.
10. T. Stricker and T. Gross. Optimizing memory system performance for communication in parallel computers. In *Proc. 22nd Intl. Symp. on Computer Architecture*, page accepted, Portofino, Italy, June 1995. ACM/IEEE.
11. J. Subhlok, J. Stichnoth, D. O'Hallaron, and T. Gross. Programming task and data parallelism on a multicomputer. In *Proceedings of 4th PPoPP*, pages 13–22, May 1993.
12. A. Sussman, G. Agrawal, and J. Saltz. A manual for the multiblock PARTI runtime primitives, revision 4.1. Tech Report CS-TR-3070.1, University of Maryland, December 1993.
13. A. Thirumalai and J. Ramanujam. Fast address sequence generation for data-parallel programs using integer lattices. In *Proceedings of 8th Workshop on Languages and Compilers for Parallel Computing*, page to appear, Columbus, Ohio, August 1995. Springer Verlag.
14. H. Zima, P. Brezany, B. Chapman, P. Mehrota, and A. Schwald. Vienna Fortran – a language specification version 1.1. Technical Report ACPC/TR 92-4, Austrian Center for Parallel Computation, March 1992.

Parallel Simulation of Data Parallel Programs*

Sundeep Prakash and Rajive Bagrodia

Computer Science Department, University of California, Los Angeles, CA 90024

Abstract. Accurate simulations of parallel programs for large datasets can often be slow; parallel execution has been shown to offer significant potential in reducing the execution time of many discrete-event simulators. In this paper, we describe the design and implementation of a parallel simulator called DPSIM that simulates the execution of data parallel programs on contemporary message-passing parallel architectures. The simulator has been implemented on the IBM SPx using a conservative synchronization algorithm. This paper also describes the use of the simulator in evaluating the impact of architectural characteristics like processor speed and message communication latency on the performance of scientific applications including Gauss Jordan elimination and matrix multiplication.

1 Introduction

Simulators for parallel programs can be effectively utilized to test, debug, and predict performance of parallel programs on a diverse set of parallel architectures. A variety of simulators have been designed[BDCW91, DGH91, RHL+93, CDJ+91, DHN94] to estimate the performance of a parallel program. Most simulators were designed to estimate the performance of asynchronous or task parallel programs. With few exceptions, these simulators fall broadly into two classes: the simulator itself is sequential and can be ported to almost any sequential workstation; or the simulator is parallel but designed to execute on a specific parallel architecture. The former category includes simulators like Proteus and Tango, which can be used to simulate the execution of a program on a very detailed model of the target parallel architecture. The primary drawback with this approach is that accurate simulations of target programs that will operate on large datasets and execute on a large number of processors, are typically slow.

Many techniques have been used to improve the execution time of program simulators, including the use of direct execution where local code is executed rather than simulated, and the use of high-level models where components of the parallel architecture are modeled at an abstract level. However, in spite of these innovations, it is not unusual to have a factor of anywhere from 10-1000 slowdown in the execution of the simulator when compared with the execution time for the actual program. This slowdown is perhaps more significant for sparse and irregular computations, where it is harder for a programmer to extrapolate the

* This research was supported in part by an ARPA/CSTO Award (No. F30602-94-C-0273)

results obtained from the execution of smaller datasets. Parallel implementations of the simulator offer significant potential for reducing the execution time for the simulator.

A data parallel program may be executed on both synchronous and asynchronous parallel architectures. In the latter case, the program is compiled into a SPMD program, with (typically) one process assigned to each processor of the target architecture. (In general, it is possible for the compiler to create multiple threads for each processor; we assume one thread/processor for simplicity in exposition). Sequential simulators interleave the simulation of each process in the target program on the single processor of the simulation engine leading to significant slowdown in its execution. Parallel simulators can use multiple available processors, such that each processor in the simulation engine interleaves a smaller number of processes from the target program. Thus given a target program with N processes, a sequential simulator must interleave N processes on one processor, whereas a parallel simulator with S, $S < N$, available processors can interleave approximately N/S processes on each processor. However, the parallel simulator must ensure that the the simulation processes executing on different processors of the simulation engine are synchronized such that all events in the model are executed in their correct global order. This synchronization can add to the overhead of parallel execution of the simulator limiting its potential benefit. This overhead can, in turn, be reduced by using a number of optimizations that exploit semantic knowledge of specific data parallel constructs.

In this paper, we describe the design and implementation of a program simulator called DPSIM. The simulator is designed for execution on both sequential workstations and parallel distributed memory architectures. The primary contributions of this paper are:

- design of a simulator for data parallel programs. To the best of our knowledge, most existing simulators are designed for asynchronous or task parallel programs.
- implementation of the simulator on a parallel distributed memory architecture (IBM SP2) using an optimized synchronization strategy that exploits the semantics of data parallel programs.
- experimental results on the performance of the simulator for a set of scientific applications that include Gauss Jordan elimination and matrix multiplication. In addition, our measurements show that the IBM SP2 implementation of our simulator can yield speedup factors as high as 11 using 16 processors.

The rest of the paper is organized as follows: the next section gives a brief description of the primary constructs found in most data parallel languages. Section 3 introduces the simulation methodology. Section 4 contains the detailed design of the simulator and experimental results that validate it and describe the speedups that can be achieved from parallel execution of the simulator compared to a sequential implementation. Section 5 discusses the relationship between this and existing program simulators and section 6 discusses future work.

2 Compilation of Data Parallel Programs

Data parallel programming is defined as single threaded, global name space, loosely synchronous parallel computation[Hig93]. A data parallel program, in order to be executed on a multicomputer, is first translated into a message passing SPMD program. The SPMD program is then compiled and run on each of (a subset of) the nodes of the multicomputer. The operations in the data parallel program that lead to communication (and synchronization) in the corresponding SPMD program may be classified into the following categories:

- Data Distribution: These are operations which specify the placement and alignment of data (relative to other data or to some template) over a set of processors. Familiar HPF primitives which perform these functions are ALIGN and REALIGN for alignment and DISTRIBUTE and REDISTRIBUTE for placement.
- Parallel data assignment: These allow parallel operations on sections of arrays with the same shape. In HPF such operations occur in the FORALL statement and construct, the INDEPENDENT statement, the WHERE statement and in array assignment statements.
- Parallel data combination: Data combination occurs in operations like reduction, prefix, suffix and combining scatter. In HPF, these operations occur as intrinsic operations.

From the point of view of communication optimization, the communication patterns resulting from these operations may be classified as predictable or unpredictable[PB]. Predictable communication patterns are those in which every processor knows which other processor needs its data. Unpredictable communication patterns are those in which a processor does not know who needs its data and hence generally need costly global synchronizations to implement them. For the purposes of this paper, we introduce another classification of communication patterns. Communication patterns may also be classified as either *deterministic* or *non-deterministic*. Just as the (un)predictable classification identifies the patterns that are easy to implement, the (non)deterministic classification identifies the patterns that are easy to *simulate*. A deterministic communication pattern is one in which every processor receives a deterministic set of messages (unchanged over executions of the program). A non-deterministic communication pattern is one in which the sequence of messages that is accepted at a processor cannot be predetermined. We next present some examples of data parallel code and their equivalent SPMD code, in order to explain the communication pattern classification. We assume the following Maisie[BtL94] like syntax for message passing calls in the SPMD code:

- (**send to** < *dest* > **message** < *msgtype* > {< *msg* >};): This statement describes the send of a message < *msg* > to a process < *dest* >. < *msgtype* > is a user defined message type, and in the programs we consider, messages can be of type data or request. < *msg* > is the body of the message. In a data message we define it to contain fields for the sender id and the data value. In a request message it contains fields for the sender id and the address of the requested value[2]. Upon execution of this statement, a message is deposited in the receive buffer of the destination process.

- (**brecv mtype**(< *msgtype1* >) **st** < *guard1* > {< *code1* >} **or mtype**(< *msgtype2* >) **st** < *guard2* > {< *code2* >}... ;): This is a a blocking selective receive statement. Upon execution, a process waits until a message of any of the listed message types (< *msgtype1* >, < *msgtype2* > etc) is deposited in its receive buffer. If the message satisfies the corresponding guard (< *guard1* >, < *guard2* >..), then it is an enabling message, and the process may resume execution. The guard is a side-effect free boolean expression that may reference local variables or message fields[3]. If more than one enabling messages are received, or already present in the receive buffer when the statement is executed, one is non-deterministically selected. The enabling message is then removed from the receive buffer of the process, and execution resumed at the corresponding point e.g < *code1* >, < *code2* > etc.
- (**recv**...): This is a non-blocking selective receive statement with essentially the same syntax as the blocking receive. The only difference in semantics is that the non-blocking receive does not wait for messages to arrive, but makes decisions based on arrived messages. If no enabling messages are present, the statement is treated as a skip statement.

We assume HPF syntax for the data parallel code. *PROCESSORS* tells us the rectilinear processors arrangement, which is mapped onto the actual physical processors. For convenience, we assume that this is the same as the number of physical processors. The *DISTRIBUTE* directive tells us how the data is mapped onto the processor arrangement. In order to simplify presentation, we assume simple block mappings for all the array data. Changing the data mapping will not affect the type of communication pattern generated, although the communication pattern itself will change. The *FORALL* statement describes a synchronous parallel assignment. Using this terminology, the following data parallel code shows a predictable communication pattern implemented as a deterministic communication pattern (henceforth referred to as Example 1):

Source Code:

```
          INTEGER a(0:7)
!HPF$     PROCESSORS procs(0:7)
!HPF$     DISTRIBUTE (BLOCK) ONTO procs:: a
          FORALL (i=0:7) a(i) = a(MOD(i+1,8));
```

SPMD code for FORALL statement for processor i (C syntax):

```
          int i,a;
```

---

[2] Both data and request messages may also contain a tag, which is used by the receiver to accept messages out of order

[3] Fields of a message are referenced as **msg**.< *msgtype* > . < *field − name* >.

```
        send to (i-1)%8 message datamsg{i, a};   /* s1 */
        brecv mtype(datamsg) st              /* s2 */
            (msg.datamsg.sender == (i+1)%8){
            a = msg.datamsg.value;
        }
```

The following is an unpredictable communication pattern (henceforth referred to as Example 2) implemented in two ways: as a deterministic and as a non-deterministic communication pattern:

Source Code:

```
        INTEGER a(0:7), b(0:7)
!HPF$   PROCESSORS procs(0:7)
!HPF$   DISTRIBUTE (BLOCK) ONTO procs:: a,b
        FORALL (i=0:7) a(i) = a(MOD(b(i),8));
```

Deterministic Implementation:

```
        int a, b, i,j, source;
        source = b%8;
        for (j=0;j<8;j++){
            if (j != i) send to j message datamsg{i,a};
        }
        for (j=0;j<7;j++){
            brecv mtype (datamsg) {
                if (msg.datamsg.sender == source)
                    a = msg.datamsg.value;
            }
        }
```

Non-deterministic Implementation:

```
        int a, b, i, source, recvd;
        source = b%8;
        send to source message rqstmsg{i,&a};
        recvd = FALSE;
        while (!recvd) {
            brecv mtype (datamsg){ ;
                a = msg.datamsg.value;
                recvd = TRUE;
            }
            or mtype (rqstmsg){
                send to msg.rqstmsg.sender
                    datamsg{i, *(msg.rqstmsg.wantaddr)};
            }
        }
        barrier;
```

In the deterministic implementation each processor broadcasts to all other processors and selects the required value from the incoming messages. Clearly, a lot of unnecessary messages are sent. In the non-deterministic implementation each processor places a request, and then waits for a reply; while waiting, it services incoming requests[4]. Since the number of incoming requests is unknown the pattern is non-deterministic.

In general, we expect data distribution operations to be predictable, as well as data combination operations. Data assignment operations may be unpredictable and hence possibly produce non-deterministic communication patterns as shown in the example above. However, to the best of our knowledge most data parallel compilers exclusively produce deterministic communication patterns. These can be simulated with relatively little overhead as shown in the next section.

3 Simulation Methodology

The standard approach to simulation of a program that consists of a number of asynchronous message-passing processes is to use a sequential discrete-event simulator. When viewed as a discrete-event model, each process of the compiled program contains only three types of events: *basic blocks*, or code that does not involve communication with another process, *send events*, and *receive events*. Although it is possible to simulate basic blocks, most simulators use direct execution[CMM+88, MF88] as this has been shown to be more efficient. In direct execution, the time to execute the basic block is either measured using the physical processor clock and scaled appropriately to model the target processor, or it is computed by counting the number of instruction cycles that will be needed to execute the basic block. The cycle count may then be directly translated to a time measure depending on the clock and statistical cache characteristics of the target processor. Send and receive events are typically simulated by estimating the transmission time for each message and including the (simulation) timestamp at which the corresponding message will be received with each message. A separate logical clock is maintained for each process that indicates the (simulation) time at which each event occurs in the corresponding process.

Thus the basic simulation methodology is as follows: the compiler that generates the SPMD program from the data parallel program is modified to instrument the resulting compiled code such that accurate timestamps for each event can be generated by the simulator:

- *Basic block*: Code is embedded by the compiler to count the number of instruction cycles needed to execute each basic block. At run-time, the cycle count is translated into a time value, say δ, and on completion of the basic block, the logical clock for this thread is advanced by δ.

---

[4] Not all requests are serviced at this statement; some may be serviced at the following barrier

- *Send event:* Each message that is generated by a process is timestamped with the (simulation) time at which this message would have been generated in the target program. When the message is generated by a thread, its logical clock is simply copied into the timestamp field of the message. The transmission time for the message on the target architecture must be estimated to determine the (simulation) time at which the corresponding message will be received by the destination process. The message latency can be estimated using analytical models, measurements on the target architecture, or a simulation model of the interconnection network, or a combination of the preceding methods. Once the latency has been estimated, the receive time is also inserted in the message.
- *Receive event* The receive time for a message is inserted by the sending process as described above.

Once the timestamps have been generated for each event in the simulation model, the model can be executed using either sequential or parallel algorithms. Model execution using a sequential algorithm is straightforward: events scheduled by all processes are stored in increasing order of their timestamps in a global event list. At each step, the event with the smallest timestamp is removed from the global list and executed; any additional events (e.g. send events) generated by the execution of this event are inserted in the global list.

However, parallel execution of the preceding model is considerably more complex. Each processor of the simulation engine simulates one or more processes from the target program. Although the processor can determine the earliest events among the processes that are mapped on it, it is harder for a processor to deduce whether its (locally) earliest event is in fact, globally the earliest. In general, a global synchronization may be required in the parallel simulator before simulation of each event (Note: simulation of an event may generate and schedule events at other processors, requiring that the globally earliest event be recomputed after each event!).

Two primary solutions have been suggested to eliminate this global periodic synchronization: *conservative* and *optimistic*. Conservative algorithms do not permit any causality error: a simulation object (also called an LP) cannot process an event until the system can guarantee that it will not subsequently receive a message (event) with an earlier timestamp. This constraint may introduce deadlocks, which are typically handled by incorporating deadlock detection[Mis86] or deadlock avoidance[Mis86, CS89a] mechanisms into the simulation algorithm. Optimistic algorithms[Jef85, CS89b] allow an LP to process messages out of order; causality errors are corrected by using rollbacks and recomputations. Implementations of optimistic algorithms are usually more difficult because they require complex mechanisms for detection and handling of causality errors, termination detection, exception handling, and memory management. A comprehensive discussion of parallel discrete-event simulations may be found in [Fuj90, Mis86]. A simulation language called Maisie[BtL94] has been designed at UCLA to support the execution of parallel discrete-event models. Maisie is a C-based discrete-event simulation language that was designed to cleanly separate a simulation model from the underlying algorithm (sequential or parallel) used for the execution of the model. With few modifications, a Maisie program may be executed using a sequential simulation algorithm, a parallel conservative algorithm or a parallel optimistic algorithm. The parallel simulator described in this paper has been written in Maisie. Some optimizations, described in the next section, have been implemented to reduce the synchronization overheads. These optimizations have resulted in significant improvement to the performance of the parallel simulator as reported in Section 4.

3.1 Optimizations

The following terms are used in the sequel:

- DP program: A dataparallel program
- Target architecture: Architecture on which the DP program will execute.
- MP program: The message passing program that results from compilation of DP.
- MPSIM program: The instrumented message passing program that simulates execution of MP.
- Host architecture: Architecture on which MPSIM will execute.
- $real_N$: Assuming some input, an execution of the MP program on N nodes of the target architecture (one process per node)
- $sim_{N:k}$: Assuming the same input, an execution of the MPSIM program on k nodes (one simulation process per process of the MP program, $>= 1$ simulation processes per processor)

As suggested in the previous subsection, a simple but inefficient simulation of an MP program would require each simulation process of the corresponding MPSIM program to synchronize with other simulation processes before executing the next event on its event list. However, the event list is basically the code of the MP program. The only points at which a remote simulation process, say A, can affect the execution of a given simulation process, say B, is when B executes a receive statement. Hence, the MPSIM program can execute send and basic block events on its event list without first synchronizing with all other processes. Upon encountering a receive statement however, the simulation process B must accept the same message that was accepted by the corresponding process of the MP program at the same point. However, receive statements in MP programs occur only in deterministic communication patterns. The following rule can then be used:

Rule 1 *If in each execution of a MP program, exactly k messages satisfy the conditions of receive R at its each invocation, then receive R can be accurately simulated by simply waiting for k messages which satisfy the conditions of the receive, and then invoking the receive.*

This rule helps us avoid a global barrier that would otherwise occur in trying to determine which message to accept at R. For instance, consider the simulation of the DP fragment in Example 1 in the preceding section. Assume that the corresponding MPSIM program is to be executed on a single processor. The simulation will proceed as follows:

1. Simulate the local block ending at statement $s1$ by using direct execution. Assume that the simulation time at statement $s1$ for process p_i in $sim_{8:1}$ is $t1[i]$.

2. Simulate the send in statement $s1$ as follows: the message sent at $s1$ is times-tamped with $t1[i] + msg\_delay[i]$; $msg\_delay[i]$ is computed by the simulator to model the transmission time for this message sent by process p_i in $real_8$.

3. The receive event in statement $s2$ is simulated as follows: on receiving the message, update local simulation time (for process p_i) as follows:
$simtime[i] = t1[i] > msg\_timestamp?t1[i] : msg\_timestamp$
In $real_8$, if the message arrives at $s2$ prior to the execution of the receive by p_i, then $msg\_timestamp$ would be greater than $t1[i]$ in $sim_{8:1}$. In contrast, if in $real_8$ the process had to wait at statement $s2$ for the message to arrive, then in $sim_{8:1}$ $t1[i]$ would be less than $msg\_timestamp$.

4. The local block following the receive statement is again simulated using direct execution.

In other words, in the compiled MP program, each process 'knows' that exactly one message will be received at each receive statement. Thus in $sim_{8:k}$, for $k > 1$, each p_i can simulate the receive event at statement $s2$ as soon as the message is received. Clearly parallel execution of the simulation will not incur additional synchronization overhead compared to the sequential execution and hence has significant potential for performance improvements.

4 Experiments

4.1 Simulator

Our results are based on a simulator written for a compiler of the data parallel language UC[BKM] on the IBM-SP2. The compiler translates UC code into Maisie[BtL94][5] with MPL calls for fast communication and synchronization over the HPS (high performance switch). The resulting program executes as one single-threaded process per processor. The simulator is simply a modified version of the same compiler, which:

- Also produces Maisie code. In the simulator, Maisie additionally provides lightweight threads (in order to put many logical simulation processes on one processor) and point-to-point communication between threads (whether they are on the same or different processors).
- Inserts code to calculate local code execution time at the beginning and end of each local code block, and to update simulation time.

---

[5] Maisie can be used both as a message passing language and as a full-fledged simulation language. We use it only as the former

– Substitutes MPL communication routines i.e. broadcasts, reduces, barriers and point-to-point communication with the respective communication simulation routines. For example, we discovered the tree algorithm used in the IBM-SP2 for broadcasts, barriers and reduces. The same algorithm is used to simulate each of those routines using point-to-point communications. It is at all these points that the simulation optimizations discussed in the previous section are inserted. Point-to-point message delays are predicted using an analytic model based on linear interpolation and extrapolation of measurements of delays for selected message sizes.

The resulting simulation program executes as one multi-threaded process per processor.

4.2 Validation

The current version of the UC compiler produces exclusively deterministic communication patterns. Hence, the simulator applies the optimization resulting from Rule 1 to all communication generated by the compiler. For a number of small programs, we verified that the actual program execution ($real_N$, according to the terminology introduced earlier) and the simulations ($sim_{N:k}$, for a number of $k < N$) gave the same output. We also compared predicted and actual execution times for a number of programs. Figure 1 shows the accuracy of the prediction for Gauss-Jordan Elimination. The curve labeled "Real Execution" shows the execution time of $real_N$ for $N = 4, 8, 16$. The curves labeled "k Processor Simulation" are the execution times of $sim_{N:k}$ for $N = 4, 8, 16$. All curves are in close agreement i.e. at all points each simulation is within 5.5% of the actual execution time and all simulations are within 4.89% of each other.

4.3 Simulator Predictions

One of the applications of the simulator is in predicting how program performance is affected by factors such as communication latency and even processor speed. Figure 2 shows these results for a matrix multiplication program. The X axis of the graph shows the scaled message latency on a logarithmic scale. So, at $x = 0$, the communication latency is that of the IBM-SP2. At $x = 1$ the latency is twice that of the SP2 and so on. The Y axis shows the scaled processor speed on a similar logarithmic scale ($x = 0$ processor speed is that of a SP2 processor, $x = 1$ is that of a processor with half the speed). Consider the 8 processor implementation. When the latency is about 16 times that of the SP2 (about the same as on an ethernet with TCP/IP), program performance becomes less sensitive to processor speed. At this point ($x = 4$), on increasing the processor speed by a factor of 16 (from $y = -2$ to $y = 2$), only a factor of 4 improvement is achieved in program performance. As message latency drops to 0 ($x = -4$ on the graph), the sensitivity increases (program performance improves exactly as processor speed). Also, the compiler does a fairly good job of overlapping communication and computation as long as the message latency remains below

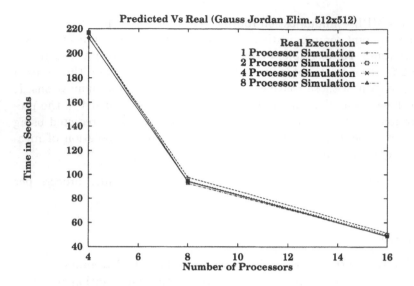

Fig. 1. Simulator Accuracy

4 times that of the SP2. This is evidenced by the fact that program execution time is totally insensitive to latency increase until $x = 2$. Also, the 32 processor implementation of the program is more sensitive to latency increase after $x = 2$, since the synchronization overheads are higher for a greater number of processors. Very similar results are obtained for the Gauss-Jordan elimination program (Figure 3). In this way, the simulator can be used to predict in what environments a program would perform well, and where performance bottlenecks exist. Also, due to the fact that the simulator can itself be run in parallel, the results can be obtained quickly. The simulator execution times for Gauss Jordan elimination, for example, are shown in Figure 4. $sim_{128:16}$ is about 11 times faster than $sim_{128:1}$, meaning that the 128 processor problem can be simulated 11 times faster using 16 processors than sequentially.

5 Related Work

A number of sequential simulators have been designed to evaluate the performance of parallel architectures and programs. Existing simulators include Proteus[BDCW91], Tango[DGH91] and the RPPT simulation engine[CDJ+91] among others. In Proteus, the application to be simulated is written in a superset of C, and constructs are provided to control the placement of data. Provided library routines are used for message passing, thread management, memory management and data collection. The target architecture is specified in terms of interconnection medium (bus, direct or indirect network), sizes of shared and private memory at each node, and other features e.g. interprocessor interrupts

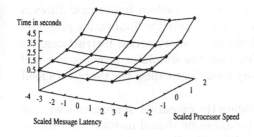

64x64 Matrix Multiply on 8 procs

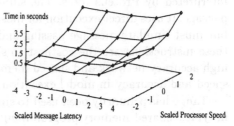

64x64 Matrix Multiply on 32 procs

Fig. 2. Matrix multiplication

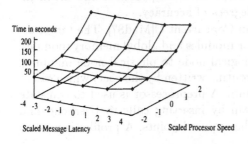

Gauss Jordan Elimination: 512x512 on 16 procs

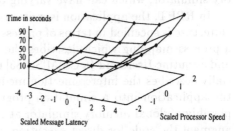

Gauss Jordan Elimination: 512x512 on 64 procs

Fig. 3. Gauss Jordan Elimination

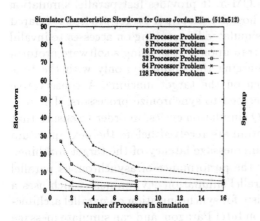

Simulator Characteristics: Slowdown for Gauss Jordan Elim. (512x512)

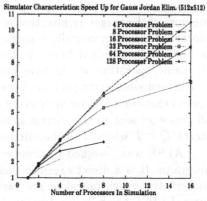

Simulator Characteristics: Speed Up for Gauss Jordan Elim. (512x512)

Fig. 4. Simulator Characteristics for Gauss Jordan Elimination

and handlers. An application- and architecture-specific simulator is created by the simulation engine, which upon execution produces a trace file that can be interpreted by Proteus tools. The simulator uses a custom lightweight threads package. It uses direct execution for most instructions of the application program, but must simulate message passing and shared memory access instructions. As these instructions are the costliest to simulate, the simulator provides low and high accuracy network and shared memory modules to allow the user to tradeoff speed and accuracy in model execution.

Tango has primarily been used to simulate the execution of programs written in typical shared-memory programming notations on shared memory computers. The target application is written in C or FORTRAN, using macros to emulate a variety of programming paradigms, such as locks, barriers, distributed loops and messages. These macros eventually expand into routines which implement equivalent primitives of the target architecture. The code is augmented for direct execution. The simulator executes as set of Unix processes. Target architecture primitives are implemented by interactions between the processes (using shared memory and semaphores), and interactions between the processes and the memory simulator, which can have varying degrees of accuracy.

In RPPT, the application is written in Concurrent C[Mad87]. The target architecture is specified in terms of processor modules and global memory modules, a process mapping which describes the logical node to physical node mapping, and a routine UserSend (a CSIM[Sch85] routine written by the user) which essentially describes the interconnection medium. A preprocessor is used to translate the application into a simulation program by inserting calls to UserSend and possibly a global memory simulator at the required points. A profiler is used to augment the code for direct execution.

Parallel simulation engines include the Wisconsin Wind Tunnel[RHL+93] (WWT) and the Large Application Parallel Simulation Environment[DHN94] (LAPSE). WWT is a simulator of cache-coherent, shared memory computers that runs on the Thinking Machines CM-5. It provides fast parallel simulation by direct execution of local code, one host processor per target processor. Shared memory of the target architecture is simulated by trapping on accesses to invalid blocks [6] This automatically causes a trap upon access, using a software protocol to obtain the required block, and charging the simulation only with the time the same operation would have taken on the target machine. A conservative distributed simulation protocol is executed to synchronize processors. The processors execute a barrier after every Q simulation cycles, in order to ensure that all messages sent in the current quantum are received before the next quantum starts. $Q < T$ where T is the minimum message latency of the target machine.

LAPSE was designed to simulate the performance of asynchronous parallel programs. It is a direct execution parallel simulation environment which uses a conservative synchronization mechanism for synchronization on parallel architectures. LAPSE has been implemented on Intel Paragon, and can simulate message passing application programs which use the Intel message passing library calls.

---

[6] An block is marked invalid by manipulating the ECC bits in the CM-5 memory.

6 Conclusions and Future Work

In this paper, we have discussed the design of parallel simulators of data parallel programs, and used a simulator, DPSIM, designed at UCLA, to prove the usefulness of the proposed techniques. We have shown that the communication patterns generated by data parallel programs can be easily simulated, without costly runtime simulation mechanisms. Hence, we have achieved excellent slow-downs which, although application dependent, have been brought to as close as 1.06 of the actual application. Also, we have shown that conservative simulation techniques can be effectively used to parallelize simulations. We have achieved a speed up of as much as 11 by increasing the processors in the simulation from 1 to 16.

A lot of work remains to be done. We intend to interface our simulator to other data parallel language compilers e.g compilers for HPF. Also, we intend to port the simulator to other platforms e.g the Intel Paragon. Since we have a simple model for predicting message latencies, we cannot simulate communication patterns that develop congestion. We want to provide the option of interfacing to a detailed interconnection network simulator in such situations.

7 Acknowledgements

All the data presented in this paper was collected on the IBM-SP2 at Argonne National Labs(MCS division) and the IBM-SP2 at UCLA's Office of Academic Computing, granted to UCLA by IBM Corporation under their Shared University Research Program. We particularly wish to express our gratitude to Paul Hoffman at OAC, UCLA for allocating resources to us whenever we requested, and for solving the numerous problems we encountered in running our simulations.

References

[BDCW91] E. A. Brewer, C. N. Dellarocas, A. Colbrook, and W. E. Weihl. PRO-TEUS: A High-Performance Parallel-Architecture Simulator. Technical Report MIT/LCS/TR-516, Massachusetts Institute of Technology, Cambridge, MA 02139, 1991.

[BKM] R. Bagrodia, K.M.Chandy, and M.Dhagat. UC: a set-based language for data parallel programming. To appear.

[BtL94] R. Bagrodia and Wen toh Liao. Maisie: A language for design of efficient discret-event simulations. *IEEE Transactions on Software Engineering*, April 1994.

[CDJ+91] R.G. Covington, S. Dwarkadas, J.R. Jump, J.B. Sinclair, and S. Madala. The efficient simulation of parallel computer systems. *International Journal in Computer Simulation*, 1:31–58, 1991.

[CMM+88] R.G. Covington, S. Madala, V. Mehta, J.R. Jump, and J.B. Sinclair. The Rice Parallel Processing Testbed. In *Proceedings of the 1988 ACM SIG-METRICS Conference on Measurement and Modeling of Computer Systems*, May 1988.

[CS89a] K.M. Chandy and R. Sherman. The conditional event approach to distributed simulation. In *Distributed Simulation Conference*, Miami, 1989.

[CS89b] K.M. Chandy and R. Sherman. Space-time and simulation. In *Distributed Simulation Conference*, Miami, 1989.

[DGH91] H. Davis, S. R. Goldschmidt, and Hennessey. Multiprocessor simulation and tracing using Tango. In *Proceedings of the 1991 International Conference on Parallel Processing (ICPP'91)*, pages II99–II107, August 1991.

[DHN94] P. Dickens, P. Heidelberger, and D. Nicol. A distributed memory lapse: Parallel simulation of message-passing programs. In *Workshop on Parallel and Distributed Simulation*, pages 32–38, July 1994.

[Fuj90] R. Fujimoto. Parallel discrete event simulation. *Communications of the ACM*, 33(10):30–53, October 1990.

[Hig93] High Performance Fortran Forum. High Performance Fortran Language Specification. Available by anonymous ftp from titan.cs.rice.edu, May 1993.

[Jef85] D. Jefferson. Virtual time. *ACM TOPLAS*, 7(3):404–425, July 1985.

[Mad87] S. Madala. Concurrent c users manual. Tech. rept. #8701, ECE Dept., Rice University, October 1987.

[MF88] I. Mathieson and R. Francis. A dynamic-trace-driven simulator for evaluating parallelism. In *Proceedings of 21st Hawaii International Conference on System Sciences*, volume 1, pages 158–166, January 1988.

[Mis86] J. Misra. Distributed discrete-event simulation. *ACM Computing Surveys*, 18(1):39–65, March 1986.

[PB] S. Prakash and R. Bagrodia. An adaptive synchronization method for unpredictable communication patterns in dataparallel programs. To appear in IPPS95.

[PDB93] S. Prakash, M. Dhagat, and R. Bagrodia. Synchronization issues in multicomputer implementation of data-parallel languages. In U. Banerjee, M.Wolfe, A. Nicolau, and D. Padua, editors, *Sixth Workshop on Languages and Compilers for Parallel Computing*, August 1993.

[RHL+93] S. K. Reinhardt, M. D. Hill, J. R. Larus, A. R. Lebeck, J. C. Lewis, and D. A. Wood. The Wisconsin Wind Tunnel: Virtual Prototyping of Parallel Computers. In *Proceedings of the 1993 ACM SIGMETRICS Conference*, May 1993.

[Sch85] H. Schwetman. Csim : A c based process oriented simulation language. Technical report, Microelectronics & Computer Technology Corp., Austin, May 1985.

A Parallel Processing Support Library
Based On Synchronized Aggregate Communication

H. G. Dietz, T. M. Chung, and T. I. Mattox

School of Electrical and Computer Engineering
Purdue University
West Lafayette, IN 47907-1285
hankd@ecn.purdue.edu
(317) 494 3357

The concept of "data parallelism" is a pervasive force throughout parallel processing. Although a certain level of processing-element autonomy can help performance, the fact is that many parallel algorithms, applications, and compiler analysis techniques focus on identifying a set of data objects that can be processed using loosely synchronous parallelism. Thus, it is not surprising that a large number of communication libraries support at least a few synchronized aggregate operations on data. In this paper, we present an overview of the parallel processing support library for PAPERS clusters.

Unlike most other systems, which construct aggregate communications by layering message-passing or shared-memory communication, the PAPERS hardware and software directly implements a model of parallel execution based on synchronized aggregate communications. Asynchronous processor operation is fully supported, but asynchronous communications are not directly supported (although they can be derived using the PAPERS parallel interrupt mechanism). Thus, PAPERS provides highly efficient aggregate communications for MIMD, SIMD, and VLIW execution modes. We demonstrate the effectiveness of this implementation by presenting detailed benchmarks for a variety of other libraries supporting dedicated parallel machines and workstation clusters.

This work was supported in part by the Office of Naval Research (ONR) under grant number N00014-91-J-4013 and by the National Science Foundation (NSF) under Parallel Infrastructure Grant number CDA-9015696.

1. Introduction

PAPERS, Purdue's Adapter for Parallel Execution and Rapid Synchronization, is inexpensive hardware designed to provide very low latency barrier synchronization and aggregate communication operations to user-level unix processes running on a cluster of personal computers or workstations. The PAPERS library is designed to provide both:

- Good support for hand-coding of parallel applications and
- An efficient target for optimizing/parallelizing compilers.

Of course, these goals can only be accomplished by avoiding the usual software interface layering and the associated increases in latency.

Thus, the PAPERS library must solve two fundamental problems. The first problem is how to avoid the usual ill effects of using a cluster, as we discuss in Section 1.1. The second, discussed in Section 1.2, is how to construct a parallel execution model that can provide the appropriate functionality without sacrificing performance.

1.1. Clustering

The use of clusters of workstations/PCs for parallel computation is an attractive idea for many reasons. However, there are also many reasons why such clusters do not make effective parallel computing platforms. The most obvious problem is that of efficiently transmitting data between the processing elements (PEs) of the cluster.

Traditional networks, ranging from Ethernet to FDDI and ATM, all focus on providing bandwidth for PE-to-PE block transfers -- but fine-grain parallel programs need low-latency communication and efficient ways to examine the global state of the computation. Actual network hardware transmission time for a small datum is generally on the order of a few microseconds; however, total latency is generally much higher. Low-level network communication protocols require packet structures and transmission logic that generally increase latency by at least an order of magnitude. OS-level protocols, such as BSD sockets, add perhaps another 100 microseconds to latency by requiring a system call and process context switch for each operation. Libraries like PVM, which introduce even more software layers, can add milliseconds of delay to each operation. Further, PE-to-PE networks require at least log N sequential transmissions to sample global state. Given such high latency, only very coarsegrain parallelism is effective.

In contrast, everything about PAPERS is designed with the goal of supporting fine-grain parallelism. Although a PAPERS cluster might use the exact same personal computers and workstations that a conventional cluster would employ, the PAPERS hardware implements a different model for interactions. PAPERS is designed to allow the library to execute as part of the user process, directly accessing the hardware using the minimum number of port I/O instructions or volatile memory references to memory-mapped device registers. Further, there is no protocol or software layering, and global state can be sampled in a single operation rather than log N or N. The only OS interaction with PAPERS is "parallel interrupt" handling to support gang-scheduled timesharing across a cluster.

Another interesting implication of the PAPERS mechanism and software interface is that the execution time of each operation is very consistent and predictable. This property makes it possible for compiler analysis to more precisely estimate the performance of alternative codings, making static scheduling far more effective than it would be for a traditional cluster. In fact, PAPERS provides such a precise time reference that it can even be used to support scheduling of hard real-time operations; latency may be a few microseconds, but timing accuracy (repeatability or clock synchronization) is typically within a single microsecond.

1.2. Parallel Computation Model

The PAPERS library is not compliant with emerging standards for message-passing libraries (e.g., PVM [GeS93] or MPI [Mes94]) because the basic operations supported by the PAPERS hardware are **not** based on a message-passing model. While interactions between PEs using message-passing systems are often asynchronous and are always initiated by individual PEs, PAPERS operations are aggregate operations which are requested and performed in unison by all PEs within a specified group. Thus, although a PAPERS cluster is not restricted to SIMD execution, all PAPERS operations are based on a model of aggregate interaction that closely resembles SIMD communication. This is not a coincidence; years of research involving Purdue University's PASM (PArtitionable Simd Mimd) prototype supercomputer have experimentally demonstrated that SIMD-like interactions are more efficient than traditional message-passing for a wide range of applications [BeS91].

The PAPERS execution model is based on the properties of the generalized barrier synchronization mechanism that we have been developing since [DiS88]. In barrier MIMD execution, each processor executes independently until it wishes to synchronize with an *arbitrary group* of (one or more) other processors. The barrier synchronization is accomplished by each processor individually informing the barrier unit that it has arrived, and then waiting to be notified that all participating processors have arrived. Once the barrier synchronization has completed, execution of each processor is again completely independent. Thus, barrier MIMD execution is a purely MIMD execution model that can, at any point desired, impose timing properties accurately emulating either a SIMD or VLIW execution model.

Suppose that, instead of executing just a barrier wait, all participating processors may additionally perform a communication operation: communication is literally a side-effect of an arbitrary set of PEs executing a barrier synchronization. This communication model is somewhat like synchronous message-passing in concept, but is much more powerful because communication need not be PE-to-PE. In this model, the PAPERS unit collects an aggregate of the data items output by each PE that participates in the current barrier. The value obtained by each PE can thus be any of a wide range of functions of the aggregated data — and these functions can be *computed in parallel within the PAPERS unit*. For example, reductions, scans (parallel prefix operations), and various other functions can yield performance comparable to or better than the cost of performing a simple permutation communication using a more traditional network. Current PAPERS hardware directly implements only a subset of all possible functions, but the high performance achieved with remarkably simple hardware clearly demonstrates the power of the model.

Despite the synchronous nature of aggregate communication, it is important to remember that only the specified group of PEs must participate in each communication, and every PE can be executing a unique program. In fact, each PE participating in a particular aggregate communication even can behave differently within that communication (e.g., one processor broadcasts while others receive). However, unlike asynchronous message-passing, the role of each processor in a synchronization or communication operation must be determined by that processor. Processors are free to dynamically alter how they interact, but only by means that preserve the static qualities of the interactions. For example, the only way for processor A to get data from processor B is for B to know that some processor might want this data, and to act accordingly in aggregate with A.

The PAPERS hardware also provides a "parallel interrupt" mechanism that can be used by any processor to signal the selected group of processors, and this device could be used to simulate asynchronous message-passing. However, the performance characteristics of asynchronous message-passing using PAPERS in this way are similar to those obtained using PVM. Thus, we do not include any such messaging operations in this paper, nor do we consider such operations to be properly part of the PAPERS library communication model. PAPERS parallel interrupts are normally used only by PEN, the Papers ENvironment that performs high-level parallel OS functions such as gang scheduling of parallel programs.

In summary, the PAPERS library model is neither message-passing nor shared memory, but is an inherently different model based on the concept of synchronously aggregating data from an arbitrary group of PEs. We suggest that this barrier MIMD based model yields simple and efficient hardware that better supports the needs of many parallel applications executing in any combination of MIMD, SIMD, and VLIW execution modes.

2. Overview

The PAPERS library discussed in this document is designed to provide all the basic components needed to support a wide range of parallel applications. The routines are intended to be called directly within C code to be compiled by the Gnu C Compiler. Thus, this library can be used:

- Directly by the application programmer using C or any language that can be translated into C (e.g., Fortran via f2c, Pascal via p2c).

- By an optimizing/parallelizing compiler generating stylized C code as a "portable assembly language" target. We have experimentally confirmed that expressing tuples as C code written using temporary variables declared with the register attribute results in an efficient, and predictable, translation to native assembly code. For example, the PAPERS MPL compiler generates code in this style. This approach allows instruction-level analysis and optimization to be easily parameterized to account for differences between machines — which is particularly important if the machines within a cluster are heterogeneous.

In this paper, the basic PAPERS library functions are described and benchmarked in detail. The PAPERS library also contains other operations such as support for parallel file I/O; however, these routines are beyond the scope of the current work.

Before describing the library routines themselves and their performance relative to comparable routines in other libraries, it is useful to review the basic data types managed by the routines. This is done in Section 2.1. Likewise, the performance evaluation requires some background discussion of the methods used to measure performance and scalability. Section 2.2 reviews these issues.

2.1. Data Types

Unlike most implementations of PVM [GeS93] or MPI [Mes94], the PAPERS hardware and interface software does not have a significant set-up time; an operation on *n* units of data generally takes nearly the same time as performing *n* single-unit data operations. This fact is clearly demonstrated by the benchmark data given in the following sections. Thus, there is no reason to pack/unpack blocks of data into a memory-based message buffer. It is actually more efficient to perform the PAPERS operations directly using processor registers, with one PAPERS operation performed for each datum being acted upon, because this saves the cost of having to read and write each datum to a local memory buffer.

Thus, unlike PVM or MPI, the PAPERS library routines focus on low-latency communication operations that can act upon individual data values within a computation. Functions that return data values have multiple versions, one for each basic data type supported by the Gnu C Compiler (i.e., each type that could be held in a processor register). Each of these types is listed in Table 1, along with the equivalent portable type definition used in the PAPERS library and the corresponding function name suffix. For example, the function that sums a 32-bit `unsigned int` value from each participating processor is called `p_reduceAdd32u()`, where the suffix `32u` identifies the type of both the operand and the return value.

Table 1: PAPERS Data Types

GCC Type	PAPERS Type	PAPERS Suffix
boolean (`unsigned int`)	`uint1`	`1u`
8-bit `char`	`int8`	`8`
8-bit `unsigned char`	`uint8`	`8u`
16-bit `short`	`int16`	`16`
16-bit `unsigned short`	`uint16`	`16u`
32-bit `int`	`int32`	`32`
32-bit `unsigned int`	`uint32`	`32u`
64-bit `long long`	`int64`	`64`
64-bit `unsigned long long`	`uint64`	`64u`
32-bit `float`	`f32`	`f`
64-bit `double`	`f64`	`d`

The portable definition of these types yields a minor complication: if the machines within a cluster are not all based on the same processor, each may use a slightly different representation for the same value. In PVM 2, for example, this was handled using the notoriously slow UNIX socket XDR (eXternal Data Representation) library routines to convert to a standard exchange format as values are moved into or out of the message buffer in local memory. However, the PAPERS unit is fed data in a way that is inherently insensitive to memory byte order; each datum is apparently sent directly from a processor register to a processor register. Thus, all integer data are inherently portable, and byte-order variations on floating point formats are also handled correctly. Currently, we assume that the floating point formats used on different machines do not differ by more than byte ordering — an assumption that holds true for the vast majority of workstations. Later versions of the PAPERS library may handle more drastic floating point format variations by sending floating point values as separate exponent and mantissa, because these can be portably obtained and sent faster than the standard XDR routine could be applied. Of course, none of these problems arise in homogeneous clusters or dedicated parallel machines.

A similar portability constraint arises with respect to taking advantage of the fact that PAPERS may be able to operate faster on lower-precision values by transmitting only the specified number of bits. Although it might be possible to, for example, send only a portion of the mantissa of a floating point value, such operations are not portable. Thus, only functions that operate on unsigned integer values can be augmented by versions that have the ability to restrict the PAPERS operations to a specific number of bits. These functions are named with the suffix `Bits` followed by the suffix that specifies the unsigned integer type from which the low bits are extracted. The benchmark data presented in this paper ignores the `Bits` operations because none of the other libraries supports any such operations.

We have also omitted benchmarks of the `lu` routines, which are used to manage 1-bit logical true/false values. Most of these routines take the same time as `p_any()`. Further, none of the other libraries directly supports such operations.

2.2. Performance Analysis

This performance analysis is given primarily to demonstrate that the PAPERS library provides an effective fine-grain target. Although the current PAPERS hardware is cheaper than Ethernet connection, and has bandwidth artificially limited by the use of a parallel port interface, the performance of the PAPERS library compares favorably to that of dedicated commercial supercomputers:

- Cray T3D [Cra93]. A 4 PE partition was benchmarked using the standard library.
- Cray T3D (PVM). A 4 PE partition was benchmarked using the PVM-compatible library.
- MasPar MP-1 MPL support library. The MasPar that we benchmarked is a 16,384 PE SIMD machine that was run with only 4 PEs enabled. It is significant, however, that most operations become only slightly slower when more PEs are enabled.
- Paragon XP/S [Int94]. The Paragon that we benchmarked is a 140 PE MIMD machine, but the benchmarks reported were run on a 4 PE partition. We found that execution time of most operations increased nearly linearly as the number of PEs in the partition is increased.

The numbers for the MasPar MP-1 and Paragon XP/S are more complete than for the Cray T3D simply because we had better access to these machines at Purdue.

For our library running on a PAPERS cluster, we actually benchmarked two different versions of the PAPERS hardware using the same four personal computers as PEs. Each PE was an IBM ValuePoint 486DX33 system running Linux 1.1.75. The PAPERS units were:

- PAPERS1. A PAL-based version of PAPERS that connects to 4 PEs via their parallel ports. This unit supports the full dynamic barrier mechanism [OKD90a] (implemented as described in [Muh95]) and provides hardware support for both `putget` and NAND aggregate operations. Because the external data path for each PE is just 4 bits wide, only operations that require each PE to obtain more data as the design is scaled to larger systems incur proportionally more delay.

- TTL_PAPERS [DiC95]. A TTL-based version of PAPERS that connects to 4 PEs via their parallel ports. This design has been greatly simplified to make it cheaper and easier to build, so performance of TTL_PAPERS generally marks the lower bound on PAPERS performance. This unit supports the full static barrier mechanism [OKD90] and provides hardware support for NAND aggregate operations. Because both the internal and external data paths are just 4 bits wide, operations that require more data to pass through the unit as the design is scaled to larger systems incur proportionally more delay.

To provide a reference for the performance of a more traditional cluster parallelism library, we also benchmarked performance using the same PEs that we used to benchmark the PAPERS units listed above. These four IBM ValuePoint 486DX33 systems running Linux 1.1.75 were connected using a standard Ethernet (with insignificant other traffic on the Ethernet). The library benchmarked was:

- PVM 3.3.7 [GeS93]. This library is the de-facto standard for parallel computing on workstation clusters, and this version generally yields significantly better benchmark times than older versions of PVM. Because communication is using Ethernet, the execution time of most operations increases nearly linearly as the number of PEs is increased.

To minimize any bias, in all cases we benchmarked 4 PEs using the standard library routine without modification for each supported operation, and indicate times obtained for operations that were not directly supported by following the time with the "*" character; a "?" character is given instead of a time in cases where the routine was not directly supported and we were unable to create an efficient implementation. We also found that some operations could not be supported without major restructuring, in which case we list a "−" character rather than an execution time.

All the tables in the remainder of this document have the same form. Each line corresponds to the system and library being measured. Each column corresponds to the operation being performed. Operations within the same table that differ only by the size and type of their operand/return value are indicated by giving the size of the integer value in bits or listing "Float for 32-bit floating-point and "Double" for 64-bit floating-point. (The timing difference between signed and unsigned integer operations is generally negligible.) **All execution times are listed in microseconds.**

3. PAPERS Management Operations

Before any program can use the PAPERS hardware, it must obtain PAPERS access permission from the operating system, confirm that the software and hardware environment is consistent, and generate an initial barrier synchronization. All of these functions are performed by simply calling p_init().

To indicate that a program has completed using PAPERS, it calls p_exit() with an argument which is used much like the argument to the ordinary UNIX exit() call. Notice, however, that calling p_exit() does not necessarily terminate the calling process — it just terminates the use of PAPERS. The routine p_error() is provided to terminate the current PAPERS parallel program with the given error message.

4. Low-Level PAPERS Operations

At the lowest level of the PAPERS library, these routines form the interface for the most direct use of the PAPERS hardware.

To set the current barrier group, p_enqueue() is called with a bit mask that has a 1 bit in each position corresponding to a member of the barrier group. Currently, by default, all available processors are in the initial barrier group. To perform a barrier wait with the current barrier group, simply call p_wait().

The remaining three functions all operate on integer flags as single-bit truth values. The p_any() and p_all() operations are familiar enough to any user of parallel processing.

The p_waitvec() operation is actually a one-bit multibroadcast that allows all processors to obtain a mask vector constructed from the one-bit votes of all processors. Processor k's vote is in bit k of the result. Enabled processors vote 1 if f is true (non-zero), 0 otherwise. Disabled processors always vote 0. This voting operation was originally devised so that processors could vote on which partition they wanted to be in when a barrier group is divided by a parallel conditional, trivially creating the new barrier mask for each processor. However, it is also used to determine things like which processors want to access a shared resource, or which have extra work to do, etc. Thus, p_waitvec() is very commonly used, for example, by code generated by compilers or translators to schedule I/O operations; however, users are not expected to directly access this type of function.

The times measured for these functions are listed in Table 2. Note that the Cray T3D hardware barrier mechanism does not support arbitrary partitioning, but only static partitioning on fixed boundaries; thus, the concept of dynamically enqueuing a new barrier grouping does not exist. Likewise, both the Paragon XP/S and PVM 3 treat groupings as essentially static. However, as a SIMD machine with enable masking hardware, the MasPar MP-1 supports runtime re-grouping of PEs very efficiently. The MasPar's completely synchronous nature explains the remarkable Wait time, and its global OR network makes the other times also very respectable.

Table 2: Timing for Low-Level Operations (microseconds)

	Enqueue	Wait	Waitvec	Any	All
Cray T3D	-	1.7	?	?	?
Cray T3D (PVM)	-	21	?	?	?
MasPar MP-1	4.7	0.1	9.4	2.7	5.1
Paragon XP/S	-	530	?	?	?
PAPERS1	3.5	3.1	3.2	3.2	3.3
TTL_PAPERS	0.1	2.5	6.3	6.3	6.3
PVM 3	-	49,000	?	?	?

5. Putget Operations

The PAPERS library putget operation is the most fundamental mechanism for supporting arbitrary communication between processors. The model is simply that each processor in the current barrier group outputs a datum, specifies which processor it wants the datum from, and returns the selected value. Logically, each processor writes to its own bus buffer within the PAPERS unit and simply snoops the value written on the bus it selects.

Although some versions of PAPERS directly implement this mechanism (e.g., PAPERS1), TTL_PAPERS does not. Instead, it must map the putget into a series of simple broadcasts (see Section 9). There are two basic approaches to this mapping. One method is to simply force every processor in the barrier group to perform a broadcast; this is simple and consistent, but is inefficient for patterns in which the values sent by some processors are not used (i.e., this technique is best for permutations). The alternative is to first collect a vote from the processors as to which PEs would be sending useful values, and then to send only those values. Surprisingly, this voting operation is just p_waitvec().

The timing of putget operations is particularly important because this operation is used to implement arbitrary communication patterns. For example, a single putget can implement any permutation or any multi-cast. There is no concept of "neighbors" or network contention for putget — every processor is just one communication away.

Table 3 gives the times for putget operations. Clearly, the MasPar's router network supports the notion of putget surprisingly well. What is not evident in this table is that even the times for the Paragon and PVM are essentially independent of the communication pattern implied by the putget.

Table 3: Timing for Putget Operations (microseconds)

	8	16	32	64	Float	Double
MasPar MP-1	33	36	44	67	44	67
Paragon XP/S	710*	700*	700*	700*	700*	700*
PAPERS1	8.5	15	27	62	29	63
TTL_PAPERS	58	111	216	434	219	467
PVM 3	97,000*	96,000*	100,000*	100,000*	96,000*	101,000*

6. Gather Operations

The PAPERS library gather operations collect a datum from each processor in the current barrier group, and fill-in the corresponding entries in each processor's local memory array whose address is passed as the first argument to the function. Array entries corresponding to processors that are not in the current barrier group are unaffected. Thus, gather is essentially either n broadcast operations (as in TTL_PAPERS) or n-1 putget operations (as in PAPERS1).

There is no scheduling overhead introduced for TTL_PAPERS to schedule the broadcasts because each processor in the group has a local copy of the barrier bit mask. Likewise, PAPERS1 putgets are scheduled without additional overhead.

The performance of these functions is summarized in Table 4.

Table 4: Timing for Gather Operations (microseconds)

	8	16	32	64	Float	Double
MasPar MP-1	125*	144*	191*	290*	191*	290*
Paragon XP/S	710*	700*	700*	700*	700*	700*
PAPERS1	33	53	89	194	95	199
TTL_PAPERS	57	110	216	439	248	444
PVM 3	96,000*	96,000*	98,000*	99,000*	98,000*	100,000*

7. Arithmetic Reduction Operations

By definition, a reduction operation is an associative operation; i.e., the order in which the component operations are performed does not significantly alter the resulting value. One way to perform these operations is to have all processors collect all the data and then serially reduce the local copy. This yields a very simple implementation suitable for clusters with up to about 8 processors, and this technique is currently used for the 4 PE TTL_PAPERS library.

The problem with this approach on larger clusters is that it executes in $O(n)$, rather than $O(\log_2 n)$, time for n processors. This is remedied by using the usual tree reduction with communication implemented by a putget operation for each of the $\log_2 n$ communication steps. However, the tree reduction is somewhat complicated by the fact that some processors might not be members of the current barrier group, in which case they do not participate in the reduction. Thus, if a tree reduction is to be used, the participating nodes must effectively be "renumbered" to determine their positions within the reduction tree. This can be done without any communication operations — each node is numbered by p_enumerate() and the tree contains p_population() leaves (see Section 11). This is the method used by PAPERS1.

Benchmark times for sum, product, minimum and maximum reductions are very similar for all but the MasPar MP-1. Times for p_reduceAdd operations are given in Table 5. Because the MasPar MP-1 processors are implemented using a 4-bit slice ALU, times for multiply reductions are markedly slower; e.g., p_reduceMuld() takes 849 microseconds. For the same reason, the MasPar MP-1 hardware is faster for comparison operations than for additions; e.g., p_reduceMin32() takes just 81 microseconds.

264

Table 5: Timing for ReduceAdd Operations (microseconds)

	8	16	32	64	Float	Double
MasPar MP-1	124	139	180	266	302	428
Paragon XP/S	700*	700*	700	700	710	680
PAPERS1	20	33	57	128	63	131
TTL_PAPERS	58	112	217	438	219	444
PVM 3	101,000*	101,000	100,000	99,000	100,000	116,000

8. Bitwise Reduction Operations

The TTL_PAPERS hardware communication mechanism is actually a 4-bit NAND of the data from all processors in the barrier group, which is accessed within the library by the in-line function p_nand(). Thus, a 4-bit bitwise OR can be implemented simply by complementing the inputs to the NAND. Likewise, a 4-bit bitwise AND is generated by complementing the result of a NAND. Similar logic is also used within PAPERS1. Timing for OR reduction is given in Table 6.

Table 6: Timing for ReduceOr Operations (microseconds)

	8	16	32	64
MasPar MP-1	9.4	12	17	31
Paragon XP/S	710*	710*	710	710
PAPERS1	9	16	30	81
TTL_PAPERS	16	30	59	137
PVM 3	104,000	99,000	100,000	103,000

9. Broadcast Operations

Although both PAPERS1 and TTL_PAPERS directly implement broadcasting, these functions are actually implemented as macros of other PAPERS library routines. For example, both the TTL_PAPERS and PAPERS1 definitions of p_bcastPut32() and p_bcastGet32() are:

```
#define p_bcastPut32(d)    ((void) p_reduceOr32(d))
#define p_bcastGet32()     p_reduceOr32(0)
```

A PE which is simply getting the broadcast value is really contributing 0 to a global OR.

Table 7 summarizes the benchmark results for paired broadcast put and get operations. The MasPar times are very low because the global OR network is used (in the guise of the MPL proc[] construct) to obtain the value from the PE that is broadcasting and the SIMD broadcast hardware is then used to transmit that value to all PEs.

Table 7: Timing for Broadcast Put/Get Operations (microseconds)

	8	16	32	64	Float	Double
Cray T3D (PVM)	?	?	?	82	?	82
MasPar MP-1	9.5	12	18	31	18	31
Paragon XP/S	210	220	210	210	210	210
PAPERS1	9	16	30	81	30	81
TTL_PAPERS	16	30	59	137	59	137
PVM 3	38,000	38,000	38,000	40,000	39,000	41,000

10. Scan Operations

A scan, or parallel prefix, computation is much like a reduction, but returns partial results to each of the processors. Like reductions, these operations can be performed in parallel or serially. For a small number of processors, using a gather operation to collect the data values in each processor and then serially computing the result for each processor in local memory works well (and is used by both TTL_PAPERS and PAPERS1), but there are many alternative implementations.

Aside from using a tree structured implementation (with the same barrier group numbering problem described for reductions in Section 7), many of the scan operations that use integer data can be implemented efficiently by methods based on p_waitvec(). In some cases, the p_waitvec() would be used for processors to vote high or low relative to the value output by one processor (e.g., for a rank operation). For the Bits variants of the scans, a series of p_waitvec() operations can be used to transmit only the desired data bits from all processors.

The timing of sum, product, AND, OR, minimum, and maximum parallel prefix operations are quite similar; for space reasons, only ScanAdd times are listed in Table 8. Although not strictly a scan operation, the ranking operation (used for sorting) behaves very much like a scan, and is thus benchmarked in Table 9.

Table 8: Timing for ScanAdd Operations (microseconds)

	8	16	32	64	Float	Double
MasPar MP-1	381	561	920	1,640	1,041	1,799
Paragon XP/S	710*	700*	700*	700*	700*	700*
PAPERS1	35	55	91	197	97	204
TTL_PAPERS	63	124	227	463	245	456
PVM 3	96,000*	96,000*	98,000*	99,000*	98,000*	100,000*

Table 9: Timing for Rank Operations (microseconds)

	8	16	32	64	Float	Double
MasPar MP-1	5,465	6,754	9,318	14,451	9,884	14,975
Paragon XP/S	710*	700*	700*	700*	700*	700*
PAPERS1	37	57	93	201	103	205
TTL_PAPERS	63	116	222	510	228	522
PVM 3	96,000*	96,000*	98,000*	99,000*	98,000*	100,000*

11. Group Property Operations

These operations compute properties of the current barrier group — without any communication. The value of p_population() is literally the population count of (number of 1 bits within) the barrier bit mask. The value of p_enumerate() can be determined in essentially the same way, but before computing the bit population, the barrier mask should be bitwise ANDed with the current processor's bit mask minus 1. Thus, each processor counts the number of participating processors in the mask that have lower processor numbers than itself. The select operations simply return the number of one PE in the current barrier group.

The benchmark results are given in Table 10. Both PAPERS1 and TTL_PAPERS implement all of these functions as table lookups based on the barrier bit mask. The MasPar yields a more costly implementation because the bit mask is spread across the PEs (i.e., each PE knows only its own enable status), and communication is required. Because the other libraries do not support partitioning into arbitrary barrier groups, these operations are not supported.

Table 10: Timing for Group Property Operations (microseconds)

	Population	Enumerate	SelectFirst	SelectOne
MasPar MP-1	147*	572	35	12
PAPERS1	0.5	1	0.7	0.8
TTL_PAPERS	0.5	1	0.7	0.8

12. Voting Operations

One of the most powerful uses of the PAPERS library involves the use of PAPERS to statically schedule operations at runtime based on precise knowledge of the global state of the computation. We have found that such scheduling often is based on determining which PEs, or how many PEs, are contending for the same resource.

The most obvious resource upon which PEs might contend is the data bus that connects each PE to the PAPERS unit. For example, suppose that we need to have the sender, rather than the receiver, determine which PE will get a datum. Unlike putget, sender-targeted communication can have conflicts if multiple PEs want to send to the same PE. The receiver can determine that this contention exists by examining the return value obtained when each PE uses p_voteCount() to register the number of the PE to which it will send a datum. If the return value is 0, no PE targets this PE. If the return value is 1, the communication can be accomplished in one operation. A higher number indicates contention.

The use of p_vote() is similar to that of p_voteCount(), but the return value is a new barrier mask containing only processors that voted for this PE. Although this barrier mask might, or might not, be used to create a new barrier group, it can be used very effectively to statically schedule the contending accesses.

The concept of the match operations is very similar to that of the vote operations, but each PE gets either the count or the barrier mask representing the set of PEs that put forth the same data value as itself.

Although future versions of PAPERS will directly implement some of these functions, both PAPERS1 and TTL_PAPERS currently implement these operations by performing a sequence of $\log_2 n$ `p_waitvec()` operations to transmit an n-bit vote or match value from all PEs. The algorithm can be summarized as follows.

For each bit in the vote or match value, use `p_waitvec()` to transmit the bit. The returned bit vector is inverted if this PE's corresponding PE number/match value bit was a 0. By anding all the resulting bit vectors together, we create a bit mask with a 1 in each position corresponding to a PE that is contending for/with us. The counts are obtained by simply performing a population count of bits in this mask.

The resulting execution times are listed in Table 11. Notice that none of the other libraries directly provides this type of scheduling support operation, although the MasPar's router network incorporates similar logic for detecting contention within its network.

Table 11: Timing for Voting Operations (microseconds)

	VoteCount	Vote	MatchCount8	Match8
PAPERS1	6.9	6.4	26	26
TTL_PAPERS	13	13	51	50

13. Conclusion

In this paper, we have presented a brief overview of the new communication model implemented by the PAPERS hardware and library. This library is suitable for use either as a vehicle for hand-coding applications or as a target for an optimizing compiler.

We have also shown that many functions provided by this library are familiar in the sense that similar functions appear in a variety of other libraries. However, as the detailed benchmarks reported in this paper show, the PAPERS library routines are consistently among the most efficient. We suggest that this efficiency is not due to our cleverness, but due to the use of a computation model which treats communication as a tightly-coupled parallel operation rather than as a bunch of seemingly independent, potentially conflicting, block-oriented, high-latency, PE-to-PE transmissions.

The benefits of synchronous aggregate communication have long been known in the SIMD world, and have been cited as a primary advantage of SIMD/MIMD mixed-mode computation. However, it is a misconception that such operations require SIMD execution. Making aggregate operations efficient simply requires the ability to efficiently achieve synchronization across a group of PEs — which is to say it requires fast hardware barrier synchronization. One also has to be careful not to bury the communication hardware under too many latency-laden layers of interface software.

All aspects of the PAPERS system design and support software are fully public domain, and a wide variety of projects involving PAPERS are underway. For more information, and more complete benchmark results than space permitted in this paper, see WWW URL:

```
http://garage.ecn.purdue.edu/~papers/Index.html
```

References

[BeS91] T.B. Berg and H.J. Siegel, "Instruction Execution Trade-Offs for SIMD vs. MIMD vs. Mixed Mode Parallelism," *5th International Parallel Processing Symposium*, April 1991, pp. 301-308.

[Cra93] Cray Research Incorporated, *Cray T3D System Architecture Overview*, Cray Research Incorporated, 1993.

[DiC95] H. G. Dietz, T. M. Chung, T. Mattox, and T. Muhammad, "Purdue's Adapter for Parallel Execution and Rapid Synchronization: The TTL_PAPERS Design," submitted to *ACM-IEEE-CS Supercomputing '95*, December 1995.

[DiS88] H. G. Dietz and T. Schwederski, *Extending Static Synchronization Beyond SIMD and VLIW*, Purdue University School of Electrical Engineering, Technical Report TR-EE 88-25, June 1988.

[GeS93] G. Geist and V. Sunderam, *Evolution of the PVM concurrent computing system*, 38th Annual IEEE Computer Society International Computer Conference, February 1993.

[Int94] Intel Corporation, *Paragon User's Guide*, Intel Supercomputer Systems Division, 1994.

[Mas91] MasPar Computer Corporation, *MasPar Programming Language (ANSI C compatible MPL) Reference Manual, Software Version 2.2*, Document Number 9302-0001, Sunnyvale, California, November 1991.

[Mes94] Message Passing Interface Forum, *MPI: A Message-Passing Interface Standard*, Rice University, Technical Report CRPC-TR94439, April 1994.

[Muh95] T. Muhammad, *Hardware Barrier Synchronization For A Cluster Of Personal Computers*, Purdue University School of Electrical Engineering, MS Thesis, May 1995.

[OKD90] O'Keefe, M.T., and Dietz, H.G., Hardware barrier synchronization: static barrier MIMD (SBM). *Proc. of 1990 Int'l Conf. on Parallel Processing*, St. Charles, IL, August 1990, pp. I 35-42.

[OKD90a] O'Keefe, M.T., and Dietz, H.G., Hardware barrier synchronization: dynamic barrier MIMD (DBM). *Proc. of 1990 Int'l Conf. on Parallel Processing*, St. Charles, IL, August 1990, pp. I 43-46.

FALCON: A MATLAB Interactive Restructuring Compiler

L. De Rose*   K. Gallivan**   E. Gallopoulos***   B. Marsolf**   D. Padua[†]

Center for Supercomputing Research and Development
and Coordinated Science Laboratory
University of Illinois at Urbana-Champaign
Urbana, Illinois 61801
{derose, gallivan, stratis, marsolf, padua}@csrd.uiuc.edu

Abstract. The development of efficient numerical programs and library routines for high-performance parallel computers is a complex task requiring not only an understanding of the algorithms to be implemented, but also detailed knowledge of the target machine and the software environment. In this paper, we describe a programming environment that can utilize such knowledge for the development of high-performance numerical programs and libraries. This environment uses an existing high-level array language (MATLAB) as source language and performs static, dynamic, and interactive analysis to generate Fortran 90 programs with directives for parallelism. It includes capabilities for interactive and automatic transformations at both the operation-level and the functional- or algorithm-level. Preliminary experiments, comparing interpreted MATLAB programs with their compiled versions, show that compiled programs can perform up to 48 times faster on a serial machine, and up to 140 times faster on a vector machine.

1 Introduction

The development of efficient numerical programs and library routines for high-performance parallel computers is a complex task requiring not only an understanding of the algorithms to be implemented, but also detailed knowledge of the target machine and the software environment. Today, few effective tools are available to help the programmer of high-performance computers perform the transformations necessary to port parallel programs and library routines across

---

* Supported by the CSRD Affiliates under grant from the U.S. National Security Agency.

** Supported by the National Science Foundation under Grant No. US NSF CCR-9120105 and by ARPA under a subcontract from the University of Minnesota of Grant No. ARPA/NIST 60NANB2D1272.

*** Supported by the National Science Foundation under Grant No. US NSF CCR-9120105.

† Supported in part by Army contract DABT63-92-C-0033. This work is not necessarily representative of the positions or policies of the Army or the Government.

machines. This task is made even more difficult by the great diversity in overall organization between the different classes of parallel computers. This difficulty holds true even when the objective is to develop code for a single target machine.

Several approaches to facilitate the development and maintenance of parallel code are currently under study. One approach is the automatic translation of conventional programming languages, notably Fortran, into parallel form. SUIF [2], a compiler developed at Stanford, and Parafrase-2 [27] and Polaris [25], developed at Illinois, are examples of this first approach. Another approach is to extend conventional languages with simple annotations and parallel constructs. This second approach also involves the development of translation techniques for the extensions. Examples include High Performance Fortran [19] and pC++ [7]. Finally, a third approach is to accept a very high-level description of the mathematical problem to be solved and automatically compute the solution in parallel. Examples of this approach are //ELLPACK [20], developed at Purdue, AL-PAL [12], developed at Lawrence Livermore Laboratories, and EXTENT [15], developed at Ohio State University.

We are developing FALCON, a programming environment that includes capabilities for interactive and automatic transformations at both the operation-level and the function- or algorithmic-level. This environment supports the development of high-performance numerical programs and libraries, combining the transformation and analysis techniques used in restructuring compilers with the algebraic techniques used by developers to express and manipulate their algorithms in an intuitively useful manner [16]. As we envision it, the development process should start with a simple prototype of the algorithm and then continue with a sequence of automatic and interactive transformations until an effective program or routine is obtained. The prototype and the intermediate versions of the code should be represented in an interactive array language. The interactive nature of the language is important to facilitate development and debugging. Array operations are the natural components of most numerical code; therefore, including array extensions in the base language should make the programs easier to develop and modify.

The ideal interactive array language should be easy to learn and capable of accessing powerful graphics and other I/O facilities. We are using an existing language in order to shorten the learning curve for our system and give us immediate access to existing support routines. APL and MATLAB [22] are the most widely used interactive array languages today. We have chosen MATLAB because it is the more popular of the two and has a conventional syntax that facilitates learning it. In MATLAB, as in any interactive array language, the type, rank and shape of variables are dynamically determined. However, for the generation of efficient code, static declarations are necessary. In our system, to facilitate code development, declarations can be inserted by the programmer or automatically by the compiler. Furthermore, in the absence of information from the programmer, or if the compiler is unable to determine type, rank, and shape automatically, code is generated to make the determination at run-time.

A major effort in this research is devoted to the development of the interactive restructuring system which, through correctness-preserving transformations, will lead to efficient code from the original prototype. Our system includes capabilities for interactive restructuring of both expressions and program statements via standard restructuring techniques, algebraic restructuring techniques, and the combination of the two. We designed a uniform transformation system, based on an extensible collection of rewriting rules. Some transformations will operate on a single expression, while others, such as data structure selection, have a global effect on the code. Also, transformations for library routine selection are part of the interactive transformation. Library selection will help the programmer take advantage of a library of routines highly tuned for a particular target machine. Many other transformations, including those to enhance locality and exploit implicit parallelism, are also being developed.

As discussed in more detail below, we take advantage of the collection of functions and operations in MATLAB to facilitate the translation process. Our programming environment incorporates knowledge of the algebraic and computational properties of many MATLAB functions. This enables us to perform complex algebraic transformations on the source program. The availability of information at this semantic level will substantially increase the chances of success where traditional high-level language restructurers fail, due to their almost exclusive focus on low-level operations. The chances of successfully transforming MATLAB programs are further increased by the simplicity of the language. In our experience, Fortran restructurers often fail because of aliasing or the undisciplined use of GO TOs.

The rest of this paper is organized as follows. In Section 2, we present a more detailed description of the system. The current status and some experimental results are presented in Section 3. Finally, our conclusions are presented in Section 4.

2 System Description

In this section, we describe the overall organization of the system as it was designed, and then present additional information about the techniques already implemented. As mentioned in the Introduction, our objective is to develop a programming environment for implementing, maintaining, and extending scientific programs and numerical library routines. Our long-term goal is to generate code for a variety of machines, including conventional workstations, vector supercomputers, shared-memory multiprocessors, and multicomputers. However, to be able to solve several difficult problems that arise in the translation of MATLAB codes, we concentrated our initial efforts on a conventional workstation.

The main target language of the system is Fortran 90, which is very convenient for our purposes because of its similarities with MATLAB. Later, we will also consider generating pC++ as a target language in order to explore object-oriented issues that arise in numerical programming.

The environment consists of four main modules, namely the Program Analysis module, the Interactive Restructuring and Routine Selection module, the

272

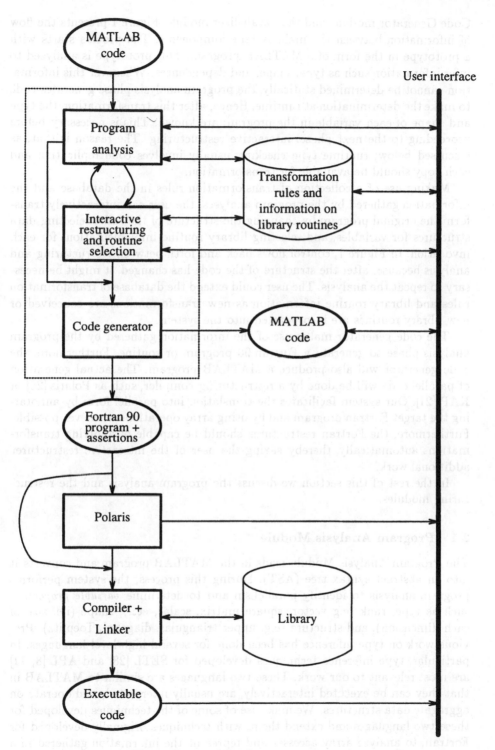

Fig. 1. Program development environment.

Code Generator module, and the Parallelizer module. Figure 1 presents the flow of information between the main system components. The process starts with a prototype in the form of a MATLAB program. This prototype is analyzed to infer information such as type, shape, and dependences. Whenever this information cannot be determined statically, the program analysis phase generates code to make the determination at runtime. Hence, after this transformation, the type and shape of each variable in the program are known. This is necessary before proceeding to the next phase: interactive restructuring. The reason is that, as discussed below, runtime type checking usually involves code replication and each copy should be available for transformation.

Making use of a collection of transformation rules in the database and the information gathered by the program analyses, the user can interactively transform the original program by changing the structure of the code, selecting data structures for variables, and selecting library routine implementations for each invocation. In Figure 1, control flows back and forth between restructuring and analysis because, after the structure of the code has changed, it might be necessary to repeat the analysis. The user could extend the database of transformation rules and library routine information as new transformations are conceived or new library routines are incorporated into the system.

The code generator makes use of the information gathered by the program analysis phase to generate a Fortran 90 program or routine. Furthermore, the code generator will also produce a MATLAB program. The actual generation of parallel code will be done by a restructuring compiler, such as Polaris [25] or KAP [21]. Our system facilitates the translation into parallel form by annotating the target Fortran program and by using array operations whenever possible. Furthermore, the Fortran restructurer should be capable of applying transformations automatically, thereby saving the user of the interactive restructurer additional work.

In the rest of this section we discuss the program analysis and the restructuring modules.

2.1 Program Analysis Module

The Program Analysis Module reads in the MATLAB program and converts it into an abstract syntax tree (AST). During this process, the system performs program analysis to identify parallelism and to determine *variable properties*, such as type, rank (e.g vector, square matrix, scalar, etc.), shape (i.e. size of each dimension), and structure (e.g. upper triangular, diagonal, Toeplitz). Previous work on type inference has been done for several high-level languages. In particular, type inference techniques developed for SETL [28] and APL [8, 11] are most relevant to our work. These two languages are similar to MATLAB in that they can be executed interactively, are usually interpreted, and operate on aggregate data structures. We make use of some of the techniques developed for these two languages and extend them, with techniques originally developed for Fortran, to analyze array accesses and represent the information gathered in a compact form [29]. These techniques are necessary for MATLAB, since arrays

are often built using Fortran-like loops and assignments that may be distributed
across several sections of the code. In contrast, the techniques developed for
APL assume that arrays are usually built by a single high-level array operation.
Determining variable properties automatically should facilitate the program development process. Even though the system also accepts user assertions, the
users may prefer to leave the determination of the properties to the system,
especially when the program under development makes use of routines whose local variables have different shapes and types, depending on the context in which
they are invoked.

To determine variable properties, we make use of *high-level summary information* on the behavior of the MATLAB built-in functions. For example, the
system considers the fact that the function lu returns lower and upper triangular matrices; using this information, it is able to utilize optimized functions,
instead of generalized methods, on these returned matrices in the compiled code.
The use of this high-level information should greatly increase the accuracy of the
analysis over the approach used in conventional high-level language compilers,
where only the information from elementary operations is used.

Use-Definition Coverage The MATLAB program is internally represented in
Static Single Assignment (SSA) form [14]. This is a convenient representation
for many of the analysis algorithms that are implemented. In the SSA representation, it is evident which definitions affect (or cover) a particular use of a scalar
variable. Using this information, it is easy to perform variable renaming and privatization. The usefulness of renaming to improve the accuracy of the analysis
is illustrated in the following pseudocode, which uses i as the imaginary unit.

```
a = 2 * i
b = exp(a)
a = pi / 4.
z = sin(a)
```

In this example, the variable a is used for two different purposes. Giving a
different name to the second use of a makes it possible to assign the type **complex**
to the first use of a, and type **real** to the second. In the absence of renaming, it
would be necessary either to perform dynamic analysis, as discussed below, or
to assume a to be **complex** all the time. While either alternative would produce
a correct program, the code would clearly be more efficient if the correct type of
every use were determined statically.

While it is easy to determine which definitions cover a given use in the case
of scalars using the SSA representation, a more complex approach is necessary
in the case of arrays. For arrays, this information is useful not only to determine
whether different types of values are assigned to array elements in different
sections of the code, but also to determine where to allocate and reallocate
arrays and how much storage is required in each case.

This last problem, which seems to be ignored by current APL compilers [8,
11], is illustrated by the pseudocode segment in Figure 2. In this case, the com-

```
A = ...                              for i=1:n
if (cond)                                k = function(i)
    k = ...                              ...
else                                     A(k) = ...
    k = ...                          end
end
A(i:k) = ...

   (a)                                  (b)
```

Fig. 2. Examples requiring use-definition coverage analysis

piler needs to determine if the partial assignment to **A** is a subrange of the previous definitions of the variable. If not, reallocating **A** may be necessary.

As a second example, consider the pseudocode segment in Figure 2(b). In this case, the compiler needs to estimate the maximum value of **k** to avoid the overhead of dynamic allocation for every iteration of the loop.

We plan to attack the problem of array memory allocation using the techniques described in [29]. These have proven quite effective in detecting privatizable arrays in Fortran programs and should be at least equally effective in this context. The strategy uses data flow analysis to determine which definitions cover the uses of array elements. It also makes use of a number of conventional analysis algorithms, including induction variable recognition [18] to compute upper and lower bounds of these variables, and propagation of the range of values of scalars and of those arrays used as subscripts [6, 13]. This analysis is performed interprocedurally whenever the modules referenced in the program are available to the system. In the case of intrinsic functions, information on the elements accessed are available in a database that is consulted during the computation of ranges. The analysis of ranges and induction variables is facilitated by the use of the SSA representation.

Type Inference To generate Fortran declarations and to support structure selection, the system infers variable properties. Although described separately here, shape and structure inference work in coordination with the coverage analysis discussed in the previous subsection. Variable properties are estimated using a forward/backward scheme [1].

For type inference, we use a *type algebra* similar to the one described in [28] for SETL. This algebra operates on the type of the MATLAB objects and is implemented using tables for all operations. Each node, of the graph representing the program, contains attribute fields to store inference information. These fields are filled during the static inference phase and propagated through the graph whenever a new attribute is synthesized. If these attributes are inferred to have different (or unknown) types, then the node is marked to be resolved during the dynamic phase, or a type that subsumes all possible types is assigned to the variable.

Array shapes are estimated using the induction variable and range propagation algorithms mentioned in the previous subsection. Structural information is computed in similar ways. Again, in the case of rank and shape, code to apply dynamic analysis is generated whenever the static analysis fails. For structural inference, the system uses semantic information to identify special matrix structures, such as diagonal and triangular. This structural information is propagated using an "algebra of structures" which defines how the different structures interact for the various operations. This information is used by the interactive restructurer to replace general methods that operate on regular dense matrices with specialized functions for structured sparse matrices. For example, consider the following MATLAB code for the solution of a linear system $Ax = b$, using a LU decomposition:

```
[L, U, P] = lu(A);
y = L \ (P * b);
x = U \ y;
```

The first statement calls a built-in function (lu) that returns a lower triangular matrix L, an upper triangular matrix U, and a permutation matrix P. For a regular compiler, the second statement should perform a matrix-vector multiplication (Pb) and solve the linear system $Ly = Pb$. Finally, the last statement should solve the linear system $Ux = y$. However, by taking into consideration the semantics of the array language and knowing the properties of L, U, and P, the system will infer that the matrix-vector multiplication (P * b) is only a permutation on the vector b, and that the two linear systems to be solved are triangular systems. Using this information, the multiplication operation and the general linear system solve can be replaced by specialized algorithms during the restructuring phase.

As mentioned above, a facility for user interaction is an important component of the analysis phase. To simplify the interaction, the system will internally record how the properties of a variable affect other variables. The objective is to create a hierarchy of information interdependence and use it to query the user only about the topmost level of the hierarchy.

Dynamic Analysis In some cases, when the static information is insufficient, the user may not be able (or willing) to provide enough information to determine variable properties. In those cases, the system generates code to determine these properties at run-time and, based on this determination, allocates the necessary space and selects the appropriate code sequence. We follow an approach similar to that used in many systems: associating tags with each array of unknown type or shape. Based on these tags that are stored in *shadow variables*, conditional statements are used to select the appropriate operations and to allocate the arrays. Similar shadow variables are generated for dynamic type inference. For example, if the type of A in an assignment of the form B = A + 0.5 were unknown at compile-time, the system would generate two variables for A ($A^{complex}$ and A^{real}) along with a shadow variable for the type of A (A_type) and similar variables for B. Then the assignment is transformed into:

```
B_type = A_type
if(A_type == t_complex)
    B^complex = A^complex + 0.5
else
    B^real = A^real + 0.5
end if
```

Clearly, such transformations cannot be indiscriminately applied. For example, if A is a scalar, it may be faster to assume throughout the program that it is a complex variable and generate code accordingly. However, if A is a large array, or if it is a scalar that is operated with large arrays, the overhead of the if statement will be minimal compared to the extra cost of the assignment, assuming that A is often a real.

Also, in the case of right-hand sides with many operands, or in the case of loops containing many statements, the number of possibilities would grow exponentially. This problem is reduced by transforming the long expressions into shorter ones, or by distributing the loop; in some cases, however, the best strategy may be to assume that the variable is complex. In any case, in our final version, a cost model that incorporates information from typical input data sets will be defined to decide the best strategy in each case. In the current version, static analysis techniques are used to minimize the number of tests applied at run-time.

2.2 Interactive Restructuring and Routine Selection Module

Code restructuring will be done within this module by applying transformations to expressions and blocks of statements. The system will have the necessary interface mechanisms to accommodate the use of automatic transformation modules. Initially, however, we are focusing on interactive transformations based on an easy-to-extend database of rewriting rules. The user will be able to mark any section of the program, including compound statements, subexpressions, and function invocations, for restructuring. The system will then determine which of the transformations in the database apply to the code segment marked by the user. To make such a determination, it will use information automatically inferred from the code, such as dependence graphs, and properties of variables and expressions in the code. The system will then allow the user to select which applicable transformations to perform.

During code restructuring, the user will select the implementation to be used for each function invocation in the final version of the program. This selection process could be done automatically, based upon target machine characteristics. When the selection is done interactively, the user will be able to target specific libraries to be used in the implementation and to select a version of the implementation to be used for a specific function invocation. There will also be a facility that allows the user to query the system's database, which contains information about the library on particular target machines. This information will include: version descriptions; performance information and tuning recommendations; the type of processing used (parallel on all processors, parallel on a subset of processors, vector, scalar); and possible rewriting of the library routine in terms of other lower-level library routines.

There has been some work on interactive program restructuring and there are some commercially available interactive Fortran restructurers, such as FORGE [3]. Also, restructuring of high-level operators has been discussed in the literature [4, 12], although there are no widely-used systems that apply these types of transformations, as no system today includes capabilities for algebraic, control structure, and library selection transformations.

We are planning on implementing several restructuring techniques for complex transformations on the code. These transformations will be used either to improve the performance of the code or to enhance the numerical properties of the algorithm. These techniques can be divided into two groups: *algebraic restructuring*, based on the algebraic information, and *primitive-set restructuring*, based on the primitives being used.

Algebraic Restructuring This part of the system will use the algebraic rules defined for the variables, whether they are scalars, vectors, or matrices, to restructure the operations performed on the variables. To perform such manipulations, symbolic computation tools, such as Maple [10], can be employed. In some cases, applying these rules may be similar to the standard loop-based restructuring strategies used by conventional restructuring compilers, such as loop blocking. However, we also want to be able to handle special matrix classes and more complex operators. Our goal in applying the algebraic rules to matrices and vectors will be to achieve better restructuring than when the rules are only applied to scalar operations. For the interactive application of transformations, algebraic restructuring may provide a more convenient form for the user than loop-based restructuring, even when the effect on the resulting code is the same.

The main rules that will be considered for these transformations are the algebraic properties of associativity, distributivity, and commutativity for vectors and matrices. These properties for vectors and matrices are not as simple as for scalars. For instance, the multiplication operations are not commutative and, with matrices, the commuted operation may not even be possible. For example, $A * B$ may be possible whereas $B * A$ may not be possible. Furthermore, the order in which matrix operations are performed can have a significant effect on the number of operations to be performed [24]. Consider the multiplication of three vectors, $v_1 * v_2^t * v_3$, where each vector contains n elements. If the matrix operations are grouped as $(v_1 * v_2^t) * v_3$, the calculation takes $\mathcal{O}(n^2)$ floating point operations whereas, if the operations are grouped as $v_1 * (v_2^t * v_3)$, it only takes $\mathcal{O}(n)$ operations.

In addition to the simpler properties, the system will attempt to understand more complex operators, such as the Gauss transform and the Householder transform. These types of transformations are used to build matrix factorization algorithms: the Gauss transform for the LU factorization and the Householder

$$x_i^T = v_i^T A$$
$$Y_i = 2v_i x_i^T$$
$$A = A - Y_i$$
$$x_j^T = v_j^T A$$
$$Y_j = 2v_j x_j^T$$
$$A = A - Y_j$$

(a)

$$x_i^T = v_i^T A$$
$$Y_i = 2v_i x_i^T$$
$$x_j^T = v_j^T A$$
$$Y_j = 2v_j x_j^T$$
$$\alpha = v_j^T v_i$$
$$Z_j = 2\alpha v_j x_i^T$$
$$A = A - Y_i - Y_j - Z_j$$

(b)

Fig. 3. Two examples of the application of two Householder transforms.

transform for the QR factorization. By examining the properties of the transformations, we can reach an understanding of how these properties can be used for restructuring. For example, consider how the Householder QR factorization could be blocked. By examining the code, the application of two Householder transforms, H_i and H_j to the matrix A, could be viewed as $H_j(H_i A)$. Using the definition of the Householder transform, $H_i = (I - 2v_i v_i^T)$, the operations normally required in the code would be as presented in Figure 3(a). This code requires the use of 6 $\mathcal{O}(n^2)$ operations. If, however, the transforms are combined before they are applied, $(H_j H_i)A$, then the operations presented in Figure 3(b) are required.

With this code there are now 8 $\mathcal{O}(n^2)$ operations and a new $\mathcal{O}(n)$ operation for the calculation of α. Although this new code requires additional operations and memory storage, in practice it provides better locality thus resulting in improved performance. These additional operations were generated by utilizing the definition of the transform; they would not have been apparent by just examining the code. This utilization of algebraic information is being performed not only by algorithm developers, but is also being explored by compiler writers [9].

The transformations will be based on patterns that the system can recognize in the code and on the replacements for these patterns. The developer will be able to select a segment of code and the system will indicate which patterns match the segment. The developer will then select which transformation to apply from those possible. For example, consider some replacement patterns for statements involving the MATLAB solve operation, "\", in Figure 4.

These patterns consist of two main parts: the pattern to be replaced and the resulting code. Within the pattern, it is important to match not only the operation, but also the characteristics of the operands. For instance, in the first pattern, the matrix M is a square matrix; but, for the second pattern, M must be a diagonal matrix. In order to reduce the number of patterns required, we will attempt to order the matrix types according to their characteristics.

The structured sparse matrix characteristics form a lattice through which properties are inherited from the original *square* matrix. For instance, operations on a *square* matrix will work on a *lower triangular* matrix, and operations on a

```
REPLACE                          REPLACE
   INTEGER n                        INTEGER n
   REAL M(n,n), b(n), x(n)          REAL M(n,n){DIAGONAL}
   x = M \ b;                       REAL b(n), x(n)
WITH                                x = M \ b;
   REAL L(n,n), U(n,n)           WITH
   REAL y(n)                        x = b ./ diag(M);
   [L, U] = lu(b);               END
   y = L⁻¹ × b;
   x = U⁻¹ × y;
END
```

Fig. 4. Sample restructuring patterns for MATLAB solve operation.

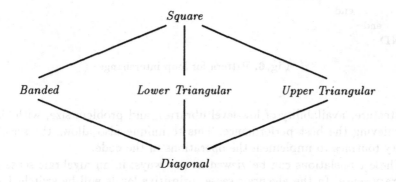

Fig. 5. Partial ordering of matrix types.

lower triangular matrix will also work on a *diagonal* matrix. A partial ordering of these types is presented in Figure 5.

In order to support complex algebraic transformations, it is sometimes necessary to match code segments according to characteristics of the operations instead of exactly matching the operations. In Figure 6, a pattern for interchanging loops shows how certain dependence conditions can be placed on the matching of the loop body. In this example, the loops can be interchanged only if the data dependences do not contain a direction vector of the form <,> [26].

Primitive-set Translation Primitive-set translation can also be used to translate the code to the level of numerical operations that work best for the target machine and application [17]. Instead of dealing with the code only at a matrix operation level, this phase will be able to decompose the algorithms to matrix-vector operations and vector–vector operations; or, in some circumstances, it will form higher-level operations by combining multiple lower-level operations. This optimization technique should be guided by factors such as the machine

```
REPLACE
    INTEGER i,j
    do i = 1:n
        do j = 1:n
            <BODY>
            WHERE
                no-match-direction-vector("<, >", dependence(<BODY>))
            END
        end
    end
WITH
    INTEGER i,j
    do j = 1:n
        do i = 1:n
            <BODY>
        end
    end
END
```

Fig. 6. Pattern for loop interchange.

architecture, availability of low-level libraries, and problem size, with the goal of achieving the best performance. This technique also allows the selection of library routines to implement the operations in the code.

These translations can be viewed in two ways: in an algebraic sense and in a library sense. In the algebraic sense, primitive levels will be switched via the combination or decomposition of matrix and vector operations. In the library sense, primitive levels will be switched via modifying the code so that it maps to the subroutines in a specific library. The end results, however, will be similar regardless of which of the two views is used.

When mapping an operation to the subroutines in a library, the subroutines may be at the same primitive level, at a lower level, or at a higher level. Switching to a lower primitive level will involve taking an operation and decomposing it into multiple operations. This will be achieved by decomposing one, or both, of the operands into substructures and then applying the operation with these substructures. For instance, matrix multiplication can be performed by: using the Level-3 BLAS subroutine DGEMM once; using the Level-2 BLAS subroutine DGEMV in a loop; or, using the Level-1 BLAS subroutine DDOT in a doubly nested loop. The code can be transformed using patterns similar to those used for the algebraic restructuring, as shown in Figure 7 for the Level-2 BLAS subroutine.

As with algebraic restructuring, it will be necessary for the code developer to specify which transformation to use when multiple patterns match the operation. It will be possible for the developer to select the patterns from a specific library to use for all operations, or to examine the code and select a pattern for each specific operation. For each library the system will support, replacement patterns must be developed to map the MATLAB operations to subroutines in the library.

```
REPLACE
 INTEGER n
 REAL A(n,n), B(n,n), C(n,n)
 C = A * B;
WITH
 INTEGER i
 SUBROUTINE DGEMV(P_IN,P_IN,P_IN,P_IN,P_IN,P_IN,P_IN,P_IN,P_IN,P_OUT,P_IN)
 for i = 1:DIM(B,2)
   C(1,i) = DGEMV('N',DIM(A,1),DIM(A,2),1.D0,A,DIM(A,1),B(1,i),1,0.D0,1);
 end
END
```

Fig. 7. Pattern for mapping matrix multiplication to level-2 of the BLAS.

Moving to a higher primitive level, therefore, would involve finding multiple primitives that can be combined into a single operation. However, for the transformation system to do this, it needs to search the program for multiple statements that fit a known pattern, typically a loop of operations, or to react to the user's directions.

2.3 Support for Parallelism

In the initial implementation, the primary support for parallelism will be the ability to place data dependence assertions within the code using directives. Such directives can be used to supply information, such as interprocedural analysis and the independence of data accesses. For instance, the calls to built-in functions in MATLAB are known to be side-effect free by the semantics of the language. However, if the calls to the built-in functions are translated to subroutine calls for a specific library, the semantics of the calls may no longer guarantee that the operation is side-effect free. Consider the example in Figure 8, where the matrix multiplication C = A * B has been decomposed into a series of independent matrix-vector products to allow parallel execution. In this example, the left side shows the original code, and the right side shows the code after it has been translated to use a level-2 BLAS primitive. A traditional compiler would not be able to determine if the loop is parallel without performing analysis of the DGEMV code. However, our system will be able to assert that the calls can be performed in parallel since the functionality of the original code was parallel.

A second example of dependence information involves the use of sparse data structures. The code in Figure 9 shows a code segment for adding two vectors together and the resulting code when one of the vectors, A, is changed to a sparse vector. A traditional compiler would not be able to determine that the indices contained in ind vector of the transformed code are unique. Our system, however, would be able to assert that the indices are unique because it understands the semantics of the nonzeros function.

```
for i = 1:n                        for i = 1:n
    C(:,i) = A * B(:,i);               call DGEMV('N',n,n,1.0D0,A,n,
end                                        B(1,i),1,0.0D0,C(1,i),1);
                                   end
```

Fig. 8. Two implementations showing the loss of dependence information.

```
for i = 1:n                        ind = nonzeros(A);
    B(i) = A(i) + B(i);            len = size(ind);
end                                for i = 1:len
                                       B(ind(i)) = A(ind(i)) + B(ind(i));
                                   end
```

Fig. 9. Two vector additions showing the loss of dependence information.

3 Current Status and Experimental Results

Presently we have a compiler that can parse MATLAB code into the AST and generate Fortran 90 for most operations and built-in functions. This current version of the compiler supports: the static analysis for type, rank, and shape; the utilization of shadow variables for dynamic inference; the generation of code for the dynamic allocation of variables; and the interactive replacement of MAT-LAB statements using simple patterns. Future work on the compiler includes: the implementation of the structural inference; an optimization of the dynamic analysis for indexed variables; and the expansion of the pattern matching system.

Currently, the primitive–set translation system supports translating simple MATLAB operations into subroutine calls for a specific library. The transformation system is being modified to support other combining rules for mapping the MATLAB operations to subroutine calls. The new rules allow one MATLAB operation to be mapped to multiple subroutine calls as well as multiple MATLAB operations to be mapped to a single subroutine call.

Figure 10 shows an example of the code generated by the transformation system which used the replacement pattern from Figure 7. In this figure, the original MATLAB code segment is presented, followed by the code segment that would utilize a level-2 BLAS library. Other libraries, such as a level-3 BLAS or a sparse library, can be supported.

The performance of this version of the compiler was initially tested using three MATLAB code segments provided in Netlib for the algorithms presented in [5]. These programs were written for general use; hence, they were not completely optimized for specific matrix structures. However, for our tests, we hand-optimized these MATLAB programs, and also wrote a Fortran 90 version of the same algorithms for comparison with the compiler generated codes. The main characteristic of these programs is that none of the variables are referenced or assigned using indices.

```
MATLAB code:              Translated Fortran 90 code:
  D = rand(4);               call RANDOM_NUMBER(D)
  F = D * D;                 do T__3 = 1,4
                               call DGEMV('N', 4, 4, 1.0D0, D, 4,
                                 D(1, T__3), 1, 0.0D0, F(1, T__3), 1)
                             end do
```

Fig. 10. Example of code translation for matrix multiplication, using level-2 BLAS.

| | | | Fortran 90 | |
Algorithm	Iterations	MATLAB	Generated	Hand coded
CG	103	11.2	4.8	4.6
QMR	54	12.3	4.8	4.4
SOR	40	15.9	6.8	2.0

Table 1. Execution times in seconds using optimized MATLAB code.

These code segments correspond to the following algorithms for the iterative solution of linear systems: the Conjugate Gradient method (CG), the Quasi-Minimal Residual method (QMR), and the Successive Overrelaxation method (SOR). The programs were tested using a 420×420 stiffness matrix from the Harwell-Boeing Test Set. To control the time required for the experiments, the tolerance was set to 10^{-5} for the CG and QMR algorithms, and 10^{-2} for the SOR. The experiments were conducted on a SPARCstation 10. The times are presented in Table 1.

When comparing the timing results presented in Table 1, we observe that the compiled programs are almost three times faster than the interpreted programs. Since both versions use BLAS and LINPACK routines to perform the numerical operations on the matrices, this difference in performance is attributed to the overhead of the interpretation of the MATLAB code. However, since most of the hand optimizations used to improve the performance of the MATLAB execution will be done automatically by the compiler with the structural inference, we can expect an even greater improvement in performance, when comparing with programs that were written for general use.

When comparing the hand-coded Fortran 90 programs with the compiler generated versions, several observations can be made. First, in the CG case, the performance of the compiled version was very close to the performance of the hand-coded program. This 5% difference is attributed to the overhead of the dynamic inference. Second, in the QMR program we observed a difference in performance on the order of 10%. This larger performance difference is because, in the current version of the static inference mechanism, operations (such as square root), that rely upon the value (in addition to the type) of the input variable to determine the resulting type, are always considered to result in a **complex** variable. Since the QMR program had a square root operation, some of the variables in the compiled program were defined to be of type **complex**. The operations with these complex variables generated a second source of overhead, due to the larger number of computations required by complex operations. We are extending our inference mechanism for this kind of function, by trying to keep track of each variable's sign.

Finally, in the SOR case, we observed that the hand-coded version is almost four times faster than the compiled code. The main reason for this difference is attributed to the computation of the following MATLAB expression inside a loop:

$$x = M \setminus (N * x + b);$$

where x and b are vectors, M is a lower triangular matrix, and N is an upper triangular matrix. The hand-coded version considers this information and calls specialized routines from the BLAS library to compute the solve operation ($\setminus$) and the matrix multiplication (N * x) for triangular matrices. The compiled version (as well as MATLAB) uses a run-time test to detect that M is a triangular matrix, and computes the solve using specialized functions. However, they pay the price of detecting the triangular structure of the matrix: it requires $\mathcal{O}(n^2)$ operations. Moreover, in both cases, the matrix multiplication is performed using a generalized function for full matrices that performs $2n^2$ operations, while the BLAS function for triangular matrix multiplication performs roughly half the number of operations. Furthermore, it would not be worthwhile to test if the matrix is triangular during runtime because, as mentioned above, the test itself has an $\mathcal{O}(n^2)$ cost. We observe again that, after the structural inference process is complete, the compiler will be able to detect the triangular structure of the matrices, and the performance of the generated code will be closer to the hand-optimized code.

A second set of test were performed using programs that contain indexed variables. A brief description of these programs is presented in Table 3. These programs were run on a SPARCstation 10, and on a Convex C-240 compiling for vector optimization.

We can classify the programs in Table 3 into three groups, depending upon certain characteristics of the MATLAB code and its execution. The first group consists of programs that spend most of their time executing built-in functions (i.e. QL, 3D-Surface, and Cholesky). In this case, the performance improvements are similar to the previous tests, and are attributed mainly to the overhead of interpretation. We place in the second group the program that requires dynamic allocation of matrices inside of a loop (i.e. Adaptive Quadrature). In this case, for the data set used, we observed an improvement for the serial execution on the order of 20. However this improvement varies considerably, depending upon the number of reallocations that are required by the program, that is in turn dependent upon the function that is being used. Finally, the third group contains loop-based programs that require element-wise access of arrays (i.e. the remaining programs). In this case, we observed a very good performance improvement, because the loop control structure of the compiled code is far more efficient than the interpreted code, especially for doubly-nested loops.

Problem	Source	Problem size
QL method for finding eigenvalues	a	50 × 50
Generation of a 3D-surface	b	41 × 21 × 11
Incomplete Cholesky factorization	b	200 × 200
Adaptive quadrature using Simpson's rule	a	1 Dim. (7)
Dirichlet solution to Laplace's equation	a	26 × 26
Crank-Nicholson solution to the heat equation	a	321 × 321
Finite difference solution to the wave equation	a	321 × 321
Computation of the inverse Hilbert matrix	c	180 × 180
Source:		
a - From [23]; b - Colleagues; c - The MathWorks Inc, as a M-File (*invhilb.m*).		

Table 2. List of test programs for indexed variables

Algorithm	SPARCstation 10			Convex C-240		
	MATLAB	F 90	Speedup	MATLAB	F 90	Speedup
QL method	8.8	3.17	2.8	NA	NA	NA
3D-Surface	17.1	2.95	5.8	NA	NA	NA
Inc. Cholesky Fact.	2.1	0.35	6.0	6.3	0.49	12.9
Adaptive Quadrature	1.4	0.07	20.0	4.5	0.06	68.8
Dirichlet Method	20.7	0.61	33.9	71.8	0.99	72.5
Crank-Nicholson	61.7	1.46	42.2	237.7	2.50	95.0
Finite Difference	25.2	0.55	45.8	98.4	0.82	120.0
Inv. Hilbert matrix	5.8	0.12	48.3	21.2	0.15	141.3

Table 3. Execution times (in seconds) for programs using indexed assignments.

4   Conclusions

This system creates an environment that is useful for researchers in computational sciences and engineering for the rapid prototyping and development of numerical programs and libraries for scientific computation, an environment that takes advantage of both the power of interactive array languages and the performance of compiled languages. This environment provides capabilities for interactive and automatic transformations at both the operation-level and the function- or algorithmic-level.

In order to generate code from the interactive array language, this system combines static and dynamic inference methods for type, shape, and structural inference. Research is also being performed into the application of high-level optimizations, that take into consideration the semantics of the array language to improve the performance of the target code.

As shown by our preliminary results, by compiling the interpreted language we can generate a code that executes faster than the interpreted code, especially for loop-based programs with element-wise access. Also, we observe that in some cases the performance of the compiled code is very close to the performance of the hand-optimized Fortran 90 program.

Finally, exploitation of parallelism will be enhanced, because the utilization of a high-level array language (Fortran 90) as output will facilitate the generation of code for a parallel machine by a parallelizing compiler. Moreover, the possibility of adding directives for parallelization, and data dependence assertions, will further improve parallelism.

References

1. AHO, A., SETHI, R., AND ULLMAN, J. *Compilers: Principles, Techniques and Tools*. Addison-Wesley Publishing Company, 1985.
2. AMARASINGHE, S. P., ANDERSON, J. M., LAM, M. S., AND LIM, A. W. An Overview of a Compiler for Scalable Parallel Machines. In *Languages and Compilers for Parallel Computing* (August 1993), U. Banerjee, D. Gelernter, A. Nicolau, and D. Padua, Eds., Springer-Verlag, pp. 253–272. 6th International Workshop, Portland, Oregon.
3. APPLIED PARALLEL RESEARCH. *FORGE 90 Baseline System User's Guide*. Placerville, California. Version 8.9.
4. BACKUS, J. Can Programming Be Liberated from the Von Newmann Style? A Functional Style and Its Algebra of Programs. *Communications of the ACM 21*, 8 (August 1978), 613–641.
5. BARRETT, R., BERRY, M., CHAN, T., DEMMEL, J., DONATO, J., DONGARRA, J., EIJKHOUT, V., POZO, R., ROMINE, C., AND VAN DER VORST, H. *Templates for the Solution of Linear Systems: Building Blocks for Iterative Methods*. SIAM, 1993.
6. BLUME, W., AND EIGENMANN, R. The Range Test: A Dependence Test for Symbolic, Non-linear Expressions. In *Proceedings of Supercomputing '94* (November 1994), pp. 528–537.
7. BODIN, F., BECKMAN, P., GANNON, D., NARAYANA, S., AND YANG, S. Distributed pC++: Basic Ideas for an Object Parallel Language. In *OON-SKI'93 Proceedings of the First Annual Object-Oriented Numerics Conference* (April 1993), pp. 1–24.
8. BUDD, T. *An APL Compiler*. Springer-Verlag, 1988.
9. CARR, S., AND KENNEDY, K. Compiler Blockability of Numerical Algorithms. In *Proceedings, Supercomputing '92* (November 1992), pp. 114–124.
10. CHAR, B. W., GEDDES, K. O., GONNET, G. H., LEONG, B. L., MONAGAN, M. B., AND WATT, S. M. *Maple V Language Reference Manual*. Springer-Verlag, New York, 1991.
11. CHING, W.-M. Program Analysis and Code Generation in an APL/370 Compiler. *IBM Journal of Research and Development 30:6* (November 1986), 594–602.
12. COOK JR., G. O. ALPAL A Tool for the Development of Large-Scale Simulation Codes. Tech. rep., Lawrence Livermore National Laboratory, August 1988. Technical Report UCID-21482.
13. COUSOT, P., AND HALBWACHS, N. Automatic Discovery of Linear Restraints Among Variables of a Program. In *Proceedings of the 5th Anual ACM Symposium on Principles of Programming Languages* (1978), pp. 84–97.
14. CYTRON, R., FERRANTE, J., ROSEN, B. K., WEGMAN, M. N., AND ZADECK, F. K. Efficiently Computing Static Single Assignment Form and the Control Dependence Graph. *ACM Transactions on Programming Language and Systems 13*, 4 (October 1991), 451–490.

15. DAI, D. L., GUPTA, S. K. S., KAUSHIK, S. D., LU, J. H., SINGH, R. V., HUANG, C.-H., SADAYAPPAN, P., AND JOHNSON, R. W. EXTENT: A Portable Programming Environment for Designing and Implementing High-Performance Block-Recursive Algorithms. In *Proceedings of Supercomputing '94* (November 1994), pp. 49–58.

16. DEROSE, L., GALLIVAN, K., GALLOPOULOS, E., MARSOLF, B., AND PADUA, D. An Environment for the Rapid Prototyping and Development of Numerical Programs and Libraries for Scientific Computation. In *Proc. of the DAGS'94 Symposium: Parallel Computation and Problem Solving Environments* (Dartmouth College, July 1994), F. Makedon, Ed., pp. 11–25.

17. GALLIVAN, K., AND MARSOLF, B. Practical Issues Related to Developing Object-Oriented Numerical Libraries. In *OON-SKI'94 Proceedings of the Second Annual Object-Oriented Numerics Conference* (April 1994), pp. 93–106.

18. GERLEK, M. P., STOLTZ, E., AND WOLFE, M. Beyond Induction Variables: Detecting and Classifying Sequences Using a Demand-driven SSA Form. *ACM TOPLAS* (to appear).

19. HIGH PERFORMANCE FORTRAN FORUM. *High Performance Fortran Language Specification*, May 1993. Version 1.0.

20. HOUSTIS, E. N., RICE, J. R., CHRISOCHOIDES, N. P., KARATHANASIS, H. C., PAPACHIOU, P. N., SAMARTIZS, M. K., VAVALIS, E. A., WANG, K. Y., AND WEERAWARANA, S. //ELLPACK: A Numerical Simulation Programming Environment for Parallel MIMD Machines. In *Proceedings 1990 International Conference on Supercomputing* (1990), pp. 96–107.

21. KUCK AND ASSOCIATES, INC. *KAP User's Guide*, 4th ed. Savoy, IL 61874, 1987.

22. THE MATH WORKS, INC. *MATLAB, High-Performance Numeric Computation and Visualization Software. User's Guide*, 1992.

23. MATHEWS, J. H. *Numerical Methods for Mathematics, Science and Engineering*, 2nd ed. Prentice Hall, 1992.

24. MURAOKA, Y., AND KUCK, D. J. On the Time Required for a Sequence of Matrix Products. *Communications of the ACM 16*, 1 (January 1973), 22–26.

25. PADUA, D., EIGENMANN, R., HOEFLINGER, J., PETERSEN, P., TU, P., WEATHERFORD, S., AND FAIGIN, K. Polaris: A New-Generation Parallelizing Compiler for MPP's. Tech. rep., Univ. of Illinois at Urbana-Champaign, Center for Supercomputing Research and Development, June 1993. CSRD Report No. 1306.

26. PADUA, D., AND WOLFE, M. Advanced Compiler Optimizations for Supercomputers. *Communications of the ACM 29*, 12 (December 1986), 1184–1201.

27. POLYCHRONOPOULOS, C., GIRKAR, M., HAGHIGHAT, M. R., LEE, C.-L., LEUNG, B., AND SCHOUTEN, D. Parafrase-2: A New Generation Parallelizing Compiler. In *Proceedings of 1989 Int'l. Conference on Parallel Processing, St. Charles, IL* (August 1989), vol. II, pp. 39–48.

28. SCHWARTZ, J. T. Automatic Data Structure Choice in a Language of a Very High Level. *Communications of the ACM 18* (1975), 722–728.

29. TU, P., AND PADUA, D. Automatic Array Privatization. In *Languages and Compilers for Parallel Computing* (August 1993), U. Banerjee, D. Gelernter, A. Nicolau, and D. Padua, Eds., Springer-Verlag, pp. 500–521. 6th International Workshop, Portland, Oregon.

A Simple Mechanism for Improving the Accuracy and Efficiency of Instruction-Level Disambiguation*

Steven Novack, Joseph Hummel, and Alexandru Nicolau

Department of Information and Computer Science
University of California, Irvine, CA 92717

Abstract. Compilers typically treat source-level and instruction-level issues as independent phases of compilation so that much of the information that might be available to source-level systems of transformations about the semantics of the high-level language and its implementation, as well as the algorithm in some cases, is generally "lost in the translation", making it unavailable to instruction-level systems of transformations. While this separation of concerns reduces the complexity of the compiler and facilitates porting the compiler to different source/target combinations, it also forces the costly recomputation at the instruction-level of much of the information that was already available to the higher level, and in many cases introduces spurious dependencies that can not be eliminated by instruction-level analysis alone.

In this paper we present a simple mechanism for retaining algorithm and source language semantics information for use in instruction-level disambiguation, while retaining the ease of porting the compiler to different source/target combinations, and without noticeably increasing the complexity of the compiler. Simulation results show that our mechanism provides a significant increase in both performance, resulting from more accurate higher level data dependence information, and efficiency, as instruction-level dependence analysis no longer needs to recompute information that was already available at the higher level.

1 Introduction

In this paper we present a mechanism for using algorithm-level and source-level (high-level language) semantics information to simplify and improve memory reference disambiguation (anti-aliasing) at the instruction-level, thus enabling improved instruction-level parallelization by removing spurious data dependencies[3]. This mechanism is motivated by the observation that ambiguities that constrain instruction-level parallelization often result, in practice, from the loss of important semantics information when translating a program from higher to lower levels of abstraction: when the programmer translates an abstract algorithm into high-level source code, any information about algorithm-level semantics that can not be expressed directly in the source language are typically lost, and then, when the compiler "front-end" translates the source code into an instruction level (e.g. 3-addr[1]) intermediate representation, there is usually further loss of algorithm-level, as well as source-level semantics information that can not be expressed directly within the instruction-level representation. For instance, algorithm level semantics may imply that two different pointer variables always refer to disjoint memory spaces; the definition of a source language may state that separately defined arrays within the same scope use disjoint pieces of memory; a particular source language implementation may imply that different kinds of variables are allocated on

* This work was supported in part by ONR grant N00014-93-1-1348.

the heap, while others are allocated on the stack; and a programmer may specify that variables of certain data types may never share memory with variables of certain other data types, even though the source language itself allows for it. While in principle these kinds of higher level semantics information could be passed through from higher to lower levels, in practice, very little, if any, of this kind of information is available for use in instruction level disambiguation. In fact, the typical approach to compilation is to completely separate front-end (algorithm-/source-level) and back-end (instruction-level) issues in order to manage the complexity of the compilation problem and to facilitate the porting of the compiler to different source/target combinations. The unfortunate consequence of such a complete separation is that *all* memory references at the instruction level that represent accesses to variables specified in the source, as well as those introduced by the compiler for temporaries, spill code, and passing parameters on the stack become potentially ambiguous at the instruction level. Thus the instruction-level parallelization engine is forced to make overly conservative assumptions regarding memory reference interdependencies or must resort to potentially very expensive analysis techniques to determine these interdependencies — a redundant and inherently incomplete exercise since in many cases we are at best re-computing dependencies that were already known at the higher level, and at worst we are forced to make overly conservative decisions anyway as some information can not be determined via instruction-level analysis, but still might have been available at the algorithm or source level.

For example, consider a typical 3-addr representation for a LOAD, "(LOAD $r1 $r2 1234)", which copies into register r1 the value stored at the memory location addressed by the sum of the contents of register r2 and the constant 1234. Without considering the context in which this LOAD exists we must assume that it could access any location in memory, since r2 might contain any value. Instruction-level disambiguation techniques typically attempt to remove this ambiguity by deriving symbolic expressions (e.g. by folding up along def-use chains leading from r2) that represent the possible locations that each LOAD or STORE might access, usually as a function of one or more irreducible variables (e.g. loop induction variables, indirections through memory, or program inputs), and then estimating solutions to systems of these equations in order to determine whether memory accesses sometimes, always, or never interfere with one another. More sophisticated symbolic analysis techniques like [8] might then be applied to further refine disambiguation. Techniques based on symbolic analysis can be fairly accurate when dealing with memory references whose access expressions are expressed in terms of the same unknowns, or can be reduced to unknowns with a known relationship (e.g. for references to different parts of the same array); however, when the expressions are too complicated for the particular technique or are expressed in terms of different unknowns with complex relationships, the instruction level disambiguator must conservatively assume that the references conflict. Whether the instruction-level disambiguator correctly determines the dependence or not, the time spent trying to disambiguate the reference is completely wasted if the dependence had been known at the algorithm or source level; if in addition, the disambiguator conservatively reported a conflict when none actually existed at the higher level, then the degree of parallelism, as well as the efficiency of parallelization, are unnecessarily, and sometimes severely, diminished.

While the need for using algorithm-level and/or source-level semantics information for coarse grain transformations and parallelization at the source level has been well established [14, 23, 2, 12, 11, 9], little attention has focused on retaining higher level semantics for use in instruction-level transformations and parallelization. For instance, source-level dependence analysis and programmer assertions regarding pointer inter-dependencies are commonly used to increase the degree of coarse-grain parallelism by enabling various loop transformations like loop interchange and strip mining [23]; however, by the time source-level data structures have been mapped to memory locations and source-level references have been converted to sequences of machine instructions for accessing that memory, the correspondence between the actual memory LOAD and STORE operations and the source-level references that they represent, as well as the dependence information that related the different source-level references is lost.

Our goal in this paper is to provide a mechanism for retaining high-level semantics for use in instruction level parallelization that both improves and simplifies memory reference disambiguation, without noticeably increasing the complexity of compilation or sacrificing the ease of porting the compiler to different source/target combinations. The mechanism we propose is based on defining a hierarchical decomposition of the address space of the program wherein all instruction level memory references (e.g. LOADs and STOREs) are associated with one or more objects in the hierarchy. References associated with disjoint objects in the hierarchy are considered independent (and references to different parts of the same object may still be determined to be independent via traditional disambiguation techniques). The hierarchical decomposition is defined by explicit and implicit assertions that embody higher level semantics: algorithm-level semantics, as explicitly specified by an analysis tool or a programmer, and source-level semantics, as specified implicitly by the definition of the source language and its implementation in a particular context, and explicitly by certain restrictions on the use of the language enforced by the programmer (including those that represent algorithm-level semantics). For example, one approach to creating the hierarchy that has worked for us when using C as the source language is to begin with default assertions provided by the compiler writer about the semantics of C and its implementation by a particular compiler (e.g., GCC), and then to refine the hierarchy using assertions about programmer enforced restrictions on the use of C and algorithm level semantics provided by an applications programmer and/or high-level analysis tool.[2] These assertions are made initially about each source-level alias, which may be an actual source-code variable or a temporary introduced by the compiler, and then are inherited by any instruction-level memory references generated to access the aliased data object.

For example, Figure 1 shows how a semantics retention hierarchy might be used to parallelize a piece of C code at the instruction level for an idealized VLIW architecture with 3 homogeneous, unicycle functional units. In this example, the arrays A, B, and C are auto variables and are therefore allocated on the stack and N is a pointer into heap memory. The 3-addr statements labelled 1-4 are the instruction-level representation of the first line of C code in the body of the loop, 5-8 represent the second line, and 9-10 represent the last line (loop control code is omitted here for conciseness). The semantics hierarchy shown was initially created based on assertions about the source-code that represent the abovementioned facts: A, B, and C are variables allocated on the stack, and whatever N points to is allocated on the heap. The 3-addr statement 5 inherits the associations of N, statements 6 and 8 inherit those of A, statements 2

---

[2] Depending on the language, algorithm, and user sophistication, some or all of this information may not be supplied. We are not advocating the use of the techniques proposed in this paper by all users and for all codes, but rather we are merely trying to show that implementation and use of this approach are not too hard and can have very significant benefits if used appropriately.

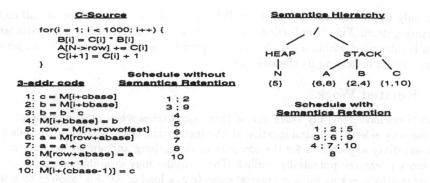

Fig. 1. Using a simple semantics retention hierarchy.

and 4 inherit those of B, and statements 1 and 10 inherit those of C. Ignoring the facts represented by the semantics hierarchy, the LOAD on line 5 must be assumed to conflict with all STOREs, and the STORE on line 8 must be assumed to conflict with all STOREs and LOADs.[3] The best schedule that can be obtained for the target architecture given these ambiguities, labelled "Schedule without" in the figure, is twice as long as the schedule achieved ("Schedule with") when the scheduler is able to examine the semantics hierarchy for conflicts.

Note that our use of assertions differs significantly from the typical "statement-based" approach in which assertions describe explicit dependence relations (especially independence) between individual source-level statements or variables.[4] Statement-based assertions have two main drawbacks. The first is the interspersing of numerous, point-specific assertions throughout the program, often resulting in sloppy and potentially error-prone code. The second is that, whether at the source-level or the instruction-level, the point-specific dependence information described by statement-based assertions generally needs to be updated when the code is changed by optimizing and parallelizing program transformations. One of the main advantages of our approach is that, rather than provide "point-specific" assertions that describe dependencies between individual statements or variables, our assertions describe, at a high level, how a program's data is structured, without any reference to the specific statements used to create, modify, or access this structure. Thus, our assertions are valid across most code optimizations and transformations (i.e., as long as the semantics of the data structures remain the same), without the costly overhead of updating asserted dependencies in response to changes in the code.

The remainder of this paper is organized as follows. Section 2 relates our work to other techniques that, to one extent or another, make use of higher level semantics during instruction-level parallelization. In Section 3 we describe our simple semantics retention mechanism that could easily be integrated into most compilers and we illustrate the importance of using semantics retention in instruction level parallelization,

---

[3] Note that better symbolic analysis will not help — the problem is not with ı, but rather is related to not knowing the values of N or N->row.

[4] Given the appropriate mechanism, statement-based assertions could also be retained at the instruction-level as explicit dependence assertions between individual 3-addr operations; however, in practice, they are typically used exclusively at the source-level.

not only to increase the degree of parallelism but also to decrease the overall cost of disambiguation. Finally in Section 4 we provide a brief outline of how semantics retention is integrated within a parallelizing compiler being developed at UCI and provide some results indicating its effectiveness.

2 Related Work

Compilers have generally taken one of three approaches when attacking the problem of memory reference disambiguation at the instruction-level. The most obvious (and conservative) approach is for the compiler to do nothing and simply assume that all memory references potentially conflict. The compiler may disambiguate a few simple references by checking for some special cases (e.g. a load of $SP + 4$ followed by a store into $SP + 8$), but applies no general technique of memory disambiguation. The *gcc* compiler falls into this category, which is unfortunate given its wide use both as a C compiler and as a back-end for other high-level languages. For instance, the GNAT project, which developed an Ada 9x compiler using *gcc*'s back-end is both an excellent motivator and candidate for semantics retention as proposed here, given its use of *gcc* as a back-end while the front-end is dealing with Ada 9x, a language with a stricter type system, parameter specifications, and pure functions.

A second approach is for the compiler to make all source-level information directly available at the instruction-level. In particular, the data structures created by the compiler during parsing and source-level analysis—which maintain, for example, def-use and alias information—are accessible from the instruction-level. This is typically done by having each instruction point back to the statement from which it originated, thereby providing access to the relevant source-level information. The advantage of course is that the instruction-level now has access to more accurate program information, thus enabling more accurate memory disambiguation. However, the disadvantages are two-fold: (1) the separation of concerns between the front-end and back-end of the compiler has been severely compromised, and (2) code movement at the instruction-level may force the costly recomputation of information at the source-level. For example, sophisticated techniques are available for computing alias information in the presence of pointers [16, 6]. Collecting such alias information can be expensive, and the resulting information is *program-point* specific. Yet the movement of a single instruction may alter not only its alias information but also that of other instructions, thereby requiring alias recomputation.

The third and last approach is the one taken by most optimizing compilers. In this case the compiler performs at least some intraprocedural disambiguation analysis at the instruction-level, but algorithm and source-level dependence information, if present, is discarded during the translation from source-level to instruction-level. The advantage of this approach is that the back-end is fairly easy to build and maintain due to its total separation from the front-end, but also retains some ability to perform memory disambiguation. The disadvantage is that the back-end may be repeating analysis previously performed at a higher level. Worse, some information simply cannot be deduced at the instruction level (or at least is too expensive to compute), such as information about types, parameters, and the algorithm.

Our approach attempts to retain the three separate advantages of each of the above-mentioned approaches — namely efficiency, separation of concerns, and retention of source-level (and algorithm level) information for increased accuracy — without incurring the disadvantages of any. We achieve this by allowing the front-end to communicate higher level, memory reference information to the back-end by associating each reference with a portion of a hierarchical decomposition of the program's address space. This information is not program-point specific, can be efficiently tested to detect potential memory conflicts, and is sufficiently concise and high-level to ensure a reasonable separation of concerns during compiler development. The information being communicated is similar in spirit to that collected by Emami et. al. [6] (and later extended by [7]), which is used to build a memory hierarchy based on pointers into the STACK and HEAP. Our approach however is not program-point specific, and goes a step further in supporting a general framework for all memory references, scalars and pointers alike. A language-based approach of similar vein was also proposed by Lucassen in [17], however, in this case the hierarchy is completely user-defined and at the granularity of entire data structures.

3 Semantics Retention

Semantics retention refers to retaining semantics from higher to lower levels of program abstraction. From the highest level of abstraction, the algorithm-level, we would think of retaining that information that is either known or can be inferred from the algorithm, but that can not typically be expressed directly in the next lower level of abstraction, the source-level. For instance, in C there is no way to specify that two pointer variables always refer to disjoint pieces of memory, however, this fact may be obvious, or determinable via sophisticated analysis engines, at the algorithm-level. Similarly, from the source-level of abstraction, we would think of retaining information at the instruction-level that is known or can be inferred about the source language, from its definition, from its implementation, or even from programmer enforced restrictions on its use (including those restrictions that represent algorithm-level semantics). For instance, in C, auto variables are typically allocated on the stack, while static variables and memory allocated by malloc are allocated on the heap, so any pointer that is known to refer to the heap is known to be independent of any auto variable; however, little if any of this information is typically expressed within the framework of an instruction level representation of the program. For instance, with a flat, unsegmented memory space, there is no reason other than the definition and/or implementation of the source language to assume that stack and heap space are disjoint. Even when it is known that the heap and stack are disjoint, instruction level representations rarely distinguish between LOADs/STOREs to the heap versus LOADs/STOREs to the stack; moreover, even when this distinction can be inferred through analysis, doing so is redundant (and potentially very time consuming) since the information was readily available at a higher level of abstraction.

In this section we will describe a simple mechanism for retaining algorithm-level and source-level semantics for use in instruction-level parallelization. This description consists of two parts. First, we will define the hierarchical decomposition of the program's address space, the levels of which will ultimately be associated with the potentially ambiguous instruction level memory references of the program, allowing for many of the ambiguities to be resolved based on the properties of the hierarchical decomposition, without the potentially very expensive analysis that might otherwise be required. Then, we will describe how algorithm-level and source-level semantics are used to guide the decomposition and to bind memory references to the objects in the decomposition.

3.1 Hierarchical Decomposition: Definition

The semantics retention mechanism is based on a hierarchical decomposition of the program's address space in which successively lower layers in the hierarchy represent a more and more refined partitioning of the program's address space. Within this framework, references to data objects that were known to be independent at the algorithm-level or source-level are associated with disjoint objects within the hierarchy. Given this information it is often possible to disambiguate instruction-level LOADs and STOREs simply by examining their associated objects within the hierarchical decomposition — when the objects are disjoint, the references are known to be independent. Thus, the hierarchy allows the instruction-level to benefit from much of the same sorts of dependence information that is often available to source-level systems of transformations, and vastly decreases the overall cost of disambiguation by allowing powerful, but often expensive, instruction-level analysis techniques to be employed only when strictly necessary (i.e. for references to possibly different parts of the same object). More formally, a hierarchical decomposition of the address space of a program is a tree of nodes, wherein each node N is associated with a set S_N having the following properties:

- $S_I \subseteq S_N$ for each successor I of N
- reference $A \in S_N \Rightarrow B \in S_N \; \forall \, B$ s.t. SPACE(A) $\bigcap$ SPACE(B) $\neq \emptyset$.
- if N is the root of the tree, then reference $A \in S_N \; \forall \, A$.

where a reference is either an explicit reference for a variable declared in the source or for a temporary introduced by the compiler, and SPACE(A) is the set of all addresses that A might access. Note that for any reference A, SPACE(A) never actually needs to be known, but rather, only whether or not it might intersect with SPACE(B) for some other reference B, which can always be answered conservatively in the affirmative, but in most cases can be answered far more precisely according to the available algorithm-level and source-level semantics.

Figure 1 shows an example decomposition for a piece of code. Notice that since membership at a leaf node implies membership at all nodes leading back from the leaf to the root of the hierarchy, we only show the S_{LEAF} sets associated with each leaf node LEAF.

It follows directly from the definition of the hierarchical decomposition that for any two memory references, A and B, A is independent of B if there exists a node N in the hierarchy such that $A \in S_N$ and $B \notin S_N$. In other words, even though A and B may refer to the same object higher in the hierarchy, at a sufficiently low level, the references are to disjoint objects in the hierarchy. It remains now to show how such a hierarchy can be constructed that embodies a useful amount of algorithm-level and source-level semantics of the program.

3.2 Hierarchical Decomposition: Instantiation

Any technique that satisfies the definition of the hierarchical decomposition as defined above can be used to decompose the address space. In this section we will describe one such technique that begins with a general structuring of the hierarchy that embodies the semantics of the C language as implemented within the GCC compiler, plus a few common restrictions on the usage of C that a programmer would likely adhere to,[5] and then ends with a discussion of how a high level dependence analysis tool is used to refine this hierarchy to include algorithm-level semantics specific to a particular program.

---

[5] Of course, the relevant refinements to the hierarchy would only be used when the programmer does indeed adhere to these restrictions.

Ultimately we want the hierarchical decomposition to associate instruction level memory references with different objects in the hierarchy, based on source-level assertions about algorithm-level and source-level semantics; however, at the source-level, instruction-level memory references are not yet known. To get around this apparent contradiction, we divide the creation of the hierarchy into two phases. During the first phase, the hierarchy is built in its entirety based on source-level assertions about *source-level* aliases and the data objects they represent, and then in the second phase, while generating the instruction-level representation of the program, each memory reference created to access the data aliased by the source-level alias X is simply added to each level in the hierarchy that X belongs to (i.e. the memory reference inherits the associations of X). For the purposes of this paper we define an alias to be any source-level variable, temporary introduced by the compiler, or a component of an aggregate variable (e.g. a field of a **struct** in C).

The first phase of decomposition proceeds as follows. We start with a trivial hierarchy consisting only of a root node containing all source-level aliases (i.e. all aliases in the program are contained within S_{ROOT}). Then, using a simple assertion mechanism we refine this initial hierarchy by adding new nodes and/or new aliases to existing nodes to represent newly acquired higher level semantics information about the program. These assertions take the form: ASSERT(ALIAS, PATH) where ALIAS is a source-level alias and PATH has the form: /$NODE_1$/$NODE_2$/.../$NODE_M$, $M \geq 1$ and represents a path of nodes from the root, denoted "/", to the node $NODE_M$. The function of ASSERT is to traverse the hierarchy, following in order the nodes on PATH while adding ALIAS to each node visited; when visiting $NODE_I$, if $NODE_{I+1}$ is not a successor of $NODE_I$, then $NODE_{I+1}$ is created and made a successor of $NODE_I$. In this fashion, a single ASSERT can completely specify one way in which an alias fits within the hierarchy. The entities making the assertions, such as a compiler writer, application programmer, and/or high-level dependence-analysis tool would be responsible for ensuring that the resulting hierarchical decomposition is correct with respect to the definition given in Section 3.1.

One approach to creating the hierarchy that has worked for us when using C as the source language[6] is to begin with default assertions provided by a compiler writer about the semantics of C and its implementation by a particular compiler (e.g. GCC), and then to refine the hierarchy using assertions about programmer enforced restrictions on the use of C and algorithm-level semantics provided by an application programmer and/or high-level analysis tool.

Figure 2 shows a basic structure for the semantics hierarchy based on a few trivial but fundamental facts about the C language as implemented by GCC (the other information in the figure will be described shortly) . The first layer in the hierarchy, which distinguishes between HEAP and STACK variables, is based on the facts that each data object is allocated on either the stack or the heap, and that auto variables are always allocated on the stack while static variables and memory returned by malloc are always allocated on the heap. The next layer in the hierarchy, which distinguishes between objects of different types, is based on the fact that a variable of type "pointer to T" will indeed usually be required to point only to objects of type T.[7] Note that unless the application programmer is known to follow this rule strictly, then no assertion

---

[6] C is merely used to provide a concrete example — any high-level language would be equally amenable to semantics retention along the lines described here.

[7] The ability in C to freely cast pointers of one type to pointers to another, means that a pointer to type T, could in fact point to an object of type T1.

is made about any particular pointer variable, i.e. the semantics of the source language alone can only imply that all pointers are associated with all nodes in the hierarchy; however, as we will see shortly, the programmer and/or a dependence analysis tool will usually be able to make specific assertions about individual pointer variables, or collections of pointer variables, that do follow this rule (or even more precise restrictions) so that those pointer variables will be associated only with paths for which the appropriate "type" node is present. Below we will show examples of using this simple "type" assertion, as well as other, more algorithm specific assertions to create a hierarchy that greatly improves disambiguation of pointer references at the instruction level.

While the first two levels in the hierarchy represent partitions that can be made for virtually all C programs, the next level in the hierarchy, which shows a different node for each variable, represents the first level that is program specific. The partitioning at this level is based on the fact that different variables in C do not share memory with one another. In fact, the existence of this level highlights one of the main problems with the conventional approach of completely separating front-end from back-end issues in compilation. At the instruction level, every LOAD and STORE is potentially ambiguous since there is typically no way to know *a priori* what it is used for. The conventional approach for dealing with this is to try to determine interdependencies between LOADs and STORE's (and other memory references for non-RISC targets) via analytical (symbolic) disambiguation techniques. Due to imperfections in these techniques and/or cost vs. performance trade-offs used to artificially constrain the amount of work done, many LOADs and STOREs that would be clearly independent if looked at in the context of the high-level references that they represent (e.g. LOADs and STOREs to different data structures), may be conservatively determined to be dependent by conventional instruction-level disambiguation techniques. Even for those dependencies that conventional analysis techniques correctly determine, the time taken to do so is completely wasted when considered in relation to the fact that most of these dependencies were already known at the higher level.

The example shown in Figure 2 illustrates how even this simple base structure for the hierarchy can by itself eliminate many potential ambiguities and much of the cost of disambiguation at the instruction level. The ASSERT's shown create a hierarchical decomposition that represents the facts that NODE and CTRL each point to objects of different types and furthermore that CNT, DATA, and NEXT are disjoint parts of *NODE (i.e. the object pointed to by node) and VEC is a field of *CTRL. These assertions can be made manually by the programmer or automatically by the compiler if the programmer is known to follow the rule that all pointers are to objects of the correct type,[8] then, when translating to the instruction-level representation, 3-addr statements 1 and 3 inherit the associations of CNT, 4 inherits those of DATA, 5 and 7 inherit those of VEC, and 8 inherits those of NEXT. For the sake of simplicity we again assume an idealized 3-wide VLIW target architecture with homogeneous, unicycle functional units. If the compiler does not exploit the facts represented by the semantics hierarchy, then the compiler must make the conservative assumption that the pointers NODE and CTRL could point anywhere in memory and therefore that the LOAD represented by the 3-addr statement 5 must be conservatively assumed to depend on the STORE in statement 3. In this case, the best schedule that can be obtained for the selected target architecture, shown under the "Schedule without" heading in the figure, takes 6 cycles. If on the other hand, the compiler exploits the properties of the hierarchical decomposition, then the 3-cycle schedule, shown under the "Schedule with" heading,

---

[8] This information would typically be imparted via a command line argument to the compiler.

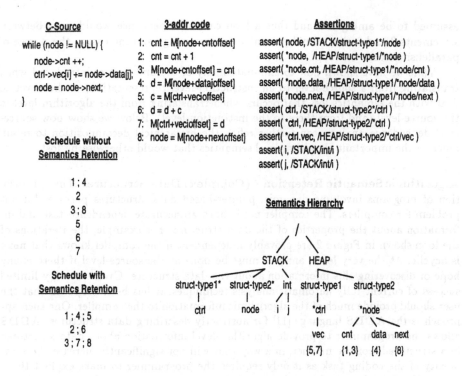

Fig. 2. Eliminating ambiguities.

can be achieved. In this case, the hierarchy indicates that NODE and CTRL can not possibly point to the same object and therefore statement 5 could be scheduled in parallel with statement 1. In addition, the hierarchy also implies that statement 4 is independent of statement 3. While this fact might be determinable via analytical instruction-level disambiguation techniques (and in fact, notice that we did assume that the references were correctly disambiguated for the "No Semantics Retention" schedule), the hierarchy obviates the need for performing such analysis for these two references; at the very least this represents improved compilation time efficiency and in cases where the analysis would fail to disambiguate the references, it would often yield improved parallelization as well. For instance, if the range of possible values for J, the variable used to index node->data, is unknown at the instruction level, and the compiler lays out data so that CNT follows DATA, then any purely analytical instruction-level disambiguation technique would still have to assume that statement 4 depends on statement 3 since, in this case, there is no way to distinguish between the end of DATA and the beginning of CNT, even though at the source-level the references are clearly independent according the semantics of the source language.

The above example shows how simply retaining some trivial semantics information about the C language can significantly improve instruction-level parallelization. The above example also shows that this is insufficient to yield maximum parallelism — if, as it seems, the "while" loop traverses an acyclic linked list of nodes, it should be possible to pipeline the loop so that successive iterations are executed in parallel; however, without some algorithm-level semantics information about what the loop is doing, the memory references to NODE from successive iterations are conservatively assumed to be ambiguous and thus a loop carried dependence would exist between statements 3 and 1 that would prevent loop pipelining from increasing the degree of parallelism within the loop.

While we have shown how to eliminate many of the ambiguities introduced when translating from a source-level to an instruction-level representation, we have yet to deal with the semantics loss that occurs when translating from the algorithm-level to the source-level (and from there to the instruction-level). Below we show how source-level dependence analysis can further refine the hierarchical decomposition to retain much of the important algorithm-level semantics that would otherwise be lost.

Algorithmic Semantic Retention – (Complex) Data Structures The optimization of programs involving dynamic, pointer-based data structures poses a difficult problem for compilers. The compiler needs both an accurate dependence test and information about the properties of the data structure. For example, the iterations of the loop shown in Figure 2 are provably independent if the compiler knows that **next** is acyclic. At the very least, analysis must be done at the source-level if there is any hope of discovering this information about the data structure. Given the very limited success of current fully automatic analysis techniques, it has been proposed that the user should provide much of the algorithmic information to the compiler. One such approach is the **ADDS** language [11] for abstractly describing data structures. **ADDS** allows the programmer to provide algorithm-level information about data structures in a structured, concise manner, in a way that will not significantly increase the complexity of the coding task as it only requires the programmer to make explicit those properties of the data structure that should be obvious to anyone who understands the algorithm. This information can easily be integrated into the approach proposed here by using it to further refine the program's memory reference hierarchy.

```
typedef struct llnode [N] {
    int cnt;
    float data[100];
    struct llnode *next forward along N;
} list;
```

(a) Supplying the property of "acyclicness".

```
while (...) {
    node->cnt++;
    ctrl->vec[i] + = node->data[j];
    node1 = node->next;
    if (...) break;
    node1->cnt++;
    ctrl->vec[i] + = node1->data[j];
    node2 = node1->next;
    if (...) break;
    node2->cnt++;
    ctrl->vec[i] + = node2->data[j];
    node = node2->next;
}
```

(b) Thus allowing more code to be exposed for parallelization at the instruction-level.

Fig. 3. Using **ADDS** to provide algorithm level semantics.

Thus, in the example shown in Figure 2, the user can use **ADDS** to provide a more informative type declaration, supplying the necessary properties to the compiler — namely that of "acyclicness". The revised declaration is shown in Figure 3a: the keyword **forward** conveys the fact that the **next** field is traversing the specified *dimension* **N** in an acyclic manner. Analysis of the loop would then reveal that the iterations are independent if for any node p, it can be shown that the path $p.next^+$ does not lead back to p. This is easily proven given the fact that **next** is acyclic. To exploit this information at the instruction-level, the compiler could, for instance, unroll the loop from

Figure 2 a few iterations at the source-level to expose more operations to be scheduled in parallel at the instruction-level.[9] This is what is shown in Figure 3b. In this case, each version of NODE from successive iterations is assigned a new compiler-generated variable, NODE$_I$, while the other, loop invariant, variables CTRL,[10] I, and J, remain the same across all iterations. The compiler would then encode the fact, derived from the **ADDS** declaration, that each NODE$_I$ is independent of the others, by generating new ASSERT's that have the cumulative effect of creating new copies of the sub-trees rooted at NODE and *NODE for each NODE$_I$ version. Given this new refinement to the hierarchy, the degree of parallelism available to the instruction level scheduler is now limited only by the length of the linked list and the rate at which the **next** fields can be traversed.

One of the advantages of dynamic data structures is their ability to be composed in complex ways, allowing more complicated relationships to be expressed. The challenge of course is for the compiler to perform accurate analysis even in the presence of such complexities. Furthermore, as indicated by the previous example, it can be critical for the results of this analysis to be available to all stages of compilation, not just to systems of source-level transformations. For example, a *Bipartite graph* is essentially two linked-lists, where each node contains a list of connections (pointers) to some of the nodes in the other linked-list. This data structure simply allows nodes in one list to be related to those in another, and since it is composed of linked-lists, the previous analysis and semantics retention techniques should apply. The difference now is that the data structure is no longer a simple tree-like structure, but a DAG.

```
typedef struct bgnode [N][E] {                  p = head;
    float coeff, value;                         while (p ≠ NULL) {
    struct bgnode *next forward along N;            for (i=0; i<max; i++) {
    struct bgnode *dests[max] forward along E;          d = p->dests[i];
} bigraph                                               p->value + = p->coeff * d->value; /* L */
where ∀ p and i, p.next* <> p.next*dests[i] ;       }
                                                    p = p->next;
                                                }
(a) ADDS declaration for the bipartite graph.  (b) The main computational loop.
```

Fig. 4. A more complex example.

Bipartite graphs are useful in real applications, as for example, in the simulation of the propagation of electromagnetic waves through objects in 3D [4]. The graph's linked-lists are composed of electric (E) nodes and magnetic (M) nodes. The most important properties of this data structure are that (1) the sets of E and M nodes are distinct, and (2) the data structure is acyclic. This is extremely difficult to deduce automatically, and yet is known to the programmer as a consequence of the algorithm. These properties can however be conveyed to the compiler using a combination of the approaches discussed in [11, 13], as shown in Figure 4a. The data structure has two dimensions, N and E, which denote traversal along the nodes and traversal along edges to the destination nodes, respectively. These fields are acyclic, which is conveyed by the **forward** keyword. The **where** clause supplies an axiom based on regular expressions

---

[9] In practice, we tend to rely on instruction-level loop pipelining techniques to expose new operations; however, in the interest of brevity we will focus here on source-level unrolling — the issues involved for refining the hierarchy at the instruction-level are essentially the same, but require a bit more terminology to describe.

[10] Recall that we already know that CTRL is independent of any value that NODE might have.

[13] to state that the sets of nodes are distinct: the set of nodes S reachable by traversing **next** (0 or more times) is disjoint from the set of nodes reached by starting from those in S and traversing along dest[i] exactly once.

Figure 4b is the main computational loop taken from the simulation program. The outer loop updates each E (or M) node based on the values in the M (or E) nodes to which it is connected. The outer loop iterates across the linked-list of E or M nodes, while the inner loop performs a sum operation using the values in its destination nodes. The inner loop is inherently sequential given the sum computation performed by statement L. However, at first glance there also appears to be a loop-carried dependence across the outer loop: unless the relationship between d and p is known, it appears that one iteration of the outer loop is writing a value (p->value) that is being read by some later iteration (d->value).

Given that the sets of E and M nodes are disjoint, our system can prove that the iterations of the outer loop are in fact independent. This would allow, for example, the while loop to be parallelized at the source-level. However, there are additional optimization opportunities at the instruction-level, which will be missed unless this information is retained. In particular, consider the inner loop once again. Unless the relationship between d and p is known, the load of d->value in iteration $i + 1$ cannot proceed until the store of p->value in iteration i is completed, thus forcing sequentiality between successive iterations of the loop. We know at the algorithm-level however that d and p refer to disjoint sets of nodes, and thus the load of d->value and the computation of p->coeff*d->value for iteration $i + c$ can proceed independently of the store p->value in iteration i. The end result is an improved instruction schedule which exploits this parallelism. The information which enables this transformation is supplied at the algorithm-level, calculated at the source-level, and easily retained at the instruction-level via ASSERT(*p, /HEAP/bigraph/*p) and ASSERT(*d, /HEAP/bigraph/*d).

4 Implementation and Results

This section provides a brief overview of how the semantics retention hierarchy is integrated within a retargetable fine-grain parallelizing compiler being developed at the University of California, Irvine,[11] and presents results that illustrate some of the advantages of semantics retention. This compiler is divided into a frond-end, based on the GNU C compiler (GCC), and a retargetable back-end responsible for performing instruction-level parallelization. GCC is responsible for translating C into an optimized 3-addr representation that becomes the input to the back-end. Higher-level semantics are communicated to the back-end via ASSERT statements embedded within the 3-addr code. These ASSERT statements may be generated by GCC itself or simply passed along from the source-level — source-level ASSERT's are implemented as macros that use the GCC ASM statement to pass the information along from source to the internal representations of GCC (i.e. TREE and RTX code), and finally to the 3-addr representation which will be read by the back-end (the 3-addr representation is based on the MIPS instruction-set).

Note that, while the selection of ASSERT's by the front-end depends entirely on algorithm level and source-level semantics, the semantics retention hierarchy constructed by the back-end is based entirely on the ASSERT's themselves, without any other information about the algorithm, the source language, or the front-end itself. Thus, given

---

[11] Details about the functionality of this compiler can be found in [19, 20, 22, 21].

this "3-addr + ASSERT's" representation, the back-end is able to construct the semantics retention hierarchy and parallelize code at the instruction-level with fairly precise algorithm level and source-level semantics that improve both the efficiency and degree of parallelization, without sacrificing the principal advantages of the traditional separation of front-end and back-end concerns, namely complexity management and the ease of porting the compiler to different source/target combinations.

	Neglecting Semantics			Retaining Semantics		
bench	speedup	disamb cost	efficiency	speedup	disamb cost	efficiency
SPARSE	1.34	0.25	5.36	4.85	0.11	44.09
EM3D	2.25	0.03	75.00	4.87	0.04	121.75
1DPP	2.18	1.46	1.49	4.35	0.43	10.12
OCTREE	3.50	0.61	5.74	6.44	0.30	21.47
CAXPY	2.39	0.11	21.73	5.90	0.05	118.00
Avg	2.33	0.49	4.74	5.28	0.19	28.40

Table 1. Neglecting vs. Retaining Higher-Level Semantics

Table 1 compares the results of compilation with and without semantics retention for a few codes actually used in some real-world applications. EM3D is the bipartite graph example discussed in Section 3.2 used for simulating the propagation of electromagnetic waves through objects in 3D [4]; SPARSE is code for scaling a sparse matrix abstract data type implemented using orthogonal linked lists [15]; 1DPP is a one-dimensional particle pusher implemented using array indirections [18]; OCTREE traverses threads in a 3-dimensional tree representation of a scene, mapping colors from RGB to CMY[10]; and finally, CAXPY is the linpack routine[5], implemented in C, for multiplying a vector by a constant and adding it to another vector (the potential instruction-level ambiguity here comes from the fact that vectors (i.e., arrays) are passed as pointers in C). The target architecture used for these results is a VLIW architecture with 32 registers and can issue two operations per cycle to any of the following functional units: 2 ALU units (which handle integer addition, subtraction, and logical operations), 2 SHIFT units (shift operations), 2 FALU units (floating point addition, subtraction), 2 MUL units (integer and floating point multiply), 1 DIV unit (floating point division), 2 MEM units (memory load and store), and, finally, 1 BRANCH unit (conditional branches). All functional units are pipelined. The ALU and SHIFT units take 3 cycles to execute an operation, the FALU and MUL units take 5 cycles, the DIV unit takes 15 cycles, the MEM units take 4 cycles for cache reads and 1 cycle for cache writes (cache misses stall the processor), and the BRANCH unit takes 4 cycles. These functional unit kinds and latencies are roughly the same as those of the Motorola 88110 Superscalar.

Speedup is the ratio of sequential to parallel cycles observed during simulation, *disamb(iguation) cost* is the total time (in seconds) spent trying to compute dependencies between memory accesses, and *efficiency* is the ratio of speedup to disambiguation cost. Notice that the speedup using semantics retention is uniformly better by more than 2.4 times on average. Similarly, even though semantics retention results in increased code motion and parallelization, the disambiguation cost is still generally lower with semantics retention by an average of 40%. Finally, the efficiency numbers show that, even when the disambiguation cost increases slightly as a result of semantics retention (as for EM3D), the time spent compiling with semantics retention is consistently better utilized, by an average efficiency improvement of 416%.

References

1. A. Aho, R. Sethi, and J.D. Ullman. *Compilers: Principles, Techniques and Tools.* Addison-Wesley, Reading, MA, 1986.

2. R. Allen and K. Kennedy. Automatic translation of FORTRAN programs to vector form. *TOPLAS*, 9(4), 1987.

3. U. Banerjee. *Dependence analysis for supercomputing.* Kluwer Academic Press, Boston, MA, 1988.

4. D. Culler, A. Dusseau, S. Goldstein, A. Krishnamurthy, S. Lumetta, T. von Eicken, and K. Yelick. Parallel programming in split-c. In *Proceedings of Supercomputing 1993*, 1993.

5. J. Dongarra, J.R. Bunch, C.B. Moler, and G.W. Stewart. *LINPACK Users's Guide.* Society for Industrial and Applied Mathematics, Philadelphia, PA, 1978.

6. M. Emami, R. Ghiya, and L. Hendren. Context-sensitive interprocedural points-to analysis in the presence of function pointers. In *PLDI*, 1994.

7. R. Ghiya. Disambiguating heap references. Technical Report Masters Thesis, School of Computer Science, McGill University, October 1994.

8. M. Girkar and C.D. Polychronopoulos. A general framework for program optimization and scheduling. *TOPLAS*, 1995. Preprint.

9. M. Haghighat and C. Polychronopoulos. Symbolic program analysis and optimization for parallelizing compilers. In *Lang. and Compilers for Par. Comp.*, volume 757 of *LNCS Series*. Springer-Verlag, 1992.

10. D. Hearn and M. Pauline Baker. *Computer Graphics.* Prentice-Hall, 1986.

11. L. Hendren, J. Hummel, and A. Nicolau. Abstractions for recursive pointer data structures: Improving the analysis and transformation of imperative programs. In *PLDI*, 1992.

12. L. Hendren and A. Nicolau. Parallelizing programs with recursive data structures. *IEEE Trans. on Parallel and Distributed Computing*, 1(1), 1990.

13. J. Hummel, L. Hendren, and A. Nicolau. A language for conveying the aliasing properties of dynamic, pointer-based data structures. In *IPPS*, 1994.

14. D. Kuck, R. Kuhn, B. Leasure, and M. Wolfe. The structure of an advanced vectorizer for pipelined processors. In *Fourth International Computer Software and Applications Conference*, 1980.

15. K. Kundert. Sparse matrix techniques. In A. Ruehli, editor, *Circuit Analysis, Simulation and Design.* Elsevier Science Publishers B.V. (North-Holland), 1986.

16. W. Landi and B. Ryder. A safe approximation algorithm for interprocedural pointer aliasing. In *PLDI*, 1992.

17. J. M. Lucassen. *Types and Effects: Towards the Integration of Functional and Imperative Programming.* PhD thesis, MIT, 1987.

18. F.H. McMahon. The livermore fortran kernels: A computer test of the numerical performance range. Technical Report UCRL-53745, Lawrence Livermore National Laboratory, 1986.

19. S. Novack and A. Nicolau. An efficient global resource constrained technique for exploiting instruction level parallelism. In *ICPP*, St. Charles, IL, August 1992.

20. S. Novack and A. Nicolau. Vista: The visual interface for scheduling transformations and analysis. In *Lang. and Compilers for Par. Comp.*, volume 768 of *LNCS Series*. Springer-Verlag, 1993.

21. S. Novack and A. Nicolau. Mutation scheduling: A unified approach to compiling for fine-grain parallelism. In *Lang. and Compilers for Par. Comp.*, volume 892 of *LNCS Series*. Springer-Verlag, 1994.

22. S. Novack and A. Nicolau. A hierarchical approach to instruction-level parallelization. *International Journal of Parallel Programming*, 23(1), February 1995.

23. D. Padua and M. Wolfe. Advanced compiler optimization for supercomputers. *CACM*, 29(12), December 1986.

Hoisting Branch Conditions –
Improving Super-Scalar Processor Performance

Bill Appelbe[1], Sri Doddapaneni[1], Reid Harmon[1], Phil May[2], Scott Wills[2], and
Maurizio Vitale[1]

[1] College of Computing
[2] School of Electrical and Computer Engineering Georgia Institute of Technology,
Atlanta, GA 30332

Abstract. The performance and hardware complexity of super-scalar
architectures is hindered by conditional branch instructions. When conditional branches are encountered in a program, the instruction fetch
unit must rapidly predict the branch predicate and begin speculatively
fetching instructions with no loss of instruction throughput. Speculative
execution has a high hardware cost, is limited by dynamic branch prediction accuracies, and does not scale well for increasingly super-scalar
architectures.

The conditional branch bottleneck would be solved if we could somehow
move branch condition evaluation far forward in the instruction stream
and provide a new branch instruction that encoded both the source and
target address of a branch. This paper summarizes the hardware extensions to support just such a Future Branch, then gives a compiler algorithm for hoisting branch evaluation across many blocks. The algorithm
is applicable to other optimizations for parallelism, such as prefetching
data.

1 Introduction

Studies have shown that from 1.6% to 22% of instructions executed are branches
or conditional branches [3], with most non-scientific programs much closer to
22%. A branch instruction interrupts the instruction pipeline unless the branch
target address is known before the branch instruction is decoded, and the direction of a conditional branch is known. Branch caches enable the branch target
address to be determined with fairly high probability at a modest hardware
cost [8]. By contrast, determining the direction of a conditional branch is far
more difficult. The most common technique is *speculative execution*, in which
the direction of the branch is predicted either statically (a bit in the branch
instruction) or dynamically (using a cache of previous branch directions). Most
modern microprocessors use dynamic prediction. Studies of the prediction accuracy of processors with sophisticated dynamic branch prediction show prediction
accuracy of around 90% (e.g., Ultra SPARC [10]: SPECint 88%, SPECfloat 94%
[10]; Power 620 [8]: SPEC composite 90% [9]).

Our simulation studies have shown that a fundamental problem with speculative execution is that the overhead of wasted cycles, due to incorrect prediction

limits processor throughput, even assuming no data dependencies and unlimited functional units.

Intuitively, conditional branches present a seemingly insuperable bottleneck to increasing superscalarity. Assuming that conditional branches are a fixed proportion of the instructions fetched, the penalty for incorrect branches, and the depth to which branches must be predicted, rises approximately linearly with the degree of superscalarity.

Our insight is that in fact, at the source level, most branches are predictable well before we reach them. In a classic `for loop` a programmer can easily determine whether the next iteration will be taken at the start of the current iteration. If the for loop test is `I <= N`, then if `I <= N-1` at the start of the iteration we know that the next iteration will be taken. The "intelligent programmer" is thus making deductions about what a *future branch* will be. It does not matter how long the loop is, or whether it contains other branches, we can determine at the start of the loop if the next iteration will be taken. To support this at the hardware level, we need a branch instruction that encodes both the source and target address.

To implement future branches work we need:

1. An architectural design of future branch hardware
2. Compiler algorithms that can hoist branch decisions

This paper first summarizes the instruction set design and architecture extensions needed to support future branches (hoisting branch decisions). Then we discuss in detail algorithms for converting regular conditional branches into future branches. Finally, we summarize the implementation status.

It is worth noting that hoisting branch decisions has a rather broader applicability than just compiling for future branches. A common optimization for NUMA parallel processors is prefetching data. We obviously want to avoid prefetching data that will not be needed (to avoid bus contention, cache pollution, and unnecessary instructions). Prefetch instructions are normally issued dozens of instructions before the data will be accessed. To be able to predict whether data will be needed, we need to be able to hoist branch decisions.

2 Future Branch Architecture

Future branch instructions are applicable as extensions to almost any instruction set. We have designed hardware implementations for the Motorola 88010[7], the Power PC 604[8], and the DLX[6]. Future branches bear some superficial similarity to delay slots[6, page 269]: instructions following a branch that are always executed. However, in practice it is hard to fill more than a couple of delay slots, and modern super-scalar microprocessors rely on speculative execution instead of delay slots. From a compiler viewpoint, the algorithm for filing delay slots is simply to find instructions in the basic block contain the branch, or its immediate successor blocks, that have no dependences on the branch. By contrast, the algorithm for hoisting branches tries to move the branch, and all its dependent instructions, forward to another basic block in the flowgraph.

The idea of decoupling the branch decision from the branch itself has been used in many architectures, ranging from those which have separate instructions for computing the branch condition to branch instructions with a variable number of delay slots[4]. However, these all have the limitation that the path and number of instructions executed between the computation of a branch condition and the branch itself is fixed and must be known at compile time. This usually limits hoisting the evaluation of the branch condition to the same basic block as the branch.

With modern superscalar architectures, and non-numerical applications, it is almost invariably necessary to calculate the branch condition in a different basic block than the branch is taken, to avoid the penalty of stalls or speculative execution. Hence future branches, together with hardware support for a queue[3] of pending branches, is needed.

2.1 Future Branch Semantics

Any conditional branch instruction can be represented as:

S..branch: branch *condition*, L..target

where the branch to the target label L..target is taken if the *condition* is true. The condition might be a condition code, a register test, a comparison of two registers, and so on. A future branch instruction has the form:

fbranch *condition*, S..branch, L..target

Its semantics are as follows: upon execution of the instruction, if *condition* is true, then a future branch is *pending*. This means that when the program counter reaches S..branch it should change to to L..target (i.e., jump).

It turns out to be useful to be able to cancel a pending future branch. For example: a branch may be pending for the next iteration of a loop before we encounter a loop exit. Hence we provide an *unbranch* instruction:

unbranch S..branch

We also provide unconditional future branches, and the ability to save/restore pending future branches. Pending future branches are part of the processor state[4], and hence must be saved and restored upon context switches[5]. Finally, we allow more than one future branch to be pending for the same address. Our experimental results show that this is very useful in small loops that have not been unrolled.

---

[3] Actually, a queue cannot be used to hold pending future branches, as they are not necessarily issued in the order that they are taken

[4] There is no indication in the object code, at the branch source, that this is the source of a branch! It is possible to implement future branches that are purely advisory[2], but this has a high space overhead.

[5] By context switches, we mean process context switches rather than procedure calls

3 Future Branch Hardware

An obvious question is whether 16 bits, the usual field size for a branch target, is enough to encode both the source and target address for a branch. Since all branch addresses that we are interested in are PC relative, we first need to determine the distribution of branch distances for a range of benchmarks. Our analysis of a suite of C benchmarks using a modified *gcc* indicates that from .2% (espresso) to 5% (gcc, spice) of branches are for a relative distance of more than 256 instructions. Hence both the relative source and target address can be encoded in the usual 16 bit displacement[6]

The implementation of future branches for the 604 is given in detail in Appelbe et al[2]. Intuitively, the hardware maintains a *future branch cache*, of pending future branches. When the program counter is advanced to fetch instructions, it is compared against branch source addresses in the future branch cache. If any of these is a hit, the contents of the program counter is replaced by the branch target address (i.e., a jump takes place), instructions are fetched from the new address, and the entry is deleted from the future branch cache.

In general, the predicate may not be known until several cycles after the future branch is decoded. This is because the future branch may depend on flags or registers set by an instruction which has not completed. If the predicate is not resolved when the branch source is reached, the branch prediction mechanisms of the PowerPC 604 (branch target address cache, branch history table) are used to best predict the branching path. In an implementation where speculative execution is not provided, instructions fetched using predicted rather than computed predicates would stall in the dispatch stage until the predicate is resolved.

The estimated increase in transistor count for this implementation is 30,000. This does not include hardware already present in the PowerPC 604 (e.g., branch target address cache). For the current PowerPC 604 die, this future branch implementation would occupy just 3.3% of the die area.

4 Compiler Algorithms for Hoisting Branches

Compiling for future branches reduces to the following problem: given a branch instruction **br**, can we *hoist*[1, page 714] this instruction so that at least **N_PIPELINE** instructions lie between the *execution* of the future branch and its target. The value of **N_PIPELINE** is chosen so to "almost guarantee"[7] that the future branch instruction will have completed before the branch target is reached. The parameter **N_PIPELINE** is hardware dependent and branch dependent. For the Power PC 604, a rough upper bound for **N_PIPELINE** is 15. We do not want

---

[6] Preliminary studies suggest the use of 8 bits signed for both the source and target offsets. The future branch instruction is often far from the branch source address in large loops. Obviously, large scale benchmarking might lead to a different division of the instruction space.

[7] "almost guarantee" implies that we may need to be optimistic about cache misses which cause unusual stalls.

to hoist branches much further than N_PIPELINE, as hoisting too far uses up resources (entries in the branch cache). However, the places where we can hoist branches to depends upon data flow and dominance analysis.

The standard use of code hoisting is to save space. For example: by moving hoisting common subexpressions out of the **then** and **else** parts of a conditional. Our use of code hoisting is quite different, and has more in common with software pipelining. The standard algorithm for code hoisting will not hoist multiple statements at once, or hoist to multiple points of the program. Both of these turn out to be necessary for hoisting branches.

Firstly, we consider the problem of hoisting a single branch. We give a general algorithm and feasibility test for hoisting any branch, then give a global algorithm for choosing branches to hoist and points to hoist them to. Finally, we point out pathological cases where we cannot achieve any significant performance improvement by hoisting branches.

Superficially, the problem of hoisting future branches resembles that of instruction scheduling: reordering machine instructions to maximize thruput. However, there is a fundamental differences

- Branch hoisting is conceptually a source level transformation, whereas instruction scheduling is done at the machine level

4.1 Hoisting a Single Branch

Branch hoisting is a rather curious program transformation that straddles both source and machine level optimization. It is possible to determine the legality of branch hoisting at the source level, but it is difficult to express the transformation in conventional source level representations such as abstract syntax trees. Hence we perform branch hoisting on a low-level form of intermediate code (such as gcc's RTX), after most standard local and loop optimizations, but before physical register allocation or instruction scheduling[8].

The standard algorithm for hoisting evaluation of an expression is to find a point at which an expression is *very busy*[1, page 713] (the operands of the expression are not subsequently defined). In practice, this needs to be modified for hoisting branches, as a branch may need to hoisted to more than one location.

Statement Hoist Criterion: A statement s can be hoisted form a point p to a set of points $\{p_0, p_1, ...p_N\}$ in the program provided:

strong domination on any path from the start of the program to p or from p to itself, that does not including p, passes *exactly once* through one and only one of the points in $\{p_0, p_1, ...p_N\}$.[9]

---

[8] Instruction scheduling must be aware of future branches, to try to ensure that no stalls occur due to a future branch that is still in the instruction pipeline

[9] Gupta[5], introduced *generalized dominators*: a set of nodes that dominate a point p. However, our *strong dominators* are "stronger", as we require uniqueness, and consider paths from p to itself. We need this as branches must be computed exactly once on each run time path to p.

availability after each point in $\{p_0, p_1, ...p_N\}$, there is no definition of the variables used in s , or use of any variable defined by s .

For branch statements that are based upon condition codes, the condition code is an anonymous variable used by the branch, and set by prior statements.

Algorithms for determining domination and availability are well known[1]. We have had to strengthen the definition of dominance so that the future branch is always at the same loop level as the branch source itself. Also, a future branch can only be issued once (otherwise there will be two future branches pending for the same jump).

Unfortunately, the above algorithm does not work well in practice. Firstly, many branch instructions are immediately preceded by a compare instruction that sets the condition code used by the branch. We could generalize the definition of a conditional branch to include with it any instruction that sets the condition code, but this is ad hoc. Further, in most loops the modification of the loop control variable comes just before the test. For example, consider the following C code fragment that computes the sum of the squares of the positive elements in a list:

```
/* List is a struct consisting of a next pointer and data */
int sumpos(struct List* np) {
    int sum = 0;
    for(; np; np=np->next) {
        if(np->data > 0)
            sum += np->data * np->data;
    }
    return sum;
}
```

Example 1

Like most loops, the increment of the loop control variable comes just before the test. Thus, the above algorithm would be unable to hoist the test far at all. Hence, we need an algorithm which can hoist the calculation condition as well as the branch.

We need to be able to hoist all statements that contribute to the calculation, while preserving all dependences. Consider the following artificial example:

```
    int sum = 0;
    int list[10]
    for(; i<10; ++i) {
        if(list[i]) {
            sum += list[i];
            ++i;
        }
    }
    return sum;
}
```

Example 2

We want to hoist the increment of i, test i<10, and future branch to the beginning of the loop iteration[10]. The first problem is that i is used in the loop: there is an anti-dependency from the use of i (in list[i]) to its definition (in ++i). Such anti-dependencies are easily eliminated by renaming: introduce a new variable i' = i+1. A far more troublesome problem is the additional, conditional, assignment to i. This is a "show stopper"[11]; in general, if there are definitions of a variable *which do not dominate other uses and definitions*, it is impossible in general to hoist the definition beyond the join of those definitions.

Given this criteria, we can define a general recursive algorithm for hoisting any branch and its associated condition.

Statement Hoist Algorithm:

INPUT: a dependence graph, a branch statement br, and a set of points $\{p_0, p_1, ...p_N\}$ which satisfy the strong domination criterion above.
OUTPUT: a transformed program or failure if the branch cannot be hoisted while maintaining dependences.

Let $\{d_0, d_1, ...d_k\}$ be the transitive closure of the set of definitions
    along paths $Paths_{\{p_0, p_1, ...p_N\}} \rightarrow p$ with dependences to br
    (including true, output, and anti-dependences).
All of these definitions will need to be hoisted if the branch is to be hoisted.
These definitions can be hoisted only if:

- For each dependence s→t, the source of the dependence dominates the sink

If this condition does not hold, return FALSE.
Otherwise, topologically sort the definitions, and hoist them in that order using **hoist-statement** and finally the branch itself.
Each definition must be hoisted to all points in $\{p_0, p_1, ...p_N\}$ which dominate that definition.
Return TRUE.

hoist-statement:
Assume that the statement is of the form: $v := f(uselist\ )$.
If their are any anti-dependences upon the definition d_i,
    in paths $Paths_{\{p_0, p_1, ...p_N\}} \rightarrow p$:
        Create a new temporary variable v_{temp}.
        Replace the statement $v := f(uselist\ )$ by $v := v_{temp}$, and
        Hoist the statement $v_{temp} := f(uselist\ )$.
otherwise
        Hoist the statement $v := f(uselist\ )$.

---

[10] Almost all C compilers convert while and for loops to the do ... while form with the increment and test at the end of the loop, as this eliminates a jump
[11] Not quite, we could pipeline the loop to calculate the condition list[i] in the previous iteration, but this is the subject of future work.

One obvious case for specialized optimization is the common case of a **for** loop, such as:

```
for(; i<10; ++i) {
    // uses of i
    }
```

Example 3

Instead of calculating i' = i+1 and testing i'<10, we can simply test i<9.

4.2 Global Algorithms

The above algorithm can be used to hoist branches, but it leaves unspecified what hoist points to choose. Also, it says nothing about unbranching in the case of exits from loops.

The following algorithm was based on hand analysis of the source code for several benchmarks. Our compiler analysis of the benchmark *gcc* indicates that it can be improved by using SSA form to determine join points for multiple definitions (page 13).

The global algorithm for hoisting branches for loops and conditional statements in structured programs can be best understood by considering a skeleton program, which is typical of a **while** loop converted to **do ... while** form:

```
// <- p0
...
if (e1) goto EXIT:  // <- b1
// <- p1
do {
    // <- p2
    ...
    if (e2) {        // <- b2
        // <- p3
        ...
    } else  {
        if (e3) ... // <- b3
    }
    // <- p4
    ...
} while (e1);        // <- b4
EXIT:
    // <- p5
```

Example 4

For each of the conditional branches above, we define the hoist points for the branch used by our algorithm.

Conditional Branches Outside Loops (b1) This branch must be hoisted to an earlier point in the subprogram (p0) which dominates the branch. If there are few instructions in the subprogram before the branch, then inline subprogram calls if possible.

Conditional Branches Within Loops (b2) This branch should be hoisted to point (p2) at the start of the loop iteration, provided that there are enough statements between p2 and e2.

If the loop is small, or the conditional statement constitutes almost all of the loop, then there may be insufficient statements. In that case, try hoisting the branch to just *after* the end of the conditional statement (p4. For the first iteration, a copy of the branch will be hoisted outside the loop (p1). If we hoisting b2 to p4, we will need an unbranch at p5, as we always predict the branch for the next iteration (which eventually will not be executed).

In some benchmarks, even this does not give us enough instructions between the future branch source and target. In that case, if no definitions from within the loop reach the branch, then we can issue several branches before the loop is entered. We call this technique *branch pipelining*.

Nested Conditional Branches (b3) As with non-nested branches, the points which dominate the branch for the next iteration are p4 and p2. We will need an unbranch at p3 in any case.

Loop Branches (b4) Again, the points which dominate the branch are p2 and p4. If the loop body contains sufficient instructions, choose p2. Otherwise, hoist the branch test for the first iteration to p1, and the branch test for subsequent iterations to p4. This will require an unbranch at p5. Short loops are often candidates for branch pipelining.

If there are any exits from the loop, then we will also require an unbranch at p5.

In the case of nested loops, first try to convert all branches in the inner loop to future branches. As noted above, procedure inlining can be used for very short procedures whose first instructions are a conditional branch. Loops with very short shortest paths cause problems if we are trying to hoist a branch more instructions ahead than are in the path. Ideally, the compiler will have done standard loop optimizations earlier to unroll such loops. If not, it is possible to pipeline future branches for subsequent iterations.

Procedure calls within loops with future branches present a problem. Architecturally, we can always provide support to save/restore the future branch state across calls, and we are investigating this in our simulator. In practice, it is probably better to just use future branches in leaf procedures, and inline small leaf procedures to create more opportunities for future branches.

A fundamental characteristic of the hardware is that the size of the future branch cache is bounded, and the compiler *must* guarantee not to overflow this buffer.

5 Implementation

The analysis above shows the feasibility of future branches. Nevertheless, validating the usefulness of future branches requires a fairly sustained research effort:

1. Build, or obtain and modify, an instrumented, reconfigurable super-scalar micro-architecture simulator, that incorporates future branch instructions as well as speculative execution for comparison.
2. Modify a production quality C compiler to perform program transformations and code generation for future branches
3. Systematic benchmarking, using standard large-scale benchmark programs.

These efforts are underway, and the results are encouraging.

5.1 Micro-Architecture Simulator

We have acquired a micro-architecture simulator, for the *DLX* instruction-set[6], from McGill university. The simulator is reconfigurable, and supports speculative execution. We have modifying it to support future branch instructions and instrumentation for these. We have extended the *SuperDLX* architecture and implementation in several ways, primarily by including support for future branches. Fortunately, the *DLX* instruction set has many holes in its opcode space, and hence we were able to easily add future branch instructions corresponding to all the conditional and unconditional *DLX* branches. We have also extended the *SuperDLX* simulator to provide better tracing and configuration of branch hardware.

5.2 Compiling for Future Branches

We are basing our implementation of a compiler to generate future branch instructions upon *gcc*. Our reason for doing so is the support that *gcc* provides for targeting almost all commercial microprocessors (including the *DLX*). Using *gcc* gives us portability should we obtain a commercial micro-architecture simulator. Also, *gcc* supports most standard compiler optimizations. Unfortunately, *gcc* does not provide a clean interface to enable manipulation of its low-level intermediate code *RTX*. Further, *gcc* provides only ad-hoc dataflow analysis.

For this and other projects, we have thus undertaken the somewhat radical approach of defining a new environment and interface to *gcc*'s internals using Scheme (a Lisp dialect).

GiL – Gcc In Lisp The fundamental reason for using Scheme for compiler prototyping is that it is a better language than C for prototyping compiler algorithms. Scheme is interpreted, supports a rich heterogeneous data structures library, pattern matching, powerful macros, and so on. GiL is a scheme environment, in which *gcc* is encapsulated as a function call which returns the intermediate code generated at any stage as a Scheme data structure. We have built an extensible set of Scheme libraries for manipulating the Scheme form of the RTX intermediate code, such as general multi-graphs and call-graphs, and are developing Scheme libraries to support scalar dependence analysis and a simplified version of the algorithm for generating future branches.

6 Benchmarks

Initially, we have been hand-coding assembler for standard benchmark kernels. One commonly used set of kernel benchmarks are the Livermore Loop, which consist of 24 kernel loops from scientific applications. Of these 24 loops, 4 contain conditional statements within loops. We have focused on these benchmarks with conditional statements, as long-running loops with large blocks of straight-line code are notoriously easy to get good performance numbers on. By contrast, loops with conditionals are common in non-scientific applications, and difficult for speculative execution to do well at. However, it is important to note that there is no penalty for using future branches in programs with regular loop structures and highly predictable branches.

The shortest of the Livermore Loops benchmarks with conditional statements within loops is benchmark #24, which calculates the minimum in an array. This type of loop is not atypical, and is clearly problematic for speculative execution. There is just no way to correctly guess whether the next element will be less than the minimum! The inner loop is very tight. After optimizing the use of registers, there are just eight or ten instructions in the inner loop, in the version which does not use future branches.

The primary questions that we are interested in answering is: how does the performance of future branches compare with the "best possible" speculative execution, and how do these results vary as the degree of superscalarity changes?

Table 1 summarizes the results:

Superscalarity	Speculative Branch Depth				Future	Percentage
	2	3	4	∞	Branches	Speedup
3	578	541	541	541	516	4.8%
4	543	526	490	490	428	14.5%
5	528	514	498	490	428	14.5%

Table 1. Cycles Required to Execute Benchmark LL #24

SuperDLX uses a fairly sophisticated two-bit dynamic branch prediction strategy, and achieved a 83.2% branch prediction accuracy. Further, there were no stores, or stalls on loads, while speculatively executing: the only overhead was lost cycles due to incorrect predictions.

However, as Table 1 shows, the use of Future Branches resulted in significant performance improvement. Table A also illustrates the need for increasingly deep, and expensive, branch prediction at higher superscalarity. If we limit branch prediction to a a maximum depth of 3, then future branches are at least 4.8%

faster than speculative execution. As the degree of superscalarity rise, future branches do better, plateauing 14.5%.

The performance gain using future branches is a little surprising because of the four extra instructions in the inner loop of the future branched version. The extra instructions are needed because the inner condition loop condition is a recurrence[14], and the loop is very short [15].

The performance of the future branch version can be improved by loop unrolling and other techniques. However, recurrences within short loops present a fundamental hurdle: most of the work in the loop is devoted to calculating conditions used in subsequent iterations. Our intuition, and the results in the previous section, suggests that such situations are atypical. To more accurately determine the frequency of such situations will require a long term study of large benchmarks, which is underway.

A simple modification of the above benchmark, without recurrences, calculates the sum of the non-negative elements in the array.

Table 2 summarizes the results:

The results for this benchmark are quite dramatic: the future branch version of the benchmark is around 40% faster.

Superscalarity	Speculative Branch Depth				Future	Percentage
	2	3	4	∞	Branches	Speedup
3	615	570	570	570	396	43.9%
4	576	570	562	550	376	46.2%
5	559	543	515	515	372	38.4%

Table 2. Cycles Required to Execute Benchmark LL #24'

The *DLX* instruction set is comparable to that of most modern RISC processors, hence we expect our results will carry over to any other superscalar architecture.

6.1 Compiler Analysis

Our initial goal was to implement the algorithm above to detect the feasibility of future branches. We analyzed 27 files in the *gcc* distribution looking for branches whose predicate can be trivially hoisted. A predicate is declared trivially hoistable if all the virtual registers needed for its evaluation are defined *exactly* once within the loop it belongs to.

---

[14] The test in each iteration on is dependent upon the test result in the previous iteration

[15] The test condition is $x[k] < xm$, but to predict ahead two iterations we need a test condition of $x[k+1] < xm$ and $x[k+1] < x[k]$

Table 3 shows the distribution of branches in the files we have analyzed. Only about one seventh of the branches are not trivially hoistable. Many of the non hoistable branches could be hoisted by a better algorithm[17]

Total number of conditional branches	4497
Total number of unconditional branches	2270
Not trivially hoistable	764

Table 3. Branch distribution in GCC

Figure 1 shows the distribution of the predicate size (number of instructions necessary to evaluate a predicate). All the instruction needed for a predicate evaluation need to be hoisted as a whole (or at least the last instructions in the chain must be moved far enough from the branch source), thus the shorter these chains are the easier it is to move them.

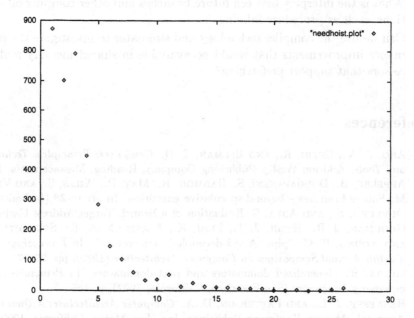

Fig. 1. Distribution of branch predicate sizes

---

[17] Hand inspection has revealed that the reason why most branches are not trivially hoistable is that there one definition is inside a conditional. The branch is usually still hoistable, to a point just after the conditional. To recognize this we need ϕ functions and SSA form, which we are now implementing.

7 Conclusion

Analysis has shown that the traditional approaches to avoiding branch delays, speculative execution, does not scale with increasingly super-scalar architectures. Future branches represent a simple but radical departure from traditional approaches to improving performance of branch instructions. Hardware support for future branches is relatively straightforward to implement. Thus, the feasibility of future branches depends upon largely upon compiler technology to hoist branch decisions sufficiently far. This paper presented an algorithm for doing just that. The algorithm is applicable to another problem in compiling for parallelism: data prefetching. Hoisting branch decisions ahead in the instruction stream uses the same compiler technology that is needed to prefetch data.

Although this paper has demonstrated the feasibility of future branches from architecture, hardware, and compiler viewpoints, there are many open questions and unresolved issues that we are actively addressing at present, including:

- What actual speedups are achieved on standard benchmarks for future branches vs speculative execution?
- What is the interplay between future branches and other compiler optimizations, such as procedure inlining
- Can we use the compiler technology and simulator to investigate the performance improvements that would be available in shared memory multiprocessors that support prefetching?

References

1. AHO, A. V., SETHI, R., AND ULLMAN, J. D. *Compilers: Principles, Techniques, and Tools.* Addison Wesley Publishing Company, Reading, Massachusetts, 1987.
2. APPELBE, B., DODDAPANENI, S., HARMON, R., MAY, P., WILLS, S., AND VITALE, M. Future branches – beyond speculative execution. In *Micro-28* ((submitted)).
3. DUVVURU, S., AND ARYA, S. Evaluation of a Branch Target Address Cache.
4. GOODMAN, J. R., HSEIH, J. T., LIOU, K., PLESZKUN, A. R., SCHECHTER, P., AND YOUNG, H. C. "pipe: A vlsi decoupled architecture". In *Proceedings of The Twelfth Annual Symposium on Computer Architecture* (1989), pp. 20–27.
5. GUPTA, R. Generalized dominators and post-dominators. In *Principles of Programming Languages* (San Francisco, California, 1992), p. 246.
6. HENNESSY, J. L., AND PATTERSON, D. A. *Computer Architecture: A Quantitative Approach.* Morgan Kaufmann Publishers, Inc., San Mateo, California, 1990.
7. SECTOR, M. S. P. *MC88110 Second Generation RISC Microprocessor Users Manual.* Motorola, Inc., Phoenix, Arizona, 1991.
8. SONG, S. P., AND DENMAN, M. The PowerPC 604 Microprocessor. *IEEE Micro* (October 1994), 8–17.
9. THOMPSON, T., AND RYAN, B. PowerPC 620 Soars. *BYTE* (November 1994), 113–120.
10. WAYNER, P. SPARC Strikes Back. *BYTE* (November 1994), 105–112.

Integer Loop Code Generation For VLIW

James Radigan
Pohua Chang
Utpal Banerjee
Intel Architecture Lab
M/S RN6-18
2200 Mission College Blvd.
Santa Clara, CA 95052-8119

Code generation for complex integer loops within the context of a VLIW architecture, has to date, been handled by several disparate methodologies. We provide an empirical study to characterize what a typical complex integer loop is and propose a general solution that optimally modifies the key control dependencies in common integer loops. This single algorithm, integrates several software techniques (assuming key architectural features) in order to provide for varying degrees of nested complex control flow. A number of techniques, including loop peeling, loop unrolling, software pipelining, if-conversion, and procedure inlining are combined cohesively to make the best transformation decisions, for a typical integer loop, before scheduling and register allocation. Optimal fusion and distribution decisions are assumed.

1. Introduction

Within the space of all integer programs the characterization of a complex integer loop can only be accomplished through empirical data as intrinsic complexity alone does not map directly to what is profitable to consider. We summarize the results of a study involving the source code for SPEC CINT92 in Appendix A. From this data, we can extract the requirements of a single cohesive code generation technique for a new architecture. Thus, the following attributes both characterize a complex integer loop and indicate functional requirements for the algorithm. The algorithm must be able to handle loops of all sizes that have: (1) short trip counts, (2) contain several nested conditionals (3) contain several data dependent loop exits (4) contain calls on infrequently executed paths and/or (5) contain second level loop nests with multiple exits

For this paper we focus on eight loops from the integer side of the spec benchmark suite. These loops cover a wide range of control flow complexities and are listed in Appendix-B. Loop 1 is a small loop, with a short trip count containing more than one exit. Loop 2 is a second level loop with two small, short trip inner loops. Loop 3 is a simple loop that initializes an array. Loop 4 is a small loop that has a conditional that can be eliminated by if-conversion. Loop 5 is a second level loop with multiple exits from the inner loop. Loop 6 has two conditionals that can be eliminated by if-conversion, with multiple exits. Loop 7 is a large loop that contains an inner loop and several nested conditionals. Loop 8 contains a macro definition, which when expanded, has a call on an infrequently executed path.

We will propose an algorithm that generates good code for all eight test loops, which were deemed important from profile information and show how one algorithm can handle these very different integer codes for a VLIW like machine architecture. Empirical data from an implementation in work will show this algorithm does not deteriorate the performance of loops that would otherwise be unaltered. The key insight is that first knowing something about likely paths through a program can aid more traditional source level transformations.

Work done at Multiflow has shown that the behavior of conditional branches can be predicted from previous runs of a program that gather probabilities from splits. Later work [13] considered execution frequencies when coupled with split probabilities to further refine a basic idea. Thus, optimizations that require the knowledge of branch probabilities clearly benefit from profiling. In the absence of profile information, smart heuristics can be used [12]. These heuristics can be derived from observing the general behavior of a large number of programs and extracting the key empirical data.

Loop unrolling is a way to extend the scope of code scheduling. It has been used in the Trace scheduling approach [14]. Software pipelining is way to overlap loop iterations [1-11]. If-conversion is a technique to convert some branch instructions into data computation instructions [20][21]. Tail duplication is a technique to isolate infrequently executed paths through a loop [22]. Procedure inlining eliminates calls by substituting them by the bodies of the callee functions [15-19].

The rest of the paper is organized as follows: Section 2 sketches the algorithm while describing loop unrolling, software pipelining, if-conversion, tail duplication, and procedure inlining in more detail. Section 3 discusses profiling issues. Section 4 presents the algorithm. Section 5 presents experimental data. Finally, in section 6, we offer some concluding remarks.

2.0 An overview

(1) Procedure calls on frequently executed paths are inlined. If there are procedure calls on frequently executed paths that cannot be inlined, then apply acyclic scheduling on the loop and stop.
(2) Tail duplication is applied to isolate infrequently executed paths from the loop.
(3) If-conversion is applied to convert the loop body into a Hyperblock [22].
(4) Unroll the Hyperblock loop by a number of times.
(5) Apply either a cyclic or acyclic scheduling algorithm on the Hyperblock loop.

We assume that, in the target architecture, all instructions can be predicated, including branch instructions. A Hyperblock is a sequence of instructions with a single control flow entry and one or more control flow exits. A DAG of basic blocks can be converted into a Hyperblock by if-conversion. We will extend the concept of Hyperblock to permit a second level loop to be software pipelined. In our definition, a Hyperblock is a sequence of nodes with a single control flow entry and one or more control flow exits, where a node can range from an instruction to an inner loop.

There are of course phase ordering problems that are either cyclic interactions between steps or basic tradeoffs. For example, whether to unroll a loop and apply acyclic scheduling, or to software pipeline a loop is a decision that must be made before loop unrolling while software pipelining often requires loop unrolling first be performed. Further, for a split in a control flow graph, a tradeoff needs to be made determining whether to apply tail duplication or if-conversion. In this paper, we will investigate heuristics for making properly ordered transformation decisions for the integer loops we listed on an architecture that has predicationation amoung other novel architectural features.

2.1. Loop Peeling/Unrolling

Consider Loop 3 and assume that *size* is a compile time constant. If *size* is small, we can peel off *size* number of iterations and the loop would execute as straight line code. If *size* is large, we can unroll the loop and exploit the resulting register temporaries.

```
for ( j = size -1; j >= 0; j -- ) {
    count[j-1] = count[j] * n;
}
```

For Loop 3, the code generation algorithm needs to know early that the loop is not optimally software pipelined (because the data dependence paths are tight and the trip count is short) ; therefore, loop peeling and unrolling should be considered. Note however, for more complex loops with tight dependencies and unknown loop bounds, the difference between loop unrolling followed by basic acyclic scheduling, and software pipelining is the start-up and wind-down thus basic acyclic scheduling suffers and we prefer the software pipeline version with early outs.

2.2. If-Conversion

Some branch instructions can be eliminated by converting to predicated instructions. Thus trading register pressure to thwart miss-predicted branches. For example, Loop 4 can be converted into

```
for (i=first_part; i<=lastbit; i++) {
    sum += count[i];
    active += (count[i] > 0);
    p = (active > maxactive);
    maxactive = active (if p); }
```

2.3. Software Pipelining

The body of Loop 4 looks like

```
L0:
        r1 = count[i];                      cycle 0
        sum = sum + r1;                     cycle 1
        r2 = r1 > 0;                        cycle 1
        active = active + r2;               cycle 2
        r3 = active > maxactive;            cycle 3
        maxactive = active (if r3);         cycle 4
        i = i + 1;                          cycle 4
        if (i <= lastbit) goto L0;          cycle 4
```

Assuming a wide issue machine, each iteration takes four cycles. Software pipelined, the code would be :

```
        r1 = count[i];
        sum = sum + r1;
        r2 = r1 > 0;
        active = active + r2;
L0:
        r3 = active > maxactive;            cycle 1
        maxactive = active (if r3);         cycle 2
        r1 = count[i+1];                    cycle 1
        sum = sum + r1;                     cycle 2
        r2 = r1 > 0;                        cycle 2
        active = active + r2;               cycle 3
        i = i + 1;                          cycle 2
        if (i <= lastbit) goto L0;          cycle 3
```

Now each iteration takes only three cycles.

2.4. Tail Duplication

Loop 8 expands into

```
        while (c==' ' || c=='\t')
                c = (--((&__iob[0]))->_cnt < 0 ? __filbuf((&__iob[0])) : (int) * ((&__iob[0]))->_ptr++);
```

This loop fills up a large character buffer and then processes one character at a time. Therefore, we expect calls to __filbuf() to be rare. We can rewrite the loop in the following way to exclude __filbuf() from being considered as a part of the iterated loop with the data dependent exit .

```
        if (c==' ' || c=='\t') {
        L0:     do {
                        p = --((&__iob[0])->_cnt < 0);
                        if (p) goto L1;
                        c = (int) * ((&__iob[0]))->_ptr++;
                } while (c==' ' || c=='\t');
        }
        L2: ;
        ...
        L1:
                c = __filbuf((&__iob[0]));
                if (c==' ' || c=='\t') goto L0;

                goto L2;
```

There is a dilemma in choosing between if-conversion and tail duplication for certain codes. To form a Hyperblock, one can eliminate a branch by if-conversion, or by tail duplication to exclude re-entries. This is a somewhat simpler problem if one has profile information. If-conversion should be applied when both sides of a branch are likely to be executed, and tail duplication should be applied when a branch is heavily biased towards one direction.

2.5. Procedure Inlining

Procedure inlining consists of two major phases. In the first phase, the call graph and potential callee routines are stored in a compiler database. From the call graph, a number of call sites are selected to be inlined. In the second phase, the selected call sites are replaced by the callee, routine bodies and parameters are properly propagated with a two versioning technique know as cloning.

3. Loop Profiling

To guide loop peeling, loop unrolling, and software pipelining, we need to know the average and variance of the number of times a loop is iterated per invocation. To guide if-conversion and tail duplication, we need to know the branch probabilities.

Profile-guided optimization is a two-step process. In the first step, the compiler adds probes into the code being compiled. Each probe is a function call or a sequence of instructions for recording execution time events. In our case, there are two kinds of probes. The first kind is for counting number of occurrences. This is used for counting the number of times a branch instruction is executed, the number of times a branch instruction is taken, the number of times a loop is entered, and the total number of times a loop is iterated. The second kind of probe is for calculating variance of the number of times a loop is iterated per invocation. After profiling, profile data is written into a database. Multiple runs can be taken and the profile data be summarized. In the second step of compilation, the compiler uses the profile information to guide code optimizations.

4. Our Approach

Our approach uses a combination of hardware and software techniques. Hardware techniques are used to support software pipelining, and enable more code motion freedom. Software techniques are a combination of procedure inlining, if-conversion, tail duplication, loop peeling, loop unrolling, and software pipelining.

4.1. Hardware Support

There are two hardware techniques that we consider. These are all traditional techniques. The first technique is rotating register files [3]. A rotating register file has N registers, r[1], r[2], ..., r[N]. Upon a rotation command (by special loop instructions), r[i+1] = r[i], for I = 1 to N-1, and r[1] = r[N]. This can be implemented by a hardware base register and register renaming hardware, which adds the register index to the contents of the hardware base register modulo the size of the rotating register file to form the register index. In software pipelining, some values that are live across iterations need to be preserved. Suppose that a value is produced in iteration k and used in iteration k+n, the value needs to be preserved between these iterations. One way to preserve the value is to keep the value in r[i+j], where j=0..n. For example, in iteration k, the value is written into r[i]. In iteration k+1, the value is moved to r[i+1] by rotating the register file. In iteration k+2, the value is moved to r[i+2]. In iteration k+n, the value appears in r[i+n]. In this fashion, it is safe to write a new value into r[i] each iteration.

The second technique is control speculation [24]. It is important to enable long latency instructions that are on critical paths to be moved up in the program order. For example, load instructions are typically on the critical path, and the load latency is typically two or three cycles for a L1 cache hit. Load instructions may trap. In order to move load instructions, that cannot be proven to be safe, above branch instructions, we need a version of load instructions that do not trap or defer exceptions until the original location of the load instructions.

4.2. Loop Code Generation Considerations

After *all* loop transformations that optimize for memory bandwidth, the goal is to either entirely eliminate a loop, software pipeline it, or unroll it an appropriately restrained amount. Thus by either eliminating a loop or transforming it we have exposed the optimal amount of instruction level parallelism. Simply put for inner most loops :

{small body , short trip count} -> loop peeling and predication
{small body, large trip count} -> loop unrolling or software pipelining(compiler implementation issue)
{large body, short trip count} -> straight forward acyclic scheduling is adequate
{large body, large trip count} -> software pipelining

For loops that contain inner loops, if the inner loop is small and has a short trip count we want to completely peel off the inner loops and then apply tail duplication on the outer loop, causing the outer loop to contain a Hyperblock. If the inner loops iterate many times, after scheduling the inner loops, we represent each inner loop as a node and apply acyclic or cyclic scheduling on the outer loop, treating the inner loops as single instructions..

For loops that contain calls on infrequently executed paths, we apply tail duplication to isolate the infrequently executed portions of the loop from being considered in scheduling.

For loops that contain calls on frequently executed paths, we like to inline the calls if possible. If not possible, we rely on inter-procedural analysis to tell us what global variables can be accessed from the calls.

For loops with side exits, if the loops are candidates for software pipelining, we would like to apply predication and multiway branch conversion to convert the Hyperblock loop into a loop containing a single basic block. If the loops have side exits and are not good candidates for software pipelining, we leave the branches intact and apply typical acyclic scheduling on the loop.

To reduce the loop exit branch penalty, especially for loops that iterate few times, the scheduler should schedule the condition code generation instructions or the prepare-to-branch instructions early.

4.3. Loop Code Generation Algorithm

We transform code inside out based upon control dependencies. Thus when processing the outermost loop as many inner loops as possible have been eliminated or optimally transformed to expose instruction level parallelism and remove as much branch overhead as possible.

Procedure Loop-Scheduling {
Step 0:
        if ((there are calls on infrequently executed paths) and
        (there are no calls on frequently executed paths) and
        (the loop is not too large) and
        (the loop iterates more than N times))
            apply Tail-Duplication;
Step 1:
        if ((the loop is small) and
        (the loop is a Hyperblock) and
        (the loop iterates less or equal to N times) and
        (the variance of loop iteration count is small)) {
            apply Loop-Peeling;
            apply If-Conversion;
            apply ILP-Transformations;
            Compute the dependence graph;
            Determine Single-Iteration-Schedule;
            goto Step 8;
        }
        if ((the loop is small) and
        (the loop is a Hyperblock) and
        (the loop iterates more than N times) and
        (the loop start-up and wind-down costs are low)) {
            apply Loop-Unrolling;
            apply ILP-Transformations;
            Compute the dependence graph;
            Determine Single-Iteration-Schedule;
            goto Step 8;
        }
Step 2:
        apply If-Conversion;
        apply ILP-Transformations;
Step 3:
        Compute the dependence graph;
Step 4:
        Determine MII (minimum initiation interval);

Step 5:

    Determine Single-Iteration-Schedule (Length is L);
    if (MII==L)
        goto Step 8;
    if ((loop is too large) or (loop contains call))
        goto Step 8;
    if (loop is not a Hyperblock)
        goto Step 8;
    if (loop does not iterate more than N times)
        goto Step 8;

Step 6:

    for (k=MII; k<L; k++) {
        Determine an Iteration-Schedule(k);
        if (possible)
            goto Step 7;
    }
    Use the result of Step 5 as the schedule;
    goto Step 8;

Step 7:

    Assign rotating registers;

}

4.3.1. Tail-Duplication

Procedure Tail-Duplication {
Step 0:

    If the current loop is a second-level loop, inline all peeled iterations of inner loops;

Step 1:

    Identify all infrequently executed nodes (from the profile information or heuristic);

Step 2:

    Mark all nodes that can be reached from an infrequently executed nodes, not including the nodes that are marked in Step 1;

Step 3:

    Duplicate all nodes that are marked in Step 2;

Step 4:

    Introduce a new loop preheader basic block;

Step 5:

    For all duplicated nodes, for all control flow to the loop header basic block, reconnect to the loop preheader basic block;

Step 6:

    From each node marked in Step 1, remove connections to nodes in the original loop body, and connect to the duplicated nodes in Step 2;

}

4.3.2. If-Conversion

For a control flow graph (A->B, A->C, B->D, C->D), where A and D are basic blocks, and B and C are sub-control flow graphs, the whole control flow graph can be converted into a single block if
(1) all instructions in B and C can be predicated,
(2) the sizes of B and C are not too large, and
(3) both B and C are likely to be executed.
To handle a nested if-structure, we apply the above transformation to the inner most if-structure first and work outward.

If-conversion can also be used to generate multiway branches. For a pair of basic blocks (A->B), if all instructions in B can be predicated, the size of B is not large, and (A->B) is the likely path, then predicate all computation instructions in B by ccA.

4.3.3. Single-Iteration-Schedule

Any global acyclic scheduling algorithm on a DAG of basic blocks can be used.

4.3.4. ILP-Transformations

After loop peeling and loop unrolling, registers typically need to be renamed to allow overlap of iterations. A few more ILP transformations are discussed in [25]. In order to derive a good software pipelining schedule, code transformations such as scalar replacement are important to reduce the cyclic path lengths. Another useful ILP transformation is to convert a load instruction

> var = ptr->flag

into

> r1 = ptr->flag
> var = r1

to allow the load instruction to be moved as early as possible. Another common ILP transformation is to exploit the address generation capability of memory instructions, so that induction variables are updated after the memory instructions rather than before the memory instructions.

4.3.5. Iteration-Schedule(k)

Any modulo scheduling algorithm can be used. For the purpose of this paper, the following procedure is used. Note that we assume that the loop is a Hyperblock.

Procedure Iteration-Schedule(II) {
Step 1: Apply extended block code scheduling. Use a lazy code scheduling approach so that instructions are scheduled
 as late as possible without increasing the critical path lengths;
Step 2: Identify the top instructions that should be moved to previous iterations. One heuristic is that we look at the
 scheduled code, starting from the bottom of the extended block schedule to the upper part of the extended
 block, for regions of code that lack parallelism. We move the code, where there are not enough parallelism,
 up to the previous loop iteration;
Step 3: Move the selected instructions to previous loop iterations and loop prologue;
Step 4: if we have not reached a saturation state, goto Step 1;
}

During scheduling, all register queues remain virtual. After scheduling, we determine if the virtual queues can be allocated of physical registers. If not, we assume that the schedule has failed. Our assumption is that there are enough physical registers most of the time.

When a load instruction is scheduled above a branch instruction, a check instruction is inserted at the home basic block for detecting deferred exceptions. Check instructions always remain in the home basic block.

4.3.6. Schedule Instructions That Are Predicated

If-conversion introduces predicated instructions. There is a flow dependence between the instruction that generates the predicate value and the predicated instruction. Sometimes we like to eliminate some of those dependencies in scheduling. One way to achieve that is by control speculation. A non-trapping or deferred-trapping version of control speculative instruction is available. For example,

> r1 = r2 > 100;
> r3 = a[r4 + 8] (if r1);
> r5 = r3 * 7 (if r1);

Note that the second instruction cannot start until the first instruction is finished. If r3 is used only as a scratch register and is not live on the (if !r1) path), then we can lift the predicate.

> r1 = r2 > 100;
> r3 = a[r4 + 8] (non-trapping version);
> r5 = r3 * 7 (if r1);

Now, the second instruction can be scheduled ahead of the first instruction. We assume that the acyclic and cyclic scheduler can perform the above transformation.

5. Experiment

Currently, our compiler can produce acyclically scheduled codes. We will apply the Loop-Scheduling algorithm by hand to the test loops and carefully analyze each code transformation step. The goal is to clarify some of the statements made in the previous section. In the analysis below, we will focus on how to generate efficient codes for integer program loops, using hardware support. We will compare the result of single-iteration scheduling to that of Loop-Scheduling.

The target machine can issue 8 instructions per cycle. We assume that there are 4 load/store units, 6 integer ALUs, and 2 branch units. We further assume that the load latency is 2 cycles, integer operation latency is 1 cycle, and branch latency is 2 cycles. We assume that all loop exit branches are miss predicted.

5.1. Loop 1

We assume that the loop iterates three times. If we apply a traditional global code scheduling algorithm to the loop, we would derive a 13 cycles schedule. We then apply Loop-Scheduling on the loop.

    Step 0:   do nothing because there is no call
    Step 1:   apply Loop-Peeling
              apply If-Conversion
              apply ILP-Transformation
              Compute the dependence graph
              Determine Single-Iteration-Schedule
              goto Step 8
    Step 8:   apply Add-Control-Speculation-Repair-Code

If-Conversion has not effect on this loop because the conversion from control dependencies to data dependencies introduces long dependence paths. But if we force If-Conversion to take effect, the schedule is 11 cycles (1.18 speedup). If If-Conversion has no effect, then the schedule is 6 cycles (2.17 speedup). Note that register renaming in the ILP-Transformation is important to achieve overlap between loop iterations.

5.2. Loop 2

Both of the inner loops iterate four times. If we apply Loop-Peeling to both of the inner loops, we achieve a 1.93 speedup.

5.3. Loop 3

We assume that the loop iterates 100 times. We apply local scheduling to the loop and the schedule is 201 cycles. We then apply Loop-Scheduling on the loop.

    Step 0:   do nothing because there is no call
    Step 1:   apply Loop-Unrolling
              apply ILP-Transformation
              Compute the dependence graph
              Determine Single-Iteration-Schedule
              goto Step 8
    Step 8:   apply Add-Control-Speculation-Repair-Code

Loop unrolling is preferred over software pipelining because the loop startup cost (the overlap region) is small. If we unroll four times and apply ILP transformations to compute the memory addresses early, the schedule is 76 cycles (2.64 speedup).

5.4. Loop 4

Assume that the branch in the middle is 50% taken, and the loop iterates 10 times. If we apply global scheduling on the loop, the schedule is 61 cycles. We then apply Loop-Scheduling.

    Step 0:   do nothing
    Step 1:   do nothing
    Step 2:   apply If-Conversion
              apply ILP-Transformation
    Step 3:   compute dependence graph
    Step 4:   determine MII

Step 5: determine Single-Iteration-Schedule
Step 6: determine Iteration-Schedule
Step 7: assign rotating registers
Step 8: apply Add-Control-Speculation-Repair-Code

The resultant schedule is 26 cycles (2.35 speedup).

5.5. Loop 5

Assume that both the inner and the outer loop iterate two times per invocation. If we apply simple local scheduling on the loops, the schedule is 43 cycles. If we apply global code scheduling on the loops, the schedule is 31 cycles. We then apply Loop-Scheduling. Loop-Scheduling decides to completely peel the inner loop and software pipeline the outer loop.

Step 0: do nothing
Step 1: do nothing
Step 2: apply If-Conversion
apply ILP-Transformation
Step 3: compute dependence graph
Step 4: determine MII
Step 5: determine Single-Iteration-Schedule
Step 6: determine Iteration-Schedule
Step 7: assign rotating registers
Step 8: apply Add-Control-Speculation-Repair-Code

The schedule is 16 cycles (1.94 speedup). The MII is only 2 cycles, but code motion is limited by branch instructions.

5.6. Loop 6

We assume that the loop iterates 30 times. If we apply if-conversion and global code scheduling to the loop, we derive a schedule of 151 cycles. We then apply Loop-Scheduling.

Step 0: do nothing
Step 1: do nothing
Step 2: apply If-Conversion
apply ILP-Transformation
Step 3: compute dependence graph
Step 4: determine MII
Step 5: determine Single-Iteration-Schedule
Step 6: determine Iteration-Schedule
Step 7: assign rotating registers
Step 8: apply Add-Control-Speculation-Repair-Code

The schedule is 61 cycles (2.48 speedup).

5.7. Loop 7

Loop-Scheduling decides to software pipeline the inner loop (probe) and to apply global acyclic scheduling on the outer loop. The speedup over non-software pipelined version is 1.45.

5.8. Loop 8

We assume that the loop iterates 100 times and the _filbuf path is never taken. If we apply global code scheduling on the loop, the schedule is 801 cycles. We then apply Loop-Scheduling.

Step 0: Tail-Duplication
Step 1: do nothing
Step 2: apply If-Conversion
apply ILP-Transformation
Step 3: compute dependence graph
Step 4: determine MII
Step 5: determine Single-Iteration-Schedule
Step 6: determine Iteration-Schedule
Step 7: assign rotating registers
Step 8: apply Add-Control-Speculation-Repair-Code

The schedule is 207 cycles (3.87 speedup)

6. Conclusion

The contributions of this paper include a Loop-Scheduling algorithm and analysis of how the Loop-Scheduling algorithm handles eight important loops of varying control flow complexities. We have shown that a number of hardware and software techniques can be integrated into the Loop-Scheduling framework. Without hardware support, it is not possible to generate efficient loop codes for integer loops.

In the future, we would like to implement the Loop-Scheduling algorithm in our prototype compiler and measure its effectiveness for entire application programs. We also like to study how to generate codes for large loops that have complex control flow structures.

References

[1]   M. Lam, "Software pipelining: an effective scheduling technique for VLIW machines," in Proceedings of the SIGPLAN'88 Conference on Programming Language Design and Implementation, pg. 318-328, June 1988.

[2]   N. J. Warter, G. E. Haab, K. Subramanian, and J. W. Bockhaus, "Enhanced modulo scheduling for loops with conditional branches," in Proceedings of International Symposium on Microarchitecture, Dec. 1992.

[3]   J. C. Dehnert, P. Y.-T. Hsu, and J. P. Bratt, "Overlapping loop support in the Cydra5," in Proc. 3rd Intl. Conf. on Arch. Support for Prog. Lang. and Oper. Syst., pg.26-38, April 1989.

[4]   Qi Ning, Guang R. Gao, "A noval framework of register allocation for software pipelining," in Proc. of Twentieth Annual ACM SIGPLAN-SIGACT Symposium on Principles of Programming Languages, pg.29-42, Jan. 1993.

[5]   Alexandre E. Eichenberger, Edward S. Davidson, and Santosh G. Abraham, "Minimum register requirements for a modulo schedule," in Proc. of 27th Annual International Symposium on Microarchitecture, Nov. 1994.

[6]   R. Ramakrishna Rau, "Iterative modulo scheduling: an algorithm for software pipelining loops," in Proc. of 27th Annual International Symposium on Microarchitecture, Nov. 1994.

[7]   B. R. Rau, M. Lee, P. P. Tirumalai, and M. S. Schlansker, "Register allocation for software pipelined loops," in Proc. of SIGPLAN'92 Conf. on Programming Language Design and Implementation, pg. 283-299, June 1992.

[8]   R. F. Touzeau, "A Fortran compiler for the FPS-164 scientific computer," in Proc. of the ACM SIGPLAN'84 Symposium on Compiler Construction, pg. 48-57, SIGPLAN Notices Vol. 19, No. 6, June 1984.

[9]   K. Ebcioglu, "A compilation technique for software pipelining of loops with conditional jumps," in Proc. of the 20th Annual Workshop on Microprogramming, pg.69-79, Dec. 1987.

[10]   P. Tirumalai, M. Lee, and M. S. Schlansker, "Parallelization of loops with exits on pipelined architecture," in Proc. of the Supercomputing'90, pg. 200-212, Nov. 1990.

[11]   D. Bernstein and Y. Lavon, "A software pipelining algorithm based on global instruction scheduling," Technical Report 88.338, Science and Technology, IBM Israel, Sep. 1993.

[12]   T. Ball and J. R. Larus, "Branch prediction for free," in Proceedings of the ACM SIGPLAN 1993 Conference on Programming Language Design and Implementation, pg. 300-313, June 1993.

[13]   J. A. Fisher and S. M. Freudenberger, "Predicting conditional branch directions from previous runs of a program," in Proceedings of 5th International Conference on Architectural Support for Programming Languages and Operating Systems, pg. 85-95, Oct. 1992.

[14] J. A. Fisher, "Trace scheduling: a technique for global microcode compaction," IEEE Transactions on Computers, Vol. C-30, pg. 478-490, July 1981.

[15] R. Allen and S. Johnson, "Compiling C for vectorization, parallelization, and inline expansion," in Proceedings of the SIGPLAN'88 Conference on Programming Language Design and Implementation, June 1988.

[16] R. W. Scheifler, "An analysis of inline substitution for a structured programming language," Communications of the ACM, Vol. 20, No. 9, Sep. 1977.

[17] C. A. Huson, "An in-line subroutine expander for Parafrase," University of Illinois, Champaign-Urbana, 1982.

[18] J. W. Davidson and A. M. Holler, "A study of a C function inliner," Software-Practice and Experience, Vol. 18(8), pg. 775-790, Aug. 1988.

[19] P. Chang, S. A. Mahlke, W. Y. Chen, and W.-M. W. Hwu, "Profile-guided automatic inline expansion for C programs," Software Practice and Experience, May 1992.

[20] J. R. Allen, K. Kennedy, C. Porterfield, and J. Warren, "Conversion of control dependence to data dependence," in Proceedings of the 10th ACM Symposium on Principles of Programming Languages, pg. 177-189, Jan. 1983.

[21] J. C. Park and M. S. Schlansker, "On predicated execution," Tech. Report. HPL-91-58, Hewlett Packard Laboratories, May 1991.

[22] S. A. Mahlke, D. C. Lin, W. Y. Chen, R. E. Hank, and R. A. Bringmann, "Effective compiler support for predicated execution using the hyperblock," in Proceedings of the 25th International Symposium on Microarchitecture, pg. 45-54, Dec. 1992.

[23] H. C. Young and J. R. Goodman, "A simulation study of architectural data queues and prepare-to-branch instruction," in Proceedings of the IEEE International Conference on Computer Design: VLSI in Computers ICCD'84, pg. 544-549.

[24] P. Chang, S. A. Mahlke, W. Y. Chen, N. J. Warter, and W.-M. Hwu, "IMPACT: an architectural framework for multiple-instruction-issue processors," in Proceedings of the 18th International Symposium on Computer Architecture, May 1991.

[25] S. A. Mahlke, W. Y. Chen, J. C. Gyllenhaal, W.-M. W. Hwu, P. Chang, and T. Kiyohara, "Compiler code transformations for superscalar-based high-performance systems," in Proceedings of Supercomputing'92, November 1992.

Appendix 0 Empirical data characterizing loops:

LOCATION	#exprs	#cond br	#side exits	#backe edges	#call	#loop level	#switch	#avg iteration
### espresso ###								
[compl.c 270]	3	1	0	1	0	0	0	2.5
[compl.c 276]	10	2	1	1	1%	1	0	100
[compl.c 310]	5	2	1	1	1%	0	0	120
[cofactor.c 67]	many	many	0	1	0	1	0	140
[cofactor.c 128]	2	1	0	1	0	0	0	100
[cofactor.c 215]	6	2	0	1	0	0	0	50
[cofactor.c 58]	10-20	3	1	1	0	1	0	1
[contain.c 216]	3	2	1	1	0	0	0	2
[cofactor.c 239]	many	9	0	1	0	1	0	30
[cofactor.c 182]	30-40	20	0	1	0	1	0	4

li

[xlsym.c 126]	10-20	3	1	1	0	1	0	3
[xlsym.c 110]	10-20	3	1	1	0	1	0	2
[xleval.c 363]	5-10	2	0	1	1*	0	0	2
[xlsym.c 126]	5-10	2	1	1	0	0	0	1
[xldmem.c 441]	20-30	5	0	1	4	0	1	1000
[xldmem.c 353]	10-20	3	2	1	0	0	0	2
[xldmem.c 386]	20	3	2	1	0	0	0	2
[xlsym.c 110]	5-10	2	1	1	0	0	0	1
[xleval.c 217]	10-20	3	0	1	1*	0	0	1.5
[xldmem.c 387]	many	6	0	1	0	1	0	3

eqntott

[pterm_ops.c 57]	10	4	1	1	0	0	0	27
[pterm_ops.c 111]	5-10	3	2	1	0	0	0	14

compress

[compress.c 807]	5-10	3	1	1	0	0	0	3
[compress.c 822]	many	10	0	3	3	1	0	100000+
[compress.c 929]	5-10	2	0	1	1*	0	0	14

sc

[sc.c 419]	large	many (not suitable for software pipelining)						
[interp.c 1003]	10	4	0	1	1	1	0	30
[interp.c 266]	10	4	0	1	0	1	0	1.5
[interp.c 266]	5	3	0	1	0	0	0	5
[sc.c 421]	large	many (not suitable for software pipelining)						
[sc.c 229]	5	2	0	2	0	0	0	60

gcc

[tree.c 411]	3	1	0	1	0	0	0	4
[c-parse.y 2177]	10-15	2	0	1	0	0	0	8
[c-parse.y 1942]	5-10	2	1	1	1*	0	1	2
[c-parse.y 2072]	3	1	0	1	0	0	0	8
[c-parse.y 2004]	10-20	8	1	1	1*	0	0	5
[tree.c 522]	3	1	0	1	0	0	0	5
[tree.c 532]	5	1	0	1	0	0	0	5
[tree.c 875]	4	1	0	1	0	0	0	20
[c-parse.y 1630]	5	3	0	1	1*	0	0	2
[c-parse.y 2183]	large	many (not suitable for software pipelining)						

% can be inlined
* infrequently called
+ data size dependent

330

Appendix-A: Loops

Loop 1
```
  i = c;
  do {
        if (a[i]&~b[i])
            break;
  } while (--i>0);\
```

Loop 2
```
  for (k=0; k<100; k++) {
        i = d;
        do {
            if (a[i]&~b[i])
                break;
        } while (--i>0);\
        if (i==0)
            break;
        i = d;
        do {
            c[i] = (a[i]&~b[i]) ;
        } while (--i>0);\
  }
```

Loop 3
```
  for (i = size - 1; i >= 0; i--)
        count[i] = 0;
```

Loop 4
```
  int active = 0;
  for(i = first_part; i <= lastbit; i++) {
        sum += count[i];
        active += (count[i] >= 0);
        if (active > maxactive)
            maxactive = active;
  }
```

Loop 5
```
  for (fp = xlenv; fp; fp = fp->cdr)
        for (ep = fp->car; ep; ep = ep->cdr)
            if (sym == ep->car->car)
                return ep->car->cdr;
```

Loop 6
```
  for (i = 0; i < ninputs; i++) {
        aa = a[i];
        bb = b[i];
        if (aa == 2)
            aa = 0;
        if (bb == 2)
            bb = 0;
        if (aa != bb) {
            if (aa < bb) {
                return (-1);
            }
            else  {
                return (1);
```

```
            }
        }
  }
```

Loop 7
```
  while ( (c = getchar()) != EOF ) {
        in_count++;
        fcode = (long) (((long) c << maxbits) + ent);
        i = ((c << hshift) ^ ent);    /* xor hashing */

        if ( htabof (i) == fcode ) {
            ent = codetabof (i);
            continue;
        } else if ( (long)htabof (i) < 0 )   /* empty slot */
            goto nomatch;
        disp = hsize_reg - i;        /* secondary hash (after G. Knott) */
        if ( i == 0 )
            disp = 1;
probe:
        if ( (i -= disp) < 0 )
            i += hsize_reg;

        if ( htabof (i) == fcode ) {
            ent = codetabof (i);
            continue;
        }
        if ( (long)htabof (i) > 0 )
            goto probe;
nomatch:
        output ( ent );
        out_count++;
        ent = c;
        if ( free_ent < maxmaxcode ) {
            codetabof (i) = free_ent++; /* code -> hashtable */
            htabof (i) = fcode;
        }
        else if ( in_count >= checkpoint && block_compress )
            cl_block ();
  }
```

Loop 8
```
  c = getc(stdin);
  while (c==' ' || c=='\t')
        c = getc(stdin);
```

Dependence Analysis in Parallel Loops with $i \pm k$ Subscripts

Samuel P. Midkiff*

IBM T.J. Watson Research, P.O. Box 704, Yorktown Height, NY 1059

Abstract. Dependence analysis in sequential loops is well understood, but little work has been done on dependence analysis in explicitly parallel loops. In this paper we describe a technique for performing dependence analysis in explicitly parallel loops when all subscripts are of form $i \pm k$, where k is an integer constant. Our technique is the only one we know of that performs subscript based dependence analysis in parallel loops.

1 Introduction

Dependence analysis of references in sequential loops is a well understood problem[9, 12, 1, 2]. In this paper we tackle the less understood problem of dependence analysis in explicitly parallel loops. Dependence analysis of parallel loops is important since, without it, optimizations cannot be performed in explicitly parallel programs that affect the access order of array elements. The techniques presented here are the only ones we know of that use subscript information to analyze subscripted references in explicitly parallel loops.

The techniques described are applicable to loops whose references have subscripts of the form $i \pm k$, where k is an integer constant. We also discuss the difficulty of analyzing loops containing general affine subscripts in one variable (e.g. $c \cdot i \pm k$).

Like dependence analysis for sequential programs, our analysis identifies all sequential orders implied by the semantics of the original program that must be enforced for executions of the program to be *sequentially consistent*[6]. A sequentially consistent execution of a program has the same outcome as some execution of the original program that honors all ordering specified by the original program.

The paper is organized as follows: Section 2 presents assumptions and definitions that hold for the rest of the paper. Section 3 gives some background results from [10]. Section 4 discusses our technique, Section 5 describes related work, and finally Section 6 gives our conclusions.

---

* This work was done was at the Center for Supercomputing Research and Development, University of Illinois at Urbana-Champaign. It was funded by DOE Grant No. DOE DE-FG02-85ER25001, The Control Data Corporation, and the NASA Ames Research Center under Grant No. NASA NCC 2-559.

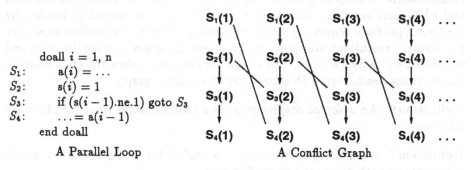

S_1:   doall $i = 1$, n
S_1:   a(i) = ...
S_2:   s(i) = 1
S_3:   if (s($i - 1$).ne.1) goto S_3
S_4:   ... = a($i - 1$)
    end doall

A Parallel Loop   A Conflict Graph

Fig. 1. An Explicitly Parallel Loop and its Instance Level Conflict Graph

2 Notation, Definitions and Assumptions

Parallelism will be expressed using explicitly parallel *doall* loops and *cobegin* statements. Each iteration of the parallel loop is a *thread* which executes asynchronously, and in parallel, with other threads. Each branch of the cobegin forms a thread. This paper does not treat dependence analysis in the presence of cobegin statements, but they are useful for describing some necessary results.

For brevity, we only consider loop nests with a single parallel loop in this paper, however the techniques are extensible to deeper loop nests.

Definition 1. A *statement instance* is the execution of a statement in an iteration of a loop. The instance of statement S_2 executed in iteration 3 is denoted $S_2(3)$.

Definition 2. Two references *conflict* if they access the same memory location, and the order of access affects the outcome of the program. For our purposes, a conflict occurs if two references access the same memory location and at least one is a write. If, e.g., both write the same value this definition is too conservative. Conflict can be tested using the *gcd* test and Banerjee's Inequalities with a $< *, *, \ldots, * >$ direction vector[1, 12].

In the program of Figure 1a, the a references conflict and the b references conflict. Since no order is assumed for the accesses, the conflict on a(i) and a(i-1) can be denoted either *(a(i), a(i-1))* or *(a(i-1), a(i))*.

Two statements are said to conflict if they contain conflicting references.

Definition 3. An order can be placed on the conflicting accesses of two references. In particular, an execution of the program orders all conflicts in the program. Conflict so ordered are *oriented conflicts*.

Definition 4. The number of iterations between the conflicting accesses of a reference is the *distance* of the conflict. Thus, for the conflict on a(i) and a($i' - 1$), the conflict distances are *1* and *-1*. Oriented conflicts have only one distance. Distances are positive if the conflict extends from a lower to a higher iteration.

Definition 5. A *conflict graph* is a graph whose nodes are statement instances and whose arcs represent conflict relations and execution orderings implied by the source program semantics. Arcs representing conflicts are *conflict arcs*. Arcs representing executions orders are *program arcs*. Program arcs are directed, and the statement instance at the tail of the arc executes before the statement instance at the head. Figure 1b shows part of a conflict graph.

Definition 6. An *oriented conflict graph* is a conflict graph whose conflicts are oriented.

Definition 7. A *mixed cycle* is a cycle in a conflict (or oriented conflict) graph that contains both program and conflict arcs.

Definition 8. A *dependence* is a program arc that must be honored at run-time by any transformation for the transformed program to produce the same results as an untransformed program. As shown in [10], this is a generalization of the definition of data dependence for sequential programs. Control dependence is beyond the scope of this paper.

3 Dependence in Explicitly Parallel Programs

In [10], Shasha and Snir present basic results concerning dependence analysis in parallel programs. They are concerned with dependences between scalar accesses, and do not consider the problem of subscript-based dependence analysis. Nevertheless, their results are fundamental to our work. In particular, they show the relationship between dependence and cycles in a program's conflict graph. This sections briefly presents results from [10] needed in the rest of the paper.

The definition of correctness for optimizing compilers for Fortran and similar languages has been that any execution of the transformed program be a *sequentially consistent execution* of the original program. Lamport [6] defines a *sequentially consistent multiprocessor* as one that:

> [t]he result of any execution is the same as if the operations [of the program] were executed in some sequential order, and the operations of each individual processor appear in this sequence in the order specified by its program.

In other words, the outcome of executing the program must be the outcome of some execution which honors all the orderings implied by the semantics of the original program. Any interleaving of statements from different threads which honors all such orderings we call a *consistent interleaving*. Thus, any topological sort on program arcs produces a consistent interleaving.

Consider the (non-determinate) parallel program of Figure 3. There are 6 consistent interleavings of statements (shown italicized) which honor the program arcs, i.e. S_2 follows S_1, and S_4 follows S_3. The program outcomes corresponding to these interleavings ($x = 0, y = 0; x = 1, y = 0$, or $x = 1, y = 1$) define the set of legal outcomes for the program.

```
        X, Y = 0
        cobegin
S₁:     X = 1
S₂:     Y = 1
        //
S₃:     y = Y
S₄:     x = X
        coend
```

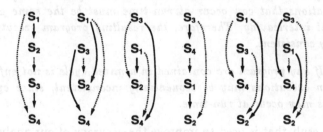

(a) A Program and its Conflict Graph

Execution Order	x =	y =	Execution Order	x =	y =
S_1, S_2, S_3, S_4	1	1	S_1, S_2, S_4, S_3	1	1
S_1, S_3, S_2, S_4	1	0	S_1, S_3, S_4, S_2	1	0
S_1, S_4, S_2, S_3	1	1	S_1, S_4, S_3, S_2	1	0
S_2, S_1, S_3, S_4	1	1	S_2, S_1, S_4, S_3	1	1
S_2, S_3, S_1, S_4	1	1	$\mathbf{S_2, S_3, S_4, S_1}$	0	1
S_2, S_4, S_1, S_3	0	1	$\mathbf{S_2, S_4, S_3, S_1}$	0	1
S_3, S_1, S_2, S_4	1	0	S_3, S_1, S_4, S_2	1	0
S_3, S_2, S_1, S_4	1	0	S_3, S_2, S_4, S_1	0	0
S_3, S_4, S_1, S_2	0	0	S_3, S_4, S_2, S_1	0	0
S_4, S_1, S_2, S_3	0	1	S_4, S_1, S_3, S_2	0	0
S_4, S_2, S_1, S_3	0	1	$\mathbf{S_4, S_2, S_3, S_1}$	0	1
S_4, S_3, S_1, S_2	0	0	S_4, S_3, S_2, S_1	0	0

(b) Outcomes of all Possible Executions of a Sequential Program

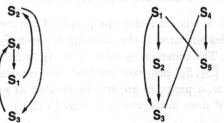

(c) Oriented Conflict Graphs for Consistent Interleavings

(d) An Oriented Conflict Graph   (e) Consecutive Program
for an Inconsistent Interleaving   Arcs Example

The oriented conflict graph for each consistent interleaving must be acyclic since:

1. program arcs are oriented from a statement to a statement that executes later;
2. conflict arcs are oriented from a statement to a statement that executes later.

Thus no back edges exist in the graph, and therefore no cycles exist.

In the oriented conflict graphs for non-consistent interleavings (see Figure 3d) cycles can exist. By definition, a non-consistent interleaving allows the order implied by program arcs to be violated at run-time. This allows orientations of conflict arcs that might not occur in a sequentially consistent interleaving. When these orientations are combined with the program arcs in an oriented conflict graph, a cycle will arise since back edges are present. The presence of a cycle indicates two things:

1. an orientation of conflicts arcs that is not possible when program arcs are enforced has occurred; and
2. that this orientation has occurred is captured in the state of the variables involved in the conflicts.

If the program arcs involved in the cycle had been enforced, the conflict orientations would have to be one of those resulting from a consistent interleaving. Thus, enforcing the program arcs involved in the cycle prevents the cycle from arising.

Result 1 *If all program arcs contained in mixed[2] cycles are enforced, the conflict orientations that can occur at run-time must be the same as occur with a consistent interleaving. Therefore, the resulting program executions must be sequentially consistent.*

Result 2 *If any program arc contained in a mixed cycle is not enforced, resulting program executions may be sequentially inconsistent, since cycle inducing orientations may occur at run-time.*

A final result that is used to improve the accuracy of our analysis is:

Result 3 *The presence of a program arc in a mixed cycle with traversals of adjacent program arcs does not imply dependence.*

To see why this is true consider the graph of Figure 3e. Conflict orientations that lead to cycles will arise if the ordering between S_1 and S_3, or S_4 and S_5 are not maintained. The order of S_2 relative to S_3 or S_1 is irrelevant. Therefore, it is the transitive (S_1, S_3) program arc that is of interest.

To summarize, a program arc will be treated as a dependence unless it can be proven that it does not occur in a mixed cycle in the conflict graph for the program.

---

[2] In [10], a stronger result involving *minimal mixed cycles* is given. The result, however, is not necessary for our purposes.

4 Dependence Analysis of Parallel Loops with $i \pm k$ Subscripts

In this section we first give a broad overview of a technique to perform dependence analysis in parallel loops, followed by a detailed discussion of these techniques. As an example, we will perform dependence analysis on the loop of Figure 1.

4.1 Dependence Analysis in Parallel Loops – An Overview

Section 3 shows that a test for dependence in explicitly parallel loops is a test for mixed cycles in the conflict graph for the loop. The straightforward approach of constructing a conflict graph for the entire loop, and finding all mixed cycles in that graph is impractical. Therefore, it is necessary to operate on a compact representation of the conflict graph. The test we describe has four major phases.

First, construct a compact representation of the conflict graph (Sections 4.2 and 4.3).

Second, determine if there is a collection of conflict arcs that could form a path from an iteration i through the graph back to iteration i (Section 4.4). This portion of the test determines if what combinations of conflicts allow the cross iteration portion of the cycle to exist.

Third, determine the constraints imposed by the lexical ordering of statements in the loop (Section 4.5). For example, to follow the (S_2, S_3) conflict arc the (S_1, S_2) program arc must be traversed. Similarly, after traversing the (S_2, S_3) oriented conflict, the (S_3, S_4) program arc must be followed.

Fourth, determine if the collection of conflicts found in the second step, and the constraints imposed by the lexical ordering of statements are consistent (Section 4.7). That is, determine if the number and distance of conflicts visited in a path can be the same as required by the set of conflicts found in step 3.

To allow the fourth step to be carried out, the representation of the collection of conflict arcs and paths through the program is of crucial importance. Collections of conflict arcs are represented as a system of parametric equations that are the solution to a diophantine equation[1]. The path from statement S to itself is represented as a system of equations found by applying Kirchoff's Laws of Flow[4] to the compact representation of the conflict graph. Representing the results of the second and third phases as systems of equations and inequalities allows the consistency check to be done by a linear system solver, e.g. a linear or integer programming system.

In this section we will give the techniques to perform the three phases of the dependence test outlined in the previous section.

4.2 Building a Compact Form of the Conflict Graph

Our goal in building a compact form of the conflict graph is to both compactly represent the original conflict graph and allow traversals of the different orientations of a conflict arcs to be distinguished. This requires splitting a statement

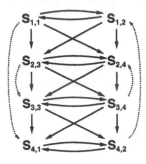

Fig. 2. An Example of a Compact Conflict Graph

adjacent to a conflict into 2 nodes – one node represents instances of the statement adjacent to one orientation of the conflict, and the other node represents instances of the statement adjacent to the other orientation. Conflict and program arcs are then added to the graph. Figure 2 shows a completed compact conflict graph.

Splitting Statements into Pairs of Nodes Number each conflict with an odd positive number. Let S_p and S_q be adjacent to conflict r. Two nodes are formed for each statement: $S_{p,r}$, $S_{p,r+1}$, $S_{q,r}$ and $S_{q,r+1}$.

Adding Conflict Arcs Let $S_{p,r}$, $S_{p,r+1}$, $S_{q,r}$ and $S_{q,r+1}$ be as above. Add the oriented conflict arcs $(S_{p,r}, S_{q,r})$ and $(S_{q,r+1}, S_{p,r+1})$ to the compact graph. Conflict arcs will be shown as dashed lines.

Adding Program Arcs Let $S_{u,*}$ be any node derived from statement S_u. If S_p reachs S_q in any iteration, add the directed program arcs $(S_{p,*}S_{q,*})$ to the graph. S_p is assumed to always reach itself in zero iterations. Program arcs will be shown as solid lines.

Note that the above construction puts the transitive closure of the program arcs on the graph. In the examples, transitive arcs are usually eliminated for clarity.

4.3 Enumerating Candidate Components in the Compact Conflict Graph

The compact conflict graph is not analyzed as a monolithic entity. Rather, a strategy similar to that employed in sequential dependence analysis is employed. In sequential dependence analysis, only a single conflict is involved in a dependence, and full analysis (e.g. Banerjees's Inequalities[1]) is brought to bear on pairs of conflicting references. A dependence in a parallel loop may involve some or all of the conflicts in the loop. Therefore, the analysis is applied to portions of the conflict graph containing various groups of conflicts. Specifically, the compact conflict graph is divided into components containing all possible combinations of orientations of the conflicts, and there is one component for each member of the power set of conflict orientations.

For example, in the conflict graph of Figure 2, there are four different oriented conflicts. One candidate component might contain the oriented conflicts $(S_{2,3}, S_{3,3})$ and $(S_{4,2}, S_{1,2})$, and testing it would test for dependence arising from cycles in the conflict graph involving exactly those orientations. Since all members of the power set of orientations are tested, all possible dependences will be tested.

The full analysis, however, need not be applied to every component, but only to those components that cannot be quickly identified as not corresponding to a mixed cycle in a full conflict graph for the loop. We use the following criteria to reduce the number of components that must be completely analyzed:

1. Oriented conflict arcs must be present that go both forward and backwards in the iteration space. This is a necessary condition for a traversal to move forwards and backward through the iteration space, which is a necessary condition for a cycle.
2. Oriented conflicts from more than one conflict must be present in the graph. This is necessary for the existence of a mixed cycle in the graph. Consider the conflict graph of Figure 1. If only oriented conflict arcs from a single conflict are in the component, all "cycles" will be of the form $S_1(1), S_4(2), S_1(1)$.
3. The component must be a strongly connected component and must contain at least one program arc. This ensures that all conflict orientations are reachable in a mixed cycle in the full conflict graph. If not, then no cycle involving these conflict orientations can exist in the full conflict graph, and therefore no dependences resulting from these conflict orientations can exist.

Figure 3 enumerates all combinations of conflict arc orientations. A "$\sqrt{}$" the column for some conflict orientation denotes its presence in the candidate component. If the full analysis need not be applied to the candidate component, the *Analyzed?* column states the number (from above) of the reason why the component need not be analyzed. Two candidate components are identified: one containing the oriented conflict arcs $(S_{4,2}, S_{1,2})$ and $(S_{2,3}, S_{3,3})$, and the other containing the oriented conflict arcs $(S_{4,2}, S_{1,2})$, $(S_{2,3}, S_{3,3})$, and $(S_{3,4}, S_{2,4})$. Figure 4 shows the compact conflict graph for each of these components.

We finish building the compact conflict graph for the candidate component by adding to the graph all program arcs whose tail is at the head of a conflict arc in the component, and whose head is at the tail of a conflict arc. Finally, if both an oriented conflict arc and a program arc join $S_{p,r}, S_{q,r}$ then either the conflict arc or the program arc can be followed to go from $S_{p,r}$ to $S_{q,r}$. Therefore, the program arc $(S_{p,r}, S_{q,r})$ should also be added to the graph. In order to apply Kirchoff's Laws of Flow to the graph, and to distinguish between traversals of the program and conflict arc joining the two statements, the program arc is

Oriented Conflict				Analysed?
$(S_{1,1}, S_{4,1})$	$(S_{4,2}, S_{1,2})$	$(S_{2,3}, S_{3,3})$	$(S_{3,4}, S_{2,4})$	
				(1), (2)
			✓	(1), (2)
		✓		(1), (2)
		✓	✓	(2)
	✓			(1), (2)
	✓		✓	(1)
	✓	✓		analyse
	✓	✓	✓	analyse
✓				(1), (2)
✓			✓	(3)
✓		✓		(1)
✓		✓	✓	(3)
✓	✓			(2)
✓	✓		✓	(3)
✓	✓	✓		(3)
✓	✓	✓	✓	(3)

Fig. 3. Candidate Cycle Enumeration

not added directly to the graph. Instead, we observe that because the graph for the component is a strongly connected component, the tail of the conflict arc is adjacent to one or more program arcs $(S_{u,v}, S_{p,r})$. Adding the transitive program arc $(S_{u,v}, S_{q,r})$ has the same affect on the flow through the conflict graph as adding the program arc $(S_{p,r}, S_{q,r})$. The program arc $(S_{1,2}, S_{3,3})$ is an example of this.

Adding the transitive arc prevents having multiple arcs $(S_{p,r}, S_{q,r})$ on the graph, which would make the application of Kirchoff's Laws of Flow more difficult.

Finally, program arcs which are adjacent only to different orientations of the same conflict arc should not be added to the graph, since they are not contained in any simple cycle in the full conflict graph. The prevents the program arc $(S_{2,4}, S_{2,3})$ from being added to the conflict graph of Figure 3a.

The result of the construction for the two candidate cycles identified in Figure 3 are shown in Figure 4.

4.4 Finding Collections of Conflict Arcs that Allow Cycles

In order for a cycle to exist in the conflict graph, it must be possible to follow a sequence of conflicts from an iteration to another iteration and back to the original iteration. This section shows how the to describe the oriented conflicts that can make up this sequence as parametric equations.

Consider the conflicts in the candidate component of Figure 4a. Three conflicts are in the cycle, one with distance 1 $((S_{2,3}, S_{3,3}))$ and two with distance -1 $((S_{3,4}, S_{2,4}$ and $(S_{4,2}, S_{1,2}))$. For the sequence described to exist, it must be the case that:

$$0 = (1) \cdot E_2 + (-1) \cdot E_6 + (-1) \cdot E_8$$

where E_2 is the number of times an instance of $(S_{2,3}, S_{3,3})$ (e_2) is traversed, E_6 is the number of times an instance of $(S_{3,4}, S_{2,4}$ $(e_6)$is traversed, and E_8 is the

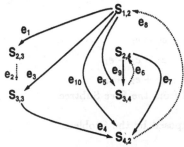

(a) The Candidate Component for the Cycle Containing Oriented Conflicts $(S_{4,2}, S_{1,2})$, $(S_{2,3}, S_{3,3})$, and $(S_{3,4}, S_{2,4})$

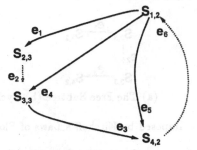

(b) The Candidate Component for the Cycle Containing Oriented Conflicts $(S_{4,2}, S_{1,2})$ and $(S_{2,3}, S_{3,3})$

Fig. 4. Candidate Components

number of times $(S_{4,2}, S_{1,2})$ (e_8) is traversed. The solutions to this diophantine equation can be expressed as the parametric equations (see [1] for details):

$$E_2 = t_2 + t_3, \quad E_6 = t_2, \quad E_8 = t_3 \tag{1}$$

For the conflicts of the candidate component of Figure 4b the equation to be solved is $0 = E_2 - E_6$ with parametric solutions:

$$E_2 = t_2, \quad E_6 = t_2 \tag{2}$$

Note that there will always be a solution to these equations. Let d_1 and d_2 be two distances. Since full analysis is being applied to the component it can be assumed that their signs are different. Then $0 = |d_1| \cdot d_2 + |d_2| \cdot d_1$ will always be true.

4.5 Finding Lexical Constraints on Conflict Graph Traversals

In this section, the lexical constraints on conflict graphs will be modeled with a system of equations. The basic idea is that in order to traverse an arc α in the graph it is necessary to traverse other arcs in the graph that form a path to α. Which other arcs must be traversed is a consequence of the lexical relationship of the statements at the endpoints of the arcs. Kirchoff's Laws of Flow give a systematic way of developing these equations. The equations express the number of times each arc is traversed in a cycle in terms of how many times other arcs in the cycle are traversed. Variable E_i represents the number of times the arc e_i is traversed.

Consider the component of Figure 4b. To apply Kirchoff's Laws of Flow, a *free subtree* is first formed. The free subtree is formed by removing arcs from the graph until the removal of any other arc will cause the graph to become disconnected. One of many possible free subtrees is shown in Figure 5a. In the

$$S_{2,3} \xleftarrow{\quad e_1 \quad} S_{1,2}$$

$$e_2 \downarrow$$

$$S_{3,3} \xrightarrow{\quad e_3 \quad} S_{4,2}$$

$$C_4 : e_4 - e_2 - e_1$$

$$C_5 : e_5 - e_3 - e_2 - e_1$$

$$C_6 : e_6 + e_1 + e_2 + e_3$$

(a) The Free Subtree   (b) Cycles Formed from the Free Subtree

Imposed by Kirchoff's Laws of Flow   Imposed by the Problem

$E_1 = -E_4 - E_5 + E_6$	(3)	$E_2 > 0$	(6)
$E_2 = -E_4 - E_5 + E_6$	(4)	$E_6 > 0$	(7)
$E_3 = -E_5 + E_6$	(5)	$E_2 = E_6$	(8)
		$E_i \geq 0, 1 \leq i \leq 6$	(9)

(c) Constraints on the Program Flow

Fig. 5. Free Trees for the Component of Figure 4b.

system of equations modeling the effect of the lexical relations of statements, variables corresponding to arcs in the free subtree will be the dependent variables of the system.

The *fundamental cycles* of the component are now found. An arc not in the free subtree is added to the free subtree, and the resulting cycle is expressed as an algebraic sum. For example, e_4 is added to the free subtree. To traverse the resulting cycle, e_4 is followed, and is added to the sum representing the cycle C_4. Next e_2 and e_1 are traversed (in reverse order), and so $-e_2$ and $-e_1$ are added to the sum. The resulting sums for the cycles are shown in Figure 5b, where C_i corresponds to the cycle formed by adding arc e_i to the free subtree.

Now the equations that model the effects of the lexical relationship on flow can be formed. For each arc e_i in the free subtree, an equation is created for the variable E_i. The procedure is to scan the cycle equations. If "$+e_i$" appears in the equation for C_j, then then E_j is added to the right hand side of the equation for E_i. If "$-e_i$" appears in the equation for C_j, then then E_j is subtracted from the right hand side of the equation for E_i. Thus, in Figure 5 "$-e_1$" appears in the cycles C_4 and C_5, and "$+e_1$" appears in cycle C_6, giving the equation $E_1 = -E_4 - E_5 + E_6$.

The system of equations for this component are shown in Figure 5c. Figure 6 gives the same information for the component of Figure 4a.

4.6   Constraints Imposed by the Program Semantics and Definitions

Testing a component determines if a mixed cycle that traverses each oriented conflict at least once might exist in the full conflict graph. Therefore, the constraint is added to the system that each conflict must be traversed one or more

(a) The Free Subtree

$C_3 : e_2 - e_1$

$C_7 : e_7 - e_4 - e_2 - e_1 + e_5 + e_6$

$C_8 : e_8 + e_1 + e_2 + e_4$

$C_9 : e_6$

$C_{10} : -e_4 - e_2 - e_1$

(b) Cycles Formed from the Free Subtree

Imposed by Kirchoff's Laws of Flow

Imposed by the Problem

$$E_1 = -E_3 - E_7 + E_8 - E_{10} \quad (10)$$

$$E_2 = -E_3 - E_7 + E_8 - E_{10} \quad (11)$$

$$E_4 = -E_7 + E_8 - E_{10} \quad (12)$$

$$E_5 = E_7 \quad (13)$$

$$E_6 = E_7 + E_9 \quad (14)$$

$$E_2 > 0 \quad (15)$$

$$E_6 > 0 \quad (16)$$

$$E_8 > 0 \quad (17)$$

$$E_2 = E_6 + E_8 \quad (18)$$

$$E_i \geq 0, 1 \leq i \leq 10 \quad (19)$$

(c) Constraints on the Program Flow

Fig. 6. Free Trees for the Component of Figure 4a.

times. Equations 6 and 7 in Figure 5c, and equations 15, 16 and 17 in Figure 6c impose this constraint.

The constraints imposed by Equation 2 are incorporated in the system of Figure 5c in Equation 8. The constraints imposed by Equation 1 are incorporated in the system of Figure 6c in Equation 18.

Finally, since statements cannot execute a negative number of times, all program and conflict arcs must be traversed zero or more times. This constraint is reflected in Equation 9 of the system of Figure 5c, and Equation 19 of the system of Figure 6c.

4.7 Testing for Dependence

We are now ready to test for dependence by determining if the system formed in the previous phases is consistent. If the system is consistent, the component may correspond to a cycle in the full conflict graph for the loop, and program arcs in the component may need to be treated as dependences. Before declaring that a program arc must be treated as a dependence, one final test is used to attempt to disprove dependence. If the program arc is in the cycle, the constraint of Section 4.6 that program arcs must be traversed zero or more times can be tightened. Instead, the program arc must be traversed. Therefore, before declaring the program arc e_i to be a dependence, the constraint $E_i > 0$ is added to the system, and the system is again tested for consistency. If the system is still consistent, the the program arc is treated as a dependence.

```
                                    doall i = 1, n
                                       cobegin
                        S₁:               a(i) = ...
                        S₂:               s(i) = 1
                                    //
                        S₃:               if (s(i).ne.1) goto S₃
  S₁        S₃          S₄:               ...= a(i-1)
  │(=)      │(=)                     end coend
  S₂        S₄                     end doall
```

(a) The Dependence Graph for (b) A Transformation Enabled by
the Loop of Figure 1   the Dependence Information

Fig. 7. The Dependence Graph for the Loop of Figure 1

We illustrate this using the example. The system of Figure 5c is consistent – one solution is $E_1 = 1$, $E_2 = 2$, $E_3 = 1$, $E_4 = 0$, $E_5 = 0$ and $E_6 = 6$. Clearly, the system is consistent if the tighter constraint $E_1 > 0$ or $E_3 > 0$ is added to the system, since their value in the solution just given fulfills the constraint. Thus $(S_{1,2}, S_{2,3})$ (e_1) and $(S_{3,3}, S_{4,2})$ (e_3) must be treated as dependences.

The situation is not so obvious for $(S_{1,2}, S_{3,3})$, i.e. arc (e_4). Adding the constraint $E_4 > 0$ to the system of Figure 5c makes the system inconsistent, as we now show. By Equation 8 $E_2 = E_6$. Substituting E_2 for E_6 in Equation 4 gives: $E_2 = -E_4 - E_5 + E_6$ which simplified gives $0 = -E_4 - E_5$. Since $E_4 \geq 0$ and $E_5 \geq 0$ (by Equation 9), this can only be true if $E_4 = E_5 = 0$. But the new constraint forces $E_4 > 0$, and so the system is not consistent.

A similar derivation shows that the system is not consistent with the constraint $E_5 > 0$. Therefore, program arcs $(S_{1,2}, S_{3,3})$ and $(S_{1,2}, S_{4,2})$ do not need to be treated as dependences.

We now show that the system for the second component, shown in Figure 6c, is inconsistent. By equation 18, $E_2 = E_6 + E_8$. Substituting $E_6 + E_8$ into the right hand side of Equation 11, we get:

$$E_6 + E_8 = -E_3 - E_6 + E_8 - E_{10},$$

and

$$E_6 = -E_3 - E_6 - E_{10}.$$

By Equation 19, all $E_i \geq 0$, therefore $E_6 = 0$, which contradicts Equation 16, and the system is inconsistent.

Therefore, dependence is disproven in the second component, and only the two program arcs identified in the first component must be treated as dependences. Figure 7 shows the resulting dependence graph, and a transformation that is enabled by the analysis.

5 Related Work

Krishnamurthy and Yelick[5] give a polynomial time algorithm for dependence analysis in parallel SPMD programs. Their approach does not, however, deal with array analysis.

Grunwald and Srinivasan[3] describe the computation of classical data flow information (use-def, kill sets, etc.) for deterministic parallel programs. Stoltz, Srinivasan, Wolfe, and Hook[11] describe computing Static Single Assignment (SSA) information for deterministic explicitly parallel programs. Our work considers both deterministic and non-deterministic programs, and concentrates on programs with array accesses.

Banerjee [1], Wolfe [12] and others have discussed the dependence analysis of sequential programs. If the program is parallel their analysis is invalid – even within a sequential loop nest[8].

Midkiff, Padua and Cytron[8], and Midkiff and Padua [7], discuss techniques for performing dependence analysis in programs with explicit *cobegin*, or *parallel section* parallelism. Their techniques relies on knowing, at compile time, the number of parallel threads that will exist at run-time.

The results of Shasha and Snir[10] form the foundation of our work, but they concentrate on straight-line programs with scalar references. Subscripted array assignments are treated like scalar assignments within a loop – an assignment to any element of the array is treated as an assignment to the entire array. Our solution builds on their results, but makes use of array subscript information to give more precise results.

6 Conclusions and Future Work

A major difficulty in the design of parallel programming languages is to allow compilers to analyze and optimize programs written in the language. Current programming languages with parallel constructs, such as Parallel Common Fortran, or HPF, restrict the type of data sharing that can occur in explicitly parallel loops. A cleaner approach is to deduce the effects of data sharing and perform transformations based on that knowledge. Dependence analysis of parallel programs is necessary to achieve that goal.

We have described a technique to perform subscript based dependence analysis in explicitly parallel loops with $i \pm k$ subscripts. This is the first technique of this kind to be demonstrated. Although the analysis is less general and more expensive than dependence analysis for sequential programs, it demonstrates that dependence analysis is possible for parallel loops. Loops containing only subscripts of the form $c \cdot i$ can also be analyzed by this method. The diophantine equation solved in Section 4.4 is replaced by a system of equations arising from the prime factorization of conflict distances, but otherwise the technique is the same.

The author is working on less expensive and more general tests. It is hoped that advances in this area will enable the development of general, parallel languages that both allow algorithms to be expressed in a natural form, and that allow compilers to optimize those expressions of algorithms for efficient execution on parallel and sequential machines.

As well, the underlying technology – i.e. the ability to find cycles in infinite graphs describable by affine functions – should prove useful for race detection, deadlock analysis and code motion in the presence of message passing operations or synchronization.

7 Acknowledgements

I would like to thank Lee Nackman, David Padua and Edith Schonberg for their support of this work. I would also like to thank the referees and workshop attendees for their insightful and helpful comments.

References

1. U. Banerjee. *Dependence analysis for supercomputing*. Kluwer Academic Publishers, Boston, Mass., 1988.
2. M. Burke and R. Cytron. Interprocedural dependence analysis and parallelization. In *Proceedings of The SIGPLAN '86 Symposium on Compiler Construction*, pages 162–175, June 1986. Also avalailable as Vol 21, No. 7, SIGPLAN Notices.
3. D. Grunwald and H. Srinivasan. Data flow equations for explicitly parallel programs. In *Conf. Record 4th ACM Symp. Principles and Practices of Parallel Programming*, May 1993.
4. D. Knuth. *Fundamental Algorithms*, volume 1 of *The Art of Computer Programming*. Addison-Wesley, Reading, Mass, 2 edition, 1973.
5. A. Krishnamurthy and K. Yelick. Optimizing parallel SPMD programs. In K. Pingali, U. Banerjee, D. Gelernter, A. Nicolau, and D. Padua, editors, *Languages and Compilers for Parallel Computing, 7th International Workshop*, pages 331–345, Ithaca, NY, USA, August 1994.
6. L. Lamport. How to make a multiprocessor computer that correctly executes multiprocess programs. *IEEE Transactions on Computers*, C-28:690–691, 1979.
7. S.P. Midkiff and D.A. Padua. Some issues in the compile-time optimization of parallel programs, 1991. Research report number RC17431.
8. S.P. Midkiff, D.A. Padua, and R.G. Cytron. Compiling programs with user parallelism. In D. Gelernter, A. Nicolau, and D. Padua, editors, *Languages and compilers for parallel computing*, pages 402–422. MIT Press, Cambridge, Mass., 1990. Available as CSRD Report no. 728.
9. William Pugh. A practical algorithm for exact array dependence analysis. *Communications of the ACM*, 35(8):102–114, Aug 1992.
10. D. Shasha and M. Snir. Efficient and correct execution of parallel programs that share memory. *ACM TOPLAS*, 10(2):282–312, April 1988.
11. E. Stoltz, H. Srinivasan, James Hook, and Michael Wolfe. Static Single Assignment form for explicitly parallel programs: Theory and practice. submitted *Journal of Programming Languages*, 1993.
12. M.J. Wolfe. *Optimizing supercompilers for supercomputers*. MIT Press, Cambridge, Mass., 1989.

Piecewise Execution of
Nested Data-Parallel Programs

Daniel W. Palmer, Jan F. Prins, Siddhartha Chatterjee, and Rickard E. Faith

Department of Computer Science
The University of North Carolina
Chapel Hill, NC 27599-3175
{palmerd,prins,sc,faith}@cs.unc.edu

Abstract. The technique of flattening nested data parallelism combines all the independent operations in nested apply-to-all constructs and generates large amounts
of potential parallelism for both regular and irregular expressions. However, the
resulting data-parallel programs can have enormous memory requirements, limiting their utility. In this paper, we present *piecewise execution*, an automatic method
of partially serializing data-parallel programs so that they achieve maximum parallelism within storage limitations. By computing large intermediate sequences
in pieces, our approach requires asymptotically less memory to perform the same
amount of work. By using characteristics of the underlying parallel architecture to
drive the computation size, we retain effective use of a parallel machine at each
step. This dramatically expands the class of nested data-parallel programs that
can be executed using the flattening technique. With the addition of piecewise I/O
operations, these techniques can be applied to generate out-of-core execution on
large datasets.

1 Introduction

1.1 Flattening nested data parallelism

Nested data parallelism is a powerful paradigm for expressing concurrent execution, especially irregular and dynamic computations. Unlike flat data-parallel languages such as
C* [11], High Performance Fortran [9], and APL [12], nested data-parallel languages
allow arbitrary functions to appear in apply-to-all constructs and provide nestable, non-
rectangular aggregates. The expressive benefits of nested data parallelism were long ago
recognized by high-level languages such as SETL [19], FP [2], and APL2, but practical parallel execution of such expressions was not achieved until Blelloch and Sabot
introduced the flattening technique [4]. Flattening combines all the independent operations in nested apply-to-all constructs into large data-parallel operations. Both NESL [5]
and Proteus [13] are high-level, nested data-parallel languages that use this technique
to provide architecture-independence by implementing the data-parallel operations with
portable vector operations [6].

1.2 Excessive memory requirements of flattened programs

The flattening technique fully parallelizes every apply-to-all construct, providing large
amounts of fine-grained potential parallelism, but introduces temporaries whose sizes

are proportional to the potential parallelism. The generality of the apply-to-all construct can easily lead to programs that have enormous potential parallelism, and hence, excessive memory requirements. Blelloch and Narlikar [3] encountered these large temporaries while comparing two algorithms for n-body simulations. They resolved the problem by manually serializing portions of their NESL code reducing the program's memory requirements so it could execute.

The following example illustrates that flattening a nested data-parallel expression can generate code with large temporary values. Consider a problem related to the n-body computation: finding the largest force between any two particles in a sequence of n particles. We express this computation in Proteus using a nesting of two data-parallel *iterators*.

```
max./[i in [1..n]:
        max./[j in [1..i-1]: force(S[i],S[j])]]          (1)
```

Here force (p, q) yields the magnitude of the force between particles p and q. The inner iterator specifies a sequence of independent applications of force and the outer iterator specifies a sequence of independent reductions. The dependence of the inner iterator variable, j, on the outer iterator variable, i, ensures that we only compute the force between any two particles once. The dependency also generates an irregular collection of arguments to force. Consequently, the computation requires an irregular data aggregate which flat data-parallel languages do not linguistically support. Flattening (1) combines the n separate inner invocations of max. / into a single, larger data-parallel maximum reduction and also combines the $\frac{n(n+1)}{2}$ nested invocations of force into a single invocation of the data-parallel version of the function. As a consequence, $O(n^2)$ applications of force are evaluated simultaneously, requiring $O(n^2)$ storage. Clearly, we could sequentially evaluate the expression using only $O(n)$ space. Note that flattening can handle arbitrary, user-defined functions in place of force and max. /. In this paper, we show how to partially serialize flattened programs to reduce their memory requirements while still retaining sufficient parallelism to fully utilize the resources of a targeted architecture.

1.3 Organization of paper

The remainder of this paper is organized as follows. In Section 2, we examine two approaches to partially serializing data-parallel operations: outer iterator serialization and piecewise execution. We further explore piecewise execution in Section 3 and present an implementation of interpreted piecewise execution. In Section 4, we identify some key issues in compiling piecewise execution programs. We present some preliminary performance results of piecewise execution in Section 5. Then, in Section 6, we identify some limitations of piecewise execution and finally, in Section 7, we discuss related work, report the status of our current system, an present our conclusions.

2   Fixed Memory Execution of Flattened Programs

2.1   Partially serialized parallelism

By combining all the operations in nested iterators, flattening exposes all the available parallelism and generates a data-parallel program that operates on sequences, potentially very large ones. A hypothetical parallel machine with an arbitrary number of processors could take advantage of all this parallelism by executing data-parallel operations in a single step (see Fig. 1a). Existing, fixed-processor parallel machines could attempt to execute the data-parallel operations with virtual processors. This approach works well for the large class of flattened programs whose memory requirements do not exceed the resources of a targeted machine. However, in general, simulating n virtual processors requires $O(n)$ memory. To realistically execute a flattened program on existing parallel machines, we must partially serialize the program to reduce its memory requirements.

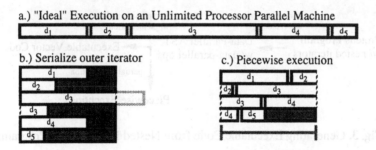

Fig. 1. Approaches to Executing Potential Parallelism

Instead of generating monolithic data-parallel operations from nested iterator expressions, we could transform outer iterators into loop structures and inner iterators into smaller data-parallel operations. This approach serializes regular parallelism well, because each loop iteration will execute the same amount of work, yielding good load balancing. However, for irregular parallel expressions, like the n-body force computation, serializing the outer iterations yields large variations in work and wastes computational resources on undersized sequences (see Fig. 1b).

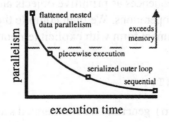

Fig. 2. Comparison of Execution Methods

To achieve load-balanced execution, we must always serialize a computation into *equal* sized pieces. To execute on many different platforms, we must select the size of these pieces based on the characteristics of the target architecture, not simply on the characteristics of the computation. Since it is much easier to serialize portions of exposed parallelism than it is to extract a specified amount of parallelism from nested iterators, we will not alter the the flattening technique. Instead, we introduce a new technique that partitions large data-parallel operations into uniformly-sized pieces (see Fig. 1c). This *piecewise execution* allows a program to retain sufficient parallelism for good performance and satisfies the memory resource restrictions shown in Fig. 2.

2.2 Piecewise execution of flattened data-parallel programs

Fig. 3 illustrates an overview of our implementation of flattening and transformation of high-level nested data-parallel programs into executable vector operations.

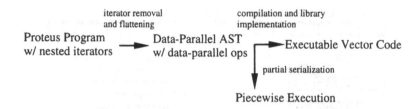

Fig. 3. Generating Executable Code from Nested Data-Parallel Programs

To present a concrete example of this process and to illustrate piecewise execution, we consider computing $n!$ using multiplication reduction on the sequence $[1,\ldots,n]$. We can write this in Proteus as `*./[i in [1..n]:i]`. We then successively apply iterator-removing transformation rules [18] [15], yielding equivalent data-parallel operations.

```
  *./[i in [1..n]:i]
= mult_reduce([i in [1..n]:i])
= mult_reduce([1..n])
= mult_reduce(range1(n))
```

These operations are part of the Data-Parallel Library (DPL) [14], a collection of routines that supports nested sequences as primitive objects and provides data-parallel execution of nested sequence operations. We then compile the functional expression into an imperative, single-assignment form with explicit temporary variables.

```
T = range1(n);
r = mult_reduce(T);
```

The function `range1(n)` generates an enumerated sequence of integers from 1 to n and `mult_reduce(T)` computes the product of the values in T. To compute several factorials simultaneously, we put the values in a sequence $D = [d_1,\ldots,d_n]$, and use [i in D: */. [j in [1..i]:j]] to yield $[d_1!,\ldots,d_n!]$. Although this algorithm is not work efficient, it provides a useful example for illustrating piecewise execution. Evaluated in this manner the Proteus code specifies a data-dependent, irregular parallel operation. Flattening yields the following data-parallel operations.

```
  [i in D: mult_reduce([j in [1..i]:j])]
= mult_reduce¹([i in D:[j in [1..i]:j]])
= mult_reduce¹([i in D:[1..i]])
= mult_reduce¹([i in D:range1(i)])
= mult_reduce¹(range1¹(D))
```

For any function f, we use f^1 to designate a data-parallel function that applies f to all elements of a sequence in parallel. In this example, range^1 computes multiple enumerations in parallel and mult_reduce^1 computes many sequence products simultaneously. As before, we rewrite the functional expression in a single-assignment form with explicit temporary values.

```
T = range1¹(D);
R = mult_reduce¹(T);
```

The data-parallel version of range1 generates results whose storage can greatly exceed that of the inputs. Conversely, mult_reduce^1 produces results whose storage requirements can be far less than that of its inputs. Fig. 4 shows the data-flow graph for the data-parallel factorial program using these operations. The trapezoid-shaped nodes indicate the relative size relation between the inputs and outputs of an operation.

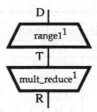

Fig. 4. Simple Data-Flow Graph

As illustrated in the maximum force example, the large temporary, T, can exhaust memory. This is of particular concern for two reasons. First, the large memory requirements are not inherent in the original program, but are introduced by the flattening process. Second, whether a program will exceed memory or not depends on the particular target architecture and on the particular problem size, both of which are determined at runtime. To resolve these problems, we must generate partially serialized code from the data-parallel abstract syntax tree. We can express the functionality of a *piecewise execution* program as a loop.

range1[1] *consumes D*
repeat
      range1[1] *generates a piece of T*
      mult_reduce[1] *consumes the piece of T producing some of R*
until *D is finished*

This approach avoids excessive memory use by never generating T in its entirety. For comparison, we also express this computation with a serialized outer iterator.

```
for (i=1;i<=#D;i++){
    T = range1(D[i]);
    R[i] = mult_reduce(T); }
```

In Table 1, we compare the execution of these two versions. In this example we have four processors and have set $D = [5, 2, 7, 3]$. For the serialized outer iterator code, if the size of T exceeds the number of processors, we must use multiple steps to complete the computation using virtual processors (see Fig. 1b).

Serialized Outer Iterator			
Step	Space	T	R
2	5	[1,2,3,4,5]	[120,]
1	2	[1,2]	[120,2,]
2	7	[1,2,3,4,5,6,7]	[120,2,5040,]
1	3	[1,2,3]	[120,2,5040,6]
Sum:6 Max:7			

Piecewise Execution			
Step	Space	T	R
1	4	[1,2,3,4	[ ]
1	4	5],[1,2],[1	[120,2,]
1	4	2,3,4,5	[120,2,]
1	4	6,7],[1,2	[120,2,5040,]
1	4	3]	[120,2,5040,6]
Sum:5 Max:4			

Table 1. Comparison of Approaches to Partial Serialization of Factorial Program

For comparison, executing the flattened program without any serialization on the four processor machine takes five steps (using virtual processors) and requires 17 memory locations. The serialized outer iterator approach does reduce the memory usage, but actually *increases* the number of steps due to undersized vectors. The piecewise execution maintains the minimal number of steps, and also significantly reduces the required memory. As the number of processors and the problem size increase, the cost of the undersized vectors increases and negates any gains made by serializing the outer iterators, while piecewise execution maintains effective memory use.

2.3 Requirements of piecewise execution

One of the key characteristics of the flattening technique is that it preserves the asymptotic work complexity of a computation, even for irregular, nested iterators. Therefore we require that piecewise execution also be work-efficient. We attempt to select a size for pieces that will keep the underlying parallel machine fully utilized. Oversized pieces exhaust memory resources, and undersized pieces fail to amortize the overhead of parallel execution or achieve a significant percentage of a parallel machine's peak performance. The proper piece size lies somewhere between $n_{1/2}$, which provides half the performance of the machine and $n_{exceeds\ memory}$ which cannot execute because of insufficient storage (See Fig. 5). Sethi [20] showed that determining whether a program can successfully execute without external memory using only k registers requires exponential time. Selecting an acceptable piece size is equivalently complex. The number of pieces, n and the piece size, p are inversely related by $n * p = M$. Since M, the total available memory for a parallel machine is fixed, selecting p determines n. Since we must select piece sizes with incomplete information, we require that the amount of serialization of piecewise execution be adjustable at runtime to support experimentation.

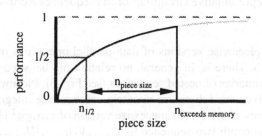

Fig. 5. Acceptable Values for the Size of Pieces

Also to maintain work efficiency, we avoid recomputing sequence values to facilitate piecewise execution. We do not require, but strive for efficient execution and minimal buffering of piecewise execution programs. In practice, there are several instances in which we cannot reach these goals. In Section 6, we examine two program configurations that may cause piecewise execution to fail. We also strive for an approach to piecewise execution that fosters chaining on a vector machine.

3 Interpreted piecewise execution

3.1 Piecewise primitive operations

Piecewise versions of the data-parallel primitive operations consume sequence inputs and generate sequence outputs in a succession of equal-sized pieces. To support fixed-memory execution of flattened programs, we must provide a piecewise version of every DPL operation. DPL consists of two types of operations: basic operations, including range1 and mult_reduce, and data-parallel extensions of the basic operations, including range1[1] and mult_reduce[1].

To implement piecewise versions of the basic operations, we straightforwardly consume pieces of input or generate pieces of output by initiating a series of calls to non-piecewise functions. For example, piecewise_range(n,m,p) enumerates of integers between n and m in pieces of size p by calling range, with the succession of values $(n, n + p - 1), (n + p, n + 2p - 1), \ldots, (n + kp, m)$. Each consecutive invocation of piecewise_range generates the next consecutive piece of the overall sequence result.

Grouping with piece size of 3

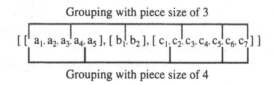

Grouping with piece size of 4

Fig. 6. Representative Groupings of Subsequences Across Pieces

Generating the piecewise versions of data-parallel operations requires a more sophisticated approach. There is, in general, no relationship between the piece size and the hierarchical boundaries of nested sequences (see Fig. 6). Piecewise versions of the data-parallel primitives must therefore maintain subsequence integrity across an arbitrary number of pieces. Consider the piecewise version of range[1] (U, V) which generates, in pieces, the depth two sequence $[[U_1, \ldots, V_1], \ldots, [U_n, \ldots, V_n]]$. We implement the function piecewise_range[1] (U, V, p) by making a series of calls to range[1], but we must carefully supply the proper input sequences.

We define r_k as the amount of space remaining within a piece after k subsequences have been generated. Whenever $V_k - U_k + 1 > r_{k-1}$, generating the kth subsequence will require multiple iterations and computation of multiple starting and ending values of pieces within the subsequence. Conversely, whenever $V_k - U_k + 1 < r_{k-1}$ multiple subsequences will fit into a single piece, requiring a sequence of starting and ending values to generate enough of the result to fill that piece. Table 1 illustrates these conditions.

Both range and range[1] are *generators* because they can produce multiple output pieces from a single set of inputs. Additionally, their results are nested one level deeper than their inputs. Other operations, such as mult_reduce are *accumulators* because they may consume multiple input pieces before producing an output. Results of accumulators are one level shallower than their inputs. Because of this structural correlation, generators that produce pieces for accumulators operate in step with each other. A third class of operations which have a one-to-one correspondence between consumption of input pieces and generation of output pieces, such as elementwise operations, are called *participants*. Table 2 provides a list and categorization of several representative data-parallel primitive operations.

Name	Action	Piecewise Behavior
arith-ops	basic arithmetic and logical operations	participant
substitute	replaces every sequence element with a supplied value	participant
distribute	replicate values to form a sequence	generator
range1	enumerate integers between 1 and a supplied value	generator
length	the number of elements in a sequence	accumulator
x_reduce	family of reduction operations ($+$, $*$, and, or, max, min)	accumulator
index	extract an element from a sequence	other
restrict	pack a sequence according to a mask	other

Table 2. Selected Nested Sequence Operations in Data Parallel Library

The operations restrict and index do not conform to any of the defined categories, so we describe their distinctive piecewise behavior individually. The restrict operation returns elements of an input sequence packed according to a boolean mask:

restrict([T,T,F,T,F],[1,2,3,4,5]) = [1,2,4]

Because the size of the result is determined by the value, and not the structure of the input (as with reduction), restrict may consume an arbitrary number of input pieces before generating a piece of result. This requires runtime size tests and eliminates the structure-based, lock-step execution of the factorial example.

Indexing operations also require special handling, because, unlike all other DPL operations, index consumes its input in a data-dependent order. Piecewise execution only works for operations that expect their inputs and generate their outputs in linear order. To satisfy arbitrary accesses, the entire source sequence must be available before indexing begins. As a result, index operations with piecewise-generated source sequences become *synchronization points*. All piecewise execution initiated prior to a synchronization point must complete before the index operation can begin. When its source sequence does not exceed the piece size, index does not require synchronization and can itself operate in a piecewise manner with respect to its indices.

Although this approach counteracts the effects of piecewise execution, Palmer, Prins and Westfold have developed another technique, *work-efficient indexing* [15], that prevents increasing the size of many source sequences during the flattening process. We expect that this will reduce the impact of index as a synchronization point on piecewise execution.

We implement piecewise versions of all primitive operations in C with explicit calls to DPL operations. These piecewise primitives comprise the Piecewise Data-Parallel Library (PDPL) which directly supports fixed-memory execution of flattened Proteus programs.

3.2 Retaining state between invocations of piecewise operations

Piecewise primitive operations behave like co-routines: many can be invoked simultaneously; only one executes at a time; they can suspend and resume execution; and they relinquish control to others after making some computational progress. To support this behavior, we introduce a new type to the Piecewise Data Parallel Library called an *engine*. Engines retain pertinent state information for piecewise operations so the operations can restart at the exact point where they previously suspended. Once restarted, the operation generates or consumes the next piece, updates the engine's state information to reflect the latest progress, and suspends (see Fig. 7).

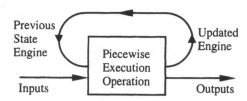

Fig. 7. Conceptual Model of an Engine

Each engine is associated with a single piecewise operation, and stores information specific to restarting that operation. Engines for generators retain the remaining portion of the operation's current piece of input which implicitly specifies the next output piece. Engines for accumulators retain the partially generated output piece and information on how to integrate the next input into the growing result. Participants directly produce an output piece from an input piece requiring no information from previous invocations and thus do not require engines.

Since engines contain all the inter-invocation information for piecewise operations, we allocate them in the heap. This allows us to achieve co-routine behavior without persistent activation records or altering the management of the stack.

3.3 Demand-driven piecewise interpretation

Pingali and Arvind [16, 17] use demand-driven interpretation to evaluate their stream-based language with infinite data structures. Unlike data-driven interpretation, this approach prevents non-termination and unbounded amounts of useless work. Although these issues do not impact Proteus, we use a modified form of demand-driven interpretation to support piecewise execution.

Ordinary demand-driven evaluation operates by demanding the output of the final node in the data-flow graph. Unable to comply without input, the final node propagates the demand to its parent nodes. Propagation continues in this manner until the demands reach to the top of the graph and can be satisfied by the inputs to the program, thus starting a cascade of node execution and generated data propagation.

Our approach differs from theirs in three significant ways. First, our data-flow graphs represent data-parallel programs, so aggregate values flow along the edges, not streams of scalar values. For efficient execution, our edges must always propagate piece-sized sequences so they can achieve a significant portion of a parallel machine's peak performance. Second, our data-flow graph contains generator nodes that can produce results without consuming any input, and it also contains accumulator nodes that can consume inputs without generating any output. To support this unusual behavior, we must handle demand propagation differently. Third, we localize the buffering of pending values to eliminate the need for unbounded storage along every edge.

The requirement to reduce memory usage of flattened nested data-parallel programs makes demand-driven interpretation attractive for piecewise execution. A generator cannot execute effectively in a data-driven style. An attempt to do so will either produce all its output pieces at once, possibly exceeding memory resources, or produce a single piece of output and relinquish control without a mechanism of regaining it. Demand-driven execution allows generators to produce single pieces in response to demands for single pieces, neither exceeding memory or abandoning results.

Our data-flow graphs have four basic types of nodes: generators, accumulators, participants and *copy nodes*. Copy nodes replicate values when a path in the dataflow graph splits. They are analogous to Pingali and Arvind's fork construct.

Node Type	Demand Action	Data Action
Generator	If possible, produce data else propagate demand upwards	Execute, and produce data
Accumulator	Propagate demand upwards	Execute, if possible produce data else propagate demand upwards
Participant	Propagate demand upwards	Execute and produce data
Copy	If data buffered for source of demand, send data, else mark source node as pending. If copy node is not waiting for a demand to be satisfied then propagate demand upwards	Send data to all pending nodes, buffer data for all other child nodes

Table 3. Demand Driven Actions for Piecewise Interpretation Nodes

Our demand-driven interpreter propagates data and demands according to the rules in Table 3. Each data produced and demand propagated is placed on an event queue. The event at the head is removed and executed, adding more events to the queue, when the queue is empty, the program is complete.

We generate a piecewise version of flattened programs from an abstract syntax tree representation of data-parallel operations. The structure of the piecewise program consists of three parts: a copy of the demand-driven interpreter, code to generate to the data-flow graph of the original program and modularized functions that encapsulate the operations of each node. This structure is analogous to the that of a table-driven parser, consisting of a general interpreter, a representation of the grammar, and action routines.

4   Piecewise Execution Loops

Interpreted piecewise execution successfully executes parallel programs in fixed memory. However, the generality of the approach incurs the overhead costs associated with interpretation. Additionally, the interpreted approach interferes with chaining sequence operations. One partial solution merges data-flow graph nodes that always execute consecutively, such as groups of participants. This provides some potential chaining of vector operations.

A more general solution compiles the data-flow graphs into *piecewise execution loops*. These loops extend between matching pairs of generators and accumulators as in Fig. 4. When generator/accumulator pairs are nested, the corresponding piecewise execution loops are also nested. An outer loop is necessary to restart the inner loop after it generates a single output piece.

```
repeat
        range1¹ consumes a piece of D
        repeat
                range1¹ generates a piece of T
                mult_reduce¹ consumes the piece of T producing some of R
        until a full piece of R has been produced or the piece of D is finished
until all of D has been consumed
```

In our early investigation into compiling piecewise execution loops, we identified several complex issues in statically producing code that emulates the behavior of demand driven execution. Identifying the generator/accumulator pairs that specify loop bounds is complicated by the possibility that multiple generators can match with a single accumulator and vice versa. Furthermore, pairs of generators/accumulators that exhibit the same piecewise structural behavior are *conformable* and should be placed in the same piecewise execution loop for best performance. Chatterjee's size inference [8] can be used to identify conforming operations. Restrict operations require the introduction of additional loops to provide the data-dependent number of input pieces necessary for restrict to generate an output piece. Finally, piecewise execution loops require a complex control-flow mechanisms to maintain small amounts of buffering, and perform the piecewise operations in the correct order. If we determine from our performance experiments that the overhead of interpreting piecewise execution programs is too costly, we will further investigate these compilation issues.

5 Experimental Results

The performance results shown in Fig. 8 illustrate piecewise execution's effective use of memory. The measured program computes multiple summations in parallel and requires 10 vectors of the maximum size to perform the computation. We impose a memory restriction of 1 Mword to highlight the differences between the direct and piecewise approaches. As a result, the direct calculation can only handle vector sizes up to 100,000 elements. For those vectors, the direct computation, as expected, yields better performance than piecewise execution. However, our results show that piecewise execution can perform the computation for dramatically larger problem sizes in the same amount of memory.

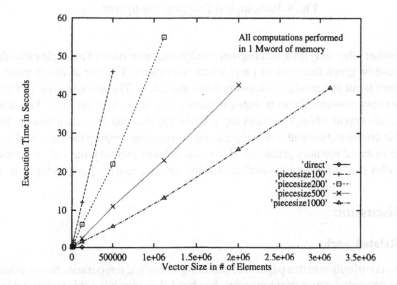

Fig. 8. Sequential Performance of Piecewise Execution

We also observe that the execution cost per element of the maximal vector size generally remains the same across the wide range of vector sizes. For small piece sizes the overhead associated with creating and maintaining an engine dominates the execution time. As the piece size increases, the effect of that cost diminishes and we start to see performance closer to that of the direct computation. We also ran this computation on the MasPar MP-1 and observed similar behavior, but the performance only got within a factor of 2 of the direct approach for piece sizes of 512K elements and larger.

6 Limitations of Piecewise Execution

Certain program configurations inherently preclude execution in a piecewise manner. Consider a program in which two generators consume the same piecewise generated input, but a data dependence between them prevents one from executing until the other completes. Because, in general, we cannot store the entire sequence, we must relax the execution constraints and allow the sequence to be recomputed. This increases the work, but allows the program to execute.

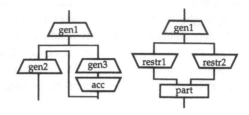

Fig. 9. Pathological Program Configurations

Another inherently difficult program configuration consists of multiple paths through the data-flow graph that contain `restrict` operations. The rate at which `restrict` consumes input and produces output is data-dependent. Therefore two `restrict` operations may consume the same input sequence at widely different rates. The slower of the *rate-divergent siblings* requires input buffering that can exhaust memory. We execute this configuration with normal piecewise execution, hoping the rates will be close enough to avoid memory problems. If they do exhaust memory, our only recourse is to again relax the "no recomputation" constraint, and execute the paths independently.

7 Discussion

7.1 Related work

Our key contribution in this paper is eliminating oversized temporaries from nested data-parallel programs, much previous work has been done applying this technique in other contexts. Reducing the memory requirements of a program by eliminating storage of temporary aggregate values is not a recent idea. In 1970, Abrams developed an interpreter system that partially compiled and sequentially executed APL programs [1]. The system postponed execution of certain operations until they could be optimized based on contextual information gathered during the postponement. These optimizations eliminated storing temporary aggregates, even those resulting from size increasing operations such as distributions and enumerations. Abrams accomplished this by processing a single element of the aggregate through an entire computation and yielding an element of the result before moving on to the next element. With this approach, he could evaluate expressions composed from a restricted set of APL operations using fixed storage equal to the larger of the expressions inputs and outputs.

In 1978, Guibas and Wyatt formalized and extended Abrams' ideas to build a system that fully compiled APL programs [10]. Using data-flow analysis techniques, they generated code that statically did the equivalent of Abrams contextual postponement. The compiled code evaluated APL's aggregate operations using fixed storage by streaming single elements of a flat aggregate through a complete computation.

Budd explored extending these ideas to the vector domain. Instead of single elements at a time, he proposed to stream a vector's worth of elements through a computation [7]. This approach not only evaluated APL expressions in space equal to the larger of the inputs and outputs, but could also make effective use of vector hardware.

Waters, generalizing the APL-based work to applicative series expressions for Common Lisp and Pascal, used data-flow analysis and program transformations to generate semantically equivalent imperative loop structures [21]. The transformations eliminated temporaries from series expressions and provided efficient single processor execution of functional programs using streaming. Although Waters speculated on extending his program transformations to handle nested series expressions, he did not implement it.

In 1993, Chatterjee compiled nested data-parallel programs to increase code granularity and relax lock-step synchrony so the programs could effectively execute on MIMD machines [8]. Although his compiler did not implement the fixed memory evaluation of Abrams, he was the first to apply temporary elimination in the context of nested data-parallel programs. His system used loop fusion to eliminate intermediate temporary storage from transformed NESL programs.

7.2 System status

We are currently building the piecewise execution system for Proteus on top of our existing execution system. We have implemented portions of PDPL and are currently working on implementing the rest. We have written the demand-driven piecewise interpreter with the modified demand driven execution and run it on small programs with large datasets. We have not yet automated the generation of piecewise programs or the compilation of piecewise execution loops. Our current research focuses on piecewise execution of user-defined functions, and our current implementation effort is aimed at reducing the memory management costs associated with creating and using engines.

7.3 Conclusions

The major drawback to the technique of flattening nested data parallelism is that it extracts so much parallelism that it often generates programs that cannot execute within the memory limitations of parallel machines. In this paper we presented piecewise execution, an approach which provides parametric runtime serialization of flattened parallel programs to overcome this obstacle. Our preliminary results confirm that piecewise execution can significantly reduce the memory requirements of a flattened, nested data-parallel program. Future results will reveal whether interpreted piecewise execution will provide sufficient performance or if we must further develop compilation techniques and generate piecewise execution loops. Regardless of our ultimate approach to implementing piecewise execution, we have demonstrated its applicability and usefulness.

References

1. P. Abrams. *An APL Machine*. PhD thesis, Stanford University, 1970.
2. J. Backus. Can programming be liberated from the von Neumann style? A functional style and its algebra of programs. *Commun. ACM*, 21(8):613–41, Aug. 1978.
3. G. Blelloch and G. Narlikar. A comparison of two n-body algorithms. In *Proceedings of DIMACS Parallel Implementation Challenge Workshop III*, Oct. 1994.
4. G. Blelloch and G. Sabot. Compiling collection-oriented languages onto massively parallel computers. *Journal of Parallel and Distributed Computing*, 8(2), Feb. 1990.
5. G. E. Blelloch. Nesl: A nested data-parallel language. Technical Report CMU-CS-92-129, Carnegie Mellon University, 1992.
6. G. E. Blelloch, S. Chatterjee, J. Hardwick, M. Reid-Miller, J. Sipelstein, and M. Zagha. Cvl: a c vector library manual, version 2. Technical Report CMU-CS-93-114, Carnegie Mellon University, 1993.
7. T. Budd. *An APL Compiler*. Springer-Verlag, 1988.
8. S. Chatterjee. Compiling nested data-parallel programs for shared-memory multiprocessors. *ACM Trans. Prog. Lang. Syst.*, 15(3):400–462, July 1993.
9. H. P. F. Forum. High Performance Fortran language specification. *Scientific Programming*, 2(1–2):1–170, 1993.
10. L. J. Guibas and D. K. Wyatt. Compilation and delayed evaluation in APL. In *Conf. Record of the Fifth Annual ACM Symp. on Princ. of Prog. Lang. (Tucson, Arizona)*, pages 1–8. ACM, Jan. 1978.
11. P. Hatcher and M. Quinn. *Data-Parallel Programming on MIMD Computers*. MIT Press, 1991.
12. K. Iverson. *A Programming Language*. Wiley, 1962.
13. G. Levin and L. Nyland. An introduction to Proteus, version 0.9. Technical report, University of North Carolina at Chapel Hill, Aug. 1993.
14. D. W. Palmer. Dpl: Data-parallel library manual. Technical Report UNC-CS-93-064, University of North Carolina at Chapel Hill, Nov. 1993.
15. D. W. Palmer, J. F. Prins, and S. Westfold. Work-efficient nested data-parallelism. In *Proc. Fifth Symp. on the Frontiers of Massively Parallel Processing (Frontiers 95)*. IEEE., 1995.
16. K. Pingali and Arvind. Efficient demand-driven evaluation. Part 1. *ACM Trans. Prog. Lang. Syst.*, 7(2):311–33, Apr. 1985.
17. K. Pingali and Arvind. Efficient demand-driven evaluation. Part 2. *ACM Trans. Prog. Lang. Syst.*, 8(1):109–39, Jan. 1986.
18. J. F. Prins and D. W. Palmer. Transforming high-level data-parallel programs into vector operations. In *Proc. 4th PPOPP. (San Diego, CA, 19–22 May 1993)*. ACM., 1993. Published in SIGPLAN Notices, 28(7):119–28.
19. J. Schwartz. Set theory as a language for program specification and programming. Technical report, Computer Science Department, Courant Institute of Mathematical Sciences, New York University, 1970.
20. R. Sethi. Complete register allocation problems. *SIAM Journal of Computing*, 4(3), 1975.
21. R. C. Waters. Automatic transformation of series expressions into loops. *ACM Trans. Prog. Lang. Syst.*, 13(1):52–98, Jan. 1991.

Recovering Logical Structures of Data [*]

Michał Cierniak and Wei Li
{cierniak,wei}@cs.rochester.edu

Department of Computer Science, University of Rochester, Rochester, NY 14627

Abstract. Many powerful parallelizing compiler techniques rely on the structures of data and code. Unfortunately, in many real applications, arrays do not have syntactic structures. In this paper, we show that logical data structures can be automatically recovered from the flat, one-dimensional arrays and accesses. We present a framework and algorithms for recovering the logical multi-dimensional data structures.

1 Introduction

Understanding the pattern of array accesses has been identified as a key element of many optimization techniques: it is necessary for achieving good locality of memory references, for deciding data distribution, and for determining data dependences.

Many powerful parallelizing compiler techniques are based on the structures of data (e.g. multiple array dimensions) and code (e.g. multiply nested loops). Intuitively, having more information about the logical structure of the data used in a computer program provides the compiler with more possibilities for optimization.

For *distributed shared-memory machines*, we often need to optimize the programs for locality by changing the array layout in memory [8, 2, 10]. Experiments have shown that unified data and loop transformations may significantly improve performance of some applications. However, data transformations are impossible without the multi-dimensional array structures, and control transformations are impossible without the multiply nested loop structures.

For *distributed memory message-passing machines*, a parallelizing compiler must decide the placement of data into the local memories of participating processing units. For every array, the compiler must compute a function mapping from data space to a processor space [11, 9, 6, 1, 3]. Such algorithms also depend on the multiple dimensionality of arrays and multiply nested loops.

Unfortunately, in many real applications [4, 5], arrays do not have interesting structures; i.e., they are plain linear arrays rather than multi-dimensional arrays, and they contain a single loop rather than multiple nested loops. For example, consider the code in Fig. 1 from the program TRFD in the PERFECT benchmark suite. This array structure leaves little room for powerful compiler optimizations based on data and code structures mentioned above. Logically, however, the array XIJRS has a nice 4-dimensional structure which can be exploited in a compiler.

---

[*] This work was supported in part by an NSF Research Initiation Award (CCR-9409120) and ARPA contract F19628-94-C-0057.

```
m=0
DO 300 i=1,n
  DO 300 j=1,i
    ...
    DO 240 r=1,n
      DO 230 s=1,r
      m=m+1
      VAL=XIJRS(m)
      ...
230      CONTINUE
240      CONTINUE
    ...
300 CONTINUE
```

Fig. 1. A loop nest from TRFD/OLDA

Array linearization, which generates linear array structure and accesses, is frequently used in scientific programs [13, 14]. Maslov [14] reports that 6 out of 8 programs in the RiCEPS [5] benchmark suite contain linearized references. In addition to the applications from RiCEPS, we have studied programs from the PERFECT Benchmarks [4] suite. The study shows that linearized array references are common in PERFECT applications.

In this paper, we show that interesting logical data structures can be automatically recovered from the flat one-dimensional arrays and accesses. We present a framework and algorithms for recovering the logical multidimensional data structures.

There has been very little work on recovering logical structures of arrays. The closest is the work by Maslov [14], where he developed a data dependence algorithm capable of detecting data dependencies in the complicated access patterns to the linear arrays. The dependence analysis for linearized references has been further refined in Maslov and Pugh [15].

In the rest of this paper, we first present the conceptual framework for our algorithm. Later, in Sects. 3 and 4 we present algorithms for recovering array structures for rectangular and non-rectangular arrays, respectively. Section 5 shows how to resolve possible conflicts for multiple references to the same array. Final conclusions are presented in Sect. 6.

2 Framework

2.1 Notation

To discover the number of dimensions and recovered subscript expressions, we use some concepts introduced in [8]. We will briefly describe them here. A simple example in Fig. 2 will be used as an illustration.

We define the following terms:

```
REAL A(0:199, 0:99)
DO i = 1, 99
  DO j = 1, 100
    DO k = 0, 99
      A(199 - 2 * k, i - 1) = ...
    END DO
  END DO
END DO
```

Fig. 2. Example 1

- **Number of data dimensions** d is the number of dimensions of an array.
- A **subscript vector** S contains subscript expressions for a given array reference.
- A **stride vector** v contains strides for every loop in the loop nest. A stride for a given loop says what is the difference in addresses generated by an array reference in consecutive iterations. The stride vector for the reference in Fig. 2 is $v = \begin{pmatrix} 200 \\ 0 \\ -2 \end{pmatrix}$.
- A **mapping vector** m defines the layout of an array in memory. In this paper we assume that all recovered array structures follow Fortran conventions, i.e., all arrays mappings are column major. An interpretation of an element of the mapping vector for dimension $i = 2, \ldots, d$ is that it represents the total size of an $(i-1)$-dimensional subarray consisting of dimensions $1, \ldots, i - 1$ of the whole array. For convenience, we will use the term *subarray size* for an element of a mapping vector. The size of a single array element is equal to m_1.
- An **offset** ζ is a number which for a given array reference describes the distance of the referenced array element from the start of the array. It can be computed as: $\zeta = S^T m$. If the subscripts do not start from zero, we may have to use *extended mapping vectors* to compute correct offsets.
- A **subscript range vector** w describes the ranges of subscripts expressions in an array. For the array declared in Fig. 2, the subscript range vector is: $w = \begin{pmatrix} 200 \\ 100 \end{pmatrix}$. Note that an array declared as C(1:200, -1:98) would have the same subscript range vector.
- An **access matrix** [12] A describes the subscripts of an array reference in terms of loop variables.
- An **offset vector** δ contains constant parts of each subscript expression.

Let u be a vector of loop variables. For our example $u = \begin{pmatrix} i \\ j \\ k \end{pmatrix}$. With this notation, the subscript vector can be computed as: $S = Au + \delta$. For our example:

$$S = Au + \delta = \begin{pmatrix} 0 & 0 & -2 \\ 1 & 0 & 0 \end{pmatrix} \begin{pmatrix} i \\ j \\ k \end{pmatrix} + \begin{pmatrix} 199 \\ -1 \end{pmatrix} = \begin{pmatrix} 199 - 2k \\ i - 1 \end{pmatrix} \ .$$

Here A is the access matrix. The mapping vector for this array is $m = \begin{pmatrix} 1 \\ 200 \end{pmatrix}$ and it can be interpreted to mean that a single element is of size 1 and a single column has the size 200.

For notational convenience, we define $\overline{S} = Au$, so that $S = \overline{S} + \delta$.

For a given reference, the mapping vector and the subscript range vector are closely related. The following is true:

$$(\forall i = 2, \ldots, d) m_i = \prod_{j=1}^{i-1} w_j \ . \tag{1}$$

Whenever necessary (mainly for code generation phase), we will include one additional element in a mapping vector representing the correction necessary to make the offset for the first element of the array equal to zero. In that case, we will also add an additional element to the subscript vector, $S_{d+1} = 1$. For the example from Figure 2, the extended vectors would be: $S = \begin{pmatrix} 199 - 2k \\ i - 1 \\ 1 \end{pmatrix}, m = \begin{pmatrix} 1 \\ 200 \\ 0 \end{pmatrix}$, so that the offset is $\zeta = S^T m = 200i - 2k - 1$. Unless explicitly stated otherwise, we use simple mapping vectors, not the extended vectors.

Many of our algorithms are based on the following simple equality [8]: $A^T m = v$.

Arrays with constant mapping vectors are called *rectangular*. This is the only kind of an array supported by type systems of programming languages like C or Fortran. We extend the notion of an array to multidimensional structures which can be represented with variable mapping vectors. We call those arrays *non-rectangular*.

For a more detailed discussion of the above terms and conditions for subscript expressions which can be expressed with this notation see [8].

2.2 A Legal Fortran Mapping

For rectangular arrays, we assume that recovered mappings must correspond to legal arrays in an existing programming language. Without loss of generality, we assume that we want to recover Fortran (i.e., column major) arrays whose subscripts start from 0. Note that we do not have enough information in the linearized reference to recover lower bounds of subscript ranges. We can only discover how many elements there are in each array dimension.

A mapping vector $m = \begin{pmatrix} m_1 \\ \vdots \\ m_d \end{pmatrix}$ represents a legal Fortran mapping if the following conditions are satisfied:

1. $m_1 = 1$
2. $(\forall i = 2, \ldots, d)\, m_i \geq m_{i-1}$, and
3. $(\forall i = 2, \ldots, d)\, m_i \bmod m_{i-1} = 0$.

3 Rectangular Arrays

3.1 An Overview

In this part of the paper we concentrate on recovering structures of affine array references. We assume that we start with a one-dimensional, affine array reference enclosed by a loop nest and we want to turn this reference into a multidimensional reference. With those assumptions, we describe a multidimensional array reference with a mapping vector, an access matrix, and an offset vector (see Sect. 2.1).

We can recover this structure in two steps:
1. First we compute the stride vector and use it to find a mapping vector and an access matrix.
2. Then we complete the subscript expressions by finding an offset vector.
We present solutions to those two steps in the following sections.

If there is more than one reference to an array in the analyzed portion of the code, we may recover different multidimensional structures for the same array. We show later how to merge those different array definitions into one consistent array type.

```
REAL A(0:19999)
DO i = 1, 99
  DO j = 1, 100
    DO k = 0, 99
      A(200i - 2k - 1) = ...
    END DO
  END DO
END DO
```

Fig. 3. A linearized reference

Throughout this section we will use the loop nest from Fig. 3 to illustrate the algorithm for recovering a multidimensional structure of an array. After each step of the algorithm, we will show how that step is applied in practice.

3.2 Computing a Mapping Vector and an Access Matrix

Finding a Stride Vector Given a one-dimensional subscript expression b and a loop nest structure, we can easily find a stride vector for an array reference by calculating the difference between values of b for subsequent iterations.

The stride vector need not be constant. Nevertheless, in practice, strides tend to be either constant or simple functions of loop variables. In some cases they may be more complex, e.g., as a result of indirection. In this section, we assume that strides are loop-invariant (more general stride vectors are discussed later in this paper). If the stride vector is constant, the recovered array is rectangular and it can be represented as a built-in array type in programming languages like C or Fortran.

Example: Consider the loop nest shown in Figure 3. The subscript expression is $b = 200i - 2k - 1$. Since $\left(b\big|_{i=x+1} - b\big|_{i=x} \right) = 200$, the stride for loop i is 200. Computing similarly strides for the other two loops, we get the stride vector: $v = \begin{pmatrix} 200 \\ 0 \\ -2 \end{pmatrix}$.

Finding a Mapping Vector In general, the solutions space for the mapping vector and the access matrix may be infinite and finding a *meaningful solution* may be difficult. We present here an algorithm which will find a solution for all linearized references to rectangular arrays which we found in existing applications.

In this approach, we first find a mapping vector and then compute an access matrix which is consistent with this mapping vector and the stride vector calculated earlier.

We observe that in many cases each subscript expression of the recovered logical array reference contains at most one loop variable and for a given reference each loop variable appears in at most one subscript expression. We call this condition the *simple subscripts condition*.

This observation leads us to a conclusion that a mapping vector found as a sorted permutation of non-zero elements of the stride vector will be a legal Fortran mapping [2].

When analyzing a linearized array reference, we do not know whether the recovered logical multidimensional reference satisfied the simple subscripts condition. Therefore, we initially assume that the condition is indeed true and try to apply the algorithm. At various points of the algorithm the validity of the solution is verified. If a solution is determined to be invalid, the algorithm fails.

The algorithm presented here assumes that in a given loop nest all non-zero strides are different. We start with computing the stride vector v. We verify that v is constant. Now, we create a vector v' by removing from v all elements equal to 0 and ordering all non-zero elements by their absolute values. Number of elements of v' is the number of dimensions, d, in the recovered array structure. The mapping vector m is created as an elementwise absolute value of v'. If the absolute value of the smallest element of v' is greater than 1, we make this element equal to one.

After computing the mapping vector, we verify that it defines a legal Fortran mapping, as explained in Sect. 2.2. If it does, we can proceed to finding an access matrix.

---

[2] As discussed later, we have to take care of a few details, but this is the basic idea of our approach.

Example: Compressing and sorting the stride vector $v = \begin{pmatrix} 200 \\ 0 \\ -2 \end{pmatrix}$ produces: $v' = \begin{pmatrix} -2 \\ 200 \end{pmatrix}$. And the mapping vector is: $m = \begin{pmatrix} 1 \\ 200 \end{pmatrix}$.

Finding an Access Matrix First, we compute the subscript range vector, w, using (1). We need w to represent the array, but it is also used to resolve potential ambiguities while building the access matrix. Note that from (1) we can compute all but the last element of the subscript range vector, i.e., w_d. The last element is not required for uniprocessor code generation (unless we want to check subscript ranges at run-time), but it may be necessary to decide data distribution. We compute it later from the subscript expression in the last dimension and the ranges of loop variables involved in that expression.

Given v and m, we want to find A which satisfies: $A^T m = v$.

Recall that we assume that the multidimensional array reference satisfies the simple subscripts condition (defined in Sect. 3.2). In that case we can construct the access matrix column by column.

Consider column i. We have:

$$v_i = \sum_{j=1}^{d} A_{j,i} m_j .$$

There are two cases:

1. $|v_i| = m_j$ for some j. In this case we make $A_{j,i} = \frac{v_i}{m_j}$ and $A_{k,i} = 0$ for all $k \neq j$. Note that the value of $\frac{v_i}{m_j}$ is either 1 or -1 depending on the sign of v_i.
2. Otherwise we choose the maximum m_j such that $m_j < |v_i|$ (given the algorithm described in Section 3.2 for finding the mapping vector, we know that $j = 1$). We make $A_{j,i} = \frac{v_i}{m_j}$ and $A_{k,i} = 0$ for all $k \neq j$.

After finding the access matrix, the only information needed to generate the multi-dimensional reference is the offset vector. We show how to find it in Sect. 3.3.

Example: For $v = \begin{pmatrix} 200 \\ 0 \\ -2 \end{pmatrix}$ and $m = \begin{pmatrix} 1 \\ 200 \end{pmatrix}$, we can find the subscript range vector: $w = \begin{pmatrix} 200 \\ ? \end{pmatrix}$ The algorithm described in this section builds the following access matrix: $A = \begin{pmatrix} 0 & 0 & -2 \\ 1 & 0 & 0 \end{pmatrix}$. The subscripts of the reference are: $S = \begin{pmatrix} -2k + \delta_1 \\ i + \delta_2 \end{pmatrix}$. We will show how to compute δ_1 and δ_2 in the next section.

3.3 Computing an Offset Vector

In Sect. 3.2 we have recovered the structure of an array, i.e., the mapping vector m and the parts of subscripts expressions which depend on loop variables, i.e., the access matrix A. Now, we have to compute constant parts of the subscripts expressions.

More formally, we want to find the vector δ as defined in Sect. 2.1. The vector δ is subject to two constraints:

1. All elements of the subscript vector $S = Au + \delta$ must be within the array bounds defined by the subscript range vector w. Recall that subscripts in the recovered array structure start from 0 (compare Sect. 2.2).
2. The value of the offset $\zeta = S^T m$ for u being a zero vector must be equal to the constant part t_1 of the one-dimensional subscript expression b.

The second constraint will be satisfied if $(A0 + \delta)^T m = t_1$ or simply $\delta^T m = \sum_{k=1}^{d} \delta_k m_k = t_1$. As $m_1 = 1$ and $w_1 = \frac{m_2}{m_1} = m_2$, we can rewrite the equation as:

$$\delta_1 + \overline{\delta}_1 w_1 = t_1 \quad \text{where} \quad \overline{\delta}_1 = \delta_2 + \frac{\sum_{j=3}^{d} \delta_j m_j}{m_2} \tag{2}$$

There are infinitely many solutions to (2). We first find an arbitrary solution δ_1', $\overline{\delta}_1'$: $\delta_1' = t_1$ and $\overline{\delta}_1' = 0$.

Then we find the value of δ_1 that satisfies the condition for the range of the subscripts in the first dimension: $0 \leq \overline{S}_1 + \delta_1 < w_1$ by subtracting a multiple of w_1 from δ_1': $\delta_1 = \delta_1' - t_2 w_1$.

The solution to (2) can be completed by setting $\overline{\delta}_1 = t_2$. It is easy to verify that the pair δ_1, $\overline{\delta}_1$ satisfies (2).

By substituting the value of $\overline{\delta}_1$ in the formula for $\overline{\delta}_1$ in (2) with t_2, we obtain an equation that can be used to compute δ_2:

$$\delta_2 + \overline{\delta}_2 w_2 = t_2 \quad \text{where} \quad \overline{\delta}_2 = \delta_3 + \frac{\sum_{j=4}^{d} \delta_j m_j}{m_3} \tag{3}$$

Notice that (3) is similar to (2). We can generalize this algorithm for any dimension. For dimension i we start with the equation:

$$\delta_i + \overline{\delta}_i w_i = t_i \tag{4}$$

where $\overline{\delta}_i = \delta_{i+1} + \frac{\sum_{j=i+2}^{d} \delta_j m_j}{m_{i+1}}$. We find $\delta_i = t_i - t_{i+1} w_i$ which satisfies: $0 \leq \overline{S}_i + \delta_i < w_i$. The value of t_{i+1} will be used to compute δ_{i+1}.

Note that for the last dimension (4) is degenerated to: $\delta_d = t_d$ and we get δ_d directly without adding the correction. However, we still have to verify that the condition: $0 \leq \overline{S}_d + \delta_d < w_d$ is satisfied.

Example: We continue recovering structure of the reference from Figure 3. We have $t_1 = -1$.

Now we compute the offsets:

- Dimension 1: $\delta_1 + 200\overline{\delta}_1 = -1$. We compute $\delta_1 = -1 - 200t_2$ such that $0 \leq \overline{S}_1 + \delta_1 < w_1$ where $\overline{S}_1 = -2k$. By computing the values of $\overline{S}_1$ for the lower and upper bound of the loop k, we can determine that we should use $t_2 = -1$. Hence $\delta_1 = 199$.

– Dimension 2: $\delta_2 = t_2 = -1$.

The subscripts vector of the recovered two-dimensional reference is $S = \begin{pmatrix} 199 - 2k \\ i - 1 \end{pmatrix}$.
We can see that the loop nest from Fig. 3 is equivalent to the loop nest from Fig. 2.

We are now able to compute the last element of the subscript range vector, w. We have already recovered all but the last elements of w. The subscript expression in the last dimension is $S_2 = i - 1$ and its range is $0..98$. Therefore the full vector is: $w = \begin{pmatrix} 200 \\ 99 \end{pmatrix}$
The recovered array: $A(0:199, 0:98)$ has one column less than the array declared in Fig. 2. This is correct as the last column of A is never referenced in this loop nest.

4 Non-rectangular Arrays

In this section we will show how to recover a multidimensional structure of a non-rectangular array. We first describe the problem and propose a solution for a general class of arrays whose subscript ranges can be described as functions of the values of other subscripts. Later, in Sect. 4.3, we discuss a special case of non-rectangular arrays: *triangular arrays* which are common in practice.

4.1 General arrays

In Sect. 3, we assumed that the stride vector is constant. In this case, if we are able to recover the structure of an array, the array will be rectangular.

```
DO i = 1, n
    DO j = 1, i*i
        A(j + (i*(i*(2*i -3) + 1)) / 6) = ...
    END DO
END DO
```

Fig. 4. Non-rectangular loop

Consider the reference in Fig. 4. The stride for loop i is not constant. To see this, let us consider the subscript expression for two consecutive iterations of loop i: $b_i = j + \frac{2i^3 - 3i^2 + i}{6}$ and $b_{i+1} = j + \frac{2(i+1)^3 - 3(i+1)^2 + (i+1)}{6}$. The difference between those expressions is the stride for loop i: $v_1 = b_{i+1} - b_i = i^2$. The stride vector is: $v = \begin{pmatrix} i^2 \\ 1 \end{pmatrix}$.
The techniques developed in Sect. 3 are not directly applicable here.

In this example, although a closer inspection reveals that the logical structure of array A seems to have two dimensions, there is no way to convert the reference in Fig. 4 into a two-dimensional array reference in a classical programming language like

Fortran. To make the logical number of dimensions explicit, we need to introduce a new notation. We allow a subscript range to be a function of the values of other subscripts.

So, a two-dimensional array would have a subscript range vector:

$$w = \begin{pmatrix} F_1 \\ F_2 \end{pmatrix} \; ,$$

where F_1 and F_2 are functions mapping a subscript vector to a positive integer, i.e., $F_1, F_2 \colon \mathbf{Z}^d \to \mathbf{Z}$

For the example given in Fig. 4, we would like to be able to recover a two-dimensional array with the following subscript ranges: $F_1 \equiv \lambda x.\lambda y.y^2$ and $F_2 \equiv \lambda x.\lambda y.n$ (or, equivalently, $F_1(x, y) = y^2$ and $F_2(x, y) = n$). In other words, the number of elements in the first dimension is equal to the square of the value of the subscript in the second dimension, and the number of elements in the second dimension is N.

In principle, functions which determine subscript ranges may be very complex, but in practice we have only encountered the following two functions:

1. A *constant* — this is the simplest case. If subscript ranges for all dimensions are constant, we have a rectangular array (see Section 3) which is allowed by existing programming languages.
2. A *linear function* of a subscript expression in another dimension (the subscript range of that dimension is constant). Usually (recall that we assume column major mapping), a linear subscript range depends on the subscript in the *next* dimension, i.e., $F_i(S_1, \ldots, S_d) = S_{i+1}$. Arrays with such subscript ranges are called *triangular*.

For non-rectangular arrays, the compiler must generate code for an array reference in a more general way than for rectangular array. Code generated for a given reference must compute a linear offset from the base address of an array. For rectangular arrays computing the offset is straightforward [8]: $\zeta = S^T m$ (for simplicity of the discussion we ignore constant terms in the subscript expressions). For non-rectangular arrays, we have to replace the simple multiplication with an operator which computes the sum of subarray sizes. For constant elements, this sum is of course equivalent to the multiplication used for rectangular arrays.

We use the symbol $\otimes$ to represent this new operator. The offset can be now computed as $\zeta = S^T \otimes m$. Because for constant mapping vectors, $\otimes$ is reduced to multiplication, we can use this new notation consistently whenever we want to compute the offset.

We will use the same symbol $\otimes$ for scalar and vector operations. Operation on vectors consists of pairwise applications of "scalar" $\otimes$ to elements of the two vectors and adding the results (being in effect an "inner product"). '

The semantics of $\otimes$ can be explained as follows. Consider a subscript vector S and a mapping vector m:

$$S = \begin{pmatrix} S_1 \\ \vdots \\ S_d \end{pmatrix}, \quad m = \begin{pmatrix} m_1 \\ \vdots \\ m_d \end{pmatrix} .$$

Let ζ_i denote a contribution to the offset in ith dimension ($\zeta = \sum_{i=1}^d \zeta_i$). For dimension 1, we trivially have $\zeta_1 = S_1$ (assuming that an array element has size 1). Consider contribution in dimension $i > 1$. We compute it as the sum of the values of m_i for all values of the subscript in the ith dimension:

$$\zeta_i = \sum_{k=1}^{S_i-1} m_i(S_1, \ldots, S_{i-1}, k, S_{i+1}, \ldots, S_d) \ .$$

Of course, we do not want to generate code which will compute the sum at run-time in a loop. The compiler must be able to symbolically compute the sum at compile-time. For more complicated functions this may be impossible. For all functions which we have encountered in real applications, computing the sum of a series is straightforward.

If m_i is a constant, this sum is equivalent to multiplication of S_i by m_i. Therefore, we can use the $\otimes$ operator for rectangular arrays (Sect. 3).

4.2 Recovering Algorithm

Recovering the structure of a non-rectangular array is considerably more difficult than for a rectangular array. For references whose subscript expressions in the recovered, multi-dimensional reference are either constants or loop variables (which is equivalent to satisfying the simple subscript condition with $\delta = 0$), we apply an approach similar to the one described in Sect. 3. Below is a sketch of such an algorithm.

First, we compute the stride vector (if the linearized subscript expression b is too complex, the algorithm fails). Then, we sort the stride vector by absolute values. The elements of the stride vector are symbolic expressions of loop variables, therefore finding the ordering of the strides is not trivial. For simple functions, we can do it by considering loop bounds. We can get a mapping vector from the sorted stride vector the same way as for rectangular arrays. Directly from the mapping vector, we can get a subscript range vector expressed in terms of loop variables. To describe the structure of the array in a way independent from this loop nest, we must find a subscript range vector expressed in terms of other subscripts. This is straightforward, because all recovered subscript expressions are either constant or loop variables. Note that every loop variable present in the the stride vector must be used in some subscript of the recovered array reference.

After we have obtained the subscripts vector, we check if the ranges of the subscripts are within appropriate ranges from the subscript range vector.

Example: Let us show how the structure of array A from Figure 4 may be recovered.

First, we compute $v' = \begin{pmatrix} 1 \\ i^2 \end{pmatrix}$, $m' = \begin{pmatrix} 1 \\ i^2 \end{pmatrix}$, and $w' = \begin{pmatrix} i^2 \\ ? \end{pmatrix}$. Now we can find an access matrix, A, which satisfies: $A^T m = v$: $A = \begin{pmatrix} 0 & 1 \\ 1 & 0 \end{pmatrix}$. Since we assume $\delta = 0$, we can compute

$$S = Au = \begin{pmatrix} j \\ i \end{pmatrix} \ .$$

Now we want to express the mapping vector and the subscript range vector in terms of subscript expressions rather than loop variables, $m = \begin{pmatrix} M_1 \\ M_2 \end{pmatrix}$ and $w = \begin{pmatrix} W_1 \\ W_2 \end{pmatrix}$, where $M_1, M_2, W_1,$ and $W_2: \mathbf{Z}^2 \to \mathbf{Z}$. It is clear that $M_1(x, y) = 1$. Because $m'_2 = i^2$ and

$S_2 = i$, we know that $M_2(x, y) = y^2$. Similarly, we have $W_1(x, y) = y^2$. To compute W_2, we have to look at the bounds for the loop variable in S_2. By examining the bounds of the i loop, we can see that $W_2(x, y) = n$.

In the code generation phase, we can compute the offset as:

$$\zeta = S^T \otimes m = (j \ \ i) \otimes \begin{pmatrix} \lambda x.\lambda y.1 \\ \lambda x.\lambda y.y^2 \end{pmatrix} = j + \sum_{k=1}^{i-1} k^2 \ ,$$

$$\zeta = j + \frac{2i^3 - 3i^2 + i}{6} \ .$$

4.3 Triangular Arrays

References like the one in Fig. 4 are of course possible. However, the most complicated non-rectangular array structure we have encountered in practice is triangular.

Recall that an array is a triangular array if all ranges are of the following two types: (1) constant, or (2) linear and depend on the subscript in the next dimension. Using the functional notation introduced in Sect. 4.1, we can write this condition as $F_i(S_1, \ldots, S_d) = S_{i+1}$ and F_{i+1} is constant.

The notation used in Sect. 4.1 is general in that it can be used to represent non-rectangular arrays with subscript ranges defined by arbitrary functions. It is also cumbersome to use and too general for triangular arrays. In [7] we have developed a specialized notation and algorithm for triangular arrays which makes the recovery of such arrays simpler and faster.

We can have more than one triangular dimensions in one array. As an example consider the reference to array XIJRS in the loop 300 of the subroutine OLDA in the TRFD benchmark. The loop nest is shown in Figure 1. By applying our algorithm, we can recover the 4-dimensional structure of the array XIJRS. This array has two triangular dimensions [7].

5 Multiple References

The algorithms presented in previous sections consider each array reference separately. The drawback of this approach is that it may happen that if there are multiple references to the same array, several different structures may be recovered for the same array. It is desirable to have exactly one type for a given object.

In our framework, we try to unify all structures for a given array, so that the same mapping vector may be used for any reference to the same array. In many cases it is possible. If the types cannot be unified, we are left with two options: we can either use linear structure for all references, or we have to deal with having inconsistent types for the same array.

We have encountered two different code patterns which result in recovering different types. The first — more common — occurs when the loop structure is linearized. The second case results if the dimensionality of an array is unknown at compile time. In the rest of this section, we give examples for both cases and propose how to unify conflicting types.

5.1 Compatible Arrays

The unification in this case may be followed by the recovery of loop structure. Intuitively, the idea is that two or more dimensions recovered from one array reference are treated as only one dimension in a second reference.

```
do i = 1, x
  do j = 1, y
    do k = 1, z
      A(k, j, i) = ...
do i = 1, x
  do j = 1, y * z
    A(j, i) = ...
```

Fig. 5. Linearized Loop Structure

Consider the example shown in Fig. 5. We assume that the 2-D and 3-D references to array A were both recovered from linearized references and the following mapping vectors were computed: $m_1 = \begin{pmatrix} 1 \\ z \\ zy \end{pmatrix}$, $m_2 = \begin{pmatrix} 1 \\ zy \end{pmatrix}$.

We see that the references are "compatible" in that the first reference could be changed to use m_2 and the second reference could be changed to use m_1. In the first case, the array A would become two-dimensional for both references. In the second case, the unification would make A three-dimensional. We can choose either of the solution. Generally, it is desirable to have as many dimensions as possible. However, in some cases, we may find it preferable to choose the lower dimensionality.

For this example if we decide that we need a 2-D structure, we keep m_2 as the mapping vector for A and replace the reference in the first loop nest with:

```
A(k + j * z, i) = ...
```

In general with vectors like m_1 and m_2 we will replace the subscript vector $S = \begin{pmatrix} S_1 \\ S_2 \\ S_3 \end{pmatrix}$ with $S = \begin{pmatrix} S_1 + S_2 m_2 \\ S_3 \end{pmatrix}$ and at the same time replace m_1 with m_2.

The alternative unification would have to take care of translating the subscript expression j in the second array reference into a pair of subscript expressions. This is possible without changing the loop structure, but it is better to recover the loop structure at the same time, i.e., to unroll loop j in the second nest into two loops.

```
      L = 0
      IF (NY.GT.1) THEN
         DO 30 K=1,NZTOP
            DO 20 J=1,NY
               DO 10 I=1,NX
                  L=L+1
                  DCDX(L)=-(UX(L)+UM(K))*DCDX(L)-(VY(L)+VM(K))*DCDY(L)
     1            +Q(L)
 10            CONTINUE
 20         CONTINUE
 30      CONTINUE
      ELSE
         DO 50 K=1,NZTOP
            DO 40 I=1,NX
               L=L+1
               DCDX(L)=-(UX(L)+UM(K))*DCDX(L)+Q(L)
 40         CONTINUE
 50      CONTINUE
      ENDIF
```

Fig. 6. An example from ADM/ADVC

5.2 Unification

In the example in Fig. 6, the array UX (and other arrays in this code fragment) is treated as *either* three-dimensional *or* two-dimensional depending on the value of NY.

From loop nest 30, we can recover the following 3-D structure: UX(NX, NY, NZTOP). The structure recovered from loop nest 50 has two dimensions only: UX(NX, NZTOP). It is desirable to have a single type for all references to one array. Because we do not know if NY has positive value, the common type for UX is: UX(NX, NY$^+$, NZTOP).

Where p^+ is defined to be p if $p > 0$ and 1 otherwise. With this array type we can access UX in both loop nests as if it was a 3-D array. The recovered references are: UX(I,J,K) for loop nest 30, and UX(I,1,K) in loop nest 50.

6 Conclusions

In this paper, we have shown that logical structures of data objects can be automatically recovered from the flat, one-dimensional arrays and accesses. We have presented a framework and algorithms for recovering the logical multi-dimensional array structures.

The recovery of multidimensional arrays and accesses can facilitate the powerful data locality optimizations and automatic data distribution.

In some programs, the loop nests are linearized as well. In many cases the logical structure of the loop nest can be recovered enabling further optimizing transformations. We present code and data recovery in [7].

References

[1] J. M. Anderson and M. S. Lam. Global Optimizations for Parallelism and Locality on Scalable Parallel Machines. In *Proceedings of the SIGPLAN '93 Conference on Programming Language Design and Implementation*, pages 112–125, Albuquerque, NM, June 1993.

[2] J. M. Anderson, S. P. Amarasinghe, and M. S. Lam. Data and Computation Transformations for Multiprocessors. In *Proceedings of the Fifth ACM Symposium on Principles and Practice of Parallel Programming*, Santa Barbara, CA, July 1995.

[3] D. Bau, I. Kodukula, V. Kotlyar, K. Pingali, and P. Stodghill. Solving Alignment using Elementary Linear Algebra. In *Proceedings of the Seventh Annual Workshop on Languages and Compilers for Parallel Computing*, Ithaca, NY, August 1994.

[4] M. Berry and others. The PERFECT Club Benchmarks: Effective Performance Evaluation of Supercomputers. *Int. Journal of Supercomputer Applications*, 3(3):9–40, Fall 1989.

[5] D. Callahan and A. Porterfield. Data Cache Performance of Supercomputer Applications. In *Supercomputer '90*, 1990.

[6] S. Chatterjee, J. R. Gilbert, R. Schreiber, and S.-H. Teng. Automatic Array Alignment in Data-Parallel Programs. In *Conference Record of the Twentieth ACM Symposium on Principles of Programming Languages*, Charleston, SC, January 1993.

[7] M. Cierniak and W. Li. Recovering Logical Data and Code Structures. TR 591, Computer Science Department, University of Rochester, July 1995.

[8] M. Cierniak and W. Li. Unifying Data and Control Transformations for Distributed Shared-Memory Machines. In *Proceedings of the SIGPLAN '95 Conference on Programming Language Design and Implementation*, La Jolla, CA, June 1995. Also available as TR 542, Computer Science Department, University of Rochester, November 1994.

[9] M. Gupta and P. Banerjee. Demonstration of Automatic Data Partitioning Techniques for Parallelizing Compilers on Multicomputers. *IEEE Transactions on Parallel and Distributed Systems*, 3(2):179–193, March 1992.

[10] Y.-J. Ju and H. Dietz. Reduction of Cache Coherence Overhead by Compiler Data Layout and Loop Transformations. In U. Banerjee, D. Gelernter, A. Nicolau, and D. Padua, editors, *Languages and Compilers for Parallel Computing*, Lecture Notes in Computer Science, pages 344–358. Springer-Verlag, August 1991. Fourth Int. Workshop, Portland, OR.

[11] J. Li and M. Chen. Index Domain Alignment: Minimizing Cost of Cross-Referencing Between Distributed Arrays. In *Proceedings of the Third Symposium on Frontiers of Massively Parallel Computation*, College Park, Maryland, October 1990.

[12] W. Li and K. Pingali. Access Normalization: Loop Restructuring for NUMA Compilers. *ACM Transactions on Computer Systems*, 11(4):353–375, November 1993.

[13] L. M. Liebrock and K. Kennedy. Parallelization of Linearized Applications in Fortran D. In *Proceedings of the Eighth International Parallel Processing Symposium*, Cancun, Mexico, April 1994.

[14] V. Maslov. Delinearization: An Efficient Way to Break Multiloop Dependence Equations. In *Proceedings of the SIGPLAN '92 Conference on Programming Language Design and Implementation*, San Francisco, CA, June 1992.

[15] V. Maslov and W. Pugh. Simplifying Polynomial Constraints Over Integers to Make Dependence Analysis More Precise. In *International Conference on Parallel and Vector Processing (CONPAR '94 — VAPP VI)*, Linz, Austria, September 1994.

Efficient Distribution Analysis via Graph Contraction

Thomas J. Sheffler [1], Robert Schreiber [1], William Pugh [2], John R. Gilbert [3],

Siddhartha Chatterjee [4]

[1] Research Institute for Advanced Computer Science
   ({sheffler,schreiber}@riacs.edu)
[2] University of Maryland (pugh@cs.umd.edu)
[3] Xerox Palo Alto Research Center (gilbert@parc.xerox.com)
[4] University of North Carolina, Chapel Hill (sc@cs.unc.edu)

Abstract. Alignment and distribution of array data should be managed by optimizing compilers for parallel computers, but current approaches to the distribution problem formulate it as an NP-complete graph optimization problem. The graphs arising in applications are large and difficult to optimize. In this paper, we improve some earlier results on methods that use graph contraction to reduce the size of a distribution problem. We report on an experiment using seven example programs that show these contraction operations to be effective in practice; we obtain from 70 to 99 percent reductions in problem size, the larger number being more typical, without loss of solution quality.

1 Introduction

Programmers expect that array parallel languages such as High-Performance Fortran (HPF) will provide high performance on distributed memory parallel computers if they pay careful attention to the distribution of arrays to the available processors. Currently, array distribution must be performed by the programmer, who annotates a program with distribution directives. This difficult task is further complicated by the fact that the optimal distribution for a program is dependent on the target machine. In the interest of simplifying the task of the programmer and enhancing the portability of array parallel programs, distribution should be handled by the compiler.

Unfortunately, distribution is a difficult combinatorial optimization problem [1]. Heuristic algorithms can be effective for small programs. For very large programs or very detailed analyses (employing inter-procedural analysis, for example) these algorithms may become less effective or unacceptably slow.

In this paper, we show how to reduce the size of a distribution problem. We recall the formulation [1, 3] of the distribution problem as a graph labeling problem, then show how the size of the graph may be reduced through graph contraction. We propose algorithms that identify regions of the program (the vertices of a subgraph) that may be performed under the same distribution. Once identified, the algorithm collapses each such subgraph into a single vertex that captures all of the information present in the

---

[1] The work of these authors was supported by the NAS Systems Division via Contract NAS 2-13721 between NASA and the Universities Space Research Association (USRA).

[4] The work of this author was supported by the NAS Systems Division via Contract NAS 2-13721 between NASA and the Universities Space Research Association (USRA) while he was a postdoctoral scientist at RIACS. Current affiliation: University of North Carolina, Chapel Hill.

original problem. The contraction operations are lossless: they do not diminish the quality of the best solutions.

We examine different strategies for applying the contraction operations and evaluate their relative merit. Initial experiments conducted with example programs show that these contraction operations are effective in practice. It is possible, moreover, that stronger contraction operations will further reduce the size of problems to the point where they can be solved exactly.

1.1 Related Work

While we are aware of no other approaches to the distribution problem through graph contraction, there is a significant amount of work done concerning other aspects of automatic distribution. Formulations of the distribution optimization problem may be categorized as either solving the *static* or *dynamic* distribution problem. Previous researchers have focused on the *static* version, in which the distribution of each array remains fixed throughout the execution of the program. Wholey [12] uses a hill-climbing procedure to successively refine the distribution parameters for a given program until the program can no longer be improved. Gupta [7] uses heuristic methods to determine the distribution parameters for each array. Our formulation of the distribution optimization problem allows the distribution of an array object to change over its lifetime. This is the *dynamic* distribution problem.

Last year, we introduced a divide-and-conquer approach to the dynamic distribution problem [3]. In this approach, the program is recursively divided into regions which are independently assigned distributions. The conquer stage merges regions when the cost of the dynamic distribution is worse than the static distribution. Recently, Gupta's techniques have been applied by Palermo to the dynamic distribution problem [10]. Palermo's is also a divide-and-conquer approach, and uses Gupta's static analyzer to assign distributions to the regions generated.

Rather than generating distribution parameters, our analysis begins with a candidate set of distributions from which to construct solutions. In this respect, our formulation is very similar to Kremer's [1]. However, we allow only a single candidate set, while he allows a different candidate set for each program operation. This difference is inconsequential since the one formulation may be easily transformed into the other.

2 Modeling Distribution

This section first describes how data mapping is specified in HPF through alignment and distribution directives. We then develop a cost model that estimates the running time of a program as a function of the alignments and distributions of its arrays. Since distribution analysis assumes that alignment analysis has already been performed, we are able to construct a greatly simplified graph model that only includes the effects of distribution on the running time of a program. This simplified model is the basis of our distribution analysis.

2.1 Alignment and Distribution

Our model of data mapping follows that of HPF: an array is aligned to a template, which is distributed over the available processors. A template is an abstract array used as a target in alignment directives. An alignment is specified by four separate components. These are *axis*, *stride*, *offset*, and *replication*. *Axis* alignment determines the correspondence of array axes to template axes. *Stride* alignment specifies the factor by which the array is stretched across the template. *Offset* is a vector specifying the distance of an array from the origin of the template, and *replication* specifies certain axes of the template over which an array might be copied.

An example of alignment and distribution as specified in an HPF program follows. The first two directives declare the template and describe the alignment of the array. The third and fourth lines together describe the distribution. The PROCESSORS directive describes the allocation of arrays to the axes of the template, while the DISTRIBUTE directive specifies how the template is divided over the processors. In this case, the BLOCK directive says that the first dimension of the template is distributed in blocks of 25 over 4 processors, and the CYCLIC directive specifies that the second dimension is distributed in blocks of 10 over 8 processors. Since the extent of the template is 200 in the second dimension, the blocks will wrap around the processors.

```
real :: a(100,100)

!hpf$ template t(100,200)
!hpf$ align a(i,j) with t(i,j+100)
!hpf$ processors p(4, 8)
!hpf$ distribute t(block, cyclic(10)) onto p
```

The alignment or distribution of an array object may change throughout its lifetime in a program. A change in alignment effectively changes the data mapping of an array and results in realignment communication. The type of communication needed to implement the realignment is determined by the component of an alignment that changes. Axis or stride realignment requires all-to-all personalized communication, offset realignment requires shift communication, and replication realignment requires a spread (broadcast) communication operation. In general, redistribution requires all-to-all personalized communication.

We choose to perform distribution analysis after alignment analysis. In our system, we first optimize axis and stride alignment, then replication alignment, followed by shift alignment. Previously, we presented algorithms that efficiently determine each of these alignment parameters [2, 11]. The order of the optimizations is motivated by the relative costs of the communication required by these types of realignment. It might be possible to find a better alignment if distribution information were known, but distribution analysis is difficult without some model of realignment communication costs. Consider the following example code fragment, typical of a finite-difference stencil computation.

```
integer, parameter :: n = 1000
real a(n), left(n-2), right(n-2), cl, cr
left = cl * a(1:n-2)
right = cr * a(3:n)
a(2:n-1) = a(2:n-1) + left + right
```

In our system, we would perform alignment first. The axis and stride alignments chosen here cause no realignment, but there is offset realignment in this fragment. Because of the necessary offset realignment, which comes to light in the alignment optimization phase, we would prefer to give the arrays a block rather than a cyclic distribution, since this reduces data traffic when shift communication is performed. It would be difficult to determine this fact about distribution without first having established alignment information.

2.2 The Alignment Distribution Graph

A data-parallel program may be modeled as a directed graph (V, E). The members of the vertex set V of the graph correspond to array operations in the program. An operation consumes one or more arrays, and produces one or more arrays as a result. A directed edge $(v, w) \in E$ connects a definition of an array object in array operation v to a use by operation w. Only true dependences are modeled by edges.

A *weight* labels each edge; it is an estimate of the number of elements in the array carried by the edge multiplied by an estimated trip-count of the edge in an execution of the program. In this way, the weight incorporates information about control flow.

Alignment is specified for the head and tail of each edge, giving the alignment of an array at its definition and use. Distribution must also be given for each vertex, specifying the distribution that is applied to each of the arrays involved in the vertex computation. The graph, along with these labels, is called an alignment-distribution graph (ADG) [4].

2.3 Modeling redistribution cost

The alignment-distribution graph (ADG) $G = (V, E)$ may be used to model the effects of distribution decisions. Our system first finds a set D of candidate distributions. Vertex costs are recorded in a matrix, C, and edge costs are recorded in a matrix, W. Entry $C(d, v)$ estimates the time required to perform operation $v \in V$ under distribution $d \in D$. Realignment costs are also incorporated in this model by adding an estimate of the cost of performing the realignment, if any, on directed edge (u, v), for each distribution d, into the cost entry $C(d, u)$. Each edge, $(u, v) \in E$, has an associated weight, $W(u, v)$, which is an estimate of the time required to redistribute the array value communicated along the edge. Even though this single weight is a simplistic measure of redistribution (since it is insensitive to the actual starting and ending layouts) experiments have shown that this discrete metric accurately reflects the cost of performing a redistribution step [8]. Furthermore, any edge that carries an axis or stride realignment has its weight changed to zero prior to distribution analysis, since redistribution of the value carried by the edge can be accomplished as part of the all-to-all personalized communication required for the realignment.

We seek to give each ADG vertex a distribution in D, *i.e.*, we seek a mapping $m : V \rightarrow D$. For a particular distribution map, we estimate the execution time of the program it models by the sum over the vertices of the cost of performing the vertex computation in its given distribution, plus the sum of the weights of all edges whose endpoints have different distributions:

$$\text{cost}(m) = \sum_{v \in V} C(m(v), v) + \sum_{(u,v) \in E, \ m(u) \neq m(v)} W(u, v).$$

The goal of distribution analysis is to map each vertex to a distribution so that this cost is minimized.

The model's vertex cost component is trivially minimized by mapping each vertex to its distribution of smallest vertex cost, but this can result in many edges carrying redistribution communication. At the other extreme, edge costs may be avoided entirely by mapping every vertex to some one distribution, the best of these being the distribution that minimizes the sum of the vertex costs. The optimal solution typically lies at neither of these extremes. The conflict between reducing vertex costs (by labeling vertices independently) and eliminating edge costs (by labeling vertices identically) makes the problem difficult. Kremer [9] in fact shows that this formulation of the distribution problem is NP-complete.

2.4 The set of distributions

A distribution $d \in D$ specifies both the deployment of processors to the axes of arrays and the blocking factor with which each axis is distributed to the processors (in a cyclic fashion). Our analysis requires a set D of candidate distributions. The set may be specified by a programmer, or may be generated by a compiler as it analyzes the program. We adopt the latter approach.

The generation of a set of distributions requires care. The achieved cost is never increased, and may be reduced, by allowing a larger set of candidate distributions, but the running time of our optimization algorithms is sensitive to the size of D. Thus we want a small set D that nevertheless includes those distributions that are best for the given program. We have previously shown how to select candidate distributions and how to limit their number [3].

2.5 Static and dynamic mappings

We introduce two terms to describe a distribution map for a subset of ADG vertices S. Let m be a given distribution map. Then S is *static* under m if m maps each member of S to the same distribution; S is *dynamic* under m otherwise. We say that the map m is static if V is static under m. Since all vertices in a static subset have the same distribution, no edge internal to a static subset can carry redistribution cost; the cost of a static distribution is completely determined by the vertex costs.

Each cost matrix entry, $C(d, v)$, gives an estimate of the time required to perform the computation of vertex v under distribution d. It is convenient to speak of the cost vector of a vertex, which is simply the column of entries $C(*, v)$ pertaining to the vertex, denoted C_v. We extend this term to sets of vertices, S, where the cost vector of a subset is simply the vector sum of the cost vectors of the vertices in S, denoted C_S. Thus, $C_S(d)$ is the cost of performing all of the operations of S in distribution d.

The way in which we attempt to reduce the size of the graph is to identify *optimally static* (O.S.) subsets of vertices in the distribution graph.

Definition 1 (Optimally Static). A subset $S \subseteq V$, is *optimally static* if for any map $m : V \rightarrow D$ there exists a map m' such that m' and m take identical values on $V - S$, S is static under m', and cost$(m') \leq$ cost(m).

Our overall plan for finding a distribution map m is this. We first determine a collection of subsets that we require to be static under m. This partially determines m. Then, we aggregate each subset into a single "super" vertex whose cost vector is the sum of the cost vectors of its members. Clearly, any O.S. subset can be so contracted, as this does not increase the cost of the best distribution. The remainder of the paper is concerned with finding O.S. subsets.

Our approach is to first find a candidate subset, and then test whether it is O.S. The next section develops a theory of O.S. subsets. Section 4 discusses heuristic strategies for finding candidate subsets.

3 Sufficient Conditions for Optimally Static Subsets

An understanding of properties of the distribution graph allows us to develop theorems that describe how subsets of vertices can be collapsed or amalgamated into super vertices, without changing the problem in an essential way. In this manner, we will reduce the size of the ADG as a first step in distribution analysis.

3.1 Definitions

In discussing whether or not a set S is O.S., we need to look at the largest and smallest entries of C_S, *i.e.* the largest and smallest aggregate vertex costs for S when it is distributed statically. Let

$$C_{min}^{(stat)}(S) \equiv \min_{d \in D} C_S(d)$$

and

$$C_{max}^{(stat)}(S) \equiv \max_{d \in D} C_S(d).$$

In contrast, we need to compare these with the smallest possible vertex cost total for S. Let

$$C_{min}^{(dyn)}(S) \equiv \sum_{s \in S} \min_{d \in D} C_s(d).$$

Last, let the difference between the maximum and minimum cost of a single vertex be called the *range* of the vertex,

$$range(v) \equiv \max_{d \in D} C_v(d) - \min_{d \in D} C_v(d).$$

Many of our proofs require consideration of the edges crossing from one set S to another set T. Define $w(S, T)$ as follows:

$$w(S, T) \equiv \sum_{v \in S, w \in T} W(v, w) + W(w, v).$$

Thus, $w(S, \bar{S})$ is the sum of the weights of all edges entering or leaving S. We will commit the obvious abuse of using $w(s, T)$ instead of $w(\{s\}, T)$ for a single vertex s. Note that w is a symmetric function of its arguments.

3.2 Optimally static subsets

We present a number of tests that may be used to verify that a subset of vertices is O.S. Each of the lemmas below gives an explicit construction showing, for a class of subsets S, how a map with dynamic S can be modified on S to make S static and not increase the cost. A following section discusses the implementation of the tests and the expected running time of each.

Lemma 2 (Accretion [3]). *Let S be O.S. and assume $v \notin S$. If*

$$w(v, \bar{S}) + range(v) \le w(v, S)$$

then $S \cup \{v\}$ is O.S.

Proof. Any map may, by assumption, be modified on S to make S static without increasing the cost of the map. Now consider a map in which S is static with distribution d and v has a different distribution d'. Changing the distribution of vertex v to d reduces the cost of the mapping by $w(v, S)$ and raises it by at most $w(v, \bar{S}) + range(v)$. By the hypotheses, this change also does not increase the cost. Hence $S \cup \{v\}$ is O.S. ∎

Corollary 3 (Edge Contraction). *Let s and v be distinct vertices. The set $\{s, v\}$ is O.S. if*

$$w(v, \{\bar{s}\}) + range(v) \le w(v, s).$$

Proof. Since any singleton vertex is an O.S. subset, the corollary follows immediately by applying Lemma 2 to $S = \{s\}$.

This simple corollary of Lemma 2 turns out to be very useful in practice: it identifies pairs of vertices that should be merged. In particular, unary operations representing SPREAD and REDUCE functions often have small ranges and have input and output edges of very different weights. Elementwise unary operations may have zero range with equal weights on their two incident edges.

Lemma 4 (Min-cut [3]). *A set S is O.S. if*

$$w(S, \bar{S}) + \left(C_{min}^{(stat)}(S) - C_{min}^{(dyn)}(S)\right) \leq \text{mincut}(S).$$

Proof. Assume that S is dynamic under a given distribution map. If the inequality holds, then the cost of this map is not increased by assigning S to its best static distribution. For we gain at least mincut(S) in edge costs, and lose at most $C_{min}^{(stat)}(S) - C_{min}^{(dyn)}(S)$ in added vertex costs and at most $w(S, \bar{S})$ in additional redistribution on edges leaving S.

The strategy of the previous lemma was to remap all of S to its preferred single location. As an alternative, we consider remapping all of S to the distribution of one of its neighbors, so as to make S static and avoid redistribution on edges connecting it to that neighbor. These results are new to this paper.

Lemma 5 (External Vertex). *A set S is O.S. if for some vertex $v \notin S$,*

$$(w(S, \bar{S}) - w(S, v)) + \left(C_{max}^{(stat)}(S) - C_{min}^{(dyn)}(S)\right) \leq \text{mincut}(S). \tag{1}$$

Proof. Let S be dynamic under some map m, and let v be connected to S by a set of edges of largest total weight. Remap all vertices in S to the distribution of vertex v. The vertex costs can increase, but not by more than the second term of the inequality (1); the edges from S except those touching v may now incur redistribution costs, but these added costs are not more than the first term of the inequality. Since, again, we gain at least mincut(S) in avoided redistribution on edges internal to S, the remapping cannot increase the total cost.

Note that although the construction in the proof guarantees that $S \cup \{v\}$ is static after the relabeling, we cannot conclude that $S \cup \{v\}$ is O.S., since we claimed a gain of mincut(S) after relabeling a map for which S is dynamic. The following reformulation allows us to conclude that S is O.S. by considering remapping S to the same distribution as one of its own vertices.

Lemma 6 (Internal Vertex). *A set S is O.S. if, for some vertex $v \in S$,*

$$w(S - \{v\}, \bar{S}) + \left(C_{max}^{(stat)}(S - \{v\}) - C_{min}^{(dyn)}(S - \{v\})\right) \leq \text{mincut}(S). \tag{2}$$

The proof is analogous to that of the External Vertex lemma.

4 Locating candidate subsets

The lemmas developed in the preceding section verify that a subset of vertices is O.S., but do not reveal how to find candidate subsets. It is not practical to consider all possible subsets of V, so we develop heuristics to locate subsets with the potential to be O.S.

Our heuristic creates a series of partitions of the graph by deleting edges whose weight falls below a given threshold. Note that a single threshold value uniquely defines a partition of the graph. To generate a large number of candidate subsets, our heuristic examines all partitions defined by a set of thresholds, T.

The set of thresholds is generated by histogramming the edge weights of the graph and then gathering the histogram points into clusters. The minimum value in each cluster becomes a threshold value in the set T. To use this algorithm, we work through the thresholds in T from heaviest to lightest. We apply the O.S. tests to each connected component at the current threshold.

This heuristic is effective because of the way the O.S. Lemmas are constructed and the way that the edge weights in the ADG are calculated. Lemmas 4, 5 and 6 prefer sets that have no small edge cut. The heuristic finds subsets that are highly connected internally (leading to a large min-cut value), with low-weight connections to vertices outside of the subset. For a given threshold value t, the mincut of any such component is not less than t, while the weight of each external edge is less than t.

The ADG tends to have clusters of heavy weight edges bordered by lighter weight edges. Recall that the ADG incorporates the effects of control flow into its edge weight calculation by multiplying the weight of an edge by its estimated trip count. In the ADG, vertices corresponding to operations within loops are connected by heavy edges, and values are communicated into and out of loops by lighter edges (because they are traversed only once). The strategy above tends to find connected components encompassing the operations inside the bodies of loops, and the threshold values correspond to different levels in loop nests.

The complexity of this subset finding algorithm is proportional to the number of edges, $|E|$, and the number of thresholds, $|T|$. The histogramming phase of the algorithm can be performed in time $O(|E|)$, and connected components can be found in time $O(|E|)$ by using depth-first search. The enumeration of all subsets using this technique can be performed in time $O(|T| \, |E|)$.

5 Implementing the O.S. tests and the contraction operation

This section suggests data structures and algorithms for implementing the tests of Section 3. We make use of basic sparse matrix techniques to keep the running times of the O.S. tests and the contraction operations low.

5.1 Data structures

The matrices C and W are stored as sparse matrices. An element in a matrix is a record structure storing its row, column, and value, and pointers threading it into two doubly-linked lists: a list of elements in the same row, and another list of elements in the same column. The elements of the lists are unordered.

Finding a particular matrix element in this data structure requires potentially searching through an entire row or column list. However, our algorithms do not require finding individual elements quickly, but rather depend on a data structure that supports unit time insertion and deletion of single elements, and finding the neighbors of a given vertex. The data structure described above supports these operations.

Our algorithms use a Sparse Accumulator (SPA) to add sparse vectors [5]. A SPA is used to compute the sum of several sparse vectors in time proportional to the number of non-zero elements in the vectors. This capability is important when contracting vertices.

5.2 Contracting vertices

The vertex contraction operation replaces a set of vertices, S, with a single vertex s in a reduced graph. The vertex cost vector C_s of the new vertex is the sum of the vertex cost vectors of its members, and the weight of each edge incident to s is the sum of the weights of all edges between the adjacent vertex and members of S. Precisely, this is written as

$$C(d, s) = \sum_{v \in S} C(d, v); \qquad W(s, w) = \sum_{v \in S} W(v, w); \qquad W(w, s) = \sum_{v \in S} W(w, v).$$

Our technique contracts S by adding the sparse vectors that encode the edge weight and adjacency information for the vertices in S. Merging the cost table entries for the vertices requires adding the corresponding columns of C. Thus, the cost table entries for a set can be computed in $O(|S| \cdot |D|)$ time.

Merging the adjacency table entries requires merging both the row and column lists for the vertices of S. When merging row lists, we treat each row as a sparse vector and use the SPA to add the vectors, deleting the elements from the matrix as we go. We then enumerate the non-zero elements of the SPA and insert these new values in the contracted matrix. Column merging proceeds the same way. By using a SPA, the modification of the adjacency matrix requires time linear in the number of non-zeros processed.

5.3 Complexity analysis

We now consider the overall complexity of the contraction algorithms we propose. These algorithms consist of application of a sequence of transformations in some pre-specified or adaptively chosen order, until some stopping criterion is satisfied. The three transformations we use follow.

Edge Contract Test all edges using Corollary 3.
Min-Cut Generate a set T of thresholds and for each, generate a set of subsets, as in Section 4. Apply the Min-Cut lemma to each subset and contract it if it is O.S.
Distinguished-Vertex Generate a set T of thresholds and for each, generate a set of subsets, as in Section 4. For each subset, and for each vertex either adjacent to or internal to the subset, apply the relevant Distinguished Vertex lemma and contract it if it is O.S.

A single pass refers to an application of the "Edge Contract" test to every edge in the graph, or an application of the "Min-Cut" and "Distinguished-Vertex" to all of the subgraphs of a partition of the graph defined by a single threshold value t. We have already shown that the modification of the data structures takes linear time; here we show that the application of the tests is efficient too.

We make the following assumption about our algorithm: The number $|T|$ of thresholds and the number $|D|$ of candidate distribution are bounded above by constants, independent of the graph.

Edge contraction Edge contraction is easy to implement. In order to facilitate it, we can store the range, the weight of all incident edges, and the weight of the heaviest incident edge in the vertex data structure. Then we can immediately tell whether a given vertex can be contracted into a neighbor. An important observation is that when a contraction occurs, vertices not adjacent to the two merged vertices are unaffected: if they could not be contracted into a neighbor before, they cannot after. Vertices adjacent to one of the merged vertices are likewise unaffected. Vertices adjacent to both *may* become contractable into the new vertex, and our implementation checks such vertices and contracts them in, if possible, immediately. Thus, we may examine the vertices, including those created by contraction, once each. When we finish, no more edges can be contracted. The total number of vertices we need to examine is therefore $O(|V|)$. The cost of the contraction of an edge is dominated by the cost of the addition of two rows and columns of W, which grows as the degree of the new vertex. Let B be the largest degree of any vertex created during the process; obviously $B < |V|$. The edge contraction algorithm runs in time $O(B \cdot |V|)$.

Min-cut based contraction Application of the min-cut and the distinguished vertex lemmas to each subset S in a partition of the graph requires knowledge of the weight of edges leaving S, mincut(S), $C_{min}^{(stat)}(S)$, $C_{max}^{(stat)}(S)$, and $C_{min}^{(dyn)}(S)$. The weight of edges leaving each subset can be computed in a single pass over the graph in $O(|E|)$ time. Clearly, the sum of the minima and the minimum and maximum of the sum of the vertex costs for each subset can be computed in $O(|V| \cdot |D|)$ time. The difficult part is computing the min-cut. There are two options: use an easily obtained lower bound on the min-cut, or compute it exactly.

If S is connected, then mincut(S) is not less than than the minimum weight edge in S. We may find the lightest one by examining all edges internal to S. For a particular partition of the graph (defined by a threshold value t), we may determine the lightest edge of each subset in $O(|E|)$ time. With this simple lower bound on the min-cut, a single pass of the "Min-Cut" test takes $O(|V| \cdot |D| + |E|) = O(|V| + |E|)$ time.

In the second case, we compute the global min-cut of each set S exactly, using an algorithm of Goldberg and Tarjan which runs in $O(|S|^4)$ time [6]. In practice, when using this option, we only invoke the min-cut procedure when the size of the set is smaller than some predefined value — because the running time of the min-cut procedure becomes unacceptable for large sets.

Distinguished vertex tests The application of the external vertex test requires finding the external vertex whose weight connecting it to a subgraph S in a partition of the graph is greater than that of any other vertex. (Computation of the other quantities is straightforward.) Using a SPA, for each subgraph S, we can compute the total weight with which it is connected to each external vertex. This operation is the same as the contraction step, except that we do not modify the matrix W. In doing this for each subset, each edge will be traversed at most twice: once from each vertex. Using the simple lower bound on the min-cut (as above), a single pass of the external vertex test takes $O(|V| + |E|)$ time.

The internal vertex test is similar to the external vertex test except that for each vertex $v \in S$ we compute $C_{max}^{(stat)}(S - \{v\})$ and $\min C_v$. This may be done in the following way to make the test efficient. Record the cost vector for the set, C_S. Now, as each vertex is visited, make use of the fact that $C_{max}^{(stat)}(S - \{v\}) = \max(C_S - C_v)$ and compute both this value and $\min C_v$ in $O(|D|)$ time. The rest of the implementation of the test is the same as the external vertex test. Thus, with the simple lower bound on the min-cut, a single pass of the internal vertex test takes $O(|V| + |E|)$ time.

6 Experiments

We now present an experimental study of the effectiveness of the contraction operations developed earlier. The process of locating subsets and verifying that they are O.S. is heuristic; such a study is therefore mandated, and we view the data below as preliminary, pending better tools and a larger base of experimental programs.

Using program analysis tools we have developed earlier [4], we constructed the distribution graphs for seven test programs and applied various combinations of the contraction operations. The contraction operations are sensitive to the adjacency structure of the graph as well as the values of the cost entries. For this reason, it is important to understand how the test cases were generated. We begin by describing the example programs and how the cost values were calculated. We then discuss contraction strategies and examine the results of these strategies.

6.1 The example programs

We chose seven example programs that represent typical scientific applications. A brief description of each of the seven follows. In addition, Table 1 describes properties of the cost and adjacency tables for each of the programs. Each of the graphs is quite sparse. With the exception of BlockLU, each program was analyzed with a relatively small number of distributions. Because BlockLU has many different feature sizes, a large number of distributions are generated by our automatic system.

ADI: A two-dimensional alternating-direction implicit algorithm. This uses cyclic reduction to solve tridiagonal systems.

BlockLU: A blocked algorithm for LU factorization of a dense matrix.

Erle: A three-dimensional alternating-direction implicit algorithm. This differs from ADI in that it uses Gaussian elimination to solve the tridiagonal systems.

LU: Unblocked LU factorization of a dense matrix.

Shallow: A benchmark weather prediction program; finite-difference approximation of the shallow water equations.

Tred: Reduction of a dense matrix to tridiagonal form using Householder transformations.

TwoZone: Solution of Poisson's equation in an L shaped domain by Schwartz alternating procedure, using a Jacobi over-relaxation method for the subdomain solver.

6.2 Cost matrix construction

In Section 2, we differentiated between three communication patterns: all-to-all personalized communication, offset communication (shift), and reduction/replication communication. When analyzing a program, we estimate the time of an elementwise operation to be proportional to the amount of data on the most heavily loaded processor. We estimate the time of a communication operation to be proportional to the maximum amount of data sent or received by any one processor, with the constant of proportionality determined by the type of operation. The three constants are ρ (for all-to-all), σ (for reduction/replication) and ν (for shift). (The names recall the now ancient and disappearing Connection Machine jargon: *router, scan, NEWS*). High-level operations

Table 1. Properties of the example program graphs. Each is quite sparse. In general, the number of distributions used in the analysis of each program is small, with the exception of BlockLU.

Properties of the Programs			
Program	$|V|$	$|E|$	$|D|$
ADI	232	308	12
BlockLU	108	131	41
Erle	666	845	7
LU	21	25	12
Shallow	445	545	3
Tred	105	124	9
TwoZone	335	411	12

Table 2. Mapping of high level HPF operations to low-level communication types. Each of the three low-level operations is modeled as requiring time proportional to the amount of data communicated, with the constant of proportionality as shown.

Coefficients of Proportionality		
High-Level Operation	Low-Level Communication Type	Constant
Redistribute	all-to-all	ρ
Stride Realign	all-to-all	ρ
Axis Realign	all-to-all	ρ
Offset Realign	shift	ν
Replication Realign	broadcast	σ
Subscript	all-to-all	ρ
Reduction	fan-in	σ

in HPF give rise to one of these three types of low-level communication. Table 2 shows the correspondence between high-level and low-level communication operations.

In general, it is impossible to predict how varying the parameters, ρ, σ, and ν, will affect the contraction operations. Even the interaction between this model of communication and the cost values generated is quite complex. Realignment costs are incorporated into the vertex cost matrix, while redistribution costs affect adjacency information. Varying the parameters by the same factor changes the relationship between elementwise computation and communication. Varying the parameter ρ can affect values in both, while varying σ or ν can only affect values in the cost matrix. Because of these complex interactions, we ran tests of the contraction operations for a number of values of the parameters to see how the results changed.

6.3 Contraction operation strategies

The contraction operations may be applied individually, or in combinations. In all, we experimented with 21 different combinations of the contraction operations. In the discussion of the combinations of contraction operations we use a shorthand. The character "e" means repeated application of edge contraction to all edges until the graph does not change. The character "m" stands for the min-cut test, and "d" for the distinguished vertex tests. By default, each of the "m" and "d" tests use the simple lower-bound on the min-cut value. We also ran these tests using the exact min-cut algorithm, but only for subsets whose size is smaller than a specified threshold. These thresholds are indicated by a number following the test combination, *e.g.* "eme:50." The contraction combinations examined are listed below.

```
m  m:25  m:50  em  em:25  em:50  eme  eme:25  eme:50
d  d:25  d:50  ed  ed:25  ed:50  ede  ede:25  ede:50
e  ememe  emedeme:50
```

6.4 Results

For each of the seven programs, we generated test data assuming a 64 processor target using these five sets of communication parameter values shown below.

Case1	$\rho = 1$	$\sigma = 1$	$\nu = 1$
Case2	$\rho = 10$	$\sigma = 1$	$\nu = 1$
Case3	$\rho = 100$	$\sigma = 1$	$\nu = 1$
Case4	$\rho = 100$	$\sigma = 10$	$\nu = 1$
Case5	$\rho = 1000$	$\sigma = 1$	$\nu = 1$

Case 1 reflects an architecture where communication costs as much as computation. There is no such machine widely available today, but such a machine would tolerate a lot of redistribution, preferring dynamic distributions over static ones. Thus, this case should thwart many of our contraction operations.

Cases 2 reflects an architecture where communication is only slightly expensive. Cases 3, 4, and 5 describe architectures with progressively more expensive communication. We expect that the cases with higher redistribution costs will encourage static solutions to the distribution problem, and thus expect our contraction operations to do well.

Rather than present tables containing all 735 data points, the contraction data is summarized in a scatter plot in Figure 1. Each of the test program and communication parameter combinations appears along the X-axis, with test programs abbreviated by the first letter of their name. A single column of points illustrates the contraction obtained by all of the various contraction combinations tried. The amount of contraction achieved by combination "eme:50" is shown as a box, and "eme" is shown as a star. All other combinations are simply shown as a dot. From this graph it is clear that combination "eme:50" achieved the best contration for almost all of the tests. For only the first two test programs of Case 5 did it not achieve the highest contraction rate.

The "eme" combination performs nearly as well as "eme:50" in many of the tests. Using the min-cut approximation ensures that the contraction tests run in linear time, and these results show that this crude approximation to the min-cut value is effective in practice. If run time is not a factor, however, then using the exact min-cut produces better results in a few of the few tests.

The overall percentage of reduction achieved by the "eme:50" combination is shown in Table 3. Initially, we did not expect to see high contraction rates for Case 1 because redistribution is inexpensive and the low edge-weights lead to small min-cut values relative to the node costs. The results show that, on the contrary, the tests are effective even when ρ is small.

7 Conclusions

When we began formulating algorithms for solving the distribution problem, we originally felt that sophisticated optimization techniques would be needed. We now believe

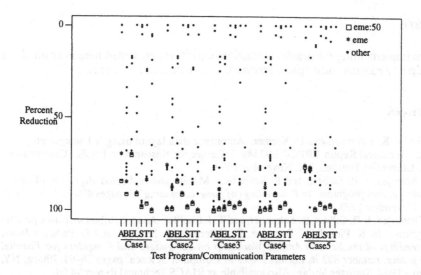

Fig. 1. Scatter plot of the contraction data. Combination "eme:50" is highlighted as a box, and "eme" appears as a star; all others are dots. Combination "eme:50" most consistently achieves the highest contraction rate.

Table 3. The amount of contraction as a percentage of the total size for the combination "eme:50." This particular combination proved the most effective overall.

Percentage Contraction using eme:50						
	ADI	Block	Erle	LU	Shal	Tred	TwoZ
Case1	83%	91%	70%	90%	98%	95%	99%
Case2	99%	98%	83%	90%	98%	95%	99%
Case3	99%	98%	99%	95%	98%	95%	99%
Case4	99%	98%	99%	90%	98%	95%	99%
Case5	75%	77%	99%	95%	98%	96%	99%

that contraction operations can dramatically reduce the size of a distribution problem without losing information. With effective contraction operations, problem sizes become so small that less powerful optimization strategies may suffice. Indeed, some problems become small enough that it may be possible to find optimal solutions exactly.

Some issues that remain open are these. If one should relax the requirement that the contraction operations remain lossless — that is, subgraphs that are not necessarily O.S. are contracted anyway — what is the tradeoff between compile time and run-time? Is it better to do a heuristic optimization of a big but exact distribution problem or an exact optimization of a small but approximate problem? We also need to reexamine our subset selection procedure. In the few cases in which the contracted graph remains large, is it because we haven't found the right subsets to test, or are our lemmas not powerful enough to prove that these subsets are indeed O.S?

Software

Software implementing the graph contraction algorithms presented here is available at URL `ftp://riacs.edu/pub/Excalibur/excalibur.html`.

References

1. R. Bixby, K. Kennedy, and U. Kremer. Automatic data layout using 0-1 integer programming. Technical Report CRPC-TR93349-S, Center for Research on Parallel Computation, Rice University, Houston, TX, November 1993.
2. S. Chatterjee, J. R. Gilbert, and R. Schreiber. Mobile and replicated alignment of arrays in data-parallel programs. In *Proceedings of Supercomputing'93*, pages 420–429, Portland, OR, November 1993.
3. S. Chatterjee, J. R. Gilbert, R. Schreiber, and T. J. Sheffler. Array distribution in data-parallel programs. In K. Pingali, U. Banerjee, D. Gelernter, A. Nicolau, and D. Padua, editors, *Proceedings of the Seventh Annual Workshop on Languages and Compilers for Parallel Computing*, number 892 in Lecture Notes in Computer Science, pages 76–91, Ithaca, NY, August 1994. Springer-Verlag. Also available as RIACS Technical Report 94.09.
4. S. Chatterjee, J. R. Gilbert, R. Schreiber, and T. J. Sheffler. Modeling data-parallel programs with the alignment-distribution graph. *Journal of Programming Languages*, 2:227–258, 1994. Special issue on compiling and run-time issues for distributed address space machines.
5. J. R. Gilbert, C. Moler, and R. Schreiber. Sparse matrices in MATLAB: Design and implementation. *SIAM J. Matrix Anal. Appl.*, 13(1):333–356, January 1992.
6. A. V. Goldberg and R. E. Tarjan. A new approach to the maximum-flow problem. *J. ACM*, 35(4):921–940, October 1988.
7. M. Gupta. *Automatic Data Partitioning on Distributed Memory Multicomputers*. PhD thesis, University of Illinois at Urbana-Champaign, Urbana, IL, Sept. 1992. Available as technical reports UILU-ENG-92-2237 and CRHC-92-19.
8. P. Hough and T. J. Sheffler. A performance analysis of collective communication on the CM-5. RIACS Technical Report in preparation.
9. U. Kremer. NP-completeness of dynamic remapping. Technical Report CRPC-TR93-330-S, Center for Research on Parallel Computation, Rice University, August 1993. Appears in the *Proceedings of the Fourth Workshop on Compilers for Parallel Computers*, Delft, The Netherlands, December 1993.
10. D. J. Palermo and P. Banerjee. Automatic selection of dynamic data partitioning schemes for distributed-memory multicomputers. Talk presented at the Workshop on Automatic Data Layout and Performance Prediction. Center for Research on Parallel Computing. April 19, 1995. Rice University.
11. T. J. Sheffler, R. Schreiber, J. R. Gilbert, and S. Chatterjee. Aligning parallel arrays to reduce communication. In *Proceedings of Frontiers '95: The Fifth Symposium on the Frontiers of Massively Parallel Computation.*, pages 324–331, February 1995.
12. S. Wholey. *Automatic Data Mapping for Distributed-Memory Parallel Computers*. PhD thesis, School of Computer Science, Carnegie Mellon University, Pittsburgh, PA, May 1991. Available as Technical Report CMU-CS-91-121.

Automatic Selection of Dynamic Data Partitioning Schemes for Distributed-Memory Multicomputers

Daniel J. Palermo and Prithviraj Banerjee

Center for Reliable and High-Performance Computing, University of Illinois at
Urbana-Champaign, 1308 West Main Street, Urbana, IL 61801
({palermo, banerjee}@crhc.uiuc.edu)

Abstract. For distributed-memory multicomputers such as the Intel Paragon, the
IBM SP-1/SP-2, the NCUBE/2, and the Thinking Machines CM-5, the quality
of the data partitioning for a given application is crucial to obtaining high performance. This task has traditionally been the user's responsibility, but in recent
years much effort has been directed to automating the selection of data partitioning schemes. Several researchers have proposed systems that are able to produce
data distributions that remain in effect for the entire execution of an application.
For complex programs, however, such static data distributions may be insufficient
to obtain acceptable performance. The selection of distributions that dynamically
change over the course of a program's execution adds another dimension to the
data partitioning problem. In this paper, we present a technique that can be used
to automatically determine which partitionings are most beneficial over specific
sections of a program while taking into account the added overhead of performing
redistribution. This system is being built as part of the PARADIGM (PARAllelizing compiler for DIstributed-memory General-purpose Multicomputers) project
at the University of Illinois. The complete system will provide a fully automated
means to parallelize programs written in a serial programming model obtaining
high performance on a wide range of distributed-memory multicomputers.

1 Introduction

Distributed-memory multicomputers such as the Intel Paragon, the IBM SP-1/SP-2, the
NCUBE/2, and the Thinking Machines CM-5 offer significant advantages over shared-
memory multiprocessors in terms of cost and scalability. However, lacking a global address space, they present a very difficult programming model in which the user must
specify how data and computations are to be partitioned across processors and determine
which sections of data need to be communicated among which processors. To overcome
this difficulty, significant effort has been aimed at source-to-source parallelizing compilers that relieve the programmer from the task of communication generation, while the
task of data partitioning remains a responsibility of the programmer.

As part of the research performed in the PARADIGM (PARAllelizing compiler for
DIstributed-memory General-purpose Multicomputers) project [2] at the University of
Illinois, automatic data partitioning techniques have been developed to relieve the pro-
grammer of the burden of selecting good data distributions. Currently, the compiler can

This research was supported in part by the National Aeronautics and Space Administration under Contract NASA NAG 1-613
and in part by the Advanced Research Projects Agency under contract DAA-H04-94-G-0273 administered by the Army Research office. We are also grateful to the National Center for Supercomputing Applications and the San Diego Supercomputing
Center for providing access to their machines.

automatically select a static distribution of data (using a constraint-based algorithm [9]) specifying both the configuration of an abstract multi-dimensional mesh topology along with how program data should be distributed on the mesh. In this paper, we present a technique which extends the static partitioning algorithm to select dynamic data distributions which can further improve the performance of the resulting parallel program.

The remainder of this paper is organized as follows: Section 2 presents a small example to illustrate the need for dynamic array redistribution; related work in automatic selection of static and dynamic data distribution schemes is discussed in Section 3; the methodology for selection of dynamic data distributions is presented in Section 4; an experimental analysis of the presented techniques is performed in Section 5; and conclusions are presented in Section 6.

2 Motivation

Figure 1 shows the basic computation performed in a two-dimensional Fast Fourier Transform (FFT). To execute this program in parallel on a machine with distributed memory, the main data array, Image, is partitioned across the available processors. By examining the data accesses that will occur during execution it can be seen that, for the first half of the program, data is manipulated along the rows of the array. For the rest of the execution, data is manipulated along the columns. Depending on how data is distributed among the processors, several different patterns of communication could be generated. The goal of automatic data partitioning is to select the distribution which will result in the highest level of performance.

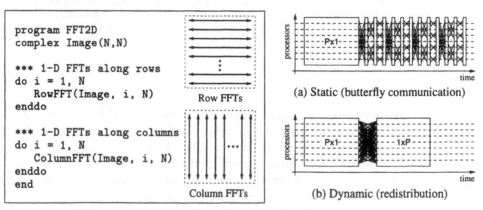

Fig. 1. Two-dimensional Fast Fourier Transform

If the array were distributed by rows, every processor could independently compute the FFTs for each row that involved local data. After the rows had been processed, the processors would now have to communicate to perform the column FFTs as the columns have been partitioned across the processors. Conversely, if a column distribution were selected, communication would be required to compute the row FFTs while the column FFTs could be computed independently. Such static partitionings, as shown in Figure 1a, suffer in that they cannot reflect changes in a program's data access behavior. When conflicting data requirements are present, static partitionings tend to be compromises between a number of preferred distributions.

Instead of requiring a single data distribution for the entire execution, program data could also be redistributed dynamically for different *phases*[1] of the program. For this example, assume the program is split into two separate phases; a row distribution is selected for the first phase and a column distribution for the second (as shown in Figure 1b). By redistributing the data between the two phases, none of the one-dimensional FFT operations would require communication. Such dynamic partitionings can yield higher performance than a static partitioning when the redistribution is more efficient than the communication pattern required by the statically partitioned computation.

3 Related Work

Static Partitioning Some of the ideas used in the static partitioning algorithm currently implemented in the PARADIGM compiler [9] were inspired by earlier work on multidimensional array alignment [14]. In addition to this work, in recent years much research has been focused on: performing multi-dimensional array alignment [5, 12, 14]; examining cases in which a communication-free partitioning exists [17]; showing how performance estimation is a key in selecting good data distributions [6, 22]; linearizing array accesses and analyzing the resulting one-dimensional accesses [20]; applying iterative techniques which minimize the amount of communication at each step [1]; and examining issues for special-purpose distributed architectures such as systolic arrays [21].

Dynamic Partitioning In addition to the work performed in static partitioning, a number of researchers have also been examining the problem of dynamic partitioning. Anderson and Lam [1] approach the dynamic partitioning problem using a heuristic which combines loop nests (with potentially different distributions) in such a way that the largest potential communication costs are eliminated first while still maintaining sufficient parallelism. Bixby, Kennedy and Kremer formulate the dynamic data partitioning problem in the form of a 0-1 integer programming problem by selecting a number of candidate distributions for each of a set of given phases and constructing constraints from the data relations [3]. Chapman, Fahringer, and Zima describe the design of a distribution tool that makes use of performance prediction methods when possible but also uses empirical performance data through a pattern matching process [4]. Hudak and Abraham have also proposed a method for selecting redistribution points based on locating significant control flow changes in a program [11]. More recently, Sheffler, Schreiber, Gilbert and Chatterjee have applied graph contraction methods to the dynamic alignment problem to reduce the size of the problem space that must be examined [19].

Bixby, Kremer, and Kennedy have also described an *operational definition* of a phase which defines a phase as the outermost loop of a loop nest such that the corresponding iteration variable is used in a subscript expression of an array reference in the loop body [3]. Even though this definition restricts phase boundaries to loop structures and does not allow overlapping phases, it can be seen that for the example in Section 2 this definition is sufficient to describe the two distinct phases of the computation.

---

[1] A *phase* can be described simply as a sequence of statements in a program over which a given distribution is unchanged.

```
program ADI2d
double precision u(N,N), uh(N,N), b(N,N), alpha
integer i, j, k                                                                         Phase
                                                              do j = 2, N - 1                31  ┐
*** Initial value for u                            Phase        uh(N - 1,j) = uh(N - 1,j) / b(N - 1,j)  32  │ VI
do j = 1, N                                          1  ┐      enddo                          33  ┘
  do i = 1, N                                        2  │      do j = 2, N - 1                34  ┐
    u(i,j) = 0.0                                     3  │        do i = N - 2, 2, -1          35  │
  enddo                                              4  │ I        uh(i,j) = (uh(i,j) + uh(i + 1,j)) / b(i,j)  36  │ VII
  u(1,j) = 30.0                                      5  │        enddo                        37  │
  u(n,j) = 30.0                                      6  │      enddo                          38  ┘
enddo                                                7  ┘
                                                              *** Forward and backward sweeps along rows
*** Initialize uh                                             do j = 2, N - 1                39  ┐
do j = 1, N                                          8  ┐      do i = 2, N - 1                40  │
  do i = 1, N                                        9  │        b(i,j) = (2 + alpha)         41  │
    uh(i,j) = u(i,j)                                10  │ II     u(i,j) = (alpha - 2) * uh(i,j) +  │ VIII
  enddo                                             11  │ &                      uh(i + 1,j) + uh(i - 1,j)  42  │
enddo                                               12  ┘      enddo                          43  │
                                                              enddo                          44  ┘
alpha = 4 * (2.0 / N)                               13         do i = 2, N - 1                45  ┐
do k = 1, maxiter                                   14           u(i,2) = u(i,2) + uh(i,1)    46  │
  *** Forward and backward sweeps along columns                 u(i,N - 1) = u(i,N - 1) + uh(i,N)  47  │ IX
  do j = 2, N - 1                                   15         enddo                          48  ┘
    do i = 2, N - 1                                 16
      b(i,j) = (2 + alpha)                          17         do j = 3, N - 1                49  ┐
      uh(i,j) = (alpha - 2) * u(i,j) +                          do i = 2, N - 1                50  │
&                       u(i,j + 1) + u(i,j - 1)     18 III        b(i,j) = b(i,j) - 1 / b(i,j - 1)  51  │ X
    enddo                                           19             u(i,j) = u(i,j) + u(i,j - 1) / b(i,j - 1)  52  │
  enddo                                             20           enddo                        53  │
  do j = 2, N - 1                                   21         enddo                          54  ┘
    uh(2,j) = uh(2,j) + u(1,j)                      22 IV       do i = 2, N - 1                55  ┐
    uh(N - 1,j) = uh(N - 1,j) + u(N,j)              23           u(i,N - 1) = u(i,N - 1) / b(i,N - 1)  56  │ XI
  enddo                                             24         enddo                          57  ┘
                                                              do j = N - 2, 2, -1            58  ┐
  do j = 2, N - 1                                   25  ┐        do i = 2, N - 1               59  │
    do i = 3, N - 1                                 26  │          u(i,j) = (u(i,j) + u(i,j + 1)) / b(i,j)  60  │ XII
·     b(i,j) = b(i,j) - 1 / b(i - 1,j)              27  │ V      enddo                         61  │
      uh(i,j) = uh(i,j) + uh(i - 1,j) / b(i - 1,j)  28  │      enddo                          62  ┘
    enddo                                           29  │    enddo                            63
  enddo                                             30  ┘    end                              64
```

Fig. 2. 2-D Alternating Direction Implicit method (ADI) with operational phases shown

4 Dynamic Distribution Selection

The technique we propose to automatically select redistribution points can be broken down into two main steps. First, the program is recursively decomposed into a hierarchy of candidate phases. Then, taking into account the cost of redistributing the data between the different phases, the most efficient sequence of phases and phase transitions is selected.

This approach allows us to build upon the static partitioning techniques [9] previously developed in the PARADIGM project. Static cost estimation techniques [8] are used to guide the selection of phases while static partitioning techniques are used to determine the best possible distribution for each phase. The cost models used to estimate communication and computation costs use parameters, empirically measured for each target machine, to separate the partitioning algorithm from a specific architecture.

To help illustrate the dynamic partitioning technique, an example program will be used. In Figure 2, a two-dimensional Alternating Direction Implicit iterative method[2] (ADI) is shown which computes the solution of an elliptic partial differential equation known as Poisson's equation [7]. Poisson's equation can be used to describe the dissipation of heat away from a surface with a fixed temperature as well as to compute the

---

[2] To simplify later analysis of performance measurements, the program shown performs an arbitrary number of iterations as opposed to periodically checking for convergence of the solution.

free-space potential created by a surface with an electrical charge.

For the program in Figure 2, a static data distribution will incur a significant amount of communication for over half of the program's execution. For illustrative purposes only, the operational definition of phases previously described in Section 3 identifies twelve different "phases" in the program. These phases exposed by the operational definition need not be known for our technique (and, in general, are potentially too restrictive) but they will be used here for comparison as well as to facilitate the discussion.

4.1 Phase Decomposition

Initially, the entire program is viewed as a single phase for which a static distribution is determined. At this point, the immediate goal is to determine if and where it would be beneficial to split the program into two separate phases such that the sum of the execution times of the resulting phases is less than the original (as illustrated in Figure 3). Using the selected distribution, a *communication graph* is constructed to examine the cost of communication in relation to the flow of data within the program.

We define a *communication graph* as the flow information from the dependence graph (generated by Parafrase-2 [16]) weighted by the cost of communication. The nodes of the communication graph correspond to individual statements while the edges correspond to flow dependencies that exist between the statements. As a heuristic, the cost of communication performed for a given reference in a statement is assigned to (*reflected* back along) every incoming dependence edge corresponding to the reference involved[3]. Since flow information is used to construct the communication graph, the weights on the edges serve to expose communication costs that exist between producer/consumer relationships within a program. The granularity of phase partitioning is also restricted to the statement level, therefore, single node cycles in the flow dependence graph are not included in the communication graph.

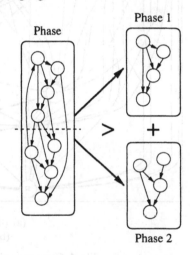

Fig. 3. Phase decomposition

In Figure 4, the communication graph is shown for ADI with some of the edges labeled with the expressions automatically generated by the static cost estimator (using a problem size of 512×512 and maxiter set to 100). Conditionals appearing in the cost expressions represent costs that will be incurred based on specific distribution decisions (e.g. $P_2 > 1$ is true if the second mesh dimension is assigned more than one processor). For reference, the communication models for an Intel Paragon and a Thinking Machines CM-5, corresponding to the communication primitives used in the cost expressions, are shown in Table 1.

---

[3] There is at most only one edge between two nodes for each array referenced in the statement. For multiple references to the same array, the edge weight is the sum of all communication for that array.

(a) $100 * (P_2 > 1) * \text{Shift}(510)$
(b) $3100 * \text{Transfer}(510)$

Fig. 4. Communication graph and example edge costs for ADI
(Statement numbers correspond to Figure 2)

	Intel Paragon	TMC CM-5
Transfer(m)	$50 + 0.018m$	$23 + 0.12m \quad m \leq 16$ $86 + 0.12m \quad m > 16$
Shift(m)		$2 * \text{Transfer}(m)$

Table 1. Communication primitives

In addition to the costs of communication generated by a statement, we also introduce the idea of *transparent* statements. These are statements for which the target of the assignment: (1) is also referenced in the assignment function with identical indexing, and (2) is not referenced again with a different indexing function. If any communication cost is reflected back to a transparent statement, it is also further reflected on any incoming dependence edges originating from statements prior to the current position. This has a net effect of encouraging redistribution as early as possible in the program text by allowing selected costs to be propagated toward the start of the program. For the ADI program, statements 22, 23, 46, and 47 can be considered transparent.

Once the communication graph has been constructed, a split point is determined by computing a maximal cut of the communication graph. The maximal cut removes the largest communication constraints from a given phase to potentially allow better individual distributions to be selected for the two resulting split phases. Since the communication graph can potentially contain edges with a zero communication cost, it is also possible to find several cuts which all have the same cost. The following algorithm is used to determine which cut to use to split a given phase:

To better describe the algorithm, view the communication graph $G = (V, E)$ in the form of an adjacency matrix (with source vertices on rows and destination vertices on columns).

1. For each statement S_i $\{i \in [1; (|V| - 1)]\}$ compute the cut of the graph between statements S_i and S_{i+1} by summing all the edges in the sub-matrices specified by $[S_1, S_i] \times [S_{i+1}, S_{|V|}]$ and $[S_{i+1}, S_{|V|}] \times [S_1, S_i]$ (an efficient implementation, which only adds and subtracts the differences between two successive cuts, takes $\mathcal{O}(E)$ time on the actual representation).

2. While computing the cost of each cut also keep track of the current maximum cut.

3. If there is more than one cut with the same maximum value, choose the first.

4. Mark the arrays involved in the cut edges to redistribute and split the phase using the selected cut.

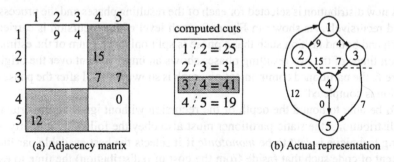

(a) Adjacency matrix   (b) Actual representation

Fig. 5. Example graph illustrating the computation of a cut

In Figure 5, the computation of the maximal cut on a smaller example graph with arbitrary weights is shown. The maximal cut is found to be between vertices 3 and 4 with a cost of 41. This is shown both in the form of the sum of the two adjacency submatrices, specified by the algorithm, and graphically as a cut on the actual representation. Since the ordering of the nodes is related to the linear ordering of statements in a program, the algorithm also guarantees that the nodes on one side of the cut will always all precede or all follow the node most closely involved in the cut. This is necessary to ensure that the cut divides the program at exactly one point.

It is interesting to note that if a cut occurs within a loop body, and loop distribution can be performed, the amount of redistribution can be greatly reduced by lifting it out of the distributed loop body and performing it in between the two sections of the loop. Also, if dependencies allow statements to be reordered, statements may be able to move across a cut boundary without affecting the cost of the cut while possibly reducing the amount of data to be redistributed. Both of these optimizations can be used to reduce the cost of redistribution but neither be examined in this paper.

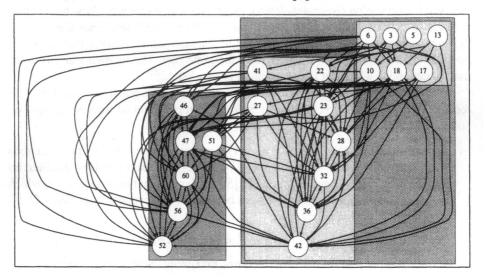

Fig. 6. Partitioned communication graph for ADI
(Statement numbers correspond to Figure 2)

A new distribution is selected for each of the resulting phases and the process is continued recursively. As shown in Figure 3, each level of the recursion is carried out in branch and bound fashion such that a phase is split only if the sum of the estimated execution times of the two resulting phases shows an improvement over the original[4]. In Figure 6, the partitioned communication graph is shown for ADI after the phase decomposition is completed.

To be able to bound the depth of the recursion without ignoring important phases and distributions, the static partitioner must also obey the following property. A partitioning technique is said to be *monotonic* if it selects the best available partition for a segment of code such that (aside from the cost of redistribution) the time to execute a code segment with a selected distribution is less than or equal to the time to execute the same segment with a distribution that is selected after another code segment is appended

---

[4] A further optimization can also be applied to bound the size of the smallest phase that can be split by requiring its estimated execution time to be greater than a "minimum cost" of redistribution.

to the first. In practice, this condition is satisfied by the static partitioning algorithm that we are using. This can be attributed to the fact that conflicts between distribution preferences are not broken arbitrarily, but are resolved based on the costs imposed by the target architecture [9].

4.2 Phase and Phase Transition Selection

After the program has been recursively decomposed into a hierarchy of phases, redistribution costs are estimated [18] and are weighted by their execution count. for each of the possible phase transitions. Since it is possible that using lower level phases may require transitioning through distributions found at higher levels (to keep the overall redistribution costs to a minimum), redistribution is allowed at the granularity of the lowest level of the phase decomposition. Edges with the resulting costs are used to connect the phases in a *phase transition graph* (as in Figure 7) to help determine which phases and transitions are necessary to obtain the best performance.

In the presence of control flow which causes iteration in the program (i.e. loops and backward branches), additional redistribution may be induced. A redistribution edge that occurs within a loop or between the source and target of a backward branch will have its cost doubled to account for a potential reverse redistribution[5]. Once costs have been assigned to all redistribution edges, the best sequence of phases and phase transitions is selected by computing the shortest path on the phase transition graph.

Using the cost models for an Intel Paragon and a Thinking Machines CM-5, the distributions and estimated execution times reported by the static partitioner for the resulting phases (described as ranges of operational phases) is shown in Table 2. The performance parameters of the two machines are similar enough that the static partitioning actually selects the same distribution at each phase for each machine. The times estimated for the static partition are a bit higher than those actually observed, resulting from a conservative assumption made by the static cost estimator, but they still exhibit similar enough performance trends to be used as estimates.

Op. Phases(s)	Distribution		Intel Paragon	TMC CM-5	
I-XII	*,block	1×32	20.588940	35.970293	Level 1
I-VIII	*,block	1×32	1.354800	2.347115	Level 2
IX-XII	block,*	32×1	0.603424	0.942850	
I-III	block,*	32×1	0.376035	0.590306	Level 3
IV-VIII	*,block	1×32	0.978784	1.529350	

Table 2. Detected phases and estimated execution times (sec) for ADI

On an Intel Paragon the cost of performing redistribution is low enough that a dynamic distribution scheme is selected (shown by the shaded area in Figure 7). For a Thinking Machines CM-5, however, the cost of redistribution is more expensive than the gains that can be made using a dynamic distribution; therefore, a static distribution is selected for this machine.

---

[5] This is a conservative estimate of the actual cost since it assumes that reverse redistribution will always occur.

Pseudo-code for the dynamic partitioning algorithm is presented in Figure 8 to briefly summarize the entire procedure.

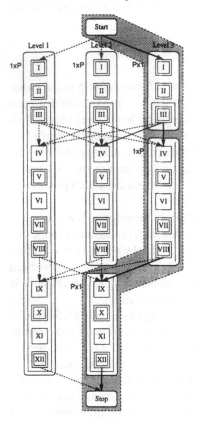

Fig. 7. Selected phases for ADI

Construct the communication graph for the *program*
Perform an initial static partitioning on the *program*
phases = Decompose_Phase(*program*)
scheme = Select_Redistribution(*phases*)

Decompose_Phase(*phase*)
    Add *phase* to list of recognized phases
    Assign new costs to the communication graph
    Compute the maximal cut
                ($phase \rightarrow phase_1, phase_2$)
    Perform static partitioning on *phase₁*
    Perform static partitioning on *phase₂*
    Mark the arrays to be redistributed
    if ($\mathrm{cost}(phase_1) + \mathrm{cost}(phase_2)) < \mathrm{cost}(phase)$
        $phase \rightarrow left$ = Decompose_Phase($phase_1$)
        $phase \rightarrow right$ = Decompose_Phase($phase_2$)
    else
        $phase \rightarrow left$ = **null**
        $phase \rightarrow right$ = **null**
    return(*phase*)

Select_Redistribution(*phases*)
    Construct the phase transistion graph
    Estimate the interphase redistribution costs
    Compute the shortest phase transition path
    return(selected phase transition path)

Fig. 8. Pseudo-code for the partitioning algorithm

Since the selection of the split point during decomposition implicitly maintains the coupling between individual array distributions, redistribution at any stage will only affect the next stage. This can be contrasted to the technique proposed by Bixby, Kremer, and Kennedy [3] which first selects a number of partial candidate distributions for each phase specified by the operational definition. Since their phase boundaries are chosen in the absence of flow information, redistribution can affect stages at any distance from the current stage. This causes the redistribution costs to become binary functions depending on whether or not a specific path is taken, therefore, necessitating the need for 0-1 integer programming. If distributions are exhaustively enumerated for every operational phase, the integer programming technique will obtain an optimal solution. Since the choice of candidate distributions can be considered somewhat of a heuristic in itself, it would be of interest to compare the quality and performance of these two techniques as more results are obtained.

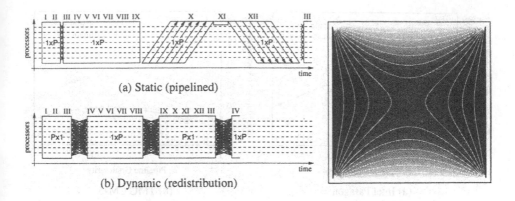

Fig. 9. Modes of parallel execution for ADI and the solution for the test data

5 Evaluation

In order to evaluate the effectiveness of dynamic distribution, the ADI program, with a problem size of 512×512[6], is compiled with both a fully static distribution (one iteration shown in Figure 9a) as well as with the selected dynamic distribution (one iteration shown in Figure 9b). These two parallel versions of the code were run on an Intel Paragon and a Thinking Machine's CM-5 to examine the performance of each on the different architectures. With initial conditions of zero within the core of the matrix and upper and lower boundaries with a value of 30, both schemes obtain the solution shown in Figure 9 (overlaid with contours along constant potentials).

The static scheme illustrated in Figure 9a performs a shift operation to initially obtain some required data and then satisfies two recurrences in the program using software pipelining [10, 15]. Since values are being propagated through the array during the pipelined computation, processors must wait for results to be computed before continuing with their own part of the computation. Depending on the ratio of communication and computation performance for a given machine, exactly how much data is computed before communicating to the next processor will have a great effect on the performance of pipelined computations.

A small experiment is first performed to determine the best pipeline *granularity* for the static partitioning. A granularity of one (fine-grain) causes values to be communicated to waiting processors as soon as they are produced. By increasing the granularity, more values are computed before communicating, thereby amortizing the cost of establishing communication in exchange for some reduction in parallelism. In addition to the experimental data, compile-time estimates of the pipeline execution [15] are shown in Figure 10. For the two machines, it can be seen that by selecting the appropriate granularity; the performance of the static partitioning can be improved. Even though the current computational model is only based on high-level instruction counts [8] and ignores

---

[6] In order to prevent poor serial performance from cache-line aliasing due to the power of two problem size, the arrays were also padded with an extra element at the end of each column. This optimization, although here performed by hand, is automated by aggressive serial optimizing compilers such as the KAP preprocessor from KAI.

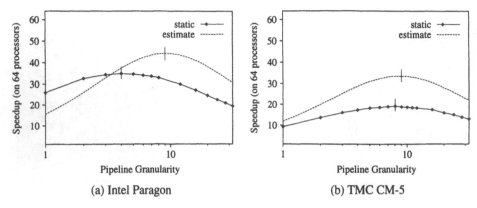

Fig. 10. Coarse grain pipelining for ADI

processor pipeline and cache effects, the trend is still modeled well enough to select a granularity at compile-time that closely approximates the optimal. Both a fine-grain and the optimal coarse-grain static partitioning will be compared with the dynamic partitioning.

The redistribution present in the dynamic scheme appears as 3 transposes[7] performed at two points within an outer loop (the exact points in the program can be seen in Figure 7). Since the sets of transposes occur at the same point in the program, the data to be communicated for each transpose can be aggregated into a single message during the actual transpose. It has been previously shown that aggregating communication improves performance by reducing the overhead of communication [15], so we will also examine aggregating the individual transpose operations here.

Also, to improve the efficiency of memory management when moving large regions of data (such as required during redistribution), the array section pack and unpack routines in the PARADIGM run-time library are optimized to use block memory operations (memcpy) when possible. Furthermore, to avoid unnecessary congestion in the communication network, the order in which communication takes place during the redistribution is scheduled such that every processor sends data to a different processor at each step in the redistribution (as opposed to each processor communicating with an identical sequence of destinations). Even though the transpose redistribution is currently part of the run-time library, these modifications will also be incorporated into the code generation techniques for automated redistribution [18] when it is integrated with the rest of the compiler.

In Figure 11, the performance of both static and dynamic partitionings for ADI is shown for an Intel Paragon and a Thinking Machines CM-5. Recall that the time for redistribution on the CM-5 was high enough that a static partitioning was predicted to perform better. On the Paragon, the cost of redistribution was low enough that a dynamic partitioning was selected. For the dynamic partitioning, both aggregated and non-aggregated transpose operations were compared. For both machines, it is apparent that

---

[7] This could have been reduced to 2 transposes at each point if we allowed the cuts to reorder statements and perform loop distribution on the innermost loops (between statements 17, 18 and 41, 42), but these optimizations are not examined here.

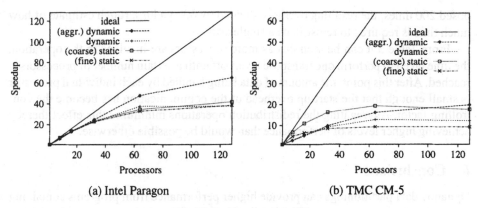

(a) Intel Paragon (b) TMC CM-5

Fig. 11. Performance of ADI

aggregating the transpose communication is very effective, especially as the program is executed on larger numbers of processors. This can be attributed to the fact that the start-up cost of communication (which can be several orders of magnitude greater than the per byte transmission cost) is being amortized over multiple messages with the same source and destination.

For the static partitioning, fine grain pipelining was compared to coarse-grain using the granularity selected earlier. The coarse-grain optimization yielded the greatest benefit on the CM-5 while still improving the performance (to a lesser degree) on the Paragon. For the Paragon, the dynamic partitioning with aggregation clearly improved performance (by over 70% compared to the fine-grain and 60% compared to the coarse-grain static distribution). On the CM-5 the dynamic partitioning with aggregation showed performance gains of over a factor of two compared to the fine-grain static partitioning but only outperformed the coarse-grain version for extremely large numbers of processors. For this reason, it would appear that the limiting factor on the CM-5 is the performance of the communication.

As a final check, in Table 3 the cost of performing a single transpose in either direction (P×1 ⇄ 1×P) is estimated from the communication overhead present in the dynamic runs. Ignoring any performance gains from cache effects, the communication overhead can be computed by subtracting the ideal run time (serial time divided by the selected number of processors) from the measured run time. Given that 3 arrays are trans-

	Intel Paragon		TMC CM-5	
processors	individual	aggregated	individual	aggregated
8	36.7	32.0	138.9	134.7
16	15.7	15.6	86.8	80.5
32	14.8	10.5	49.6	45.8
64	12.7	6.2	40.4	29.7
128	21.6	8.7	47.5	27.4

Table 3. Empirically estimated time (ms) to transpose a 1-D partitioned
512 × 512 double precision matrix

posed 200 times, the resulting overhead divided by 600 yields a rough estimate of how much time is required to redistribute a single array.

From Table 3 it can be seen that as more processors are involved in the operation, the time taken to perform one transpose levels off until a certain number of processors is reached. After this point, the amount of data being handled by each individual processor is small enough that the start-up overhead of the communication has become the controlling factor. Aggregating the redistribution operations minimizes this effect thereby achieving higher levels of performance than would be possible otherwise.

6 Conclusions

Dynamic data partitionings can provide higher performance from programs containing competing data access patterns. The distribution selection technique presented in this paper provides a means of automatically determining the best distribution scheme to use for a particular machine in an efficient manner. A key requirement in automating this selection process is to be able to obtain estimates of communication and computation costs which accurately model the behavior of the program under a given distribution. Furthermore, by building upon existing static partitioning techniques the number of phases examined as well as the amount of redistribution considered is kept to a minimum.

Further investigation into the application of statement reordering and loop distribution to reduce the amount of required redistribution is currently under way. We are also in the process of applying interprocedural analysis along with the techniques presented in this paper to investigate possible redistribution at procedure boundaries.

Acknowledgements: We would like to thank the reviewers for their comments, Amber Roy Chowdhury for his assistance with the coding of the serial ADI algorithm, John Chandy, Amber Roy Chowdhury, and Eugene Hodges for discussions on algorithm complexity, Steven Parkes for his suggestions on improving the efficiency of the memory management routines in the PARADIGM run-time library, as well as Christy Palermo for her suggestions and comments on this paper.

The figures used in this paper for the communication graphs were also generated using a software package known as "Dot" developed by Eleftherios Koutsofios and Steven North with the Software and Systems Research Center, AT&T Bell Laboratories [13].

References

1. J. M. Anderson and M. S. Lam. Global Optimizations for Parallelism and Locality on Scalable Parallel Machines. In *Proc. of the ACM SIGPLAN '93 Conf. on Prog. Lang. Design and Implementation*, pages 112–125, Albuquerque, NM, June 1993.
2. P. Banerjee, J. A. Chandy, M. Gupta, E. W. Hodges IV, J. G. Holm, A. Lain, D. J. Palermo, S. Ramaswamy, and E. Su. An Overview of the PARADIGM Compiler for Distributed-Memory Multicomputers. to appear in *IEEE Computer*, 1995.
3. R. Bixby, K. Kennedy, and U. Kremer. Automatic Data Layout Using 0-1 Integer Programming. In *Proc. of the 1994 Int'l Conf. on Parallel Archs. and Compilation Techniques*, pages 111–122, Montréal, Canada, Aug. 1994.
4. B. Chapman, T. Fahringer, and H. Zima. Automatic support for data distribution on distributed memory multiprocessor systems. In *Proc. of the 6th Work. on Langs. and Compilers for Parallel Computing*, pages 184–199, Portland, OR, Aug. 1993. Springer-Verlag.

5. S. Chatterjee, J. R. Gilbert, R. Schreiber, and S. H. Teng. Automatic Array Alignment in Data-Parallel Programs. In *Proc. of the 20th ACM SIGPLAN Symp. on Principles of Prog. Langs.*, pages 16–28, Charleston, SC, Jan. 1993.

6. T. Fahringer. *Automatic Performance Prediction for Parallel Programs on Massively Parallel Computers*. PhD thesis, Univ. of Vienna, Vienna, Austria, Sept. 1993. TR93-3.

7. G. Golub and J. M. Ortega. *Scientific Computing: An Introduction with Parallel Computing*. Academic Press, San Diego, CA, 1993.

8. M. Gupta and P. Banerjee. Compile-Time Estimation of Communication Costs on Multi-computers. In *Proc. of the 6th Int'l Parallel Processing Symp.*, pages 470–475, Beverly Hills, CA, Mar. 1992.

9. M. Gupta and P. Banerjee. PARADIGM: A Compiler for Automated Data Partitioning on Multicomputers. In *Proc. of the 7th ACM Int'l Conf. on Supercomputing*, Tokyo, Japan, July 1993.

10. S. Hiranandani, K. Kennedy, and C. Tseng. Compiling Fortran D for MIMD Distributed Memory Machines. *Communications of the ACM*, 35(8):66–80, Aug. 1992.

11. D. E. Hudak and S. G. Abraham. *Compiling Parallel Loops for High Performance Computers – Partitioning, Data Assignment and Remapping*. Kluwer Academic Pub., Boston, MA, 1993.

12. K. Knobe, J. Lukas, and G. Steele Jr. Data Optimization: Allocation of Arrays to Reduce Communication on SIMD Machines. *J. of Parallel and Distributed Computing*, 8(2):102–118, Feb. 1990.

13. B. Krishnamurthy, editor. *Practical Reusable UNIX Software*. John Wiley and Sons Inc., New York, NY, 1995.

14. J. Li and M. Chen. The Data Alignment Phase in Compiling Programs for Distributed-Memory Machines. *J. of Parallel and Distributed Computing*, 13(2):213–221, Oct. 1991.

15. D. J. Palermo, E. Su, J. A. Chandy, and P. Banerjee. Compiler Optimizations for Distributed Memory Multicomputers used in the PARADIGM Compiler. In *Proc. of the 23rd Int'l Conf. on Parallel Processing*, pages II:1–10, St. Charles, IL, Aug. 1994.

16. C. D. Polychronopoulos, M. Girkar, M. R. Haghighat, C. L. Lee, B. Leung, and D. Schouten. Parafrase-2: An Environment for Parallelizing, Partitioning, Synchronizing and Scheduling Programs on Multiprocessors. In *Proc. of the 18th Int'l Conf. on Parallel Processing*, pages II:39–48, St. Charles, IL, Aug. 1989.

17. J. Ramanujam and P. Sadayappan. Compile-time Techniques for Data Distribution in Distributed Memory Machines. *IEEE Trans. on Parallel and Distributed Systems*, 2(4):472–481, Oct. 1991.

18. S. Ramaswamy and P. Banerjee. Automatic Generation of Efficient Array Redistribution Routines for Distributed Memory Multicomputers. In *Frontiers '95: The 5th Symp. on the Frontiers of Massively Parallel Computation*, pages 342–349, McLean, VA, Feb. 1995.

19. T. J. Sheffler, J. R. Gilbert, R. Schreiber, and S. Chatterjee. Aligning Parallel Arrays to Reduce Communication. In *Frontiers '95: The 5th Symp. on the Frontiers of Massively Parallel Computation*, pages 324–331, McLean, VA, 1995.

20. H. Sivaraman and C. S. Raghavendra. Compiling for MIMD Distributed Memory Machines. Tech. Report EECS-94-021, School of Electrical Enginnering and Computer Science, Washington State Univ., Pullman, WA, 1994.

21. P. S. Tseng. Compiling Programs for a Linear Systolic Array. In *Proc. of the ACM SIGPLAN '90 Conf. on Prog. Lang. Design and Implementation*, pages 311–321, White Plains, NY, June 1990.

22. S. Wholey. Automatic Data Mapping for Distributed-Memory Parallel Computers. In *Proc. of the 6th ACM Int'l Conf. on Supercomputing*, pages 25–34, Washington D.C., July 1992.

Data Redistribution
in an Automatic Data Distribution Tool *

Eduard Ayguadé, Jordi Garcia, Mercè Gironès,
M. Luz Grande and Jesús Labarta

Computer Architecture Department, Polytechnic University of Catalunya
cr. Gran Capità s/núm, Mòdul D6, 08071 - Barcelona, Spain

Abstract. Data distribution is one of the key aspects to consider in
a parallelizing environment for Massive Parallel Processors. Automatic
data distribution proposals may be categorized as either static or dynamic, depending on whether the distribution of the arrays is allowed to
change throughout the execution of the program. This paper describes
the features and implementation of the intra-procedural data remapping
module implemented in our automatic data distribution research tool.
The solution to the remapping problem for a sequence of computational
phases consists in selecting a mapping among the possible candidates for
each phase and introduce remapping actions between consecutive phases.
Control flow information is used to identify how phases are sequenced
during the execution of the application.

1 Introduction

Data distribution is one of the key aspects to consider in a parallelizing environment for Massive Parallel Processors. In these systems, data distribution
dramatically affects performance because of the non-uniformity of the memory
system. The cost of accessing a local (or close) memory location can be more
than one order of magnitude lower than the cost of accessing a remote memory
location.

Mapping data into the distributed memory has to be done according to the
access patterns within computational intensive phases and parallelism exploitation out of them. There has been a significant amount of work concerning static
mappings, where the mapping of each array remains fixed along the execution
of the whole program ([LC90], [KLS90], [LC91], [Gup92], [Who92], [CGSS94b],
[AGG+94]). Our work focuses on dynamic mappings in which the mapping of
an array may change over its lifetime. Data remapping is one of the topics in
this area subject of current research ([CP93], [BKK94], [CGSS94a], [PB95]). The
main objective of this work has been to devise an algorithm to automatically
detect points in the code where to realign or redistribute arrays in order to reduce the total data movement and thus improve performance of the application.
Deciding the granularity of the computational phases executed with a static
mapping, and among which remapping may be done is also one of the aspects
to consider.

* This research was partially supported by Convex Computer Corporation, CONVEX
Supercomputers S.A.E, CEPBA (European Center for Parallelism of Barcelona) and
by the Ministry of Education of Spain under contracts TIC-880/92 and TIC-429/95.

[BKK94] considers the profitability of data remapping between computational phases. Each phase has a set of candidate mapping schemes. Selecting a mapping scheme for each phase in the entire program is done by representing the problem with the Data Layout Graph. Each possible mapping for a phase is represented with a node. Edges between two nodes in different phases represent the remapping that has to be carried out to execute each phase with the associated mapping. Nodes and edges have weights representing the overall cost of executing a phase with a mapping and remapping costs respectively, in terms of execution time. The problem is translated into a 0-1 integer programming problem suitable to be solved by a state-of-the-art general purpose integer programming solver.

The FCS system [CP93] considers the problem in the framework of a data distribution tool for Fortran90 source codes. In this scope, array-syntax assignment statements and WHERE masks are examined to determine candidate data mappings. A phase is basically a DO-loop containing array-syntax assignment statements or WHERE masks in its body. It uses a tree-exhaustive algorithm with some heuristics to prune the search space. A Conflict Table storing the conflicts between the mappings of the arrays from one phase to the other is the basis of the remapping algorithm. This table determines which remapping options are worth considering at each transition. From this information, a tree showing all the different alternatives of remapping is built. The aim is to determine the path in the tree with the lowest cost. The full remapping tree can easily grow to intractable proportions.

[CGSS94b] represent the problem as an alignment-distribution graph and use a divide-and-conquer approach to the dynamic mapping problem [CGSS94a]. It initially assigns a static mapping to all the nodes and then recursively divides it into regions which are assigned different mappings. Two regions are merged when the cost of the dynamic mapping is worse than the static mapping taking computation, data movement and remapping costs into account. [PB95] also use a divide-and-conquer approach in which the program is recursively decomposed into a hierarchy of candidate phases. Then, taking into account the cost of remapping between the different phases, the sequence of phases and phase transitions with the lowest cost is selected. It uses [Gup92] to assign mappings to the phases generated.

2 Overview of Our Approach

In this section we outline the major aspects of the intra-procedural remapping module implemented in DDT and introduce the working example that is used along the paper. For this example and for simplicity, we only consider one-dimensional distributions; the algorithm in Section 3 deals with the general case.

The intra-procedural data remapping module groups, for each routine, the statements in the original source code into a collection of phases. A phase is either the outermost non-iterative loop in a nest or a call to a routine. For each phase, a set of candidate mappings is obtained for it: if the phase is a loop nest, the candidate mappings are obtained by performing an analysis of reference patterns within the nest; if the phase is a call, the candidate mappings are imported from the DDT inter-procedural database. The inter-procedural analysis module of DDT is based on the call graph for the entire program. In a bottom-up pass over it, each routine is analyzed when all the routines called by it have already been processed. From an analysis of compatibility between the candidate mappings of the different phases, a set of candidate mappings are generated for the whole routine and stored in the inter-procedural database. Details about the inter-procedural data mapping module are described elsewhere [AGG+95].

2.1 An Example: Alternate Direction Implicit

In this section we introduce the Alternating Direction Implicit (ADI) integration kernel to show the main features of the DDT intra-procedural data remapping module. The source code of ADI defines a two-dimensional data space of size 256 in each dimension; it has a sequence of loops that initialize the data space followed by an iterative loop that performs the computation. In each iteration of this loop, forward and backward sweeps along rows and columns are done in sequence. The source code is shown in Figure 1 for completeness. DDT identifies 9 phases in this program. Each phase corresponds to one of the nested loops (labeled from 1 to 9) in Figure 1.

DDT evaluates data mappings and parallelization strategies for each phase in the program. For each of them, it estimates the data movement and the computation time costs. From the analysis, a set of candidate solutions is selected. The target machine considered along the example is a NUMA architecture with local and remote accesses. Each processor has its own memory hierarchy and it is connected to other processors through an interconnection network. Data movement costs are estimated as the number of remote accesses multiplied by the remote access time (one microsecond along the paper). Given a parallelization strategy, computation costs are estimated from a profile of the sequential execution on a workstation based on the same processor and with the same memory hierarchy than the target parallel machine.

For instance, after analyzing phase 4 the two candidate solutions shown in Table 1 could be selected. For each solution we have the mapping for the arrays used in the phase (second column) and the associated parallelization strategy (fourth column). For each of them, an estimate of the data movement costs is performed by matching reference patterns within the phase with a predefined set of data movement patterns. The third column in the same table shows the data movement cost estimated by DDT; this estimation for phase 4 reflects the cost of two shift-like data movements in the second dimension needed to perform the remote accesses to arrays x and b. According to the data dependences in this loop and the parallelization strategy, the computation time for the phase is estimated (fifth column assuming 16 processors along the example).

Once the candidate mappings for each phase are obtained, an algorithm to check their compatibility is used. We say that the mappings of an array in two different phases are compatible when no data movement has to be performed when sequencing from one phase to the other. For instance, consider the sequence

```
      program adi
        double precision x(256,256)
        double precision a(256,256), b(256,256)

        do 1 i = 1,  256                                    Phase 1
          a(i, 1) = 0.0
          b(i, 1) = 3.0
          x(i, 1) = 4.0
   1    continue
        do 2 j = 2, 255                                     Phase 2
          do 2 i = 1,  256
            a(i, j) = 1.0
            b(i, j) = 3.0
            x(i, j) = 5.0
   2    continue
        do 3 i = 1,  256                                    Phase 3
          a(i, 256 ) = 1.0
          b(i, 256 ) = 3.0
          x(i, 256 ) = 4.0
   3    continue
        do 10 iter = 1, 10
C ADI forward & backward sweeps along rows
        do 4 j = 2,   256                                   Phase 4
          do 4 i = 1,  256
            x(i, j) = x(i, j) - x(i, j - 1) * a(i, j) / b(i, j - 1)
            b(i, j) = b(i, j) - a(i, j) * a(i, j) / b(i, j - 1)
   4    continue
        do 5 i = 1,  256                                    Phase 5
          x(i, 256 ) = x(i, 256 ) / b(i, 256 )
   5    continue
        do 6 j = 255 , 1, -1                                Phase 6
          do 6 i = 1,  256
            x(i, j) = (x(i, j) - a(i, j + 1) * x(i, j + 1)) / b(i, j)
   6    continue
C ADI forward & backward sweeps along columns
        do 7 j = 1,  256                                    Phase 7
          do 7 i = 2,  256
            x(i, j) = x(i, j) - x(i - 1, j) * a(i, j) / b(i - 1, j)
            b(i, j) = b(i, j) - a(i, j) * a(i, j) / b(i - 1, j)
   7    continue
        do 8 j = 1,  256                                    Phase 8
          x(256 , j) = x(256 , j) / b(256 , j)
   8    continue
        do 9 j = 1,  256                                    Phase 9
          do 9 i = 255 , 1, -1
            x(i, j) = (x(i, j) - a(i + 1, j) * x(i + 1, j)) / b(i, j)
   9    continue
  10    continue
        end
```

Fig. 1. Source code for ADI.

	Mapping	Movement Cost	Loop Parallelization	Computation Cost
Solution 1	a(BLOCK,*) b(BLOCK,*) x(BLOCK,*)	0	dopar 4 i=1,256 do 4 j=1,256	0.0493
Solution 2	a(*,BLOCK) b(*,BLOCK) x(*,BLOCK)	0.000768	do 4 j=1,256 do 4 i=1,256	0.7264

Table 1. Data mapping alternatives and associated parallelization strategies with their respective costs in terms of data movement and computation time. t is the template used to specify the alignment of arrays.

{4, 5, 6} of phases. From the source code in Figure 1, one can see that these three phases have the same best mapping $(BLOCK, *)$ and loop parallelization strategy (execute the i loop in parallel). Similarly, one can conclude that the best mapping for each phase in the sequence {7, 8, 9} is $(*, BLOCK)$ and the parallelization of the j loop. Table 2 shows the costs of the different candidate mappings for the phases within the iterative loop *do iter*.

Phase	Solution 1 Movement	Solution 1 Computation	Solution 2 Movement	Solution 2 Computation
4	0	0.049302	0.000768	0.726395
5	0	0	0	0
6	0	0.023155	0.000512	0.370482
7	0.000768	0.620246	0	0.038765
8	0	0.049302	0	0
9	0.000512	0.330937	0	0.020684

Table 2. Costs for the different data mapping alternatives and associated parallelization strategies for each phase in the program.

In conclusion, the solutions for the two subsequences of phases are not compatible in their mapping and parallelization strategies. Three different alternatives are evaluated by DDT:

- Assign Solution 1 to all the phases. In this case the cost per iteration is 1.024 and estimated cost for the outer iterative loop 10.24.
- Assign Solution 2 to all the phases. In this case the cost per iteration is 1.157 and the estimated cost for the outer iterative loop 11.57.
- Assign the preferred solution to each phase. In this case we have to remap the arrays between incompatible phases. In particular, arrays a, b and x have to be remapped from row to column distribution before the execution of phase 7, with an approximated cost of $(256 * 256)/16$ array elements each. This remapping action is performed 10 times during the execution of the iterative loop. Due to the same loop, after executing phase 9 phase 4 is executed again. So we have to consider the compatibility between these two phases and the possible remapping costs if their mappings are not compatible. In particular, arrays a, b and x have to be remapped from column to row distribution before the execution of phase 4, with the same approximated cost. However, this remapping action is performed 9 times (since in the last iteration of the iterative loop forces the execution to exit it). The total cost for this sequence of phases within the iterative loop is estimated as:

$$(0.131906 + 3 * 0.004096) * 10 + (3 * 0.004096) * 9) = 1.552,$$

which is lower than the cost of the two previous alternatives.

3 Intra-procedural Remapping Algorithm

In this section we describe the implementation of the algorithm that performs the intra-procedural data remapping. For the sake of clarity we consider the problem when the application is composed of a single module (main program). The presence of routine calls is described elsewhere [AGG+95]. In this section we also consider that a simple control flow between phases exists (phases are executed lexicographically). Section 4 describes the main control-flow structures considered and how they modify the functionality of the main algorithm. An outline of the remapping algorithm is shown in Figure 2.

```
1. phases_list = Identify_Phases (routine_id);
   phase_id = First_Phase(phases_list);
2. while (phase_id != NIL ) {
       Generate_Local_Mappings (phase_id);
       phase_id = Next_Phase (phases_list, phase_id);
       }
   phase_id = First_Phase (phase_list);
3. if (phase_id != NIL) {
       local_M = First_Mapping (phase_id);
       while (local_M != NIL ) {
           combinations_list = Analyze_Compatibility (global_M, local_M);
           combination = First_Combination (combinations_list);
           while (combination != NIL) {
           global_M = Compute_Cost (global_M, local_M, combination);
           phase_id = Next_Phase (phases_list, phase_id);
           recursively go to 3;
           combination = Next_Combination (combinations_list, combination));
           }
       local_M = Next_Mapping (phase_id, local_M);
       }
   }
```

Fig. 2. Intra-procedural remapping algorithm.

3.1 Identification of Phases and Generation of Candidate Solutions

Function *Identify_Phases* tags each loop in the main data structure of DDT as phase or not according to the following definition of phase by [BKK94]:

"A phase is a loop nest such that for each induction variable occurring in a subscript position of an array reference in the loop body, the phase contains the surrounding loop that defines the induction variable."

This function analyzes the internal structure of DDT where loop information is stored. If any of the loop control or induction variables is used to subscript arrays in the loop body, the loop is tagged as a candidate for phase. Once tagged, all those outermost loops that have been tagged as candidates are included in the list of phases *phases_list*.

Once phases are identified, procedure *Generate_Local_Mappings* generates a set of candidate local mappings for each one and stores them in the DDT internal data structure. The types of mappings currently handled by DDT include inter- (permutations and embeddings) and intra-dimensional (shift) alignments and

BLOCK and CYCLIC distributions. In the process of mapping generation, it is important to keep suboptimal solutions in the list of candidate mappings because sometimes it is better to execute a phase with one of them instead of the optimal one. In fact, a solution for a phase is better than another when not only its cost is smaller but also the remapping cost to execute it with the associated mapping. Each of the local mappings specifies only the relative alignment and distribution between the variables referenced within the phase, but not an absolute alignment over a global virtual target array for the application.

More details about the implementation of this procedure within DDT can be found elsewhere [AGG+94].

3.2 Compatibility Between Phases

In progressing from one phase to another, we are faced with the problem of deciding which arrays are remapped and which ones are kept with the same mapping. Assume a sequence of phases $\{p_0, p_1, ..., p_i, ..., p_{n-1}\}$. Each phase p_i has an associated set of n_i candidate local mappings $LM_i^{1..n_i}$. In addition to the local mappings, we have a global mapping GM_i specifying the reaching mapping of all the arrays that have been used until phase p_{i-1} with respect to a global virtual target array. Three different alternatives could be considered when analyzing any phase p_i with a given local mapping LM_i^k with respect to the global mapping GM_i:

- To remap all the arrays for which LM_i^k conflicts with GM_i.
- To remap some of the arrays for which LM_i^k conflicts with GM_i.
- Do not remap any of the arrays in phase p_i.

The philosophy behind the first alternative is that each phase should be executed with its preferred local mapping and so data should be remapped if necessary before executing the phase. The cost is estimated as the cost of executing phase p_i with LM_i^k plus the cost of remapping. In the second alternative, some of the arrays are not remapped and as a consequence the phase is not executed with the preferred mapping. In addition to the cost of remapping some arrays, the cost of executing phase p_i with a non-optimal $LM_i^{k'}$ should be evaluated. In the third alternative, the assumption is that it is not worth trying to adapt to the preferred mapping of an phase, and thus the cost of executing phase p_i with mapping GM_i has to be evaluated. The second alternative has not been considered in the implementation since the search space can easily grow to intractable proportions. This alternative is considered by [CP93], and they realize this problem. One heuristic they propose is to cut the search space by limiting the number of arrays that can be simultaneously remapped between two phases.

When trying to adapt the actual global mapping GM_i to a solution LM_i^k in phase p_i, one of the following actions will take place for each array used in p_i:

- If the array is not included in GM_i, this means that it has not yet been used in the previous phases and it is not included in the initial global mapping GM_0. Therefore, this array can be included in GM_i with any desirable mapping, as it will be assumed the initial one.

- If the array is included in GM_i, and the mapping for it in GM_i and LM_i^k differs either in the number of distributed dimensions or in the dimensions actually distributed, then the array should be redistributed.
- If the array is already included in GM_i, and its mapping in GM_i has the same distributed dimensions than in LM_i^k (no matter is they are transposed or not), then the array is candidate to be realigned. If only one array fits in this case, then no realignment is necessary. Realignment is only necessary when two or more candidate arrays in the LM_i^k need a different permutation of their distributed dimensions to fit into the GM_i. In this case, we propose to keep one of them by turn in the GM_i, and realign the rest, in order to maintain the relative alignment that is specified in the LM_i^k. All these solutions are generated recursively and the algorithm proceeds with the next phase.

In the current implementation, the initial global mapping GM_0 is considered empty; however it could be possible to initialize it with either a mapping specified by the user in the source code or a mapping inherited from a caller routine.

The algorithm in Figure 2 performs a recursive exploration of all different alternatives of candidate solutions $LM_i^{1..n_i}$ for each phase $p_{0..n-1}$ and remapping alternatives between each LM_i^k and GM_i. The actual algorithm reduces the search space based on the cost of the different combinations of all these alternatives. Once we know the cost for a complete sequence of phases (combination), we can decide to leave the exploration of another (complete or incomplete) combination if we detect that its current cost is worse than the cost of a previous one.

Remapping costs are estimated by DDT from the specification of the global GM_i and a local mapping LM_i^k. Details about the implementation of function $Compute\_Cost$ in Figure 2 can be found elsewhere [AGG+95].

We will devote the rest of this section in describing a practical example where the previous algorithm is applied. Consider a fictitious subroutine with the initial mapping and local mappings shown in Figure 3 (specified in HPF and assuming 16 processors). In the example we assume that there exists a single candidate mapping for each phase.

The initial mapping for arrays A, B, and C defines the global mapping GM_0. This information is stored internally as shown below:

$$GM_0 : \quad \begin{array}{c|c|c|c} A & 1_{B(4)} & 2_{B(4)} & 3_* \\ \hline B & 1_{B(4)} & 2_{B(4)} & - \\ \hline C & 2_{B(4)} & 1_{B(4)} & 3_* \end{array}$$

The first row reflects that the first and second dimensions of array A are block distributed with 4 processors allocated to each one. In addition, there is a perfect alignment between the dimensions of array A and the dimensions of the virtual global template (each column of the table represents a dimension of the template). All the dimensions of array B are distributed with the same alignment than array A, and some dimensions of array C are transposed with respect to the ones of the template.

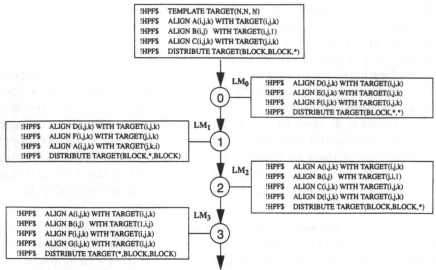

Fig. 3. Initial and local mappings for a synthetic sequence of phases.

From the specification of the mapping for phase p_0 shown in Figure 3, we have the following local mapping LM_0:

$$LM_0 : \begin{array}{|c|c|c|c|} \hline D & 1_{B(16)} & 2_* & 3_* \\ \hline E & 1_{B(16)} & 2_* & 3_* \\ \hline F & 1_{B(16)} & 2_* & 3_* \\ \hline \end{array}$$

Note that these three arrays are not included in GM_0, and therefore they can be directly included in GM_1:

$$GM_1 : \begin{array}{|c|c|c|c|} \hline A & 1_{B(4)} & 2_{B(4)} & 3_* \\ \hline B & 1_{B(4)} & 2_{B(4)} & - \\ \hline C & 2_{B(4)} & 1_{B(4)} & 3_* \\ \hline D & 1_{B(16)} & 2_* & 3_* \\ \hline E & 1_{B(16)} & 2_* & 3_* \\ \hline F & 1_{B(16)} & 2_* & 3_* \\ \hline \end{array}$$

The algorithm proceeds with phase p_1, whose local mapping is:

$$LM_1 : \begin{array}{|c|c|c|c|} \hline D & 1_{B(4)} & 2_* & 3_{B(4)} \\ \hline F & 2_{B(4)} & 1_* & 3_{B(4)} \\ \hline A & 2_{B(4)} & 3_* & 1_{B(4)} \\ \hline \end{array}$$

If we compare this mapping with the actual global mapping GM_1, we can see that we have to redistribute arrays D and F, since the number of distributed dimensions in LM_1 and GM_1 is different. Notice that the distributed dimensions for array A in both mappings are the same, but transposed. So array A is candidate to be realigned. However, since it is the only array that is candidate to realignment, it is not necessary to perform it because there are no conflicts with any other array in the global mapping. This is possible because LM_1 can be transposed, and the relative alignment of arrays D and F with respect to array A remains the same. So the insertion of arrays D and F into GM_2 must only keep their relative alignment with array A as indicated by LM_1 and thus it has to be transposed with respect to the global virtual target. Now the global mapping for the next phase is:

$$GM_2:$$

A	$1_{B(4)}$	$2_{B(4)}$	3_*
B	$1_{B(4)}$	$2_{B(4)}$	-
C	$2_{B(4)}$	$1_{B(4)}$	3_*
D	$3_{B(4)}$	$1_{B(4)}$	2_*
E	$1_{B(16)}$	2_*	3_*
F	$3_{B(4)}$	$2_{B(4)}$	1_*

Next we consider phase p_2, whose local mapping is shown below:

$$LM_2:$$

A	$1_{B(4)}$	$2_{B(4)}$	3_*
B	$2_{B(4)}$	$1_{B(4)}$	-
C	$1_{B(4)}$	$2_{B(4)}$	3_*
D	$1_{B(4)}$	$2_{B(4)}$	3_*

If we compare this local mapping with the actual global one, we can see that array D has to be redistributed since it has the same number of distributed dimensions but they are different, and that arrays A, B, and C are candidate to be realigned since the distributed dimensions are the same. Now with all the candidates, we have to decide which arrays will effectively be realigned. Since arrays B and C have the same relative alignment in both GM_2 and LM_2, two different alternatives can be considered:

 − To keep array A as it is in GM_2 and transpose arrays B and C according to LM_2.
 − To keep arrays B and C as they are in GM_2 and transpose array A according to LM_2.

Although at first sight it seems less expensive to only transpose array A, it is possible that the other alternative leads to a lower overall cost for the whole sequence of phases. So let us explore the two alternatives in turn.

In the first alternative, when we keep array A with the same alignment and transpose arrays B and C, then we obtain the following global mapping:

$$GM_3:$$

A	$1_{B(4)}$	$2_{B(4)}$	3_*
B	$2_{B(4)}$	$1_{B(4)}$	-
C	$1_{B(4)}$	$2_{B(4)}$	3_*
D	$1_{B(4)}$	$2_{B(4)}$	3_*
E	$1_{B(16)}$	2_*	3_*
F	$3_{B(4)}$	$2_{B(4)}$	1_*

If we compare this mapping to the local mapping for the last phase p_3:

$$LM_3:$$

A	1_*	$2_{B(4)}$	$3_{B(4)}$
B	-	$1_{B(4)}$	$2_{B(4)}$
F	1_*	$2_{B(4)}$	$3_{B(4)}$
G	1_*	$2_{B(4)}$	$3_{B(4)}$

we find that array A has to be redistributed, and arrays B and F are candidate to realignment. Since array G is new, it will be included in the global mapping according to the local mapping LM_3. The relative alignment of arrays B and F in the LM_3 and GM_3 is the same, so we conclude that they do not have to be realigned. So in this case, the final global mapping is

$$GM_4 :$$

A	$3_{B(4)}$	$2_{B(4)}$	1_*
B	$2_{B(4)}$	$1_{B(4)}$	-
C	$1_{B(4)}$	$2_{B(4)}$	3_*
D	$1_{B(4)}$	$2_{B(4)}$	3_*
E	$1_{B(16)}$	2_*	3_*
F	$3_{B(4)}$	$2_{B(4)}$	1_*
G	$3_{B(4)}$	$2_{B(4)}$	1_*

In conclusion, this solution leads to four redistributions and two realignments along the execution of the sequence of phases.

In the second alternative of phase 2, when we keep the alignment specified in the global mapping for arrays B and C, then we obtain the following GM_3

$$GM_3 :$$

A	$2_{B(4)}$	$1_{B(4)}$	3_*
B	$1_{B(4)}$	$2_{B(4)}$	-
C	$2_{B(4)}$	$1_{B(4)}$	3_*
D	$2_{B(4)}$	$1_{B(4)}$	3_*
E	$1_{B(16)}$	2_*	3_*
F	$3_{B(4)}$	$2_{B(4)}$	1_*

If we compare this mapping with the local mapping LM_3 shown before, we can see that array A has to be redistributed and arrays B and F are candidate to realignment. Since array G is new, it will be included in the global mapping according to the local mapping LM_3. Notice that only one of the two arrays has to be realigned. So for instance, if we realign array B then we obtain the same final global mapping GM_4 shown before. In conclusion, in this case we have performed 4 redistributions and two realignments. Notice that although one of the alternatives was locally worst, the cost of the whole sequence of phases has become similar in terms of number of redistributions and realignments.

4 Control Flow

In this section we describe the aspects that have to be considered when control statements (like conditional or iterative statements) appear in the source code. These statements provoke a sequencing of the phases in the program different than the lexicographical order. In this section we present how the algorithm in Figure 2 is used when these statements appear.

The phase control flow graph is built for each routine and main program analyzed. In this graph, nodes represent phases and edges link nodes when there is a flow of control between the associated phases. There are other nodes that represent statements in the source code that provoke changes in the flow of phases. From the information in the control flow graph, the different sequences of phases that might appear during the execution of a routine are generated. For each sequence, the same algorithm described in the previous section is applied.

In the rest of this section we detail how iterative loops and conditional statements are handled by DDT and how they influence the generation of sequences of phases. Other control flow structures, such as entry points and multiple exits are also handled by DDT but not explained in this paper.

4.1 Outer Loops

Phases might be included within loops whose loop control variable or induction variables generated by it are not used to subscript arrays. In this case control flow indicates that after executing the last phase inside the loop, the first phase inside it will be executed again.

For instance, Figure 4.a shows the control-flow graph between the phases that appear in the ADI program shown in Figure 1. Notice that compatibility has to be analyzed between phases $\{9, 4\}$ since there is a flow of control due to the outer *do iter* loop.

When outer iterative loops are found in the source code, DDT generates a sequence of phases that try to resemble what happens during the actual execution. As shown in Figure 4.c, DDT repeats twice the phases in the body of the outer loop. Phases $\{4, 5, 6, 7, 8, 9\}$ are assumed to be executed once but phases $\{4', 5', 6', 7', 8', 9'\}$ are assumed to be executed N-1 times, where N is the number of times the outer loop is executed. Notice that now, possible remapping between phases $\{3, 4\}$ is accounted once, remapping between any pair of phases within the loop body is accounted N, and remapping between phases $\{9, 4'\}$ is accounted N-1. The algorithm ensures that the same solution is selected for each pair of phases p_i and p_i'.

If the loop only contains a phase, then it is not necessary to duplicate the phase, since remapping between a phase and itself will never occur.

In our running example (ADI), DDT would choose a dynamic data layout that is changed twice at every iteration of the iterative loop. An outline of the solution generated by DDT is shown in Figure 4.b.

4.2 Conditional Statements

Conditional statements generate alternative sequences of phases that are executed depending on the condition evaluated in the statement. The probability of taking one of the alternative branches is used to compute the probability of each sequence of phases.

The different sequences are analyzed iteratively, starting from the most probable one. Since sequences may have phases in common, different solutions may be suggested for a given phase in different sequences. The algorithm we propose ensures that each phase is always executed with the same solution. To ensure that, the solution for a phase is chosen in the first sequence it appears (i.e. the most probable sequence where the phase is used). Other less probable sequences where the same phase appears have the solution for the phase fixed.

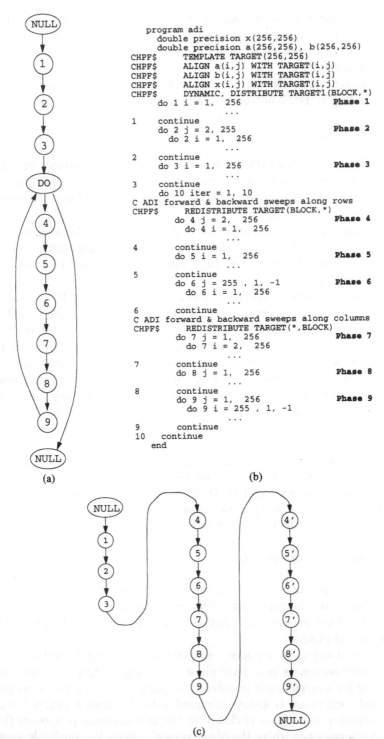

```
     program adi
        double precision x(256,256)
        double precision a(256,256), b(256,256)
CHPF$     TEMPLATE TARGET(256,256)
CHPF$     ALIGN a(i,j) WITH TARGET(i,j)
CHPF$     ALIGN b(i,j) WITH TARGET(i,j)
CHPF$     ALIGN x(i,j) WITH TARGET(i,j)
CHPF$     DYNAMIC, DISTRIBUTE TARGET1(BLOCK,*)
        do 1 i = 1,  256                        Phase 1
           ...
1       continue
        do 2 j = 2, 255                         Phase 2
          do 2 i = 1,  256
           ...
2       continue
        do 3 i = 1,  256                        Phase 3
           ...
3       continue
        do 10 iter = 1, 10
C ADI forward & backward sweeps along rows
CHPF$     REDISTRIBUTE TARGET(BLOCK,*)
        do 4 j = 2,  256                        Phase 4
          do 4 i = 1,  256
           ...
4       continue
        do 5 i = 1,  256                        Phase 5
           ...
5       continue
        do 6 j = 255 , 1, -1                    Phase 6
          do 6 i = 1,  256
           ...
6       continue
C ADI forward & backward sweeps along columns
CHPF$     REDISTRIBUTE TARGET(*,BLOCK)
        do 7 j = 1,  256                        Phase 7
          do 7 i = 2,  256
           ...
7       continue
        do 8 j = 1,  256                        Phase 8
           ...
8       continue
        do 9 j = 1,  256                        Phase 9
          do 9 i = 255 , 1, -1
           ...
9       continue
10      continue
        end
```

(a)   (b)

(c)

Fig. 4. (a) Control-flow graph for ADI. (b) Source code for ADI with directives specifying mapping and remapping of arrays. (c) Sequence of phases analyzed by DDT.

To illustrate this aspect, we analyze the main program in the SPEC swm256 benchmark. As shown in Figure 5.a, there is a conditional statement in the main program that selects either the execution of one phase (call to *calc3*) or the execution of another one (call to *calc3z*). The control flow (Figure 5.b) for the main program generates two sequences of phases. In this case, if the *then* path has less probability than the *else* path, then compatibility will be first analyzed for phases $\{1, 2, 3, 5\}$. From this analysis, a solution among the possible candidate ones is selected for each phase in the sequence. Once selected, compatibility between phases on the other sequence $\{1, 2, 3, 4\}$ is analyzed and as a result, the mapping for phase 4 is selected according to the previously fixed mappings for phases 1, 2 and 3.

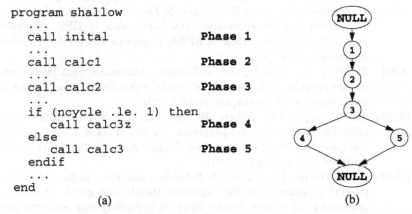

```
      program shallow
      ...
         call inital          Phase 1
      ...
         call calc1           Phase 2
      ...
         call calc2           Phase 3
      ...
         if (ncycle .le. 1) then
            call calc3z        Phase 4
         else
            call calc3         Phase 5
         endif
      ...
      end
            (a)                              (b)
```

Fig. 5. (a) Outline of the main program in the SPEC swm256 benchmark. (b) Control-flow graph.

5 Conclusions and Remarks

In this paper we have presented one of the key modules in our automatic data distribution tool (DDT). This module detects computational phases in the source Fortran77 code and selects data mappings and parallelization strategies for them with the aim of improving the performance of the application by reducing data movement and computation costs.

DDT generates both static and dynamic HPF data distributions for a given Fortran 77 routine and for a whole application with inter-procedural analysis. In the static solutions, the mapping (alignment and distribution) of each array in the program does not change during the execution. Dynamic solutions include executable statements in the source code that change the mapping of specific arrays when necessary. DDT performs a cost analysis of profitability in order to include them. The algorithm explores a rich set of combinations although it is not exhaustive. It includes mechanisms to cut down the search space so that the quality of the solutions generated depends on how far the algorithm goes into this space.

We are currently working on the porting of this technology to generate efficient code for hierarchical Global Shared Memory architectures. In these architectures a number of CPUs can simultaneously access data anywhere in the system. However, the non-uniformity of the memory accesses is still an important issue to consider and may require an appropriate mapping of data in the non-uniform memory in order to achieve performance. The remapping algorithm presented can be used to track data movement during program execution and thus parallelize loops with higher locality of references.

References

[AGG+94] E. Ayguadé, J. Garcia, M. Gironès, J. Labarta, and M. Valero. Detecting and using affinity in an automatic data distribution tool. In *7th Workshop on Languages and Compilers for Parallel Computing*, August 1994.

[AGG+95] E. Ayguadé, J. Garcia, M. Gironès, M.Luz Grande, and J. Labarta. DDT: A research tool for automatic data distribution in HPF. Technical Report UPC-CEPBA-1995-20, CEPBA European Center for Parallelism of Barcelona, April 1995.

[BKK94] R. Bixby, K. Kennedy, and U. Kremer. Automatic data layout using 0-1 integer programming. In *International Conference on Parallel Architectures and Compilation Techniques*, August 1994.

[CGSS94a] S. Chatterjee, J.R. Gilbert, R. Schreiber, and T.J. Sheffler. Array distribution in data parallel programs. In *7th Workshop on Languages and Compilers for Parallel Computing, Lecture Notes in Computer Science 892*. Springer-Verlag, August 1994.

[CGSS94b] S. Chatterjee, J.R. Gilbert, R. Schreiber, and T.J. Sheffler. Modeling data-parallel programs with the alignment-distribution graph. *Journal of Programming Languages, Special issue on compiling and run-time issues for distributed address space machines*, (2), 1994.

[CP93] P. Crooks and R.H. Perrot. An automatic data distribution generator for distributed memory mimd machines. In *4th Workshop on Compilers for Parallel Computers*, December 1993.

[Gup92] M. Gupta. *Automatic Data Partitioning on Distributed Memory Multicomputers*. PhD thesis, Center for Reliable and High-Performance Computing, University of Illinois at Urbana-Champaign, 1992.

[KLS90] K. Knobe, J.D. Lukas, and G.L. Steele. Dataoptimization: Allocation of arrays to reduce communication on SIMD machines. *Journal of Parallel and Distributed Computing*, 8, February 1990.

[LC90] J. Li and M. Chen. Index domain alignment: Minimizing cost of cross-referencing between distributed arrays. In *Frontiers90: 3rd Symposium on the Frontiers of Massively Parallel Computation*, October 1990.

[LC91] J. Li and M. Chen. Compiling communication-efficient programs for massively parallel machines. *IEEE Trans. on Parallel and Distributed Systems*, 2(3), July 1991.

[PB95] D.J. Palermo and P. Banerjee. Automatic selection of dynamic data partitioning schemes for distributed-memory multicomputers. In *2nd Workshop on Automatic Data Layout and Performance Prediction, Center for Research on Parallel Computing Research Report CRPC-TR95548*. Rice University, April 1995.

[Who92] S. Wholey. Automatic data mapping for distributed-memory parallel computers. In *ACM International Conference on Supercomputing*, July 1992.

General Purpose Optimization Technology

Thomas Cheatham*
Amr Fahmy**
Dan C. Stefanescu*
Aiken Computation Laboratory
Harvard University
33 Oxford St, Cambridge MA 02138
Email:cheatham, amr, dan@das.harvard.edu

Abstract

A necessary condition for the establishment, on a substantial basis, of a parallel software industry would appear to be the availability of technology for generating transportable software, i.e. architecture independent software which delivers scalable performance for a wide variety of applications on a wide range of multiprocessor computers. We are in the process of developing H-BSP – a general purpose parallel computing environment for developing transportable algorithms. H-BSP is based on the Bulk Synchronous Parallel Model (BSP), in which a computation involves a number of supersteps, each having several parallel computational threads that synchronize at the end of the superstep. The BSP Model deals explicitly with the notion of communication among computational threads and introduces parameters g and L that quantify the ratio of communication throughput to computation throughput, and the synchronization period, respectively. These two parameters, together with the number of processors and the problem size, are used to quantify the performance and, therefore, the transportability of given classes of algorithms across machines having different values for these parameters. Recently algorithm designers have developed algorithms for a number of regular problems that are provably optimal as functions of g and L, but for many irregular problems developing optimal solutions will depend on the compiler and the run-time system taking advantage of the g and L values for the intended target. This paper describes the unbundled compiler technology and, particularly, the optimization technology it provides, that facilitates the development of such a parallel computer environment.

* Research supported in part by ARPA Contract Nr. F19628-92-C-0113.
** Research supported in part by ARPA Contract Nr. F19628-92-C-0113 and a grant from the National Science Foundation, NSF-CDA-9308833

1 Introduction

For a parallel software industry to establish itself on a substantial scale a necessary condition would appear to be that the problem of creating transportable software be solved. A solution to this problem has to encompass two vital issues: it has to accommodate a variety of high level programming styles as is found essential in sequential computing, and it has to offer a technology for compiling programs efficiently onto parallel machines as these continue to evolve. Three aspects of parallelism need to be addressed. One is that of providing a computational model to serve as an alternative to the von Neumann Model that has served us so well in transportability with sequential computations. Another is developing programming language constructs that are appropriate for hosting parallel computations. The final one is developing compilers that produce highly efficient code appropriate for a variety of parallel target architectures.

We propose to address these issues as part of a solution to this problem that takes the view that standardization sufficient to ensure success is unlikely to be achieved at either the language or the architecture level, but does appear to be feasible at the level that the von Neumann model plays in sequential computation, one that is intermediate between language and architecture, and tolerates broad variations in both.

Our proposed solution is based on the Bulk Synchronous Parallel Model (the BSP model for short) ([25, 13]), in which a computation involves a number of *supersteps*, each having several parallel computational threads that synchronize at the end of the superstep. The BSP Model deals explicitly with the notion of communication among computational threads and introduces parameters g and L that quantify the ratio of computational throughput to communication throughput, and the synchronization period, respectively. These parameters, together with the number of processors and the problem size, are used to quantify the performance and, therefore, the transportability of a given class of algorithms. In order to produce efficient code that is transportable to a variety of machines, programmers working in this framework may make explicit how the execution of the program should depend on these parameters. In other respects, the programming style supported may be more or less conventional.

This paper describes H-BSP (see Figure 1) – a proposed general purpose parallel computing environment for transportable software which subscribes to the BSP Model and consists of:

- BSP-L, an experimental higher level programming language, that serves as a testbed for linguistic constructs appropriate to transportable programs, and whose constructs will be usable for extending parallel Fortran, C or other higher level parallel programming languages.
- A collection of compiler tools (optimizers, code generators, etc.) which, based on the parameters of the computational model, will generate efficient code for a large range of parallel computers([4, 24, 7]).

– A collection of library operations for communication and synchronization
appropriate for a BSP runtime system.

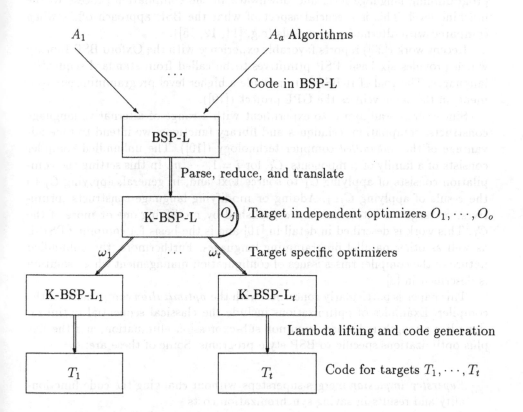

Fig. 1. A schematic diagram for H-BSP.

For a number of significant computational problems algorithms can be found
that are provably efficient on the BSP model for specified ranges of the parameters of the model ([13, 25, 3]). For many other algorithms such static analysis may
not be feasible because the communication requirements are less predictable. In
these cases simulations will be needed ([23]) to determine the algorithms' behavior over a range of parameter values. The efficiency of the algorithms not
optimized for the BSP model by the programmer will depend upon the BSP-
style optimizations provided by the compiler. We note that in the special case
that communication and computation are well balanced in the machine, i.e. g
is close to 1, compilation techniques for simulating shared memory models with
provable efficiency are known([25, 26]). While these techniques may be used as
a default for machines with large values of g, one expects that in many cases

better performance can be achieved by explicit use of the parameters by either the programmer or the compiler.

Transportability among machines with widely different values of p, g and L appears to necessitate that these parameters permeate both upwards to the programming language level and downward in the compilation process to the machine level. This is a crucial aspect of what the BSP approach offers when compared with alternative proposals (e.g. [11, 12, 15]).

Recent work ([20]) reports favorable experience with the Oxford BSP Library which provides six basic BSP primitives to be called from standard sequential languages. The goal of H-BSP is to provide a higher level programming environment, in the same vein as the GPL project ([19]).

Since our overall aim is to experiment with a range of alternative language constructs, compilation techniques and library functions, we intend to take advantage of the *unbundled* compiler technology ([10]). The unbundled compiler consists of a family of components, C_i, for $i = 1, \cdots, m$. In this setting the compilation consists of applying C_1 to source text and, in general, applying C_j to the result of applying C_{j-1}. Adding or modifying language constructs, primitives, or target architectures is accomplished by modifying one or more of the C_j. This work is described in detail in [10] and is the basis for compiling BSP-L as well as other parallel programming languages. Furthermore, the unbundled nature of the compiler raises issues of configuration management whose solution is described in [6].

This paper is particularly concerned with the *optimization* components of the compiler. Examples of optimizations include the classical sequential optimizations like strength reduction, common sub-expression elimination, and the like plus optimizations specific to BSP style programs. Some of these are:

- *Superstep implosion* merges supersteps without changing the code functionality and results in saving synchronization costs.
- *Superstep explosion* is an optimization typical for code implementing combining/dispersion operations.
- *Data pre-fetching* is an optimization performed in order to reduce communication costs (by overlapping communication and computation) as well as to improve load balance.
- *Superstep promotion* is a generalization of data pre-fetching and is applied when supersteps can be scheduled earlier than specified in the program and their rescheduling results in a reduction in the number of supersteps.
- The *early put* optimization is applicable when some subset of the elements computed in a superstep are communicated to other processors and this subset can be computed first and shipped out with the result that the communication cost may be covered by the compuation of the elements not in the subset.

The next section identifies several sorts of optimizations we want to perform. The section following sketches the control flow analysis component of the unbundled compiler and the behavior graph produced by that analysis that is central to the optimizer technology. It is followed by a description of one particular optimizer, the "early put" optimizer. We close with a discussion of status and future plans.

2 Optimizations

There has been considerable work done in developing optimizations for parallel target architectures. For example, [15] discusses message aggregation, message pipelining as well as various optimizations of communications. In [14] there is an algorithm for labeling statements with sync ranks which are used in producing optimized programs with less barrier synchronization. Reference [2] gives an algorithm for communication optimization by solving a set of inequalities.

As described in [25, 18] a BSP program is a sequence of supersteps separated by barrier synchronizations. This organization induces a natural dichotomy on the performance evaluation of a BSP program, and, as a result, on the optimization opportunities for BSP programs.

At a first level of abstraction (the BSP level) the cost of a program is given as the sum of the costs of its supersteps. Each superstep cost is defined[3] to be CMP+COMM+L, where:

- CMP is the maximum computation cost for any process assuming a one-level memory
- COMM is the maximum communication and is computed as hg, where h is the maximum number of messages sent or received by any process and g is a machine parameter denoting the ratio of the number of computation steps/communication steps.
- L, a machine parameter, is the barrier synchronization cost.

The next level of abstraction (the sequential level) details the computation cost of CMP in terms of a register/cache/local memory hierarchy model for the respective platform.

This "separation of concerns" view can be extended naturally to optimization opportunities by distinguishing between BSP-style and sequential-style optimizations.

Superstep explosion is an example of a BSP level optimization. This optimization is typical for code implementing dispersing/combining operations. For example, suppose that we want to multiply the arrays A and B and that they reside on the same processor. Then the compiler must generate code to ship certain blocks of A and B to several processors. One possibility is to use straight message sending at a cost of $C_1 = L + mdg$, for messages of size m, which in this case equals $N^2/p^{2/3}$ (see [5] for details of optimal BSP style matrix multiplication). An alternative to this approach is to broadcast using a binary tree in

---

[3] This definition is a slight variant of the ones used in [25, 18, 21].

which case the cost is $C_2 = log_2(d)(L+2mg)$. The compiler can choose which of these codes to generate by comparing C_1 and C_2. For example, if $L/g = 200$, as reported in [21] for one measurement, the compiler will choose code implementing straight message broadcast for the case that $d = p^{1/3} = 8$ and $N \leq 112$. Note that this optimization depends only on the values of g and L for the particular target architecture and thus is a trivial addition to any compiler so long as g and L are exposed.

As another example of a BSP-level optimization, we consider the "early put" optimization that is often appropriate for computations like iterative solution of PDEs. For this computation each processor would have a block of the array for the complete domain that is, for some processor p, pictorially:

Here the inside box contains the elements that a particular processor is to update and the borders contain elements that are the results of updates done by the neighbors to the north, east, south, and west to their bottom row, left column, top row, and right column, respectively, that must be communicated to processor p.

Consider the following code fragment that abstracts a small part of the behavior of a PDE solver (and ignores swapping A and B between updates and the east/west communication):

```
Let r be 10
Let c be 10
Let h be 1.0
Let A: array(<0 .. r + 1, 0 .. c + 1>, real)
Let B: array(<0 .. r + 1, 0 .. c + 1>, real)
While not done
  For i in 1 to r; j in 1 to c do
    A[i, j] <- h +
                0.25 * (B[i - 1, j] + B[i + 1, j] +
                        B[i, j + 1] + B[i, j - 1])
  put(A, <1 .. 1, 1 .. c>, north)
  put(A, <r .. r, 1 .. c>, south)
  get(A, <0 .. 0, 1 .. c>, north)
  get(A, <r + 1 .. r + 1, 1 .. c>, south)
```

The early put optimization is to transform such computations so that we first compute just the array elements that are to be sent out, send them, and then compute the remaining elements. For the above example this is very simple because there are no dependencies among the array elements being computed: We can thus first compute rows 1 and r, send them, and then compute rows 2 to r - 1. In general, however, there may be various dependencies among the array elements being computed and these must be taken into account. Thus this optimization requires an optimizer that can determine whether such dependencies exist.

As an example of sequential-style optimization, consider the block matrix multiplication performed in each processor during the multiplication, for example:

```
For s in 1 to tsize do
  For q in 1 to tsize do
    For r in 1 to tsize do
      CO[s, r] <- CO[s, r] + A[s, q] * B[q, r]
```

Based on the cache size of the sequential platform, the compiler can choose a block size *b* and generate instead the following code:

```
For qq in 1 to tsize step b
  For rr in 1 to tsize step b
    For s in 1 to tsize do
      For q in qq to qq+b-1 do
        For r in rr to rr+b-1 do
          CO[s, r] <- CO[s, r] + A[s, q] * B[q, r]
```

whose use induces a significant enhancement in performance ([28]).

3 Control Flow Analysis and the Behavior Graph

The representation that we use for programs is essentially the Lambda Calculus augmented with constants including data constants like integers and reals. Additionally, is includes function constants like **real-add** that takes two reals and returns their sum, **put** that takes a processor id, some data structure, a specification of a slice of that data structure, and a tag and sends the slice of the data structure and tag to the processor identified, and **cond** that takes a boolean and two values and return the first (second) value if the boolean is true (false). The reason for using kernel terms is their sufficiency and simplicity.

Control flow analysis seeks to determine which abstractions can be in the operator position of each application. The results of flow analysis are represented as a *behavior graph*, a structure that is crucial to the optimization technology to be discussed below.

A behavior graph has nodes that correspond to *flows* of program terms, where by the flow of some term we mean the behavior of that term with respect to some set of abstract values. If t is a program term then Φ_t denotes the flow of t. The arcs of a behavior graph correspond to a $\geq$ relation between flows and the graph fragment $\Phi_t \rightarrow \Phi_u$ is interpreted as $\Phi_t \geq \Phi_u$. For example, if f is bound to $\lambda x.B$ then the behavior graph encodes the relation $\Phi_f \geq \lambda x.B$. If $(f\ 1)$, the application of f to 1 is also a program term, then we can infer that Φ_x can be, among other things, 1, or that its type includes int, or that it may be a candidate for a set of basic induction variables (variables bound to integers and to other members of the set plus or minus an integer), and so on.

The node of the behavior graph corresponding to the primitive p applied to arguments $t_1, \cdots, t_k$ is called a *surrogate* and is denoted $F_p(\Phi_{t_1}, \cdots, \Phi_{t_k})$. Its interpretation depends upon the the particular analysis task being performed. For flow analysis, the set of abstract values that are of interest is the set of all subsets of abstractions that appear in a program term and the only primitives that have interpretations of interest are those, like cond, that can return an abstraction. Details of the control flow analysis and behavior graph construction can be found in [4].

4 Constructing Optimizers

We think of an optimizer as having three components. The first does an analysis of a program term. The second can be thought of as a *solver* — about which we will say more presently — that uses the results of the analysis step to develop annotatations for the program term and its sub-terms. The third transforms the program term to produce an optimized term based on the annotations of its sub-terms. The first step in doing a particular analysis, α, is to determine the set of abstract values that are appropriate for that analysis. These values form a lattice, $\mathcal{L}^\alpha$, in the sense that if $\Phi_t \geq \Phi_u$ and $\Phi_t \geq \Phi_v$ then $\Phi_t \geq \Phi_u \sqcup \Phi_v$ where $\sqcup$ is the join operation for $\mathcal{L}^\alpha$. The second step is to define a function, F_p^α, for each primitive p, that returns the interpretation of $F_p(\Phi_{t_1}, \cdots, \Phi_{t_k})$ appropriate for the analysis α. The third is to define a function, τ^α, such that $\tau^\alpha(\Phi_t)$ returns the set of abstract values that can be reached on all non-cyclic paths through the graph starting at node Φ_t, where the surrogate nodes are interpreted via F_p^α.

The solver that is required for some optimization can range from something that is essentially trivial (as is the case with the example presented below) to something that is quite hard. An example of the latter arises in attempting to determine whether some array subscript is within the appropriate range (so that index checking can be eliminated) and that requires a solver that reasons about conjuncts of linear equalities, disequalities, and inequalities.

5 The Early Put Optimization

One type of optimization that we want to do is to transform loops such as the one mentioned above so that we first compute just the array elements that are to be sent out, send them, and then compute the remaining elements. For the above example this is very simple because there are no dependencies among the array elements being computed. In general, however, there may be various dependencies among the array elements being computed and these must be taken into account.

The analysis component of the early put optimizer determines what dependencies exist that might prohibit the transformation of the loop. The solver component is trivial and the transformation component modifies the program so as to split the loop into two parts, placing the calls on **put** between the two parts.

Some fragments of the behavior graph for the above program are as follows:

$$\Phi_{\mathtt{i}} \rightarrow F_{\mathtt{to}}(\Phi_1, \Phi_r)$$

$$\Phi_{\mathtt{j}} \rightarrow F_{\mathtt{to}}(\Phi_1, \Phi_c)$$

$$\phi_1 \rightarrow \cdots \rightarrow F_{\mathtt{assign-array-element}}(\Phi_{\mathtt{A}}, \Phi_{\mathtt{i}}, \Phi_{\mathtt{j}}, \phi_k)$$

The arc from $\Phi_{\mathtt{i}}$ to $F_{\mathtt{to}}(\Phi_1, \Phi_r)$ indicates that the parameter i takes values in the range $[1, r]$, and similarly for $\Phi_{\mathtt{j}}$. The path from ϕ_1 to the node $F_{\mathtt{assign-array-element}}(\Phi_{\mathtt{A}}, \Phi_{\mathtt{i}}, \Phi_{\mathtt{j}}, \phi_k)$ indicates that the body of the program sets the i, j element of A to whatever is computed by application k, the application for the right hand side of the assignment. Tracing this application reveals no mention of any element of A nor any variable being changed in the loop (other than i and j) and we can therefore conclude that any order of computation of the elements of A is acceptable.

In general, suppose that some computation is organized as follows:

1. *Ds* — zero or more declarations and some *prelude*,
2. *Loop* — a loop that sets elements of one or more arrays $A_1, A_2, \cdots, A_a$,
3. *Puts* — one or more **puts** of slices of the arrays $A_1, A_2, \cdots, A_a$, and
4. *Rest* — the remainder of the computation.

For the above example, the declarations introduce r, c, h, A, and B. The *Rest* is empty, the *Loop* is the **For** i **in** 1 **to** r ... construct and *Puts* is comprised of the two **puts**.

What we want to do is to transform this to a computation in which the *Loop* is split into two loops, the second of which follows the *Puts*.

5.1 The Loop Dependencies

The analysis task that is required in order that the above transformation is valid is to determine that the computation of the values for elements of A_j in *Loop* are independent of $A_1, A_2, \cdots, A_a$, for $j = 1, \cdots, a$ and any other values (except for the loop index values) that may change in the loop[4].

Suppose that the computation in the loop *Loop* is done by the application ϕ_ℓ. We need to determine the sets $\mu = \{v_1, \cdots, v_c\}$, — the arrays whose elements ϕ_ℓ depends on plus the set of variables whose values can be changed in ϕ_ℓ and $As = \{A_1, \cdots, A_k\}$ — the set of arrays whose elements are being set in the loop. If $\mu \cap As$ is not empty, then the transformation is not valid (without some deeper analysis).

A lattice, $\mathcal{L}^{dep}$, that would be appropriate for this dependency analysis would be the set of all subsets of pairs $< t, r >$ where $t \in \{\mu, A\}$ and r is the name of a parameter in the program term being analyzed.

The "tracing" function, τ^{dep} for this analysis is as follows:

- $\tau^{dep}(\varphi) = \{< \mu, v >\}$ if φ is the flow of a variable,
- $\tau^{dep}(\varphi)$ is the result of calling $F_p^{dep}(\Phi_{\mathbf{t}_1}, \cdots, \Phi_{\mathbf{t}_k})$ if φ is the surrogate $F_p(\Phi_{\mathbf{t}_1}, \cdots, \Phi_{\mathbf{t}_k})$, and
- $\tau^{dep}(\varphi)$ returns null otherwise.

Some examples of the functions F_p^{dep} for the surrogates $F_p(\Phi_{\mathbf{t}_1}, \cdots, \Phi_{\mathbf{t}_k})$ are:

- $F_{\mathtt{integer-add}}^{dep}(\varphi_1, \varphi_2)$: Return $\tau^{dep}(\varphi_1) \cup \tau^{dep}(\varphi_2)$.
- $F_{\mathtt{select}}^{dep}(\Phi_{\mathbf{A}}, \varphi_1, \cdots, \varphi_k)$: The primitive **select** returns the element of its first (array) argument indexed by its remaining arguments. Thus $F_{\mathtt{select}}^{dep}(\Phi_{\mathbf{A}}, \varphi_1, \cdots, \varphi_k)$ returns $\{< \mu, a >\} \cup \tau^{dep}(\varphi_1) \cup \cdots \cup \tau(\varphi_k)$, where a names the array referenced.
- $F_{\mathtt{assign-array-element}}^{dep}(\Phi_{\mathbf{A}}, \varphi_1, \cdots, \varphi_k, \varphi)$: The primitive **assign-array-element** assigns the element of its first (array) argument indexed by the next k arguments the value of its final argument. Thus $F_{\mathtt{assign-array-element}}^{dep}(\Phi_{\mathbf{A}}, \varphi_1, \cdots, \varphi_k, \varphi)$ returns $\{< A, a >\} \cup \tau^{dep}(\varphi_1) \cup \cdots \cup \tau(\varphi_k) \cup \tau^{dep}(\varphi)$, where a names the array referenced.

The computation of these sets is done by calling $\tau^{dep}(\phi_\ell)$ and sorting its results into the appropriate of μ and As.

For the example discussed earlier, these sets will be:

$$\mu = \{\mathtt{B}\}$$

$$As = \{\mathtt{A}\}$$

---

[4] Obviously there are dependencies that could be tolerated but for the moment we do not propose to do the deeper analysis required to deal with these.

6 Conclusions

One of the major challenges in parallel computing is the creation, on a substantial scale, of an industry for general purpose parallel software. As a result of intensive efforts, there is now a continuous stream of new parallel computers that provide decreasing price performance ratios. Much work is left to be done, however, before parallel software that is efficient, architecture independent and scalable will be available to fully utilize these machines.

This paper describes an approach to this problem that provides for a variety of high level programming styles and that promises technologies for efficient compilation on a wide variety of existing and evolving machines.

Our tenet is that the optimal area for activity ensuring broad transportability is neither the language nor the architecture levels, but rather the in-between *bridging* level which tolerates significant variations in both. Our approach proposes to adopt the BSP model as the computational model for this level and to generate transportable software by permeating its features in the areas of efficient algorithms, linguistic constructs and compilation techniques.

References

1. A.Aggarwal, A.Chandra and M.Snir *Communication Complexity of PRAMs*, Theoretical Computer Science, 71(1990), pp 3-28.
2. S. P. Amarasinghe and M. Lam *Communication Optimization and Code Generation for Distributed Memory Machines* Proceedings of the ACM SIGPLAN'93, Conference on Programming Language Design and Implementation, June 1993
3. R.H. Bisseling and W. F. McColl *Scientific Computing on Bulk Synchronous Parallel Architectures* Preprint 836, Dept. of Mathematics, Utrecht University, December 1993
4. T. Cheatham, H. Gao, and D. Stefanescu *A Suite of Analysis Tools Based on a General Purpose Abstract Interpreter*, Proceedings of the International Conference on Compiler Construction, Edinburgh, April 1994
5. T. Cheatham, A. Fahmy, D. Stefanescu, and L. Valiant *Bulk Synchronous Parallel Computing — a Paradigm for Transportable Software*, Proceedings HICSS95, Vol II, pp 268-275.
6. T. Cheatham, A. Fahmy, and D. Stefanescu *Supporting Multiple Evolving Compilers*, SEKE'94, Riga, June 1994
7. T. Cheatham, *Models, Languages, and Compiler Technology for High Performance Computers*, Workshop on Mathematical Foundations of Computer Science, Kosice, Slovakia, Lecture Notes on Computer Science, Springer Verlag, August 1994.
8. T. Cheatham, A. Fahmy, and D. Stefanescu *H-BSP - A General Purpose Parallel Computing Environment*, Proceedings of IFIP World Congress, Vol. 1, pp 515-520, Hamburg, August 1994
9. T. Cheatham, A. Fahmy, and D. Stefanescu *A Compiler for BSP-L, A Programming Language for the Bulk Synchronous Processing Model*, Proceedings of IEEE TENCON'94, Singapore, August 1994
10. T.Cheatham *The Unbundled Compiler*, Technical Report, Harvard University, 1993

11. D. E. Culler, et al. *Introduction to Split-C* EECS, UC Berkeley, Berkeley, CA 94720, April 1993

12. A. Geist, et al. *PVM3 Users Guide and Reference Manual* ORNL/TM-12187, Oak Ridge National Laboratory, Tennessee, May 1993

13. A.V.Gerbessiotis and L.G.Valiant *Direct bulk-synchronous parallel algorithms*, Third Scandinavian Workshop on Algorithm Theory, vol. 621, pages 1-18, Springer Verlag, 1992. Extended version in Journal of Parallel and Distributed Computing, 22, pp. 251-267, 1994

14. E. Heinz, M. Phillipson *Synchronization Barrier Elimination in Synchronous FORALLs* TR13/93 University of Karlsruhe, April 1993

15. S. Hiranandani, K.Kennedy, C.Tseng *Compiling Fortran D for MIMD Distributed-Memory Machines* Communications of the ACM, August 1992

16. J.W.Hong and H.T.Kung *I/O Complexity: The Red-Blue Pebble Game* Proceedings of the 13-th ACM Symposium on Theory of Computing, pp 326-333, 1981

17. V.Kathail and D. Stefanescu *A Data Mapping Parallel Language* TR-21-89, Center for Research in Computing Technology, Harvard University, December 1989

18. W. F. McColl *General Purpose Parallel Computing*, In A.M. Gibbons and P.Spirakis, editors, Lectures on Parallel Computation, Proc. 1991 ALCOM Spring School on Parallel Computation, vol 4 of Cambridge International Series on Parallel Computation, Cambridge University Press, 1993

19. W. F. McColl *BSP Programming* In DIMACS Series of Discrete Mathematics and Theoretical Computer Science, 1994. To appear.

20. W. F. McColl *Scalable Parallel Computing: A Grand Unified Theory and its Practical Development* Proceedings of IFIP World Congress, Vol. 1, pp 539-546, Hamburg, August 1994

21. R. Miller and J. Reed *The Oxford BSP Library. Users Guide. Version 1.0*, Oxford University, 1994

22. M. Paterson. Manuscript. 1994

23. J. P. Singh, E. Rothberg, and A. Gupta *Modeling Communication in Parallel Algorithms: A Fruitful Interaction Between Theory and Systems* Proceedings of the ACM Symposium on Parallel Algorithms and Architectures, 1994.

24. D. Stefanescu and Y. Zhou *An Equational Framework for the Abstract Analysis of Functional Programs*, Proceedings of ACM Conference on Lisp and Functional Programming, Orlando, 1994.

25. L. G. Valiant *A Bridging Model for Parallel Computation* Communications of the ACM, 33(8):103-111, 1990

26. L. G. Valiant *A combining mechanism for parallel computers.* In Parallel Architectures and Their Efficient Use, Proceedings of First Heinz Nixdorf Symposium, Paderborn,Germany, November 1992. Lecture Notes in Computer Science Vol678, Springer-Verlag, 1-10.

27. L. G. Valiant *Why BSP Computers?* Proceedings of the 7-th International Parallel Processing Symposium, pp 2-5, IEEE Computer Society Press, Los Alamitos, CA, 1993

28. M.E.Wolf and M.Lam *A Data Locality Optimizing Algorithm*, Conference on Programming Languages Design and Implementation'91, 1991

Compiler Architectures for Heterogeneous Systems

Kathryn S. McKinley, Sharad K. Singhai, Glen E. Weaver, Charles C. Weems

Department of Computer Science
University of Massachusetts
Amherst, MA 01003-4610
{mckinley, singhai, weaver, weems}@cs.umass.edu
(413) 545-1249 (fax)

Abstract. Heterogeneous parallel systems incorporate diverse models of parallelism within a single machine or across machines and are better suited for diverse applications [25, 43, 30]. These systems are already pervasive in industrial and academic settings and offer a wealth of un-derutilized resources for achieving high performance. Unfortunately, het-erogeneity complicates software development. We believe that compilers can and should assist in handling this complexity. We identify four goals for extending compilers to manage heterogeneity: exploiting available resources, targeting changing resources, adjusting optimization to suit a target, and allowing programming models and languages to evolve. These goals do not require changes to the individual pieces of existing compil-ers so much as a restructuring of a compiler's software architecture to increase its flexibility. We examine six important parallelizing compilers to identify both existing solutions and where new technology is needed.

1 Introduction

Heterogeneous processing

Current parallel machines implement a single homogeneous model of paral-lelism. As long as this model matches the parallelism inherent in an application, the machines perform well. Unfortunately, large programs tend to use several models of parallelism. By incorporating multiple models of parallelism within one machine (e.g., Meiko CS-2, IBM SP-2, and IUA [42]) or across machines, creating a virtual machine (e.g., PVM [38], p4 [9], and MPI [28]), heterogeneous systems provide consistent high performance.

Heterogeneous processing [36, 40, 41, 24, 18] is the well-orchestrated use of heterogeneous hardware to execute a single application [24]. When an appli-cation encompasses subtasks that employ different models of parallelism, the

We are designing a new compiler architecture to meet the needs of heterogeneity. Another paper [27] has a preliminary description of our design along with an expanded survey section.

This work was supported in part by the Advanced Research Projects Agency under contract N00014-94-1-0742, monitored by the Office of Naval Research.

application may benefit from using disparate hardware architectures that match the inherent parallelism of each subtask. For example, Klietz et al. describe their experience executing a single application, a simulation of mixing by turbulent convection, across four machines (CM-5, Cray-2, CM-200, and an SGI)[25]. The four machines form a single virtual machine, and the authors leverage the strengths of each machine for different tasks to achieve high performance.

Their experience illustrates that although heterogeneous processing offers improved performance, it increases the complexity of software development. The complexity arises from three important features of heterogeneity: variety, variability, and high performance. First, heterogeneous systems consist of a *variety* of hardware. For an application to take advantage of heterogeneity, it must be partitioned into subtasks, and each subtask mapped to a processor with a matching model of parallelism. Variety also opens up opportunities to trade local performance for overall performance. Second, virtual heterogeneous systems experience *variability* as their makeup changes from site to site or day to day or based on load. This variability of hardware resources requires rapid adaptation of programs to new configurations at compile and run time. Furthermore, variability deters programmers from using machine specific code (or languages) to improve performance. Third, heterogeneous systems can achieve *high performance*. If the execution time of a program does not matter, it could run on a homogeneous processor with less trouble. The demand for high performance precludes simple solutions such as adding layers of abstraction that obscure heterogeneity.

Compilers for heterogeneous systems

Developing software for heterogeneous systems would be overwhelming if each application needed to handle the complexity caused by variety, variability, and high performance. In Kleitz et al., they hand-parallelized each task specifically for its target machine in that machine's unique language dialect. If the hardware configuration changes, they must rewrite parts of the program. Instead of manually modifying programs, the variability of heterogeneous systems should be automatically handled at least in part by a compiler. With certain modifications to their software architecture, compilers can use transformations[1] to adjust a program to execute efficiently on a heterogeneous system.

Extending compilers to manage heterogeneity must address four goals: *exploiting available resources, targeting changing resources, adjusting optimizations to suit a target*, and *allowing programming models and languages to evolve*. (Sect. 3 explains why these goals are important.) Meeting these goals does not require changes to the individual pieces of a compiler so much as a restructuring of the compiler's software architecture to increase its *flexibility*. Current compilers, including retargetable compilers, tightly couple the compiler with both the source language and the target machine. This coupling is natural for homogeneous machines, where a single compilation can only target a single machine. However, this coupling limits the compiler's flexibility in dealing with diversity in targets, optimization strategies, and source languages. Heterogeneity is the first compiler application that requires and therefore justifies this level of flexibility.

---

[1] For brevity, "transformations" refers to both optimizations and transformations.

Overview

This paper surveys optimizing compilers and compiler frameworks for parallel machines and examines their potential contributions to a compiler for heterogeneous systems. In this section, we have motivated compiler support for heterogeneous systems, and distilled the impact of heterogeneity into four goals for an ideal compiler: exploiting available resources, targeting changing resources, adjusting optimization to suit a target, and allowing programming models and languages to evolve. Sect. 2 reviews six well-known parallelizing compilers. Sect. 3 discusses the applicability of techniques found in our survey to heterogeneity and the impact of heterogeneity on the overall architecture of the compiler. For each goal and compiler, we identify where existing technology can be adapted to meet the needs of heterogeneity.

We find that heterogeneity's variety and variability of available resources requires a compiler architecture that is much more flexible than current ones.

2 High Performance Parallelizing Compiler Survey

This section compares six existing compilers and frameworks: Parafrase-2, ParaScope, Polaris, Sage++, SUIF, and VFCS. We selected these systems because of their significant contributions to compiler architectures and because they are well documented. Since it is not feasible to change each system to handle heterogeneity and compare the efforts, we instead describe each system's architecture, and discuss their potential benefits and drawbacks for compiling for heterogeneous systems (see Section 3). This section describes the general approach, programming model, organization, intermediate representation, optimizations and transformations of the six systems and summarizes them in Table 1.[2]

System Overviews and Goals

Parafrase-2 is a source-to-source translator from the University of Illinois [19, 33]. Its design goal is to investigate compilation support for multiple languages and target architectures. It easily adapts to new language extensions because its IR emphasizes data and control dependences, rather than language syntax.

Rice University's ParaScope is an interactive parallel programming environment built around a source-to-source translator [12, 23]. It provides sophisticated global program analyses and a rich set of program transformations. Here we concentrate on the D System which is a specialized version of ParaScope for Fortran-D [17]. The output of the D System is an efficient message-passing distributed memory program [21, 22, 39].

Polaris is an optimizing source-to-source translator from the University of Illinois [4, 31, 15]. The authors have two major goals for Polaris: to automatically parallelize sequential programs and to be a near-production quality compiler. The authors focus on parallelization for shared memory machines. Polaris is written in C++ and compiles Fortran 77. Programmers may convey extra information, such as parallelism, to the compiler by embedding assertions in source code.

---

[2] We give more detailed descriptions in [27].

Table 1. Comparison table for surveyed systems.

Properties	Parafrase-2	ParaScope/D System	Polaris	Sage++/pC++	SUIF	VFCS
			General			
Goals	Multiple Languages and Target Architectures, Extensibility	Automatic and Interactive Parallelization	Production Quality Translator for Automatic Parallelization	Framework for Building Source-To-Source Translators	Tool for Research in Compilation Techniques, especially Automatic Parallelization	Compiling for Distributed Memory Systems
Source-to-Source	√	√	√	√	√	√
Source Languages	C, Fortran 77, Cedar Fortran	Fortran 77, Fortran 90[3], Fortran D	Fortran 77	C, C++, Fortran 77, Fortran 90, pC++	C, Fortran 77[4]	Fortran 77, Fortran 90[3], HPF, Vienna Fortran
Code Generation	Tuples	Tuples	—	—	MIPS Assembly	—
			Programming Model			
Input	Sequential or Control Parallel	Sequential or Data Parallel	Sequential	*NA*	Sequential	Sequential or Data Parallel
Output	Task/Loop Parallel	SPMD, Loop Parallel	Loop Parallel	*NA*	Loop Parallel	SPMD
Target Architectures	Multithreaded, SM, DSM	Uniprocessor, SM and DM	SM, DSM	*Not Specified*	Uniprocessor, SM, DSM	DM
Intermediate Representations	HTG, Linear Tuples	AST	AST[5]	AST	Hybrid of AST and Linear Tuples[6]	AST

SM Shared Memory   DSM Distributed Shared Memory   √ Yes   — No or None
DM Distributed Memory   HTG Hierarchical Task Graph   √+ Exceptional Implementation   NA Not Applicable

[3] Language subset.   [4] Preprocesses Fortran with f2c.   [5] Has pattern matching language for manipulating IR.
[6] Single IR has two levels of abstraction.

Table 1. Comparison table for surveyed systems, continued...

Properties	Parafrase-2	ParaScope/ D System	Polaris	Sage++/ pC++	SUIF	VFCS
Analyses						
Data Dependence	√	√	√	√	√	√
Control Depend.	√+	√	√	—	√	—
Symbolic[7]	√+	√+	√	—	√	√
Interprocedural	Alias, MOD, REF, Constant Propagation	Alias, MOD, REF, Constant Propagation	Inlining (for analysis), Constant Propagation	—	MOD, REF, GEN, KILL, Constant Propagation, Array Summary, Array Reshape, Reductions[8], Induction Variables, Cloning[8]	USE, DEF, Alias, Overlap, Constant Propagation, Communication, Dynamic Distribution
Incremental	—	√	*In Progress*	—	—	—
Optimizations and Transformations						
Traditional	√	√	√	—	√+	√
Loop	√	√	√	√	√	√
Comm/Sync	—	√[9]	√	—	√	√+
Interprocedural	Inlining	Inlining, Cloning	Inlining, Cloning	—	Parallelization, Data Privatization, Inlining, Cloning, Reductions	Inlining, Cloning
Data Partitioning	—	√	√	—	√	√
Task Partitioning	√	—	—	—	—	—
Applicability Criteria	√	√	√	—	√	√
Profit. Criteria	Queries User	Queries User	Fixed for Arch.	—	Fixed for Arch.	Static Measure

[7] Intraprocedural. [8] Used for both analysis and optimization. [9] Only for D System compiler.

Sage++ is a toolkit for building source-to-source translators from Indiana University [6]. The authors foresee optimizing translators, simulation of language extensions, language preprocessors, and code instrumentation as possible applications of Sage++ [7, 46, 26, 5]. Sage++ is written in C++ and provides parses for C, C++, pC++, Fortran 77, and Fortran 90. Because Sage++ is a toolkit instead of a compiler, it is not limited to particular hardware architectures.

SUIF from Stanford University is a compiler framework that can be used as either a source-to-C translator or a native code compiler [44, 1, 20, 37]. SUIF is designed to study parallelization for both shared memory and distributed shared memory machines as well as uniprocessor optimizations. SUIF accepts source code written in either Fortran 77 or C, however a modified version of f2c [16] is used to convert Fortran code to C code.

The Vienna Fortran Compilation System (VFCS) from the University of Vienna is an interactive, source-to-source translator for Vienna Fortran [10, 11, 48, 49]. VFCS is based upon the data parallel model of computation with the Single-Program-Multiple-Data (SPMD) paradigm. VFCS outputs explicitly parallel, SPMD programs in message passing languages, Intel features, PARMACS, and MPI.

General

Reflecting their common mission of compiling for parallel machines, the systems are similar in their general approach. All the systems (except Sage++) are designed for automatic parallelization, and Sage++ supports features necessary for building a parallelizing compiler (e.g., data dependence). All the systems parse some variation of Fortran and half of them also handle C, the traditional languages for high performance computing. Except for Sage++, the systems in our survey can operate as source-to-source translators, and Sage++ facilitates the construction of source-to-source translators. In addition, SUIF compiles directly into assembly code for the MIPS family of microprocessors, and Parafrase-2 and ParaScope generate tuples.

Programming model

SUIF accepts only sequential C and Fortran 77 programs, and therefore must extract all parallelism automatically. Polaris parses only Fortran 77 but interprets assertions in the source code that identify parallelism. ParaScope allows programmers to use data parallel languages as well as sequential languages, and attempts to find additional loop and data parallelism. VFCS accepts data parallel languages and requires that programmers supply the data distribution and the assignment of computation to processors, following the *owner-computes* rule as in ParaScope. Parafrase-2 inputs Cedar Fortran which offers vector, loop, and task parallelism.

Most of the compilers in our survey generate data parallel programs, but Parafrase-2 produces control parallel code as well. SUIF and Polaris take a classic approach to parallelization by identifying loop iterations that operate on independent sections of arrays and executing these iterations in parallel. For scientific applications, loop-level parallelism has largely equated to data parallelism. The D System and VFCS, on the other hand, output programs that follow the

SPMD model; the program consists of interacting node programs. Parafrase-2 is unique in that it exploits task parallelism as well as loop parallelism.

Most of the systems use an abstract syntax tree (AST) as an intermediate representation. ASTs retain the source level syntax of the program which makes them convenient for source-to-source translation. SUIF's AST is unique because it represents only select language constructs at a high-level; the remaining constructs are represented by nodes that resemble RISC instructions. These low-level nodes are also used in SUIF's linear tuple representation. Parafrase-2 uses the hierarchical task graph (HTG) representation instead of an AST. HTGs elucidate control and data dependencies between sections of a program and are convenient for extracting control parallelism.

Analyses

All the systems in our survey provide the base analyses necessary for parallelism, but beyond that their capabilities diverge. Data dependence analysis is central to most loop transformations and is therefore built into all the systems. Instead of using traditional dependence analysis, Polaris builds symbolic lower and upper bounds for each variable reference and propagates these ranges throughout the program using symbolic execution. Polaris' range test then uses these ranges to disprove dependences[3].

Polaris, Parafrase-2, ParaScope, and SUIF perform control dependence analysis, albeit in a flow-insensitive manner. Parafrase-2 has additional analyses to eliminate redundant control dependences.

All the systems (except Sage++) perform intraprocedural symbolic analysis to support traditional optimizations, but ParaScope and Parafrase-2 have extensive interprocedural symbolic analysis such as forward propagation of symbolics. VFCS provides intraprocedural irregular access pattern analysis based on PARTI routines [35]. Parafrase-2, ParaScope, Polaris, SUIF, and VFCS provide interprocedural analysis. Polaris recently incorporated interprocedural symbolic constant propagation [32]. Parafrase-2, ParaScope, and VFCS [47] perform flow-insensitive interprocedural analysis by summarizing where variables are referenced or modified. SUIF's FIAT [20] tool provides a powerful framework for both flow-insensitive and flow-sensitive analysis [20].

Optimizations and Transformations

The organization of analyses and transformations varies among the systems. SUIF has a flexible organization, with each analysis and transformation coded as an independent pass and the sole means of communication between passes being the annotations attached to the IR. Polaris also organizes its analyses and transformations as separate passes that operate over the whole program, but a pass may call the body of another pass to operate over a subset of the program. Programmers can affect the operation of passes in both systems through command line parameters. All of the systems support batch compilation and optimization. However, Parafrase-2, ParaScope, and VFCS also provide a graphical interface that enables users to affect their transformation ordering. Moreover, ParaScope and Polaris support incremental updates of analysis data. Though incremental analysis is not more powerful than batch analysis, it dramatically increases the speed of compilation and therefore encourages more extensive optimization.

Transformations performed by uniprocessor compilers are termed *traditional*. Except Sage++, all the systems provide traditional optimizations. In addition, Polaris and SUIF perform array privatization and reductions [34]. Because SUIF generates native code, it also includes low-level optimizations such as register allocation.

All six systems provide loop transformations. ParaScope has a large set of loop transformations. SUIF too has a wide assortment of traditional and loop transformations including unimodular loop transformations (i.e., interchange, reversal, and skewing) [45].

All systems except Sage++, include inlining as one of their interprocedural optimizations. ParaScope, Parafrase-2, SUIF and VFCS also perform cloning. SUIF exploits its strong interprocedural analyses to provide data privatization, reductions and parallelization.

Communication and synchronization transformations, though not always distinct from loop transformations, refer to the transformations specifically performed for distributed memory machines, like message vectorization, communication selection, message coalescing, message aggregation, and message pipelining. VFCS, designed exclusively for distributed memory machines, has a richer set of communication transformations than the others. SUIF is able to derive automatic data decompositions for a given program. ParaScope and VFCS do this to some degree, however, the default computation partitioning mechanism for them is the *owner computes* rule and data partitioning is specified by programmers (recent work in ParaScope addresses automatic data partitioning [2]).

Parafrase-2 is unique in that it exploits *control* parallelism by partitioning programs into separate tasks. The other compilers use only data parallelism.

All compilers include *applicability* criteria for the transformations since a transformation may not be legal, (e.g., loop interchange is illegal when any dependence is of the form $(\cdots, <, >, \cdots))$. Sage++ is unique in the respect that although it has a few loop transformations, it does not have any applicability criteria built in. Sage++ developers argue that in a preprocessor toolkit applicability should be defined by the compiler writer for individual implementations.

Though a transformation may be applicable, it may not be *profitable*. The six compilers surveyed in this article take varying approaches to this issue. Parafrase-2 and ParaScope rely on user input. ParaScope also offers a small amount of feedback to the user based on its analysis. SUIF and Polaris use a fixed ordering of transformations for each target, and therefore perform valid transformations according to a predefined strategy. VFCS relies on static performance measurement by an external tool, P^3T, to determine profitability [13, 14].

Closely related to profitability is ordering criteria. Transformations applied in different orders can produce dramatically different results. In interactive mode, ParaScope and Parafrase-2 allow users to select any ordering of transformations. All support fixed transformation ordering via their command lines.

Interaction with users

Most of the surveyed compilers have additional tools to assist users in writing and understanding their parallel programs. ParaScope strives to provide a parallel programming environment, including an editor, debugger and an automatic data partitioner. Polaris allows programmers to provide instructions to the compiler through source code assertions. Sage++ provides a rich set of tools for pC++ named *Tuning and Analysis Utilities*, TAU [8, 29]. TAU includes tools for file and class display, call graph display, class hierarchy browsing, routine and data access profile display, and event and state display. Almost all of these systems are research tools that encourage user experimentation. Experimentation is further facilitated by having a graphical user interface in Parafrase-2, ParaScope, Sage++, and VFCS which display various aspects of the compilation process in windows so the user can request more details or provide inputs to the compiler.

3 Criteria of a Compiler for Heterogeneous Systems

In Sect. 1, we introduced four goals that a compiler for heterogeneous systems must meet: exploiting available resources, targeting changing resources, adjusting optimization to suit a target, and allowing programming models and languages to evolve. This section expounds upon these goals by determining their implications with respect to the compiler, and finding where technology from Sect. 2 is applicable or new technology is needed.

3.1 Exploiting Available Resources

As with any computer system, compilers for heterogeneous systems should generate programs that take maximum advantage of available hardware. However, variability in resources complicates this task. To account for variability, programs could simply be recompiled. Recompiling whenever the hardware configuration changes works well when the configuration is stable but is inefficient if the configuration changes frequently. Recompiling at runtime adjusts for the current workload of a heterogeneous system, but may negate performance benefits.

Multiple object modules for different targets

Instead of recompiling when the configuration changes, the compiler could precompile for several machines. Hence, the compiler produces the building blocks for a program partitioning, but the linker assembles the final partitioning. The compiler generates alternate versions of subtasks (or routines), and passes along enough information for the linker to select a final partitioning. None of the existing compilers provide this level of flexibility. All the compilers perform partitioning and mapping within the compiler.

Compiler communicates with run-time environment

Another approach to exploiting varying resources is for the compiler to embed code that examines its environment at run time and dynamically decides how to execute. For example, VFCS has transformations that dynamically decide their applicability at run-time. These transformations, along with delayed binding of subtasks to specific processors, increase communication between the compiler and the run time system. This approach can be adapted to accommodate variations in hardware resources without the cost of recompilation.

3.2 Targeting Changing Resources

The variety and variability of hardware complicates code generation for individual components. Unlike existing compilers, a compiler for heterogeneous systems must generate code for diverse processors during a single compilation, which not only requires flexible instruction selection but also flexible transformation selection. The compiler must choose the transformations that suit the target processor.

IR supports code generation for diverse hardware

A compiler transforms a program through a series of representations from source code to object code. The final step, selection of object code instructions, is facilitated by an intermediate representation that resembles the target instruction set. The more accurately the IR reflects the hardware, the greater the opportunity for optimization. On the other hand, including more hardware specific detail in the IR decreases its generality. All of the surveyed systems, except SUIF, do a source-to-source translation and leave code generation to native compilers, thus avoiding code generation issues. These compilers lose the benefits of intertwining their high-level transformations with machine-level optimizations. SUIF's unique representation allows it to capture RISC hardware specific details (for most source language constructs) and still perform high-level transformations on the program.

Compiler accepts an extensible description of the target

Another concern for generating efficient code is exploiting details of the target hardware. Even high-level transformations can benefit from exploiting features such as the number of registers, memory access latencies, and cache line size. The variety of hardware in a heterogeneous system precludes embedding hardware knowledge in the compiler. Instead, there must be some way to provide target descriptions to the compiler. The Memoria compiler, which is part of ParaScope and is only for uniprocessors, uses hardware parameters such as latency, but none of the compilers for parallel machines accept hardware parameters as input. Memoria accepts only a limited hardware description, but this approach can be extended to accept a richer description.

Compiler detects/accepts programming model

In order to assign code to a processor with the appropriate model of parallelism, the compiler must know the model of parallelism used by the programmer. Programmers could annotate programs with this information, or analysis techniques might be able to detect the model of parallelism. None of the surveyed systems automatically determine the source program's model of parallelism because they assume it is one of a small set of models. For example, Polaris and SUIF assume a sequential model, and ParaScope assumes the program is either sequential or data parallel. Thus, new technology is needed to both accept and extract the programming model.

Compiler converts programming models with user assistance

Because of the variability of resources in a heterogeneous system, a compiler must be able to target code that uses one model of parallelism for a machine that implements a different model of parallelism. Thus, the compiler must convert, to some extent, the model of parallelism that a code module uses. Extensive effort has gone into developing methods for converting sequential programs into parallel programs (i.e., automatic parallelization), and some forms of parallel code can be readily converted to other forms. All the compilers in our survey transform programs to execute on a different model of parallelism, and they represent the state of the art in automatic parallelization. Their techniques should be included in a compiler for heterogeneous systems. Yet, automatic techniques have had limited success because they make conservative assumptions. Parafrase-2 and ParaScope address this issue with an interactive interface that allows programmers to guide code transformation. Unfortunately for heterogeneous systems, this approach requires programmers to edit their programs each time the system's configuration changes because the programmer's deep understanding of a program remains implicit in the code. Instead programmers should convey their insights about the program to the compiler and allow it to determine how to apply these insights.

Annotating source programs with additional semantic knowledge is appropriate only when the algorithm changes slightly for a new target. Sometimes a change in the target requires a radical change in the algorithm to obtain good performance. Programmers currently have two choices: write generic algorithms with mediocre performance on all processors or rewrite the algorithm when the target changes. A compiler for heterogeneous systems should provide a third choice by managing multiple implementations of a routine.

3.3 Adjusting optimization to suit a target

Current compilers have a limited number of targets and therefore apply their analyses and transformations in a fixed order (or under user control). Because of the variety of hardware in heterogeneous systems, a compiler must be able to reorder transformations to suit a particular target. Moreover, because heterogeneous systems have variable configurations, new analyses and transformations may need to be added. Thus, a compiler for heterogeneous systems should encode analyses and transformations in a form that facilitates reordering and addition.

Modular analyses, optimizations, and transformations

One implication of needing to reorder analyses and transformations as well as include new ones is that they should be modular. Parafrase-2, Sage++, and SUIF break transformations into individual passes which communicate through the IR. This approach to modularity works well if the entire program needs the same ordering and is destined for the same model of parallelism. Because optimization strategies for subtasks vary depending on the target processor and a heterogeneous system has a variety of targets, the compiler must also be able to apply an analysis or transformation to individual sections of code. Polaris supports this capability directly; passes may call the bodies of other passes as needed. ParaScope, Parafrase-2, and to some extent VFCS also provide this capability through their interactive interface. New technology should use the flexibility these systems provide to automatically adapt the ordering of transformations based on varying models of parallelism and a target's hardware features.

Compiler maintains consistency of analysis data

Though the compilers in our survey have modular implementations of their analyses and transformations, most of them still have strong ordering constraints. Ideally, transformations would be written such that the compiler infrastructure would manage these constraints by ensuring that necessary analysis data is accurate and up-to-date. Not only would this capability prevent errors, but it would also simplify the addition of new transformations. Polaris already supports incremental update of flow information. ParaScope can identify when analysis data is not current, but incremental update is the responsibility of individual transformations. Extensions of these techniques can simplify the compiler developer's task in ordering transformations.

3.4 Allowing Programming Models and Languages to Evolve

The inherent complexity of a compiler for heterogeneous systems along with the variety of targets favors a single compiler with multiple source languages and targets. Because languages typically evolve in response to new hardware capabilities and virtual machines allow the introduction of new hardware, a compiler should include two capabilities to support changes in the source languages it accepts. The first capability is already common: a clean break between the front and back ends of the compiler. The second capability is much harder: despite the separation, the front end must pass a semantic description of new language features to the back end.

IR hides source language from back end

The separation of front and back ends protects the analyses and transformations in the back end from details of the source language's syntax. Compilers separate their front and back ends by limiting their interaction to an intermediate representation. To the extent that the IR is unaffected by changes in the language, the back end is insulated. Unfortunately, ParaScope, Polaris, Sage++, SUIF, and VFCS use an AST representation, which inherently captures the syntax of the source language. SUIF attempts to overcome the limitations of ASTs by immediately compiling language constructs it considers unimportant to RISC-like IR nodes. Parafrase-2 uses an HTG which does not necessarily represent the syntax of the source language, and can therefore hide it. Extending this approach of reducing source language syntax dependences in the IR can improve the separation of front and back ends.

IR is extensible

To pass a semantic description of new language features through the intermediate representation, the IR must be extended. Some simple changes to a

Table 2. Compiler Goals for Heterogeneous Systems.

1. Exploiting available resources:
   - Compiler generates multiple object code modules for different targets to support load balancing and maximize throughput.
   - Compiler communicates with Run-time environment.
2. Targeting changing resources:
   - IR supports code generation for diverse hardware.
   - Compiler accepts an extensible description of the target.
   - Compiler detects (or accepts from user) the code's programming model.
   - Compiler accepts user assistance in converting programming models.
3. Adjusting optimization to suit a target:
   - Modular analyses, optimizations, and transformations.
   - Compiler maintains consistency of analysis data.
4. Allowing programming models and languages to evolve:
   - IR hides source language from back end.
   - IR is extensible (via new constructs or annotations).

language (e.g., a new loop construct) may be expressible in terms of the existing IR, but others (e.g., adding message passing to C) require new IR nodes. Sage++, Parafrase-2, SUIF, and Polaris allow extension of their respective IRs through object-oriented data structures. Their IRs can be extended to include new features of an evolving language or to reuse parts of the IR for a completely different language. Note that a new IR node may require new or enhanced transformations to process that node. Object-oriented features improve extensibility but they may not be sufficiently flexible for unanticipated extensions.

4 Summary and Conclusions

Compiling for heterogeneous systems is a challenging task because of the complexity of efficiently managing multiple languages, targets and programming models in a dynamic environment. In this paper, we survey six state-of-the-art high-performance optimizing compilers. We present four goals of an ideal compiler for heterogeneous systems and examined their impact on a compiler summarized in Table 2. Existing compilers satisfy some of these goals, but they lack the flexibility needed by heterogeneous systems because homogeneous systems do not require it. We identify areas from which existing technology can be borrowed and areas in which these compilers lack the necessary flexibility for heterogeneity. Achieving this flexibility does not require substantial changes to core compiler technology, e.g., parsers and transformations, but rather the way that they work together, i.e., the compiler's software architecture.

Acknowledgements: We want to thank the development teams of each compiler in our survey for their comments and feedback, especially John Grout, Jay Hoeflinger, David Padua, Constantine Polychronopoulos, Nicholas Stavrakos, Chau-Wen Tseng, Robert Wilson, and Hans Zima.

References

1. S. Amarasinghe, J. Anderson, M. Lam, and A. Lim. An overview of a compiler for scalable parallel machines. In *Proceedings of the Sixth Workshop on Languages and Compilers for Parallel Computing*, Portland, OR, August 1993.
2. R. Bixby, K. Kennedy, and U. Kremer. Automatic data layout using 0-1 integer programming. In *International Conference on Parallel Architectures and Compilation Techniques (PACT)*, pages 111–122, Montreal, August 1994.
3. W. Blume and R. Eigenmann. The range test: A dependence test for symbolic, non-linear expressions. CSRD 1345, Center for Supercomputing Research and Development, University of Illinois at Urbana-Champaign, April 1994.
4. W. Blume et al. Effective Automatic Parallelization with Polaris. *International Journal of Parallel Programming*, May 1995.
5. F. Bodin et al. Distributed pC++: Basic ideas for an object parallel language. *Scientific Programming*, 2(3), Fall 1993.
6. F. Bodin et al. Sage++: An object-oriented toolkit and class library for building Fortran and C++ restructuring tools. In *Second Object-Oriented Numerics Conference*, 1994.
7. F. Bodin, T. Priol, P. Mehrotra, and D. Gannon. Directions in parallel programming: HPF, shared virtual memory and object parallelism in pC++. Technical Report 94-54, ICASE, June 1994.
8. D. Brown, S. Hackstadt, A. Malony, and B. Mohr. Program analysis environments for parallel language systems: the TAU environment. In *Proceedings of the 2nd Workshop on Environments and Tools For Parallel Scientific Computing*, pages 162–171, Townsend, Tennessee, May 1994.
9. R. Butler and E. Lusk. Monitors, messages, and clusters: the p4 parallel programming system. *Parallel Computing*, 20(4):547–564, April 1994.
10. B. Chapman, P. Mehrotra, and H. Zima. Programming in Vienna Fortran. *Scientific Programming*, 1(1):31–50, Fall 1992.
11. B. Chapman, P. Mehrotra, and H. Zima. Vienna Fortran - a Fortran language extension for distributed memory multiprocessors. In J. Saltz and P. Mehrotra, editors, *Languages, Compilers, and Run-Time Environments for Distributed Memory Machines*. North-Holland, Amsterdam, 1992.
12. K. Cooper et al. The ParaScope parallel programming environment. *Proceedings of the IEEE*, 81(2):244–263, February 1993.
13. T. Fahringer. Using the P^3T to guide the parallelization and optimization effort under the Vienna Fortran compilation system. In *Proceedings of the 1994 Scalable High Performance Computing Conference*, Knoxville, May 1994.
14. T. Fahringer and H. Zima. A static parameter based performance prediction tool for parallel programs. In *Proceedings of the 1993 ACM International Conference on Supercomputing*, Tokyo, July 1993.
15. K. Faigin et al. The polaris internal representation. *International Journal of Parallel Programming*, 22(5):553–586, Oct. 1994.
16. S. Feldman, D. Gay, M. Maimone, and N. Schryer. A Fortran-to-C converter. Computing Science 149, AT&T Bell Laboratories, March 1993.
17. G. Fox et al. Fortran D language specification. Technical Report TR90-141, Rice University, December 1990.
18. A. Ghafoor and J. Yang. A distributed heterogeneous supercomputing management system. *Computer*, 26(6):78–86, June 1993.

19. M. B. Girkar and C. Polychronopoulos. The hierarchical task graph as a universal intermediate representation. *International Journal of Parallel Programming*, 22(5), 1994.

20. M. Hall, B. Murphy, and S. Amarasinghe. Interprocedural analysis for parallelization. In *Proceedings of the Eighth Workshop on Languages and Compilers for Parallel Computing*, Columbus, OH, August 1995.

21. S. Hiranandani, K. Kennedy, and C. Tseng. Compiler support for machine-independent parallel programming in Fortran D. Technical Report TR91-149, Rice University, Jan. 1991.

22. S. Hiranandani, K. Kennedy, and C. Tseng. Compiling Fortran D for MIMD distributed-memory machines. *Communications of the ACM*, 35(8):66–80, August 1992.

23. K. Kennedy, K. S. McKinley, and C. Tseng. Analysis and transformation in an interactive parallel programming tool. *Concurrency: Practice & Experience*, 5(7):575–602, October 1993.

24. A. Khokhar, V. Prasanna, M. Shaaban, and C. Wang. Heterogeneous computing: Challenges and opportunities. *Computer*, 26(6):18–27, June 1993.

25. A. E. Klietz, A. V. Malevsky, and K. Chin-Purcell. A case study in metacomputing: Distributed simulations of mixing in turbulent convection. In *Workshop on Heterogeneous Processing*, pages 101–106, April 1993.

26. A. Malony et al. Performance analysis of pC++: A portable data-parallel programming system for scalable parallel computers. In *Proceedings of the 8th International Parallel Processing Symposium*, 1994.

27. K. S. McKinley, S. Singhai, G. Weaver, and C. Weems. Compiling for heterogeneous systems: A survey and an approach. Technical Report TR-95-59, University of Massachusetts, July 1995. http://osl-www.cs.umass.edu/~oos/papers.html.

28. Message Passing Interface Forum. MPI: A message-passing interface standard, v1.0. Technical report, University of Tennessee, May 1994.

29. B. Mohr, D. Brown, and A. Malony. TAU: A portable parallel program analysis environment for pC++. In *Proceedings of CONPAR 94 - VAPP VI*, University of Linz, Austria, September 1994. LNCS 854.

30. H. Nicholas et al. Distributing the comparison of DNA and protein sequences across heterogeneous supercomputers. In *Proceedings of Supercomputing '91*, pages 139–146, 1991.

31. D. A. Padua et al. Polaris: A new-generation parallelizing compiler for MPPs. Technical Report CSRD-1306, Center for Supercomputing Research and Development, University of Illinois at Urbana-Champaign, June 1993.

32. D. A. Pauda. Private communication, September 1995.

33. C. Polychronopoulos et al. Parafrase-2: An environment for parallelizing, partitioning, synchronizing, and scheduling programs on multiprocessors. *International Journal of High Speed Computing*, 1(1), 1989.

34. W. Pottenger and R. Eigenmann. Idiom recognition in the Polaris parallelizing compiler. In *Proceedings of the 1995 ACM International Conference on Supercomputing*, Barcelona, July 1995.

35. J. Saltz, K. Crowely, R. Mirchandaney, and H. Berryman. Run-time scheduling and execution of loops on message passing machines. *Journal of Parallel and Distributed Computing*, 8(2):303–312, 1990.

36. L. Smarr and C. E. Catlett. Metacomputing. *Communications of the ACM*, 35(6):45–52, June 1992.

37. Stanford Compiler Group. The SUIF library. Technical report, Stanford University, 1994.

38. V.S. Sunderam, G.A. Geist, J. Dongarra, and P. Manchek. The PVM concurrent computing system: Evolution, experiences, and trends. *Parallel Computing*, 20(4):531–545, April 1994.

39. C. Tseng. *An Optimizing Fortran D Compiler for MIMD Distributed-Memory Machines*. PhD thesis, Rice University, January 1993.

40. L. H. Turcotte. A survey of software environments for exploiting networked computing resources. Technical Report MSSU-EIRS-ERC-93-2, NSF Engineering Research Center, Mississippi State University, February 1993.

41. L. H. Turcotte. Cluster computing. In Albert Y. Zomaya, editor, *Parallel and Distributed Computing Handbook*, chapter 26. McGraw-Hill, October 1995.

42. C. Weems et al. The image understanding architecture. *International Journal of Computer Vision*, 2(3):251–282, 1989.

43. C. Weems et al. The DARPA image understanding benchmark for parallel processors. *Journal of Parallel and Distributed Computing*, 11:1–24, 1991.

44. R. Wilson et al. The SUIF compiler system: A parallelizing and optimizing research compiler. *SIGPLAN*, 29(12), December 1994.

45. M. E. Wolf and M. Lam. A loop transformation theory and an algorithm to maximize parallelism. *IEEE Transactions on Parallel and Distributed Systems*, 2(4):452–471, October 1991.

46. S. Yang et al. High performance fortran interface to the parallel C++. In *Proceedings of the 1994 Scalable High Performance Computing Conference*, Knoxville, TN, May 1994.

47. H. Zima. Private communication, September 1995.

48. H. Zima and B. Chapman. Compiling for distributed-memory systems. *Proceedings of the IEEE*, 81(2):264–287, February 1993.

49. H. Zima, B. Chapman, H. Moritsch, and P. Mehrotra. Dynamic data distributions in Vienna Fortran. In *Proceedings of Supercomputing '93*, Portland, OR, November 1993.

Virtual Topologies: A New Concurrency Abstraction for High-Level Parallel Languages

(Preliminary Report)

James Philbin[1], Suresh Jagannathan[1], Rajiv Mirani[2]

[1] Computer Science Division, NEC Research Institute, 4 Independence
Way, {philbin | suresh}@research.nj.nec.com
[2] Department of Computer Science, Yale University, New Haven, CT
mirani@cs.yale.edu

Abstract. We present a new concurrency abstraction and implementation technique for high-level (symbolic) parallel languages that allows significant programmer control over load-balancing and mapping of fine-grained lightweight threads. Central to our proposal is the notion of a *virtual topology*. A virtual topology defines a relation over a collection of *virtual processors*, and a mapping of those processors to a set of physical processors; processor topologies configured as trees, graphs, butterflies, and meshes are some well-known examples. A virtual topology need not have any correlation with a physical one; it is intended to capture the interconnection structure best suited for a given algorithm. We consider a virtual processor to be an abstraction that defines scheduling, migration and load-balancing policies for the threads it executes. Thus, virtual topologies are intended to provide a simple, expressive and efficient high-level framework for defining complex thread/processor mappings that abstracts low-level details of a physical interconnection.

1 Introduction

Abstractions used by designers of parallel algorithms [12] are very different from those available to implementors of these algorithms. High-level parallel languages [11, 19, 15] often provide no mechanism for programmers to specify the mapping, scheduling and locality properties of a computation; policy decisions of this kind are usually hard-wired as part of the language implementation. The efficiency of a parallel algorithm, however, is typically dictated precisely by how well it optimizes these concerns. Moreover, the abstract process graph manipulated by an algorithm is often dissimilar to the physical topology of the machine on which implementations of the algorithm execute; in general, there is no well-defined, machine independent mechanism to reconcile these differences.

In this paper, we present a new concurrency abstraction and implementation technique for high-level (symbolic) parallel languages that address these issues. Central to our proposal is the notion of a *virtual topology*. A virtual topology defines a relation over a collection of *virtual processors*; processor topologies configured as trees, graphs, hypercubes, and meshes are some well-known examples. A virtual topology need not have any correlation with a physical one; it is intended to capture the interconnection structure best suited for a given algorithm. We consider a virtual processor to be an abstraction over a physical processor that defines scheduling, migration and load-balancing policies for the threads it executes. Thus, virtual topologies are intended to provide a simple and expressive high-level framework for defining complex thread/processor mappings that abstracts low-level details of a physical interconnection.

There need be no *a priori* correlation between the number of virtual processors in a topology, and the number of physical processors in the machine on which the computation will run. Because virtual processors are first-class, virtual topologies can be specified on a per-application basis. Threads created by a computation are mapped to processors in the virtual topology via mapping functions associated with the topology. These mapping functions are user definable.

Virtual topologies also permit significant performance gains for many high-level parallel programs. Our benchmark results indicate that using virtual topologies *even on physically shared-memory machines* can yield performance benefits ranging from 1.5 to over a factor of 6 relative to an identical system that uses a simple round-robin or random thread scheduling policy. The performance gains are due primarily to improved locality and load-balancing. Thus, virtual topologies are not only an expressive language abstraction, but also an important efficiency tool. To our knowledge, this is the first implementation of virtual topologies that seriously addresses efficiency and programmability on real multiprocessor platforms.

A high-level parallel program is thus parameterized over a virtual topology. Because programs no longer need to rely on details of physical processors and their interconnection, code becomes machine independent and highly portable. All concerns related to thread mapping and locality are abstracted in the specification of the virtual topology used by the program, and the manner in which nodes in the topology are traversed during program execution.

2 Implications

Using virtual topologies leads to several important benefits; we enumerate them here, and elaborate in the following sections:

1. *Portability:* Implementations of parallel algorithms need not be specialized for different *physical* topologies. An implementation is defined only with respect to a given *virtual* topology.

2. *Control over Thread Placement:* Since the mapping algorithm used to associate threads with processors is specified as part of a virtual topology, programmers have fine control over how threads should be mapped to virtual processors.

3. *Load Balancing:* If the computation requirements of the threads generated by a program are known in advance, the ability to explicitly allocate these threads onto specific virtual processors can lead to better load balancing than an implicit mapping strategy.

4. *Exploiting Algorithmic Structure:* The structure of a control and dataflow graph defined by a parallel algorithm can be exploited in a number of ways:

   (a) *Improved Data Locality:* If a collection of threads share common data, we can construct a topology that maps the virtual processors on which these threads execute to the same physical processor. Virtual processors are multiplexed on physical processors in the same way threads are multiplexed on virtual processors.

   (b) *Improved Communication Locality:* If a collection of threads have significant communication requirements, we can construct a topology that maps threads which communicate with one another onto virtual processors near each other in the virtual topology.

   (c) *Improved Thread Granularity:* If thread T_1 has a data dependency with the value yielded by another thread T_2, we can map T_1 and T_2 on the same virtual processor. In fine-grained programs where processors are busy most of the time, the ability to schedule data-dependent threads on the same processor leads to opportunities for improved thread granularity [10, 14, 23].

5. *Dynamic Topologies:* Certain algorithms have a process structure that unfolds as the computation progresses; adaptive tree algorithms [12] are a good example. These algorithms are best executed on topologies that permit dynamic creation and destruction of virtual processors.

The remainder of the paper is structured as follows. Section 3 describes a simple parallel program used to motivate the use of virtual topologies. Section 4 introduces virtual topologies. Section 5 describes virtual and physical processors. Section 6 reformulates the example given in Section 3 to use virtual topologies. Section 7 gives a concrete specification of a virtual tree topology. Benchmark results are given in Section 8. Conclusions and comparison to related work are presented in Section 9.

Our discussion and examples use Scheme [4] as the base language, but virtual topologies and first-class virtual processors are language independent abstractions.

3 An Example

To help motivate the utility of virtual topologies, consider the program fragment shown in Figure 1. This program is written in a parallel dialect of Scheme that uses *futures* [6] to create parallel threads of control. The expression, (future E), returns a future object. Associated with this future is a thread responsible for computing E. When the thread finishes, it stores the result of E in the future. The future is then said to be *determined*. An expression that *touches* a future either blocks if E is still being computed or yields v if the future is determined.

D&C defines a parallel divide-and-conquer procedure; when given a merge procedure M, and a list of data streams as its arguments, it constructs a binary tree that uses M to

```
(define (D&C merge streams)
  (let loop ((streams streams))
    (future
      (if (null? (cdr s))
          streams
          (let ((output-stream (make-stream)))
            (merge (loop (left-half streams))
                   (loop (right-half streams))
                   output-stream))))))
```

Fig. 1. A divide-and-conquer parallel program parameterized over a merge procedure.

merge pairs of streams. Each pair of leaves in the tree are streams connected to a merge node that combines their contents and outputs the results onto a separate output stream. The root of the tree and all internal nodes are implemented as separate threads.

There is significant data and communication locality in this program since data generated by child streams are accessed exclusively by their parents. Load-balancing is also an important consideration. We would like to avoid mapping internal nodes at the same depth to the same processor whenever possible since these nodes operate over distinct portions of the tree and have no data dependencies with one another. For example, a merge node N with children C_1 and C_2 ideally should be mapped onto a processor close to both C_1 and C_2, and should be mapped onto a processor distinct from any of its siblings.

4 Virtual Topologies

To address the issues highlighted in the previous section, we define a high-level abstraction that allows programmers to specify how threads should be mapped onto a virtual topology corresponding to a logical process graph. In general, we expect programmers to use a library of topologies that are provided as part of a thread system; each topology in this library defines procedures for constructing and accessing its elements. Figure 2 enumerates some of the topologies we have implemented, along with their interface procedures. The cognitive cost of using topologies is thus minimal for those topologies present in the topology library.

However, because virtual processors are first-class objects, building new topologies is not cumbersome. Programmers requiring topologies not available in the library, can construct their own using the abstractions described in the next section.

For example, a tree is an obvious candidate for the desired thread/processor map in the example shown in Figure 1. A tree, however, may not correspond to the physical topology of the system; virtual topologies provide a mechanism for bridging the gap between the algorithmic structure of an application and the physical structure of the

Topology	Interface Procedures
Array	(make-array-topology *dimensions*) (get-node *dim₁ dim₂ ...dimₙ*) (move-up-in-nth-dimension *n*) (move-down-in-nth-dimension *n*)
Ring	(make-ring-topology *size*) (get-vp *n*) (move-right *n*) (move-left *n*)
Static Tree Dynamic Tree	(make-static-tree-topology *depth*) (make-dynamic-tree-topology *depth*) (get-root) (left-child) (right-child)
Butterfly	(make-butterfly-topology *levels*) (move-straight-left) (move-straight-right) (move-cross-left) (move-cross-right)

Fig. 2. Interfaces for built-in topologies.

machine on which it is to run. Mapping a tree onto a physical topology such as a bus or hypercube is defined by a topology that relates virtual processors to physical ones.

The implementation of a virtual tree topology on a physical ring as implemented in our system is given in Section 7. Figure 3 illustrates such a virtual topology.

5   The Abstractions

5.1   Virtual Processors

In instances where a desired virtual topology is not available, programmers can build their own using two basic abstractions. The first is a *virtual processor*. A virtual processor is a first-class object that abstracts policy decisions related to thread scheduling, mapping, and migration. Threads execute on a virtual processor. There may be many threads mapped to the same processor, and no constraints are imposed by the abstraction on how these threads are scheduled. There are five simple operations on virtual processors:

(make-vp *pp*)   returns a new virtual processor mapped onto physical processor *pp*.

(current-vp)   returns the virtual processor on which this operation is evaluated.

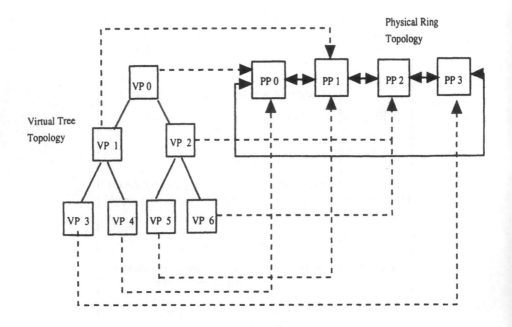

Fig. 3. A virtual topology that embeds a tree onto a ring.

(vp->address *vp*) returns the address of *vp* in the topology of which it is a part.

(set-vp->address *vp addr*) sets *vp*'s address in a virtual topology to be *addr*.

Each virtual processor implements a very simple control logic: it repeatedly removes a thread from its thread ready queue for evaluation or, if the queue is empty, calls a policy procedure. This procedure may choose to migrate a new thread from some other virtual processor, or initiate a context-switch to the underlying physical processor (PP). The PP may at this point choose to run any other VP in its VP ready queue, migrate VPs from other processors, or perform bookkeeping operations. Running a new VP is tantamount to shifting the locus of control to a new node in a virtual topology.

Notice that two levels of context-switching takes place in this design. Threads context-switch among VPs either because of preemption or because of synchronization constraints imposed by the application. VPs context switch among PPs to improve load-balancing and overall efficency; for example, a VP will choose to initiate a context-switch if its thread queue is empty, thereby allowing threads resident on another (currently idle) VP to run.

5.2 Physical Processors

The second abstraction necessary to construct topologies are *physical processors*. A physical processor is a software abstraction of a physical computing device. Each of these physical processors exist in a physical topology that reflects an underlying hardware interconnection structure. Operations analogous to those available on virtual processors exist for physical ones.

A set of physical processors along with a specific physical topology form a *physical machine*. Each physical machine provides a set of topology dependent primitive functions to access physical processors. For example, a machine with a ring topology may provide: (a) (current-pp) which returns the physical physical processor on which this operation executes; (b) (pp->address *pp*) that returns the address in the physical topology to which pp is associated; (c) (move-left *i*) which returns the pp *i* steps to the left of (current-pp); and, (d) (move-right *i*) which behaves analogously. Given procedures for accessing virtual and physical processors, topology mappings can be expressed using well-known techniques [5, 12].

6 Example Revisited

```
(define (D&C merge streams)
  (let* ((depth (log (length streams)))
         (root  (make-static-tree-topology depth)))
    (let loop ((streams streams)
               (node (current-node)))
      (future
        (if (null? (cdr s))
            streams
            (let ((output-stream (make-stream)))
              (merge (loop (left-half streams) (left-child))
                     (loop (right-half streams) (right-child))
                     output-stream)))
        node)))))
```

Fig. 4. A divide-and-conquer procedure using virtual topologies.

We use topologies in parallel programs by allowing virtual processors to be provided as explicit arguments to thread creation operators. Consider the merge stream example shown in Figure 1. Using topologies, this program fragment could be rewritten as shown in Figure 4.

The changes to the code from the original are shown in italics. Although the changes all small, they lead to potentially significant gains in efficiency and expressivity. Each application of a future now takes as its argument a virtual processor that specifies where the thread created by the future should evaluate on the virtual topology. Left-child and right-child return the left and right child of the current VP in the virtual topology created by tree.

7 A Virtual Tree Topology

The code shown in Figure 5 defines procedures for constructing a static tree topology of some depth. A physical topology accessor procedure is passed as an argument to `child` in `make-tree`; the definition of these accessors is given in Figure 6. The call to `make-tree-node` returns a tree node structure that contains fields for traversing trees; the `define-structure` special form provides accessor and setter procedures on structure fields.

The `left-child` accessor procedure returns the left child of the virtual processor on which this operation is executed. A call to a tree accessor procedure performed by some thread whose virtual processor V is mapped to a leaf node in this topology simply returns V.

7.1 Mapping Trees onto Rings

The code shown in Figure 6 demonstrates how a tree virtual topology may be embedded in a ring physical topology. Given a virtual processor `vp`, `pp-map-left-child` returns the physical processor on which `vp`'s left child should execute.

8 Benchmarks

The benchmarks shown in this section were implemented on an eight processor Silicon Graphics 75MHz MIPS-R3000 shared memory machine. The machine contains 256 MB of main memory and a one MB unified secondary cache; each processor has a 64KB data and a 64KB instruction primary cache.

Offhand, it might appear that the benefits of virtual topologies would be nominal on a shared-memory machine since the cost of inter-processor communication is effectively the cost of accessing shared memory. However, even in this environment, virtual topologies can be used profitably. Communication locality effects easily observable on a distributed memory system are modeled on a shared-memory machine in terms of memory locality. For example, programs can exhibit better cache behavior if communicating threads (or threads with manifest data dependencies) are mapped onto the same processor when possible, provided that such mappings will not lead to poor processor utilization. A system that supports fast creation and efficient management of threads and virtual processors would thus benefit from using virtual topologies regardless of the underlying physical topology.

8.1 Baseline Costs

Since there may be many virtual processors executing on a single physical one, implementations of virtual topologies must ensure that the cost of creating and managing

```
(define-structure node
  vp
  left-child
  right-child)

(define (make&init-node vp)
  (let ((node (make-node)))
    (set-node-vp node vp)
    (set-node-left-child! node nil)
    (set-node-right-child! node nil)
    (set-vp->address vp node)
    node))

(define (make-tree depth)
  (let ((root (make&init-node (make-vp (current-pp)) 0)))
    (let loop ((node root)        ;; local recursion
               (cur-depth 0))
      (cond ((= cur-depth depth) node)
            (else
             (let* ((child
                     (lambda (pp-mapper)
                       (make&init-node
                        (make-vp (pp-mapper (node-vp node))))))
                    (left  (loop (child pp-map-left-child)
                                 (+ cur-depth 1)))
                    (right (loop (child pp-map-right-child)
                                 (+ cur-depth 1))))
               (set-node-left-child!  node left)
               (set-node-right-child! node right)))))))

(define (left-child)
  (node-left-child (vp->address (current-vp))))
(define (right-child)
  (node-right-child (vp->address (current-vp))))
```

Fig. 5. The specification of a tree topology.

virtual processors on a physical one is small. In the implementation described here, the cost of creating a virtual processor is roughly comparable to the cost of creating a thread; a VP is represented by a data structure whose size is approximately 20 long words. Encapsulated in this data structure are fields containing the physical processor to which this VP is mapped, and references to exception handlers, scheduler procedures, and various thread queues.

Figure 7 gives some baseline costs for creating and managing virtual processors. Our implementation of virtual topologies was built as part of Sting [10, 16] intended to serve as a high-level operating system for high-level programming languages such as

```
(define (pp-map-left-child vp)
  (let* ((index (vp->address vp))
         (pos (+ (* 2 index) 1))
         (shift (mod pos num-pps)))
    (if (> pos num-pps)
        (move-left shift)
        (move-right shift))))

(define (pp-map-right-child vp)
  (let* ((index (vp->address vp))
         (pos (+ (* 2 index) 2))
         (shift (mod pos num-pps)))
    (if (> pos num-pps)
        (move-right shift)
        (move-left shift))))
```

Fig. 6. Embedding a virtual tree onto a physical ring.

Scheme [4], ML [13], or Haskell [8].

Operation	Times (μ-seconds)
Creating a VP	31
Adding a VP to a VM	5.4
Fork/Tree	25
Fork/Vector	20
VP Context Switch	68
Dynamic Tree	207

Fig. 7. Baseline times for managing virtual processors and threads.

"Creating a VP" is the cost of creating, initializing, and adding a new virtual to a virtual machine; note that it is roughly the cost of creating a thread on a tree or vector processor topology. "Adding a VP to a VM" is the cost of updating a virtual machine's state with a new virtual processor. "Fork/Tree" is the cost of creating a thread on a static tree topology; "Fork/Vector" is the cost of creating a thread on a static vector topology. "VP Context Switch" is the cost of context-switching two virtual processors on the same physical processor; it also includes the cost of starting up a thread on the processor. "Dynamic Tree" is the cost of adding a new VP to a dynamic tree topology.

8.2 Applications

We consider three benchmarks to highlight various aspects of our design. All times derived using a particular topology mapping are compared relative to a round-robin global FIFO scheduler on a simple processor configuration in which there is a one-to-one map between virtual and physical processors. All benchmarks were structured so as not to trigger garbage collection. All times are given in seconds.

Details of the benchmarks are given below. Since all these benchmarks were executed on a physically shared-memory platform, we expect the performance benefits to increase significantly on disjoint memory architectures.

1. **MinMax.** The topology of a program cannot always be determined statically. For many algorithms, the process structure is dependent on the computation itself. Virtual topologies are well suited to these problems since virtual processors are dynamic objects: they may be created at run time, assigned to a physical processor and garbage collected when no longer needed. In addition, virtual topologies can be reconfigured dynamically by moving virtual processors from one physical processor to another.

   As an example, consider the minmax algorithm for game trees. Typically, the depth to which a branch of the game tree is explored depends on the perceived potential of the game positions along that branch. Thus, the process tree is skewed and its structure cannot be determined statically.

   A naive implementation of this algorithm on a complete tree topology may result in poor performance. For example, one may choose to map all virtual processors in a subtree below a certain depth to the same physical processor (arguing that this gives the best locality) and then find that most of the computation takes place along one long branch in that subtree. An alternate method would delay the creation of the topology until the computation requires allocating a thread on some portion of the topology that does not yet exist. At this point, the topology can be extended with the addition of a new virtual processor. Since more information is available when this happens, better load balancing may result. It is worth emphasizing that, since virtual processors are very light weight, the cost of dynamic manipulation is small. To test this functionality, we measured the performance of a static topology mapping versus a dynamic one using a tree of depth 150 with varying cutoff depths on 8 processors; these cutoff depths indicate the point at which no new virtual processors are added:

Cutoff	2	3	4	5	6	7	8
Static	5.88	5.87	5.76	5.71	5.67	5.71	5.78
Dynamic	5.92	6.05	5.69	5.40	5.26	4.96	5.15

   At a depth cutoff of 7, for example, minimax performed approximately 14% faster using a dynamic topology than a static one. Using a simple round-robin scheduler, this program took 10.23 seconds to execute on 8 processors, roughly 50% slower than the dynamic tree topology.

2. **Quicksort** sorts a vector of 2^{18} integers using a parallel divide-and-conquer strategy. We use a tree topology that dynamically allocates virtual processors; the maximum depth of the topology tree in this problem was 6; calls to left-child and

`right-child` result in the creation of new virtual processors if required. The virtual to physical topology mapping chooses one child at random to be mapped onto the same physical processor as its parent in the virtual topology. Internal threads in the process tree generated by this program yield as their value a sorted sub-list; because of the topology mapping used, more opportunities for thread absorption [10], or task stealing [14] present themselves relative to an implementation that performs round-robin or random allocation of threads to processors. This is because at least one child thread is allocated on the same virtual processor as its parent; since the child will not execute before the parent unless migrated to another VP, it will be a strong target for thread absorption. The impact of improved cache locality and greater absorption is evident in the wallclock times shown below – on eight processors, the mapped version was roughly 1.4 times faster than the unmapped one; roughly 14% more threads were absorbed in the topology mapped version than in the unmapped case (201 threads absorbed vs. 171 absorbed with a total number of 239 threads created).

	Processors			
	1	2	4	8
Dynamic Tree (depth 6)	8.57	4.51	2.45	1.7
Round-Robin	8.49	4.95	3.16	2.51

3. **Hamming** computes the extended hamming numbers up to 10000 for the first 16 primes. The extended hamming problem is defined thus: given a finite sequence of primes $A, B, C, D, \ldots$ and an integer n as input, output in increasing magnitude without duplication all integers less than or equal to n of the form

$$(A^i) \times (B^j) \times (C^k) \times (D^l) \times \ldots$$

This problem is structured in terms of a tree of mutually recursive threads that communicate via streams. The program example shown in Figure 1 captures the basic structure of this problem. There is a significant amount of communication locality exhibited by this program. A useful virtual topology for this example would be a static tree of depth equivalent to the depth of the process tree. By mapping siblings in the tree to different virtual processors, and selected children to the same processor as their parent, we can effectively exploit communication patterns evident in the algorithm. On eight processors, the implementation using topologies outperformed an unmapped round-robin scheduling policy by over a factor of six:

	Processors			
	1	2	4	8
Static Tree (Depth 5)	143.5	108.3	46	15.3
Round-Robin	140.4	118.24	100	96.5

9 Conclusions and Comparison to Related Work

Concurrent dialects of high-level languages such as Scheme [9, 11], ML [15, 17], or Concurrent Prolog [3, 21] typically encapsulate all scheduling, load-balancing and thread management decisions as part of a runtime kernel implementation. Consequently, locality and communication properties of an algorithm must often be inferred by a runtime system, since they cannot be specified by the programmer even when readily apparent.

Concurrent computing environments such as PVM [22] permit the construction of a type of virtual machine; such machines, however, consist of heavyweight Unix tasks that communicate exclusively via message-passing. In general, it is expected that there will be as many tasks in a PVM virtual machine as available processors in the ensemble. Systems such as Linda [1] that provide operations for dynamically creating and synchronizing threads provide no high-level mechanism to specify how threads should be load-balanced or mapped onto processors since virtual topologies are not part of their abstract machine model.

Our work is closely related to *para-functional* programming [7]. Para-functional languages extend implicitly parallel, lazy languages such as Haskell [8] with two annotations: *scheduling expressions* that provide user-control on evaluation order of expressions that would otherwise be evaluated lazily, and *mapping expressions* that permit programmers to map expressions onto distinct virtual processors.

While the goals of para-functional programming share much in common with ours, there are numerous differences in the technical development. First, we subsume the need for *scheduling expressions* by allowing programmers to create lightweight threads wherever concurrency is desired; thus, our programming model assumes explicit parallelism. Second, because VPs are closed over their own scheduling policy manager and thread queues, threads with different scheduling requirements can be mapped onto VPs that satisfy these requirements; in contrast, virtual processors in the para-functional model are simply integers. Third, there is no distinction between virtual and physical processors in a para-functional language; thus virtual to physical processor mappings cannot be expressed. Finally, para-functional languages, to our knowledge, have not been the focus of any implementation effort; by itself, the abstract model provides no insight into the efficiency impact of a given virtual topology in terms of increased data and communication locality.

Schwan and Bo[20] describe a topology abstraction for programming distributed memory machines. A topology in their system "represents a distributed object as an arbitrary communication graph with nodes that contain the object's distributed representation and execute the object's operations." While the motivation for topologies is similar to ours, the designs of the two systems are very different. Our topologies are first-class objects built using virtual processors. As a result, virtual topologies can be dynamically reconfigured or extended. Furthermore, the implementation of topologies is given via first-class procedures, rather than in terms of a separate abstract data type representation. Finally, our primary goal in defining virtual topologies was to exploit communciation and data locality, and to provide mechanism for customization of diverse scheduling policies. In contrast, the system described in [20] focuses on synchronization, message-passing, and global communication abstractions.

Finally, there has been much work in realizing improved data locality by sophisticated compile-time analysis [18, 24] or by explicit data distribution annotations [2]; the focus of these efforts has been on developing compiler optimizations for implicitly parallel languages. Outside of the fact that we assume explicit parallelism, our work is distinguished from these efforts insofar as virtual topologies require annotations on threads, not on the data used by them. Deriving efficient data distributions is straightforward given a topology that provides a relation over these threads.

While our results are still preliminary, they support our hypothesis that topology mapping and first-class processors will have significant benefit in optimizing communication and data locality for many high-level parallel applications.

References

1. Nick Carriero and David Gelernter. Linda in Context. *Communications of the ACM*, 32(4):444 – 458, April 1989.

2. Marina Chen, Young-il Choo, and Jingke Li. Compiling Parallel Programs by Optimizing Performance. *Journal of Supercomputing*, 1(2):171–207, 1988.

3. K.L Clark and S. Gregory. PARLOG: Parallel Programming in Logic. *ACM Transactions on Programming Languages and Systems*, 8(1):1–49, 1986.

4. William Clinger and Jonathan Rees, editors. Revised⁴ Report on the Algorithmic Language Scheme. *ACM Lisp Pointers*, 4(3), July 1991.

5. David Saks Greenberg. *Full Utilization of Communication Resources*. PhD thesis, Yale University, June 1991.

6. Robert Halstead. Multilisp: A Language for Concurrent Symbolic Computation. *Transactions on Programming Languages and Systems*, 7(4):501–538, October 1985.

7. Paul Hudak. Para-functional Programming in Haskell. In Boleslaw K. Szymanski, editor, *Parallel Functional Languages and Compilers*. ACM Press, 1991.

8. Paul Hudak *et.al.* Report on the Functional Programming Language Haskell, Version 1.2. *ACM SIGPLAN Notices*, May 1992.

9. Takayasu Ito and Robert Halstead, Jr., editors. *Parallel Lisp: Languages and Systems*. Springer-Verlag, 1989. LNCS number 41.

10. Suresh Jagannathan and James Philbin. A Customizable Substrate for Concurrent Languages. In *ACM SIGPLAN '91 Conference on Programming Language Design and Implementation*, June 1992.

11. David Kranz, Robert Halstead, and Eric Mohr. Mul-T: A High Performance Parallel Lisp. In *Proceedings of the ACM Symposium on Programming Language Design and Implementation*, pages 81–91, June 1989.

12. F. Thomas Leighton. *Introduction to Parallel Algorithms and Architectures*. Morgan-Kaufmann, 1992.

13. Robin Milner, Mads Tofte, and Robert Harper. *The Definition of Standard ML*. MIT Press, 1990.

14. Rick Mohr, David Kranz, and Robert Halstead. Lazy Task Creation: A Technique for Increasing the Granularity of Parallel Programs. In *Proceedings of the 1990 ACM Conference on Lisp and Functional Programming*, June 1990.

15. J. Gregory Morrisett and Andrew Tolmach. Procs and Locks: A Portable Multiprocessing Platform for Standard ML of New Jersey. In *Fourth ACM Symposium on Principles and Practice of Parallel Programming*, pages 198–207, 1993.

16. James Philbin. *An Operating System for Modern Languages*. PhD thesis, Dept. of Computer Science, Yale University, 1993.

17. John Reppy. CML: A Higher-Order Concurrent Language. In *Proceedings of the SIGPLAN'91 Conference on Programming Language Design and Implementation*, pages 293–306, June 1991.

18. Anne Rogers and Keshave Pingali. Process Decomposition Through Locality of Reference. In *SIGPLAN'89 Conference on Programming Language Design and Implementation*, pages 69–80, 1989.

19. Vijay Saraswat and Martin Rinard. Concurrent Constraint Programming. In *Proceedings of the 17th ACM Symposium on Principles of Programming Languages*, pages 232–246, 1990.

20. Karsten Schwan and Win Bo. Topologies – Distributed Objects on Multicomputers. *ACM Transactions on Computer Systems*, 8(2):111–157, May 1990.

21. Ehud Shapiro, editor. *Concurrent Prolog Collected Papers*. MIT Press, Cambridge, Mass., 1987.

22. V.S. Sunderam. PVM: A Framework for Parallel Distributed Computing. *Concurrency: Practice & Experience*, 2(4), 1990.

23. M. Vandevoorde and E. Roberts. WorkCrews: An Abstraction for Controlling Parallelism. *International Journal of Parallel Programming*, 17(4):347–366, August 1988.

24. Michael Wolfe. *Optimizing Supercompilers for SuperComputers*. MIT Press, 1989.

Interprocedural Data Flow Based Optimizations for Compilation of Irregular Problems

Gagan Agrawal and Joel Saltz

Department of Computer Science
University of Maryland
College Park, MD 20742
(301)-405-2756
{gagan,saltz}@cs.umd.edu

Abstract. Data parallel languages like High Performance Fortran (HPF) are emerging as the architecture independent mode of programming distributed memory parallel machines. In this paper, we present the interprocedural optimizations required for compiling applications having irregular data access patterns, when coded in such data parallel languages. We have developed an Interprocedural Partial Redundancy Elimination (IPRE) algorithm for optimized placement of runtime preprocessing routine and collective communication routines inserted for managing communication in such codes. We also present two new interprocedural optimizations: placement of scatter routines and use of coalescing and incremental routines.

1 Introduction

In recent years, significant effort has been made to compile applications having irregular and/or dynamic data accesses (possibly with the help of additional language support) [4, 8, 10, 13]. For such codes, the compiler can analyze the data access pattern and insert appropriate communication and communication preprocessing routines. It is clear that sophisticated compilation techniques are required for getting optimized performance from irregular codes [4, 8]. These techniques have been implemented in prototype compilers for HPF like languages, however the experiences and experimental results reported have been from small code templates. For large applications, various optimizations will need to be applied across procedure boundaries to generate optimized code.

In this paper, we discuss the interprocedural analysis and optimizations for compiling irregular applications. Specifically, we concentrate on applications in

---

[1] This work was supported by NSF under grant No. ASC 9213821, by ONR under contract Numbers N00014-93-1-0158 and N000149410907, by ARPA under the Scalable I/O Project (Caltech Subcontract 9503) and by NASA/ARPA contract No. NAG-1-1485. The authors assume all responsibility for the contents of the paper.

which data is accessed using indirection arrays. Such codes are common in computational fluid dynamics, molecular dynamics, in Particle In Cell (PIC) problems and in numerical simulations.

The commonly used approach for compiling irregular applications is the inspector/executor model [10]. Conceptually, an *inspector* or a *communication preprocessing statement* analyses the indirection array to determine the communication required by a data parallel loop. The results of communication preprocessing is then used to perform the communication. CHAOS/PARTI library provides a rich set of routines for performing the communication preprocessing and optimized communication for such applications [12]. The Fortran D compilation system, a prototype compiler for distributed memory machines, initially targeted regular applications [9] but has more recently been extended to compile irregular applications [4, 8]. In compiling irregular applications, the Fortran D compiler inserts calls CHAOS/PARTI library routines to manage communication [4, 8].

An important optimization required for irregular applications is placement of communication preprocessing and communication statements. Techniques for performing these optimizations within a single procedure are well developed [6, 8]. The key idea underlying these schemes is to do the placement so that redundancies are removed or reduced. These schemes are closely based upon a classical data flow framework called Partial Redundancy Elimination (PRE) [5, 11]. PRE encompasses traditional optimizations like loop invariant code motion and redundant computation elimination.

We have worked on an Interprocedural Partial Redundancy Elimination framework (IPRE) [1, 3] as a basis for performing interprocedural placement. In this paper, we discuss various practical aspects in applying interprocedural partial redundancy elimination for placement of communication and communication preprocessing statements. We also present two other interprocedural optimizations useful in compiling irregular applications, these are placement of scatter operations and use of incremental and coalescing routines.

We have carried out a preliminary implementation of the schemes presented in this paper using the Fortran D system as the necessary infrastructure. Experimental results from our implementation have been presented elsewhere [2].

The rest of the paper is organized as follows. In Section 2, we discuss the basic IPRE framework. In Section 3, we present two new optimizations required for compiling irregular applications. We conclude in Section 4.

2 Partial Redundancy Elimination

Most of the interprocedural optimizations required for irregular applications involve some kind of redundancy elimination or loop invariant code motion. Partial Redundancy Elimination (PRE) is a unified framework for performing these optimizations intraprocedurally [5, 11]. It has been commonly used intraprocedurally for performing optimizations like common subexpression elimination and strength reduction. More recently, it has been used for more complex code placement tasks like placement of communication statements while compiling for parallel machines [6, 8]. We have extended an existing intraprocedural partial redundancy scheme to be applied interprocedurally [1, 3]. In this section, we describe the functionality of the PRE framework, key data flow properties associated with it and briefly sketch how we have extended an existing intraprocedural scheme interprocedurally.

Consider any computation of an expression or a call to a pure function. In the program text, we may want to optimize its placement, i.e. place the computation so that the result of the computation is used as often as possible and, redundant computations are removed. For convenience, we refer to any such computation whose placement we want to optimize as a *candidate*. If this candidate is an expression, we refer to the operands of the expression as *influencers* of the candidate. If this candidate is a pure function, we refer to the parameters of the pure function as the *influencers* of the candidate.

There are three type of optimizations which are performed under PRE: .

- *Loop invariant Code Motion:* This means that if the influencers of a candidate are all invariant in the loop, then the candidate can be computed just once, before entering the loop.
- *Redundant Computation Elimination:* Consider two consecutive occurrences of a computation, such that none of influencers of the candidate are modified along any control flow path from the first occurrence to the second occurrence. In this case, the second occurrence is redundant and is deleted as part of the PRE framework.
- *Suppressing Partial Redundancies:* Consider two consecutive occurrences of a computation such that one or more influencers are modified along some possible control flow path (but not all flow paths) from the first occurrence to the second occurrence. In this case, the second occurrence of the candidate is called partially redundant. By placing candidates along the control flow paths associated with the modification, the partially redundant computation can be made redundant and thus be deleted.

We now introduce the key data flow properties that are computed as part of this framework. We use these terms for explaining several new optimizations later in the paper. The properties are:

Availability. Availability of a candidate C at any point p in the program means that C lies at each of the paths leading to point p and if C were to be placed at point p, C will have the same result as the result of the last occurrence on any of the paths.

Partial Availability. Partial availability of a candidate C at a point p in the program means that C is currently placed on at least one control flow path leading to p and if C were to be placed at the point p, C will have the same result as the result of the last occurrence on at least one of the paths.

Anticipability. Anticipability of a candidate C at a point p in the program means that C is currently placed at all the paths leading from point p, and if C were to be placed at point p, C will have the same result as the result of the first occurrence on any of the paths.

A *basic block* of code in a procedure is a sequence of consecutive statements in a procedure in the flow enters at the beginning and leaves at the end without possibility of branching expect at the end.

Transparency. Transparency of a basic block with respect to a candidate means that none of the influencers of the candidate are modified in the basic block.

If a candidate is placed at a point p in the program and if it is available at the point p, then the occurrence of the candidate at the point p is redundant. If a candidate is placed at a point p in the program and if it is partially available at the point, then it is considered to be partially redundant. Anticipability of a computation is used for determining if the placement will be *safe*. A *Safe* placement means that at least one occurrence of the candidate will be made redundant by this new placement (and will consequently be deleted). Performing safe placements guarantees that along any path, number of computations of the candidate are not increased after applying optimizing transformations.

By solving data flow equations on the Control Flow Graph (CFG) of a procedure, the Availability, Partial Availability and Anticipability properties are computed at the beginning and end of each basic block in the procedure. Transparency is used for propagating these properties, e.g. if a candidate is available at the beginning of a basic block and if the basic block is transparent with respect to this candidate, then the candidate will be available at the end of the basic block also.

Based upon the above data flow properties, another round of data flow analysis is done to determine properties PPIN (possible placement at the beginning) and PPOUT (possible placement at the end). These properties are then used for determining final placement and deletion of the candidates. We do not present the details of data flow equations in the paper.

Our interest is in applying the PRE framework for optimizing placement of communication preprocessing statements and collective communication statements. The first step in this direction was to extend the existing PRE framework interprocedurally. For applying this transformation across procedure boundaries, we need a full program representation. We have chosen a concise full program representation, which will allow efficient data flow analysis, while maintaining sufficient precision to allow useful transformations and to ensure safety and correctness of transformations.

2.1 Program Representation

In traditional interprocedural analysis, program is abstracted by a *call graph* [7]. In a call graph $G = (V, E)$, V is the set of procedures and directed edge $e = (i, j)$ ($e \in E$) represents a call site in which procedure i invokes procedure j. The limitation of call graph is that no information is available about control flow relationships between various call sites within a procedure. We have developed a new program representation called Full Program Representation (FPR). In this subsection we describe how this structure is constructed for any program.

We define a basic block to consist of consecutive statements in the program text without any procedure calls or return statements, and no branching except at the beginning and end. A procedure can then be partitioned into a set of basic blocks, a set of procedure call statements and a set of return statements. A return statement ends the invocation of procedure or subroutine call.

In our program representation, the basic idea is to construct *blocks of code* within each procedure. A block of code comprises of basic blocks which do not have any call statements between them. In the directed graph we define below, each edge e corresponds to a block of code $B(e)$. A block of code is a unit of placement in our analysis, i.e. we initially consider placement only at the beginning and end of a block of code. The nodes of the graph help clarify the control flow relationships between the blocks of code.

Full Program Representation: (FPR) is a directed multigraph $G = (V, E)$, where the set of nodes V consists of an entry node and a return node for each procedure in the program. For procedure i, the entry node is denoted by s_i and the return node is denoted by r_i. Edges are inserted in the following cases:

1. Procedures i and j are called by procedure k at call sites cs_1 and cs_2 respectively and there is a path in the CFG of k from cs_1 to cs_2 which does not include any other call statements. Edge (r_i, s_j) exists in this case. The block of code $B(e)$ consists of the basic blocks of procedure k which may be visited in any control flow path p from cs_1 to cs_2, such that the path p does not include any other call statements.
2. Procedure i calls procedure j at call site cs and there is a path in the CFG of i from the *start* node of procedure i to cs which does not include any other call statements. In this case, edge (s_i, s_j) exists. The block of code $B(e)$ consists of the basic blocks of procedure i which may be visited in any control flow path p from start of i to cs, such that the path p does not include any other call statement.
3. Procedure j calls procedure i at call site cs and there is a path in the CFG of j from call site cs to a return statement within procedure j which does not include any other call statements. In this case, edge (r_i, r_j) exists. The block of code $B(e)$ consists of the basic blocks of procedure j which may be visited in any control flow path p from cs to a return statement of j, such that the path p does not include any call statements.
4. In a procedure i, there is a possible flow of control from start node to a return statement, without any call statements. In this case, edge (s_i, r_i) exists. The block of code $B(e)$ consists of the basic blocks of procedure i which may be visited in any control flow path p from start of i to a return statement in i, such that the path p does not include any call statements.

470

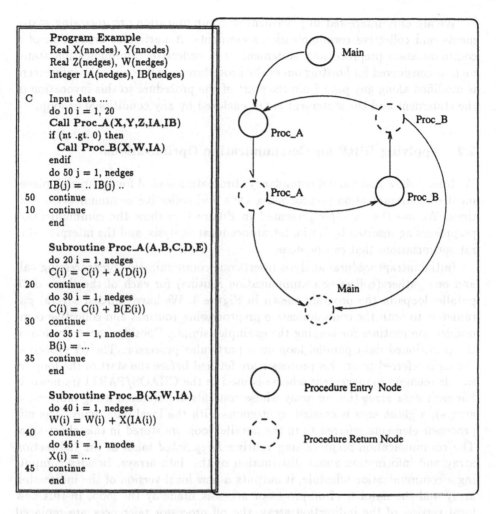

```
        Program Example
        Real X(nnodes), Y(nnodes)
        Real Z(nedges), W(nedges)
        Integer IA(nedges), IB(nedges)

C       Input data ...
        do 10 i = 1, 20
        Call Proc_A(X,Y,Z,IA,IB)
        if (nt .gt. 0) then
          Call Proc_B(X,W,IA)
        endif
        do 50 j = 1, nedges
        IB(j) = .. IB(j) ..
50      continue
10      continue
        end

        Subroutine Proc_A(A,B,C,D,E)
        do 20 i = 1, nedges
        C(i) = C(i) + A(D(i))
20      continue
        do 30 i = 1, nedges
        C(i) = C(i) + B(E(i))
30      continue
        do 35 i = 1, nnodes
        B(i) = ...
35      continue
        end

        Subroutine Proc_B(X,W,IA)
        do 40 i = 1, nedges
        W(i) = W(i) + X(IA(i))
40      continue
        do 45 i = 1, nnodes
        X(i) = ...
45      continue
        end
```

Main

Proc_B

Proc_A

Proc_A

Proc_B

Main

Procedure Entry Node

Procedure Return Node

Fig. 1. An Irregular Code   **Fig. 2.** *FPR* for the example program

In Figure 1, we show an example program (which involves irregular accesses to data). The program represenation *FPR* for this program is shown in Figure 2.

For performing partial redundancy elimination on the full program, we apply data flow analysis on *FPR*, rather than the CFG of a single procedure. Instead of considering transparency of each basic block, we consider transparency of each edge or the block of code. The data flow properties are computed for the beginning and the end of each edge in the *FPR* program representation. The details of the data flow analysis required for computing the above properties and then determining placement and deletion based on these has been given elsewhere [1, 3]. There are several difficulties in extending the analysis interprocedurally, this includes renaming of influencers across procedure boundaries, saving the calling context of procedures which are called at more than one call sites and further intraprocedural analysis in each procedure to determine final local placement. These details have been presented elsewhere and are not the focus of this paper.

We are only interested in placement of communication preprocessing statements and collective communication statements. A particular invocation of a communication preprocessing statement or a collective communication statement is considered for hoisting out of the procedure only if none of the influencers is modified along any path from the start of the procedure to this invocation of the statement and the statement is not enclosed by any conditional or loop.

2.2 Applying IPRE for Communication Optimizations

We briefly show how partial redundancy elimination is used for optimizing placement of communication preprocessing calls and collective communication routines. We use the example presented in Figure 1 to show the communication preprocessing inserted by initial intraprocedural analysis, and the interprocedural optimizations that can be done.

Initial intraprocedural analysis inserts one communication preprocessing call and one gather (collective communication routine) for each of the three data parallel loops in the program shown in Figure 3. We have omitted several parameters to both the communication preprocessing routines and collective communication routines for keeping the examples simple. Consider the execution of the partitioned data parallel loop on a particular processor. The off-processor elements referred to on this processor are fetched before the start of the loop. A simple memory management scheme is used in the CHAOS/PARTI framework. For each *data array* (i.e. an array whose contents are accessed using indirection arrays), a ghost area is created, contiguous with the local data array. The off-processor elements referred to in the parallel loop are stored in this ghost area. The communication preprocessing routine *Irreg_Sched* takes in the indirection array and information about distribution of the data arrays. Besides computing a communication schedule, it outputs a new local version of the indirection array and the number of off-processor accesses made by the loop. In this new local version of the indirection array, the off-processor references are replaced by appropriate references to the elements in the ghost area. The collective communication calls also need the starting position of the ghost area as one of the parameters. For simplicity, this detail is omitted in all the examples.

In Figure 3, we also show the program after interprocedural optimization of communication preprocessing routines and gather routines. We refer to the loop in the main of the program (which encloses the calls to the routines Proc_A and Proc_B) as the *time step* loop. Initially, interprocedural partial redundancy elimination is applied for communication preprocessing statements. Since the array IA is never modified inside the time step loop in the main procedure, the schedules $Sched1$ and $Sched3$ are loop invariant and can be hoisted outside the loop. Further, it can be deduced that the computation of $Sched1$ and $Sched3$ are equivalent (since their influencers, after renaming across procedure boundaries, are the same). So, only $Sched1$ needs to be computed, and the gather routine in Proc_B can use $Sched1$ instead of $Sched3$. For simplicity, $Sched1$ is declared to

Program Example

```
        Real X(nnodes), Y(nnodes)
        Real Z(nedges), W(nedges)
        Integer IA(nedges), IB(nedges)
C       Input data ...
        do 10 i = 1, 20
        Call Proc_A(X,Y,Z,IA,IB)
        if (nt .gt. 0) then
           Call Proc_B(X,W,IA)
        endif
        do 50 j = 1, nedges_local
        IB(j) = .. IB(j) ..
50      continue
10      continue
        end
```

Subroutine Proc_A(A,B,C,D,E)

```
        Sched1 = Irreg_Sched(D)
        Call Gather(A,Sched1)
        do 20 i = 1, nedges_local
        C(i) = C(i) + A(D(i))
20      continue
        Sched2 = Irreg_Sched(E)
        Call Gather(B,Sched2)
        do 30 i = 1, nedges_local
        C(i) = C(i) + B(E(i))
30      continue
        do 35 i = 1, nnodes_local
        B(i) = ...
35      continue
        end
```

Subroutine Proc_B(X,W,IA)

```
        Sched3 = Irreg_Sched(IA)
        Call Gather(X,Sched3)
        do 40 i = 1, nedges_local
        W(i) = W(i) + X(IA(i))
40      continue
        do 45 i = 1, nnodes_local
        X(i) = ...
45      continue
        end
```

Program Example

```
        Real X(nnodes), Y(nnodes)
        Real Z(nedges), W(nedges)
        Integer IA(nedges), IB(nedges)
C       Input data ...
        Sched1 = Irreg_Sched(IA)
        do 10 i = 1, 20
        Call Proc_A(X,Y,Z,IA,IB)
        if (nt .gt. 0) then
           Call Proc_B(X,W,IA)
        endif
        do 50 j = 1, nedges_local
        IB(j) = .. IB(j)..
50      continue
10      continue
        end
```

Subroutine Proc_A(A,B,C,D,E)

```
        Call Gather(A,Sched1)
        do 20 i = 1, nedges_local
        C(i) = C(i) + A(D(i))
20      continue
        Sched2 = Irreg_Sched(E)
        Call Gather(B,Sched2)
        do 30 i = 1, nedges_local
        C(i) = C(i) + B(E(i))
30      continue
        do 35 i = 1, nnodes_local
        B(i) = ...
35      continue
        end
```

Subroutine Proc_B(X,W,IA)

```
        do 40 i = 1, nedges_local
        W(i) = W(i) + X(IA(i))
40      continue
        do 45 i = 1, nnodes_local
        X(i) = ...
45      continue
        end
```

Fig. 3. Result of Intraprocedural Compilation (left), and Code after Interprocedural Optimizations (right)

be a global variable, so that it does not need to be passed along as parameter at different call sites. After placement of communication preprocessing statements is determined, we apply the IPRE analysis for communication routines. The gather for array IA in routine Proc_B is redundant because of the gather of array D in routine Proc_A. Note that performing IPRE on communication preprocessing statements before applying IPRE on communication statements is critical, since it is important to know that $Sched3$, one of the influencers of gather for array IB can be replaced by $Sched1$.

3 Other Optimizations for Compiling Irregular Problems

In this section, we discuss two new interprocedural optimizations which are useful in compiling irregular applications. These optimizations are: placement of scatter operations and use of incremental and coalescing routines. While none of these optimizations can be directly achieved by the interprocedural partial redundancy elimination scheme we have so far described, they can be achieved through extending the IPRE scheme or using a variation of the basic IPRE analysis.

3.1 Placement of Scatter Operations

Collective communication routines can be broadly classified to be of two kinds: *gathers* and *scatters*. By gather, we mean a routine which, before entering a data parallel loop, collects the off-processor elements referred to in the loop. By scatter, we mean a routine which, after a data parallel loop, updates the off-processor elements modified by the loop.

In distributed memory compilation, a commonly used technique for loop iteration partitioning is *owner computes rule* [9]. In this method, each iteration is executed by the processor which owns the left hand side array reference updated by the iteration. If the owner computes rule is used, then no communication is required after the end of a data parallel loop, since no off-processor element is modified by the loop.

Owner computes rule is often not best suited for irregular codes. This is because of two reasons: Use of indirection in accessing left hand side array makes it difficult to partition the loop iterations according to the owner computes rule, secondly, because of the use of indirection in accessing right hand side elements, total communication may be reduced by using heuristics other than the owner computes rule.

If a method other than owner computes is used for loop partitioning, there is need for routines *scatter_op*, which will perform an *op* on the off-processor data, using the values computed in the loop. In Figure 4, we show an example of a code requiring scatter_op routines. In the two data parallel loops, loop iteration i is executed by processor owning $Z(i)$ and $W(i)$ respectively. Further suppose

Program Example
Real X(nnodes)
Real Z(nedges), W(nedges)
Integer IA(nedges)
C   Input data ...
     do 10 i = 1, 20
     Call Proc_A(X,Z,IA)
     Call Proc_B(X,W,IA)
10   continue
     end

Proc_A(A,B,C)
     do 20 i = 1, nedges
     A(C(i)) = A(C(i)) + B(i)
20   continue
     end

Proc_B(X,W,IA)
     do 40 i = 1, nedges
     X(IA(i)) = X(IA(i)) + W(i)
40   continue
     do 45 i = 1, nnodes
     X(i) = ...
45   continue
     end

Program Example
Real X(nnodes)
Real Z(nedges), W(nedges)
Integer IA(nedges)
C   Input data ...
     Sched1 = Irreg_Sched(IA)
     do 10 i = 1, 20
     Call Proc_A(X,Z,IA)
     Call Proc_B(X,W,IA)
10   continue
     end

Proc_A(A,B,C)
     do 20 i = 1, nedges_local
     A(C(i)) = A(C(i)) + B(i)
20   continue
     end

Proc_B(X,W,IA)
     do 40 i = 1, nedges_local
     X(IA(i)) = X(IA(i)) + W(i)
40   continue
     Call Scatter_add(X,Sched1)
     do 45 i = 1, nnodes_local
     X(i) = ...
45   continue
     end

Fig. 4. Compilation and optimization of a code involving scatter operations: Original sequential code (left) and compiled code after Interprocedural Optimizations (right)

that the arrays W, X and Z are identically distributed. Array element X(IA(i)) is modified (an addition operation is performed) in such an iteration, and in general, this can be an off-processor reference. The communication preprocessing routine generates a new local version of the array IA, in which the references to the off-processor elements are changed to references to the elements in the ghost area. Modifications to the off-processor references are stored in the ghost area. (Before the loops, the elements of the ghost area need to be initialized to 0, this detail is omitted from our example). After the end of the loop, the collective communication routine *scatter_add* is used to update the off-processor elements.

In the example presented in Section 2, the collective communication routine involved were the gather operations. For performing optimized placements, gather operations were treated in the same way as the communication preprocessing routines. We now discuss what kind of analysis is required to determine optimized placement of scatter_ops.

There are two differences in dealing with scatters_ops as compared to gathers. We have seen so far, how the placement of a gather operation can be moved earlier, if this can reduce redundant communication. The required condition is that the placement must be done after the last modification of the array whose data is being gathered. Thus, we need to check if the array whose data is being gathered is modified.

In the case of scatter_ops, the placement can be done later, if this can reduce redundancies. The required condition is that the array whose data is being scattered must not be *referred* to or *modified*. If the array being scattered is referred to, then the reference made may be incorrect because the modifications made in an earlier loop have not been updated. Similarly, if the array being scattered is modified, then the updates made later may be incorrect.

Optimization of scatter_ops is therefore done by applying IPRE scheme with three differences:

- We consider a scatter operation for interprocedural placement only if none of the influencers are modified or referred to along any control flow path from the scatter's invocation to the end of the procedure, and if this invocation of scatter operation is not enclosed by any conditional or loop.
- We change the definition of Transparency, to check if the influencers of the candidate are neither referred to nor modified.
- We consider our graph, as defined in Section 2, with the notion of source and sink reversed. Thus, we tend to move the scatter_ops downwards, if there is any redundancy to be eliminated this way.

In Figure 4, the result of interprocedural optimization is shown in the right. In the procedure Proc_A, the scatter operation can be deleted, since this scatter is subsumed by the scatter done later in Proc_B.

Scatter operations have also been used by distributed memory compilers in compiling regular applications. The HPF/Fortran 90D compiler developed at Syracuse University uses scatter operations (called *post-comp writes*) whenever the subscript in the left hand side array reference is a complex function of the index variable. The optimization described above will therefore be applicable in compiling regular applications also.

3.2 Using Incremental and Coalescing Communication Routines

Consider an occurrence of a communication statement. While this communication statement may not be redundant (the same candidate may not be directly available), there may be some other communication statement, which may be gathering at least a subset of the values gathered in this statement. The execution time of the code can be reduced by disallowing redundant gathering of certain data elements.

Consider the program shown in Figure 5. The same data array X is accessed using an indirection array IA in the procedure Proc_A and using another indirection array IB in the procedure Proc_B. Further, none of the indirection arrays or the data array X is modified between flow of control from first loop to the second loop. The set of data elements to be communicated between the processors can only be determined at runtime, however it is very likely that there will be at least some overlap between the set of off-processor references made in these two loops. At the time of schedule generation, the contents of the array IA and IB can be analyzed to reduce the net communication required by these two loops.

PARTI/CHAOS library provides two kinds of communication routines for reducing communication in such situations. *Coalescing* preprocessing routines take more than one indirection array, and produce a single schedule, which can be used for generating the communication required by different loops. In the example mentioned above, a coalescing communication preprocessing routine will take in arrays IA and IB and produce a single communication schedule. If a gather operation is done using this schedule, then all off-processor elements referred to through indirection arrays IA and IB will be gathered. *Incremental* preprocessing routine will take in indirection arrays IA and IB, and will determine the off-processor references made uniquely through indirection array IB and not through indirection array IA (or vice-versa). While executing the second loop, communication using an incremental schedule can be done, to gather only the data elements which were not gathered during the first loop.

Use of both incremental and coalescing routines reduces the net communication volume. The advantage of using coalescing routines over incremental routines is that only one message is required for communication. This further reduces the communication latency involved.

The following analysis is done to determine use of coalescing and incremental communication preprocessing routines. After the placement of communication preprocessing and communication statements has been determined, consider two communication statements $L1$ and $L2$, which do gathers for the same data array.

Recall the definition of *Availability* and *Anticipability*, as presented in Section 2. The communication done by the statements $L1$ and $L2$ can be done by using a single coalescing routine if the following holds:

- The communication done in $L1$ is available at the point $L2$ in the program, **and**
- The communication done in $L2$ is anticipable at the point $L1$ in the program.

In this case, the communication at $L2$ can be deleted and the communication at $L1$ can be replaced by a coalesced communication. The first condition above ensures that the elements communicated at the point $L1$ in the program will still be valid at the point $L2$ in the program. If the communication at $L1$ is replaced by a coalesced communication, then the second condition above ensures that, along any control flow path starting from $L1$, the additional data communicated will be used.

```
          Program Example                              Program Example
          Real X(nnodes)                               Real X(nnodes)
          Real Z(nedges), W(nedges)                    Real Z(nedges), W(nedges)
          Integer IA(nedges), IB(nedges)               Integer IA(nedges), IB(nedges)
    C     Input data ...                          C    Input data ...
          do 10 i = 1, 20                              Sched1 = Irreg_Sched(IA)
          Call Proc_A(X,Z,IA)                          Sched2 = Irreg_Sched_Inc(IB,IA)
          if (nt .gt. 0) then                          do 10 i = 1, 20
          Call Proc_B(X,W,IB)                          Call Proc_A(X,Z,IA)
          endif                                        if (nt .gt. 0) then
    10    continue                                     Call Proc_B(X,W,IB)
          end                                          endif
                                                 10    continue
                                                       end
          Subroutine Proc_A(A,B,C)
          do 20 i = 1, nedges
          B(i) = B(i) + A(C(i))                        Subroutine Proc_A(A,B,C)
    20    continue                                     Call Gather(A,Sched1)
          end                                          do 20 i = 1, nedges_local
                                                       B(i) = B(i) + A(C(i))
                                                 20    continue
          Subroutine Proc_B(X,W,IB)                    end
          do 40 i = 1, nedges
          W(i) = W(i) + X(IB(i))
    40    continue                                     Subroutine Proc_B(X,W,IB)
          do 45 i = 1, nnodes                          Call Gather(X,Sched2)
          X(i) = ...                                   do 40 i = 1, nedges_local
    45    continue                                     W(i) = W(i) + X(IB(i))
          end                                    40    continue
                                                       do 45 i = 1, nnodes_local
                                                       X(i) = ...
                                                 45    continue
                                                       end
```

Fig. 5. Use of incremental schedules. Original code is shown in left and the SPMD code (after Interprocedural Optimizations) is shown in right

The second communication can be replaced by an incremental communication if the following conditions hold:

- The communication done in $L1$ is available at the point $L2$ in the program, **and**
- The communication done in $L2$ is **not** anticipable at the point $L1$ in the program.

In this case, the communication statement at $L1$ remains as it is and the communication at $L2$ can be replaced by an incremental communication. In Figure 5, we show the use of incremental routines. Note that the call to the procedure Proc_B is enclosed inside a conditional, so the second communication is not anticipable at the point of the first communication. If this conditional was not there, then the second communication could be removed all together and the first communication could be replaced by a coalesced communication.

The analysis described above can be performed at two stages. After calls to communication preprocessing routines and communication statements have been inserted by initial intraprocedural analysis, the above analysis can be done intraprocedurally. For this purpose, availability and anticipability must be computed intraprocedurally on the CFG of the single routine. Next, after optimization of communication preprocessing routines and communication statements has been done through IPRE, another round of the analysis described above can be done on the *FPR*. In this case, availability and anticipability is computed on the *FPR*.

The scatter operations can also be optimized further using coalescing and incremental routines. The difference in analysis would be to consider the graph with notion of source and sink reversed and the definition of transparency changed to use both Mod and Ref information instead of just the Mod information.

4 Conclusions

In this paper, we have presented interprocedural optimizations for the compilation of irregular applications on distributed memory machines. In such applications, runtime preprocessing is used to determine the communication required between the processors. We have developed and used Interprocedural Partial Redundancy Elimination for optimizing placement of communication preprocessing and communication statements. We have further presented two other optimizations which are useful in the compilation of irregular applications. These optimizations include placement of scatter operations and placement of incremental schedules and coalesced schedules.

References

1. Gagan Agrawal and Joel Saltz. Interprocedural communication optimizations for distributed memory compilation. In *Proceedings of the 7th Workshop on Languages and Compilers for Parallel Computing*, pages 283–299, August 1994. Also available as University of Maryland Technical Report CS-TR-3264.
2. Gagan Agrawal and Joel Saltz. Interprocedural compilation of irregular applications for distributed memory machines. In *Proceedings Supercomputing '95*. IEEE Computer Society Press, December 1995. To appear. Also available as University of Maryland Technical Report CS-TR-3447.
3. Gagan Agrawal, Joel Saltz, and Raja Das. Interprocedural partial redundancy elimination and its application to distributed memory compilation. In *Proceedings of the SIGPLAN '95 Conference on Programming Language Design and Implementation*, pages 258–269. ACM Press, June 1995. ACM SIGPLAN Notices, Vol. 30, No. 6. Also available as University of Maryland Technical Report CS-TR-3446 and UMIACS-TR-95-42.

4. Raja Das, Joel Saltz, and Reinhard von Hanxleden. Slicing analysis and indirect access to distributed arrays. In *Proceedings of the 6th Workshop on Languages and Compilers for Parallel Computing*, pages 152–168. Springer-Verlag, August 1993. Also available as University of Maryland Technical Report CS-TR-3076 and UMIACS-TR-93-42.

5. D.M. Dhamdhere and H. Patil. An elimination algorithm for bidirectional data flow problems using edge placement. *ACM Transactions on Programming Languages and Systems*, 15(2):312–336, April 1993.

6. Manish Gupta, Edith Schonberg, and Harini Srinivasan. A unified data flow framework for optimizing communication. In *Proceedings of Languages and Compilers for Parallel Computing*, August 1994.

7. Mary Hall, John M Mellor Crummey, Alan Carle, and Rene G Rodriguez. FIAT: A framework for interprocedural analysis and transformations. In *Proceedings of the 6th Workshop on Languages and Compilers for Parallel Computing*, pages 522–545. Springer-Verlag, August 1993.

8. Reinhard von Hanxleden and Ken Kennedy. Give-n-take – a balanced code placement framework. In *Proceedings of the SIGPLAN '94 Conference on Programming Language Design and Implementation*, pages 107–120. ACM Press, June 1994. ACM SIGPLAN Notices, Vol. 29, No. 6.

9. Seema Hiranandani, Ken Kennedy, and Chau-Wen Tseng. Compiling Fortran D for MIMD distributed-memory machines. *Communications of the ACM*, 35(8):66–80, August 1992.

10. C. Koelbel and P. Mehrotra. Compiling global name-space parallel loops for distributed execution. *IEEE Transactions on Parallel and Distributed Systems*, 2(4):440–451, October 1991.

11. E. Morel and C. Renvoise. Global optimization by suppression of partial redundancies. *Communications of the ACM*, 22(2):96–103, February 1979.

12. Shamik D. Sharma, Ravi Ponnusamy, Bongki Moon, Yuan-Shin Hwang, Raja Das, and Joel Saltz. Run-time and compile-time support for adaptive irregular problems. In *Proceedings Supercomputing '94*, pages 97–106. IEEE Computer Society Press, November 1994.

13. Janet Wu, Raja Das, Joel Saltz, Harry Berryman, and Seema Hiranandani. Distributed memory compiler design for sparse problems. *IEEE Transactions on Computers*, 44(6):737–753, June 1995.

Automatic Parallelization of the Conjugate Gradient Algorithm

Vladimir Kotlyar, Keshav Pingali, and Paul Stodghill

Department of Computer Science
Cornell University
Ithaca, New York 14853

Abstract. The conjugate gradient (CG) method is a popular Krylov space method for solving systems of linear equations of the form $Ax = b$, where A is a symmetric positive-definite matrix. This method can be applied regardless of whether A is dense or sparse. In this paper, we show how restructuring compiler technology can be applied to transform a sequential, dense matrix CG program into a parallel, sparse matrix CG program. On the IBM SP-2, the performance of our compiled code is comparable to that of handwritten code from the PETSc library at Argonne.

1 Introduction

Sparse matrix computations are ubiquitous in computational science applications because they arise naturally when numerical techniques like the finite element and finite difference methods are used to solve partial differential equations approximately. In most applications, these matrices are very large and very sparse. Since there is also a lot of parallelism in these computations, it is natural to use parallel computers in this context.

Unfortunately, parallelizing sparse matrix codes is much more challenging than parallelizing dense matrix codes. One problem is keeping the computation to communication ratio high. For example, in a matrix-vector product $M * v$, the number of floating-point operations that are performed if M is sparse is a small fraction of the corresponding number when M is dense. Unless there are commensurate reductions in the communication overhead, parallel performance will suffer. A second problem is *fill* — during the computation, zero entries in matrices may become non-zero either temporarily or permanently. Since one tries not to store zeros explicitly, fill must be handled by techniques like dynamic storage allocation. Fill is not an issue for dense matrix programs, of course. Furthermore, from the viewpoint of automatic parallelization, sparse matrix programs are challenging because array subscripts are usually not affine functions of loop indices, so standard tools for dependence analysis, which are based on integer linear programming, break down.

---

[1] This research was supported by an NSF Presidential Young Investigator award CCR-8958543, NSF grant CCR-9008526, ONR grant N00014-93-1-0103, and a grant from Hewlett-Packard Corporation.

In this paper, we focus on the *conjugate gradient method* (CG), a Krylov space method for solving systems of linear equations of the form $Ax = b$ where A is a symmetric positive-definite matrix, b is a vector of constants and x is the vector of unknowns. From our perspective, this algorithm has three attractions. First, it is very popular; for example, it is the primary solver in Macsyma's PDEase finite element package [Mac94]. Therefore, this problem is of real interest. Second, matrix computations in CG do not cause fill. Finally, there are many handwritten versions of this code available for study. The CG algorithm can be applied regardless of whether A is dense or sparse. *Our objective in this paper is to use restructuring compiler technology to transform a sequential, dense matrix CG program into a parallel, sparse matrix CG program for a distributed memory machine (the IBM SP-2).* We do not assume that the non-zeros have any particular structure like bandedness (this assumption is true in the case of unstructured finite element problems, for example).

How does our work compare to other efforts in this area? The 'inspector-executor' approach of Saltz and co-workers generates parallel sparse matrix code from sequential sparse matrix programs [WDS+95]. They do not have our problem of 'sparsification' — that is, converting dense matrix code into sparse matrix code. However, they give up the ability to analyze and restructure codes at compile-time. Wijshoff and co-workers have studied the problem of sparsification in the context of sequential and uniform memory access computers [BW93]. In contrast, we deal with distributed memory parallel machines in which locality of data is the driving concern.

How well do we actually do? The performance of our compiled code on the IBM SP-2 is comparable to that of handwritten code in the PETSc library from Argonne [SG94]. This is encouraging, but much more work is needed to solve the sparse matrix parallelization problem in general.

2   Generating parallel, sparse CG by hand

When writing parallel, sparse matrix code, the programmer is responsible for deciding on how data and work are distributed to processors, and for choosing a proper data structure to represent the sparse matrices. Once these decisions have been made, the programmer must manually specialize the original code for the particular parallelism and sparsity.

```
while not converged do
    for i = 1 ... n do
        x[i] = f(y[i])
    for j = 1 ... n do
        for i = 1 ... n do
            y[i] += A[i, j] × x[j]
```

colindex

rowindex
values

Fig. 2. Compressed Column Storage of A

Fig. 1. Sequential, dense CG

A stylized sequential, dense CG is shown in Figure 1. The key operations in this code are matrix-vector multiply, and vector scaling and summation. We have not shown the entire algorithm, just one of several scaling loops and the matrix-vector multiply (MVM). Also, we have written this code as one might write it in FORTRAN. In particular, the MVM loop nest accesses A in a column-major fashion, and the reference to $x[j]$ is invariant to the inner loop.

To specialize the program for sparsity, the programmer must select a compressed data structure for storing the non-zero elements of A, and then modify the code to iterate over the data structure. A data structure that is appropriate for this sequential code is the Compressed Column Storage layout, shown in Figure 2. The non-zero entries of each column of A are compressed and stored in a single vector, *values*. The row index of each value is stored in the vector *rowindex*, and the index of the first non-zero entry for each column is stored in *colindex*. The MVM loop nest must be modified to walk over this data structure, as shown below. The i index variable is renamed to ii to emphasize that it is no longer the row index of the element being accessed.

How should we parallelize this code? Most of the work is performed in the MVM loop nest, but effective parallelization of this loop nest is hindered by the fact that the outer loop of the loop nest is not parallel. A better strategy is to change the original dense code by interchanging the i and j loops so that the parallel loop is outermost. To sparsify this code, we observe that in this new code, the matrix A is being traversed by rows, so a different layout is called for. We use Compressed Row Storage (CRS) instead. The resulting code is in Figure 4.

```
while not converged do
    for i = 1 ... n do
        x[i] = f(y[i])
    for j = 1 ... n do
        for ii = colindex[j] ...
                 colindex[j + 1] - 1 do
            y[rowindex[ii]] +=
                 values[ii] × x[j]
```
Fig. 3. CCS, sequential, sparse CG

```
while not converged do
    for i = 1 ... n do
        x[i] = f(y[i])
    for i = 1 ... n do
        for jj = rowindex[i] ...
                 rowindex[i + 1] - 1 do
            y[i] += values[jj] ×
                 x[colindex[jj]]
```
Fig. 4. CRS, sequential, sparse CG

The meaning of the *colindex* and *rowindex* vectors in CRS is reversed from that in CCS storage: *colindex* holds the column indices of the *values*, and *rowindex* holds the index of the first non-zero entry for each row.

The transformed code is better suited for parallelization. It has been demonstrated in [Bas95] that an effective and scalable means of parallelization is to distribute sets of rows of A and the corresponding elements of x and y to processors. Once this is done, the scaling loop can be executed in

```
determine what needs to be communicated
while not converged do
    for i = 1 ... n_local do
        x[i] = f(y[i])
    communicate x
    for i = 1 ... n_local do
        for jj = rowindex[i] ... rowindex[i + 1] - 1 do
            y[i] += values[jj] × x[colindex[jj]]
```

Fig. 5. Parallel, sparse CG

parallel, without communication. However, the reference to x in the MVM loop will access non-local values and communication must be placed to handle these references. It is pointless to broadcast all values of x to all processors, since a processor needs $x(j)$ only if $A(i,j)$ is non-zero for some row i mapped to it. If the matrix is not available to the compiler, the exact set of values that need to be communicated cannot be determined statically. Therefore, the programmer will insert code immediately before the "while" loop to examine A and schedule the communication. The resulting code is shown in Figure 5.

Parallelizing programs by hand is a time consuming and error prone process. Specializing for sparsity makes this difficult task even worse. As a result, many programmers chose not to spend the effort developing parallel, sparse codes, and use prewritten codes, or libraries, instead. An example of such a library is KSP, which is part of PETSc ([SG94]). This library provides "templates" of algorithms, which, when combined with implementations of the sparse data structures, produce complete Krylov space solvers. The library writers have taken care of the details of these solvers and have provided implementations of important sparse layouts, but the user of the library remains responsible for selecting the data structures and distributing the data across the processors.

3   Using a parallelizing compiler

To simplify the process of developing parallel, sparse codes, the programmer could take the sequential, sparse code and try to parallelize it using a parallelizing compiler. Some examples of this approach are found in work that has been done on the Rice and Syracuse Fortran D compilers in combination with the PARTI and Chaos runtime systems ([DUSH94], [WDS+95]).

The problem with this this approach is that it will not generate good code if the original sequential, sparse program is not well-suited for parallelization. For example, if the programmer started from the code that used the CCS layout (Figure 3), the parallelizing compiler would fail to produce good parallel code for two reasons. First, the compiler would not be able to perform loop transformations in order to exploit the parallelism present in the code. Second, and more importantly, the compiler would not be able to transform the code to use the CRS layout, which is more appropriate for the transformed loops.

The inability to perform code or layout transformations is a profound failing, not just because parallel performance suffers, but also because the compiler is unable to address other performance issues, like cache locality. So, we are back to where we started: the programmer is still saddled with the responsibility of making transformations for parallelism, locality, and vectorization. Using a parallelizing compiler has saved the programmer some effort, but not much. Most of the parallelizing technology that the compiler can bring to bear on dense codes goes unused.

4   Using a parallelizing sparse compiler

In an attempt to kill these two birds with one stone, our compiler specializes for sparsity (we call this "sparsification") as well as parallelizes. This makes the programmers' job easier because they no longer have to worry about the details of sparsity or parallelism. Also, by relieving the programmer of the burden of sparsification, the compiler is able to do analysis and code restructuring that is otherwise impossible.

Another way to put this is the following. Our compiler assumes responsibility for parallelization and sparsification, and in return it gets the ability to do dependence analysis and loop transformations. We will see that the issues of parallelization and sparsification are intertwined, and that it makes of sense to delegate both to the compiler, instead of just one.

Our compiler takes sequential, dense code and programmer-supplied annotations as input, and produces parallel, sparse code as output. That is, we start with code that contains "for" loops and dense arrays, and annotations that describe the sparsity of the arrays. In the case of conjugate gradient, the sequential, dense code might look something like the code shown in Figure 1, and there is an annotation telling the compiler that A is the only sparse array.

Our compiler has the following four phases,

1. Dependence Analysis,
2. Loop Transformations,
3. Alignment, and
4. Code Generation.

```
while not converged do
    for i = 1 ... n do
        x[i] = f(y[i])
    for i = 1 ... n do
        for j = 1 ... n do
            y[i] += A[i, j] × x[j]
```

Fig. 6. After loop interchange

We do not discuss the first two, because they are conventional parallelizing compiler problems and very well studied. This is one of the big advantages of the parallelizing sparse compiler approach over the parallelizing compiler approach: since we are starting with sequential, dense code, we are able to do dependence analysis and loop transformations in a conventional manner and without intervention from the programmer.

In the case of CG, dependence analysis tells us that the dependence vector for the MVM loop is $[1\ 0]^T$. Loop transformations can be used to move the parallel loop (i.e., the i loop) in the MVM loop nest outermost. The resulting code is shown in Figure 6.

5 Alignment and Distribution

We use the following framework for assigning work and data to processors,

A "template" is a space of virtual processors.

An "alignment function" is a linear (actually, affine works too) function from iterations or array elements to template points. Alignment maps are represented using integer matrices. Computation (loop) alignments are denoted using C, and data (array) alignments using D.

A "distribution function" is a function from template points to physical processors. M is used to denote distributions. Distributions can be non-linear.

The meaning of these is given by these two properties,

- Processor p executes iteration i of a loop iff $M(Ci) = p$.
- Processor p stores element a of an array iff $M(Da) = p$.

Given an array access Fi in a loop i, the access is "aligned" if $Ci = DFi$, or more simply if $C = DF$. In this case, the data being accessed by the processor executing the iteration is local. That is, no communication is required to resolve the reference. A reference that is not aligned is called "misaligned". A reference that is misaligned *may* require communication. Communication is only required iff $M(Ci) \neq M(DFi)$.

The alignment equations for the transformed program are the following.

$$
\begin{aligned}
C_i &= D_x[1] \quad & C_i &= D_y[1] \\
C_{i,j} &= D_x[0\ 1] \quad & C_{i,j} &= D_y[1\ 0] \\
C_{i,j} &= D_A I
\end{aligned} \tag{1}
$$

5.1   Computing an alignment

We wish to relieve the programmer of the burden of deciding which alignment to use by determining it automatically. In particular, we seek to find alignment functions that,

- maximize parallelism, and
- minimize the communication caused by the misaligned references.

This is a constraint problem, where there is a constraint of the form, $C = DF$, for each array reference for which alignment is desired, and where we are interested only in solutions that exhibit some degree of parallelism, or non-trivial solutions.

There are two alignments used in practice for CG. The one with the highest degree of parallelism is an alignment with a 2D template space. This alignment is most appropriate when either A is dense or when the non-zeros are uniformly distributed in A. However, the 2D alignment is not the most appropriate for the sorts of sparsities that arise from FEM problems. So, in our case, a 1D alignment, where rows of A are collocated with values of x and y, is desired.

The full set of alignment constraints specified in Equations 1 does not have a non-trivial solution. So, in order to arrive at either the 1D or 2D alignment, it is necessary to ignore some of these constrains. The problem of deciding which constraints to ignore in order to maximize parallelism, while minimizing communication, is known to be NP-hard, so an automatic alignment system must either perform an exhaustive search, or use a heuristic technique.

We have not yet investigated heuristic techniques, but, assuming that we had a technique for eliminating references, we do have a technique for finding the communication-free solution with the maximum degree of parallelism ([BKK+94]). In the future, we hope to automatically determine a good alignment, but at the moment we use an unsophisticated heuristic, or user annotations.

5.2 Distribution

After computing alignments, we have,

- a set of template points that must be assigned to physical processors, and
- a set of misaligned references.

We wish to compute a distribution function mapping template points to physical processors that

- minimizes the amount of communication, and
- minimizes load imbalance.

In dense codes, block/cyclic distributions are used and do a good job of minimizing these two. But, in unstructured sparse problems, these regular distributions do not do as good a job as irregular distributions. In unstructured sparse problems, the best distributions are usually found by explicitly constructing a graph representing the communication, and using node partitioning techniques like recursive spectral bisection [MTTV93, LRT79, PSL90] to compute the distribution function.

However, the irregularity of the resulting distribution creates some problems for the compiler. The first is that, because the resulting distribution is irregular, it is unlikely to have a nice linear closed form, like the block/cyclic distributions do. As a result, the distribution function must be stored explicitly. Moreover, this function is known only at runtime. Therefore, either the programmer must provide the distribution function explicitly, or the compiler must generate code to compute it at runtime. We have not implemented the later approach, and, at present, we require that the programmer provide the distribution function explicitly.

The second problem with irregular distribution functions is the generation of efficient code. We address this problem in the next section.

6 Code Generation

At this point, we have performed dependence analysis and loop transformations, and have determined the alignment of computation and data. It remains for us to

- specialize the computation and data for parallelism,
- specialize the computation and data for sparsity, and
- insert communication to preserve data dependences to misaligned references.

In this section we will develop a general technique for generating code that is specialized in these ways. We will also point out improvements that can be made. We will discuss regular and irregular distributions and structured and unstructured sparsity patterns.

6.1 Naively specializing for sparsity and parallelism

We first discuss an extremely simple method for specializing the code and data for sparsity and parallelism. This method is not actually used in the compiler, but it serves as a platform upon which the optimizations and improvements used by our compiler are built.

The Runtime System We assume the existence of a runtime system (abbreviated to RTS) whose primary responsibility is handling data storage and communication. In particular, the runtime system will ensure the following.

- Zero array elements are not explicitly stored (more precisely, zero elements, as specified by the array's sparsity, are not stored).
- Only those array elements that have been assigned to a processor by alignment and distribution are stored on that processor.
- References to elements that do not reside on the local processor result in communication with the processors on which the values resides.

We imagine that each array in the program will be implemented using a set of objects, one object residing on each processor. Each object will be responsible for storing only the non-zero elements of the array that are assigned by alignment and distribution to the processor on which it resides. The methods implemented by these objects are,

double &global_ref(integer i) Returns a reference to the ith element of the array.

boolean nonzero?(integer i) Returns true iff the ith element of the array is non-zero.

When a reference is made to an array element that does not reside on the local processor, the local object must determine in which remote object the reference resides. The local object must then communicate with the remote object in order to resolve the reference. The overhead of this type of communication will be high, because short messages are used, and because the remote processor will be interrupted during other computation to handle the communication.

Specializing the code We wish to transform the code in order that

- exactly those iterations that have been assigned to a processor by alignment and distribution, are executed by that processor,
- exactly those iterations that contribute to the final result, in the presence of sparsity, are executed, and
- zero elements of sparse arrays are not directly accessed.

Parallelism The first requirement is most easily accomplished by placing guards, or conditionals, into the code in order to govern which iterations are executed. For instance, if a particular loop has an alignment of C and distribution of M, then we can ensure that iterations of the loop are executed on their assigned processor by placing the appropriate guard around the body of the loop. This is shown in Figure 7. This method of using guards to assign work to processors is called "runtime resolution" ([RP89]).

```
for i = ...
    if M(Ci) = #me then
        ... body ...
```

Fig. 7. Linear Alignment, Irregular Distribution

```
for i = 1 ... n do
    for j = 1 ... n do
        if A[i, j] ≠ 0 then
            y[i] += A[i, j] × x[j]
```

Fig. 8. MVM with sparsity guard

Sparsity We can use a similar method to specialize the code for sparsity. The technique of introducing sparsity guards and simplifying the code using algebraic properties has been developed by Bik and Wijshoff ([BW93]). In the MVM loop nest, since the increment to $y[i]$ is non-zero only when $A[i, j]$ is non-zero, we can introduce a guard that will perform the increment only when this is so. We get the code shown in Figure 8.

The data references In order to interface the resulting code with the runtime system, each array reference, $A[i, j]$ should be changed to a method invocation. For instance, the code in Figure 9 becomes the code in Figure 10.

if $A[i, j] \neq 0$ then   if A.nonzero?(i, j) then
$\ldots = \ldots A[i, j] \ldots$ $\ldots = \ldots A$.global_ref$(i, j) \ldots$

Fig. 9. Before replacement   **Fig. 10.** After replacement

Distinguishing between local and non-local accesses Recall that a reference is aligned when $C = DF$, where F is the access function of the reference, and that a reference is misaligned when it is not aligned. Since aligned references always access local data, we can have a method just for accessing local data,

double &ref(integer i) Returns a reference to the ith element of the array. The element is required to be local to the processor.

An invocation of ref is cheaper than an invocation of global_ref because the check to see if the reference is local is not required.

Taking advantage of regular distribution or structured sparsity Much has been done to address the problem of specializing code and data for regular distribution (e.g., block or cyclic). These sorts of distributions can be expressed in terms on integer linear inequalities, which can be folding directly into the bounds of loops using such methods as Fourier-Motzkin variable elimination. This approach is referred to as "compile-time" resolution.

Since some forms of structured sparsity can also be expressed as integer linear inequalities (e.g., "$A[i, j] \neq 0$ where A is tridiagonal" can be expressed as $-1 \leq i - j \leq 1$), these techniques could also be used to fold the sparsity guards into the bounds of loops. When the sparsities predicates can be expressed as integer linear inequalities, sophisticated dependence analysis may be able to exactly determine the dependences in the program, and because the alignment and distribution functions can be expressed as integer linear inequalities, it is possible to express the communication requirements in a closed form. It is then possible to insert efficient communication code into the program.

We have investigated these ideas briefly, and they appear promising, but, since we are more interested in handling irregular distributions and unstructured sparsity, we have not pursued them.

6.2 Using invariance to handle unstructured sparsity and distribution

The problem with irregular distributions and unstructured sparsities is that they make it is impossible to fold guards into the bounds of the loops. This is not only because these distributions and sparsities cannot be expressed in a nice linear manner, but also because they are often not known until runtime. As was pointed out earlier in this paper, these sorts of programs are very common in scientific computing, and it is these programs that we are most interested in generating code for.

However, as is the case in compiling dense matrix programs, it is useful to lift communication out of loops and block it wherever possible. This is possible in many scientific codes because the sparsity of the arrays and the distribution of data is fixed for large portions of the program. In a sense, the guards being evaluated are "invariant", and can be lifted so that the cost of evaluating them can be amortized over many executions of the loop. This is the key idea behind the inspector/executor approach of Saltz and co-workers. The idea is to determine the non-local references that a loop will make, to use this information to efficiently schedule communication, and to use the resulting communication schedule for many executions of the original loop nest.

To do this, a copy of a loop containing a misaligned reference is made. Then, the body of the clone loop is modified so that the loop no longer reads or writes to memory, or produces any other sort of side-effect, but the computation of array references is still performed. Procedure calls are inserted so that these references are passed to the runtime system. Thus, when this clone loop is executed, the runtime system is given the entire stream of references that the original loop would have made. This clone loop is called the "inspector".

With the stream of references, it is possible for the runtime system to determine exactly which non-local locations are referenced. The runtime system can group these references by their owner processor, and schedule a few large messages to resolve the references. This message aggregation results in less communication overhead than the many small messages that were previously required. Also, communication schedules can be shared with the data's owner processors. Then, the owner can send the data without the processor making the reference having to request it.

The inspector loop should be placed at the earliest point in the program where all of its controlling predicates are valid. That is, if the inspector loop contains a sparsity guard on, say, A, then the inspector cannot be placed any earlier than the last write than might change the sparsity of A. If the programmer indicates that A's sparsity cannot change, then perhaps the inspector can be placed very early in the program.

Next, dependence analysis can be used to determine the earliest point in the program at which the values to be communicated are available. At this point, a call to the runtime system can be placed to cause the communication to occur. Since this communication is explicitly present in the resulting code, processors don't have to worry about handling unexpected, asynchronous communication at runtime. Also, since the values are sent earlier than they are required, there is a greater chance that they will be available when they are needed. This reduces the chance that a processor will stall waiting for data.

```
while ...do
   for i = ...
      x.ref(i) = ...
   for i = ...
      for j = ...
         if A.nonzero?(i,j) then
            y.ref(i) += A.ref(i,j)
               ×x.global_ref(j)
```

Fig. 11. Before placing inspector

```
for i = ...
   for j = ...
      if A.nonzero?(i,j) then
         pass the reference "x[j]"
            to the RTS.
RTS can compute the communication
   schedule and allocate non-local
   buffers for "x[j]".
while ...do
   for i = ...
      x.ref(i) = ...
   Communicate "x[j]".
   for i = ...
      for j = ...
         if A.nonzero?(i,j) then
            y.ref(i) += A.ref(i,j)
               ×x.global_ref(j)
```

Fig. 12. After placing inspector

To make this concrete, suppose that the original code is shown in Figure 11. The only misaligned reference and, therefore, the only reference that might required communication is, $x[j]$, in the second "for" loop nest. After creating and placing the inspector loop and placing the communication, we have the code shown in Figure 12.

Using inspector loops to precompute sparsity guards and local object addresses There are still severe performance problems remaining. Consider, for instance, a program, like the one above, that accesses an aligned array with arbitrary sparsity, for which the distribution function is only known at runtime. The evaluation of the sparsity predicate $A.$**nonzero?**(i,j) is expensive because it requires performing a search within A's local object. Furthermore, the overhead of enumerating all possible values of $< i, j >$ in order to test the sparsity predicate is also very high.

But all is not lost. We have shown that it is possible to preschedule the communication; it should be clear that we can precompute and cache the sparsity predicate, as well as the location of references within the local object. As with communication, once these have been computed, it is often possible to use these cached results many times.

For instance, in our previous example, the i,j loop nest does not have the sparsity guard folded into the bounds of the loops. As a result, the number of i and j values enumerated by the "for" loops are much greater than the number of times the body of the loop is actually executed. Since we already have an inspector that performs the sparsity test in order to generate the stream of references to x, it should be fairly easy to modify it to generate the stream of valid iterations as well! We will store this stream in a vector S. Then, the original loop nest can be modified to walk S, and thus enumerate the set of valid iterations. The resulting code is shown in Figure 13.

```
n = 0;  S = φ
for i = ...
    for j = ...
        if A.nonzero?(i,j) then
            pass the reference "x[j]" to
                the RTS.
            S[n] =< i,j >;  n++
RTS can compute the communication
    schedule and allocate non-local
    buffers for "x[j]".
while ... do
    for i = ...
        x.ref(i) = ...
    Communicate "x[j]".
    for ii = 0 ... n - 1
        < i,j >= S[ii]
        y.ref(i) += A.ref(i,j)×
            x.global_ref(j)
```

Fig. 13. Inspector computes valid iterations

```
x̂_i = φ
for i = ...
    x̂_i[i] = &x.ref(i)
n_2 = 0;  S_2 = ŷ = Â = x̂_j = φ
for i = ...
    for j = ...
        if A.nonzero?(i,j) then
            pass the reference "x[j]" to
                the RTS.
            S_2[n_2] =< i,j >
            ŷ[n_2] = &y.ref(i)
            Â[n_2] = &A.ref(i,j)
            x̂_j[n_2] = &x.global_ref(j)
            n_2 ++
RTS can compute the communication
    schedule and allocate non-local
    buffers for "x[j]".
while ... do
    for i = ...
        *x̂_i[i] = ...
    Communicate "x[j]".
    for ii = 0 ... n_2 - 1
        < i,j >= S_2[ii]
        *ŷ[ii] += *Â[ii] × *x̂_j[ii]
```

Fig. 14. Inspector computes pointers

One remaining problem with this code is the searches of the local object required to resolve the references $y.\mathtt{ref}(i)$, $A.\mathtt{ref}(i,j)$, and $x.\mathtt{global\_ref}(j)$. Not surprisingly, these can be folded into the inspector as well. In the inspector, we will compute the addresses of the references, and save them as pointers in the vectors $\hat{y}$, $\hat{A}$, and $\hat{x}_j$, respectively. A second inspector in required to precompute the $x.\mathtt{ref}(i)$ reference in the i "for" loop nest, and save the addresses into $\hat{x}_i$. The resulting code is shown in Figure 14.

To summarize, the precomputed information about the set of valid iterations of a particular loop nest will consist of a set of vectors, which we call the "iteration storage". The length of these vectors will be the number of valid iterations of the loop. Some vectors will be used to store the loop indices of the valid iterations. Some will be used to store pointers to the array elements accessed by each iteration. The code of the original loop nest is modified to walk these vectors and to use the information stored within them.

Non-local buffers and local storage We have said that the runtime system, with information from the inspector loops, can efficiently schedule communica-

tion. In order to do this, it will be necessary for the runtime system to allocate buffers into which non-local values are received, and from which non-local values are sent. The runtime system must now be able to de-
termine whether a reference
resides in the local object or
one of the non-local buffers

Fortunately, this deter-
mination can be made once
by the runtime system during the inspector loop. In
particular, in the previous
example, the reference to

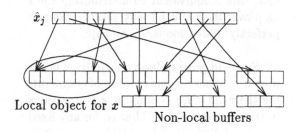

Fig. 15. Iteration storage for the reference $x[j]$

$\hat{x}_j[n_2] = \&x.\texttt{global\_ref}(j)$ in the second loop nest's inspector should be interpreted as a call to the runtime system that returns a pointer to the location in either the local object or a non-local buffer where the reference $x.\texttt{global\_ref}(j)$ will eventually be found.

6.3 Reducing the number of inspectors required

As we have presented the technique above, every loop nest in the original code will have its own inspector. But consider the code in Figure 16. In this case, it is clear that only one inspector is required.

```
for i = 0 ... n do
    for j = 0 ... n do
        if A.nonzero?(i,j) then
            ...A.ref(i,j)...
for i = 0 ... n do
    for j = 0 ... n do
        if A.nonzero?(i,j) then
            ...A.ref(i,j)...
```

Fig. 16. Two similar loops

```
n = 0;  S = φ
for i = 0 ... n do
    for j = 0 ... n do
        if A.nonzero?(i,j) then
            S[n] =< i,j >;  n ++
for ii = 0 ... n − 1 do
    < i,j >= S[ii]
    ...A.ref(i,j)...
for ii = 0 ... n − 1 do
    < i,j >= S[ii]
    ...A.ref(i,j)...
```

Fig. 17. Only one inspector

The most obvious case where it is possible to reduce the number of inspectors is when two loops have the same bounds, direction, alignment, sparsity guards, etc. What can be done when these conditions are not satisfied? This is an area where more work is needed.

6.4 Handling imperfectly nested loops

Suppose that we have an imperfectly loop nest with sparsity guards, like the code in Figure 18. What should the inspectors for this loop nest look like? One possibility is to have one inspector for i,j loop and one for the i,k loop. Then, the original loops would be modified to, first execute all valid iterations of the i,j loop, and then all iterations of the i,k loop.

If there are no dependences between the j and k loops, then this is not a problem. In fact, this is equivalent to distributing the i loop over the j and k loops, resulting in two perfectly nested loops, i,j and i,k.

Since, in general, loop distribution is not possible, we need some method of enumerating the valid $< i, j >$ and $< i, k >$ iterations in their original order. That is, for any fixed value of $\tilde{\imath}$, first all of the valid $< \tilde{\imath}, j >$ iterations are enumerated, and then all of the valid $< \tilde{\imath}, k >$ iterations. If we do compute two different sets of iteration storage, one for the i,j loop and one for the i,k loop, then we need a way of finding iterations that correspond to a particular value of $\tilde{\imath}$ within each set of iteration storage.

```
while ... do
    for i = ... do
        for j = ... do
            if A.nonzero?(i,j) then
                ...
        for k = ... do
            if B.nonzero?(i,k) then
                ...
```

Fig. 18. Imperfect loop nest

```
n_j = n_k = 0;  S_j = S_k = φ        while ... do
start_j[0] = start_k[0] = 0              for i = ... do
for i = ... do                               for jj = start_j[i] ...
    for j = ... do                               start_j[i+1] - 1 do
        if A.nonzero?(i,j) then                  j = S_j[jj]
            S_j[n_j] = j; n_j ++                 ...
    for k = ... do                           for kk = start_k[i] ...
        if B.nonzero?(i,k) then                  start_k[i+1] - 1 do
            S_k[n_k] = j; n_k ++                 k = S_k[kk]
    start_j[i+1] = n_j                           ...
    start_k[i+1] = n_k
```

Fig. 19. Inspector for imperfect loop nest

This can be done by recording, for each iteration of $\tilde{\imath}$, the location of the first and last valid iterations of j and k. For instance, we could record in $start_j[\tilde{\imath}]$ the index of the first valid iteration of $< \tilde{\imath}, j >$ in S_j, similarly with $start_k[\tilde{\imath}]$ for S_k. The first and last valid iterations of the j loop for iteration $\tilde{\imath}$ of the i loop can be found at index $start_j[\tilde{\imath}]$ and index $start_j[\tilde{\imath}+1] - 1$, respectively of the iteration storage. The resulting code is shown in Figure 19. Notice that one more index is stored in $start_j$ and $start_k$ than there are iterations of loop i. The last values mark the end of two sets of iteration storage.

A similar approach can be used to handle other types of imperfectly nested loops. Suppose that we have a loop nest in which one of the guards in invariant to the inner loop, as shown in Figure 21. This gets transformed into the code in Figure 22.

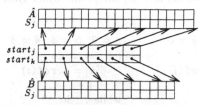

Fig. 20. Iteration storage for imperfect loops

```
while ... do
  for i = ... do
    if M(i) = #me then
      for j = ... do
        if A.nonzero?(i,j) then
          ...
```

Fig. 21. Invariant guard

```
n_i = n_j = 0;  S_i = S_j = φ
start_j[0] = 0
for i = 0 ... n - 1 do
  if M(i) = #me then
    S_i[n_i] = i
    for j = 0 ... n - 1 do
      if A.nonzero?(i,j) then
        S_j[n_j] = j;  n_j ++
    n_i ++;  start_j[n_i] = n_j
while ... do
  for ii = 0 ... n_i - 1 do
    i = S_i[ii]
    for jj = start_j[ii] ...
            start_j[ii + 1] - 1 do
      j = S_j[jj]
      ...
```

Fig. 22. Inspector for invariant guard

Fig. 23. Iteration storage for invariant guards

6.5 Accessing local storage efficiently

We have already said that aligned references do not require checks to see whether or not they are accessing non-local data. However, we still require that an inspector compute their addresses within a local object, that these addresses be saved for future use, and that the final reference to the location be made by dereferencing these pointers. All of these, but particularly the dereferences which occur within inner loops, incur substantial overhead. It is often possible to improve upon these accesses to local storage.

Suppose for instance, that we have the code shown in Figure 24, Assuming that the bounds, guards, etc. of each of the i "for" loops is the same, then we insert one inspector and get the code shown in Figure 25.

If

- all of the references to y in the program, or at least this region of the program, are precomputed in the same inspector loop,
- all the references are aligned and have the same access function, and
- the access function of the original reference is invertible (i.e., every iteration of the original i "for" loops access a different location in y),

then the map $\hat{y}$ is a one-to-one and onto map from iterations to all locations of y that are accessed by the local processor. In this case, $\hat{y}$ need not be the addresses of the locations; it can be the actual locations. That is, instead of being pointers to the values of y, $\hat{y}$ can be the values of y. The resulting code is shown in Figure 26. Since there are no pointers into it, the local object that was used to store y can be eliminated.

while ... do
  for $i = \ldots$ do
    $\ldots = \ldots y.\texttt{ref}(i)\ldots$
  for $i = \ldots$ do
    $\ldots = \ldots y.\texttt{ref}(i)\ldots$

Fig. 24. Identical refs

$n = 0;\ S = \phi;\ \hat{y} = \phi$
for $i = \ldots$ do
  $\hat{y}[n] = \&y.\texttt{ref}(i)$
  $n\texttt{++}$
while ... do
  for $ii = 0 \ldots n - 1$ do
    $\ldots = \ldots {}^{*}\hat{y}[ii]\ldots$
  for $ii = 0 \ldots n - 1$ do
    $\ldots = \ldots {}^{*}\hat{y}[ii]\ldots$

Fig. 25. As pointers

$n = 0;\ S = \phi;\ \hat{y} = \phi$
for $i = \ldots$ do
  $\hat{y}[n] = y.\texttt{ref}(i)$
  $n\texttt{++}$
while ... do
  for $ii = 0 \ldots n - 1$ do
    $\ldots = \ldots \hat{y}[ii]\ldots$
  for $ii = 0 \ldots n - 1$ do
    $\ldots = \ldots \hat{y}[ii]\ldots$

Fig. 26. As locations

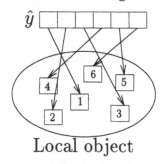

$\hat{y}$ | 1 | 2 | 3 | 4 | 5 | 6

Fig. 28. $\hat{y}$ holds the values

Fig. 27. $\hat{y}$ points into the local object

while ... do
  for $i = \ldots$ do
    $\ldots = \ldots y.\texttt{ref}(i)\ldots$
  for $i = \ldots$ do
    $\ldots = \ldots y.\texttt{ref}(i)\ldots$
  for $j = \ldots$ do
    $\ldots = \ldots y.\texttt{global\_ref}(j)\ldots$

Fig. 29. Identical refs with misaligned ref

$n_i = 0;\ S_i = \phi;\ \hat{y}_i = \phi$
for $i = \ldots$ do
  $\hat{y}_i[n_i] = y.\texttt{ref}(i);\ n_i\texttt{++}$
$n_j = 0;\ S_j = \phi;\ \hat{y}_j = \phi$
for $j = \ldots$ do
  $\hat{y}_j[n_j] = \&y.\texttt{global\_ref}(j);\ n_j\texttt{++}$
while ... do
  for $ii = 0 \ldots n_i - 1$ do
    $\ldots = \ldots \hat{y}_i[ii]\ldots$
  for $ii = 0 \ldots n_i - 1$ do
    $\ldots = \ldots \hat{y}_i[ii]\ldots$
  for $jj = 0 \ldots n_j - 1$ do
    $\ldots = \ldots {}^{*}\hat{y}_j[jj]\ldots$

Fig. 30. As locations and pointer

Actually, it is possible to relax these restrictions somewhat: we require that all *aligned* references have the same invertible access function, and allow other misaligned references. Since the runtime system already generates addresses for misaligned references, we can simply require that these addresses point into this new iteration storage, instead of into the local object.

For instance, suppose that the previous example had a misaligned reference to y, $y.\mathtt{global\_ref}(j)$, as shown in Figure 29. In this case, it is possible to store the values of $y.\mathtt{ref}(i)$ directly in $\hat{y}_i[ii]$. A second vector, $\hat{y}_j$ will hold the addresses of the references $y.\mathtt{global\_ref}(j)$, which will point into either

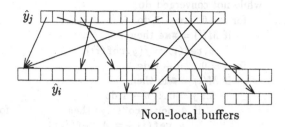

Fig. 31. Iteration storage for the reference $y.\mathtt{global\_ref}(j)$

$\hat{y}_i[ii]$ or the non-local buffers allocated by the runtime system for communication. The resulting code is shown in Figure 30.

6.6 Conjugate gradient

After inserting the guards for sparsity and parallelism and replacing array references with method invocations, we have the code shown in Figure 32. We insert a inspector before the "while" loop to schedule the communication and compute the iteration information. Since all of the aligned references to x, y, and A have the same invertible access functions, the values, and not just the addresses, of these locations can be stored in $\hat{x}_i$, $\hat{y}$, and $\hat{A}$. The resulting code is shown in Figure 33.

6.7 "Peephole" optimizations

There are two additional optimizations that we can apply to this code. First, notice that the inspector loop in Figure 34 enumerates all iterations of i in order to test which ones are aligned with template points assigned to the local processor. A better approach, in this case, would be to enumerate all of the template points assigned to the local processor, and test whether the corresponding iterations falls within the bounds of the original loop nest. The resulting code is shown in Figure 35. This results in lower loop overhead in the inspector, and is safe because dependence analysis tells us that the iterations of the original loop can be executed in any order.

There is a similar optimization that can be used to reduce the cost of finding the non-zeros in each row of A. Notice that the inspector in Figure 36 tests every entry in the row $A[i, *]$ to see if it is non-zero. Perhaps instead the local object could provide the inspector with exactly the non-zero entries in the row. Then the inspector would iterate over this set and tests to see if each element corresponds to an access that occurred within the original loop. Again, this results in lower loop overhead in the inspector, and is safe because dependence analysis tells us that the iterations of the original loop can be executed in any order.

```
while not converged do
    for i = 0 ... n − 1 do
        if M(i) = #me then
            x.ref(i) = f(y.ref(i))
    for i = 0 ... n − 1 do
        if M(i) = #me then
            for j = 0 ... n − 1 do
                if A.nonzero?(i, j) then
                    y.ref(i) += A.ref(i, j)
                        ×x.global_ref(j)
```

Fig. 32. Runtime resolution CG

```
ni = nj = 0;  Si = Sj = φ
Â = ŷ = x̂i = x̂j = φ
startj[0] = 0
for i = 0 ... n − 1 do
    if M(i) = #me then
        Si[ni] = i
        x̂i[ni] = x.ref(i)
        ŷi[ni] = y.ref(i)
        for j = 0 ... n − 1 do
            if A.nonzero?(i, j) then
                Sj[nj] = j
                Â[nj] = A.ref(i, j)
                pass the reference "x[j]"
                    to the RTS.
                x̂j[nj] = &x.global_ref(j)
                nj ++
        ni ++;  startj[ni] = nj
RTS can compute the communication
    schedule and allocate non-local
    buffers for "x[j]".
while not converged do
    for ii = 0 ... ni − 1 do
        i = Si[ii]
        x̂[ii] = f(ŷ[ii])
    Communicate "x[j]".
    for ii = 0 ... ni − 1 do
        i = Si[ii]
        for jj = startj[ii] ...
            startj[ii + 1] − 1 do
            j = Sj[jj]
            ŷ[ii] += Â[jj] ×* x̂[jj]
```

Fig. 33. Final CG

```
for i = 0 ... n − 1 do
    if M(i) = #me then
        ...
```

Fig. 34. Before distr. optimization

```
for t ∈ M⁻1(#me) do
    i = t
    if 0 ≤ i ≤ n − 1 then
        ...
```

Fig. 35. After distr. optimization

```
for t ∈ M⁻1(#me) do
    i = t
    if 0 ≤ i ≤ n − 1 then
        for j = 0 ... n − 1 do
            if A.nonzero?(i, j) then
                ...
```

Fig. 36. Before row nzs. opt.

```
for t ∈ M⁻1(#me) do
    i = t
    if 0 ≤ i ≤ n − 1 then
        for a₂ ∈ non-zeros indices
            of A[i, ∗] do
            j = a₂
            if 0 ≤ j ≤ n − 1 then
                ...
```

Fig. 37. After row nzs. opt.

6.8 The current implementation

Although our current implementation of the code generation techniques is able to compile conjugate gradient into the form described above, it does not implement all of the techniques discussed in this paper. Instead of generating the general inspectors and then applying optimizations, our implementation checks to see that certain properties of the code are true, and then generates the optimized inspectors directly. This is not completely satisfying, but it is sufficient to demonstrate the soundness and efficiency of our ideas.

7 Performance

Figure 1 shows the performance of the sparse CG code generated by our compiler, compared with the spare CG code found in the PETSc version 2.0 beta 2. Times include the execution of an inspector and 16 iterations of the *while* loop. The codes were run on 1 through 64 nodes of the Cornell Theory Center SP-2. Both codes used the vendor supplied MPI implementation as the communication layer. The matrix A was determined from a 64,000 node 3D mesh. In other words, A had 64,000 rows and columns, and an average of 27 non-zeros per row. A 3D mesh was used so that the template points could be optimally

Procs.	Compiler	PETSc
1	22.11	—
2	9.95	7.48
4	4.86	4.16
8	2.40	2.20
16	1.26	1.42
32	0.70	1.01
64	0.44	0.47

Table 1. Wall clock times for CG, in seconds

partitioned, thus eliminating the effects of heuristic partitioning techniques. The performance of the compiled code is respectable, and can probably be improved by overlapping communication and computation more aggressively. These issues require more work.

8 Related work

Our ideas on parallel, sparse compiling have been influenced most heavily by the work by Bik, et al. on the Sparse Compiler and Saltz, et al. on PARTI/Chaos.

Bik's Sparse Compiler takes sequential, dense code, as in our case, and produces sequential, sparse code. The Sparse Compiler has a fairly general annotation language for describing the sparsity of the data structures, and the compiler's job is to introduce sparsity guards into the code, to optimize these guards, and to select and generate an appropriate compressed data layout. In [BKW94], loop transformations are done to try to align array references so that access to the selected compressed data layout is more efficient. Some work has been done to parallelize the sparse code ([BW93]), but this was done within the context of a UMA multiprocessor, so the issues are different than those that we considered.

The idea of using an inspector to pass information to the runtime system, was developed by Saltz, et al.([DUSH94]) in the context of handling communication in the presence of irregularity in Fortran codes. The big difference with our approach, as was observed earlier, is that they assume that the programmer sparsifies the code before compiling.

9 Conclusions

We have shown that it is possible and advantageous to automate both the processes of sparsification and parallelization for NUMA parallel machines. We have developed a compiler that is able to produce, for the conjugate gradient method, parallel code that is comparable to hand-written code in both function and performance. This is encouraging but much more work remains to be done to solve the problem in general.

References

[Bas95]   Achim Basermann. Parallel sparse matrix computations in iterative solvers on distributed memory machines. In *Proceedings of the SIAM Conference on Parallel Processing for Scientific Computing*, San Francisco, February 1995. SIAM Press.

[BKK+94]   David Bau, Induprakas Kodukula, Vladimir Kotlyar, Keshav Pingali, and Paul Stodghil. Solving alignment using simple linear algebra. In K. Pingali, U. Banerjee, D. Gelernter, A. Nicolau, and D. Padua, editors, *Languages and Compilers for Parallel Computing. Seventh International Workshop.*, LNCS. LNCS, Springer-Verlag, 1994.

[BKW94]   Aart J.C. Bik, Peter M.W. Knijnenburg, and Harry A.G. Wijshoff. Reshaping access patterns for generating sparse codes. In *Proceedings of the Seventh Annual Workshop on Languages and Compiler for Parallel Computing*, Ithaca, New York, August 8–10, 1994. Springer-Verlag. LNCS #892.

[BW93]   Aart Bik and Harry Wijshoff. Advanced compiler optimizations for sparse computations. In *Proceedings of Supercomputing 93*, pages 430–439, November 1993.

[DUSH94]   Raja Das, Mustafa Uysal, Joel Saltz, and Yuan-Shin Hwang. Communication optimizations for irregular scientific computations on distributed memory architectures. *Journal of Parallel and Distributed Computing*, 22(3):462–479, September 1994. Also available as University of Maryland Technical Report CS-TR-3163 and UMIACS-TR-93-109.

[LRT79]   R. J. Lipton, D. J. Rose, and R. E. Tarjan. Generalized nested dissection. *SIAM Journal on Numerical Analysis*, 16:346–358, 1979.

[Mac94]   PDEase Programmer's Manual. Macsyma Inc., 20 Academy Street, Arlington, MA 02174., 1994.

[MTTV93]   G. L. Miller, S.-H. Teng, W. Thurston, and S. A. Vavasis. Automatic mesh partitioning. In A. George, J. Gilbert, and J. Liu, editors, *Graph Theory and Sparse Matrix Computation*, volume 56 of *IMA Volumes in Mathematics and its Applications*. Springer-Verlag, Berlin, 1993.

[PSL90]   A. Pothen, H. D. Simon, and K.-P. Liou. Partitioning sparse matrices with eigenvectors of graphs. *SIAM Journal of Matrix Analysis and Applications*, 11:430–452, 1990.

[RP89]   Anne Rogers and Keshav Pingali. Process decomposition through locality of reference. In *Proceedings of the SIGPLAN '89 Conference on Programming Language Design and Implementation*, pages 69–80, Portland, Oregon, June 21–23, 1989. Published as ACM SIGPLAN Notices 24(7).

[SG94]   B. Smith and W. Gropp. Portable, parallel, reusable krylov space codes. In *Colorado Conference on Iterative Methods*, Colorado, April 1994.

[WDS+95]   Janet Wu, Raja Das, Joel Saltz, Harry Berryman, and Seema Hiranandani. Distributed memory compiler design for sparse problems. *IEEE Transactions on Computers*, 44(6), 1995.

Annotations for a Sparse Compiler*

Aart J.C. Bik and Harry A.G. Wijshoff

High Performance Computing Division
Department of Computer Science, Leiden University
P.O. Box 9512, 2300 RA Leiden, the Netherlands
ajcbik@cs.leidenuniv.nl

Abstract. In an attempt to avoid the inherent complexity of developing and maintaining sparse codes, an existing prototype restructuring
compiler MT1 is being extended to support the automatic generation of
sparse codes. A program operating on 2-dimensional arrays is converted
automatically into semantically equivalent code exploiting the sparsity
of some of the matrices that are stored in these arrays. This approach
requires some kind of mechanism to supply the compiler with information that cannot be expressed in the dense description of the program.
In particular, we discuss how to enable the compiler to select a suitable
reordering method that e.g. preserves sparsity or increases the amount
of exploitable parallelism in an algorithm.

1 Introduction

In many fields of science and engineering applications arise that operate on sparse
matrices, i.e. matrices having many zero elements. The storage requirements
and computational time of these applications can be reduced substantially if
advantage of the zero elements is taken [14, 18, 22, 23, 26]. Obviously, storage
is saved if only the nonzero elements of a sparse matrix are stored explicitly.
Moreover, less computations are performed if useless operations on zeros are
avoided. However, in order to exploit the sparsity of matrices, sparse storage
schemes must be used for these matrices, which complicates the development and
maintenance of sparse codes. Moreover, the complexity of these data structures
usually disables most standard compiler optimizations.

These observations gave rise to the following approach to the development
of sparse codes. Instead of dealing with the sparsity of matrices at programming level, this issue is dealt with at the compilation level. Hence, programming
can be done as for dense computations, i.e. all matrices are stored in simple 2-
dimensional arrays. Thereafter, the compiler selects an appropriate sparse storage scheme of each sparse matrix, and converts the code accordingly. For details
of this kind of sparse code generation, which is being incorporated in an existing
prototype restructuring compiler MT1 [6], we refer to [7, 9, 10, 11].

---

* Support was provided by the Foundation for Computer Science (SION) of the Dutch
  Organization for Scientific Research (NWO) and the EC Esprit Agency DG XIII
  under Grant No. APPARC 6634 BRA III.

This approach has a number of advantages. First, it enables inexperienced programmers to generate sparse codes having acceptable performance in a relatively simply way. Additionally, the compiler can be used as a tool to develop advanced sparse codes more rapidly, since the output of the compiler can be used as a first version which is further extended and hand optimized. Moreover, because the compiler is presented with the computation on enveloping data structures, standard compiler optimizations and regular dependence analysis [5, 20, 21, 24, 25] can be performed. This frequently increases the amount of concurrency in the resulting sparse code that can be detected automatically [9]. Furthermore, since the compiler can account for both the characteristics of the target machine and the data operated on, one original dense program can be converted into several sparse versions specifically suited for a particular instance of the same problem. Finally, just as traditional restructuring compilers enable the re-use of existing serial software on parallel target architectures, MT1 enables the re-use of parts of existing dense codes to develop sparse applications.

This approach has potential limitations though. The compiler must rely on powerful strategies to prevent the generation of sparse codes with poor performance. Furthermore, since already much effort has been put in the development of efficient sparse packages solving a particular problem, it will be extremely difficult to be competitive with such heavily specialized codes, even if all peculiarities of the sparse matrices could be supplied to the compiler and sophisticated reordering methods would be incorporated.

In this paper, we discuss how information that cannot be expressed in the dense description of a program can be supplied to the compiler using annotations.

2 An Overview of MT1

A brief overview of sparse code generation is given and some sparse methods are reviewed to determine the kind of annotations required.

2.1 Terminology

For each matrix of which the sparsity is not explicitly dealt with, the following three concepts can be distinguished:

- A $m \times n$ **implicitly sparse matrix** A, used at a logical level.
- An array REAL A(M,N), used as **enveloping data structure** of A.
- A **sparse storage scheme**, selected by the compiler.

The concept of an implicitly sparse matrix is introduced to reason about programs at a logical level (e.g. perform the operation $\mathbf{b} = A\mathbf{x}$, where A is an implicitly sparse matrix). At the programming level, all operations on an implicitly sparse matrix are defined on the enveloping data structure of this matrix, for which a 2-dimensional array of appropriate size will be used. Hence, an implicitly sparse matrix is an ordinary sparse matrix for which a simple storage scheme is used to reduce the complexity of the program.

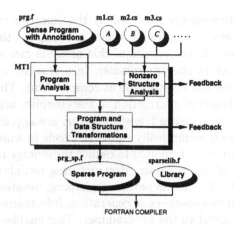

Fig. 1. Overview of Sparse Code Generation

The burden of sparse code generation is placed on the compiler, which selects a suitable sparse storage scheme for each implicitly sparse matrix and transforms all occurrences of the corresponding enveloping data structure in the dense program accordingly.

2.2 Sparse Code Generation

As illustrated in in figure 1, the input of MT1 consists of an ordinary FORTRAN program stored in, for instance, the file 'prg.f'. In this program, 2-dimensional arrays are used as enveloping data structures of all the implicitly sparse matrices. Obviously, the use of arrays simplifies both the development and maintenance of the code, provided that all alterations are applied to the original code. In addition, regular data dependence checking and standard restructuring techniques can be applied to the original dense program.

Information that cannot be expressed in the dense description of an algorithm is supplied to the compiler by means of annotations. There are, for instance, annotations to identify the enveloping data structures or to incorporate techniques that are specific for sparse applications. All annotations have the form of comments, which enables direct compilation and testing of the original dense program (cf. [16]).

The original dense code is analyzed by MT1 to detect the statements that can exploit sparsity and to determine the way in which the enveloping data structures are accessed. Furthermore, as indicated by annotations, the input of MT1 may consist of some implicitly sparse matrices that at compile-time are available on file (cf. 'm1.cs', 'm2.cs', and so on). To impose little constraints on programmers not familiar with sparse applications, the compiler expects all matrices in a very simple storage format, namely coordinate scheme. In this scheme, values together with the row and column indices of all nonzero elements appear in arbitrary order.

The files are automatically analyzed by the compiler to determine characteristics of the nonzero structures [8], which are supplied to the transformation phase of MT1. If desired, the results of this analysis can also be prompted to provide some feedback to the programmer. In a realistic application, however, not all sparse matrices will be available at compile-time. Therefore, annotations to supply nonzero structure information to the compiler are available.

Program and data structure transformations are applied to the dense program in order to obtain semantically equivalent code in which the sparsity of all implicitly sparse matrices is exploited to reduce the storage requirements and the computational time of this program. Restructuring techniques required include procedure cloning [12, 13], access pattern reshaping, iteration space partitioning and eventually the actual sparse code generation. Information about this restructuring phase is prompted to the programmer. This enables the programmer to fix the parts of the original dense program that are transformed into inefficient sparse code.

Finally, the resulting sparse program is saved in a file with the additional extension '_sp' to indicate the sparse character of this program (cf. 'prg_sp.f'). This file together with a library file 'sparselib.f' containing some useful primitives are used as input for a FORTRAN compiler producing machine code for a particular target machine.

2.3 Incorporation of Sparse Methods

In addition to methods developed for dense matrices, a vast amount of methods have been developed specifically for sparse matrix applications. In particular, these sparse applications differ from their dense counter parts by using sparse storage schemes, and reordering methods. Obviously, the automatic generation of efficient sparse codes is only possible if the compiler can incorporate both methods in the generated code.

The most efficient *sparse storage scheme* for a sparse matrix A heavily depends on the operations performed on this matrix, and the peculiarities of the nonzero structure of A. If A may change, the sparse storage scheme must deal with situations in which zero elements become nonzero (fill-in or creation) or nonzero elements become zero (cancellation). Usually, a static storage scheme is used if the matrix remains unaltered or a conservative approximation of elements that may fill-in can be computed before initialization. A dynamic storage scheme is used otherwise. To enable the selection of an appropriate sparse storage scheme, information about the kind of operations performed is gathered from the original program by analysis of the code, while nonzero structure information is either obtained from annotations or automatic analysis of matrices on file. MT1 allows for the compile-time selection of a hybrid storage scheme with static dense storage of regions which are (or become) rather dense, and dynamic storage in a 'pool of sparse vectors' of entries in sparse regions. The layout of vectors over these regions may be different for each region and depends on the most frequently used access direction in that region.

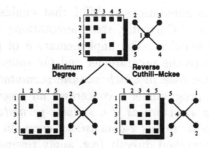

Fig. 2. The Importance of Reordering Methods

Hence, to support this kind of data structure selection, annotations are available to specify a file that may be analyzed at compile-time, or to identify the dense or sparse regions in a matrix. Regions that are completely zero, and will remain so at run-time, can also be identified. No storage is selected by the compiler for these regions. Moreover, an attempt is made to remove code performing useless operations on the regions at compile-time [11]. If zero regions are detected by automatic nonzero structure analysis, the compiler first inquires the user whether these regions remain zero at run-time before the previous optimizations are applied.

Reordering methods are used to enable the use of certain data structures, to increase the amount of exploitable parallelism, or to enhance data locality or vector performance (see e.g. [1, 2, 15]). In the context of solving a sparse system of linear equations, two different kinds of heuristics have been developed to preserve the sparsity of the original system [14, 18, 22, 23]. In *local strategies*, at each stage of the elimination, a pivot is selected locally minimizing some sparsity related objective. In *a priori reordering methods*, the matrix is permuted into a form in which zeros are isolated, confining fill-in to particular regions.

Reordering methods improve the efficiency of a sparse application and reduce storage requirements substantially. For example, factorization of the matrix shown in figure 2 without pivoting causes complete fill-in, while application of minimum degree [17, 19] or reverse Cuthill-Mckee yields a factorization in which no fill-in occurs (cf. [14, p.96-98,p.153-157]). Consequently, it is very important to incorporate reordering methods in the automatically generated sparse code. One possibility would be to let the programmer deal with all permutations explicitly, e.g. by means of permutation arrays or physical data movement. In fact, this approach is taken in dense applications where, for instance, partial or complete pivoting are explicitly implemented in the code. However, this solution is unsuited for the automatic generation of sparse codes, since it obscures the functionality of the code, disables regular dependence analysis, and reduces the flexibility of the program since only one reordering method can be implemented. Moreover, it is difficult to express sparsity related decisions in the dense code, and much programming effort is wasted since a completely different implementation is required in the resulting sparse code.

Therefore, there are annotations in MT1 that enable the permutation of implicitly sparse matrices. Currently, these annotations are focused on the *a priori* permutation of matrices. The implementation of permutations is kept completely transparent to the programmer and *the compiler is responsible for the generation of sparse code in which suitable permutations are applied and recorded.* As far as the programmer is concerned, *all programming can be done on the enveloping data structure as if a suitable permutation is performed by physically moving elements in this 2-dimensional array.* In addition, rather than specifying a particular method directly (e.g. apply reverse Cuthill-Mckee), the programmer merely informs the compiler that a matrix may be permuted. After analyzing the program, the compiler selects a suitable reordering method that, for instance, reduces the amount of fill-in or increases the amount of exploitable parallelism.

We will see that the incorporation of such permutation annotations alone is not sufficient and that we also need annotations to deal with the *mathematical consequences* of a permutation. Therefore, permutations are also recorded, and can be applied to other arrays using so-called induction annotations.

3 Declarative Part

In this section, annotations that may appear in the declarative part of the dense program are discussed.

3.1 Declaration Annotations

Because the compiler cannot distinguish between ordinary arrays and arrays that are used as enveloping data structures of implicitly sparse matrices, a mechanism to provide the compiler with this kind of information must be available.

The identification of enveloping data structures is done by means of annotations. All annotations in the declarative part start at the beginning of a line with 'C_SPARSE'. In this manner, the annotations are simply handled as comments by other compilers, so that the original dense program can be compiled and tested without any modifications, provided that the implicitly sparse matrices are not too large. In each declaration annotation, a parenthesized list of enveloping data structures is given, separated by semi-colons.

The following annotation, for instance, informs the compiler about the fact that arrays A and B are used as enveloping data structures of two implicitly sparse matrices A and B of size 100×100 and 20×50 respectively:

```
REAL A(100,100), B(20,50)
C_SPARSE(A ; B)
```

Each annotation that identifies a particular enveloping data structure must appear after the actual declaration of the corresponding array in the main program (although sparsity information is propagated automatically to subroutines and functions).

Furthermore, the enveloping data structure must be a 2-dimensional array having the index set [1..M] × [1..N] for suitable constants M and N. If any of these constraints is violated, an appropriate warning is generated and the corresponding part of the annotation is ignored.

Consider, for instance, the following program:

```
PROGRAM ANNOT                        SUBROUTINE PROC
   REAL A(-5:5,10), B(10)               REAL E(10,10)
   C(10,10), D(100)                  C_SPARSE(E)
C_SPARSE(A ; B ; C)                     ...
   ...                                  END
CALL PROC(C)
CALL PROC(D)
END
```

In this program, the annotations involving the arrays A, B and E are ignored. Hence, only the 2-dimensional array C is handled as an enveloping data structure. Procedure cloning is used to generate a clone of PROC, called 'PROC_A', in which there is a unique association between C and E. Hence, we propagate the sparsity of C to the array E in this clone. The original subroutine PROC having a 'dense' local array E is preserved to handle the call with argument D.

3.2 File Annotations

Within a declaration annotation, we can specify the file in which an implicitly sparse matrix resides.

If several files are specified for one enveloping data structure, only the first one is associated with the corresponding implicitly sparse matrix. In case the environment variable SPARSEDIR is set, the directory supplied in this variable is searched for the file. Otherwise, the current directory is examined. If the file is available at compile-time, then this file is automatically analyzed. If the size of the stored matrix does not match the declaration of enveloping data data structure, a warning is generated and the results of the analysis are ignored. Because the compiler expects all matrices in coordinate scheme, sparse matrices that are generated in a program or stored in alternative storage schemes must be converted into coordinate scheme to enable this automatic analysis.

The following annotation, for example informs the compiler about the fact that the nonzero structure of the implicitly sparse matrix A having array A as enveloping data structure can be found in the file 'm1.cs'. We also show the contents of this file and the nonzero structure of A, annotated with the block form detected by automatic nonzero structure analysis:

PROGRAM INFO		contents of file 'm1.cs'
INTEGER	N	5 5
PARAMETER (N = 5)		11
REAL	A(N,N)	1 1 5.0 2 2 5.0 3 3 5.0
C_SPARSE(A:_FILE('m1.cs'))		4 4 5.0 5 5 5.0 2 1 1.0
...		3 4 1.0 1 4 1.0 2 5 1.0
END		5 4 1.0 4 5 1.0

Nonzero Structure of A

Because during writing of the original dense program, the programmer is unaware of the sparse storage scheme that will be selected by the compiler, the compiler is responsible for the generation of appropriate initialization code for each selected data structure. Independent of the fact whether a file specified in an informative declaration is available at compile-time or not, this file will be used in the initialization code of the selected sparse storage scheme, which is generated before the first executable statement in the main program. Note that, in contrast with automatic analysis of the nonzero structure, this code will only read the file at run-time when the generated sparse code is executed.

If no file is specified, the compiler inquires the user about the file that must be used in the initialization code during the actual sparse code generation.

3.3 Nonzero Structure Information Annotations

Because usually not all implicitly sparse matrices are available at compile-time, nonzero structure information can also be supplied directly to the compiler by means of annotations. If a particular region in an implicitly sparse matrix is either dense (or will become so), completely zero (*and will remain so at run-time*) or sparse, then this information can be supplied to the compiler by specifying the property and index set of the region.

The index set of a region is described using a number of simple boundary pairs. In this manner, we can specify regions having an index set that can be expressed in terms of a 2-dimensional simple section [3, 4]. Symbolic constants may be used in all expressions to increase the flexibility of a program.

For example, the following annotations inform the compiler about the fact that the nonzero structure of an implicitly sparse matrix B has the characteristics shown in figure 3:

```
        INTEGER   N
        PARAMETER (N = 100)
        REAL      B(N,N)
C_SPARSE(B : _DENSE(-5 <= I-J <= 5)                    )
C_SPARSE(B : _ZERO(1-N <= I-J <= 20-N)                 )
C_SPARSE(B : _DENSE(N-4 <= I <= N, 6 <= I-J <= N-1))
```

It is likely that MT1 selects a storage scheme in which the band and border are stored statically in two rectangular arrays. Furthermore, attempts to eliminate useless operations on the upper right corner will be made. The compiler assumes that all remaining regions are sparse. Entries in these regions will probably be stored in a 'pool of sparse vectors'.

We can also specify a preferred access direction for an implicitly sparse matrix. During restructuring, the compiler will try to reshape the access patterns of all occurrences of the corresponding enveloping data structure along this access direction, before the actual sparse code is generated:

```
        REAL A(10,10)
      C_SPARSE(A : _ACCESS(1,2))
```

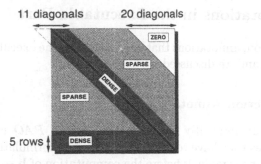

Fig. 3. Nonzero Structure of B

3.4 Permutation Annotations

A permutation annotation can be used to specify that before initialization, an implicitly sparse matrix A may be permuted arbitrarily into PAQ, or into a symmetric permutation PAP^T. An example is shown below:

```
REAL A(100,100), B(10,10)
C_SPARSE(A : _PERM ; B: _SYMPERM)
```

If the identifier specified in a permutation annotation does not correspond to an enveloping data structure, this annotation is ignored since there is no support to reorder dense data structures. The kind of permutation that will be applied and the way in which this permutation is actually implemented are kept transparent to the programmer. *The compiler is responsible for the generation of sparse code in which a suitable permutation is applied and recorded in some manner.* As far as the programmer is concerned, *data in the enveloping data structure is physically moved according to a selected permutation.*

With respect to the file in which the implicitly sparse matrix resides, there are two possibilities:

(1) This file is already available at compile-time.
(2) This file will only be available at run-time.

In case (1), the reordering method is already applied to this file at compile-time, and the permutation is only recorded to deal with the mathematical consequences of the permutations (see section 4.1). Moreover, nonzero structure analysis is applied to the permuted matrix in order to account for the characteristics of the nonzero structure that will be seen at run-time.

In case (2), the compiler generates code that will apply a suitable permutation during initialization of the selected sparse storage scheme. At compile-time, no nonzero structure information is available and code for a general sparse matrix will be generated.[2]

---

[2] In a future implementation, we could generate multiple versions of the code, each of which is tailored to a specific kind of nonzero structures, and let the results of the reordering determine which version is executed.

4 Annotations in the Executable Part

In this section, annotations that may appear in the executable part of the original dense program are discussed.

4.1 Induction Annotations

Permuting an implicitly sparse matrix A into PAQ may have mathematical consequences that have to be dealt with in the formulation of the original dense program. For example, if before the computation of $\mathbf{b} \leftarrow A\mathbf{x}$, we permute A into PAQ, we must permute the original vector $\mathbf{x}$ into $\mathbf{x}' \leftarrow Q^T\mathbf{x}$ before the product, and permute the computed vector $\mathbf{b}'$ into the desired result $\mathbf{b} \leftarrow P^T\mathbf{b}'$ after the product has been computed. This is implied by the following formula, where the part $(*)$ is computed by an implementation that assumes that elements are physically moved in the enveloping data structure:

$$P\mathbf{b} = \underbrace{\mathbf{b}' = PAQ\mathbf{x}'}_{(*)} = PAQ(Q^T\mathbf{x}) = PA\mathbf{x}$$

Likewise, if before factorization of A to solve a system $A\mathbf{x} = \mathbf{b}$, we permute A into PAQ, then any subsequent implementation of LU-factorization effectively computes the factorization $PAQ = LU$. Hence, before forward substitution is applied we must permute the right-hand side $\mathbf{x}$ into $\mathbf{x}' \leftarrow P\mathbf{x}$. After back substitution, the computed $\mathbf{x}'$ is permuted into the desired solution $\mathbf{x} \leftarrow Q\mathbf{x}'$. This is implied by the following formula, where $(*)$ is solved by an implementation assuming physically data movement:

$$PA\mathbf{x} = PAQQ^T\mathbf{x} = LU(Q^T\mathbf{x}) = \underbrace{LU\mathbf{x}' = \mathbf{b}'}_{(*)} = P\mathbf{b}$$

Induction annotations are used to deal with such consequences. The implementation of recording and applying permutation matrices are kept transparent to the programmer, i.e. *the compiler is responsible for implementing induction annotations*. However, *it is the responsibility of the programmer to correctly deal with all mathematical consequences of a permutation using induction annotations*, because it would be very hard for the compiler, if not impossible, to determine the mathematical consequences automatically. Since incorrect use of induction annotations may affect the semantics of the original program, using these annotations must be done with care.

In an induction annotation, the identifier of a 1-dimensional array that must be permuted,[3] an action, and the row or column permutation matrix that is associated with an implicitly sparse matrix are specified. If an implicitly $m \times n$ matrix A having A as enveloping data structure has been permuted into PAQ, then the following actions affects a column vector $\mathbf{x} = (x_1, \ldots, x_m)^T$ and a row vector $\mathbf{y} = (y_1, \ldots, y_n)$ stored in the array X and Y as shown in table 1.

---

[3] This restriction is imposed to simplify the implementation in the current prototype.

annotation	result	(alternative)
C_EXEC _INDUCE X < ROW (A)	$x \leftarrow Px$	$x^T \leftarrow x^T P^T$
C_EXEC _INDUCE Y < COLUMN(A)	$y \leftarrow yQ$	$y^T \leftarrow Q^T y^T$
C_EXEC _INDUCE X > ROW (A)	$x \leftarrow P^T x$	$x^T \leftarrow x^T P$
C_EXEC _INDUCE Y > COLUMN(A)	$y \leftarrow yQ^T$	$y^T \leftarrow Q y^T$

Table 1. Operations Defined by Induction Annotations

The alternative result arises from the fact that transposition has no impact on the FORTRAN array representation (viz. X and Y interpreted as row and column vector). The method of recording permutation matrices and the actual implementation of the computations specified in an induction annotations are kept transparent to the programmer. If the number of elements in the 1-dimensional array and the order of the permutation matrix differ, a warning is generated and the annotation is ignored. If the code generated for an induction annotation is executed before any permutation is applied or if a permutation matrix of a dense data structure is specified, then the results are as expected for $P = I$ and $Q = I$: the 1-dimensional array remains unaffected.

Because MT1 enforces a unique association between enveloping data structures and formal arguments, the annotations discussed in this section are also allowed in subroutines and functions (in contrast with declaration annotations).

4.2 Example

Consider the following main program, in which the system $Ax = b$ is solved in-place by calls to subroutines performing the factorization, forward substitution, and back substitution respectively:

```
PROGRAM SOLVE             SUBROUTINE FACT(A, N)
                          INTEGER I, J, K, N
REAL A(10,10), B(10)      REAL    A(N,N)
C_SPARSE (A : _PERM)      DO K = 1, N - 1
...                         DO I = K + 1, N
CALL FACT(A,    10)          A(I,K) = A(I,K) / A(K,K)
CALL FORW(A, B, 10)          DO J = K + 1, N
CALL BACK(A, B, 10)            A(I,J) = A(I,J) - A(I,K)*A(K,J)
...                           ENDDO
END                         ENDDO
                          ENDDO
                          RETURN
                          END
```

The programmer assumes that data in A is physically moved according to PAQ, so that eventually this enveloping data structure is overwritten with elements of the factors L and U satisfying $PAQ = LU$ for the original A.

In-place implementations of forward and back substitution are shown below. First, the right-hand side is permuted into $P\mathbf{b}$ to account for possible row permutations applied to the matrix stored in A. After back substitution, the contents of array B is permuted into $Q\mathbf{b}$ to obtain the desired solution:

```
      SUBROUTINE FORW(A, B, N)              SUBROUTINE BACK(A, B, N)
      INTEGER I, J, N                       INTEGER I, J, N
      REAL    A(N,N), B(N)                  REAL    A(N,N), B(N)
C_EXEC _INDUCE B < _ROW(A)                  DO I = N, 1, -1
      DO I = 1, N                             DO J = I + 1, N
        DO J = 1, I - 1                         B(I) = B(I) - A(I,J)*B(J)
          B(I) = B(I) - A(I,J)*B(J)           ENDDO
        ENDDO                                 B(I) = B(I) / A(I,I)
      ENDDO                                 ENDDO
      RETURN                          C_EXEC _INDUCE B > _COLUMN(A)
      END                                   RETURN
                                            END
```

Because MT1 generates the clones 'FACT_A0', 'FORW_A00', and 'BACK_A00', the enveloping data structure A is uniquely associated with the formal arguments A (and 10 with N, enabling constant folding within the clone), so that the annotations uniquely define the permutation matrices associated with the matrix A. Note that is the subroutines are also called with other sparse implicitly sparse matrices, more clones are generated with unique correspondences between formal arguments and enveloping data structures. The original subroutine is preserved for all calls with 'dense' arguments, in which the annotations have no effect.

5 Some Simple Experiments

In this section, we illustrate the potential of selecting a suitable reordering method with some simple experiments.

5.1 A Sparse Matrix

Assume that in the main program SOLVE presented in the previous section, the following declarations are given:

```
      REAL A(1000,1000), B(1000)
      C_SPARSE((A:_PERM ; A:_ACCESS(0,1) ; A:_FILE('d_blocks.cs'))
```

Furthermore, assume that the matrix stored in the file 'd_block.cs', available at compile-time, has the nonzero structure shown in figure 4. Application of a standard reordering method [14, p.105-126] reveals that the matrix can be permuted into block upper triangular from, with blocks of size 500×500.

First, a clone 'FACT_A0' is generated in which a unique correspondence between A and the first formal argument of the clone holds, and the call in the main program is altered accordingly. Thereafter, we can safely apply transformations to the clone without interference with calls to FACT having other arguments.

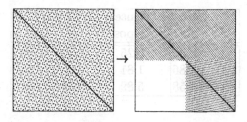

Fig. 4. Block Upper Triangular Form

We interchange the K and I-loop to increase the number of row-wise access patterns, since the preferred access direction is $(0,1)^T$. Zero regions are isolated and a compile-time elimination of useless operations is performed.

```
DO I = 1, 500
  DO K = 1, I - 1
    A(I,K) = A(I,K) / A(K,K)
    DO J = K + 1, 1000
      A(I,J) = A(I,J) - A(I,K)*A(K,J)
    ENDDO
  ENDDO
ENDDO
DO I = 501, 1000
  DO K = 501, I - 1
    A(I,K) = A(I,K) / A(K,K)
    DO J = K + 1, 1000
      A(I,J) = A(I,J) - A(I,K)*A(K,J)
    ENDDO
  ENDDO
ENDDO
```

Since dependences between the two fragments are broken [9], the compiler records that these fragments can be executed in parallel. Moreover, to economize on storage, the compiler selects separate dense storage of the first and last 500 rows and adapts the code accordingly:

```
REAL ADNS1(1:500,1:1000), ADNS2(501:N,501:N)
```

5.2 Some Timings

In table 2, we present some timings on a Cray C98/4256 for the original dense implementation and the serial block upper triangular version, and the corresponding parallel version on 2 CPUs (parallelism is indicated by 'CMIC$ case'). Wall-clock time is given for the parallel version. In all codes, storage of the matrix is transposed to enhance vector performance.

| | Initial | Dense | BUTF | BUTF |
N	NNZ	(transposed)	(ser.)	(par.)
500	4166	0.25	0.11	0.08
1000	15686	1.81	0.80	0.54
1500	34558	5.89	2.59	1.81

Table 2. Factorization Time in seconds on a Cray C98/4256

Permuting the matrix at-compile time to isolate zero blocks has enabled the use of a static storage scheme, in which fill-in is easily dealt with,[4] and a reasonable exploitation of parallelism. Similar transformations are possible in the clone FORW_A00, while only data structure transformations are done in BACK_A00.

6 Conclusions

In this paper we have presented the annotations that have been incorporated in MT1 to support the automatic generation of sparse codes. Annotations in the declarative part can be used to identify enveloping data structures in the original dense program, to supply nonzero structure information to the compiler, and to enable the incorporation of reordering methods. Annotations in the executable part can be used to deal with the mathematical consequences of permutations.

Current research is focused on the development of analysis techniques that support the incorporation of useful reordering methods in the generated sparse code. Some simple experiments have revealed the potential of this incorporation.

References

1. R.C. Agarwal, F.G. Gustavson, and M. Zubair. A high performance algorithm using pre-processing for the sparse matrix-vector multiplication. In *Proceedings of the International Conference on Supercomputing*, pages 32–41, 1992.
2. Edward Anderson and Youcef Saad. Solving sparse triangular linear systems on parallel computers. *International Journal of High Speed Computing*, Volume 1:73–95, 1989.
3. Vasanth Balasundaram. *Interactive Parallelization of Numerical Scientific Programs*. PhD thesis, Department of Computer Science, Rice University, 1989.
4. Vasanth Balasundaram. A mechanism for keeping useful internal information in parallel programming tools: The data access descriptor. *Journal of Parallel and Distributed Computing*, Volume 9:154–170, 1990.
5. U. Banerjee. *Dependence Analysis for Supercomputing*. Kluwer, Boston, 1988.
6. Aart J.C. Bik. A prototype restructuring compiler. Master's thesis, Utrecht University, 1992. INF/SCR-92-11.

---

[4] Due to much fill-in, all versions outperform a general sparse implementation.

7. Aart J.C. Bik, Peter M.W. Knijnenburg, and Harry A.G. Wijshoff. Reshaping access patterns for generating sparse codes. In K. Pingali, U. Banerjee, D. Gelernter, A. Nicolau, and D. Padua, editors, *Lecture Notes in Computer Science, No. 892*, pages 406–422. Springer-Verlag, Berlin/New York, 1995.

8. Aart J.C. Bik and Harry A.G. Wijshoff. Nonzero structure analysis. In *Proceedings of the International Conference on Supercomputing*, pages 226–235, 1994.

9. Aart J.C. Bik and Harry A.G. Wijshoff. Advanced compiler optimizations for sparse computations. *Journal of Parallel and Distributed Computing*, 1995. To Appear.

10. Aart J.C. Bik and Harry A.G. Wijshoff. Automatic data structure selection and transformation for sparse matrix computations. *IEEE Transactions on Parallel and Distributed Systems*, 1995. To Appear.

11. Aart J.C. Bik and Harry A.G. Wijshoff. Construction of representative simple sections. In *Proceedings of the International Conference on Parallel Processing*, 1995. To Appear.

12. Keith D. Cooper, Mary W. Hall, and Ken Kennedy. Procedure cloning. In *Proceedings of the IEEE International Conference on Computer Language*, pages 96–105, 1992.

13. Keith D. Cooper, Ken Kennedy, and Linda Torczon. The impact of interprocedural analysis and optimization in the R^n programming environment. *ACM Transactions on Programming Languages and Systems*, Volume 8:491–523, 1986.

14. Iain S. Duff, A.M. Erisman, and J.K. Reid. *Direct Methods for Sparse Matrices*. Oxford Science Publications, Oxford, 1990.

15. Jocelyne Erhel and Bernard Philippe. Multiplication of a vector by a sparse matrix on supercomputers. In M. Cosnard, M.H. Barton, and M. Vanneschi, editors, *Parallel Processing*, pages 181–187. Elsevier Science Publishers B.V., North-Holland, 1988.

16. Dennis Gannon et al. SIGMA II: A tool kit for building parallelizing compilers and performance analysis systems. Department of Computer Science, Indiana University, 1992.

17. Alan George and Joseph W.H. Liu. A fast implementation of the minimum degree algorithms using quotient graphs. *ACM Transactions on Mathematical Software*, Volume 6:337–358, 1980.

18. Alan George and Joseph W.H. Liu. *Computer Solution of Large Sparse Positive Definite Systems*. Prentice-Hall, Englewoord Cliffs, New York, 1981.

19. Alan George and Joseph W.H. Liu. The evolution of the minimum degree ordering algorithm. *SIAM Review*, Volume 31:1–19, 1989.

20. David J. Kuck. *The Structure of Computers and Computations*. John Wiley and Sons, New York, 1978. Volume 1.

21. David A. Padua and Michael J. Wolfe. Advanced compiler optimizations for supercomputers. *Communications of the ACM*, Volume 29:1184–1201, 1986.

22. Sergio Pissanetsky. *Sparse Matrix Technology*. Academic Press, London, 1984.

23. Reginal P. Tewarson. *Sparse Matrices*. Academic Press, New York, 1973.

24. Michael J. Wolfe. *Optimizing Supercompilers for Supercomputers*. Pitman, London, 1989.

25. H. Zima. *Supercompilers for Parallel and Vector Computers*. ACM Press, New York, 1990.

26. Zahari Zlatev. *Computational Methods for General Sparse Matrices*. Kluwer, Dordrecht, 1991.

Connection Analysis: A Practical Interprocedural Heap Analysis for C *

Rakesh Ghiya and Laurie J. Hendren

School of Computer Science, McGill University
Montréal, CANADA
{ghiya,hendren}@cs.mcgill.ca

Abstract. This paper presents a practical heap analysis technique, *connection analysis*, that can be used to disambiguate heap accesses in C programs. The technique is designed for analysing programs that allocate many disjoint objects in the heap such as dynamically-allocated arrays in scientific programs.

The method statically estimates connection matrices which encode the connection relationships between all heap-directed pointers at each program point. The results of the analysis can be used by parallelizing compilers to determine when two heap-allocated objects are guaranteed to be disjoint, and thus can be used to improve array dependence and interference analysis.

The method has been implemented as a context-sensitive interprocedural analysis in the McCAT optimizing/parallelizing C compiler. Experimental results are given to compare the accuracy of connection analysis versus a conservative estimate based on points-to analysis.

1 Introduction and Background

Optimizing and parallelizing compilers rely upon accurate static disambiguation of memory references i.e. determining at compile-time, if two given memory references always access disjoint memory locations. Although there has been a long history of developing methods for disambiguating array references, there has been an increasing interest in a variety of methods for disambiguating pointer references. This is becoming more important as optimizing and parallelizing compilers are being developed for languages supporting pointers such as C and FORTRAN90.

The pointer analysis problem can be divided into 2 distinct subproblems: (1) disambiguating pointers that point to objects on the stack, and (2) disambiguating pointers that point to objects on the heap. There has been a considerable amount of work in both of these areas [JM81, JM82, LH88, Lar91, Gua88, HPR89, Har89, CWZ90, HN90, LR92, CBC93, Deu92, Deu94, PCK93, EGH94, WL95, Ruf95], although more attention has been paid to actually implementing methods that work well for stack-allocated objects [LR92, CBC93, EGH94, Ruf95, WL95]. A complete discussion and comparison of these methods can be found in [Ghi95].

Stack-directed pointers exhibit the important property that their targets always possess a name (the name of the variable allocated to that location on the stack). Using this property, pointer relationships can be conveniently captured in the form of *points-to* pairs where the points-to pair (p,x) denotes that pointer variable p points to the data object x.

---

* This work supported by NSERC, FCAR, and the EPPP project (financed by Industry Canada, Alex Parallel Computers, Digital Equipment Canada, IBM Canada and the Centre de recherche informatique de Montréal).

Unfortunately this nice property of having a static name for all targets does not hold for heap-allocated data items. In fact, all the objects in the heap are allocated via a memory allocation function and are *anonymous*. Heap objects cannot be referenced by their name, they can only be accessed through pointer dereferences like *r, r->item and a[i], where r and a are heap-directed pointers. One might imagine that one could generate symbolic names for heap objects, but this is also difficult as a potentially infinite number of them can be created. To further complicate the problem, objects in the heap are dynamically linked, and more importantly delinked. Hence, there is no natural way of naming even collections of objects (e.g. linked structures). Unlike arrays, both the number of linked structures and the number of objects belonging to a given linked structure, vary dynamically. Thus, in order to estimate more accurate information about heap-directed pointers, a different approach is required.

In addition to designing the heap analysis itself, it is also important to determine how the heap analysis interacts with the stack analysis, and to design an analysis that can be effectively implemented in real C or FORTRAN90 compilers. It is interesting to examine three recently implemented strategies. Landi and Ryder have reported on an implementation of an interprocedural strategy for C that estimates alias information in terms of pairs of *object names* [LR92]. An object name consists of a variable and a (possibly empty) sequence of dereferences and field accesses. Typical alias pairs are: (**a, *b), (*(a->next), *(b->next)). In the presence of recursive data structures, the number of object names is infinite. To avoid this, they k-limit object names. Choi, Burke and Carini [CBC93] have been implementing a method for FORTAN90, and they also compute aliases of pairs of *access paths*. Their access paths are similar to object names [LR92]. However, they do not use access paths to name heap objects. Instead, they use the place (statement) in the program, where an anonymous heap object is created, to name it, as in [CWZ90]. To avoid giving the same name to heap objects created at the same statement, but along different call-chains, they qualify the names with procedure strings. A recent approach for C is the implementation of a context-sensitive method for the SUIF compiler system [WL95]. In this approach, a points-to representation is used, however, they use the concept of *location sets* to specify both a block of memory, and a set of positions within that block. Blocks of memory that are heap-allocated are labeled by their allocation context.

In all three of these approaches the stack-directed and heap-directed pointer problems are solved together. In contrast, our approach is to decouple the problems and to first solve the stack-directed pointer problem using points-to analysis [EGH94, Ema93], and then use the result of points-to analysis as a starting point to solve the heap-directed pointer problem. The motivation for decoupling the problems is that the solutions for the two problems are quite different, and by concentrating on each problem separately we can design appropriate abstractions and analysis rules. For the stack-directed pointer problem we calculate direct pointer relationships between *named* locations, whereas for the heap-directed pointer problem we need to collect more general relationships (such as which heap-directed pointers possibly lead to a common node). This decoupling is also beneficial from a software development point of view. By using a simple model for the heap in points-to analysis, we can simplify the points-to analysis rules, and reduce the number of objects that must be abstracted (we have only one object called *heap*, whereas the other combined approaches must use many names for objects in the heap). This leads to a faster and more space-efficient points-to analysis. Similarly, our heap analysis is simplified and faster because we can use the result of points-to analysis to locate only those pointers that point to the heap, and then run the heap analysis using this subset of pointers.

In fact, we have a hierarchy of analyses that abstract *relationships* between heap-directed pointers. As one goes up the hierarchy, a more precise solution is obtained, but at the cost of a more complex and expensive analysis. The *level-0* analysis is simply the points-to analysis that treats the entire heap as one named location. For programs with few heap objects, this is enough. This paper focuses on the *level-1* heap analysis: *connection analysis*. Connection analysis is targeted towards programs that allocate a number of disjoint data structures in the heap. Scientific applications written in C typically exhibit this feature, as they use a number of disjoint dynamically allocated arrays. Connection analysis can also be used to distinguish between different linked data structures. The analysis was designed to provide a simple, but useful, analysis that would provide accurate results for its intended domain of applications. The rest of the paper is organized as follows. In Section 2 we introduce the analysis and give some high-level analysis rules assuming a simple model where stack-directed pointers and heap-directed pointers are clearly separated. The method has been fully implemented in the McCAT compiler as a context-sensitive interprocedural analysis. In Section 3 we give a brief overview of our implementation of this method and we discuss the most pertinent features. We present some empirical data in Section 4, to demonstrate the cost and effectiveness of this abstraction for its intended domain of applications. Section 5 gives our conclusions and briefly describes our future work.

2 Connection Analysis

Connection analysis uses a simple, *storeless* [Deu92], abstraction designed to disambiguate heap accesses at a coarse level, but in an efficient and cost-effective manner. For each program point the analysis computes a *connection matrix*, which is a boolean matrix summarizing the connectivity of heap objects. A *heap object* is defined as an object allocated in the heap memory. Our connection analysis is performed with respect to a connection matrix abstraction that is designed to disambiguate heap accesses at the data structure level. The term *data structure* in this context represents a connected region in the heap i.e. if the heap is viewed as an undirected graph with heap objects as nodes and links between them as edges, each connected component forms a separate data structure. Two disjoint data structures contain no common heap objects. For example in Figure 1, the heap consists of two data structures: one pointed to by pointers p and q and the other pointed to by pointers r, s and t. Note that we cannot give names to these data structures, we can only refer to them as being pointed to by a given set of pointers.

With the above definitions, given any two heap-directed pointers say p and q, connection matrix abstracts the following *program-point-specific* relationships:

C[p,q] = 1: Pointers p and q *possibly* point to heap objects belonging to the same data structure. In our terminology, pointers p and q are considered to be *connected*, or to have a *connection* relationship.

C[p,q] = 0: The heap objects pointed to by pointers p and q *definitely* belong to different data structures. In other words, pointers p and q are *not* connected.

The useful information is the negative information. If pointers p and q are not connected, then heap accesses originating from them will always lead to disjoint heap locations, and thus not interfere. It is *safe* to report two heap-directed pointers to be connected, when they are not. However, if they can point to the same data structure, they should always be reported to be connected.

We illustrate the abstraction in Figure 1. Part (a) shows the structure of heap at a program point, while part (b) shows its abstraction as a connection matrix. The zero in entry C[p,r] indicates that pointers p and r point to disjoint data structures. The one in the entry C[s,r] indicates that s and r point to objects belonging to the same data structure. Note that the entry C[r,t] is set to one, despite the fact that pointers r and t point to disjoint subpieces of the same data structure. This is because connection matrix is designed to disambiguate heap accesses at the data structure level. More sophisticated abstractions, which can distinguish between subpieces of a data structure itself, are defined in higher levels in the hierarchy of heap analyses.

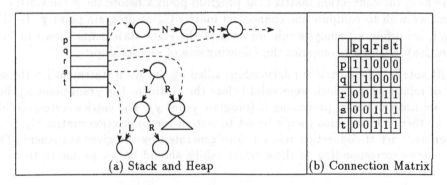

	p	q	r	s	t
p	1	1	0	0	0
q	1	1	0	0	0
r	0	0	1	1	1
s	0	0	1	1	1
t	0	0	1	1	1

(a) Stack and Heap   (b) Connection Matrix

Fig. 1. An example Connection Matrix

The following are some other important characteristics of the connection matrix abstraction:

- It abstracts relationships only between *stack-resident* heap-directed pointers. As all heap accesses originate from these pointers, their relationships effectively capture the structure of the heap. For example in Figure 1(b), the information that pointers p and s point to disjoint data structures also simultaneously implies that pointers p->N and s->L point to disjoint structures.

- For each function in the program, the connection matrix abstracts relationships between all stack-resident pointers which can be heap-directed at some point in the program and are directly or indirectly (through an indirect reference) accessible from the function. Names are naturally available from the program, for directly-accessible pointers. For indirectly-accessible pointers, special symbolic names are generated by points-to analysis and these names are reused by connection matrix analysis. To know which pointers ever point to heap, the existing points-to information is used. If p points-to the heap, then the entry *(p,heap)* will appear in the points-to set.

- If a pointer, say p, does not point to a heap location at a given program point, the connection matrix entry C[p,p] is set to zero at that program point. In this case the pointer points to **NULL** or to a stack location.
- The connection matrix relationship is symmetric i.e. for any two heap-directed pointers say p and q, we always have C[p,q] = C[q,p]. The connection relationships shown in Figure 1(b) illustrate this property. It is used in the actual implementation to reduce the storage requirement by half.

The complete list of the basic statements that can affect heap relationships is given in Figure 2(a). Variables p and q and the field f are of pointer type, variable k is of integer type, and op denotes the + and − operations. In this section we give the analysis rules for these eight *basic heap* statements with the restriction that pointers p and q can only point to heap objects. These rules are simple to describe and clearly illustrate the basic principles of connection analysis. In the next section we discuss the extensions that must be made to handle complete C programs where the effect of stack-based points-to relationships must also be taken into account. The overall structure of the analysis is shown in Figure 2(b). We have the connection matrix C at program point x before the given statment, and we wish to compute the connection matrix C_n at program point y. To this end, we define an analysis rule for each of the eight statements shown in Figure 2(a). Each rule computes the following sets of relationships:

kill_set: Set of connection relationships killed by the given statement i.e. the set of relationships which were valid before the statment (program point x), but are not valid after processing it (program point y). The entries corresponding to these relationships should be set to zero in the connection matrix C_n.

gen_set: Set of connection relationships generated by the given statement. The entries corresponding to these relationships should be set to one in the new matrix C_n.

Let H be the set of pointers whose relationships are abstracted by the connection matrix C. Let p, q, r and s represent pointers in this set. Assume that pointers can only point to heap objects or to **NULL**. Further, assume that updating an entry C[p,q] also implies identically updating the entry C[q,p]. This assumption is required due to the symmetric nature of connection relationships. The new connection matrix C_n is computed as shown in Figure 2(c). First, the old connection matrix C is copied over to C_n. Next, the entries in the kill_set are set to zero in the matrix C_n. Finally, the entries in the gen_set are set to one in the matrix C_n, to get the complete new connection matrix.

We now present the analysis rules for the eight basic statements. For each statement, we give the rules for computing their kill and gen sets. The new connection matrix can then be computed as shown in Figure 2(c).

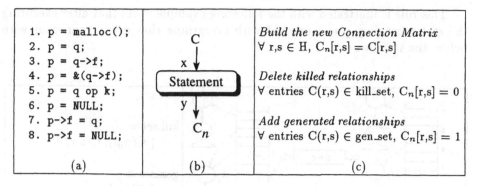

Fig. 2. Computing Connection Matrix C_n from C for Basic Statements

2.1 Allocating new heap cells

p = malloc(): In this case pointer p points to a newly allocated heap object. All the existing connection relationships of p get killed. Also as no other pointer can point to this object, p will only have connection relationship with itself. This is stated with the following rule.

$$\text{kill\_set} = \{\ C(p,s)\ |\ s \in H \wedge C[p,s]\ \}$$
$$\text{gen\_set} = \{\ C(p,p)\ \}$$

The rule is illustrated with the following example. Note that after executing the p = malloc() statement, p is only connected with itself.

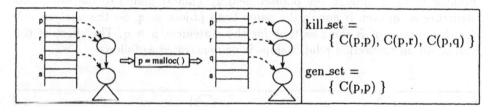

2.2 Pointer assignments

Basic heap statements 2 through 5 in Figure 2(a) (p = q, p = q->f, p = &(q->f) and p = NULL), have a common attribute: all of them update the stack-resident pointer p, and make it point to a new data structure. They do not modify the structure of the heap itself. Their effect on connection matrix information can be summarized using a general rule, as discussed below.

p = q : Pointer p now points to the same heap object as q, and hence to the same data structure as q. All the existing relationships of p get killed, and p gets connected to all pointers connected to q. If q is presently heap-directed ($C[q,q]$ = 1), then p is also heap-directed after the statement. So the entry $C(p,p)$ is added to the gen_set, if we have $C[q,q] = 1$. We present the overall rule for this statement below.

$$\text{kill\_set} = \{\ C(p,s)\ |\ s \in H \wedge C[p,s]\ \}$$
$$\text{gen\_set} = \{\ C(p,s)\ |\ s \in H \wedge C[q,s]\ \} \cup \{\ C(p,p)\ |\ C[q,q]\ \}$$

This rule is illustrated with the following example. Note that after executing the statement p=q, p is connected with everything that q was connected with before the statement.

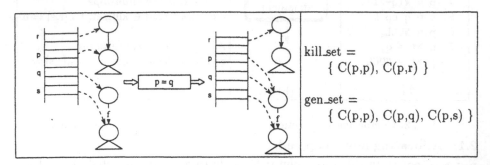

Note that if q presently points to NULL, p should also point to NULL after the statement. In this case all entries C[q,s] will be zero, resulting in an empty gen_set. Consequently all entries C_n[p,s] will also be zero after the statement, indicating p to be pointing to NULL, as desired. Similarly if q happens to be pointer p itself, resulting in the statement p = p, the gen and kill sets would be identical. In this case the connection matrix would remain unchanged, as required. Thus the above rule is general enough to take into account various special cases.

p = q->f: Pointer p now points to the heap object connected to the object pointed to by q through the pointer field f. Thus it points to the same data structure as q, even if not to the same heap object as q. So the analysis rule for this statement is same as that for the statement p = q. The effect of this statement on connection relationships is demonstrated as follows.

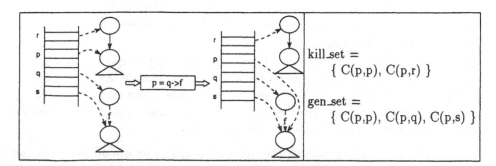

This rule incurs some imprecision, when the pointer q->f points to NULL. In this case, pointer p should also point to NULL after the statement. However we would report it be pointing to the same data structure as q. This information is *safe* but less precise. This happens because we cannot determine if q->f presently points to NULL, and not to a heap object. In other words, q->f is a heap-resident pointer, while connection matrix only abstracts the relationships (and nilness) of stack-resident pointers.

If pointers p and q are not distinct, the statement can be of the form p = p->f. The rule for this case is same as for the statment p = p, which does not change any connection relationships, as required.

p = &(q->f) : Pointer p now points to the field f of the heap object pointed to by q, as shown in the following illustration. For the purpose of our analysis we consider a pointer pointing to a specific field of a heap object, to be pointing to the object itself. Thus, this statement is equivalent to the statement p = q for connection matrix analysis.

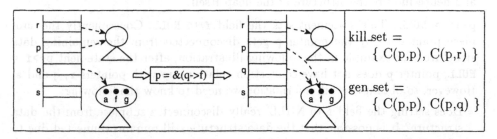

$$kill\_set = \{ C(p,p), C(p,r) \}$$
$$gen\_set = \{ C(p,p), C(p,q) \}$$

p = q op k: This rule represents pointer arithmetic. After the arithmetic operation, q continues to point to the same heap-object, though at a different offset, as shown in the following illustration. We assume that a heap-directed pointer does not cross the boundary of the heap object, when pointer arithmetic is performed on it. Otherwise, it can potentially point to memory not allocated by the program, and cause an execution error on being dereferenced. With this assumption about pointer arithmetic, this statement is equivalent to the statement p = q for connection matrix analysis.

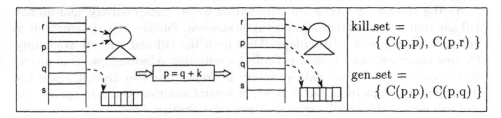

$$kill\_set = \{ C(p,p), C(p,r) \}$$
$$gen\_set = \{ C(p,p), C(p,q) \}$$

p = NULL: Pointer p now does not point to any heap object allocated by the program, as shown in the following illustration. It does not have any connection relationship with any pointer, including itself. Thus the effect of this statement is to simply kill all the relationships of p, as presented below:

$$kill\_set = \{ C(p,s) \mid s \in H \wedge C[p,s] \}$$
$$gen\_set = \{\}$$

As illustrated in the following example, after executing the statement p = NULL we have C[p,p] = 0, indicating that p presently points to NULL.

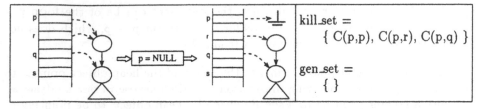

2.3 Structure Updates

The statements discussed so far update a stack-resident heap-directed pointer. The following two statements update a pointer field residing in a heap object, and hence modify the structure of the heap itself.

p->f = NULL: This statement sets the field **f** to **NULL**. Consequently the subpiece pointed to by the pointer **p** gets disconnected from the remaining data structure. For example in the following illustration, after the statement **p->f = NULL**, pointer **p** does not have connection relationship with pointers **r**, **q** and **s**. However, to obtain this kill information we need to know the following:

- Does setting the field **f** to NULL, really disconnect a subpiece from the data structure? It is possible that the data structure still remains connected due to other links. For example in the following illustration, if pointers **p** and **r** are also connected through a **g** link, the subpiece pointed to by **r** would not get disconnected by the statement **p->f = NULL**.
- In case a subpiece gets disconnected, which pointers point to it?

Unfortunately, connection matrix information is not sufficient to answer these questions. To answer the first question we need to have some approximation for the shape of the underlying data structure. The second question requires knowledge about the possible path relationships between the various pointers pointing to the data structure. As such information is expensive to abstract, we do not collect it for level-1 heap analysis.

In the absence of precise kill information we err conservatively, and do not kill any connection relationships for this statement. Further, this statement does not generate any new relationships. Thus both the kill and gen sets are empty for this statement, and it does not affect connection relationships. This means that even though the real data structure is broken into two disjoint pieces (as illustrated in the picture), our connection matrix analysis cannot recognize this and will not be able to kill any connection relationships.

`p->f = q`: This statement has two effects. First it potentially disconnects a subpiece of the data structure pointed to by p, like the previous statement `p->f = NULL`. Next, it connects the data structures pointed to by p and q. As already discussed, precise kill information due to potential disconnection cannot be obtained. However new connection relationships are generated due to the interlinking of data structures pointed to by p and q. All pointers connected to p now get connected to all pointers connected to q (which include q itself). So we have the following analysis rule for this statement:

$$kill\_set = \{\}$$
$$gen\_set = \{ C(r,s) \mid r,s \in H \land C[p,r] \land C[q,s] \}$$

This rule is illustrated in the following figure. In the real data structure, before the statement, pointers p and r are connected to p. After the assignment p is no longer connected to r, but it is now connected to q and s. However, note that the gen and kill sets for connection analysis cannot model this precisely. We cannot kill the connection between p and r and we also will generate a spurious connection between r and s. This happens because the disconnection of r from p cannot be inferred from the information available.

$$kill\_set = \{ \}$$

$$gen\_set = \{ C(p,q), C(p,s), C(r,q), C(r,s) \}$$

3 Implementing Connection Analysis in the McCAT C compiler

The connection matrix analysis has been implemented as a context-sensitive interprocedural analysis in the McCAT parallelizing/optimizing C compiler. The analysis is performed on the SIMPLE intermediate representation which is a simplified, compositional subset of C [Sri92, HDE+92, EH94]. The analysis is performed after points-to analysis and is implemented in a similar framework [Ema93, EGH94].

The implementation of connection matrix analysis is structured as a simple analysis for each basic statement of the form presented in Section 2, a compositional rule for each control construct, and an interprocedural strategy that uses an unfolded invocation graph to capture all calling contexts. Recursion is handled via special recursive and approximate nodes in the invocation graph, and an interprocedural fixed-point computation is performed at each recursive node.

Recursive nodes correspond to each point in the program where a recursive function is first called, and the approximate nodes correspond to all recursive calls that follow.

There are several important points in actually implementing this analysis. Firstly, one must be careful about how to apply the simple analysis rules presented in Section 2. The subtle point is that references of the form p->f may refer to the stack, the heap, or to both the stack and heap. For example, in one calling context, p may point to a stack-allocated object that has a name, while in another calling context p may point to a heap-allocated object. Consider a statement of the form p->f = q. If p points-to a stack-allocated object with the name x, then the appropriate connection analysis rule is x.f = q, whereas if p points-to a heap-allocated object, the appropriate rule is p->f = q. Thus, the actual implementation first uses the points-to information to resolve all references of the form p->f into a set of possible stack and heap locations, and then applies the appropriate simple connection analysis rules, merging the results of all the outputs.

The second important point is that a function f may change the connection relationships between variables that are not visible inside f. Thus, symbolic names must be generated to capture all such invisible locations. A method similar to the one used in the points-to analysis is used for this purpose.

The final important point relates to minimizing the overhead in getting an efficient context-sensitive analysis. We have currently implemented a simple memoization scheme that stores previously computed input and output values at each invocation graph node, and avoids recomputing the output values when a previously computed input/output pair can be reused. The usefulness of this scheme is discussed in Section 4.

4 Experimental Results

In this section, we present the experimental results obtained from connection matrix analysis of a set of 13 C programs. We chose programs that use a significant amount of dynamic allocation, as benchmarks for our study. In Table 1, we summarize the following characteristics for each program.

- Source lines including comments, counted using the *wc* utility.
- Number of statements in the SIMPLE intermediate representation. This number gives a good estimate of program size from the analysis point of view.
- Minimum, maximum and average number of variables abstracted by the connection matrices over all functions in the program (this includes symbolic variables introduced by our analysis). These numbers indicate the size of the abstraction and the memory requirements of the analysis for a given program.
- Total number of indirect references in the program, and the number of indirect references where the dereferenced pointer can point to a stack location, to a heap location and to both a stack and a heap location. The number of indirect references in a program, provides a measure for the relevance of pointer analysis to its optimization. The number of indirect references referring to stack and heap locations, respectively represent the significance of stack-based points-to analysis and heap-based data structure analyses for the given program.

The number of SIMPLE statements for the given benchmark set varies from 476 for *chomp* to 4909 for *volrend*, with an overall average of 2028 statements per program. The maximum number of variables abstracted by the connection matrix of a function is 133 for *pug*, followed by 114 for *cholesky*. The maximum of the average number of variables abstracted, is 89 for *cholesky* followed by 43 for *sim*. All the benchmarks have substantial number of indirect references, with maximum 822 for *pug* followed by 718 for *assembler*. Further, all of them have indirect references referring to both stack and heap locations, with the majority of indirect references referring to heap locations (except for the two benchmarks: *assembler* and *loader*). This makes the given benchmark set well-suited for evaluating a heap analysis.

As the analysis may become conservative when a pointer can point to both a stack and heap location, it is interesting to note that the right-most column indicates that this situation does not happen very often. We inspected the analysis output for programs *genetic*, *volrend* and *pug*, to detect the indirect references where this happens. We found that these indirect references mostly dereference formal parameters (of pointer type), to which both heap-directed and stack-directed pointers are passed as actuals, in different invocations of the given function.

Program	Source Lines	SIMPLE stmts	Min vars	Max vars	Avg vars	Ind Refs	To Stack	To Heap	Stack/ Heap
genetic	506	479	6	14	7	54	28	30	4
sim	1422	1760	38	69	43	374	34	340	0
blocks2	876	1070	28	54	33	373	98	275	0
ear	4953	3476	38	51	39	290	143	147	0
assembler	3361	3071	12	26	14	718	666	52	0
loader	1539	1055	7	20	10	170	106	64	0
cholesky	1899	2217	76	114	89	488	22	466	0
mp3d	1687	1849	18	28	20	490	25	465	0
water	2703	2418	8	65	27	581	32	549	0
volrend	4207	4909	18	45	20	190	63	128	1
chomp	430	476	20	27	22	127	45	82	0
sparse	2859	1495	12	40	18	468	3	465	0
pug	2400	2089	16	133	30	822	147	688	13

Table 1. Characteristics of Connection Matrix Benchmarks

4.1 Measurements for Heap Related Indirect References

In Table 2, we present empirical measurements for connection matrix analysis of the above benchmarks. Our measurements focus on indirect references in the program that refer to heap locations. We motivate our measurements using the following example program:

```
main()
    { p = my_malloc(N); q = my_malloc(M);
      ...
S:    *p = INIT_VAL;
T:    *q = INIT_VAL;
      ... }
```

This program allocates two disjoint heap structures and then initializes them. Before connection analysis, the only information available from points-to analysis is: both the indirect references *p and *q (at statements S and T respectively) refer to the location *heap*, and thus the statements S and T interfere. After connection matrix analysis, we know that the data structures pointed to by p and q are never connected (are disjoint), and hence the statements S and T do not interfere.

Our experimental measurements attempt to quantify the improvement in resolution of heap data structures provided by connection matrix information over that obtained from the conservative approximation of points-to analysis. With only points-to analysis one must assume that each heap-directed pointer is possibly connected with all other other heap-directed pointers, while with connection matrix analysis one can identify a more precise set. Thus, the effectiveness of connection matrix analysis can be evaluated by comparing the total number of heap-directed pointers at an indirect reference (the conservative estimate provided by points-to analysis), with the total number of pointers connected with the dereferenced pointer (the more precise estimate available from connection matrix analysis). For example, in the above program, at statement S, the total number of heap-directed pointers is two (both p and q are heap-directed), while the number of pointers connected with the dereferenced pointer p is only one (p itself). The same situation holds at statement T.

Following this strategy, we have calculated the following metrics for each benchmark program (presented in Table 2):

refs: Total number of indirect references in the program that can refer to heap locations.

cavg: Average number of pointers that are connected with the dereferenced pointer at an indirect reference. This average is calculated as follows. At each indirect reference we determine the total number of pointers connected with the dereferenced pointer. Let us call this number cn_tot_i for the ith indirect reference in the program (as per lexical order). We do not include symbolic variables in this count as we generate them only to facilitate interprocedural mapping, and they cannot be accessed or dereferenced by the program. Further if the dereferenced pointer is only connected with itself, the count cn_tot_i will be one for the given indirect reference. We then sum up the numbers cn_tot_i for all indirect references, and divide this sum total denoted as cn_sum_tot by the total number of heap related indirect references in the program (**refs**), to obtain the average **cavg**.

havg: Average number of pointers that are heap-directed at an indirect reference. This average is calculated in the same fashion as **cavg**. First, at each indirect reference the total number of heap-directed pointers is calculated as heap_tot_i. Next, this number is summed up for all indirect references, and the sum total heap_sum_tot is divided by **refs** to obtain the average **havg**.

decr: A measure to approximate the percentage decrease in the number of connection relationships provided by connection matrix information over points-to information. It is calculated using the following formula: ((heap_sum_tot -

`cn_sum_tot) * 100.0)/ (heap_sum_tot).`

Without connection matrix analysis, the conservative approximation for the number `cn_sum_tot` would be simply `heap_sum_tot`, resulting in zero percentage decrease. With connection analysis, the more precise the analysis, the fewer the number of connection relationships reported, and the larger is the decrease. Thus, the metric **decr** provides a reasonable measure for the effectiveness of connection matrix analysis. For our small example program (given above): **refs** is 2, `cn_sum_tot` is 2 and hence **cavg** is 1.0; `heap_sum_tot` is 4, **havg** is 2.0 and **decr** is (((4 - 2) * 100.0) / 4) or 50%.

In Table 2, the left and middle parts present these measurements separately for indirect references of the type `*a/(*a).b`, and of the type `a[i]` where `a` is of pointer type. The right part of Table 2 gives the overall results. We discuss each case below.

Program	*a / (*a).b				a[i]				*a / (*a).b / a[i]			
	refs	cavg	havg	% decr	refs	cavg	havg	% decr	refs	cavg	havg	% decr
genetic	0	0.0	0.0	0.00	30	1.7	5.2	67.74	30	1.7	5.2	67.74
sim	96	3.4	23.2	85.55	244	1.6	20.4	92.41	340	2.1	21.2	90.29
blocks2	119	8.8	22.9	61.36	156	5.2	22.3	83.74	275	6.8	22.5	69.86
ear	42	2.7	3.8	27.22	105	2.4	7.1	66.26	147	2.5	6.1	59.40
assembler	45	4.4	7.8	42.98	7	6.0	9.4	36.36	52	4.6	8.0	41.93
loader	55	5.1	6.5	21.07	9	1.0	4.1	75.66	64	4.5	6.1	26.21
cholesky	82	14.9	34.3	56.46	384	3.7	20.7	82.27	466	5.7	23.1	75.53
mp3d	391	2.5	8.6	70.42	74	1.9	7.1	73.86	465	2.4	8.4	70.88
water	250	15.4	31.2	50.69	299	14.7	24.1	38.94	549	15.0	27.3	45.05
volrend	96	7.4	22.2	66.73	32	9.8	18.8	47.59	128	8.0	21.3	62.52
chomp	56	5.2	7.2	27.65	26	1.6	3.9	59.00	82	4.1	6.2	33.86
sparse	384	9.3	10.1	7.23	0	0.0	0.0	0.00	384	9.3	10.1	7.23
pug	514	36.8	36.9	0.30	174	47.6	47.7	0.11	688	39.5	39.6	0.24

Table 2. Empirical Measurements for Connection Matrix Results

Indirect References of type `a[i]`: The percentage decrease (**decr**) is, in general, higher for indirect references of this type. This happens because most of these references represent stack-based pointers that point to dynamically allocated memory and access it as an array (of non pointer type). For example, the statement `a = (int *) malloc(8 * sizeof(int))` dynamically allocates an array of eight integers. Such array structures are, in general, not pointed to by many other pointers. In SIMPLE, the above statement is *simplified* as `temp_0 = malloc(8 * sizeof(int)); a = (int *) temp_0`, resulting in both a and `temp_0` pointing to the allocated structure. In case the allocation is done through a user-defined routine (for example `a = my_malloc(size)`) where type casting is not performed, the temporary variable is not generated, and pointer `a` alone points to the allocated structure. So the number of connection relationships of pointers like `a` tends to be close to 2.0 on an average. In Table 2, **cavg** for indirect array references is in the range of 1.0 to 3.7 for most of the benchmarks.

For some benchmarks **cavg** tends to be much larger. The benchmarks *volrend* and *blocks2* use arrays of pointers. Since we represent the entire array by the array name, connection relationships of pointers representing different indices of the array get merged. This results in large number of relationships for the single name representing them in the connection matrix. The benchmarks *assembler*, *water* and *pug* have pointers to arrays as fields of dynamically allocated structures (as opposed to being located on the stack). These pointers are reported to be connected with all other pointers that point to the given data structure. This results in larger overall **cavg** for these benchmarks. Actually **cavg** for *pug* is almost same as **havg**, as it builds only a single complex data structure, providing effectively no decrease in connections.

Indirect References of type $*a/(*a).b$: For indirect references of this form, the percentage decrease is, in general, not as high as for indirect array references. Such indirect references commonly access big aggregate data structures that consist of a large number of heap objects, specially if the data structure is recursive. Several pointers point to any such data structure, and all of them have connection relationships with each other.

In our benchmark set, *sim* and *mp3d* primarily use structures with no pointer fields. The percentage decrease for them is quite high, as these structures are also stand-alone entities in the heap, like dynamic arrays of non pointer type.

The benchmarks *ear* and *cholesky* primarily allocate structures with non-recursive pointer fields. For *ear*, **cavg** is quite small, though the percentage decrease is not very high as not many pointers are heap-directed in this program. For *cholesky* we have more than 50 percent decrease.

The benchmark *volrend* allocates integers and floats in the heap and accesses them through indirect references of the form $*a$. The percentage decrease for it could be even higher, but it uses arrays of pointers to point to heap-allocated integers and floats. The benchmark *blocks2* allocates several disjoint arrays of pointers to dynamically-allocated objects of type **int** and user-defined structure types with both recursive and non-recursive pointer fields. So it has higher **cavg**, but still shows substantial percentage decrease.

The benchmarks *assembler* and *loader* use two disjoint linked list data structures, *chomp* uses a linked list and a tree structure, while *water* uses arrays of linked lists several of which are disjoint at different points in the program. The percentage decrease statistics for these benchmarks show the following expected trend: the greater is the number of disjoint data structures used by a program, the better are the connection matrix results for it.

Finally, the programs *sparse* and *pug* use a single complex recursive data structure, and all heap-directed pointers point to it. Consequently, connection matrix analysis provides negligible improvement for them.

Overall results: In the third section of Table 2, we present the overall measurements for all the benchmark programs. The percentage decrease is highest for programs that primarily use dynamic arrays (of non pointer type) and structures without pointer fields (*sim, cholesky* and *mp3d*). For some programs (*genetic* and *ear*) the percentage decrease is not very high, but **cavg** is quite small which indicates that connection matrix analysis provides effective information for them. Overall, the results show that if the given program uses disjoint data structures, connection matrix analysis can always provide more accurate information for resolving heap related indirect references (as compared to the information provided by points-to analysis). Thus, the connection matrix abstraction works well for its target domain of applications, and more powerful and more costly analyses are required for other applications.

4.2 Interprocedural Measurements

Connection matrix analysis is a context-sensitive interprocedural analysis. In Table 3 we present some measurements demonstrating the interprocedural characteristics of the analysis. In Table 3(a), we provide some *static* interprocedural characteristics of the benchmarks. The first three columns in this table give the number of functions, call-sites, and nodes in the invocation graph. The last three columns give the number of recursive and approximate nodes, and the number of invocation graph nodes per call-site.

In Table 3(b), we provide some *dynamic* interprocedural measurements. The column labeled Tot gives the total number of procedure calls analyzed during the analysis. Our interprocedural algorithm analyzes a procedure once for each invocation context. Hence one might expect that the number of procedure calls analyzed would be equal to the number of nodes in the invocation graph. However, this is not true, since a procedure call can be analyzed several times for a single invocation context, if the call is involved in a loop or recursion fixed-point approximation. The column labeled Memo shows the number of procedure calls that get memoized using our simple memoization scheme, and the column labeled Actual gives the number of procedure calls that are not memoized. The last three columns, labeled Avgf, Avgc and Avgi, give the average number of calls actually analyzed (given in the column labeled Actual) per function, per call-site and per invocation graph node. These averages are calculated by dividing the number in the Actual column, with the appropriate number from the first three columns in Table 3(b). In other words, Avgf, Avgc and Avgi give the average number of times: (i) a function gets analyzed, (ii) a call-site is encountered during the analysis, and (iii) a call-chain in the program (possibly ending in recursion) is traversed during the analysis.

There are several interesting observations to be made from the results in Table 3. The first is that for these benchmarks, the size of the invocation graph does not explode, and we can do a complete context-sensitive analysis with reasonable cost. There are, however, other benchmarks that do have very large invocation graphs, so we are exploring more aggressive memoization techniques for handling these programs. It is also interesting to note that a large number of procedure calls get memoized, even with our simple scheme.

5 Conclusions

In this paper we have presented our approach to practical heap analysis for C. In contrast to other approaches that solve the stack-directed and heap-directed pointer problems simultaneously, we separate the two problems. The stack-based

Program	fns	call sites	ig nodes	Recur nodes	Appr nodes	nodes/ call	Calls Analyzed Tot	Memo	Actual	Avgf	Avgc	Avgi
genetic	17	32	45	0	0	1.41	55	8	47	2.76	1.46	1.04
sim	14	26	44	2	8	1.70	71	10	61	4.36	2.35	1.39
blocks2	20	28	28	1	2	1.00	371	221	150	7.50	5.36	5.36
ear	64	144	235	2	2	1.63	268	30	238	3.72	1.86	1.01
assembler	52	263	642	0	0	2.44	767	101	666	12.80	2.53	1.04
loader	30	82	125	2	2	1.52	312	132	180	6.00	2.20	1.44
cholesky	47	72	93	2	2	1.29	132	35	97	2.06	1.35	1.04
mp3d	23	28	32	0	0	1.14	47	0	47	2.04	1.68	1.47
water	15	21	26	0	0	1.24	98	73	25	1.67	1.19	0.96
volrend	53	108	169	2	2	1.56	192	21	171	11.40	1.58	1.01
chomp	22	47	98	7	7	2.09	219	92	127	5.77	2.70	1.30
sparse	28	76	121	0	0	1.59	168	47	121	4.32	1.60	1.00
pug	41	69	101	0	0	1.46	160	47	113	2.75	1.64	1.12

(a) Invocation graph characteristics   (b) Interprocedural measurements

Table 3. Invocation graph characteristics and interprocedural measurements

problem is solved with points-to analysis. A hierarchical approach to the heap-directed pointer problem is used. For programs with few heap references, points-to analysis can be used directly (level-0 heap analysis). Points-to analysis gives a very conservative answer by treating the entire heap as one named location. For programs that allocate many disjoint structures, such as scientific programs with dynamically-allocated arrays, connection matrix analysis (level-1 heap analysis) provides useful information about the disjointness of the heap-allocated structures.

We have implemented the method in the McCAT compiler, and we provided experimental results to show that connection matrix analysis gives a substantially more precise answer than points-to analysis. The results are very good for the target application domain. For applications that use structures that are heavily linked, connection matrix analysis is not enough, and our approach has been extended to provide a more expensive direction/interference/shape analysis that allows us to estimate structure interference and estimate the shape (tree/dag/graph) of each structure allocated in the heap [Ghi95].

As the other implemented methods give experimental results for the stack and heap pointers combined, we do not have an empirical comparison. However, it is clear that connection analysis is much less sensitive to the location of `malloc` sites than any approach that uses these sites as names[CBC93, WL95]. In order to distinguish between different allocations, "malloc-site" based approaches must use call sites or call strings. This can easily result in a very large set of names in the abstraction, and thus slow down the analysis. In our case, we make use of the fact that each newly-allocated node is disjoint from all other heap-directed pointers live at that point in the program. Thus, we do not have to include many extraneous names in the abstractions.

Compared to Landi and Ryder's k-limiting approach [Lan92, LR92], we should get results similar to their analysis with k=1. The differences, if measured, would result from differences in where conservative approximations must be made in each method. Since the two approaches use different context-sensitive interprocedural approaches, there will be some variation. However, in our case we have the advantage of solving the heap problem separately, and thus the heap analysis operates on a relatively small set of pointers. Furthermore, our analysis fits cleanly into our hierarchical model where we have a family of heap analyses.

Our overall strategy is to use the analysis that is most appropriate for the target application program. If the program has no (or very little) dynamic allocation, then there is is no advantage to running the heap analysis, and points-to analysis is enough. For programs that allocate mostly non-recursive data structures, connection matrix analysis is simple and relatively inexpensive, while at the same time it provides useful results. We intend to continue working on the connection matrix analysis in order to further improve its efficiency, and to examine the benefit of context-sensitive vs. context-insensitive versions. We are also building tools for using connection matrix analysis to provide good interference analysis, particularly with respect to disambiguating arrays for array dependence analysis.

References

[CBC93] J. Choi, M. Burke, and P. Carini. Efficient flow-sensitive interprocedural computation of pointer-induced aliases and side-effects. In *Conf. Rec. of the Twentieth Ann. ACM SIGPLAN-SIGACT Symp. on Principles of Programming Languages*, pages 232–245, Charleston, South Carolina, Jan. 1993.

[CWZ90] David R. Chase, Mark Wegman, and F. Kenneth Zadeck. Analysis of pointers and structures. In *Proc. of the SIGPLAN '90 Conf. on Programming Language Design and Implementation*, pages 296–310, White Plains, N. Y., Jun. 1990.

[Deu92] Alain Deutsch. A storeless model of aliasing and its abstractions using finite representations of right-regular equivalence relations. In *Proc. of the 1992 Intl. Conf. on Computer Languages*, pages 2–13, Oakland, Calif., Apr. 1992.

[Deu94] Alain Deutsch. Interprocedural may-alias analysis for pointers: Beyond *k*-limiting. In *Proc. of the ACM SIGPLAN '94 Conf. on Programming Language Design and Implementation*, pages 230–241, Orlando, Flor., Jun. 1994.

[EGH94] Maryam Emami, Rakesh Ghiya, and Laurie J. Hendren. Context-sensitive interprocedural points-to analysis in the presence of function pointers. In *Proc. of the ACM SIGPLAN '94 Conf. on Programming Language Design and Implementation*, pages 242–256, Orlando, Flor., Jun. 1994.

[EH94] Ana M. Erosa and Laurie J. Hendren. Taming control flow: A structured approach to eliminating goto statements. In *Proc. of the 1994 Intl. Conf. on Computer Languages*, pages 229–240, Toulouse, France, May 1994.

[Ema93] Maryam Emami. A practical interprocedural alias analysis for an optimizing/parallelizing C compiler. Master's thesis, McGill U., Montréal, Qué., Jul. 1993.

[Ghi95] Rakesh Ghiya. Practical techniques for interprocedural heap analysis. Master's thesis, School of Computer Science, McGill University, May 1995.

[Gua88] Vincent A. Guarna, Jr. A technique for analyzing pointer and structure references in parallel restructuring compilers. In *Proc. of the 1988 Intl. Conf. on Parallel Processing*, volume II, pages 212–220, St. Charles, Ill., Aug. 1988.

[Har89]   W. Ludwell Harrison III. The interprocedural analysis and automatic parallelization of Scheme programs. *Lisp and Symbolic Computation*, 2(3/4):179–396, 1989.

[HDE+92] L. Hendren, C. Donawa, M. Emami, G. Gao, Justiani, and B. Sridharan. Designing the McCAT compiler based on a family of structured intermediate representations. In *Proc. of the 5th Intl. Work. on Languages and Compilers for Parallel Computing*, number 757 in Lec. Notes in Comp. Sci., pages 406–420, New Haven, Conn., Aug. 1992. Springer-Verlag. Publ. in 1993.

[HN90]   Laurie J. Hendren and Alexandru Nicolau. Parallelizing programs with recursive data structures. *IEEE Trans. on Parallel and Distrib. Systems*, 1(1):35–47, Jan. 1990.

[HPR89]   Susan Horwitz, Phil Pfeiffer, and Thomas Reps. Dependence analysis for pointer variables. In *Proc. of the SIGPLAN '89 Conf. on Programming Language Design and Implementation*, pages 28–40, Portland, Ore., Jun. 1989.

[JM81]   N. D. Jones and S. S. Muchnick. *Program Flow Analysis, Theory and Applications*, chapter 4, Flow Analysis and Optimization of LISP-like Structures, pages 102–131. Prentice-Hall, 1981.

[JM82]   Neil D. Jones and Steven S. Muchnick. A flexible approach to interprocedural data flow analysis and programs with recursive data structures. In *Conf. Rec. of the Ninth Ann. ACM Symp. on Principles of Programming Languages*, pages 66–74, Albuquerque, N. Mex., Jan. 1982.

[Lan92]   William A. Landi. *Interprocedural aliasing in the presence of pointers*. PhD thesis, Rutgers U., 1992.

[Lar91]   J. R. Larus. Compiling Lisp programs for parallel execution. *Lisp and Symbolic Computation*, 4:29–99, 1991.

[LH88]   James R. Larus and Paul N. Hilfinger. Detecting conflicts between structure accesses. In *Proc. of the SIGPLAN '88 Conf. on Programming Language Design and Implementation*, pages 21–34, Atlanta, Georgia, Jun. 1988.

[LR92]   William Landi and Barbara G. Ryder. A safe approximate algorithm for interprocedural pointer aliasing. In *Proc. of the ACM SIGPLAN '92 Conf. on Programming Language Design and Implementation*, pages 235–248, San Francisco, Calif., Jun. 1992.

[PCK93]   J. Plevyak, A. Chien, and V. Karamcheti. Analysis of dynamic structures for efficient parallel execution. In *Proc. of the 6th Intl. Work. on Languages and Compilers for Parallel Computing*, number 768 in Lec. Notes in Comp. Sci., pages 37–56, Portland, Ore., Aug. 1993. Springer-Verlag. Publ. in 1994.

[Ruf95]   Erik Ruf. Context-insensitive alias analysis reconsidered. In *Proc. of the ACM SIGPLAN '95 Conf. on Programming Language Design and Implementation*, pages 13–22, La Jolla, Calif., Jun. 1995.

[Sri92]   Bhama Sridharan. An analysis framework for the McCAT compiler. Master's thesis, McGill U., Montréal, Qué., Sep. 1992.

[WL95]   Robert P. Wilson and Monica S. Lam. Efficient context-sensitive pointer analysis for C programs. In *Proc. of the ACM SIGPLAN '95 Conf. on Programming Language Design and Implementation*, pages 1–12, La Jolla, Calif., Jun. 1995.

Language and Run-Time Support for Network Parallel Computing

Peter A. Dinda   David R. O'Hallaron   Jaspal Subhlok
Jon A. Webb   Bwolen Yang
{pdinda, droh, jass, webb+, bwolen}@cs.cmu.edu

School of Computer Science
Carnegie Mellon University
Pittsburgh PA 15213

Abstract. Network parallel computing is the use of diverse computing resources interconnected by general purpose networks to run parallel applications. This paper describes NetFx, an extension of the Fx compiler system which uses the Fx model of task parallelism to distribute and manage computations across the sequential and parallel machines of a network. A central problem in network parallel computing is that the compiler is presented with a heterogeneous and dynamic target. Our approach is based on a novel run-time system that presents a simple communication interface to the compiler, yet uses compiler knowledge to customize communication between tasks executing over the network. The run-time system is designed to support complete applications developed with different compilers and parallel program generators. It presents a standard communication interface for point-to-point transfer of distributed data sets between tasks. This allows the compiler to be portable, and enables communication generation without knowledge of exactly how the tasks will be mapped at run-time and what low level communication primitives will be used. The compiler also generates a set of custom routines, called address computation functions, to translate between different data distributions. The run-time system performs the actual communication using a mix of generic and custom address computation functions depending on run-time parameters like the type and number of nodes assigned to the communicating tasks and the data distributions of the variables being communicated. This mechanism enables the run-time system to exploit compile-time optimizations, and enables the compiler to manage foreign tasks that use non-standard data distributions. We outline several important applications of network parallel computing and describe the NetFx programming model and run-time system.

1 Introduction

Network parallel computing is the use of diverse computing resources interconnected by general purpose networks to run parallel applications. The domain of effective network parallel applications is rapidly expanding because of considerable improvements in the

This research was sponsored in part by the Advanced Research Projects Agency/CSTO monitored by SPAWAR under contract N00039-93-C-0152, in part by the National Science Foundation under Grant ASC-9318163, and in part by a grant from the Intel Corporation.

latency and bandwidth characteristics of networks such as HiPPI and ATM. It is becoming practical to run applications such as scientific simulations, real-time applications and real-world modeling on network parallel computing environments. However, standard parallel languages like High Performance Fortran (HPF) [9] offer little support for network parallel computing. Further, multiple languages and programming paradigms may be necessary to fully realize the potential of the network parallel computing environment — yet there is little support for interoperability in today's parallel languages and paradigms. Without such support, the construction of an efficient, scalable, and environment–independent network parallel application is a difficult and error–prone task in which the applications programmer must wear many hats, including that of the network specialist.

The goal of our research is to make it easy to build efficient network parallel applications. This paper presents a programming model, a compiler, and a run–time system for the efficient generation and execution of network parallel applications.

Our programming model allows the programmer to express task parallelism among parallel tasks. Tasks are invocations of parallel procedures, called task procedures. The programmer specifies the interface of each task procedure, but may implement it in any language. Tasks are mapped onto the computing environment either by the compiler or the programmer. The compiler generates communication between tasks to satisfy data dependencies.

The most challenging part of compilation for a network is generating efficient communication. In a network parallel computing, multiple communication mechanisms must be supported for efficient communication. For example, crossing a HiPPI network requires different mechanisms than communicating between the nodes of an MPP. More important, the network environment is expected to be dynamic. Run–time load balancing is important even for applications with a static computation structure since the external load on different machines can vary. This means the compiler has limited information about the run–time environment during code generation.

For generating efficient and portable communication in a dynamic run–time environment, it is important to distinguish between the aspects of the communication that are constant for the duration of the execution and those that are varying and may be known only at run–time. The communication steps between tasks are a property of the program and are determined at compile time, while the actual low–level communication calls may depend on the run–time environment.

Our solution to generating efficient communication involves defining an inter–task communication interface. This interface provides mechanisms for transferring data between tasks that are mapped on groups of nodes. The compiler generates code for this communication interface and the run–time system ensures that appropriate communication calls are generated. The compiled program is portable across the machines and network protocols supported by the run–time system.

The key new idea is that the interface decouples the compilation from generation of low level communication, which is essential for a network environment, yet it provides a mechanism for the compiler to customize or extend the behavior of the run–time communication system. This mechanism allows the run–time system to exploit compile–time communication optimizations, and allows the run–time system to be painlessly extended to support new kinds of data distributions. The run–time system itself is not tied to the compiler, but may be used by other clients.

We are extending the Fx compiler system [7] to support the programming model and the run–time system. Fx already extends a data parallel language based on HPF with task parallelism. The extended version of Fx is called NetFx. We begin by motivating the need for network parallel computing with a set of example applications and then describe the NetFx language extensions, compiler strategy and the extensible run–time system.

2 Motivation for network parallel computing

The components of a large application typically have different requirements for resources like I/O devices, sensors, processing power, communication bandwidth, memory, and software tools. Further, each component may be best expressed in a different language or paradigm. Attempting to satisfy all of these resource requirements in a single computing platform utilizing a single language can be impractical or even impossible. An attractive alternative is to build each component of the application using the appropriate language or programming paradigm and run it on the appropriate platform using high speed networks to communicate with other components. This is the essence of network parallel computing.

This section illustrates the motivation for network parallel computing with three applications: (1) a *real–world modeling* application where inputs are acquired from a camera system, processed on a large parallel system, and displayed remotely, (2) an *air quality modeling* application where different steps of the computation have different processing and communication requirements, and (3) an *earthquake ground motion modeling* application where the results are computed on a large parallel system and visualized on a graphics workstation.

Many common network computing environments, such as heterogeneous workstation clusters, or embedded systems constructed from commercially–available rack–mounted array processor boards also motivate network parallel computing because exploiting them may demand multiple languages and programming paradigms.

2.1 Real–world modeling

High performance computers and their programming tools have traditionally been applied to problems in scientific modeling, including simulation analysis. A group of researchers at Carnegie Mellon is applying these same systems and tools to problems in *real–world modeling*, which means three–dimensional shape modeling of objects and environments in the real world by direct observations using computer vision techniques. Success of this approach could lead to, for example, replacement of complex and specialized sensory systems based on laser range–finding technology by simpler, more flexible and scalable, but computationally more expensive, systems like stereo vision. In real–world modeling applications the sensor system plays a key role. In some situations it is necessary to capture imagery at high rates, while in others, speed is less important than the portability of the imaging system.

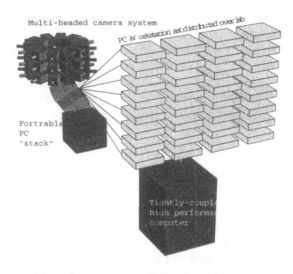

Fig. 1. Real-world modeling system

The system we envision is illustrated in Figure 1. The camera system is a detachable unit, and can be attached either to a large number of workstations, giving a high frame capture rate, or to a smaller number of portable workstations or PCs, giving portability at the expense of speed. Once the images are captured, they are transformed into stereo vision data through the application of parallel stereo vision programmed in HPF [9] or Fx [7], which can then be executed on the workstations themselves or on powerful tightly–coupled high performance computers. The resulting range imagery is then transformed into a three–dimensional model, which is another Fx program, and the resulting model can then be stored to disk or displayed remotely. NetFx will allow us to program the entire framework including communication across the network in a uniform portable manner.

2.2 Air quality modeling

Researchers at Carnegie Mellon developed a parallel implementation of the airshed environmental modeling application [14]. A goal of this work is to exploit heterogeneous systems. The application consists of repeated application of three data parallel steps. The first step, reading input data from storage and preprocessing it, is I/O intensive. The second step, computing the interaction of different chemical species in the atmosphere, exhibits massive parallelism and little communication. The third step, computing the wind–blown transport of chemical species, has significant parallelism and communication. Each of these steps is suited to a different class of machine. For example, an Fx implementation of the chemistry step runs as fast on four Ethernet–connected DEC Alpha workstations as on 32 nodes of an Intel Paragon since the relatively slow communication is not an important factor, but the transport step is expected to be more sensitive to the parameters of the communication system. Further, the input step is best run concurrently with the other stages. A NetFx implementation will allow us to use a single high level program for the entire application and the ability to use different mappings for execution.

2.3 Earthquake ground motion modeling

To address an earthquake modeling "grand challenge," researchers at Carnegie Mellon are developing techniques for predicting the motion of the ground during strong earthquakes. The computation consists of two distinct steps: simulation and visualization. The simulation step uses a large, sparse, and irregular finite element model to generate a sequence of displacement vectors, one vector per time step. The visualization step manipulates the displacement vectors and produces a graphical display. The simulation step requires access to large amounts of memory, computational power, and low–latency high–bandwidth communications, while the visualization step requires access to a bit-mapped display and, for the more complex 3D models, a graphics accelerator. The natural partitioning of this application is to run the simulation step on a large tightly–coupled parallel system, and to run the visualization step on a graphics workstation.

3 Approach to network parallel computing

This section describes our approach to network parallel computing. Our goal is a compiler and run–time system that makes it possible to use multiple parallel languages and paradigms to effectively utilize the heterogeneous network parallel computing environment. The model of a network parallel application is a set of communicating tasks. Tasks are invocations of parallel task procedures, which may be written in any language. The data communicated between tasks is in the form of distributed data sets.

Figure 2 shows how a network parallel application is built. First, appropriate compilers and programming tools are used to generate task procedures and interoperability information. Each of these tools can also generate routines for a custom distribution management library, which will be discussed later. In addition to the task procedures, a tasking program, which describes how the tasks interact, is written. A special tool, the network task parallel compiler, combines the tasking program, task interoperability information, and information about the computing environment to produce a task management program, which is then linked to the task procedures, the custom distribution management library, a standard library, and the run–time system. The task management program orchestrates the different tasks of the application, and performs inter–task communication on their behalf by calling the run–time system.

Because both the distribution of data within a task and the mapping of tasks to nodes can be dynamic, much of the work involved in communicating distributed data sets between tasks is done by the run–time system, which presents the abstraction of a task–to–task communication of distributed data sets to the task management program. A major part of communicating distributed data sets is mapping from one distribution to another. While the standard library provides many methods for doing this, the run–time system can also exploit compile–time knowledge in the form of the custom distribution management library. This mechanism also allows the run–time system to be extended to support new kinds of data distributions. The run–time system is also responsible for global load balancing and miscellaneous utilities. The extensible run–time system for network parallel computing is the main contribution of this paper.

The run–time system is currently being used to support the NetFx compiler system, which can map data parallel Fx tasks onto different sequential and parallel machines over a network.

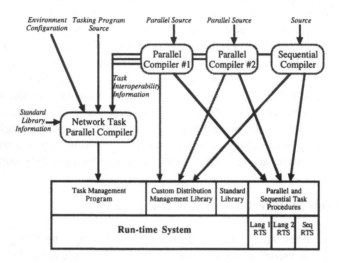

Fig. 2. Compilers and Run–time system for Network Parallel Computing

4 Programming model for NetFx

The current NetFx compiler uses the basic Fx programming model of integrated task and data parallelism [7, 18]. The main extension is that a data parallel task can be mapped to any sequential and parallel machines on a network. Support for data parallelism is similar to that provided in High Performance Fortran (HPF) and is described in [17, 20]. Task parallelism is used to map data parallel tasks onto different, possibly heterogeneous, groups of nodes. In the following, we briefly outline how task parallelism is expressed and compiled in NetFx.

4.1 Task parallelism

Task parallelism is expressed using compiler directives and no new language extensions are introduced. The current version of Fx relies on the user to identify and specify the side effects of the task procedures. Directives are also used to guide mapping of the tasks. This is important for performance and also to ensure that tasks execute on computers for which compiled versions are available. We describe the task parallelism directives and illustrate their use.

Parallel sections: Calls to task procedures are permitted only in special code regions called *parallel sections*, denoted by a begin parallel/end parallel pair. For example, the parallel section for a 2D FFT program has the following form:

```
c$        begin parallel
          do i = 1,m
             call colffts(A)
c$          input/output and mapping directives
             call rowffts(A)
c$          input/output and mapping directives
          enddo
c$        end parallel
```

The code inside a parallel section can only contain loops and task procedure calls. Every call to a task procedure inside a parallel section corresponds to a data parallel *task* that can execute in parallel with other tasks subject to dependence constraints. Outside the parallel section, the program executes as a single data parallel thread. The execution of a parallel section is consistent with the sequential execution of its contents.

Input/output directives: The user includes input and output directives to specify the side–effects of executing a task procedure, i.e., the data space that the procedure accesses and modifies.

For example, the input and output directives for the call to rowffts have the form:

```
          call rowffts(A)
c$        input (A), output (A)
c$        mapping directives
```

This tells the compiler that the task procedure rowffts can potentially use values of, and write to the parameter array A. Similarly, the input and output directives for the call to colffts have the form:

```
          call colffts(A)
c$        output (A)
c$        mapping directives
```

This tells the compiler that the task procedure colffts does not use the value of any parameter that is passed but can potentially write to array A.

Mapping: Labeling task procedure calls and supplying input/output information is sufficient for the compiler to generate a correct parallel program. However, the performance of the program largely depends on how the tasks are mapped onto the available computation resources on the network. The possible mappings are constrained by the availability of data parallel implementations of different task procedures for different architectures, the memory requirements of the task procedures, and the physical locations of devices like frame buffers. Ideally NetFx should be able to automatically map the program for correct execution and best possible performance, but that is a hard problem and NetFx is not able to do it except in some relatively simple situations [19]. In general, the programmer has to supply the mapping information.

The mapping information specifies where each task executes. Mapping information is given for each call statement in a parallel section. Thus all executions of a particular task procedure call statement (i.e., each task associated with the statement) are mapped in the same way. Currently, the mapping information is static and all mapping is done at compile–time. However, the run–time system is designed to support dynamic task mapping as well. The details of the mapping directives are somewhat cumbersome and machine specific and we will not describe them here. For example, when mapping a task to a network of workstations, it may be necessary to specify the names of the workstations to be used as a node, but when mapping to a part of a massively parallel machine like the Intel Paragon, it may be sufficient to specify the number of nodes to be used. For the purpose of this paper, we will assume that a mechanism for mapping any task to any group of available processors exists.

4.2 Compilation

The compiler uses a data flow algorithm to analyze the dependences caused by input/output variables and precisely determines the data movement between tasks. The basic paradigm is that the results obtained must always be consistent with sequential execution. It then uses the mapping information to map each task procedure call to a set of nodes. At run–time, executing the call statement amounts to receiving input data sets, executing the task procedure (i.e., invoking a task), and sending output data sets. These steps are identical for compiling for a single massively parallel machine (as in Fx) or for a heterogeneous network (as in NetFx).

Currently, the NetFx programming model and compiler are the same as Fx: the placement of all tasks, the distribution of data inside each task, and the characteristics of the communication network are fixed and known at compile time. The programming model and compiler are being extended so a wider variety of of network parallel applications can be programmed efficiently. The NetFx run–time system is designed to address the realities of network parallel computing: the network is inherently a shared resource whose usage pattern changes dynamically, the mapping of the tasks can change at run–time, and data distributions may not be known at compile time. This dynamicity means the NetFx compiler does not have all the information to generate optimal inter–task communication. Instead, communication is managed jointly by the compiler and the run–time system. The compiler generates calls to the run–time system for communication between tasks, and may also generate address computation functions (section 5.3) that the run–time system uses to translate between data distributions. The details of the communication are managed by the run–time system, and are discussed in the next section.

5 Run–time support for task parallelism

The main function of the run–time system is the efficient transfer of distributed data sets between tasks with few constraints on processors, networks, languages, tasks, or data. In this section, we first describe the design challenges of the run–time system and our approach to meeting them. Next, we explain the details of inter–task communication, and the programming interface exported to the compiler. This is followed by a discussion of the internal structure of the run–time system. Finally, we give an example of how an inter–task communication step is accomplished using the run–time system.

5.1 Design challenges

The run–time system is designed for very general network computing, although it is presently being used mainly to manage data parallel NetFx tasks on a network. To meet this goal, several design challenges must be overcome. These include multiple languages and programming paradigms, dynamic program and data mappings, and processor and network heterogeneity. Each of these challenges is discussed separately.

Multiple languages and programming paradigms: Each task procedure in the program may be written in a different parallel language or paradigm. There are two major motivations for this. First, the heterogeneity of the network parallel computing environment means that no one language or paradigm is "best." For example, the environment may include both shared memory and distributed memory computers. The second motivation is multidisciplinary applications. Each component of a multidisciplinary application may be best expressed using a particular language or paradigm. For example, one component may require the sparse matrix support available in Archimedes [16], while another may require the fast dense matrix support available in Γx, and a third may be best expressed with nested data parallelism in NESL [4].

Regardless of what language or paradigm is used to implement the tasks, it should always be possible to transfer data between two tasks as long as the *abstract* data types are compatible. For example, it should be possible to send a vector from an Fx task, where it is implemented as a set of local Fortran subvectors distributed over the processors, to a DOME [1] task, where it is implemented as a distributed C++ object. The challenge is to translate between the two implementations. In general, if there are n implementations of an abstract data type, there are n^2 combinations of implementations that must be supported. Furthermore, it should be easy to extend the range of implementations.

Dynamic program and data mappings: In many languages and paradigms, the distribution of data can change dynamically. For example, DOME load balances vectors by shifting elements between processors. At another level, the assignment of processors to tasks may change due to global load balancing or to support a run–time automatic mapping tool. The run–time system must support data transfer under these conditions.

Processor and network heterogeneity: Processor and network heterogeneity make efficient communication difficult. There are several reasons for this. First, processor heterogeneity may require that the data representation be changed. Communication systems such as PVM [6] deal with this by converting to and from the XDR format, but this usually means additional copy steps. The second reason is that routing is complicated by an essentially arbitrary topology and many different link types and access mechanisms. A common solution is to rely on internet (TCP/IP) routing [15], but this mechanism cannot make use of the parallel nature of inter–task communications because there is no notion of a parallel connection in TCP/IP. Furthermore, TCP/IP communication over a high speed network adaptor may be significantly less efficient than native communication. Finally, MPPs typically do not support TCP/IP internally, resulting in a store–and–forward stop at an interface node, which increases latency.

5.2 Meeting the design challenges

Our approach to these design challenges described in has three components: a standard run–time system interface, run–time system extensibility, and run–time system modularity.

Standard run–time system interface: The run–time system exports a standard interface to program generators. The main abstraction is that of communicating distributed data sets between tasks mapped to groups of nodes.

Run–time system extensibility: To support multiple languages and paradigms, we provide a standard method for a compiler or programmer to extend the run–time system to support new combinations of data distributions. This is similar to how a generic sort routine allows an application to pass in compare and swap functions for a particular data type, but on a larger scale. This mechanism also provides a way for compile–time knowledge to be used by the run–time system for better performance.

Run–time system modularity: The run–time system is composed of three subsystems with clearly defined interfaces between them. This allows each subsystem to be developed and optimized independent of the others, and reduces overall complexity. For example, the communication subsystem, which actually performs parallel data transfers, can be developed independently by the network specialists since it is related to the other subsystems only through a well defined interface. Similarly, the development of distribution mapping methods is simplified because it is separated from actual data transfer.

5.3 Inter–task communication details

The goal of inter–task communication is to transport a distributed data set from a source task to a destination task. The elements of the data set are partitioned across the processes of a task according to some rule. This rule is identified by the data set's distribution type and distribution. A *distribution type* identifies a class of similar rules, while a *distribution* identifies a specific member of the class. For example, the distribution type of HPF_ARRAY includes the distribution $(*, BLOCK)$. The run–time system assumes that the distribution type of the data set on each task is constant throughout the execution of the program, but its distribution may change. If the distribution can change, we say that its *binding* is *dynamic*, otherwise it is *static*.

To send a data set from a source task to a destination task, it is necessary to be able to translate between the distributions at the two end–points. It is only possible to translate between distributions whose abstract data types are compatible. For example, if the source abstract data type is an array, then the destination abstract data type must be an array of the same size and shape. The two end–point distribution types define a method for translating between the two member distributions. This method is called an *address computation function* and the process of executing it is *address computation*. Given two distributions of the appropriate type and a process pair, the address computation function returns an *offset relation* between offsets into the chunk of elements owned by each process, for corresponding global array elements. This architecture–independent relation can be trivially converted to an architecture–dependent *address relation*, which maps memory addresses on one machine to memory addresses on the other.

The address computation function operates under the abstraction that a data set's elements are distributed over a consecutively numbered group of processes of the task. Once an address relation has been computed for each pair of processes, the abstract process numbers must be mapped to the actual nodes of the machines on the network. The properties of these task bindings are similar to those of the distribution bindings discussed above. Specifically, the bindings may be static or dynamic. Once the mappings are known, actual data transfer can begin.

5.4   Run–time system interface

This section describes the programming interface between a program generator and the run–time system. It is a two way interface: the program generator emits calls to the run–time system, and the run–time system may itself call procedures produced by the program generator. The interface has three components as shown in Figure 3. The first two of these are exported by the run–time system, while the third is exported by the program itself.

Inter–task communication interface: This interface consists of simple, high–level, non–blocking collective send and receive calls for transporting whole distributed data sets between tasks. It is required that if more than one data set is transferred between a pair of tasks, the order of the sends and receives on the tasks be the same. The arguments of the send and receive calls include: source or target task IDs, the address of the first data set element local to the calling process, the data type of each element, the sender and receiver distribution types and distributions, and an implementation specific hint. There is a single call to wait for all outstanding receives to complete, which allows a task to complete input communication before executing.

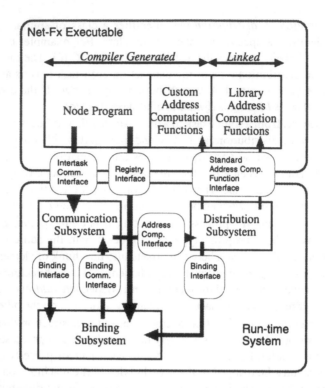

Fig. 3. The run–time system: subsystems, interfaces, and relation to the NetFx Executable

Registry interface: Before performing sends and receives, the program must describe the characteristics of relevant tasks, distribution types, and custom address computation functions to the run–time system using the registry interface. The program explicitly registers the initial task mapping and whether it is static or dynamic. Registration of a distribution type is required if the distribution type is not library-supported, or if the distribution is dynamic. Dynamic bindings are updated implicitly by examining send and receive calls. There are two main reasons why a program may want to register its own distribution types. One reason is extensibility — the distribution type may not be supported by the library. Another is efficiency — the compiler may be able to generate a specialized address computation function for a particular communication step. In either case, the program must also register custom address computation functions for any communication that involves a new distribution type. For example, suppose task 1 communicates from a new distribution type DTX to predefined types $DT2$ on task 2 and $DT3$ on task 3. All three tasks must register distribution type DTX. Task 1 must register new address computation functions $\lambda(DTX, DT2)$ and $\lambda(DTX, DT3)$, task 2 must register $\lambda(DTX, DT2)$, and task 3 must register $\lambda(DTX, DT3)$.

Standard address computation function interface: All address computation functions must conform to this interface. Each address computation function must provide two functionalities. First, it must be able to generate an offset relation between a source and destination processor. Additionally, it should be able to directly assemble and disassemble messages between the two.

5.5 Internal structure

The run–time system presents the abstraction of inter–task communication of a distributed data set between uniquely labeled tasks. Such communication requires task and data distribution binding, to establish the current state of the computation, address computation, to determine what data to send and where to send it, and efficient low level communication over heterogeneous networks. These tasks are segregated into three subsystems — binding, distribution, and communication — with well defined interfaces between them. The intention is to decouple the implementations of the subsystems so that each can be specialized for particular network computing environments. For example, we would like to encourage the development of communication subsystems by members of the networking community. By encapsulating address computation and binding for them, we greatly simplify their task. The relationships of the subsystems are shown in Figure 3 and discussed below.

Communication subsystem: The communication subsystem is the heart of the run–time system and exports the previously discussed inter–task communication interface to the program. The subsystem drives the run–time system by making use of the binding subsystem to resolve task and distribution bindings and the distribution subsystem to compute address relations. In return, it supplies a simple *binding communication interface* to the binding subsystem. The communication subsystem performs all actual data transfer.

Binding subsystem: The binding subsystem resolves task, distribution, and address computation function bindings and supplies them to the communication subsystem and the distribution subsystem through the *binding interface*. It uses the communication subsystem's binding communication interface if it is necessary to perform an inter–task communication step to determine a binding (for example, to bind the distribution of an irregular data structure). The binding subsystem supplies the registry interface to the executable.

Distribution subsystem: The distribution subsystem translates between sender and receiver distributions. It supplies the *address computation interface* to the communication system for this purpose. The binding subsystem is used to bind pairs of distribution types and distributions to the appropriate address computation function. This function may be one of the *library address computation functions* linked to every NetFx executable, or a compiler–generated *custom address computation function*. In either case, the address computation function must conform to the standard address computation function interface discussed earlier. After finding the appropriate address computation function, it dispatches it, and conforms the resulting offset relation to the format desired by the communication subsystem and converts it to an address relation. The communication system can request that a message be directly assembled or disassembled instead.

5.6 Example

We illustrate how an inter–task send using a custom address computation function is performed. Figure 4 shows the steps graphically using figure 3. On the right are the actual calls performed by the node program and those performed internally for the inter–task send. The calls are numbered to correspond to the steps discussed in this section. There is a dependence from task $T1$ to task $T2$ and the compiler has generated a send from $T1$ to $T2$ (and a matching receive in $T2$, which is not discussed here.) The compiler also produced a custom address computation function $ADXFUNC$ for this communication. At run–time, $T1$'s first step is to use the registry interface to register the initial values of all relevant bindings. The task bindings for $T1$ and $T2$ are registered as static, as are the distribution types $DT1$ and $DT2$. Finally, $T1$ registers $ADXFUNC$ as the address computation function for $DT1$ and $DT2$.

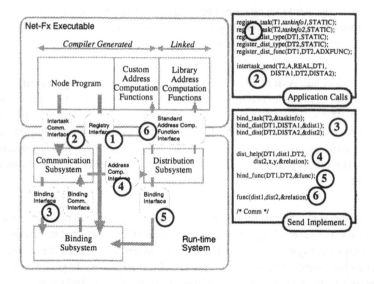

Fig. 4. Example of the steps followed for an inter–task send using a custom address computation function.

The second step (which may be repeated many times) is to invoke a send of the distributed data set A to $T2$. The inter–task send call includes the target task number, $T2$, the first element of A that is local to the process, the data type of A's elements (REAL), the sender and receiver distribution types, $DT1$ and $DT2$, and the current sender and receiver distributions, $DISTA1$ and $DISTA2$. The third step is to bind the two tasks to their current physical mappings, and the distribution types and distributions to their current distributions. Both of these steps are simple in this case because the bindings are static — they amount to local lookups. In the fourth step, the communication subsystem calls the distribution subsystem to build an address relation between each pair of sender and receiver processes $P1$ and $P2$. The distribution subsystem accomplishes this by binding the two distribution types, $DT1$ and $DT2$, to their corresponding address computation function, $ADXFUNC$ (step 5) and calling the function for each pair (step 6). The offset relations returned are conformed to the format the communication subsystem wanted, and converted to address relations. Finally, the relations are used to perform the actual communication in a environment–dependent manner. The communication subsystem may decide to cache the address relations to avoid steps 4–6 in future inter–task sends.

6 Status and implementation

The Fx compiler currently supports task parallelism on the Intel iWarp, Intel Paragon, and on DEC Alpha workstations running PVM. Compiler analysis of parallel sections (although not mapping directive support or code emission) is the same for each target. The run–time system used on the Paragon and the Alphas was initially developed for the Alphas with an eye towards portability and serves as a prototype for the system discussed above. The prototype essentially has three components: a component that computes offset relations for any pair of (static) HPF distributions, a component that conforms these relations to a particular format and caches them, and a component that does communication using the relations. Porting this run–time system to the Paragon (and achieving good performance) required rewriting only the communication component. Further details of the library are available in [5].

The main target network for NetFx is Gigabit Nectar [2] developed at Carnegie Mellon. A variety of communication interfaces have been developed for Nectar and we are incorporating them in the run–time system. Currently we are able to execute heterogeneous Fx programs across Alpha workstations using Nectar as well as simple heterogeneous Fx programs on Alphas and Suns. The full heterogeneous run–time system described in the paper is currently under development.

7 Related work

An overview of the issues involved in heterogeneous computing, especially compiler–based application mapping, is provided in [12]. In [13], the authors identify four goals for extending compilers to support and exploit heterogeneity and review six compilers using these criteria.

High level run–time support for communicating data parallel tasks is a fairly new research area. Most comparable to our work is the Schooner system [10]. Schooner combines a type specification language, a heterogeneous RPC mechanism, and a run–time system to permit procedures written in arbitrary languages to interact in a heterogeneous machine environment. A parallel procedure must be encapsulated in a sequential procedure, which acts as a proxy for communication, therefore Schooner can not perform parallel data transfers like our system. Also, the Schooner run–time system is not extensible and so cannot take advantage of compiler knowledge.

The goal of Converse [11] is to allow tasks written in different parallel languages to be linked together. Language run–time systems implemented on top of Converse can coexist. The core functionality is based on message–driven execution: run–time systems register handlers that are executed when properly tagged messages arrive. A well defined machine interface layer makes Converse itself highly portable. We feel that Converse and our system are orthogonal.

Opus [8] supports communication between tasks using *shared data abstractions* (SDAs). An SDA is essentially an independent object class whose private data is distributed over a set of threads and whose methods are protected with monitor semantics. For example, one could define a queue SDA whose elements are block–distributed vectors. To send a vector to another task, it is first sent to an SDA queue object (which requires an address computation) using the enqueue method. The receiving task would invoke the dequeue method which would cause the SDA queue object to send a data set (again requiring address computation computation). SDAs can support more general tasking paradigms than our scheme, but appear to significantly increase the communication volume and result in unnecessary synchronization between tasks due to monitor semantics.

The library described in [3] supports communication between data parallel tasks with collective sends and receives. Sends (and receives) are split between an initialization step which performs address computation and builds communication schedules, and an execution step that actually performs the send. An initialization step synchronizes sending and receiving tasks, and can be amortized over many executions. Only static task bindings and static HPF distributions are supported. All address computation is done with general purpose library routines.

8 Summary and conclusions

We address programming support for high performance networks which are emerging as an increasingly important form of parallel computing. We have presented NetFx, a compiler system that supports network parallel computing. The NetFx programming model is based on integrated support for task and data parallelism originally developed for the Fx compiler system. The NetFx run–time system presents a simple abstraction for task-to-task transfer of distributed data sets so that the compiler does not have to deal with the dynamic nature of the network computing environment. The run–time system allows the compiler and other tools that generate data parallel tasks to customize execution behavior. A clean interface between the compiler and the run–time system also allows independent development and retargetting of both. We believe that NetFx is the first tool to provide practical programming support for networks and will make network computing easier for non-specialists.

References

1. ARABE, J., BEGUELIN, A., LOWEKAMP, B., E. SELIGMAN, M. S., AND STEPHAN, P. Dome: Parallel programming in a heterogeneous multi-user environment. Tech. Rep. CMU-CS-95-137, Carnegie Mellon University, April 1995.
2. ARNOULD, E. A., BITZ, F. J., COOPER, E. C., KUNG, H. T., SANSOM, R. D., AND STEENKISTE, P. A. The design of nectar: A network backplane for heterogeneous multicomputers. In *Proceedings of the Third International Conference on Architecutural Support for Programming Languages and Operating Systems* (Apr. 1989), ACM.

3. AVALINI, B., CHOUDHARY, A., FOSTER, I., KRISHNAIYER, R., AND XU, M. A data transfer library for communicating data–parallel tasks. Case center tech report, Syracuse University, December 1995. To Appear.

4. BLELLOCH, G. Nesl: A nested data-parallel language. CMU-CS 92-103, School of Computer Science, Carnegie Mellon University, 1992.

5. DINDA, P. A., AND O'HALLARON, D. R. The impact of address relation caching on the performance of deposit model communication. In *Third Workshop on Languages, Compilers, and Run-Time Systems for Scalable Computers* (1995). To appear.

6. GEIST, A., BEGUELIN, A., DONGARRA, J., JIANG, W., MANCHECK, R., AND SUNDERAM, V. *PVM: Parallel Virtual Machine*. MIT Press, Cambridge, Massachusetts, 1994.

7. GROSS, T., O'HALLARON, D., AND SUBHLOK, J. Task parallelism in a High Performance Fortran framework. *IEEE Parallel & Distributed Technology*, 3 (1994), 16–26.

8. HAINES, M., HES, B., MEHROTRA, P., AND ROSENDALE, J. V. Runtime support for data parallel tasks. In *Fifth Symposium on the Frontiers of Massively Parallel Computation* (1995).

9. HIGH PERFORMANCE FORTRAN FORUM. *High Performance Fortran Language Specification, Version 1.0*, May 1993.

10. HOMER, P. T., AND SCHLICHTING, R. D. A software platform for constructing scientific applications from heterogeneous resources. *Journal of Parallel and Distributed Computing 21*, 3 (June 1994), 301–315.

11. KALE, L. V., BHANDARKAR, M., JAGATHESAN, N., AND KRISHNAN, S. Converse: An interoperable framework for parallel programming. Tech. rep., University of Illinois, 1995. http://charm.cs.uiuc.edu/research/interop.html.

12. KHOKHAR, A., PRASANNA, V., SHAABAN, M., AND WANG, C. Heterogeneous computing: Challenges and opportunities. *Computer 26*, 6 (June 1993), 18–27.

13. MCKINLEY, K. S., SINGHAI, S. K., WEAVER, G. E., AND WEEMS, C. C. Compiler architectures for heterogeneous systems. In *Eighth International Workshop on Languages and Compilers for for Parallel Computing* (1995). To appear.

14. MCRAE, G., RUSSELL, A., AND HARLEY, R. *CIT Photochemical Airshed Model - Systems Manual*. Carnegie Mellon University, Pittsburgh, PA, and California Institute of Technology, Pasadena, CA, Feb. 1992.

15. NARTEN, T. Internet routing. In *Proceedings of SIGCOMM'89* (September 1989), Austin, TX.

16. SHEWCHUK, J. R., AND GHATTAS, O. A compiler for parallel finite elemeent methods with domain–decomposed unstructured meshes. In *Proceedings of the Seventh International Conference on Domain Decomposition Methods in Scientific and Engineering Computing* (1994), College Park, PA.

17. STICHNOTH, J., O'HALLARON, D., AND GROSS, T. Generating communication for array statements: Design, implementation, and evaluation. *Journal of Parallel and Distributed Computing 21*, 1 (1994), 150–159.

18. SUBHLOK, J., STICHNOTH, J., O'HALLARON, D., AND GROSS, T. Exploiting task and data parallelism on a multicomputer. In *ACM SIGPLAN Symposium on Principles and Practice of Parallel Programming* (San Diego, CA, May 1993), pp. 13–22.

19. SUBHLOK, J., AND VONDRAN, G. Optimal mapping of sequences of data parallel tasks. In *Proceedings of the Fifth ACM SIGPLAN Symposium on Principles and Practice of Parallel Programming* (Santa Barbara, CA, July 1995), pp. 134–143.

20. YANG, B., WEBB, J., STICHNOTH, J., O'HALLARON, D., AND GROSS, T. Do&merge: Integrating parallel loops and reductions. In *Sixth Annual Workshop on Languages and Compilers for Parallel Computing* (Portland, Oregon, Aug 1993).

Agents: An Undistorted Representation of Problem Structure

J. Yelon and L. V. Kalé

Dept. of Computer Science, University of Illinois, Urbana Illinois 61801,
jyelon@cs.uiuc.edu, kale@cs.uiuc.edu

Abstract. It has been observed that data-parallel languages are only suited to problems with "regular" structures. This observation prompts a question: to what extent are other parallel programming languages specialized to specific problem structures, and are there any truly general-purpose parallel programming languages, suited to all problem structures? In this paper, we define our concept of "problem structure". Given this definition, we describe what it means for a language construct to "directly reflect" a problem structure, and we argue the importance of using a language construct which reflects the problem structure. We describe the difficulties that arise when the language construct and the problem structure do not fit each other. We consider existing language constructs to identify the structures they fit, and we note that language constructs are often designed with little regard for such generality. Finally, we describe a parallel language construct which is designed specifically with the goal of being able to reflect arbitrary problem structures.

1 The Importance of Problem Structure

It has often been noted that problems have "structures". Problem structure is made concrete in the dataflow graph, which is defined as follows. When executing, a program performs many primitive operations. Each operation uses one or more values as input, and produces one or more values as output. In the dataflow graph, each primitive operation is represented as a vertex. Wherever a value is transmitted from one operation to another, an arc exists in the dataflow graph. Therefore, the dataflow graph is a representation of an execution showing only the operations performed and how the values computed flowed from operator to operator.

We observe that the more closely the shape of the language construct fits the shape of the dataflow graph, the more comprehensible the program turns out to be, and the more feasible it becomes to perform macroscopic optimizations (section 1). We then consider many common notations for problem representation, and discuss the limitations of those approaches from the point of view of how well they reflect the shape of the dataflow graph (section 2). We discuss a set of constructs we have developed to make it possible to write programs whose data structures directly mirror the shape of the dataflow graph, for arbitrary graph structures (section 3).

1.1 Optimization: Extracting Knowledge about Problem Structure

Optimizers rely on data-dependency knowledge, which is essentially knowledge of the *relationship between the data structures in the program and the nodes in the dataflow graph*. Optimizations that involve multiple procedures, multiple objects, or multiple threads will often require knowledge of how the dataflow graph spans the procedure, object, or thread boundaries. For example: a parallelizer proving that two subroutines are independent is proving that there are no dataflow arcs connecting the dataflow subgraph of the first subroutine with the dataflow subgraph of the second. A load balancer which wishes to preserve locality must move objects around such that distant objects are working on (relatively) unconnected regions of the dataflow graph. A scheduler that wishes to prioritize tasks on the critical path must be able to predict the existence of critical dataflow arcs between tasks. In general, there are a tremendous number of intelligent large-scale manipulations that could be performed on parallel programs, if only the data dependency relationships between the elements in the program could be predicted.

The simpler the relationship between the dataflow graph and the elements of the program, the more likely an optimizer is going to be able to predict those relationships. For example, consider a divide-and-conquer implementation of Factorial. In this formulation, Factorial(N) is defined as the result of multiplying all the numbers in the range 1 to N. A parallel version can be achieved by splitting the range in two, generating the products of each subrange, and multiplying them together. The dataflow graph for this algorithm turns out to be an initially branching, then collapsing, tree (Fig. 1), wherein the top half computes the subranges over which to multiply, and the bottom half performs the actual multiplication.

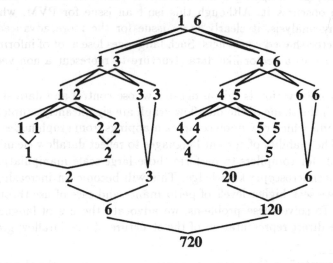

Fig. 1. dataflow graph for factorial(6) using recursive formulation

The simplest implementations of this algorithm will utilize constructs that also have a branching-then-collapsing tree structure. Perhaps the best example of such a construct is function invocation in a parallel functional language. Each function invocation can in turn spawn more function invocations. Eventually, a large tree of invocations form. As the invocations return, the tree collapses. Since the construct fits the shape of the dataflow graph so well, the implementation is trivial.

The close fit between the graph shape and the program structures yields a program that is easy to manipulate. Indeed, compilers for functional languages usually do such manipulation, effectively parallelizing, load-balancing, and scheduling tree-structured problems, all without user intervention.

Attempting to implement an algorithm with a construct that does not "fit" can be a disaster. Consider the familiar example, the data-parallel languages, as they apply to this factorial algorithm. It might be possible to express this recursive algorithm concurrently using arrays, do-loops, and barrier synchronization. However, doing so would require transformations which, as other researchers have noted, tend to leave the actual problem structure completely obscured [5]. The program would run in parallel (perhaps with poor speedups), but only because humans gritted their teeth and did the necessary convoluted analyses on behalf of the compiler.

However, the data-parallel languages are by no means the only ones that tend to distort problem structures. Many languages heavily utilize constructs which are vector-shaped.[1] For example, to process a 1000x1000 matrix on a 32-node machine using PVM, the matrix must be decomposed into a vector —– in this case, a 32-element vector of irregularly-sized rectangles. Representing a 1000x1000 square as a vector of irregular rectangles almost totally obscures its otherwise simple structure. Variable-sized vectors help in rectilinear problems like this one, but mapping a non-rectilinear problem structure onto a vector of any size obscures it. Although this isn't an issue for PVM, which doesn't attempt any analysis, it clearly *is* an issue for the more advanced languages utilizing vector-shaped constructs. Such languages lose a lot of information if the programmer uses a vector-like data structure to represent a non-vector-shaped problem.

The key observation is this: programs whose control and data structures directly match the shape of the dataflow graph are significantly simpler to analyze than programs which rely upon complex mappings from graph nodes to program elements. The inability of current languages to reflect dataflow cleanly will make it impossible for compilers to perform those large-scale manipulations that demand much macroscopic knowledge. This will become an increasingly onerous burden as we seek higher levels of performance and ease of use through smarter compilers. To solve these problems, we advocate the use of language features that enable direct representation of the structure of the dataflow graph.

---

[1] The "aggregates" in Concurrent Aggregates [4] are vectors, the "branch offices" in Charm [10] are vectors, the "replicated nodes" in TDFL [15] are vectors, etc.

1.2 Programming: Trying to Express Problem Structure

Optimizers benefit from clear expression of the problem structure. But perhaps more importantly, the programmer benefits as well. If the problem and the language constructs do not match, then the programmer must be concerned with two different structures: the shape of the problem, and the shape of the data structures used to represent it. While programming, he must continually perform mental translations between the two representations.

For example, in the case of the 1000x1000 matrix computation, the programmer thinks of the computation as being performed on a square matrix. He mentally conceives of operations such as "multiply this row times this column". However, to implement these operations, he must translate between his simple mental representation of the problem and the physical representation: instead of fetching a row or column of the matrix, he must fetch the Jth row owned by processor K, where J and K depend on some formula expressing how the rows of the matrix were distributed among the processors.

It is a great boon to be able to express problem structure directly. The programmer benefits from such a representation in exactly the same manner that the optimizer benefits: simply put, the absence of a convoluted transformation between the problem and its representation makes the program easier to understand.

1.3 Constructs that Simplify the Dataflow Graph

If the relationship between the program constructs and the dataflow graph must be simple in order for the optimizer to unravel it, then one might be tempted to search for programming constructs that yield the simplest dataflow graphs. Such a search proves futile — the dataflow graph is an inherent property of the algorithm chosen, it cannot be restructured by changing one's choice of data structures or control structures.

For example, suppose that a programmer wishes to compute Fibonacci 5. The dataflow graph will always contain the same six nodes shown in Fig. 2. The graph may contain other nodes as well, which may vary from implementation to implementation, but those six nodes will always be present.

Actually, this is only partially true: there are other algorithms for Fibonacci, and those algorithms have entirely different dataflow graphs. However, for many problems, only one or two algorithms are known. One is essentially stuck with a small choice of problem structures. Since one cannot affect these problem structures by choosing a different language or by making different implementation decisions, it instead makes sense to choose constructs based on the principle of *clearly expressing* the *inherent* shape of the dataflow graph.

2 Evaluations of Existing Languages

In this section, we consider some existing programming languages, and evaluate their programming constructs according to how well they reflect the shape of the dataflow graphs they express.

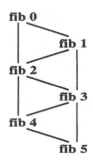

Fig. 2. dataflow graph for Fibonacci(5) using linear-time method.

2.1 Dataflow Languages

It seems intuitive that the dataflow languages would contain constructs that naturally reflect the shape of the dataflow graph. By "dataflow languages" we refer not to those languages with ordinary functional language semantics but unusual runtime systems. (Clearly, such languages are no more or less analyzeable than their non-dataflow counterparts). Instead, we refer to languages that explicitly reveal their dataflow underpinnings at the language level. Probably the best examples of such languages are the visual dataflow languages like TDFL [15], PFG [14], and Poker [13].

These languages are loosely based on the Petri net programming model. If one were to base a language on a restricted class of Petri nets, with the limitations that the net be finite, contain no cycles, process only scalars, and that arcs be used only once, then the programs would be perfect representations of their dataflow graphs. On the other hand, the language would only support finite problem structures. Therefore, languages like the ones named above necessarily extend the model: for example, TDFL adds "replicated nodes" to support vector-shaped problem structures, and recursive nets to support branching-and-collapsing problem structures.

The restricted Petri net model by itself is capable of representing (and ideally reflecting) a small class of dataflow graphs. Each extension adds the ability to express (and again, very directly reflect) another class of problem structures. The resulting language is capable of very naturally and directly expressing those problem structures for which it has constructs. Other problem structures become problematic. As a result, the temptation is present to continue adding new features for new problem structures. We now discuss the effects of such a philosophy.

2.2 Agglomerate Languages

Many languages are being created containing a collection of constructs, each construct appropriate to a different problem structure. We term these languages the "agglomerate" languages. Such languages seem to be quite popular right now: consider Charm [10], HPC++ [2] [3], and HPF+Fortran-M [6]. By including different constructs for different problem structures, these languages aim to support a broader class of problems than their predecessors.

Some would say that designers of agglomerate languages are haphazardly adding constructs, each of which is only useful for one problem structure. Others, however, might argue that the objective in adding constructs is to create a "basis set", eventually covering the entire space of problem structures. The reasoning is sound. If an agglomerate is built with sufficient constructs, it may indeed achieve a basis set.

Unfortunately, achieving a basis set requires more than the simple ability to encode arbitrary problems: it requires the ability to encode problems *without* mapping their dataflow graphs onto dissimilarly-shaped data structures or control structures. Thus, a basis set is unlikely to be achieved very quickly through haphazard addition of constructs. To our knowledge, no existing agglomerates contain a basis set; for example, no languages of which we are aware can represent both a reduction tree (which grows from the leaves up, not the top down) and a 2D matrix without mapping either onto a vector of data elements. Rather than randomly adding constructs and hoping they eventually form a basis set, it makes sense to be more critical, accepting only a set of constructs that offer us some concrete reassurance that they cover the entire space of possible problem shapes.

Such concrete reassurance is offered by the linked data structures, which can obviously be connected into any shape imaginable. Therefore, linked structures promise to singlehandedly cover the entire space of possible problem shapes.

2.3 Object-Based Languages and Linked Structures

Parallel Object-based languages (Actors [1], ABCL/1 [16], Mentat [8], etc.) rely on linked data structures to represent problem structure. Linked data structures, because of their incredibly flexible shape, are the sequential programmer's tool of choice for clear representation of complicated shapes such as trees and graphs. Unfortunately, linked data structures have two flaws which, from our point of view, make them undesirable constructs for parallelism.

The first flaw of linked structures is that their shapes are hard to predict. For example, in an object-parallel implementation of Jacobi relaxation, the compiler can easily see that the code declares objects of type jacobi_node, each containing four fields called left_neighbor, right_neighbor, and so on; yet the compiler remains oblivious to the fact that those objects form a two-dimensional rectangular grid. The challenge of predicting the shape that linked structures will form tends to be as great an impediment to optimizers (if not greater) than a complex relationship between problem structure and program stucture[2].

---

[2] Some researchers have attempted to predict the shapes of linked structures which will form at runtime. Such work has seen some success, although only certain kinds of information are made available through these techniques. [12]

The second flaw in linked structures is that they are quite difficult to construct concurrently. Consider the problem of adding a single object to an existing linked structure in such a way that the new object is accessible from (pointed to by) several old objects. One of the older objects must create the new object, obtaining a pointer to it. The creator must then deliver the pointer to all locations where it is needed — and the delivery process is the problem. Potential difficulties in delivering the pointer include identifying the other objects that need the pointer, routing the pointer through the older parts of the graph, and inventing some addressing scheme to get the pointer to the correct destination. The effort involved ranges from significant to extraordinary, even for problems as simple as building a 2D grid. The problem of routing a pointer to a destination in a graph is sufficiently difficult that linked structures are convenient only when such routing is not necessary. Routing can usually be bypassed by storing the pointers in a concurrent array or hash-table... but this, of course, maps the problem structure onto a vector again, obscuring it from the compiler. The only case where such routing is not necessary is when an object is only connected to its parent and its children — in other words, in tree-structured problems. Indeed, the fact that pure objects seem to be best for tree-processing has been noted by other researchers [9].

Both limitations of linked structures are rooted in a single property: dynamic creation. Both can therefore be eliminated by doing away with dynamic creation. Allowing the programmer to statically declare the entire problem structure would relieve him of the burden of creating it, while simultaneously making the structure far more visible to the optimizer. Therefore, our constructs are based on this fundamental principle: *whenever possible, represent problem structure declaratively.*

3   Agents: Undistorted Representation of Structure

We have devised constructs that enable the programmer to declaratively express arbitrary problem structures. Our constructs define a graph of "agents". Individually, these "agents" are very similar to objects: they are small entities that have state, and have code associated with them. Unlike objects, though, they conceptually "exist" in a prespecified pattern from the instant the program begins. In this static layout, they are much like Petri nets. However, unlike the specific patterns allowed by Petri net languages, agent networks can be infinitely large, with arbitrary numbers of connections between agents, in unrestricted patterns.

Agents are declared in groups:

```
AGENT identifier[ indices... ] RUNS function(arguments...);
```

In our model, each agent is a tiny process running a function. On a more theoretical level, agents could have been expressed using any representation of behavior and state, for example, agents could have been C++ objects. We emphasize that the means of expressing agents and their internal behaviors is orthogonal to our ideas on problem structure.

The agent identifier names a set of agents. Indices are similar to array indices, they can be used to select an individual element in the set. However, unlike array indices, they are not bounded, so the set of agents may be of unbounded size, and it may be sparse. To understand the need for unbounded, sparse sets of agents, one need only recall their purpose: each active agent intends to represent a single node in the dataflow graph[3]. The entire set of agents is intended to represent the space of possible nodes that could be used during the execution. The indices to the set of agents need not be integers, they may be any other type that can reasonably be used as an index into a table.

To accommodate unbounded sets of agents, we impose this constraint: each agent is completely passive until it receives its first message. Passive agents send nothing, compute nothing, and have uninitialized state. No memory is allocated to an agent which has not yet received its first message. Likewise, an agent which has finished executing its code it is returned to its passive state.

Our model does not assume shared memory: it is assumed that agents cannot access each other's variables without sending explicit messages to each other.

Every agent can send and receive messages. In our notation, messages are tuples of values with a symbolic tag at the front[4]. We use the notation **tag(value1, value2, ...)** to denote such a tuple. The tag is a single identifier. The **SEND** statement is used to transmit tuples:

```
SEND tag(value1, value2, ...) TO agent[index1, index2, ...];
```

Two special agent identifiers are recognized, **SELF** and **PARENT**. Sending a tuple to one's parent is defined as follows: if an agent A1 is running a function F1, and function F1 contains a declaration of an agent A2, then agent A1 is the parent of agent A2. An index can be a range of integers **low...high**, indicating a multicast. Finally, note that agent identifiers are first-class objects, so the **TO** clause can contain an expression.

The **HANDLE** declaration and **WAIT** statement are used to receive tuples:

```
HANDLE <tuple> FROM <source> { code }
WAIT <boolean-expression>;
```

Once started, agents execute uninterrupted until they reach a **WAIT** statement. When they reach the **WAIT** statement, they block, and their handlers become active. The agent begins receiving tuples, executing the appropriate handler code when each message is received. After a handler fires, the **WAIT** condition is reevaluated, and the agent may unblock and continue execution.

In the **HANDLE** declaration, the **tuple** and **source** fields are both patterns. The **tuple** field is matched against the contents of the tuple. The **source** field is

---

[3] One will often want to decrease the "resolution" or grainsize of the data flow graph by merging small sets of adjacent nodes. This does not affect our constructs.

[4] The use of the word "tuple" to describe messages should not be construed to imply that such messages enter a "tuple-space", as they do in Linda. It simply means that messages contain a short sequence of values.

matched against the name of the originating agent. Both patterns may contain variables, which are bound to the contents of the tuple or the indices of the originating agent. The **FROM** field can specify **SELF**, **PARENT**, or it can be omitted to accept tuples from anywhere. Note the following subtlety: if a tuple matches more than one handler, both fire, and if it matches no handlers, nothing fires, although the tuple still "awakens" the agent that receives it.

Note that every function invocation created by a function call is an unnamed agent, so functions can declare handlers and send and receive messages regardless of whether or not they are explicitly declared as agents.

We begin with a simple example, a Fibonacci program. This problem has the structure shown in Fig. 2. It begins with a function that acts like a binary adder:

```
void binadder()
{
   int total=0, count=0;
   handle value(int v) from parent { total+=v; count++; }
   wait (count==2);
   send value(total) to parent;
}
```

Any agent running **binadder** will receive two **value** tuples from its parent. After adding them, it sends the total back to its parent. Note that it is normal for an agent to receive its inputs from its parent, much like a function receives its arguments from its caller. The parent of the **binadders** will link them together:

```
1:int fib(int n)
2:  {
3:     int result; int done=0;
4:     agent calcfib[int i] runs binadder();
5:     handle value(int i) from calcfib[j] {
6:        send fib_eq(j, i) to self;
7:     }
8:     handle fib_eq(int i, int j) from self {
9:        if (i+1<=n) send value(j) to calcfib[i+1];
10:       if (i+2<=n) send value(j) to calcfib[i+2];
11:    }
12:    handle fib_eq(int i, int j) from self {
13:       if (i==n) { result=j; done=1; }
14:    }
15:    send fib_eq(0, 0) to self;
16:    send fib_eq(1, 1) to self;
17:    wait (done==1);
18:    return result;
19: }
```

The **fib** function declares a number of **calcfib** agents. The **calcfib** agents form a chain in which **calcfib[i]**'s job is to add fib(i-2)+fib(i-1) yielding fib(i).

The process is initiated by the **sends** on line 15-16, which trigger the handler on lines 8-11. This causes **value** tuples containing fib(0) and fib(1) to be sent to `calcfib[1]` through `calcfib[3]`. These in turn produce **value** tuples, which are received by the handler on lines 5-7, are forwarded as **fib_eq** tuples to the handler on lines 8-11, which again feeds them back to the **calcfib** agents as **value** tuples. The chain continues until the conditions (i+1<=n) and (i+2<=n) on lines 9-10 cause it to terminate. Meanwhile, the handler on lines 12-14 is looking for the final **fib_eq** tuple. When it catches this tuple, it stores the result, and sets the **done** flag. This causes the **wait** statement on line 17 to terminate, and the **fib** function returns.

I now show a more interesting example: an SLD refutation engine. SLD theorem provers start with a single assertion, and by combining that assertion with a database, generate more assertions. These new assertions are in turn combined with the database, and so on recursively, until finally an assertion is derived that is known to be false. This refutes the original assertion. The problem would be tree-structured, if not for the fact that assertions frequently get re-derived, but they must not be re-processed. The prover consists of a **refute** function, which uses many **tryrefute** children. Each **tryrefute** agent has the task of trying to refute one assertion. A **tryrefute** agent either sends **refuted** immediately, or it derives a set of assertions, transmitting **begin** tuples to initiate their recursive expansion. It then sleeps forever, thereby refusing to try to refute something twice.

```
1:   typedef string assertion, database;
2:   void refute(assertion goal, database dbin)
3:   {
4:     int refuted=0;
5:     agent dbholder runs store_string();
6:     agent tryrefute[assertion A] runs {
7:       string DB = fetch(dbholder);
8:       if (obviously_false(A)) send refuted(A) to parent;
9:       else
10:        for all assertions D derived from A and DB do
11:          send begin() to tryrefute(D);
12:      wait 0;
13:    }
14:    handle refuted(assertion a) { refuted=1; }
15:
16:    store(dbin, dbholder);
17:    send begin() to tryrefute(goal);
18:    wait (refuted==1);
19:  }
```

A few minor points: 1. Note that agents can send to agents defined in surrounding scopes, this presents no particular new issues. 2. **store_string** in line 5 is a library function defining a replicated storage agent. The string is stored in the agent using **store**, and retrieved using **fetch**. **store_string** distributes a copy of the string to all processors to eliminate copying at read-time. We therefore use it as an efficient means to distribute the database. 3. The **begin** tuples, since they are not handled, cause no effect other than to wake up the agents to which they are sent.

Note that the **fib** agent is serving as a dispatcher for large numbers of messages. As pointed out by Chien [4], any individual object acting as a dispatcher or interface for a large number of other objects can be a bottleneck. We avoid this bottleneck: when a handler does not access any local variables, it can be executed on any processor, and is in fact executed by the processor which originated the tuple. This optimization technique guarantees that tuples always go straight from their origin processor to the first agent they actually affect — in the **fib** case, straight from **calcfib** to **calcfib**. Handlers that do nothing but forward tuples are particularly relevant to understanding problem structure, so we give them a special name: "relay handlers".

3.1 Demonstrations: Analyzing an Agents-Based Program

Our new programming constructs were designed to make it easier for both the user and the optimizer to understand the problem structure. We now show two optimizations made possible by these constructs. Keep in mind this caveat: these demonstrations are not very complex. There are merely intended to show the relative ease with which optimizations can be performed in a model where problem structure is declared explicitly and statically.

Static Load Placement By Tiling In this demonstration, the optimizer notices that agents in the program form a 2D matrix. It notices that the communication is nearest-neighbor, and decides that the best alignment scheme for the agents in the matrix is to tile it into subsquares. The optimizer then implements the tiling.

To determine whether tiling a set of agents is desirable, the optimizer first checks whether the set actually forms a 2D matrix. This is done by examining the agent declaration: if they it has two integer indices, then it is a (possibly infinite) 2D matrix. If not, tiling is aborted.

Second, the optimizer checks whether communication is local; if not, tiling is undesirable and is aborted. Locality can thus be verified by checking the **SEND** statements in the matrix agents, plus the **SEND** statements in any relay handlers affecting the matrix agents. If the **TO** clauses all designate agents whose indices differ by only a small constant from the sending agent, then communication is local.

Third, the optimizer must determine the ranges of the indices. Identifying the used subrange is often possible through mathematical induction using the **TO** clauses of the send statements, and the **FROM** clauses of the relay handlers. Agents can (usually) only be awakened (receive their first message) by their parents. So we check the send-statements in the parent to identify the range of agents used.

As an example, consider the `calcfib` agents. There are two **send** statements that are not in relay handlers, these send to constant locations: `calcfib[1..3]` are accessed. There are also the sends in the relay handlers on lines 5-11. Together they provide two induction hypotheses, one of which is: if `calcfib[i]` is used, and (`i+1<=n`), then `calcfib[i+1]` is used. Therefore, the range of agents that is used is `calcfib[1]` through `calcfib[n]`. Similar inductive proofs can be made for 2D agent matrices, to verify that they are finite, and to determine the ranges of the indices. If the indices are not finite, tiling is aborted.

Finally, tiling is implemented by choosing a size for each tile. The system then generates a function that maps agent names to processors. This function is used by the runtime system to allocate the agents to processors.

Note that it is the compiler's knowledge of which agents may exist, what shape they form (a 2D matrix), and what their communication patterns are (nearest-neighbor) that makes it possible to statically and intelligently distribute the load in a reasonable fashion. Note that even smarter methods, such as following this initial placement by dynamic balancing, are quite feasible.

Vectorization Across Objects In this demonstration, the optimizer notices that a multicast to a range of objects triggers each object to perform a few simple mathematical operations. The optimizer converts the multicast code such that it can take advantage of the CPU's vector units.

To deliver a multicast to a range of objects existing on the same processor, the system uses a loop over the range of agents. Agents' state variables are stored in C **structs**. If the structs for the range of agents are allocated in a contiguous block of memory, then the delivery loop is a loop over a vector of agent **structs**. Each iteration of the multicast-delivery loop executes a handler on behalf of one agent. The handler generally modifies the agent struct of one agent. So the delivery loop is actually a loop modifying an array of structs, each struct in the same manner. If the handler code is sufficiently simple, then the delivery-loop will probably be vectorizable using traditional methods.[5]

In addition to vectorizing the handler itself, it is sometimes possible to vectorize the code after the wait statement. If it can be proved that all agents receiving the multicast are blocked at the same wait statement (for example, if all the agents are running a function that only contains one wait statement), and if it can be proved that all will unblock upon receiving the message, then the delivery loop can also include the code after the wait statement.

Again, it is the system's knowledge that certain ranges of objects form vectors that makes it possible to perform this optimization. In a linked language, the system would not know to allocate the objects in vectors, nor would it be able to express the multicast.

---

[5] The actual success of such vectorization depends upon the what code the handler contains.

4   Comparisons to Other Work

Superficially, Agents bears a close similarity to the languages based on linked objects, such as Actors, ABCL/1, Mentat, and many others. There is apparent similarity since individual agents are more or less equivalent to objects. However, in object-based languages, the structures formed by the objects must be created dynamically. In a sequential program this is no problem, but creating linked structures with any degree of concurrency is quite clumsy, except in special cases such as when creating tree-structures (see sec. 2.3). Therefore, dynamically created objects are best suited to certain specific problem structures, notably, those which are tree shaped. Also importantly, the structures formed by dynamically-created objects is hard to predict, thereby concealing the problem structure from the optimizer. Agents and the relationships between them are declared statically, alleviating both problems.

Agents is far more closely related to the parallel Petri net languages like TDFL and Poker, which are also based upon statically-declared dataflow patterns. Most Petri net languages necessarily extend the basic Petri net model. (The unextended model only supports a finite, unchanging set of nodes, which is impractical for expressing massive concurrency.) Languages like TDFL extend the Petri net model by adding several specialized constructs: for example, replicated nodes are added to support vector-shaped problem structures, and recursive nets are added to support branching-and-collapsing structures. Each of these extensions is naturally suited for one class of problem structures. Agents also extends the Petri net model, however, it extends it in a manner specifically designed to handle arbitrary problem structures: it allows arbitrarily-sized networks, having arbitrarily large numbers of arcs, with arbitrary connectivity.

One parallel programming system, Concert [4], attempts to predict inter-object data relationships *despite* its programming model, in which every structure must either be built dynamically of linked objects or mapped onto a vector of objects. As a result, Concert relies on sophisticated techniques to extract structural knowledge about linked structures [12]. This is a significant accomplishment. However, we feel that the Concert programming model is not as expressive as it could be, given its requirement that all problems be mapped onto vectors or built from linked structures, and we feel that this limitation hinders both the programmer and the optimizer. Given this consideration, we feel it would be advantageous both to the Concert programmer and to the Concert optimizer to upgrade to a programming model which is more reflective of problem structure.

Some languages deal with arbitrary problem structures by providing shared memory, fast sync variables, M-Structures, or some similar abstraction. Although shared memory doesn't make it any easier for the compiler to extract knowledge of the problem structure from the program, true hardware-based shared-memory does make it less *important* for the compiler to do so. For example, with hardware-based shared memory, the compiler can more or less ignore questions of data layout, load-balancing, scheduling, and other difficult questions. (Or at least, it needs less reliable strategies for these tasks). Since problem structure is less important to the compiler, it can be dealt with at the user-level, encapsulating the implementation details inside ADT's that neither the programmer nor the compiler need care about.

Although data-parallel languages are not generally intended for all problems, they *do* clearly show off the benefits of matching problem structure to the language construct when they are applied to the right problems. It is widely acknowledged that coding regular problems is easy in data-parallel languages (quite an accomplishment, given the widespread feeling that parallel programming is difficult). Also importantly, compiler technology for data-parallel languages is advancing by leaps and bounds, since it is possible to extract quite a bit of knowledge about the problem structure from the language constructs.

Two parallel programming systems, Linda [7] and Distributed Memo [11], can represent data of arbitrary structure without mapping or distortion. Both have a globally-accessible storage space for data items wherein items can be accessed by name. In both languages, the naming scheme is infinite. Therefore, one can store data of arbitrary shape in the space without having to force it into a predefined structure. However, though the languages have facilities for *storing* data without distorting its shape, neither languages have any facilities for expressing the computation itself as anything other than a vector of processors. It is impossible to infer the structure of the computation from the structure of the storage space, since the structures in storage space are created dynamically. Even so, both languages gain a significant degree of representational clarity from their ability to store and access data without distortion.

5 Conclusions

We started with the observation that problem structure is embodied in the shape of the dataflow graphs produced by that problem. We also pointed out that the more directly the shape of the dataflow graph is reflected in the data and control structures of the program, the easier the program is to understand, and the easier it is to analyze and optimize. We noted that for maximum predictability, the direct representation of the problem's structure must be declared statically, not created dynamically.

We defined the AGENT construct, which makes it possible to express arbitrary computation graphs without distortion. Individual agents are like C++ objects, except that they form a static mesh whose structure is declared, not linked together with pointers. An interconnected set of agents can directly reflect the shape of the computation graph. We demonstrated through two examples the ease with which optimizations can be performed in this framework.

We are currently engaged in the work of implementing our compiler, which is an aggressive implementation with tight control of overhead. This compiler will be complete in late 1995. After completion of the compiler, efforts will be shifted towards performance analysis and the implementation of optimizations.

References

1. Gul Agha and Carl Hewitt. *Concurrent Programming Using Actors: Exploiting Large-Scale Parallelism*, volume 206 of *Lecture Notes in Computer Science*, pages 19–40. Springer-Verlag, Berlin-Heidelberg-New York, October 1985.
2. F. Bodin, P. Beckman, D. B. Gannon, S. Narayana, and S. X. Yang. Distributed pC++: Basic ideas for an object parallel language. In *Proceedings of Supercomputing '91*, pages 273–282, 1991.
3. K. M. Chandy and C. Kesselman. *CC++: A declarative concurrent object-oriented programming notation*. MIT Press, 1993.
4. A. A. Chien. *Concurrent Aggregates: Supporting Modularity in Massively-Parallel Programs*. MIT Press, Cambridge, MA, 1993.
5. A. A. Chien, M. Straka, J. Dolby, V. Karamcheti, J. Plevyak, and X. Zhang. A case study in irregular parallel programming. *DIMACS Workshop on the Specification of Parallel Agorithms*, May 1994.
6. I. Foster, B. Avalani, A. Choudhary, and M. Xu. A compilation system that integrates high performance fortran and fortran M. In *Proceedings 1994 Scalable High Performance Computing Conference*, 1994.
7. David Gelernter, Nicholas Carriero, S. Chandran, , and Silva Chang. Parallel programming in Linda. In *International Conference on Parallel Processing*, pages 255–263, Aug 1985.
8. A. S. Grimshaw and J. W. Liu. Mentat: An object-oriented data-flow system. *Proceedings of the 1987 Object-Oriented Programming Systems, Languages and Applications Conference*, pages 35–47, October 1987.
9. A. Gursoy and L.V. Kale. High-level support for divide-and-conquer parallelism. In *Proceedings of Supercomputing '91*, pages 283–292.
10. L. V. Kale. The Chare Kernel parallel programming language and system. In *Proceedings of the International Conference on Parallel Processing*, volume II, pages 17–25, 1990.
11. W. O'Connell, G. Thiruvathukal, and T. Christopher. Distributed Memo: A heterogenously distributed parallel software development environment. In *Proceedings of the 23rd International Conference on Parallel Processing*, Aug 1994.
12. J. Plevyak, V. Karamcheti, and A. Chien. Analysis of dynamic structures for efficient parallel execution. *Languages and Compilers for Parallel Machines*, 1993.
13. Lawrence Snyder. Introduction to the Poker programming environment. *Proceedings of the 1983 International Conference on Parallel Processing*, pages 289–292, August 1983.
14. P. David Stotts. The PFG language: Visual programming for concurrent computation. *Proceedings of the 1988 International Conference on Parallel Processing*, II, Software:72–79, August 1988.
15. Paul A. Suhler, Jit Biswas, and Kim M. Korner. TDFL: A task-level data flow language. *Journal of Parallel and Distributed Computing*, 9(2), June 1990.
16. A. Yonezawa, J.-P. Briot, and E. Shibayama. Object-oriented concurrent programming in ABCL/1. *ACM SIGPLAN Notices, Proceedings OOPSLA '86*, 21(11):258–268, Nov 1986.

Type Directed Cloning for Object-Oriented Programs

John Plevyak and Andrew A. Chien

University of Illinois at Urbana-Champaign

Abstract. Object-oriented programming encourages the use of small functions, dynamic dispatch (virtual functions), and inheritance for code reuse. As a result, such programs typically suffer from inferior performance. The problem is that *polymorphic* functions do not know the exact types of the data they operate on, and hence must use indirection to operate on them. However, most polymorphism is parametric (e.g. templates in C++) which is amenable to elimination through code replication. We present a cloning algorithm which eliminates parametric polymorphism while minimizing code duplication. The effectiveness of this algorithm is demonstrated on a number of concurrent object-oriented programs. Finally, since functions and data structures can be parameterized over properties other than type, this algorithm is applicable to general forward data flow problems.

1 Introduction

Object-oriented (OOP) and concurrent object-oriented (COOP) programming languages have gained popularity because they provide programmers with useful tools for organizing programs. However, object-oriented programming techniques change the structure of programs significantly, typically incurring a performance degradation as a result. The reasons are fundamental to the programming models and include: encouraging programmers to use small functions, express new functionality by derivation from previous solutions (inheritance), share code (dynamic dispatch), and to separate use of operations from their implementation (data abstraction). Together, these techniques result in programs with high function call frequencies, and data dependent control flow.

These characteristics of object-oriented programs can result in poor performance on modern computers with high degrees of parallelism. Modern microprocessors rely on effective use of registers and instruction scheduling to achieve good performance. Object-oriented programs make frequent calls which, in addition to their own cost, disrupt instruction scheduling and register usage. To make matters worse, such programs allow the target of function calls to be data dependent, making inlining difficult or impossible[1] and compicating parallelization and concurrency optimization [30].

The key to eliminating the overhead of dynamic calls is *concrete type information*, knowledge of the implementation types that actually occur at function call sites. Such information can be obtained through global flow analysis [27, 26, 1, 28, 25] (across function boundaries and even across compilation units). These algorithms infer flow sensitive parameterizations for functions and data in the form of concrete type information. This information describes the pattern of

---

[1] Run time approaches are described in Section 5.

reuse of general (polymorphic) code for particular (monomorphic) situations. For example, a Set class might be able to contain any type of object, but a particular instance of Set might contain only Circle objects. The code operating on such instances could be optimized for the type of contents. Unfortunately, flow analysis results cannot be used directly for cloning, because the natural candidates for replication, contours [31], are too numerous and because standard dispatch mechanisms cannot select between them at runtime.

We present a cloning algorithm which minimizes the number of clones by replicating functions based on optimization criteria such as minimization of dynamic dispatch, unboxing opportunities and data layout. This is coupled with a call site specific dispatch mechanism to enable the selection of the appropriate clone by any remaining dynamic dispatches. We illustrate the efficiency and effectiveness of this algorithm through application to a suite of programs. Its efficiency is reflected in the modest code size increases (a range from -20% to +70%). The effectiveness is demonstrated by the elmination of dynamic dispatches resulting from parametric polymorphism in these programs. In our suite of pure concurrent object-oriented programs this results in static binding of approximately 99% of all calls and, through inlining, elimination of 45% to 99% of these calls. Thus, cloning reduces the number of dynamic and static calls executed at runtime, producing larger code regions for optimization.

Specific contributions of this paper include:

- A cloning algorithm for object-oriented languages which removes dynamic dispatches resulting from parametric polymorphism while minimizing the number of clones.
- An empirical evaluation of the efficiency and effectiveness of the cloning techniques on a suite of program.

The remainder of the paper is organized as follows. In Section 2 we describe the difficulties of optimizing object-oriented programs and introduce our compilation framework. Section 3 describes how global information is enhanced through cloning and how the number of clones is minimized. In Section 4 we report the results of our application of these techniques. Related work is discussed in Section 5 and we summarize in Section 6.

2 Background

In this section we examine characteristics of object-oriented programs which affect their efficiency. Then we briefly discuss the flow analysis techniques from which the cloning algorithm proceeds.

2.1 Efficiency of OOP and COOP Languages

Object-oriented programming provides tools for data abstraction and type-dependent dispatch, supporting both increased program modularity and code reuse. It supports polymorphism, late binding (dynamic dispatch or virtual functions calls), and inheritance, enabling programmers to organize their programs hierarchically as special cases based on general solutions, and to hide the details of operations. Likewise, concurrent object-oriented programming enables programmers to abstract and encapsulate consistency mechanisms, parallelization and data layout decisions. This, in turn, makes the programs easier to understand and modify. Object-oriented programs differ greatly in structure from procedural code [5], and there is every indication that these differences increase as programmers develop an "object-oriented" programming style.

Though they have desirable software engineering advantages, OOP and COOP typically have an adverse impact on performance. Due to high levels of hardware parallelism (deep pipelines and multiple issue), modern processors are heavily dependent on instruction scheduling and register allocation to achieve good performance. However, these optimizations require unbroken sequences of instructions, or, at the very least, good control flow information. Since object-oriented programs tend to have very small functions, inlining is required to enable these optimizations. Unfortunately, dynamic dispatch confounds control flow, seriously complicating or preventing inlining. Likewise, parallelization, data layout, blocking and other high level transformation rely on interprocedural control flow information [19].

To inline functions a compiler for object-oriented languages must know the exact type of an object (as opposed to the declared type of which it may be a subclass). This *concrete type information* is precisely the detail the programmer wishes to hide, via encapsulation and code reuse. Concrete types can be used to generate efficient code sequences which manipulate the representations of data types. For example, a sort algorithm is described in terms of comparing and moving elements. However, comparing and moving numbers as opposed to character strings, is very different and subject to different optimizations. In the absence of concrete type information, an implementation must use run time checks or dynamic dispatches, which can lead to poor performance.

2.2 Polymorphism

Polymorphism refers to the ability of a function or variable to operate on or contain objects of different types. We are concerned with two types of polymorphism: *parametric* and *true*. Parametric polymorphism occurs when a function invocation or instance of a class can be parameterized by types it uses, much like templates in C++. One popular use of parametric polymorphism is for "container" classes for sets, lists, hash tables etc. True polymorphism occurs when a specific function invocation or object contains a single reference which might be of more than one type. A typical use of such polymorphism is in a simulator, where the configuration of simulated elements is data dependent and cannot be determined at compile time. Our algorithm eliminates the parametric polymorphism exposed by the analysis which, as we will see in Section 4, is a major cause of dynamic dispatch. It is important to note that true polymorphism often cannot be eliminated since it represents a choice point in the program which would require a `case` or `switch` statement in a procedural language.

2.3 Global Program Analysis

In many object-oriented programs, the information necessary for optimization is still present in the program structure, but it is divided across module boundaries or even compilation units. Global program analysis can be an efficient and effective way of recovering information such as global control flow, global data flow, and concrete type information. In the sorting example, the type of data being sorted may not be specified at the definition of the sort, but is determined at call site of a sort operation. Global analysis recovers this concrete type information, linking the caller and callee and breaking through abstraction boundaries to enable optimization.

Recently, global program analysis frameworks have been developed for object-oriented languages which can efficiently derive global control flow and concrete type information [27, 26, 1, 28]. These algorithms simultaneously infer the interwoven global control and data flow of object-oriented programs. They do so by a combination of flow analysis and abstract interpretation and by modeling the different environment in which a function is invoked by a set of "contours" [31]. Typical analyses create for each function a number of contours polynomial in the size of the program. Moreover, these contours often do not represent useful optimization opportunities.

2.4 Implementation Context and Applications

This cloning algorithm has been implemented in the Illinois Concert system which includes a complete development environment for irregular parallel applications. The Concert system supports a concurrent object-oriented programming model and includes a globally optimizing compiler, efficient runtime, symbolic debugger, and an emulator for program development. This system compiles ICC++ [18], a parallel C++ dialect, and Concurrent Aggregates [11, 10] for execution on the Cray T3D [15] and Thinking Machines CM-5 [32] as well as uniprocessor workstations.

Cloning is used in our system to enable unboxing and register allocation of integer and floating point numbers, unboxing of integer and floating point arrays, and inlining and static binding of functions, enabling us to obtain sequential efficiency comparable to C [30]. On parallel machines, the more precise control flow information has enabled us to specialize the calling conventions in our hybrid execution model [29]. We are also in the process of using it to create and optimize call graph subtrees based the location of data in parallel machines.

3   The Cloning Algorithm

The idea of cloning is to create specialized versions of data structures and methods (which we call concrete types and clones respectively) for the different ways in which they are used by the programmer. These versions are then shared across the program by ensuring that the appropriate one is called for each use. The cloning algorithm starts with the results of global analysis. First, we describe the pertinent information provided by this analysis. Next, we present a modified dynamic dispatch mechanism for finding the appropriate clones. Then, we show how to select clones to maximize optimization opportunities and ensure that the resulting call graph is realizable via the dispatch mechanism. Once the clones have been selected they are created by constructing new concrete types, duplicating methods and rebuilding the call graph including the dispatch tables.

3.1   Contours and Clones

Flow analysis of object-oriented programs produces information about data flow values for methods based on the contours (calling environments) in which they are invoked and for instance variables based on the statement and contour at which they were created [26, 28]. We will call the contours for methods *method contours* and the statement and method contour at which objects with distinguished instance variables are created *class contours.*[2] Since these contours were created by the analysis to distinguish potentially different uses of methods or classes they roughly correspond to potential clones and concrete types. However, the analysis may distinguish method contours by any aspect of the calling environment including the contours from which they were invoked [26], the types of all the arguments [1] as well as other criteria [25]. Thus, a call graph on the contours cannot, in general, be realized by the standard dispatch mechanism.

3.2 Modified Dynamic Dispatch Mechanism

Cloning modifies the call graph by replicating subgraphs the methods of which are then called by only a subset of the previous callers. If a call site is statically bound (resolves to a single target method) it can be connected directly to the appropriate clone. However, if the call site requires a dynamic dispatch, the standard dispatch mechanism used by C++ or Smalltalk is, in general, insufficient to distinguish the correct callee clone. The problem is that this dispatch mechanism determines the method to be executed based on the selector (virtual function name) and runtime class of the target object $< selector, class >$, and these are identical for all clones of a given method. The example in Figure 1 illustrates this limitation.

```
class Stream;
class StringStream : Stream;
class Shape;
class Square : Shape;
class Circle : Shape;

Stream::print(Shape * o) – ... "

CLONE Stream:print(Square * o) – ... "
CLONE Stream:print(Circle * o) – ... "
CLONE StringStream:print(Square * o) – ... "
CLONE StringStream:print(Circle * o) – ... "
```

```
main() –
  Object * o = new Circle;
  Stream * s;

  if (...) s = new StringStream;
  else s = new Stream;
  s-¿print(o);
  o = new Square;
  s-¿print(o);
  ...
```

Fig. 1. Limitation of Standard Dispatch Mechanism

In Figure 1 the **print()** method in the **Stream** class takes a single argument o which is either a **Circle** or a **Square**. Since the variable s can be either a **Stream** or a **StringStream**, the invocation requires dynamic dispatch. However, the the standard dispatch mechanism only dispatches on the selector and the class of the target, and hence cannot select between the versions of **Stream::print()** cloned based on the type of parameter o (one for **Square** and one for **Circle**). Thus, a more powerful dispatch mechanism is required.

To address this problem we propose a call site specific dispatch mechanism. Each call site is given an identifier which is used during dynamic dispatch to distinguish the appropriate callee clone for each selector and target object type pair. In our example, the call site information would allow us to select the version

---

[2] Method contours and class contours correspond to entry sets and creation sets in [28].

of **print** for **Circle** at the first call site and that for **Square** at the second. Since only a single dimension is added, this mechanism is the smallest extension sufficient to select the correct clone, and, unlike multiple-dispatch, is independent of the number of arguments.

Cloning partitions the objects in user defined classes into concrete types which have more precise type signatures. From the point of view of the dispatch mechanism these are identical to user defined classes. Thus the modified mechanism uses the *concrete type* of the target object instead of the *class* during dispatch. Since the concrete type must be available at run time, objects are tagged when they are created with their concrete type (just as they would have been tagged with their class). Thus, the final modified dispatch mechanism uses < *call site, selector, concrete type* > to select the method to be executed. Even if using this mechanism incurs additional overhead[3], the number of dynamic dispatches is greatly reduced, more than compensating for a slightly higher resolution cost.

3.3 Selecting Clones

Clones are selected by partitioning method and concrete types by partitioning class contours.[4] The initial set of partitions is determined by optimization criteria such as minimization of dynamic dispatch or unboxing. These partitions represent concrete types and versions of methods (clones) amenable to special optimization. Then, we iteratively refine the partitions until the cloned call graph is realizable by the dispatch mechanism.

```
clone selection() -
  initial method contour partition =  new Partition;
  initial class contour partition = new Partition;
  forall m in method contours do
    m.partition = initial method contour partition;
  forall c in class contours do
    c.partition = initial class contour partition;
  while (!fixed point) -
    repartition(method contours,
               method contours equivalent);
    check class contours required for dispatch();
    repartition(class contours,
               class contours equivalent);

repartition(set,equivalent)-
  result = new Set;
  result.add( new Set(set.first()));
  forall e in set.rest() do
    forall s in result do
      if (forall r in s do
          equivalent(e,r))
        s.add(e);
      else result.add( new Set(e));
```

Fig. 2. Cloning Selection Drivers (pseudocode)

The overall algorithm is presented in Figure 2. It is based on two functions, one which determines if two method contours can share a clone (are *equivalent*) and another for class contours. Using these functions (shown in Figure 3) we first compute a partition of method contours then compute a partition of class contours. The **repartition** function for partitions by grouping the contours such that all the contours in a partition are equivalent. Since a finer partition of class

---

[3] The modified dispatch mechanism is amenable to optimizations such as folding the call site id into the selector to form a single index into the virtual function table, or the use of multi-dimensional dispatch tables.

[4] Some analyses use contours which cannot be differentiated by our modified dispatch mechanism. For such analysis a set of minimum partitions is precomputed.

contours can induce a finer partition of method contours (to ensure realizability) and vice versa we repeat the process until a fixed point is reached. Since the number of contours is finite and the partitioning proceeds monotonically (see Figure 3 under the comment **monotonicity**) termination is ensured.

```
boolean method·contours·equivalent(a,b) –
  return
      &&((a.partition == b.partition)           /* monotonicity */
      && (foreach s in callsites(method(a)) do  /* optimization criteria */
      binding(s,a)==binding(s,b))
      && (foreach v in variables(method(b)) do
      boxing(v,a)==boxing(v,b))
      && (foreach c in creation·points(method(a)) do   /* realizability */
      class·contour(c,a)==class·contour(c,b));
  "

boolean class·contours·equivalent(a,b) –
  return
      ((a.partition == b.partition)             /* monotonicity */
      && (foreach v in instance·variables(class(b)) do  /* optimization criteria */
      boxing(v,a)==boxing(v,b))
      && (! b in a.not·equivalent);             /* realizability */
  "

check·class·contours·required·for·dispatch() –
  foreach s in callsites do
    foreach e1,e2 in call·graph·edges(s) do
      if ((method·partition(e1.callee) != (method·partition(e2.callee)))
          && (e1.selector == e2.selector)
          && (class·partition(e1.target) == (class·partition(e2.target))))
        make·not·equivalent(class·contour(e1.target),
                            class·contour(e2.target));
  "

make·not·equivalent(a,b) –
  a.not·equivalent.add(b);
  b.not·equivalent.add(a);
```

Fig. 3. Contour Equivalence Functions (pseudocode)

The initial partitions are built based on optimization criteria used by the contour equivalence functions. For example, to maximize static binding we examine each call site in the method for the two contours, and if they would bind to different clones (method contour partitions) or different sets of clones we declare the two contours not equivalent. Similarly for representation optimizations, if a variable within two method contours or an instance variable within two class contours has different efficient representations (unboxed or inlined objects) grouping the contours would prevent optimizations, so we declare them not equivalent. The code to check these optimization criteria appears in Figure 3 under the comments: **optimization criteria**. Standard techniques for profiling or frequency estimation [34] can be used to maximize the benefits of optimization while limiting code expansion.

To ensure that the call graph is realizable by the modified dispatch mechanism, further refinement of the partitions may be required. This affects both method and class partitions. The dispatch mechanism uses concrete type (class contour partition) to select the target method, so call sites can require two class contours to be in different partitions in order be able to resolve the appropriate method. This occurs when the $< call\ site, selector >$ pair does not resolve to a unique target clone (method contour partition). For example, in Figure 4 we have decided to optimize the binding of print() in the method print_contents() to Circle::print() for circle containers and Square::print() for square containers. Now, at site 3 the dispatch mechanism would like to select the appropriate specialized versions. Since the call site and selector are identical, it must use the concrete type of c to distinguish the correct version. Thus, the method contour partition of print_contents() has induced a class contour partition of Container to distinguish those instances for which o is a Circle from those for which o is a Square. The function which checks this condition and ensures that two class contours will be non-equivalent is check_class_contours_required_-for_dispatch in Figure 3.

```
class Container – Object * o; ... ";
void Container::print contents()– this-¿o-¿print(); "
Container * create() – return new Container; "

main() –
  Container *a = create(); /* site 1 */
  Container *b = create(); /* site 2 */
  a-¿o = new Circle;
  b-¿o = new Square;
  Container *c = a;
  if (...) c = b;
  c-¿print contents();      /* site 3 */
"
```

Fig. 4. Example Requiring Repartitioning of Contours

Similarly, class contour partitions can induce method contour partitions. Class contours are defined by their creation point (creating statement and surrounding method contour). Since the partitions of class contours will be the concrete types which are used by the dispatch mechanism, objects must be tagged at their creation points with their concrete type. This means that two method contours cannot be in the same partition if they define different class contour partitions. For example, in Figure 4, we have partitioned the class contour for Container based on the type of o (Circle or Square). In order to tag circle containers and square containers as different concrete types, enabling the dispatch mechanism to select between them, we must repartitioning the method contours for create(), separating those called from site 2 from those called from site 3. Thus, the class contour partition of Container has induced a method contour partition of create(). This is checked in Figure 3 by the function method_contours_equivalent under the comment realizability.

3.4 Making Clones

When the fixed point is reached, we create method clones for the method contour partitions and concrete types for the class contour partitions. For each method clone, we duplicate the code and update the data flow information so that it reflects only the information stored in the contours for its partition. The call sites and variables will now have the more precise information dictated by the optimization criteria. Statically bound call sites are connected to the appropriate clone and are now amenable to inlining. Methods which contain creation points are modified so that the created objects are tagged with the appropriate concrete type instead of the original class. Finally, the modified dispatch tables are constructed. Call sites which require dynamic dispatch are assigned identifiers. For each edge in the interprocedural call graph from these sites, an entry is made into the dispatch table mapping the $< call\ site, selector, concrete\ type >$ to the appropriate clone.

4   Experimental Results

We have implemented these cloning techniques in the Illinois Concert compiler and tested them on tens of thousands of lines of Concurrent Aggregates programs [10]. In this section we present results from a representative sample of those programs. These test programs are concurrent object-oriented codes written by a variety of authors of differing levels of experience with object-oriented programming. They range in size from kernels to small applications. They all make use of code sharing through polymorphism, and several also contain true polymorphism, for example using dynamic dispatch (instead of conditional tests) to differentiate data dependent situations.

Program	ion	network	circuit	pic	mandel	tsp	richards	mmult	poly	test
User Lines	1934	1799	1247	759	642	500	378	139	49	39
Total Lines	2384	2249	1697	1209	1092	950	828	589	499	489

The first three programs simulate the flow of ions across a biological membrane (**ion**), a queueing network **network** and an analog circuit (**circuit**). **pic** performs a particle-in-cell calculation, and **man** computes the Mandelbrot set using a dynamic algorithm. The **tsp** program solves the traveling salesman problem. **richards** is an operating system simulator used to benchmark the SELF system [8, 24]. The last three programs are kernels representing uses of polymorphic libraries. **mmult** multiplies integer and floating point matrices, **poly** evaluates integer and floating point polynomials and **test** is a synthetic code which uses multi-level polymorphic data structure. All the programs were compiled with the standard CA prologue of 450 lines of code.

4.1   Clone Selection

To evaluate, the clone selection algorithm we generated initial contour partitions using optimization criteria for removing all dynamic dispatches resulting from parametric polymorphism regardless of the number of invocations. In addition, we optimized the representation of all arrays and local integer and floating point variables by unboxing. We applied these criteria to cloning of our test suite and evaluated the number of concrete types and method clones produced.

In order to demonstrate that clone selection was able to combine contours not required for optimization we report the number of contours produced by our analysis. However, it should be noted that the number of contours produced by an analysis is only superficially related to the quality of information it produces and the difficulty of selecting clones based on that information. In theory, flow analyses produce $O(N)$, $O(N^2)$, $O(N^6)$ or more contours for a program of size N [27, 26, 1, 25]. The number of contours seen in practice can require large amounts of space [2]. The particular analysis we use is an iterative algorithm which creates contours in response to imprecisions discovered in previous iterations [28]. As a result, it is much more conservative in the number of contours it creates than other analyses.

Selection of Concrete Types The number of user classes, analyzed class contours, and the number of concrete types produced by the selection algorithm are reported below:

Program	ion	network	circuit	pic	mandel	tsp	richards	mmult	poly	test
Program Classes	11	30	15	11	11	12	12	7	6	10
Class Contours	64	43	30	27	26	17	27	13	17	18
Concrete Types	11	32	15	11	11	12	13	7	6	10

The data shows that the number of class contours is much greater than the number of user-defined classes. However, the number of concrete types finally selected is closer the number of user classes. This is because not all those distinguished by the analysis are required for optimization. In particular, when all invocations on objects corresponding to some class contour are statically bound, the dispatch mechanism does not need a concrete type for dispatch and no distinct concrete type is created. Methods for such objects are simply specialized for the class contour and statically bound.

Selection of Method Clones The number of user defined methods actually used in the program (as determined by conservative global flow analysis), analyzed method contours, clones selected by our algorithm, and the final number of methods after inlining appear below. The inlining criteria is based on the size of the source and target methods as well as simple static estimation of the call frequency. When all calls to a method are inlined, that method is eliminated from the program.

Program	ion	network	circuit	pic	mandel	tsp	richards	mmult	poly	test
User Methods	348	330	143	157	108	103	129	48	42	40
Method Contours	720	555	511	271	168	153	280	139	189	87
Clones Selected	445	342	173	195	115	108	138	64	54	40
Clones After Inlining	347	181	101	148	63	71	65	42	26	22

Again, the analysis creates many more method contours than user defined methods. However, the selection algorithm chooses only those required for optimization; in most cases ending with only somewhat more than the number of user defined methods. Moreover, since many call sites can be statically bound after cloning, many of the smaller methods can be inlined at all their callers. Thus, the number of clones which remain after inlining is actually smaller than the number of methods in the original programs.

Code Size One important measure of the effectiveness of clone selection is the final code size. Figure 5 compares the resulting code size before and after cloning.

The cloned programs usually increase in size by some modest amount, and always by less than 70%. The relatively large increase in **ion** is the result of extensive use of first class selectors (virtual function pointers in C++) during the output phase of the program. Code size expansion can be reduced by using

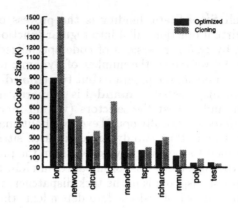

Fig. 5. Effect of Cloning on Code Size

profiling or frequency estimation to restrict cloning to the parts of the program which execute the most. Since the output phase is only executed once, such restrictions would have helped for **ion**.

4.2 Effect on Optimization

We evaluated the impact of cloning on optimization through its effect on the static and dynamic counts of dynamic dispatch as well the total number of calls. We three different runs of our compiler. The base case *baseline* copies out inheritance (customization [6]) but does no cloning and inlines only accessors and operations on primitive types (like **integers** and **floats**). This corresponds roughly to the optimization level for a hybrid language like C++. The *optimized* version includes global flow analysis and inlining and the *cloning* version includes the analysis, cloning and inlining.

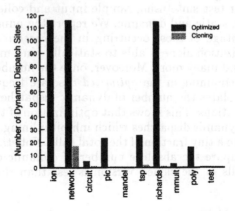

Fig. 6. Dynamic Dispatch Sites In Code

Dynamic Dispatch Sites Static binding is the process of transforming dynamic dispatches (virtual function calls) into regular function calls. Cloning enables static binding by creating versions of code specialized to the types they operate on. In Figure 6 we report the number of dynamic dispatch sites in the final code. Without cloning all the programs but two (**mandel** and **test**) contain a number of dynamic dispatch sites. **mandel** is primarily numerical with only token polymorphism and in **test** the selectors (virtual functions) have unique names, enabling them to be statically bound even without analysis. With cloning, only one program has more than two dynamic dispatch sites. Those dispatches which remain correspond to the true polymorphism in the programs, and cannot be statically bound to single methods. For instance, in **richards** (the OS simulator) the single remaining dispatch is in the task dispatcher, where the simulated task is executed. Since the set of tasks is data dependent, this dynamic dispatch cannot be eliminated.

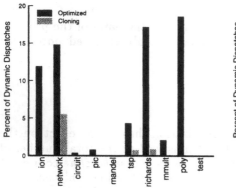 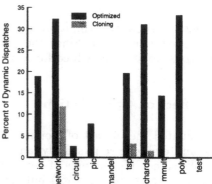

Fig. 7. Percent of Total Dynamic   **Fig. 8.** Percent of Remaining Dynamic

Dynamic Dispatch Counts The runtime counts in Figure 7 demonstrate the effectiveness of cloning for elimination of dynamic dispatch during program execution. We ran our test suite using sample input and collected the number of calls executed, both static and dynamic. We report the number of dynamic dispatches as a percentage of those occurring in the *baseline* code. While global analysis and optimization alone is able to statically bind many calls, cloning is able to statically bind many more. Moreover, once the number of calls is reduced by inlining, those remaining in the *optimized* case are frequently dynamic dispatches. Figure 8 isolates the number of dynamic dispatches as a percentage of the remaining invocations. This shows that optimization of the *optimized* code is largely limited by dynamic dispatches which inhibit inlining. In contrast, cloning keeps that number to a tiny fraction of the total calls. Note that this graph should not be used to compare the absolute number of dynamic dispatches since the total number of calls in the cloned version is less than that in the optimized version.

Number of Calls In Figure 9 we report the total number of calls (static and dynamic) after optimization. For the baseline (100%) we use the number of calls in the **baseline** version. Global analysis and inlining eliminate between 35% and

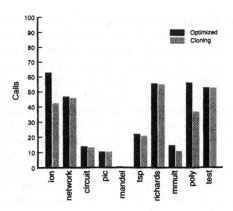

Fig. 9. Total Number of Calls

99% of the calls, and in some cases cloning eliminates 20% more. We expect that better use of frequency information (which in our current compiler is limited), combined with the greater number of statically bound methods in the *cloning* version will enable us to reduce the number of calls even further.

5 Related Work and Discussion

Cooper [12] presents general interprocedural analysis and optimization techniques. Whole program (global) analysis is used to construct the call graph and solve a number of data flow problems. Transformation techniques are described to increase the availability of this information through linkage optimization including cloning. However, this work does not address clone minimization. Cooper and Hall [19, 21, 13, 14, 20, 22] present comprehensive interprocedural compilation techniques and cloning for FORTRAN. This work is general over forward data flow problems, and presents mechanisms for preserving information across clones and minimizing their number. However, concrete types are not a forward data flow problem. Hall determines initial clones by propagation of *clone vectors* containing potentially interesting information which are merged using *state vectors* of important information into the final clones. We handle forward flow problems in a similar manner, but rely on global propagation to determine the final clones for recursive functions.

Several different approaches have been used to reduce the overhead of object-orientation. *Customization* [6] is a simple form of cloning whereby a method is cloned for each subclass which inherits it. This enables invocations on self (or this in C++ terminology) to be statically bound. Another simple approach is to statically bind calls when there is only one possible method [3]. This idea was extended by Calder and Grunwald [4] through 'if conversion', essentially a static version of polymorphic inline caches [23]. Our work also shares some similarities with that done for the SELF [33] and Cecil [9] languages. Chambers and Ungar [7], used *splitting*, essentially an intraprocedural cloning of basic blocks, to preserve type information within a function. Early work on Smalltalk used inline caches [17] to exploit type locality. Hölzle and Ungar [24] have shown the information obtained by polymorphic inline caches can be used to speculatively inline methods. While run time tests are still required, various techniques are presented to preserve the resulting type information. None of these approaches uses globally analyzes and transformation to eliminate the run time checks nor to preserve general global data flow information. More recently, Dean, Chambers, and Grove [16] have used information collected at run time to specialize methods with respect to argument types. While this can remove dynamic dispatches across method invocations, it does not handle polymorphic instance variables. Finally, Agesen and Hölzle have recently used the results of global analysis in the SELF compiler [2]. However, the information for all the contours for each customized method is combined before being used by the optimizer.

The cloning algorithm we have presented is general enough to enable optimization based on any data flow information provided by global flow analysis. All that is required is that the contour equivalence functions be modified to reflect the new optimization criteria. We have used optimization criteria for increasing the availability of interprocedural constants successfully with our cloning algorithm. However, efficient cloning for such information requires estimating its potential use for optimization which we have not yet implemented. Interested readers are referred to [19] for a discussion of the issues.

6 Summary and Future Work

Object-oriented programming is rapidly becoming a standard in program development. Traditional optimization techniques are severely hampered by the small methods and data dependent control flow of object-oriented programs. Cloning techniques can help resolve these problems, enabling object-oriented programs to achieving good performance on modern processors. We have shown that cloning can be used to eliminate dynamic dispatch and reduce the number of function calls. In effect, this removes the overhead of object-orientation, by enabling the compiler to undo the effects of information hiding and code sharing. We have demonstrated the effectiveness of cloning for optimization on a collection of object-oriented programs. We have also shown that the benefits can be achieved at modest cost; the code size growth required to accrue full optimization potential is relatively small.

To continue this work, we are examining alternatives for extending the idea of equivalence of portions of storage maps of concrete types across classes. This will allow further clone elimination, removing additional redundancies in the final code. We are also examining optimization opportunity estimation metrics for cloning with respect to other types of data flow information.

References

1. O. Agesen, J. Palsberg, and M. Schwartzbach. Type inference of Self: Analysis of objects with dynamic and multiple inheritance. In *Proceedings of ECOOP '93*, 1993.
2. Ole Agesen and Urs Hölzle. Type feedback vs. concrete type analysis: A comparison of optimization techniques for object-oriented languages. Technical Report TRCS 95-04, Computer Science Department, University of California, Santa Barbara, 1995.
3. Apple Computer, Inc., Cupertino, California. *Object Pascal User's Manual*, 1988.
4. Brad Calder and Dirk Grunwald. Reducing indirect function call overhead in C++ programs. In *Twenty-first Symposium on Principles of Programming Languages*, pages 397–408. ACM SIGPLAN, 1994.
5. Brad Calder, Dirk Grunwald, and Benjamin Zorn. Quantifying differences between C and C++ programs. Technical Report CU-CS-698-94, University of Colorado, Boulder, January 1994.
6. C. Chambers and D. Ungar. Customization: Optimizing compiler technology for Self, a dynamically-typed object-oriented programming language. In *Proceedings of SIGPLAN Conference on Programming Language Design and Implementation*, pages 146–60, 1989.
7. C. Chambers and D. Ungar. Iterative type analysis and extended message splitting. In *Proceedings of the SIGPLAN Conference on Programming Language Design and Implementation*, pages 150–60, 1990.

8. Craig Chambers. *The Design and Implementation of the Self Compiler, an Optimizing Compiler for Object-Oriented Programming Languages.* PhD thesis, Stanford University, Stanford, CA, March 1992.
9. Craig Chambers. The Cecil language: Specification and rationale. Technical Report TR 93-03-05, Department of Computer Science and Engineering, University of Washington, Seattle, Washington, March 1993.
10. Andrew A. Chien. *Concurrent Aggregates: Supporting Modularity in Massively-Parallel Programs.* MIT Press, Cambridge, MA, 1993.
11. Andrew A. Chien, Vijay Karamcheti, John Plevyak, and Xingbin Zhang. Concurrent aggregates language report 2.0. Available via anonymous ftp from cs.uiuc.edu in /pub/csag or from http://www-csag.cs.uiuc.edu/, September 1993.
12. K. Cooper, K. Kennedy, and L. Torczon. The impact of interprocedural analysis and optimization in the R^n environment. *ACM Transactions on Programming Languages and Systems*, 8(4):491–523, October 1986.
13. K. D. Cooper, M. W. Hall, and K. Kennedy. Procedure cloning. In *Proceedings of the IEEE Computer Society 1992 International Conference on Computer Languages*, pages 96–105, April 1992.
14. K. D. Cooper, M. W. Hall, and K. Kennedy. A methodology for procedure cloning. *Computer Languages*, 19(2):105–118, April 1993.
15. Cray Research, Inc., Eagan, Minnesota 55121. *CRAY T3D Software Overview Technical Note*, 1992.
16. Jeffrey Dean, Craig Chambers, and David Grove. Identifying profitable specialization in object-oriented languages. Technical Report TR 94-02-05, Department of Computer Science and Engineering, University of Washington, Seattle, Washington, February 1994.
17. L. Peter Deutsch and Allan M. Schiffman. Efficient implementation of the smalltalk-80 system. In *Eleventh Symposium on Principles of Programming Languages*, pages 297–302. ACM, 1984.
18. The Concurrent Systems Architecture Group. The ICC++ reference manual, version 1.0. Technical report, University of Illinois, Department of Computer Science, 1304 W. Springfield Avenue, Urbana, Illinois, 1995. Also available from http://www-csag.cs.uiuc.edu/.
19. M. W. Hall. *Managing Interprocedural Optimization.* PhD thesis, Rice University, 1991.
20. M. W. Hall, S. Hiranandani, and K. Kennedy. Interprocedural compilation of Fortran D for MIMD distributed memory machines. In *Supercomputing '92*, pages 522–535, 1992.
21. Mary W. Hall, Ken Kennedy, and Kathryn S. McKinley. Interprocedural transformations for parallel code generation. In *Proceedings of the 4th Annual Conference on High-Performance Computing (Supercomputing '91)*, pages 424–434, November 1991.
22. Mary W. Hall, John M. Mellor-Crummey, Alan Clarle, and René G. Rodríguez. FIAT: A framework for interprocedural analysis and transformation. In *Proceedings of the Sixth Workshop for Languages and Compilers for Parallel Machines*, pages 522–545, August 1993.
23. Urs Hölzle, Craig Charmbers, and David Ungar. Optimizing dynamically-typed object-oriented languages iwth polymorphic inline caches. In *ECOOP'91 Conference Proceedings*. Springer-Verlag, 1991. Lecture Notes in Computer Science 512.
24. Urs Hölzle and David Ungar. Optimizing dynamically-dispatched calls with run-time type feedback. In *Proceedings of the 1994 ACM SIGPLAN Conference on Programming Language Design and Implementation*, pages 326–336, June 1994.
25. Suresh Jagannathan and Stephen Weeks. A unified treatment of flow analysis in higher-order languages. In *Twenty-second Symposium on Principles of Programming Languages*, pages 393–407. ACM SIGPLAN, 1995.
26. N. Oxhøj, J. Palsberg, and M. Schwartzbach. Making type inference practical. In *Proceedings of OOPSLA '92*, 1992.
27. J. Palsberg and M. Schwartzbach. Object-oriented type inference. In *Proceedings of OOPSLA '91*, pages 146–61, 1991.
28. John Plevyak and Andrew A. Chien. Precise concrete type inference of object-oriented programs. In *Proceedings of OOPSLA*, 1994.
29. John Plevyak, Vijay Karamcheti, Xingbin Zhang, and Andrew Chien. A hybrid execution model for fine-grained languages on distributed memory multicomputers. In *Proceedings of Supercomputing '95*, 1995.
30. John Plevyak, Xingbin Zhang, and Andrew A. Chien. Obtaining sequential efficiency in concurrent object-oriented programs. In *Proceedings of the ACM Symposium on the Principles of Programming Languages*, pages 311–321, January 1995.
31. Olin Shivers. *Topics in Advanced Language Implementation*, chapter Data-Flow Analysis and Type Recovery in Scheme, pages 47–88. MIT Press, Cambridge, MA, 1991.
32. Thinking Machines Corporation, 245 First Street, Cambridge, MA 02154-1264. *The Connection Machine CM-5 Technical Summary*, October 1991.
33. David Ungar and Randall B. Smith. Self: The power of simplicity. In *Proceedings of OOPSLA '87*, pages 227–41. ACM SIGPLAN, ACM Press, 1987.
34. Tim A. Wagner, Vance Maverick, Susan L. Graham, and Michael A. Harrison. Accurate static estimators for program optimization. In *Proceedings of the ACM SIGPLAN Conference on Programming Language Design and Implementation*, pages 85–96, Orlando, Florida USA, June 1994.

The Performance Impact of Granularity Control and Functional Parallelism*

José E. Moreira†   Dale Schouten‡ Constantine Polychronopoulos‡
`moreira@watson.ibm.com`   `{schouten,cdp}@csrd.uiuc.edu`

† IBM T. J. Watson Research Center
Yorktown Heights, NY 10598-0218

‡ Center for Supercomputing Research and Development,
Coordinated Science Laboratory
University of Illinois at Urbana-Champaign
1308 W. Main St. Urbana, IL 61801-2307

Abstract. Task granularity and functional parallelism are fundamental issues in the optimization of parallel programs. Appropriate granularity for exploitation of parallelism is affected by characteristics of both the program and the execution environment. In this paper we demonstrate the efficacy of dynamic granularity control. The scheme we propose uses dynamic runtime information to select the task size of exploited parallelism at various stages of the execution of a program. We also demonstrate that functional parallelism can be an important factor in improving the performance of parallel programs, both in the presence and absence of loop-level parallelism. Functional parallelism can increase the amount of large-grain parallelism as well as provide finer-grain parallelism that leads to better load balance. Analytical models and benchmark results quantify the impact of granularity control and functional parallelism. The underlying implementation for this research is a low-overhead threads model based on user-level scheduling.

Keywords: dynamic scheduling, functional parallelism, task granularity, parallel processing, threads.

1 Introduction

The magnitude to which runtime overhead affects performance has been widely demonstrated [2, 3, 12]. In order to alleviate this problem [12] and other subsequent studies provided an environment that allows the user to control the number of parallel tasks a given parallel application generates. Given a fixed number of resources, a user or compiler can restrict the maximum number of parallel tasks of a parallel application to less than or equal to a predetermined amount.

---
* This work was supported by the Office of Naval Research under grant N00014-94-1-0234. Computational facilities were provided by the National Center for Supercomputing Applications. José Moreira was at the University of Illinois during the development of this research.

This paper reports on an implementation which employs the notion of dynamic granularity control. At any given time, the number of parallel activities a process generates is proportional to the number of physical resources allocated to that process. This allows the operating system to dynamically allocate a varying number of processors to different processes. In fact, the number of processors allocated to a particular process may vary over its lifetime.

The immediate impact of granularity control is the elimination of unnecessary overhead due to frequent context switching, creation and scheduling of tasks, additional interprocessor communication, and increased memory latency. Our method relies on a program representation which encapsulates the hierarchy of computations inherent in a parallel application. This allows for parallelism to be exploited first at the highest level of this hierarchy which corresponds to the outermost loops and the first-level function calls. Subject to resource availability, inner levels of parallelism are exploited by decomposing nested parallelism. A related focus of this work is the performance implications of the exploitation of functional (nonloop) parallelism. Our experiments indicate that functional parallelism can improve performance by a significant margin, even in situations where data (loop) parallelism is in abundance.

This paper is organized as follows: Section 2 describes the programming model and target machine architecture. Section 3 describes an autoscheduling threads model, *nano*Threads. Queue management and granularity control issues are addressed in Sections 4 and 5 respectively. The environment used for our measurements is described in Section 6. An analytical model showing the benefits of the exploitation of functional parallelism and experimental results from synthetic benchmarks are presented in Section 7. The set of benchmarks used for more general measurements is listed in Section 8, and the results from these measurements are shown in Section 9. Finally, related work is discussed in Section 10 and concluding remarks are given in Section 11.

2 Machine and Programming Model

The target machine model is a shared address space multiprocessor with a multiprogramming environment. Therefore only a subset of the machine's processors will be allocated to a particular program. We call this subset of processors a *partition* and let this partition be *time-variant*, meaning that processors may be added or removed by the operating system during the execution of the job.

The program model is the *hierarchical task graph* [10], or HTG, combined with *autoscheduling* [19]. The HTG is an intermediate program representation that encapsulates data and control dependences at various levels of task granularity. This structure is used to generate autoscheduling code, which includes the scheduling operations directly within the program code. The HTG represents a program in a hierarchical structure, thus facilitating task-granularity control. Information on control and data dependences allows the exploitation of functional (task-level) parallelism, in addition to data (loop-level) parallelism. A brief summary of the properties of the HTG is given here and details can be found in [3, 8, 9, 10, 19].

The hierarchical task graph is a directed acyclic graph $HTG = (HV, HE)$ with unique nodes START and STOP $\in HV$, the set of vertices. Its edges, HE, are a union of control (HC) and data dependence (HD) arcs: $HE = HC \cup HD$. The nodes represent program tasks and can be of three types: *simple*, *compound*, and *loop*. A simple node represents the smallest schedulable unit of computation. A compound node is an acyclic task graph (ATG) comprised of smaller nodes, each recursively defined as an HTG. A loop node represents a task that is either a serial loop (in which case all iterations must be executed in order) or a parallel loop (in which case the iterations may be executed simultaneously in any order). The body of a loop can be an HTG. An HTG may have local variables that can be accessed by any task in the HTG. In the general model, each task may have internal task-local variables.

Each HTG is associated with a set of boolean flags (local variables) that mark the execution of nodes and arcs in the HTG. As a task executes, its autoscheduling *drive code* at the exit block of the task updates the values of these boolean flags. Each node is associated with an *execution tag*: an expression on the boolean flags that is derived from the data and control dependences and represents the execution condition for that node. Let $\varepsilon(x)$ denote the execution tag of node x. Whenever the values of the boolean flags cause $\varepsilon(x)$ to evaluate to TRUE, node x will be *enabled* and ready to execute. This evaluation of $\varepsilon(x)$ is also performed by the drive code for all the successors of a task and the enabled tasks are placed in a task queue. Autoscheduling and the HTG effectively implement a *macro dataflow* model of execution on a conventional multiprocessor.

3 *Nano*Threads

*Nano*Threads [18] is a threads architecture that combines low-overhead threads and autoscheduling. Each *nano*Thread corresponds to an HTG task. Since the tasks effectively schedule themselves, via the exit blocks of the HTG, the user-level scheduler is a simple loop. Given a pointer to a task queue, it retrieves tasks from the queue and executes them directly rather than performing a context switch. Each processor in the partition allocated to a job runs such a scheduling loop. Only one system-level thread or shared memory process per processor is needed, and it only has to be created at the beginning of the job execution. As soon as the system-level thread starts running, it enters the scheduling loop and then all the user-level scheduling is done by the drive code of autoscheduling. We call these system-level threads *virtual processors* since they are doing the actual work. Every virtual processor attached to a particular job accesses the same task queue.

Each task in the queue contains two pieces of information: a code pointer (program counter) and a pointer to an activation frame (AF) containing the data local to that task. The activation frames are organized in a tree-structure called the *cactus-stack*. This is illustrated in Figure 1, together with the main scheduling loop. An entire parallel loop is represented by a single task descriptor which, in addition to the above information, contains a loop iteration counter. This allows the processors to perform dynamic loop scheduling.

The overhead associated with task dispatch is small, consisting of loading a register with the activation frame pointer and jumping to the beginning of the code for the task. Other overhead of enqueueing tasks and allocating activation frames is incurred in the program code, specifically in the entry and exit blocks of the nodes of the HTG.

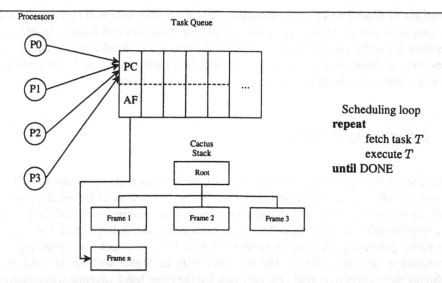

Fig. 1. Task queue, cactus stack, and main scheduling loop for a *nano*Threaded program.

4 Queue Management

Processors dispatch ready tasks and enqueue new tasks from and onto a task queue respectively. A centralized queue provides good load balancing, but it can also be a source of contention. In addition, a centralized queue does not facilitate preferential assignment of tasks to processors. A distributed task queue is used to address both the contention and the locality issues. Each processor has its own local queue, and the enqueueing and dequeueing policies work as follows:

- *Enqueueing:* When a processor determines that a new task has become ready for execution, the corresponding task descriptor is placed in the processor's local queue.
- *Dequeueing:* A processor first tries to fetch a task from its own local queue. If its queue is empty, it then searches the local queues of other processors for work.

On a heavily loaded system, local tasks tend to cluster on the same processor, enhancing locality of access. Consider the loop nest:

doall $I = 1, N$
    doall $J = 1, M$
        Body
    end
end

Assume the descriptor for the **doall** I is in the local queue of processor P_0. Other idle processors will fetch from P_0's queue and participate in the execution of **doall** I. The execution of one iteration of **doall** I by processor P_i will create the corresponding descriptor for one instance of **doall** J in the local queue of P_i. While there are enough iterations of **doall** I to keep all processors busy, each processor will be fetching from its own local queue. Thus, contention is kept to a minimum and locality inside each iteration of **doall** I can be preserved. When the iterations of **doall** I are exhausted (i.e. they have all been *issued*) idle processors will start participating in the execution of remote instances of **doall** J, thus trading locality for load balance.

5   Granularity Control

Determining the best task granularity is one of the fundamental optimization problems in parallel processing. The granularity or *grain size* of a task is informally used to indicate the size of the task. Typically the overhead of creating and scheduling a task is approximately the same regardless of its execution time. A large grain task spends a smaller percentage of time performing system functions such as scheduling and allocating its activation frame. The efficiency may be higher with larger tasks, thus reducing the relative overhead of parallelism. On the other hand, maximum exploitation of parallelism naturally leads to fine granularity tasks which can facilitate load balancing and increased utilization at the expense of efficiency. The smaller the overhead, the finer the granularity that can be exploited effectively. However, even in systems that support fine granularity, such as *nano*Threads, adjusting task granularity dynamically may be beneficial, and in fact necessary, under certain conditions, as supported by our experimental results.

Granularity control in *nano*Threads is based on hybrid scheme, part static and part dynamic, as explained below. The main goal of the static part is to guarantee a minimum task size at all times, while the dynamic part uses runtime information to select the appropriate level of granularity to exploit (i.e. above the minimum set by the compiler, and up to the maximum present in the application).

5.1   Static Granularity Control

Compile-time analysis can be used to guarantee that no task in the HTG is smaller than a certain size. The minimum size depends on the per task overhead of the system. The details of selecting an appropriate minimum size are beyond the scope of this paper. Static minimum granularity control can be implemented through *task merging*, a process described in [3].

Another aspect of static granularity control is to help prevent unnecessarily conservative dynamic granularity control decisions. When the overhead for task scheduling is negligible, as compared to the task size, there is little advantage in serializing the task. On the other hand, a dynamic granularity control decision that inhibits the parallelism of such a large task can only have a negative effect. Using static granularity control to prevent serialization can enhance performance. Our current implementation does not include automatic static granularity control, but does include facilities for specifying it manually.

5.2 Dynamic Granularity Control

Compile-time preconditioning of a program enforces a minimum granularity. In our scheme, however, the exact task size is determined at runtime and depends on program properties as well as runtime conditions. The latter depends largely on workload characteristics. Modern processor scheduling systems, such as Process Control [12] and Scheduler Activations [2], space-share the processors in a multiprocessor to improve utilization and locality of reference. In this case, the number of processors allocated to a particular job depends on other jobs running at the same time.

Dynamic granularity control works by exploiting parallelism beginning with very coarse tasks (outermost loops or first-level calls) and progressively moving to the inner subtasks. The granularity control decision is made when a new level of hierarchy in the HTG is about to be exploited, that is, at the entry block of a parallel task (ATG or parallel loop). The decision will result in setting the execution mode for a particular task: serial or parallel. If the serial mode is chosen, then the tasks comprising this parallel task will be executed sequentially by the processor assigned to the task. If the parallel mode is chosen, then the subtasks will be made available for parallel execution. The decision is local to each parallel task and does not restrict the decisions made at a lower level of the hierarchy.

An ideal granularity control scheme decomposes parallel tasks into subtasks only to the extent that all processors are utilized. Generating more tasks creates unnecessary overhead. Generating fewer task results in underutilization. The heuristics for granularity control presented and evaluated in this paper attempt to approach this ideal behavior with very simple operations so that granularity control does not become a significant overhead by itself. In our current implementation, when execution enters a parallel task its execution mode is set by the following:

$$mode = \begin{cases} \textbf{parallel} & \text{if } Q_n/P \leq \alpha \\ \textbf{serial} & \text{otherwise} \end{cases} \tag{1}$$

where Q_n is the number of tasks in the queue, P is the number of processors currently assigned to the process, and α is a given threshold. This mechanism responds to the runtime change in the number of processors appropriately. As the number of processors P increases, the ratio $\frac{Q_n}{P}$ decreases and more tasks are created, making more work available for the processors. Conversely, as the number of processors decreases, fewer tasks are made available. In general, the best value for α is machine and application dependent, but experience indicates that values like $\alpha = 1$ or $\alpha = 2$ work well for a variety of cases.

5.3 Distributed Task Queues

If the task queue is physically distributed, the total number of tasks on all queues is a valid measure of the system load. However, maintenance of this information requires updates of a centralized counter with each task enqueueing or dequeueing operation. This creates the same type of contention that the distributed queue seeks to avoid.

A fully distributed scheme involves each processor checking only its local queue. The same criteria as in the centralized queue is used (Expression 1), but Q_n now represents the size of a processor's local queue and $P = 1$. Since idle processors fetch tasks from the queue of other processors, the local queue of a processor contains some information about the state of the entire system. However, information is less accurate than in the case of a centralized queue. A fully distributed queue was employed in the *nano*Threads library.

6 Measurements Environment

*Nano*Threads was implemented on an SGI Challenge shared-memory multiprocessor [7]. The machine on which measurements were obtained was configured with 32 R4400 processors and 2 Gigabytes of main memory. Each processor had a local cache with hardware support for cache coherence.

Two different versions of *nano*Threads were implemented on the SGI Challenge. One is a C++ *nano*Threads library that allows the user to describe the HTG structure of a program as a collection of C++ classes. The actual body of the tasks can be coded either in C++ or in Fortran.

The other implementation is a *nano*Threads compiler based on the Parafrase-2 compiler [17]. This compiler uses the HTG representation of a Fortran program to automatically generate C++ code with an embedded scheduler. In both cases, system-level shared-address processes are created at the beginning of the program execution to implement the virtual processors, while all the *nano*Threads operations are performed by user-level code.

The benchmark suite used to evaluate the performance impact of granularity control and functional parallelism consists of 1) synthetic benchmarks designed to produce specific behaviors of parallelism, and 2) application kernels that are representative of the behavior of actual programs. The SGI Challenge timer facilities were used to measure wall-clock execution times. The measurements were made in single user time whenever possible, or when the machine was lightly loaded.

7 Benefits of Functional Parallelism

In this section we present performance models that quantify the improvements delivered by the exploitation of functional parallelism, even in the presence of abundant data or loop-level parallelism. We use the task graphs in Figure 2 to develop our models.

We first consider the task graph shown in Figure 2(a), which illustrates functional parallelism with internal loop parallelism. All n tasks can execute concurrently. Let each task be identically composed of a sequential part of size q and a parallel part of size p. Assume that the overhead for parallel processing is negligible. The serial execution time of task T_i (t_{T_i}) and of the entire task graph (t_S) are given by:

$$t_{T_i} = q + p, \quad t_S = n(q + p). \tag{2}$$

If only loop parallelism is exploited the tasks are executed in sequence and the total parallel execution time is:

$$t_{P(\text{loop})} = n(q + \frac{p}{P}) = qn + \frac{pn}{P}. \tag{3}$$

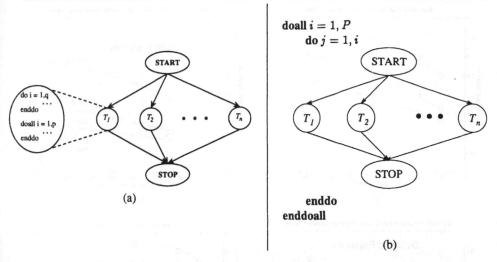

Fig. 2. Task graphs used in the performance models. (a) Each task has a serial part and a parallel part and the tasks are independent. (b) Parallel loop with internal functional parallelism.

Alternatively, the set of P processors could be distributed uniformly among the n tasks executing concurrently. Assuming that n divides P, the parallel execution time on P processors is the same as the execution time of a task on P/n processors:

$$t_{P(\mathrm{fp})} = q + \frac{p}{P/n} = q + \frac{pn}{P}. \tag{4}$$

We define the *functional speedup* $S_{P(\mathrm{fp})} = t_{P(\mathrm{loop})}/t_{P(\mathrm{fp})}$, and by normalizing $q + p = 1$ we compute:

$$S_{P(\mathrm{fp})}(n, p) = \frac{t_{P(\mathrm{loop})}}{t_{P(\mathrm{fp})}} = \frac{(1-p)n + \frac{pn}{P}}{(1-p) + \frac{pn}{P}} = \frac{Pn(1-p) + pn}{P(1-p) + pn}. \tag{5}$$

Figure 3(a) is a plot of functional speedup for varying numbers of processors when $n = 4$ and $p = (0.5, 0.8, 0.9)$. Experimental points from a synthetic benchmark that implements the task graph of Figure 2(a) are also shown.

We now use the same task graph of Figure 3(a) but we make the parallel part of task i be of size ip. The serial execution times for task T_i and the entire task graph are given by:

$$t_{T_i} = q + ip, \quad t_S = \sum_{i=1}^{n}(q + ip) = nq + p\frac{n(n+1)}{2}. \tag{6}$$

We can exploit loop and functional parallelism as before, dividing the P processors into static partitions of size P/n. The functional parallelism time is given by the time to execute the longest task and we obtain:

$$t_{P(\mathrm{loop})} = \sum_{i=1}^{n}(q + \frac{ip}{P}) = nq + \frac{p}{P}\frac{n(n+1)}{2}, \tag{7}$$

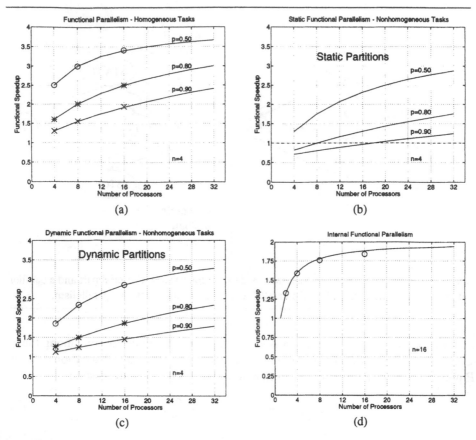

Fig. 3. Functional speedup as a function of the number of processors and fraction of parallelism p. In the above plots the lines represent results from the analytical models and the points are actual measurements of synthetic benchmarks. Parameter n is the degree of functional parallelism.

$$t_{P(\text{fps})} = q + \frac{pn}{P/n} = q + \frac{p}{P}n^2, \tag{8}$$

$$S_{P(\text{fps})}(n, p) = \frac{t_{P(\text{loop})}}{t_{P(\text{fps})}} = \frac{2Pn(1-p) + pn(n+1)}{2(P(1-p) + pn^2)}. \tag{9}$$

The functional speedup is less than 1 for $q < \frac{pn}{2P}$, in which case the exploitation of functional parallelism is detrimental to performance. The problem is the *static* partitioning of processors. Further performance improvements can be obtained by allowing dynamic assignment of processors to task. As the smaller tasks finish, their processors are reassigned to other tasks. With a uniform distribution of work among all P processors the parallel execution time and functional speedup are given by:

$$t_{P(\text{fpd})} = q + \frac{p}{P}\frac{n(n+1)}{2}, \tag{10}$$

$$S_{P(\text{fpd})}(n, p) = \frac{t_{P(\text{loop})}}{t_{P(\text{fpd})}} = \frac{2Pn(1-p) + pn(n+1)}{2P(1-p) + pn(n+1)}. \tag{11}$$

$S_{P(\text{fpd})}(n,p)$ is always greater than 1 and greater than $S_{P(\text{fps})}(n,p)$. Analytical curves and experimental points from a synthetic benchmark can be seen in Figures 3(b) and 3(c) for static and dynamic partitions, respectively.

We now consider the parallel loop in Figure 2(b), which illustrates loop parallelism with internal functional parallelism. Let each task T_i be strictly serial with execution time t. The serial and loop parallel execution times of the loop nest are given by:

$$t_S = \frac{P(P+1)}{2}nt, \quad t_{P(\text{loop})} = Pnt. \tag{12}$$

When the functional parallelism inside each loop iteration is exploited, processors that finish their iterations early become available to execute tasks of iterations from other processors. Ideally, the tasks are uniformly distributed among the processors. In this case the execution time and functional speedup are given by:

$$t_{P(\text{fp})} = \frac{P(P+1)}{2} \frac{n}{P} t. \tag{13}$$

$$S_{P(\text{fp})} = \frac{t_{P(\text{loop})}}{t_{P(\text{fp})}} = \frac{Pnt}{\frac{(P+1)n}{2}t} = \frac{2P}{P+1}. \tag{14}$$

A plot of this speedup and experimental points for $n = 16$ are shown in Figure 3(d).

8 Description of Benchmarks

In order to demonstrate the efficiency of *nano*Threads in real programs, several benchmarks have been tested. The time measured is the time actually required to perform the requisite calculations, excluding the time required to initialize the system or read in data. We give here a quick description of each benchmark.

Matrix Multiply (MM): The matrix multiply application is written in C++ using the *nano*Threads library. The code simply performs a straightforward implementation of the definition of matrix multiply ($c_{ij} = \sum_k a_{ik}b_{kj}$). The two outermost loops are run in parallel as doall loops.

Strassen's Matrix Multiply (SMM): An implementation of Strassen's matrix multiply algorithm [11] was also written in C++ using the *nano*Threads library. Strassen's algorithm is a recursive algorithm that breaks down a matrix into four quadrants, recursively performs multiplies on the quadrants and performs a combination of matrix adds and subtracts. The corresponding task graph is shown in Figure 4. Where a traditional matrix multiply of two $n \times n$ matrices is $O(n^3)$, Strassen's algorithm is $O(n^{2.807})$. Because the overhead is high, our implementation uses Strassen's algorithm only for large ($>= 64 \times 64$) matrices. When the quadrant size drops below 64, then the traditional parallel matrix multiply is used.

Complex Matrix Multiply (CMM): A C++ implementation using the *nano*Threads library. A complex multiply is equivalent to four real multiplies and two real adds. As shown in the corresponding task graph of Figure 4, these matrix operations represent functional parallelism. Each matrix A is represented by two matrices, one real and one imaginary, $A = A_r + jA_i$. The matrix $C = A \times B$ is calculated according to the equation:

$$C = (A_r B_r - A_i B_i) + j(A_r B_i + A_i B_r). \tag{15}$$

All of the measurements with the matrix multiplies in this paper were taken with matrices of size 256×256.

Two Dimensional Fast Fourier Transform (FFT2): Fortran code that performs a two dimensional fast Fourier transform was obtained from CMU's Task Parallel Suite [5] and hand-parallelized with the C++ *nano*Threads library. There are two nested parallel loops that are exploited. There is also one routine performing matrix transpose that exploits functional parallelism.

Perfect Benchmark TRFD (TRFD): A C++ version of the Perfect Club benchmark TRFD was implemented with the *nano*Threads library. This code was written from a high-level description of the functionality of TRFD. The code operates on four-dimensional triangular matrices, performing several multiplies and rearrangements. Only three loops were parallelized. Two of the parallel loops are perfectly nested.

Quicksort (QUICK): Quicksort[14] is a recursive "divide and conquer" algorithm that sorts a vector of elements. It does so by partitioning the vector into two parts, based on the value of the elements, and recursively applying the same technique to both parts. In the average case, Quicksort is $O(n \log n)$. Because of high fixed overhead, vectors below a certain size (256 elements) are sorted using a conventional nonrecursive sorting technique. The two recursive calls are independent and parallelized using functional parallelism. This benchmark was coded in Cedar Fortran, and the autoscheduling compiler automatically generated C++ autoscheduling code. The measurements were taken with a vector of size 1048576 elements.

Computational Fluid Dynamics (CFD): This is the kernel of a Fourier-Chebyshev spectral computational fluid dynamics code [15]. The task graph representing this code is shown in Figure 4. It consists of 4 stages that operate on matrices of size 128×128. The first stage involves six 2-dimensional FFTs, the second stage six element by element matrix multiplies, the third stage three matrix subtracts, and the fourth and final stage three 2-dimensional FFTs. The parallelism at the task graph level is exploited, as is the loop parallelism inside each matrix operation $(\times, -, \text{FFT})$. This benchmark was coded in Cedar Fortran, and translated by the autoscheduling compiler.

9 Results

The results presented in this section are compiled from a set of execution times for each benchmark. The experimental points were obtained by running each program three times on a given number of processors and selecting the minimum execution time observed. For the *nano*Threads library benchmarks, a distributed queue was used. For the autoscheduling compiler benchmarks, a centralized queue was used. In all cases, the granularity control parameter α was set to 1 (see Section 5).

9.1 Measurements of Speedup

Figure 5 contains speedup plots for the seven benchmarks. In each case the speedup S_P on P processors is computed as the ratio of serial execution time (for a serial version of the benchmark) to the parallel execution time on P processors. Different versions of parallel code are tested for each benchmark.

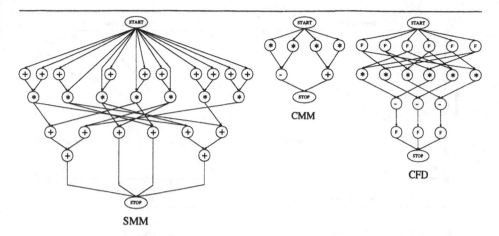

Fig. 4. Task graphs for SMM, CMM, and CFD. F, *, +, and − stand for 2D FFT, matrix multiply (element-by-element multiply in the case of CFD), matrix add, and matrix subtract, respectively.

For the real and complex matrix multiplies, MM and CMM, speedups are shown for the cases with (GC) and without (No GC) granularity control. Both benchmarks contain two nested parallel loops, thus each contains enough loop parallelism to occupy all available processors. In addition, CMM exploits an outer level of functional parallelism. The effect of granularity control is noticeable in reducing the overhead of exploiting too many loops in parallel. This benefit increases with the number of processors, since the overhead for fetching iterations from a parallel loop is proportional to the number of processors.

For Strassen's algorithm (SMM) and the two-dimensional FFT (FFT2), four versions are compared: with functional parallelism and granularity control (FP and GC), with functional parallelism but without granularity control (FP), with granularity control but without functional parallelism (GC), no granularity control and no functional parallelism (No FP or GC). The exploitation of functional parallelism in Strassen's algorithm is particularly important because it is a recursive algorithm and the loop parallelism occurs only at a smaller granularity. Because the recursive calls result in an exponential number of successively smaller tasks, granularity control has a significant effect as well. Only the version with functional parallelism and granularity control achieved reasonable speedup.

The body of the innermost parallel loop of benchmark FFT2 is very small. As a result, granularity control has a significant effect on its performance since it avoids unnecessary small grain parallelization. With granularity control, the version without functional parallelism generally achieves better performance than the version that exploits functional parallelism. The only functional parallelism in FFT2 that was exploited is in a matrix transpose function which causes bad cache performance. By using a profiler, *pixie*, we found that the number of instructions performed by the FP version is less than the number of instructions performed by the No FP version, since less time is spent by the schedulers spin waiting while there is no work to do. This indicates that the performance in a perfect memory system would be better with functional parallelism.

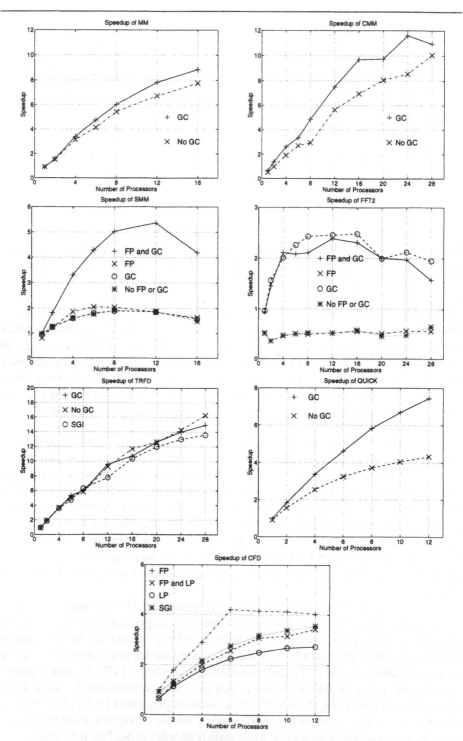

Fig. 5. Speedup plots for the various benchmarks.

Speedups of TRFD are shown for the cases of *nano*Threads with granularity control (GC), *nano*Threads without granularity control (No GC), and parallel loop constructs provided by the SGI compiler (SGI). This benchmark has no functional parallelism, but still *nano*Threads performs better than the SGI parallel loops. The granularity control version does not perform as well as the version without this control. This is a result of poor load balance resulting from the inhibited parallelism due to granularity control. This is an example of the case in which the smallest tasks are much larger than the scheduling overhead. TRFD has a limited amount of large grain parallelism and, therefore, the cost of unrestricted parallelism (no granularity control) is negligible. On the other hand, granularity control restricts some of the parallelism, in detriment of load balance. The SGI compiler restricts parallelism even more since it does not exploit nested parallelism, thus further hampering load balance.

Quicksort (QUICK) only has functional parallelism. Versions with (GC) and without (No GC) granularity control are compared. We observe a 75% improvement on the speedup for 12 processors when granularity control is used. As with Strassen's algorithm, granularity control here avoids an exponential explosion of tasks.

For CFD we compared four versions: autoscheduling compiler with loop parallelism only (LP), autoscheduling compiler with functional parallelism only (FP), autoscheduling compiler with loop and functional parallelism (LP and FP), SGI compiler with loop parallelism only (SGI). We note that the best performance was obtained by exploiting functional parallelism only. This is mainly the result of a better cache behavior in the functional parallel version. Each task operates on entire independent matrices and therefore there is little cache interference between processors. In the loop parallel versions, processor operate concurrently on the same matrices. The SGI compiler was better than the autoscheduling compiler in exploiting loop parallelism.

9.2 Improvements due to Granularity Control

Figure 6 lists the improvement in execution time as a function of the number of processors when granularity control is used for six of the benchmarks. Let t_{PG} be the execution time on P processors with granularity control and t_{PN} be the execution time on P processors without granularity control. The percentage improvement for P processors is defined as:

$$I_{\%P} = \frac{t_{PN} - t_{PG}}{t_{PN}} \times 100 \tag{16}$$

The effect of granularity control varies significantly depending on the characteristics of the algorithm and the size of the smallest task. Granularity control can make a large difference in performance, especially when the available parallelism is not large (FFT2, SMM). In the case where granularity control performs worse (TRFD), the difference is small.

10 Related Work

A variety of thread management issues and implementation alternatives are considered in [1]. It includes analysis and implementation results for different types of queue management and lock synchronization techniques.

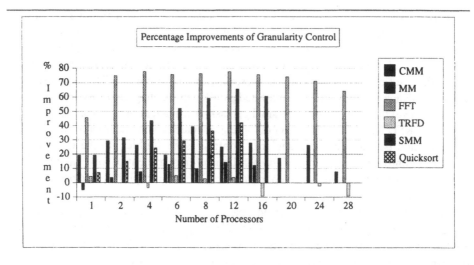

Percentage Improvement Due To Granularity Control									
Number of processors	1	2	4	6	8	12	16	20	24	28
CMM	19.6	29.0	26.7	19.6	39.5	25.0	28.2	17.2	26.3	8.2
MM	-5.2	3.3	7.9	12.8	9.8	14.0	12.4	–	–	–
FFT2	45.7	75.2	78.1	75.7	76.5	78.2	76.0	74.6	71.4	64.3
TRFD	4.6	-0.1	-3.6	5.1	3.2	3.5	-9.1	0.0	-2.0	-9.2
SMM	19.2	31.7	43.9	52.2	59.5	65.5	61.0	–	–	–
Quicksort	6.96	15.04	24.64	29.39	36.11	41.79	–	–	–	–

Fig. 6. The effect of granularity control.

Scheduler Activations [2] and Process Control [12] both offer user-level scheduling and dynamic adaptation to changing environments. Scheduler activations supply an execution context that may be manipulated by a user-level scheduler or the kernel to allow for user-level scheduling with the flexibility and power of kernel-level threads. Allowed kernel manipulations include the granting or removing of scheduler activations. The process control approach allows the user to request processors and gives the user control over when to release processors. Processors are released by the user on request of the kernel at *safe points* to prevent deadlock and similar problems.

Considerable work has been done on the exploitation of functional and loop parallelism by the Paradigm [20] group at the University of Illinois. They rely on a *Macro Dataflow Graph* which is a directed acyclic task graph in which the nodes are weighted with the communication and computation time. Their approach performs static partitioning for data and computations on a distributed system to minimize total runtime.

Jade [21] is a high-level language designed for the exploitation of coarse-grain task (functional) parallelism. Concurrency is detected dynamically from data access specifications in each task. The language also supports the declaration of hierarchical tasks.

Techniques to exploit nested parallelism include switch-stacks [4] and process control blocks (PCBs) [13]. A PCB for a parallel loop is used to schedule the iterations of that loop. Reference [13] discusses heuristics that strike a balance between efficient allocation of PCBs versus load balancing problems that arise from barrier synchronization in nested parallel loops. Switch-stacks handle nested parallelism by actually swapping stacks between processors so no one processor is left idle waiting for another to finish.

The *Psyche* [16] system has facilities for user-level threads in which many tasks normally performed by the kernel, such as interrupt handling and preemptions, are handled at the user-level. Like *nano*Threads, it relies on multiple virtual processors sharing the same address space.

Chores [6] is a paradigm for the exploitation of loop and functional parallelism. It allows dynamic scheduling at the user-level and the expression of dependences between tasks without explicit synchronization.

11 Conclusion

In this paper we have demonstrated the benefits of exploiting functional parallelism and performing dynamic granularity control. Our implementation is based on a user-level threads model that performs dynamic task scheduling.

In particular, we have shown that the exploitation of nested functional parallelism is beneficial both in terms of increasing the amount of high-level parallelism and improving the load balance of parallel loops. We have also shown the potential for significant improvements by dynamically controlling the granularity of exploited parallelism.

Results from synthetic benchmarks were used to verify analytical models of performance. Measurements with application kernels demonstrated the efficiency of our approach for real scientific computations on an existing commercial shared-memory multiprocessor.

References

1. Thomas Anderson, Edward Lazowska, and Henry Levy. The performance implications of thread management alternatives for shared-memory multiprocessors. *IEEE Transactions on Computers*, 38(12), December 1989.

2. Thomas E. Anderson, Brian N. Bershad, Edward D. Lazowska, and Henry M. Levy. Scheduler activations: Effective kernel support for the user-level management of parallelism. In *13th ACM Symposium on Operating Systems Principles*, pages 95–109. ACM Sigops, October 1991.

3. Carl J. Beckmann. *Hardware and Software for Functional and Fine Grain Parallelism*. PhD thesis, Department of Electrical and Computer Engineering, University of Illinois at Urbana-Champaign, 1993.

4. Jyh-Herng Chow and Williams Ludwell Harrison. Switch-stacks: A scheme for microtasking nested parallel loops. In *Supercomputing 90*, pages 190–199, Nov. 1990.

5. Peter Dinda, Thomas Gross, David O'Hallaron, Edward Segall, James Stichnoth, Jaspal Subhlok, Jon Webb, and Bwolen Yang. The CMU task parallel program suite. Technical Report CMU-CS-94-131, School of Computer Science, Carnegie-Mellon University, March 1994.

6. Derek Eager and John Zahorjan. Chores: Enhanced run-time support for shared-memory parallel computing. *ACM Transactions on Computer Systems*, 11(1), February 1993.

7. Mike Galles and Eric Williams. Performance optimizations, implementation, and verification of the SGI Challenge multiprocessor. Silicon Graphics Technical Report. Available from http://www.sgi.com.

8. M. Girkar and C. D. Polychronopoulos. The HTG: An intermediate representation for programs based on control and data dependences. Technical Report 1046, Center for Supercomputing Research and Development, University of Illinois at Urbana-Champaign, May 1991.

9. Milind Girkar. *Functional Parallelism: Theoretical Foundations and Implementation*. PhD thesis, Department of Computer Science, University of Illinois at Urbana-Champaign, 1992.

10. Milind Girkar and Constantine Polychronopoulos. Automatic detection and generation of unstructured parallelism in ordinary programs. *IEEE Transactions on Parallel and Distributed Systems*, 3(2), April 1992.

11. Gene H. Golub and Charles F. Van Loan. *Matrix Computations*. The Johns Hopkins University Press, Baltimore, MD, 1989.

12. Anoop Gupta, Andrew Tucker, and Luis Stevens. Making effective use of shared-memory multiprocessors: The process control approach. Technical Report CSL-TR-91-475A, Computer Systems Laboratory, Stanford University, 1991.

13. S. F. Hummel and E. Schonberg. Low-overhead scheduling of nested parallelism. *IBM J. Res. Develp.*, 35(5/6):743–765, Sept/Nov 1991.

14. D. E. Knuth. *The Art of Computer Programming, Vol. 3 Sorting and Searching*. Addison-Wesley, Reading, Mass., 1973.

15. S. L. Lyons, T. J. Hanratty, and J. B. MacLaughlin. Large-scale computer simulation of fully developed channel flow with heat transfer. *International Journal of Numerical Methods for Fluids*, 13:999–1028, 1991.

16. Brian D. Marsh, Michael L. Scott, Thomas J. LeBlanc, and Evangelos P. Markatos. First-class user-level threads. In *Proceedings of the 13th ACM Symposium on Operating Systems Principles*, pages 110–121, October 1991.

17. C. D. Polychronopoulos, M. B. Girkar, Mohammad R. Haghighat, C. L. Lee, B. Leung, and D. A. Schouten. Parafrase-2: An environment for parallelizing, partitioning, synchronizing, and scheduling programs on multiprocessors. *International Journal of High Speed Computing*, 1(1):45–72, May 1989.

18. Constantine Polychronopoulos, Nawaf Bitar, and Steve Kleiman. *nano*threads: A user-level threads architecture. In *Proceedings of the ACM Symposium on Principles of Operating Systems*, 1993.

19. Constantine D. Polychronopoulos. Autoscheduling: Control flow and data flow come together. Technical Report 1058, Center for Supercomputing Research and Development, University of Illinois at Urbana-Champaign, 1990.

20. Shankar Ramaswamy and Prithviraj Banerjee. Processor allocation and scheduling of macro dataflow graphs on distributed memory multicomputers by the PARADIGM compiler. In *International Conference on Parallel Processing*, pages II:134–138, St. Charles, IL, August 1993.

21. Martin C. Rinard, Daniel J. Scales, and Monica S. Lam. Jade: A high-level machine-independent language for parallel programming. *IEEE Computer*, 26(6):28–38, June 1993.

Author Index

Agrawal G. 465
Altman E. R. 16
Amarasinghe S. P. 61
Appelbe B. 304
Ayguadé E. 407
Bagrodia R. 239
Banerjee P. 392
Banerjee U. 318
Bik A. J. C. 500
Blume W. 141
Bodík R. 1
Chang P. 318
Chatterjee S. 346,
377
Cheatham T. 422
Chien A. A. 566
Choi L. 81
Chung T. M. 254
Cierniak M. 362
Creusillet B. 46
Dechering P. F. G. 111
Dietz H. G. 254
Dinda P. A. 534
Dinechin B. D. de 31
Doddapaneni S. .. 304
Eigenmann R. 141
Fahmy A. 422
Faith R. E. 346
Gallivan K. 269
Gallopoulos E. ... 269
Gao G. R. 16
Garcia J. 407
Ghiya R. 515
Gilbert J. R. 377
Gironès M. 407
Govindarajan R. .. 16
Gre M. L. 407

Gross T. 224
Gu J. 96
Gupta R. 1
Hall M. W. 61
Harmon R. 304
Hendren L. J. 515
Huang C.-H. 209
Hummel J. 289
Irigoin F. 46
Ishizaki K. 176
Jagannathan S. 450
Kalé L. V. 551
Kaushik S. D. 209
Kelly W. 126
Kennedy K. 161
Komatsu H. 176
Kotlyar V. 480
Labarta J. 407
Lam M. S. 61
Li W. 362
Li Z. 96
Liao S.-W. 61
Marsolf B. 269
Mattox T. I. 254
May P. 304
McKinley K. S. 434
Mellor-Crummey J. 161
Midkiff S. P. 331
Mirani R. 450
Moreira J. E. 581
Murphy B. R. 61
Nguyen T. 96
Nicolau A. 289
Novack S. 289
O'Hallaron D. R. .. 534
Padua D. 269
Palermo D. J. 392

Palmer D. W. 346
Philbin J. 450
Pingali K. 480
Plevyak J. 566
Polychronopoulos C. 581
Prakash S. 239
Prins J. F. 346
Pugh W. 126
Radigan J. 318
Ramanujam J. 191
Rose L. De 269
Rosser E. 126
Roth G. 161
Sadayappan P. 209
Saltz J. 465
Schouten D. 581
Schreiber R. 377
Sheffler T. J. 377
Shpeisman T. 126
Singhai S. K. 434
Sips H. J. 111
Stefanescu D. C. ... 422
Stichnoth J. M. 224
Stodghill P. 480
Subhlok J. 534
Thirumalai A. 191
Trescher J. A. 111
Vitale M. 304
Vreught J. P. M. de 111
Weaver G. E. 434
Webb J. A. 534
Weems C. C. 434
Wijshoff H. A. G. .. 500
Wills S. 304
Yang B. 534
Yelon J. 551
Yew P. -C. 81

Lecture Notes in Computer Science

For information about Vols. 1–957

please contact your bookseller or Springer-Verlag

Vol. 958: J. Calmet, J.A. Campbell (Eds.), Integrating Symbolic Mathematical Computation and Artificial Intelligence. Proceedings, 1994. X, 275 pages. 1995.

Vol. 959: D.-Z. Du, M. Li (Eds.), Computing and Combinatorics. Proceedings, 1995. XIII, 654 pages. 1995.

Vol. 960: D. Leivant (Ed.), Logic and Computational Complexity. Proceedings, 1994. VIII, 514 pages. 1995.

Vol. 961: K.P. Jantke, S. Lange (Eds.), Algorithmic Learning for Knowledge-Based Systems. X, 511 pages. 1995. (Subseries LNAI).

Vol. 962: I. Lee, S.A. Smolka (Eds.), CONCUR '95: Concurrency Theory. Proceedings, 1995. X, 547 pages. 1995.

Vol. 963: D. Coppersmith (Ed.), Advances in Cryptology - CRYPTO '95. Proceedings, 1995. XII, 467 pages. 1995.

Vol. 964: V. Malyshkin (Ed.), Parallel Computing Technologies. Proceedings, 1995. XII, 497 pages. 1995.

Vol. 965: H. Reichel (Ed.), Fundamentals of Computation Theory. Proceedings, 1995. IX, 433 pages. 1995.

Vol. 966: S. Haridi, K. Ali, P. Magnusson (Eds.), EURO-PAR '95 Parallel Processing. Proceedings, 1995. XV, 734 pages. 1995.

Vol. 967: J.P. Bowen, M.G. Hinchey (Eds.), ZUM '95: The Z Formal Specification Notation. Proceedings, 1995. XI, 571 pages. 1995.

Vol. 968: N. Dershowitz, N. Lindenstrauss (Eds.), Conditional and Typed Rewriting Systems. Proceedings, 1994. VIII, 375 pages. 1995.

Vol. 969: J. Wiedermann, P. Hájek (Eds.), Mathematical Foundations of Computer Science 1995. Proceedings, 1995. XIII, 588 pages. 1995.

Vol. 970: V. Hlaváč, R. Šára (Eds.), Computer Analysis of Images and Patterns. Proceedings, 1995. XVIII, 960 pages. 1995.

Vol. 971: E.T. Schubert, P.J. Windley, J. Alves-Foss (Eds.), Higher Order Logic Theorem Proving and Its Applications. Proceedings, 1995. VIII, 400 pages. 1995.

Vol. 972: J.-M. Hélary, M. Raynal (Eds.), Distributed Algorithms. Proceedings, 1995. XI, 333 pages. 1995.

Vol. 973: H.H. Adelsberger, J. Lažanský, V. Mařík (Eds.), Information Management in Computer Integrated Manufacturing. IX, 665 pages. 1995.

Vol. 974: C. Braccini, L. DeFloriani, G. Vernazza (Eds.), Image Analysis and Processing. Proceedings, 1995. XIX, 757 pages. 1995.

Vol. 975: W. Moore, W. Luk (Eds.), Field-Programmable Logic and Applications. Proceedings, 1995. XI, 448 pages. 1995.

Vol. 976: U. Montanari, F. Rossi (Eds.), Principles and Practice of Constraint Programming — CP '95. Proceedings, 1995. XIII, 651 pages. 1995.

Vol. 977: H. Beilner, F. Bause (Eds.), Quantitative Evaluation of Computing and Communication Systems. Proceedings, 1995. X, 415 pages. 1995.

Vol. 978: N. Revell, A M. Tjoa (Eds.), Database and Expert Systems Applications. Proceedings, 1995. XV, 654 pages. 1995.

Vol. 979: P. Spirakis (Ed.), Algorithms — ESA '95. Proceedings, 1995. XII, 598 pages. 1995.

Vol. 980: A. Ferreira, J. Rolim (Eds.), Parallel Algorithms for Irregularly Structured Problems. Proceedings, 1995. IX, 409 pages. 1995.

Vol. 981: I. Wachsmuth, C.-R. Rollinger, W. Brauer (Eds.), KI-95: Advances in Artificial Intelligence. Proceedings, 1995. XII, 269 pages. (Subseries LNAI).

Vol. 982: S. Doaitse Swierstra, M. Hermenegildo (Eds.), Programming Languages: Implementations, Logics and Programs. Proceedings, 1995. XI, 467 pages. 1995.

Vol. 983: A. Mycroft (Ed.), Static Analysis. Proceedings, 1995. VIII, 423 pages. 1995.

Vol. 984: J.-M. Haton, M. Keane, M. Manago (Eds.), Advances in Case-Based Reasoning. Proceedings, 1994. VIII, 307 pages. 1995.

Vol. 985: T. Sellis (Ed.), Rules in Database Systems. Proceedings, 1995. VIII, 373 pages. 1995.

Vol. 986: Henry G. Baker (Ed.), Memory Management. Proceedings, 1995. XII, 417 pages. 1995.

Vol. 987: P.E. Camurati, H. Eveking (Eds.), Correct Hardware Design and Verification Methods. Proceedings, 1995. VIII, 342 pages. 1995.

Vol. 988: A.U. Frank, W. Kuhn (Eds.), Spatial Information Theory. Proceedings, 1995. XIII, 571 pages. 1995.

Vol. 989: W. Schäfer, P. Botella (Eds.), Software Engineering — ESEC '95. Proceedings, 1995. XII, 519 pages. 1995.

Vol. 990: C. Pinto-Ferreira, N.J. Mamede (Eds.), Progress in Artificial Intelligence. Proceedings, 1995. XIV, 487 pages. 1995. (Subseries LNAI).

Vol. 991: J. Wainer, A. Carvalho (Eds.), Advances in Artificial Intelligence. Proceedings, 1995. XII, 342 pages. 1995. (Subseries LNAI).

Vol. 992: M. Gori, G. Soda (Eds.), Topics in Artificial Intelligence. Proceedings, 1995. XII, 451 pages. 1995. (Subseries LNAI).

Vol. 993: T.C. Fogarty (Ed.), Evolutionary Computing. Proceedings, 1995. VIII, 264 pages. 1995.

Vol. 994: M. Hebert, J. Ponce, T. Boult, A. Gross (Eds.), Object Representation in Computer Vision. Proceedings, 1994. VIII, 359 pages. 1995.

Vol. 995: S.M. Müller, W.J. Paul, The Complexity of Simple Computer Architectures. XII, 270 pages. 1995.

Vol. 996: P. Dybjer, B. Nordström, J. Smith (Eds.), Types for Proofs and Programs. Proceedings, 1994. X, 202 pages. 1995.

Vol. 997: K.P. Jantke, T. Shinohara, T. Zeugmann (Eds.), Algorithmic Learning Theory. Proceedings, 1995. XV, 319 pages. 1995.

Vol. 998: A. Clarke, M. Campolargo, N. Karatzas (Eds.), Bringing Telecommunication Services to the People – IS&N '95. Proceedings, 1995. XII, 510 pages. 1995.

Vol. 999: P. Antsaklis, W. Kohn, A. Nerode, S. Sastry (Eds.), Hybrid Systems II. VIII, 569 pages. 1995.

Vol. 1000: J. van Leeuwen (Ed.), Computer Science Today. XIV, 643 pages. 1995.

Vol. 1001: M. Sudan, Efficient Checking of Polynomials and Proofs and the Hardness of Approximation Problems. XIV, 87 pages. 1995.

Vol. 1002: J.J. Kistler, Disconnected Operation in a Distributed File System. XIX, 249 pages. 1995.

VOL. 1003: P. Pandurang Nayak, Automated Modeling of Physical Systems. XXI, 232 pages. 1995. (Subseries LNAI).

Vol. 1004: J. Staples, P. Eades, N. Katoh, A. Moffat (Eds.), Algorithms and Computation. Proceedings, 1995. XV, 440 pages. 1995.

Vol. 1005: J. Estublier (Ed.), Software Configuration Management. Proceedings, 1995. IX, 311 pages. 1995.

Vol. 1006: S. Bhalla (Ed.), Information Systems and Data Management. Proceedings, 1995. IX, 321 pages. 1995.

Vol. 1007: A. Bosselaers, B. Preneel (Eds.), Integrity Primitives for Secure Information Systems. VII, 239 pages. 1995.

Vol. 1008: B. Preneel (Ed.), Fast Software Encryption. Proceedings, 1994. VIII, 367 pages. 1995.

Vol. 1009: M. Broy, S. Jähnichen (Eds.), KORSO: Methods, Languages, and Tools for the Construction of Correct Software. X, 449 pages. 1995. Vol.

Vol. 1010: M. Veloso, A. Aamodt (Eds.), Case-Based Reasoning Research and Development. Proceedings, 1995. X, 576 pages. 1995. (Subseries LNAI).

Vol. 1011: T. Furuhashi (Ed.), Advances in Fuzzy Logic, Neural Networks and Genetic Algorithms. Proceedings, 1994. (Subseries LNAI).

Vol. 1012: M. Bartošek, J. Staudek, J. Wiedermann (Eds.), SOFSEM '95: Theory and Practice of Informatics. Proceedings, 1995. XI, 499 pages. 1995.

Vol. 1013: T.W. Ling, A.O. Mendelzon, L. Vieille (Eds.), Deductive and Object-Oriented Databases. Proceedings, 1995. XIV, 557 pages. 1995.

Vol. 1014: A.P. del Pobil, M.A. Serna, Spatial Representation and Motion Planning. XII, 242 pages. 1995.

Vol. 1015: B. Blumenthal, J. Gornostaev, C. Unger (Eds.), Human-Computer Interaction. Proceedings, 1995. VIII, 203 pages. 1995.

VOL. 1016: R. Cipolla, Active Visual Inference of Surface Shape. XII, 194 pages. 1995.

Vol. 1017: M. Nagl (Ed.), Graph-Theoretic Concepts in Computer Science. Proceedings, 1995. XI, 406 pages. 1995.

Vol. 1018: T.D.C. Little, R. Gusella (Eds.), Network and Operating Systems Support for Digital Audio and Video. Proceedings, 1995. XI, 357 pages. 1995.

Vol. 1019: E. Brinksma, W.R. Cleaveland, K.G. Larsen, T. Margaria, B. Steffen (Eds.), Tools and Algorithms for the Construction and Analysis of Systems. Selected Papers, 1995. VII, 291 pages. 1995.

Vol. 1020: I.D. Watson (Ed.), Progress in Case-Based Reasoning. Proceedings, 1995. VIII, 209 pages. 1995. (Subseries LNAI).

Vol. 1021: M.P. Papazoglou (Ed.), OOER '95: Object-Oriented and Entity-Relationship Modeling. Proceedings, 1995. XVII, 451 pages. 1995.

Vol. 1022: P.H. Hartel, R. Plasmeijer (Eds.), Functional Programming Languages in Education. Proceedings, 1995. X, 309 pages. 1995.

Vol. 1023: K. Kanchanasut, J.-J. Lévy (Eds.), Algorithms, Concurrency and Knowlwdge. Proceedings, 1995. X, 410 pages. 1995.

Vol. 1024: R.T. Chin, H.H.S. Ip, A.C. Naiman, T.-C. Pong (Eds.), Image Analysis Applications and Computer Graphics. Proceedings, 1995. XVI, 533 pages. 1995.

Vol. 1025: C. Boyd (Ed.), Cryptography and Coding. Proceedings, 1995. IX, 291 pages. 1995.

Vol. 1026: P.S. Thiagarajan (Ed.), Foundations of Software Technology and Theoretical Computer Science. Proceedings, 1995. XII, 515 pages. 1995.

Vol. 1027: F.J. Brandenburg (Ed.), Graph Drawing. Proceedings, 1995. XII, 526 pages. 1996.

Vol. 1028: N.R. Adam, Y. Yesha (Eds.), Electronic Commerce. X, 155 pages. 1996.

Vol. 1029: E. Dawson, J. Golić (Eds.), Cryptography: Policy and Algorithms. Proceedings, 1995. XI, 327 pages. 1996.

Vol. 1030: F. Pichler, R. Moreno-Díaz, R. Albrecht (Eds.), Computer Aided Systems Theory - EUROCAST '95. Proceedings, 1995. XII, 539 pages. 1996.

Vol.1031: M. Toussaint (Ed.), Ada in Europe. Proceedings, 1995. XI, 455 pages. 1996.

Vol. 1032: P. Godefroid, Partial-Order Methods for the Verification of Concurrent Systems. IV, 143 pages. 1996.

Vol. 1033: C.-H. Huang, P. Sadayappan, U. Banerjee, D. Gelernter, A. Nicolau, D. Padua (Eds.), Languages and Compilers for Parallel Computing. Proceedings, 1995. XIII, 597 pages. 1996.

Vol. 1034: G. Kuper, M. Wallace (Eds.), Constraint Databases and Applications. Proceedings, 1995. VII, 185 pages. 1996.

Vol. 1035: S.Z. Li, D.P. Mital, E.K. Teoh, H. Wang (Eds.), Recent Developments in Computer Vision. Proceedings, 1995. XI, 604 pages. 1996.